Power BI Tools Volume 5: Learning Power BI Desktop Made Easy

By Indera E. Murphy

Tolana Publishing
Teaneck, New Jersey

Power BI Tools Volume 5: Learning Power BI Desktop Made Easy

Published By:
Tolana Publishing
PO Box 719
Teaneck, NJ 07666 USA

Find us online at www.tolanapublishing.com
Inquiries may be sent to the publisher: tolanapub@yahoo.com

Our books are available online at www.barnesandnoble.com. They can also be ordered from Ingram.

ISBN-13: 978-1-935208-34-1
ISBN-10: 1-935208-34-9

Library of Congress Control Number: 2016910217

Printed and bound in the United States Of America

v1.0

This book is dedicated to my mother.

Even though she did not use a computer, she asked me to make the book size and print larger.

I gave in and did what she wanted.

Words cannot express how much I miss my mother.

As always, Thank you mommy.

I love you.

About The Series

Power BI Tools Volume 5: Learning Power BI Desktopl Made Easy, is part of the growing series of computer software books that are designed to be used as a self-paced learning tool, in a classroom setting or in an online class. The books in this series contain an abundance of step-by-step instructions and screen shots to help reduce the "stress" often associated with learning new software. Some of the titles in the series are shown below.

ISBN-13: 978-1-935208-36-5

ISBN: 978-1-935208-35-8

ISBN: 978-1-935208-18-1

ISBN: 978-1-935208-21-1

ISBN: 978-1-935208-29-7

ISBN: 978-1-935208-27-3

ISBN: 978-1-935208-28-0

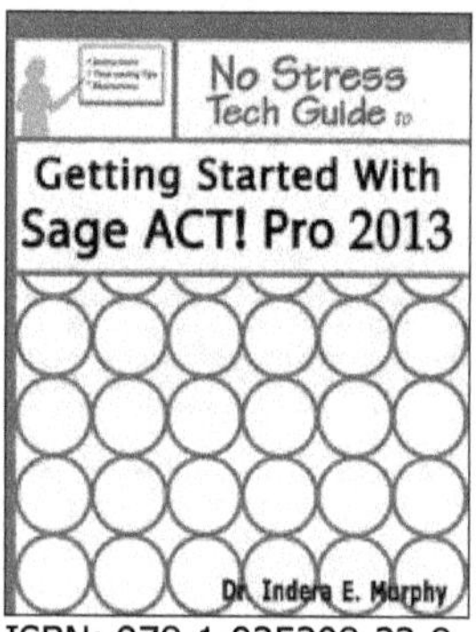

ISBN: 978-1-935208-22-8

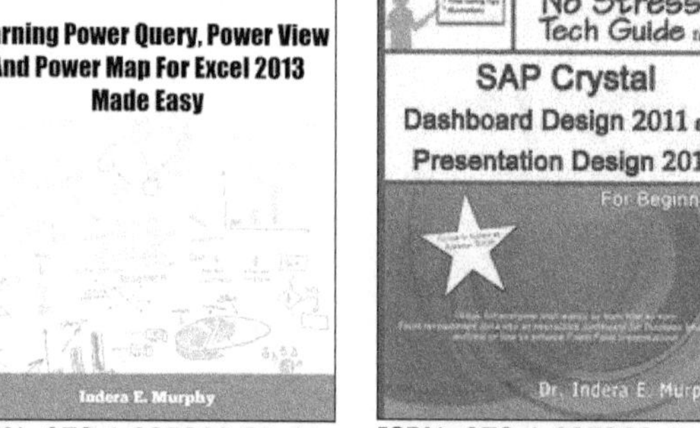

ISBN: 978-1-935208-19-8

ISBN: 978-1-935208-20-4

ISBN: 978-1-935208-11-2

ISBN: 978-1-935208-26-6

Visit us online at www.tolanapublishing.com for more titles and information

CONTENTS

GETTING STARTED WITH POWER BI DESKTOP 1-1
How This Book Is Organized 1-2
Conventions Used In This Book 1-3
Self-Service Business Intelligence 1-5
What Can Power BI Desktop Do? 1-6
Step 1: Find The Data 1-6
Step 2: Load The Data To The Data Model 1-6
Step 3: Create The Reports Or Dashboards 1-6
Step 4: Share The Data 1-6
Exercise 1.1: Download And Install Power BI Desktop 1-6
Exercise 1.2: Create A Folder For Your Files 1-8
Data Concepts 1-10
Power BI Desktop Workspace 1-11
Options Dialog Box 1-13
Global Options 1-13
Data Load Options 1-13
Query Editor Options 1-14
Current File Options 1-15
Customize The Quick Access Toolbar 1-21

LOADING DATA INTO POWER BI DESKTOP 2-1
Importing Data 2-2
External Data Options 2-2
Getting Data 2-4
Exercise 2.1: Import Data From A Web Site 2-5
Import Data From Excel 2-8
Exercise 2.2: Import Data From Multiple Sources Into One Workbook 2-9
Import Data Using Named Ranges 2-9
Import Multiple Sets Of Data 2-9
Text And CSV File Connector Import Options 2-9
Exercise 2.3: Import Data From Different Text File Types 2-10
Import Data From A CSV File 2-10
Import Data From An XML File 2-11
Import Data From A Text File 2-12
Import Data From A JSON File 2-13
Exercise 2.4: Use An Access Database As The Data Source 2-14
Load Data From Another Source 2-15
Selecting Related Tables 2-15
How To Get Data From The Azure Marketplace 2-16
What Is A Data Feed? 2-18
Exercise 2.5: Import Data From An OData Data Feed 2-18

GETTING STARTED WITH THE QUERY EDITOR 3-1
Query Editor Overview 3-2
What Is The Query Editor Designed To Do? 3-2
What Is ETL? 3-3
Understanding The "Query" In Power BI Desktop 3-3
What Is A Query? 3-3
Using A Query As A Data Source 3-8
Query Settings Panel 3-15
Query Properties Dialog Box 3-15
Applied Steps 3-16
Source Step 3-18
Navigation Step 3-19
Promoted Headers Step 3-20

Home Tab 3-21
Close & Apply Options 3-22
Sorting On Multiple Columns 3-25
Group By Options 3-27
Exercise 3.1: Use The Remove Columns And Rows Options 3-31
Use The Choose Columns Option 3-32
Use The Remove Columns Option 3-32
Use The Remove Errors Option 3-32
Use The Remove Bottom Rows Option 3-32
Exercise 3.2: Remove Duplicate Records 3-32
Exercise 3.3: Loading A List Of Tables 3-33
Exercise 3.4: Import Data From The Data Model In Excel 3-34

CREATING FILTERS, CUSTOM COLUMNS AND FORMULAS 4-1
Filter Options 4-2
Basic Filter Criteria 4-3
Text Functions 4-4
Numeric Functions 4-4
Date And Time Functions 4-4
Shaping The Data 4-6
Exercise 4.1: Use The Filter Options In The Query Editor 4-6
Create Date And Text Filters 4-7
Create Filters For More Than One Column 4-7
Exercise 4.2: Create A Custom Filter 4-7
Advanced Filter Criteria 4-8
Exercise 4.3: Create Advanced Filter Criteria 4-8
Create Advanced Date Filters 4-8
Create Advanced Text And Numeric Filters 4-9
Custom Columns 4-9
Exercise 4.4: Add Columns To A Table 4-10
Create A Total Calculated Column 4-10
Combine Columns Of Data 4-11
Combine The First Initial And Last Name 4-11
Use The IF Function To Create A Formula With Conditional Logic 4-12

USING THE QUERY EDITOR TO TRANSFORM DATA 5-1
Transforming The Data 5-2
Data Type Options 5-5
What Is The Any Data Type? 5-5
Structured Data Types 5-6
Tables 5-6
Records 5-6
Lists 5-7
Exercise 5.1: Use The Transform Tab Options 5-9
Use The Split Column By Delimiter Option 5-9
Use The Split Column By Number Of Characters Option 5-10
Use The Group By Option 5-10
Use The Replace Values Option 5-10
Exercise 5.2: Create Calculations Using Options On The Add Column Tab 5-12
Merge Columns 5-12
Calculate A Total Using Two Columns Of Data 5-13
Calculate The Line Item Total 5-13
Calculate The Sales Tax Amount 5-13
Use More Than Two Columns To Create A Calculated Column 5-14
How To Calculate The Age In Years 5-16
How The Trim And Clean Functions Work 5-16
Exercise 5.3: Use Functions On The Transform And Add Column Tabs 5-18
Use The Count Distinct Values Function 5-18
Use The Round Up Function 5-18
Use The Quarter Of Year Function 5-19
Use The Subtract Days Function 5-19
Creating Percents 5-19

Conditional Columns ... 5-20
Exercise 5.4: Create A Conditional Column ... 5-20
Create The Duration Custom Column ... 5-20
Create The Shipped On Time Conditional Column ... 5-20
Create The Else If Portion Of The Condition ... 5-21
Create The Otherwise Portion Of The Condition ... 5-21
View Tab ... 5-23

USING THE QUERY EDITOR TO MASHUP DATA ... 6-1
Why Would I Need To Combine Data From Different Tables? ... 6-2
Merging Data ... 6-2
Appending Data ... 6-3
Exercise 6.1: Use The Merge And Append Queries Options ... 6-5
Use The Merge Queries Option ... 6-5
Aggregate The Data, Then Merge It ... 6-5
Use The Append Queries Option ... 6-6
Grouping Data ... 6-7
Exercise 6.2: Merging Data To Group By ... 6-7
Add A Year Field To The Orders Table ... 6-8
Merge The Sales Rep Name Column ... 6-8
Merge The Customer Name Column ... 6-9
Merge Columns From A Date Table ... 6-9
Group The Order Records By Year ... 6-10
Group The Order Records By Sales Rep ... 6-11
Change The Sort Options ... 6-11
Group The Order Records By State ... 6-12
Add Currency Formatting To Numeric Data ... 6-12
Create A Calculated Column ... 6-14
Create And Merge Aggregations ... 6-14
Exercise 6.3: Create A New Table By Merging Queries ... 6-15
Exercise 6.4: Use The Merge And Append Options ... 6-17
Create A Many-To-Many Merge ... 6-17
Create A New Table From Appended Queries ... 6-18
Appending Queries With Different Column Names ... 6-18
Append Three Or More Tables At One Time ... 6-19
Discover The Top Selling Product By Year ... 6-19
Create The Group ... 6-20
Discover The Top Selling Products By Dollar Amount ... 6-20
Add Columns From The Record With The Largest Value ... 6-21
Calculate The Best Seller Percent ... 6-22
Add Percent Formatting To Numeric Data ... 6-22
Pivot Column Options ... 6-23
Exercise 6.5: Use The Pivot Column And Reverse Rows Options ... 6-24
Create A Pivot Table ... 6-24
Use The Reverse Rows Option ... 6-24
Unpivoting Data ... 6-25
Exercise 6.6: Use Data In Non Tabular Format ... 6-25
Unpivot The Other Columns And Transform The Data ... 6-26
Create Averages In A Pivot Table Layout ... 6-26
Exercise 6.7: Import An Unlimited Number Of CSV Files From A Folder At One Time ... 6-28
Step 1: Select The Folder With The Data ... 6-28
Step 2: Prepare The Files To Be Combined ... 6-29
Step 3: Import And Transform The Data ... 6-30
Step 4: If Necessary, Fix The Errors ... 6-31
Step 5: Import Data From Other Folders ... 6-32
Exercise 6.8: Import An Unlimited Number Of Excel Files From A Folder At One Time ... 6-33
Load An Excel File ... 6-33
Create The Function That Will Select The Files To Load ... 6-34
Create The Query To Import The Workbook Files ... 6-35

USING THE RELATIONSHIPS VIEW 7-1
What Is A Data Model? 7-2
What Is The Star Schema? 7-2
Supported Data Types In The Data Model 7-3
What Is A Relationship? 7-5
Relational Databases 7-5
Understanding Relationships In Power BI Desktop 7-7
Relationships View 7-8
Exercise 7.1: Create Relationships 7-10
Manage Relationships 7-11
Use The Auto Detect Option 7-11
Delete Relationships 7-11
Create A New Relationship 7-12
Edit An Existing Relationship 7-13

USING THE DATA VIEW 8-1
Data View Options 8-2
Fields Panel 8-3
Data Type Icons 8-5
Data View vs Query Editor 8-6
Exercise 8.1: Import The Data And Reports 8-6
Modify Some Of The Table Options 8-6
Understanding Hierarchies 8-7
Exercise 8.2: Create A Hierarchy 8-7
Exercise 8.3: Create Calculated Columns 8-8
Create A Formula To Check For Duplicate Records 8-8
Create A Formula To Calculate The Order Processing Time 8-9
What Is A Date Table? 8-10
Date Table Requirements 8-10
Sorting Columns In The Date Table 8-10
What Is Time Intelligence? 8-11
Exercise 8.4: Create A Date Table 8-11
Add More Columns To The Date Table 8-12
Calculated Tables 8-12
Create A Table 8-12
Displaying Month Names In Calendar Order 8-13
What Is A Measure? 8-14
Exercise 8.5: Create Measures 8-15
Create A Total Order Amount Measure 8-15
Create A Count Of Orders Measure 8-15
Create A Measure To Rank Sales Reps By Their Total Sales 8-15
Query Parameters 8-16
Exercise 8.6: Create Parameters 8-17
Create The Year Parameter 8-17
Create The Country Parameter 8-19
Create The List Query 8-19
Create A Parameter That Uses A List Query 8-20
Manage Parameters 8-20
Exercise 8.7: Use A Parameter With A Query 8-21

GETTING STARTED WITH THE REPORT VIEW 9-1
What Type Of Reports Do You Need To Create? 9-2
Data Analytics 9-2
What Is A Visualization? 9-3
Understanding Tables In The Report View 9-3
Report View Workspace 9-3
Visualizations Panel 9-5
Field Well Panel 9-6
Fields Panel 9-7
Exercise 9.1: Modify The Report Data File 9-8
Table Visualization Options 9-10
Exercise 9.2: Create A Customer List Report 9-10

Aggregations ... 9-11
Exercise 9.3: Add A Field To An Existing Table Visualization ... 9-12
How To Change The Summary Type ... 9-13
Exercise 9.4: Use Quick Calc ... 9-13
Exercise 9.5: Create A Table Using A Hierarchy ... 9-14
Conditional Formatting ... 9-14
Exercise 9.6: Apply Conditional Formatting To Cells ... 9-15

FILTER AND SORT DATA IN A REPORT ... 10-1
Filters Section ... 10-2
Filter Options ... 10-2
Exercise 10.1: Create Visual Level Filters ... 10-4
Advanced Filter Options ... 10-4
Date Hierarchy Fields ... 10-6
Exercise 10.2: Create A Date Filter ... 10-6
Exercise 10.3: Create A Date Range Filter ... 10-6
Exercise 10.4: Create A Year Filter ... 10-7
Sorting The Data Displayed In A Table Visualization ... 10-8
Using Date Table Fields To Filter Data ... 10-8
Exercise 10.5: Create A Table Visualization Using Fields From Multiple Data Tables ... 10-8
Exercise 10.6: Use Hierarchy Fields To Filter Data ... 10-9
Exercise 10.7: Add Another Visualization To The Page ... 10-9
Add An Image To The Page ... 10-10
Numeric Filter Options ... 10-10
Exercise 10.8: Create Table Level Filters ... 10-11
Advanced Filters For Text Fields ... 10-12
Exercise 10.9: Use The Text Field Advanced Filter Options ... 10-12
Exercise 10.10: Use A Calculated Column To Filter Records ... 10-13
Exercise 10.11: Use The OR Operator To Filter Records ... 10-13
Exercise 10.12: Create A Page Level Filter ... 10-14
Exercise 10.13: Create A Report Level Filter ... 10-14
Exercise 10.14: Use The Power BI Template Options ... 10-15

TABLE VISUALIZATIONS ... 11-1
Visualization Formatting Options ... 11-2
Page Formatting Options ... 11-2
Page Information Options ... 11-2
Page Size Options ... 11-2
Page Background Options ... 11-3
Table Formatting Options ... 11-3
General Options ... 11-3
Table Style Options ... 11-4
Grid Options ... 11-4
Column And Row Headers Options ... 11-5
Values Options ... 11-5
Total Options ... 11-5
Title Options ... 11-6
Background Options ... 11-6
Lock Aspect Option ... 11-6
Border Options ... 11-6
Formatting Options For Other Page Elements ... 11-6
Exercise 11.1: Apply Formatting Options To A Table ... 11-8
Other Table Types ... 11-8
Matrix Table Formatting Options ... 11-9
Exercise 11.2: Create A Row Matrix Table ... 11-10
Exercise 11.3: Summarize The Customer Orders By Sales Rep ... 11-11
Adding A Count Field ... 11-11
Exercise 11.4: Add Totals To The Matrix Table ... 11-11
Exercise 11.5: Create A Column Matrix Table ... 11-12
Exercise 11.6: Create A Row And Column Matrix Table ... 11-13
Multi-Row Card Table ... 11-14
Exercise 11.7: Create A Multi-Row Card Table ... 11-15

Cards ... 11-15
Card Formatting Options ... 11-15
Exercise 11.8: Use A Card To Display The Total Order Amount ... 11-16
Create A Card With A Filter ... 11-16

INTRODUCTION TO CHARTS ... 12-1
Creating Charts ... 12-2
Selecting A Chart Type ... 12-5
Chart Formatting Options ... 12-7
Exercise 12.1: Create A Basic Bar Chart ... 12-11
Using The Color Saturation Option ... 12-12
Exercise 12.2: Apply Formatting To A Chart ... 12-12
Exercise 12.3: Sort The Data On A Chart ... 12-14
Exercise 12.4: Change The Data Displayed On A Chart ... 12-14
Exercise 12.5: Change The Colors On Bar And Column Charts ... 12-15
Exercise 12.6: Create Chart Level Filters ... 12-15
Create The Page Level Filter ... 12-16
Use The Categorical Option To Load More Data ... 12-17
Exercise 12.7: Load Data While Scrolling ... 12-17
Exercise 12.8: How To Customize Tooltips ... 12-18
Exercise 12.9: Export Chart Data ... 12-18

CHARTS AND INTERACTIVE OPTIONS ... 13-1
Analytics Panel ... 13-2
Constant Line Options ... 13-2
Min, Max, Average, Median And Percentile Reference Line Options ... 13-3
Visual Tools ... 13-3
Exercise 13.1: Add Drill Down Functionality To A Chart ... 13-6
Create The Chart ... 13-7
Use The Drill Down Functionality ... 13-7
Exercise 13.2: Create A Line Chart ... 13-9
Exercise 13.3: Create A Line Chart With Two Series Of Data ... 13-9
Exercise 13.4: Drill Down On A Line Chart ... 13-10
Exercise 13.5: Create An Area Chart ... 13-11
Scatter Charts ... 13-12
Scatter And Bubble Chart Analytics Options ... 13-13
Exercise 13.6: Create A Scatter Chart ... 13-15
Exercise 13.7: Create A Scatter Chart With Drill Down Functionality ... 13-15
Exercise 13.8: Another Way To Display Drill Down Data On A Scatter Chart ... 13-16
Bubble Charts ... 13-16
Exercise 13.9: Create A Bubble Chart ... 13-16
Exercise 13.10: Add A Play Axis To A Bubble Chart ... 13-17
Exercise 13.11: Create A Stacked Column Chart ... 13-18
Exercise 13.12: Filter Chart Data With Parameters ... 13-19
Create The Month Parameter ... 13-19
Create The Filter ... 13-19
Create The Relationship For The Parameter Orders Table ... 13-20
Create The Chart ... 13-20
Exercise 13.13: Import More Data ... 13-21
Modify The Balance Sheet Table ... 13-21
Modify The Financial Data Table ... 13-21
Modify The Sales vs Market Growth Table ... 13-22
Multiple Series Of Data Formatting Options ... 13-22
Exercise 13.14: Display Multiple Series Of Data In Percent Format ... 13-24
Create The Percent Calculations ... 13-24
Exercise 13.15: Display Two Series Of Data On An Area Chart ... 13-25
Exercise 13.16: Display Homes For Sale Data On A Bubble Chart ... 13-26
Exercise 13.17: Display Balance Sheet Data On A Stacked Column Chart ... 13-27
Fix The Month Order ... 13-27
Combined Line Charts ... 13-28
Line And Column Chart Formatting Options ... 13-29

Exercise 13.18: Create A Line And Stacked Column Chart 13-30
Exercise 13.19: Create A Line And Clustered Column Chart 13-31

CHARTS, MAPS AND CUSTOM VISUALS 14-1
Pie Charts 14-2
Exercise 14.1: Create A Pie Chart To Display A Count Of Orders By Customer Type 14-2
How Pie Charts Are Sorted 14-3
Exercise 14.2: Use A Hierarchy Field To Create A Pie Chart 14-3
Handling Negative Values In Pie, Donut And Funnel Charts 14-4
Exercise 14.3: Create A Donut Chart 14-5
Exercise 14.4: Create A Funnel Chart 14-7
Exercise 14.5: Create A Waterfall Chart 14-7
Exercise 14.6: Create A Waterfall Chart Using Negative Values 14-8
Adding Drill Down Functionality To A Waterfall Chart 14-9
Exercise 14.7: Create A Gauge Chart 14-11
Exercise 14.8: Create A Tree Map 14-12
KPI's 14-13
KPI Chart Formatting Options 14-14
Exercise 14.9: Create A KPI Chart 14-15
Maps 14-15
How Maps Work In Power BI Desktop 14-16
Geographical Information 14-16
Exercise 14.10: Create A Basic Map 14-17
Exercise 14.11: Filter Data On A Map 14-18
Creating Maps That Display More Than One Series Of Data 14-18
Exercise 14.12: Add A Legend And Highlighting To A Map 14-18
Exercise 14.13: Add Drill Down Functionality To A Map 14-18
Exercise 14.14: Create A Map Using Coordinates 14-19
Exercise 14.15: Create A Filled Map Chart 14-20
Exercise 14.16: Create A Cross Filter Chart Using A Map 14-20
Shape Map 14-21
Using Custom Maps 14-22
Custom Visuals 14-22
How To Download A Custom Visual File 14-22
How To Install A Custom Visual 14-23
Gantt Charts 14-23
Exercise 14.17: Create A Gantt Chart 14-24
Box And Whisker Charts 14-25
Exercise 14.18: Create A Stock Chart 14-26
Radar Charts 14-27
Exercise 14.19: Create A Radar Chart 14-28

CREATING AND USING SLICERS 15-1
Slicers 15-2
Slicer Formatting Options 15-2
Exercise 15.1: Create A Year Slicer 15-4
Format The Slicer 15-4
Slicer Options 15-4
Exercise 15.2: Using More Than One Slicer 15-4
Exercise 15.3: Use Multiple Slicers With A Matrix Table 15-5
Create And Customize Slicers 15-6
Exercise 15.4: Add A Slicer To A Chart 15-8
Exercise 15.5: Use Two Slicers With Two Tables 15-8
Exercise 15.6: Use Bar And Pie Charts As Slicers 15-9
Use A Bar Chart As A Slicer 15-9
Use A Stacked Column Chart As A Slicer 15-10
Use A Pie Chart As A Slicer 15-11
Detach A Visual From A Slicer 15-11
Exercise 15.7: Detach A Visual From A Slicer 15-11
Highlighting Data 15-12
Exercise 15.8: Highlight A Chart Using The Legend 15-12

Exercise 15.9: Use One Chart To Highlight Data In Another Chart 15-13
Create A Pie Chart 15-13
Create A Column Chart 15-14
Highlight Data Displayed On The Column Chart Using The Pie Chart 15-14
Exercise 15.10: Highlight Data In A Bubble Chart 15-15
Exercise 15.11: Display Sales Reps By Total Order Amount 15-16
Create A Year Slicer 15-16
Timelines 15-17
Exercise 15.12: Use The Timeline Custom Visual 15-17
Add The Timeline Visual To The Page 15-18

GETTING STARTED WITH POWER BI DESKTOP

After reading this chapter and completing the exercises you will:

- ☑ Know what Power BI Desktop can be used for
- ☑ Understand the difference between the 32 and 64-bit versions of Power BI Desktop
- ☑ Have downloaded the practice files used in this book
- ☑ Understand terms related to Power BI Desktop
- ☑ Have learned about the Options dialog box, which is used to customize Power BI Desktop

CHAPTER 1

Welcome To Power BI Desktop!

Microsoft created a set of tools called Power BI Tools for Excel. This toolset includes Power Pivot, Power Query, Power View and Power Map. Power BI Desktop has the functionality of all of these Excel tools, in one interface. If you have used any of these tools for Excel, Power BI Desktop will be familiar. Power BI Desktop is a free stand alone software package, which means that you do not have to have Excel to use it.

Power BI Desktop has functionality that Excel does not have, including, creating multi dimensional reports, table support for more than one million rows of data, using data from more than one data source in the same report file and the ability to automate the process of cleaning the data. Additionally, Excel features like slicers and conditional formatting are available in Power BI Desktop.

While BI enterprise solutions have their place, it is easy for them to become outdated quickly because business needs change, and much of this ad-hoc analysis is currently being created in Excel, using static data. To aid in the various types of analysis that needs to be performed, Power BI Desktop is available. This software allows more people in a company to perform Business Intelligence analysis tasks. Microsoft is raising the Business Intelligence bar with its Power BI Desktop and Power BI software. These tools can be used as part of the decision making process.

While "Desktop" is in the name of the software, the reports that are created can be viewed on smart phones, iOS and Android tablets and in Windows. Power BI Desktop can also connect to a vast and growing set of data sources, including popular cloud services like Google Analytics™.

Sit back and lets get started!

How This Book Is Organized

This book is a visual guide that has over 730 illustrations that practically eliminates the guess work. I don't know about you, but it can be frustrating when you need to emulate something that you have "read" is possible, for a software package to do, and you try it on your own and it doesn't work! It is at that very moment that you realize how helpful it would be to have step-by-step instructions.

Learning tips and shortcuts will let you work faster and smarter. The more that you know about Power BI Desktop, the easier your day to day data analysis experiences will be, which will make you more productive.

The order that the topics are covered in this book, is not an accident on my part. They are in the order that I think makes the most sense, from a data flow perspective to learn them in, whether or not you have a need to use all of the components.

To get the most out of this book, it is not advised that you skip around. The first reason is because some of the files used in later chapters are created in earlier exercises. Working through the exercises in the order that they are presented will provide a better understanding of the concepts, because you can see first hand what Power BI Desktop is capable of and understanding the hand off, if you will, from one component to another.

The other reason skipping around in the book is not a good idea is that a topic or option may have been covered in more detail earlier in the book. If you decide to skip around and cannot complete an exercise because there is something that you do not understand, you will have to go back and find the section that covers the topic that you have a question about. Below is an overview of what is covered in each chapter.

Chapter 1, Getting Started With Power BI Desktop covers information about the software, installing the software and relevant terminology. This chapter also covers the default options that can be set in Power BI Desktop.

Chapter 2, Loading Data Into Power BI Desktop covers the data source options, the options in the External section of the Home tab. Discovering and importing data is also covered.

Chapter 3, Getting Started With The Query Editor covers the basics of using the Query Editor.

Chapter 4, Creating Filters, Custom Columns And Formulas covers using the Query Editor to create formulas to add data to a table, creating filters for different data types. Creating custom calculations is also covered.

Chapter 5, Using The Query Editor To Transform Data picks up where Chapter 3 left off. The options on the Transform, Add Column and View tabs on the Query Editor are covered.

Chapter 6, Using The Query Editor To Mashup Data covers the merge, append, grouping and summarize options.

Chapter 7, Using The Relationships View covers explaining relationships and the data model, including their importance in Power BI Desktop.

Chapter 8, Using The Data View covers the options on the Data view and the Modeling tab. Creating a new table and formatting data that will be displayed on a visualization are also covered.

Chapter 9, Getting Started With The Report View covers options on the Home tab that are for the Report view. The Fields panel, Visualizations panel, creating table visualizations and applying conditional formatting to table visualizations are also covered.

Chapter 10, Filter And Sort Data In A Report covers the Visual, Page and Report level filter options. Creating filters and sorting data in a table report is also covered.

Chapter 11, Table Visualizations covers table visualizations formatting options, creating matrix, multi-row card and card table visualizations.

Chapter 12, Introduction To Charts covers creating and modifying bar and column charts, creating filters for charts and exporting chart data.

Chapter 13, Charts And Interactive Options covers the Analytics panel, creating Scatter, Bubble and Line charts. Drill down functionality and using parameters to filter data displayed on a chart is also covered.

Chapter 14, Charts, Maps And Custom Visuals covers creating a chart that uses a KPI and several types of map charts. Cross filtering functionality and using Custom Visuals is also covered.

Chapter 15, Creating And Using Slicers covers creating, customizing and using slicers.

Objectives

An overall objective of this book is to enhance your knowledge of Power BI Desktop. This book provides the skills required to create analysis solutions efficiently. While the process may be considered technical or "geeky", I explain the terms and concepts in a manner that is hopefully easy to understand. After completing the exercises in this book, you will be able to perform the following tasks and more:

- ☑ Learn how to discover data needed for analysis and reports
- ☑ Load data from a variety of sources into the data model
- ☑ Use the Query Editor to transform data
- ☑ Create new tables of data in Power BI Desktop
- ☑ Create hierarchies, use date tables and summarize data
- ☑ Create reports that use a variety of visualization types

Conventions Used In This Book

I designed the following conventions to make it easier for you to follow the instructions in this book.

- ☑ The `Courier font` is used to indicate what you should type.
- ☑ **Drag** means to press and hold down the left mouse button while moving the mouse.
- ☑ **Click** means to press the left mouse button once, then release it immediately.
- ☑ **Right-click** means to press the right mouse button once, which will open a shortcut menu.
- ☑ Click **OK** means to click the OK button on the dialog box.
- ☑ Press **Enter** means to press the Enter key on your keyboard.
- ☑ **SMALL CAPS** are used to indicate an option to click on or to bring something to your attention.
- ☑ [Text in brackets] references a section, table or figure, that has more information about the topic being discussed. If the reference is in a different chapter, the chapter number is included, like this: [See Chapter 2, Update Options]
- ☑ Some toolbars or ribbons have a lot of options. When displayed, it can be hard to see each option on the toolbar or ribbon. When that is the case, I split the toolbar into two figures, so that it is easier to see all of the options.

- ☑ This icon indicates a shortcut or another way to complete the task that is being discussed. It can also indicate a tip or additional information about the topic that is being discussed.
- ☑ This icon indicates a warning, like a feature that has been removed or information that you need to be aware of. This icon can also represent what I call a quirk, meaning a feature that did not work as I expected it to.
- ☑ This icon indicates that some of the screen shot has been removed because it does not provide any value.
- ☑ When you see the phrase "**YOU SHOULD HAVE THE OPTIONS SHOWN IN FIGURE X-X**", or something similar in the exercises, check to make sure that your screen does look like the figure. If it does, continue with the next set of instructions. If your screen does not look like the figure, redo the steps that you just completed so that your screen does match the figure. Not doing so may cause problems when trying to complete exercises later in the book.
- ☑ Many of the dialog boxes in Power BI Desktop have OK, Cancel and Help buttons. Viewing these buttons on all of the figures adds no value, so for the most part, they are not shown.
- ☑ The section heading **EXERCISE X.Y:** (where X equals the chapter number and Y equals the exercise number) represents exercises that have step-by-step instructions that you should complete. You will also see sections that have step-by-step instructions that are not an exercise. They are not meant to be completed as you go through the book. They are for future reference, which is indicated.
- ☑ **HOME TAB ⇒ GET DATA ⇒ EXCEL**, means to click on the **HOME** tab in Power BI Desktop, then click the Get Data button, then select the Excel option, shown in Figure 1-1.

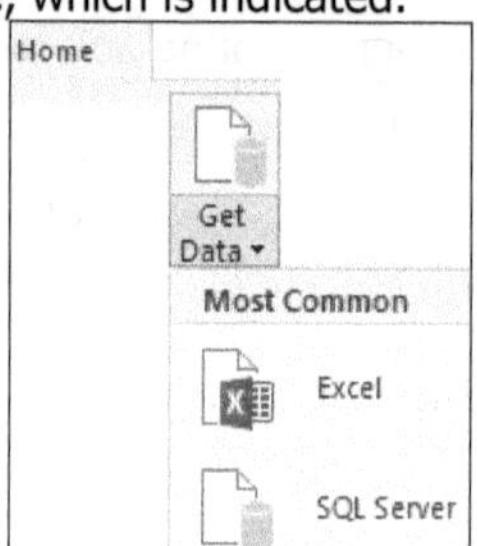

Figure 1-1 Navigation technique

- ☑ "E2.4 File Name" is the file naming convention for many of the files that you will create. E2.4 stands for Chapter 2, Exercise 4. You may consider some of the file names long. I did this on purpose, so that it will be easier to know what topic the file covers. If you do not want to type the entire file name, type E2.4, as the file name. This will still let you find the correct files when needed.

Assumptions

Yes, I know one should never assume anything, but the following assumptions have been made. It is assumed that . . .

- ☑ You know that this book is written from the perspective that you have little to no experience with Power BI Desktop.
- ☑ You know that the operating system used to write this book is Windows 8.1. If you are using a different version of Windows, some of the screen shots may have a slightly different look.
- ☑ You know to click OK or the appropriate button to close a dialog box and know to save the changes (to the file) before going to the next section or exercise. Instructions like these are omitted, as much as possible.
- ☑ When you see <smile>, you know that signifies my attempt of adding humor to the learning process.
- ☑ You know that the phrase "end user" refers to the person that will use the pivot tables that you create. If you will create and use the reports, in the context of this book, you are also the end user.
- ☑ You know that when I use the words "field" and "column", that they are one in the same. These words are interchangeable because the data is in a field in the database that you import data from and then it's called a column in Power BI Desktop.
- ☑ You know that I used the words "query" and "table" interchangeably, as they both refer to data.
- ☑ You know that I use the words "report", "visual" and "visualization" interchangeably. Why? Because I am from the old school, where the only word used to describe data presentation was report.
- ☑ You know that the end of each chapter in this book has a summary section. In addition to providing a recap of the topics covered, some summaries contain new information, like explaining another way to accomplish a task that was already covered. I did this to not interrupt the flow of the chapter.
- ☑ You know that the links (to other web sites) in this book worked when the book went to print and that I have no control over when or if the web site owners change or remove web pages.

☑ You know the difference between the **SAVE** option (saves the file with the same file name) and the **SAVE AS** option (saves the file with a different file name or with the same file name in a different folder). Power BI Desktop has buttons for both of these options on the File tab. [See Figure 1-9]. The Save As button can be added to the **QUICK ACCESS TOOLBAR**, as illustrated in Figure 1-2.

Many exercises instruct you to save an existing file with a new file name. This is when you would use the Save As button. If you want to use the Save As button, but it is not currently displayed on your Quick Access Toolbar, you will learn how to add it at the end of this chapter.

Figure 1-2 Save and Save As options illustrated

Self-Service Business Intelligence

Business Intelligence, is often called BI for short. Even though the concept of business intelligence has been around for over a decade, there are still different schools of thought in the business community on what it is, what it isn't and how it should be implemented. BI is the first topic discussed in this book because it is a primary reason that people use tools like Power Pivot, Tableau and Power BI Desktop. All of these tools allow you to perform some, if not all, of the analysis needed to make business decisions.

BI, in the broad sense, is a collection of technology and applications that are used to gather, store, access and analyze data, often in an enterprise environment. Generally speaking, business intelligence is the process of analyzing data, raw or otherwise and converting the analysis into knowledge. This process is usually used to make business decisions or track business trends and changes. This decision making process requires the raw data to be transformed, so that it can be presented accurately and usually the data is presented in real-time. The typical business intelligence process includes querying, forecasting, data mining, statistical analysis and reporting.

During my corporate IT career, business intelligence solutions were designed and developed by IT people like me. These solutions took months, sometimes years to complete and were often complex. And lets not talk about the cost <smile>. Things are changing, especially for ad-hoc reporting and analysis needs. Self service business intelligence tools, like Power BI Desktop, are making it possible for business people to create their own reports, often with very little or no help from the IT department.

These tools are often used with what is known as "big data" (a process that companies use to store massive amounts of information electronically). Data Scientists, go through the data using these tools to find business insights (also known as discovering data), to find services, products and programs to offer their customers.

BI, especially self-service or personal (do it yourself) business intelligence, is gaining a lot of momentum because companies are looking to bring more decision making tools to their employees. One goal of BI solutions is to bring data from all over the company and place it in what came to be known as a "data warehouse". This repository of data, should be accurate and not redundant. This allows employees at several levels in the company to gain access to data that will help them make more accurate business decisions in a timely manner. And yes, a major goal is to make a company more profitable.

Who Will Benefit From Using Power BI Desktop?

There are several categories of people that can benefit from using Power BI Desktop, as explained below.

DATA ANALYSTS While people that fall into this category may not have this job title, they will use the software to import data needed to create data models, transform data, use DAX as needed to create formulas, create reports and dashboards, either for their own use or for other people to use.

END USERS often benefit from the work of Data Analysts. They tend not to create the reports or dashboards that they use in their decision making process. At most, some end users will create reports, but not import or create data models. People that often fall into this category are managers and executives in the company.

DEVELOPERS create Enterprise BI solutions. People in this category are usually in the IT department. They understand concepts like data warehouses, big data and cubes. People in this category know how to design and create the infrastructure needed to support and maintain the BI initiatives. They can also create any new databases that may be needed. Job titles that are in the category are Programmer and Data Architect.

What Can Power BI Desktop Do?

As stated earlier, Power BI Desktop has the Excel Power Tools combined in one interface. The goal of this section is to explain Power BI Desktop functionality and which component is used to complete the task. You can use this section as a pseudo project plan for each visualization that you need to create.

Step 1: Find The Data

Each visualization needs data. In this step you need to find, connect to, clean and transform the data as needed. If you know that the data is clean and in the right layout, you may be able to skip parts of this step.

Step 2: Load The Data To The Data Model

The data should be clean by the time you get to this step. The goal of this step is to get the data ready for the creation of the visualization. Calculations that are needed for the visualization (charts or maps for example) are created in this step.

Step 3: Create The Reports Or Dashboards

Power BI Desktop offers a wide variety of visualization options that can be used to create and enhance a report, including charts, maps and slicers. There are also custom visualizations that you can use.

Step 4: Share The Data

Depending on the environment, this step may or may not be needed. This step can be used to load the visualization to the cloud or to a server, so that other people can view and use it. In Power BI Desktop, this functionality is known as **PUBLISHING DATA**. Reports can be used on a tablet that has Windows 8.1 or higher, if the Power BI App for Windows is installed.

What Is The Difference Between The 32 And 64-Bit Versions Of Power BI Desktop?
① If you know that you will be working with large data sets (millions of records in a table), you should consider installing the 64-bit version of Power BI Desktop.
② The 32 and 64 bit version can be installed on a computer that has a 64 bit processor.

Exercise 1.1: Download And Install Power BI Desktop

If you have not already installed Power BI Desktop, follow the steps in this exercise.

Minimum Prerequisites To Install The Software
To install Power BI Desktop, your computer needs to have the following installed: Internet Explorer 10 or higher, Windows 7 or higher or Windows Server 2008 R2 or higher.

Download The Software

If you have Microsoft Office installed, you should install the same version (32 or 64 bit) of Power BI Desktop, especially if you will be importing Excel .xls files or Access databases, because both of these file types use the Access database engine. The Access database engine bit version has to be the same as the Power BI Desktop bit version.

1. Go to https://www.microsoft.com/en-us/download/details.aspx?id=45331 This link has the 32 and 64 bit versions, as shown below in Figure 1-3.

2. Click the **DOWNLOAD** button ⇒

   Check one of the options shown in Figure 1-3.

   The first file shown in the figure is the 32-bit version ⇒ Click Next.

Choose the download you want

☐ File Name	Size
☐ PBIDesktop.msi	74.8 MB
☑ PBIDesktop_x64.msi	84.1 MB

Download Summary
1. PBIDesktop_x64.msi
Total Size: 84.1 MB

Figure 1-3 File options to select from

3. On the Opening dialog box, click the Save File button and save the file to your hard drive. The most convenient location to save the file to is the desktop <no pun intended>, so that it is easy to find when you install the software. Once the installation is complete, you can move the file to another location or delete it.

Install The Software

1. Double-click on the file that you downloaded to install the software. Follow the instructions.

2. When the installation is complete, double-click on the yellow Power BI Desktop icon. If you checked the **LAUNCH MICROSOFT POWER BI DESKTOP OPTION** on the last screen of the installation dialog box, the software will automatically open, when the installation is completed. You should see the workspace shown in Figure 1-4.

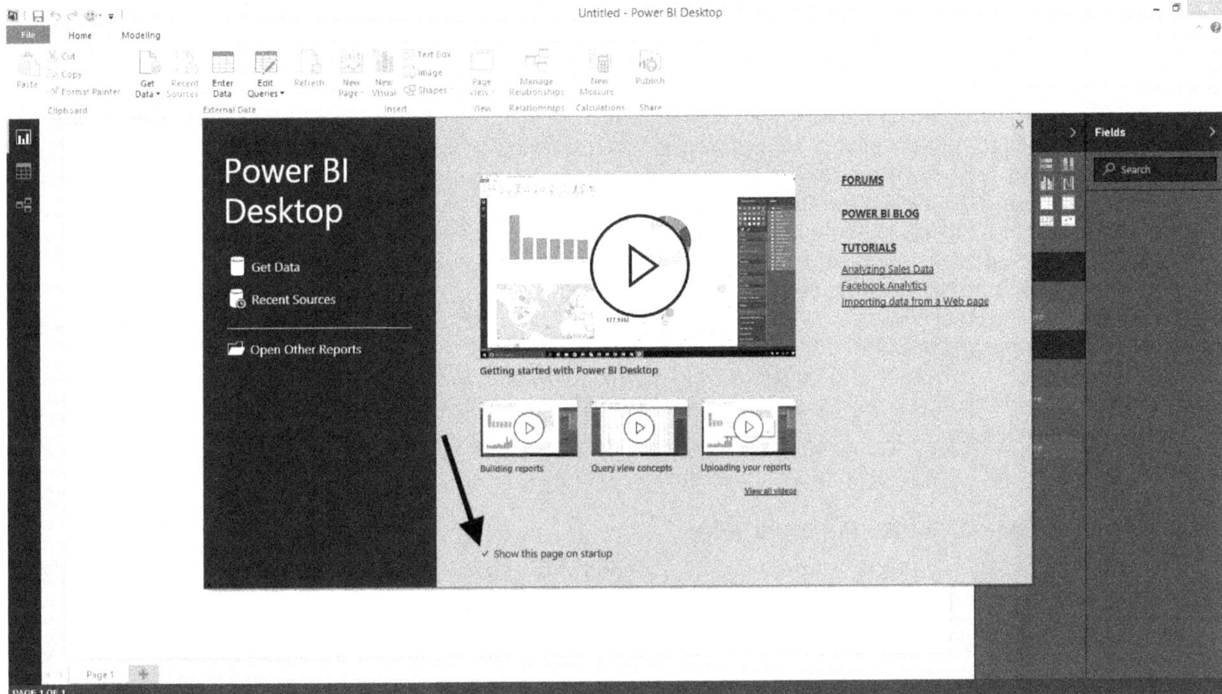

Figure 1-4 Power BI Desktop workspace

3. If you do not want to see the yellow splash screen every time you open the software, clear the check mark illustrated above in Figure 1-4.

Unlike most splash screens, this one lets you get to work right away. The **GET DATA OPTION**, opens a new report file and displays the Get Data dialog box. [See Chapter 2, Figure 2-3]

Splash Screen Warning
When I first started using Power BI Desktop, the splash screen displayed the option illustrated above in Figure 1-4, to not display the splash screen. This option is only available now, if you have a Power BI account and log in. Why this change was made is beyond me.

The **RECENT SOURCES OPTION** displays a list of data sources that you have already connected to. You can select from this list to import more data.

Once you have saved report files, the most recent four, including pinned reports, will be displayed below the Recent Sources option on the splash screen. This is useful when you need to open an existing file. By default, pinned files are displayed here first, whether or not they were recently used. If there is a file that you are not currently using, you can unpin it from this list.

Files that are displayed below the Recent Sources list have the shortcut menu shown in Figure 1-5. The options are explained in Chapter 2, Table 2-3.

Open
Copy path to clipboard
Unpin from list
Remove from list
Clear unpinned items

Figure 1-5 Recent files shortcut menu

The **OPEN OTHER REPORTS OPTION** displays the last folder that you saved a report file to. This lets you select the file that you need.

Support

There are several online tools that you can use to get help and learn more about Power BI Desktop. They are listed below.

① The **FORUM** is used to post questions, get answers and learn how other people are using the software. The forum is also a great way to keep current on the latest trends and for getting ideas on how to enhance the reports that you need to create. The link is http://community.powerbi.com [Select the Desktop section]

② **BLOG** In addition to information about new features in the software, this blog also provides information on the monthly software updates. The posts for the monthly updates, also has videos that explain new and updated features. The link is https://powerbi.microsoft.com/en-us/blog

③ **DOCUMENTATION** This tool is like an online help file. It contains descriptions of features, instructions on how to use features and sample practice files. Click on the question mark button in the upper right corner of the Power BI Desktop workspace to display the documentation. The link below also displays the documentation. https://powerbi.microsoft.com/en-us/documentation/powerbi-desktop-get-the-desktop/

④ The **SPLASH SCREEN** shown earlier in Figure 1-4 has links to download the latest version, view the blog, forums and tutorials.

Exercise 1.2: Create A Folder For Your Files

You will create and modify several files in this book. It is a good idea to store all of them in the same folder on your computer, so that you can find them easily. Many of the topics discussed in this book have step-by-step exercises. If you want to follow along, you can download the practice files used in this book.

1. To obtain the files used in this book, send an email to bidesktop@tolanapublishing.com. If you do not receive an email in a few minutes with the subject line Power BI Desktop Book Files, check the spam folder in your email software. When you receive the email, follow the steps below.

2. Open Windows Explorer ⇒ Right-click on the C drive ⇒ New ⇒ Folder. Type `BI Desktop Book` as the folder name. I will refer to this folder as **YOUR FOLDER** throughout this book.

Using A Different Drive Letter
Using a different drive letter will cause problems completing some exercises in this book. The path to files is saved in the Power BI Desktop files that you will create. If you absolutely, positively, cannot use the C drive, you will have to manually change the path in some files on the Advanced Query Editor or Data Sources Settings dialog box in Power BI Desktop, if you see a message like the one shown in Figure 1-6.

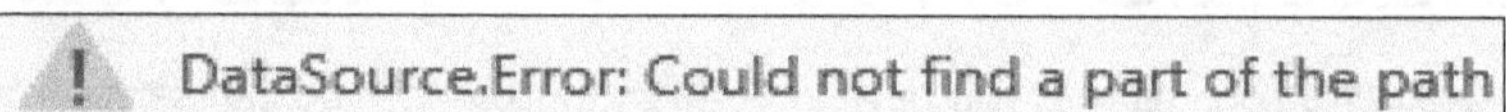

Figure 1-6 File not found message

3. From the web page listed in the email that you received, and download the zip file into your folder ⇒
Once the zip file is downloaded, extract the files to your folder.

   Your folder structure should look like the one shown in Figure 1-7.

Figure 1-7 BI Desktop Book folder structure

Vol 5 Links.txt File
This file is in the zip file that you just downloaded. When you go through this book, there are links that you may need to type in. In case you do not want to type them in, you can copy and paste them from this file into your web browser. You're welcome! <smile>

Power BI Desktop Software Updates

Many software companies have changed to a faster update release schedule for some of their software titles. Power BI Desktop falls into this category. The core functionality of this software does not change frequently. A large portion of the updates are new features, modifications to existing functionality or name changes of existing options.

One of my favorite features of Power BI Desktop is that an updated version (interface changes, new features and bug fixes) is released monthly. For users, that is great. For authors that write books based on the software, the frequent updating presents a problem. By the time you read this book, or any book on Power BI Desktop for that matter, some parts of the book will be out of date. Sadly, there isn't anything that I can do about this, other then what I am doing right now, and that is to be up front about the situation.

Monthly Update Files
I tend to keep the previous two installation update files, in case the current one has a problem that interferes with what I am working on. I do this because I couldn't not find an archive of the prior months update files on the powerbi.com web site.

Database Terminology

Below are key terms that you should understand about databases in order to work with Power BI Desktop efficiently.

Field A field contains one piece of information and is stored in a record. Examples of fields include customer name and order amount. A column in a Power BI Desktop query/table is the same as a field in a database.

Record A record has one or more fields. Each of the fields in a record are related. A record looks like a row of data in a spreadsheet.

Table A table is stored in a database and is a collection of records. Most databases have more than one table. Tables are linked on fields. Tables may remind you of a spreadsheet, because SQL databases have rows and columns. Each table contains information about a specific topic. For example, a well designed customer table would only contain information about customers. The customer table would not contain information about products.

Primary Key is a unique identifier for each row of data in the table. Primary keys are usually numeric and system generated, sequentially. They are usually used to create relationships (links) between tables.

Database A database is a collection of information that is stored in one or more tables, in the database. It is important to note that there are different types of physical database structures.

Relational Database A relational database is a collection of **RELATED** information that is stored in one or more tables in the database.

Relationship A relationship is a connection between two tables. It is how two or more tables are joined (linked). Tables can be joined when they have at least one field in each table, that has the same value. Tables can have more than one relationship. For example, an invoice table can be joined to a products table because each invoice will have at least one item from the products table.

Data Dictionary A data dictionary contains detailed information about the database and includes the following types of information: Database, table and view names, field names, field types, field sizes, indexes and related files. A data dictionary can be handwritten or typed. It can also be generated by some database software packages. When using Power BI Desktop, this document or file is very helpful if you are not familiar with the data.

Data Concepts

Before you go any further, there are some terms that you need to understand to get a better idea of how Power BI Desktop can aid in the decision making process, display trends in data and much more. These terms will also help you start to understand how powerful Power BI Desktop is. These are terms that you may have heard before, but are not exactly sure what they mean. The goal of this section is to briefly explain them and their relationship to Power BI Desktop.

Aggregation Is a way to summarize or group data.

Dashboards The intended goal is to display large amounts of data in a clear, consolidated and meaningful way. Dashboards usually contain two or more visuals on the same page. A dashboard should allow the person viewing it to see the information at a glance. Sadly, out in the workplace, you will see dashboards that have animation and gauges that are hard to figure out what the data represents. Try not to join this group <smile>.

Data Analysis Expressions (DAX) Is a programming language that Power BI Desktop supports. It contains a collection of functions that are used to create formulas. These formulas are used to manipulate data that is stored in tables, in the data model.

Data Refresh This feature is used to copy (re-import) the most recent version of data into the tables in Power BI Desktop, from the original data source.

Data Source A data source is what the data is stored in. Examples of data sources are databases, text files, OLAP cubes and spreadsheets.

Data Source Connection Contains instructions that Power BI Desktop can use to connect to a data source, so that data can be imported into Power BI Desktop.

Structured Query Language (SQL) Is the programming language that is most used to interact with databases. It is used to create and populate tables with data, modify data and retrieve data from a database. This is also known as a **QUERY**. Before you start to frown, the answer is no, you do not have to write SQL code to retrieve the data that you need for the reports that you create in this book. At some point, you may have the need for functionality that Power BI Desktop can't provide, in terms of retrieving data to import. If that is the case, you will have to write code to get the data that you need or get someone in the IT department to write the code to get the data for you.

xVelocity This database engine allows millions of rows of data to be processed quickly because the processing of data in the tables is done in the computers memory, instead of processing data on a hard drive. This engine uses a **COLUMNAR DATABASE** that compresses the data, thus using less space then what would be used for the same amount of data in a different type of database. This is why tables with millions and millions of rows of data can be imported into Power BI Desktop. This is the same data model database that Power Pivot for Excel uses.

Power BI Desktop Concepts

Below are some terms that are used in Power BI Desktop that you should understand.

.pbix This is the file extension for Power BI Desktop report files. This is the file type that is used most. It is the one that you import data into and create reports. It is often referred to as "the file".

.pbit This is the file extension for Power BI Desktop template files. This template files does not work like template files that you may have used in other software. For example, in some other software, if you make and save changes to the template file, you are given the option of updating any file that was created based on the template. The "template" file in Power BI Desktop, does not work like that.

Report is a series of pages (that have charts and tables) and data used in a .pbix file.

Visuals or **Visualizations** are items used to create a report. Examples are tables, images and charts.

Other Power BI Tools

In addition to Power BI Desktop, there are currently two other Power BI tools that are available. They are explained below.

① **POWER BI** (also known as PowerBI.com and Power BI Service) This is a cloud-based solution for sharing data via dashboards, reports and more. It also has functionality built-in to create reports and dashboards, like Power BI Desktop has.

② **POWER BI MOBILE** This is a free set of apps that allow mobile devices to view and interact with reports and dashboards that have been uploaded to PowerBI.com.

Power BI Desktop Workspace

Figure 1-8 shows the Power BI Desktop workspace. Table 1-1 briefly explains the illustrated options. They are covered in more detail throughout this book.

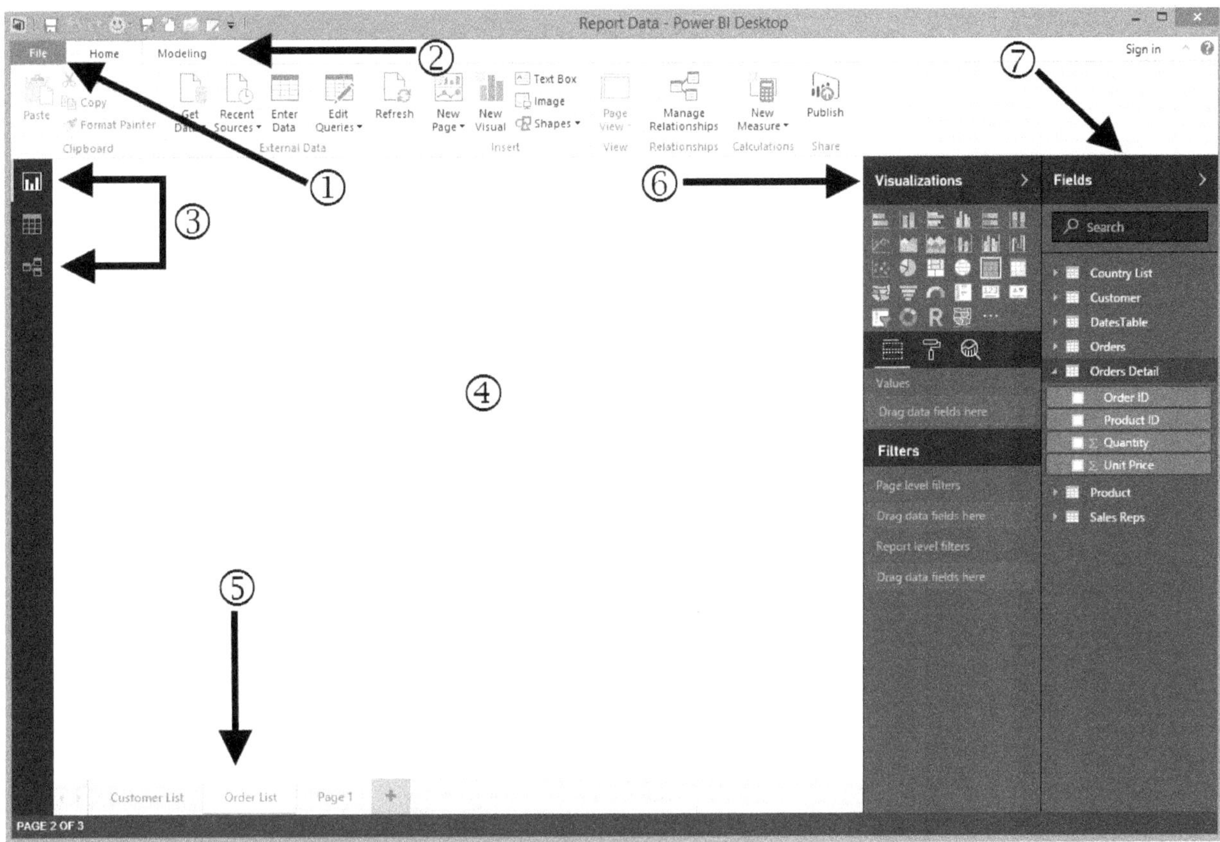

Figure 1-8 Power BI Desktop workspace

Option	Description
①	**FILE TAB** [See File Tab Options]
②	The **POWER BI DESKTOP RIBBON** has options that are used to get and manage data and create reports. The options on the Modeling tab change, depending on the view that is selected.
③	The **VIEW** options are used to switch between the **REPORT VIEW** (the default view when Power BI Desktop is first opened), the **DATA VIEW** and the **RELATIONSHIPS VIEW**. [See Views]
④	The **CANVAS** (the white space) is used to create reports and dashboards.
⑤	The **PAGE OPTIONS** are used to view different pages in the report and add new pages to the report.
⑥	The **VISUALIZATIONS PANEL** has options to select a table or chart style to use to create and modify reports and dashboards. The options in the Field Well section, at the bottom of this panel change, based on the visualization that is selected. This panel is only available when the Report view is selected.
⑦	The **FIELDS PANEL** displays the tables and fields in the data model. This panel is available on the Data and Report views. The fields are used to create reports.

Table 1-1 Workspace options explained

Views

If you have used Excels BI Tools, these views will be familiar. There are three views, as described below.

The **REPORT VIEW** most resembles Power View, in terms of functionality, because it is used to create and view reports.

The **DATA VIEW** most resembles Power Pivot in terms of functionality. It is used to manage the data model.

The **RELATIONSHIPS VIEW** most resembles the Diagram View in Power Pivot, in terms of functionality. It displays the tables in the data model in a graphical layout. It is used to create and manage relationships. Relationships can also be created and managed from the other views.

File Tab Options

Figure 1-9 shows the options on the File tab.

The Import and Export options are explained below.

The **OPTIONS AND SETTINGS** options are covered in Chapter 2. [See Chapter 2, Options Dialog Box and Data Source Settings]

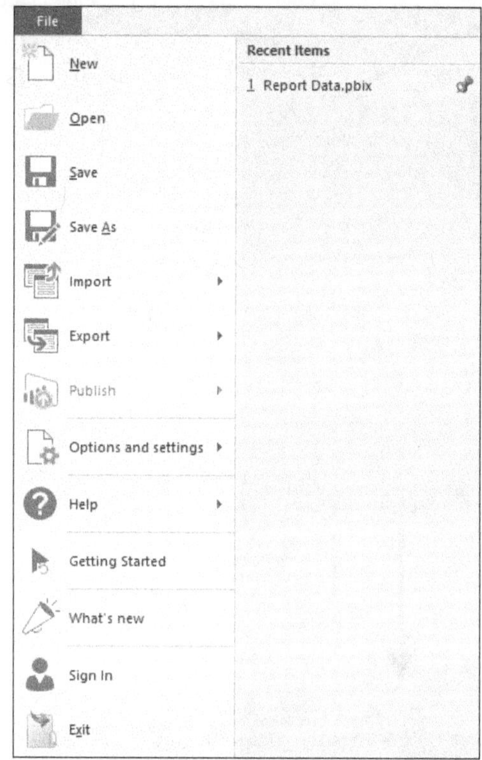

Figure 1-9 File tab options

Import Options

The right side of Figure 1-10 shows the types of files that can be imported.

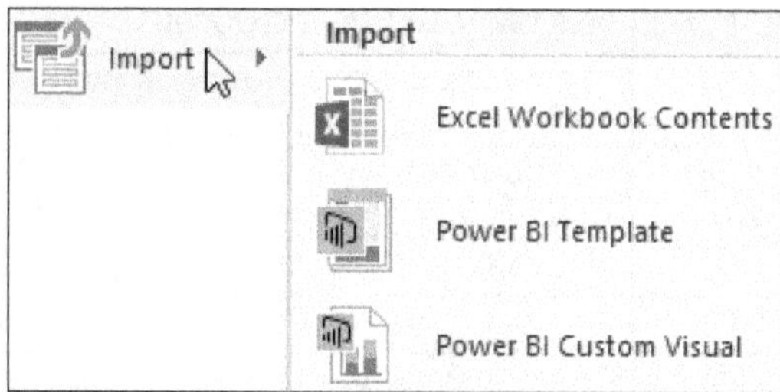

Figure 1-10 Import options

EXCEL WORKBOOK CONTENTS Select this option to import data models (including relationships, KPI's measures and data categories that were created in Power Pivot), Power View reports, queries created in Power Query, linked tables and external data connections.

This option should be helpful if you have created data models in Power Pivot, cleaned the data in Power Query or created visuals in Power View that you want to use in Power BI Desktop.

POWER BI TEMPLATE Select this option to open a **.PBIT** template file. Once opened, save the template file with a new (.pbix) file name. This option makes a copy of the template file (same as using File - Save As). It does not import the contents of the template file into the report file that you have open.

POWER BI CUSTOM VISUAL [See Chapter 14, Custom Visuals]

Export Option

The **POWER BI TEMPLATE** option is used to save the current report file (.pbix) as a template (.pbit) file. This is helpful if you have created a file that has data sources, relationships, DAX formulas, transformations or report layouts already set up, that you need to use as the basis for another report file. An example that comes to mind is creating a template file that has a date table, because many reports are date driven, and parameter fields for tables in the template.

Publish Options

The options shown in Figure 1-11 are used to copy the report file to a location where it can be used (shared) by other people.

Figure 1-11 Publish options

PUBLISH TO POWER BI This option is used to upload the current file to PowerBI.com. Using this option is beyond the scope of this book.

PUBLISH TO PYRAMID ANALYTICS This option is used to publish a report file, that you want to share, to a Pyramid Analytics private cloud server, if you have purchased their service.

Load vs Import Terminology
By default, Power BI Desktop uses the word **LOAD** to reference the process of copying data from one location to another. Other software packages use the word **IMPORT** to reference the same functionality. I use these terms interchangeably.

Options Dialog Box

The options on this dialog box are used to customize the software by selecting the default options for Power BI Desktop (the **GLOBAL** options), and the current file (the **CURRENT FILE** options).

Global Options

As applicable, the options in this section are applied to every report file.

Data Load Options

The global and current file categories shown in Figure 1-12 are used to select the default options. Categories are added from time to time.

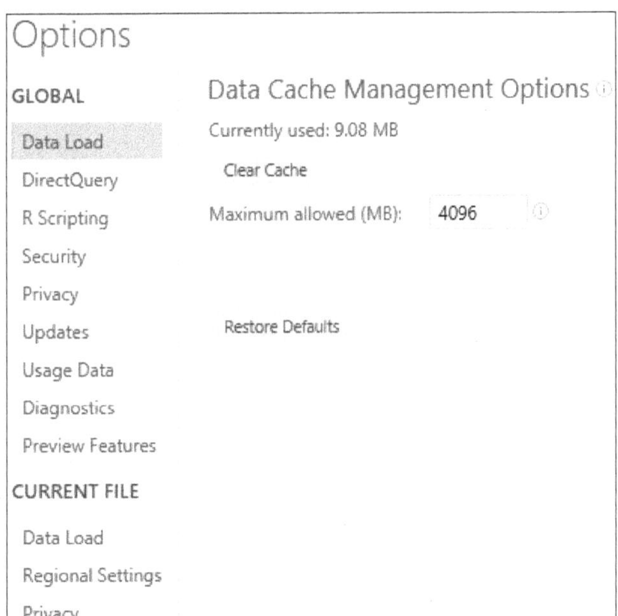

Figure 1-12 Global Data Load options

The **DATA CACHE MANAGEMENT OPTIONS** are used to select the maximum amount of hard drive space to allocate for copies of the query preview results that are stored on the computers hard drive. This feature makes it possible for the queries to load faster.

As shown in Figure 1-12, more than 9 MB has been used. This number grows each time you preview data in the Query Editor. Clear the cache when you are close to the maximum allowed amount.

If a copy or subset of the dataset is stored in the cache, that is what you are viewing, until the cache is cleared or you refresh the data. If you always want to use current data, make the **MAXIMUM ALLOWED** option a smaller number, like 32 MB, which is the smallest amount recognized. If that does not meet you needs, you will have to click the **CLEAR CACHE** button on a regular basis or raise the maximum allowed (MB).

The **DIRECT QUERY OPTION** is used to select whether or not DAX measures are restricted when using the Direct Query options to connect to a data source.

The **R SCRIPTING OPTIONS** are used to select options so that R Scripts can be used in Power BI Desktop.

The **SECURITY OPTIONS** are used to select whether or not:

☑ Approval is needed to create to create native database queries or web previews.
☑ A warning should be displayed when a custom visual is added to a report.

Query Editor Options

The options shown in Figure 1-13 are used to select features that are enabled on the Query Editor. You can also select whether or not the option to create a new parameter is available on data source dialog boxes, like the Web connector [See Chapter 2, Figure 2-5] or an option like the Replace Values transformation option.

If you plan to create parameters, enabling the parameter option will be useful.

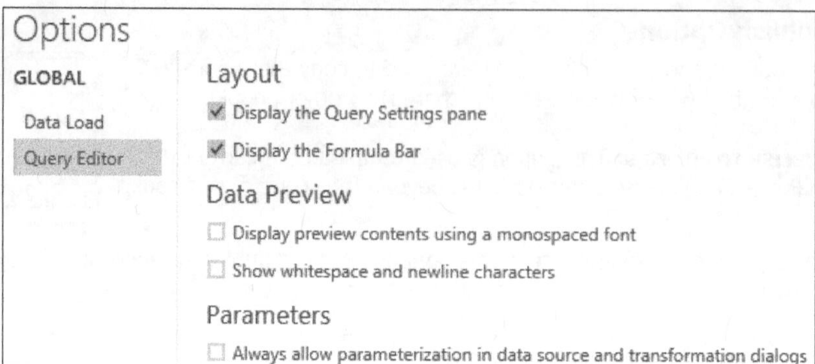

Figure 1-13 Query Editor options

Privacy Options

The global **PRIVACY LEVEL** options shown in Figure 1-14, are used to select whether or not the privacy level settings for each data source are used. The privacy level option selected on this screen overrides the Current File Privacy options, shown later in Figure 1-26.

The **COMBINE DATA ... OPTION** is the default option.

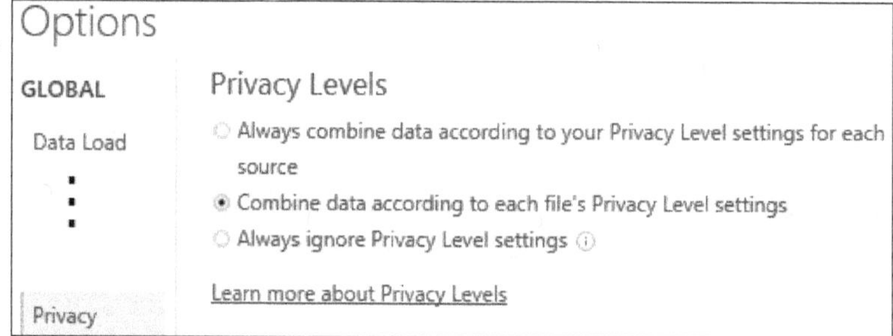

Figure 1-14 Global privacy options

The **UPDATES OPTION**, if checked, will display a message in Power BI Desktop, that lets you know that there is an update for the software. The left side of Figure 1-15 shows the message that will pop up in the Taskbar, when a new version of the software is available.

The link shown on the right side of the figure is displayed in the lower right corner of the Power BI Desktop workspace. Click on either option to download the latest version.

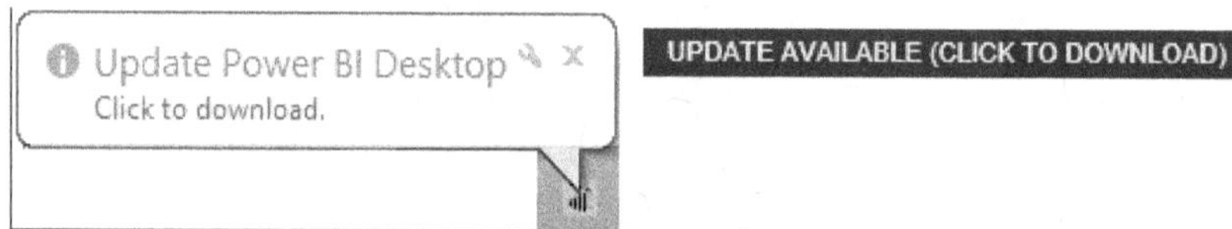

Figure 1-15 Update messages

The **USAGE DATA OPTION**, if checked, will collect information about how you are using Power BI Desktop. The collected information is sent to Microsoft.

The **DIAGNOSTICS OPTION**, if checked, will create a file that logs your actions in Power BI Desktop. This can be helpful if you are having issues with the software, because you can send the trace file to Microsoft, so that they can help resolve the problem. The screen also displays the version of Power BI Desktop that is installed.

The **PREVIEW FEATURES SCREEN**, shown in Figure 1-16, lists features that you can try out. The features on this screen usually change from month to month.

At some point, features on this screen will be released and be part of the Power BI Desktop.

Figure 1-16 Preview Features screen

The first two **AUTO RECOVERY OPTIONS** shown in Figure 1-17, if enabled, will recover your files if Power BI Desktop crashes or if you close the software without saving changes that you made to any file that was open.

The **AUTO RECOVERY FILE LOCATION OPTION** can be changed. This is where the files are stored that can be recovered. I changed this to a folder that I could easily find.

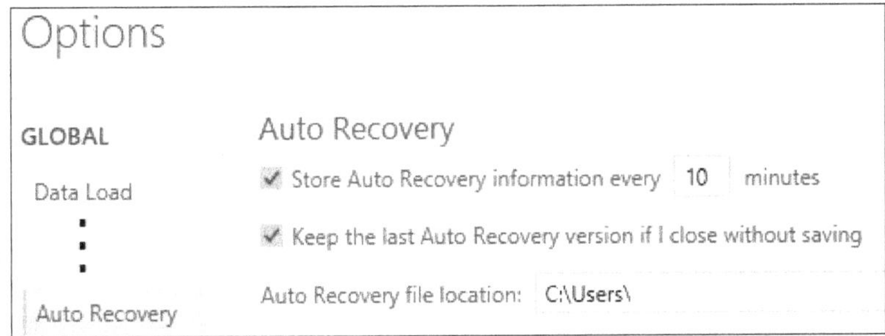

Figure 1-17 Global Auto Recovery options

When either of the scenarios mentioned above happens and you reopen a file, you will see the message shown at the top of Figure 1-18.

Click the **VIEW AUTO RECOVERY BUTTON**, in the upper right corner of the dialog box, to display the dialog box shown in the figure. If you want to recover a file shown, select it, then click the Open button to open the recovery file.

If you click the Close button or click the X on the dialog box, you will see the dialog box shown in Figure 1-19. This lets you select whether or not you want to keep the files that can be recovered and make a decision later about what to do with the files.

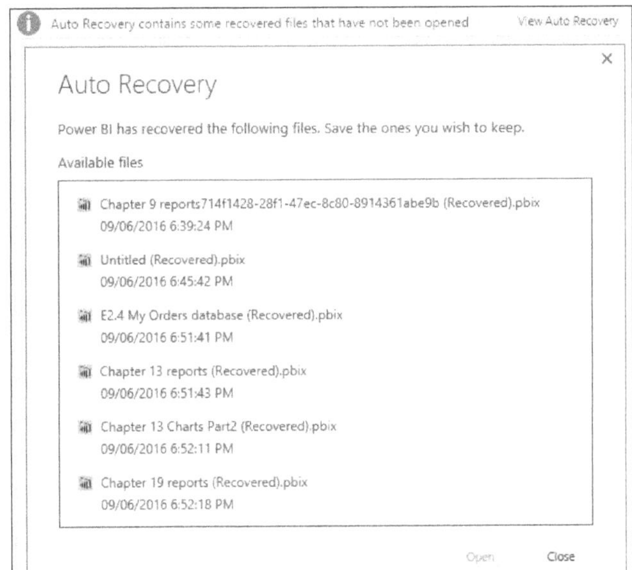

Figure 1-18 Auto recovery messages

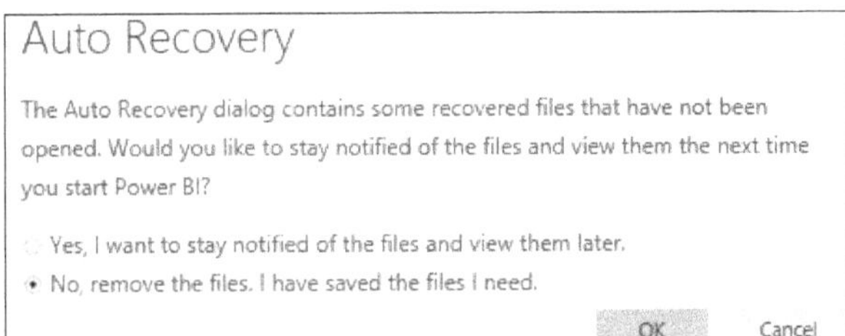

Auto Recovery
The Auto Recovery dialog contains some recovered files that have not been opened. Would you like to stay notified of the files and view them the next time you start Power BI?
Yes, I want to stay notified of the files and view them later.
No, remove the files. I have saved the files I need.
OK
Cancel

Figure 1-19 Options to select what to do with the auto recovery files

When you open Power BI Desktop and you have files that can be recovered, you will see a link called **SHOW RECOVERED FILES** on the splash screen. Clicking on the link will display at least one of the files that can be recovered.

Current File Options

As its name suggests, options in this section are only applied to the file that the Options dialog box was opened from. What is important to know is that these options override the corresponding global options, at the top of the Options dialog box.

If you make changes in this section, you should save the file as soon as you have finished making the changes, so that they will be applied to the file.

Data Load Options

Figure 1-20 shows the current file options, which are explained below.

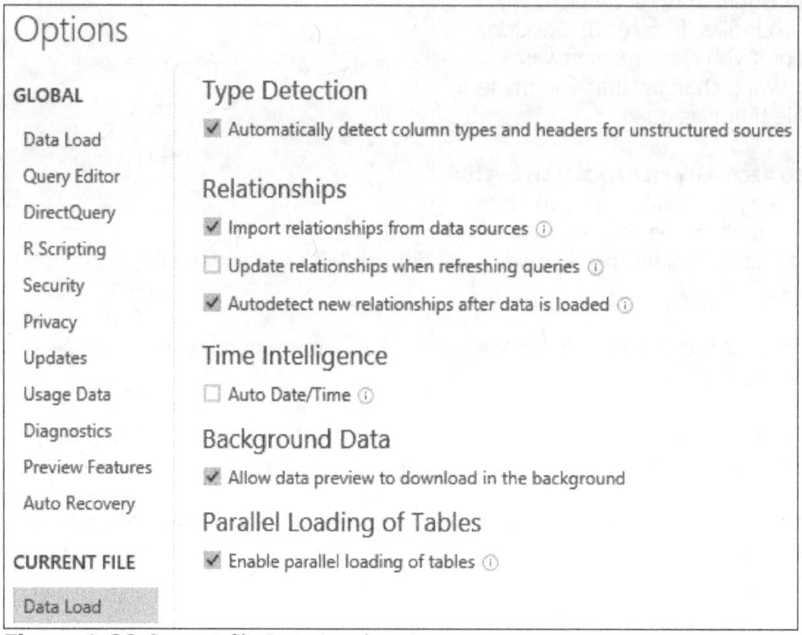

Figure 1-20 Current file Data Load options

① **TYPE DETECTION** [See How Type Detection Works]

② **RELATIONSHIPS** [See Relationships Options]

③ **TIME INTELLIGENCE** If checked, the **AUTO DATE/TIME OPTION** is used to automatically create a hidden date table for each field that has a Date or Date/Time data type. More then likely, you can uncheck this option if you have a date table.

④ **BACKGROUND DATA** By default, this option allows a preview of the data to be downloaded in the background, so that it can be previewed on the Navigator window. Clearing the check mark reduces the amount of data that is processed, which increases performance.

⑤ **PARALLEL LOADING OF TABLES** Checking this option allows more than one table of data to be loaded into Power BI Desktop at the same time. Depending on the amount of data in the tables, the import can take longer to complete. When I have tables that have millions of rows of data, I clear this option, so that they can be loaded individually.

How Type Detection Works

As far as I can tell, this option is for the Excel Workbook connector, which includes the import options on the **FILE** category on the Get Data button. If this option is checked, each column of data imported from a data source in the File category is automatically converted to the correct data type. This means that changing the data type manually should not have to be done as much.

The feature that I like best is that before this option is applied, data in a CSV file that was imported, looked like the data shown in Figure 1-21, in the Query Editor. Yes, I know that applying the **USE FIRST ROW AS HEADER OPTION** would fix this, but one less step is one less step, for us to do <smile>.

Additionally, when the Type Detection option is enabled, the same data is automatically displayed in the Query Editor, as shown in Figure 1-22. The formula at the top of the figure shows how some of the columns were transformed, which in this case is selecting a data type for each column. Most of the time, the correct data type is selected, but it is a good idea to at least look at the formula. This is easier (for me) then clicking on each column in the query to view the data type. Being from the old school though, I do not enable this option because I prefer to change the data type myself.

	Column1	Column2	Column3	Column4	Column5	Column6
1	Order ID	Employee ID	Customer ID	Order Date	Shipped Date	Shipper ID
2	30	9	27	1/15/2006	1/22/2006	2
3	31	3	4	1/20/2006	1/22/2006	1
4	32	4	12	1/22/2006	1/22/2006	2

Figure 1-21 Imported CSV file without Type Detection enabled

```
= Table.TransformColumnTypes(#"Promoted Headers",{{"Order ID", Int64.Type}, {"Employee ID", Int64.Type}, {"Customer ID", Int64.Type}, {"Order
Date", type date}, {"Shipped Date", type date}, {"Shipper ID", Int64.Type}, {"Ship Name", type text}, {"Ship Address", type text}, {"Ship
```

	Order ID	Employee ID	Customer ID	Order Date	Shipped Date	Shipper ID	Ship Name	Ship Address	Ship City	Ship State/Province
1	30	9	27	1/15/2006	1/22/2006	2	Karen Toh	789 27th Street	Las Vegas	NV
2	31	3	4	1/20/2006	1/22/2006	1	Christina Lee	123 4th Street	New York	NY
3	32	4	12	1/22/2006	1/22/2006	2	John Edwards	123 12th Street	Las Vegas	NV

Figure 1-22 Imported CSV file with Type Detection enabled

Relationships Options

The options in this section are designed to auto detect relationships. The options are explained below.

① **IMPORT RELATIONSHIPS FROM DATA SOURCE** Check this option if you want relationships that have been created in the data source (tables in a database for example) to be included when the data is imported. This option is implemented before the data is imported.

② **UPDATE RELATIONSHIPS WHEN REFRESHING QUERIES** Check this option if you want relationships to be checked for and updated each time you refresh the data. If you manually created relationships in Power BI Desktop for the same tables, it is possible that they will be removed. Most of the time, you will probably want to check this option, unless you have created a lot of relationships manually.

③ **AUTO DETECT NEW RELATIONSHIPS AFTER THE DATA IS LOADED** Check this option if you want to check for relationships after the data is loaded in the data model. This is helpful if new tables are loaded to the data model, as there may be a relationship with tables already in the data model. When that is the case, the relationships will automatically be created.

Regional Settings Option

The **LOCALE** option, shown in Figure 1-23 is used to select regional settings for Power BI Desktop to use. The options in the drop-down list contain the regions and countries.

The region selected will be used to format dates, times, numbers and text data, when it is imported. The option selected here is the default for all of the data imported into the file. If you need to override this setting for specific columns, you can, on the Query Editor after the data is loaded. [See Chapter 3, Change Type With Locale Options]

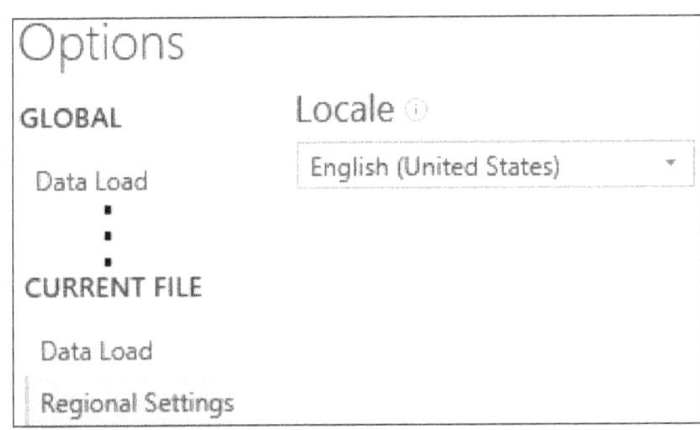

Figure 1-23 Regional Settings option

Also keep in mind that the system settings on your computer contain formatting options that are used by most other software on your computer. Figures 1-24 and 1-25 show you some of the Windows system settings that you can change, if they are the cause of the date or numeric data not being displayed as needed. Changing these options, affect all software on your computer that use them, not just Power BI Desktop.

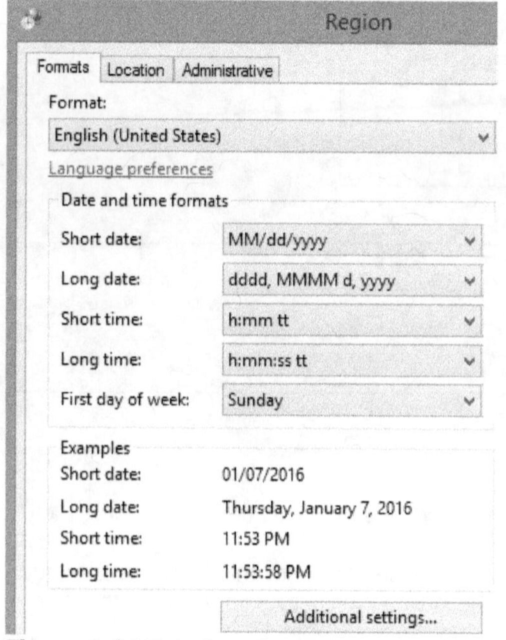

Figure 1-24 Date format options

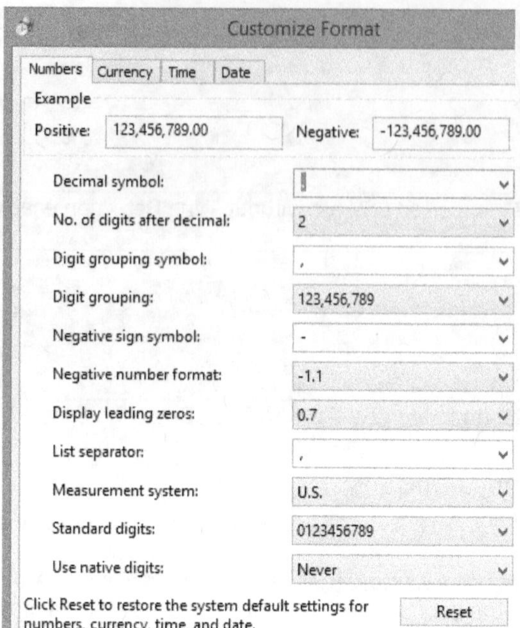

Figure 1-25 Number format options

Privacy Options

Figure 1-26 shows the options that can be used to make loading data faster, by bypassing security.

The **PRIVACY LEVELS** options are used to select whether or not the firewall and privacy settings are ignored when you combine data from more than one source.

A reason people use this option is to improve the queries performance, even though the option can make the data less secure.

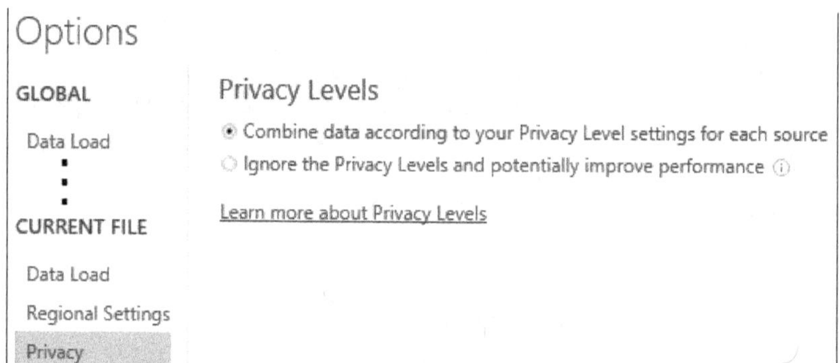

Figure 1-26 Privacy options

The first option is referring to the privacy options shown earlier in Figure 1-14.

The **AUTO RECOVERY OPTION** shown in Figure 1-27 is used to disable the global auto recovery options, covered earlier in this chapter, for the current report file.

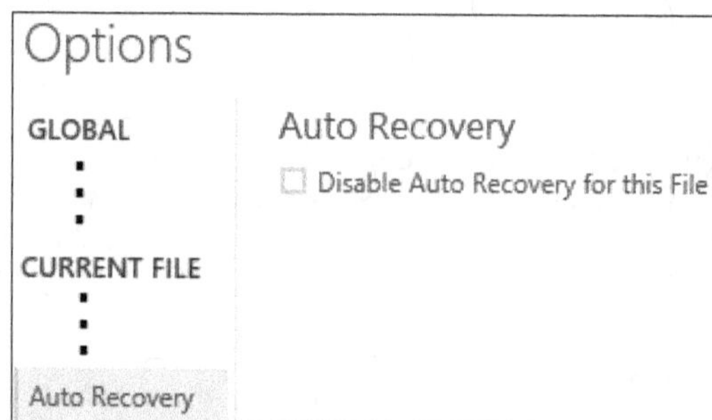

Figure 1-27 Current file Auto Recovery options

Data Source Settings

Selecting the **DATA SOURCE SETTINGS OPTION** on the File tab, displays the options shown in Figure 1-28. This window displays a list of the recent data sources that you have used. This information is stored (cached) on your computer. Having this information cached means that you do not have to recreate the connection, each time you need to refresh the data.

The options on this dialog box are used to manage and configure settings for all queries that are connected to the selected data source, in the report file that is currently open.

Data source locations, privacy levels, credentials and more can be changed. The data source location of the selected file can be changed for all queries at the same time. Examples would be a database that requires you to logon to gain access to it or the location of the database file has changed.

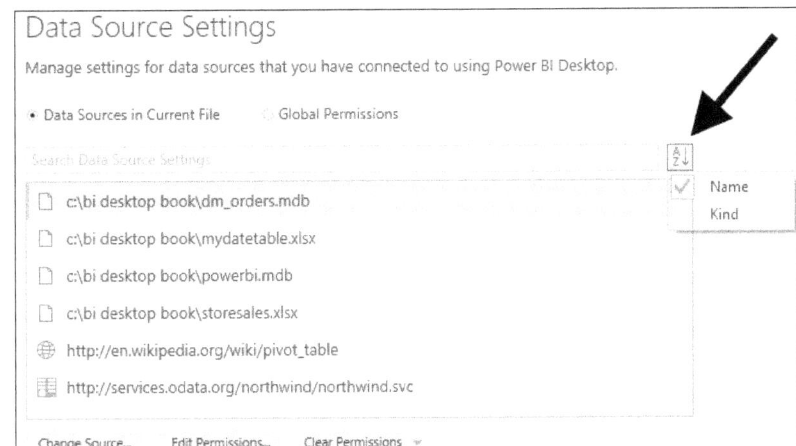

Figure 1-28 Data Source Settings (current file) options

Select the **DATA SOURCES IN CURRENT FILE OPTION** to only display data sources that are used in the current file.

The list of data sources can be sorted by **NAME** (the default) or by **KIND** (the data sources are grouped by the data source type), by selecting the option on the Sort button, illustrated above in Figure 1-28.

The **CHANGE SOURCE BUTTON** displays the connection information for the data source, so that changes, like the location of the data source file, can be made. Chapter 3, Figures 3-31, 3-32 and 3-34, show the options to change some data sources.

The **GLOBAL PERMISSIONS OPTION** displays the screen shown in Figure 1-29.

If there are a lot of entries on this dialog box, you can type in the name of the data source that you are looking for in the Search field, to help narrow down the list. This will make it easier to find the data source that you need.

The **EDIT PERMISSIONS BUTTON** displays the dialog box shown in Figure 1-30 or 1-31. The options shown in Figure 1-31 are for web data sources. Right-clicking on a data source and selecting Edit Permissions, also opens this dialog box. Depending on the type of data source that was selected, you will see slightly different options. The options on this dialog box are used to change the credentials for the selected data source.

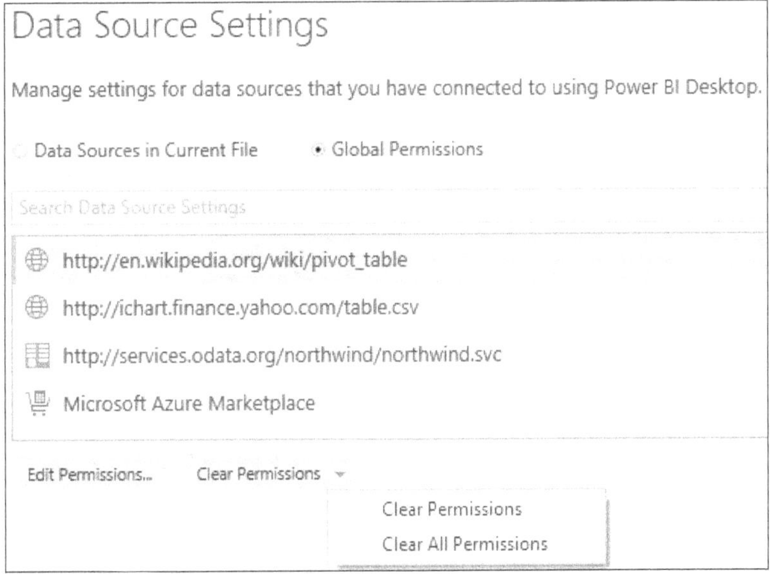

Figure 1-29 Global Permission options

The **DELETE BUTTON** is used to delete the selected data source (or all data sources) and its credentials. If you delete a query that uses credentials, the data source settings are not deleted.

The **CLEAR PERMISSIONS BUTTON** displays the options shown above, at the bottom of Figure 1-29. You can remove the permissions for the selected data source or all data sources.

The options in the **PRIVACY LEVEL** drop-down list, shown at the bottom of Figure 1-30, are used to select what level of privacy, if any, the selected data source should have.

Selecting two or more data sources, then clicking the Edit button, opens the dialog box shown in Figure 1-32. The options are used to set the privacy level for the selected data sources.

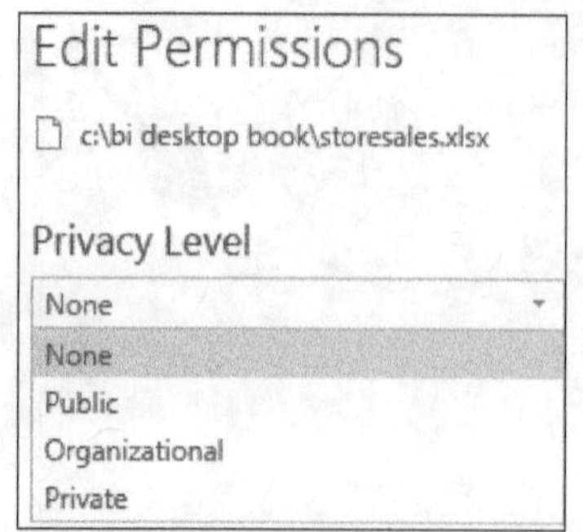

Figure 1-30 Settings for one data source

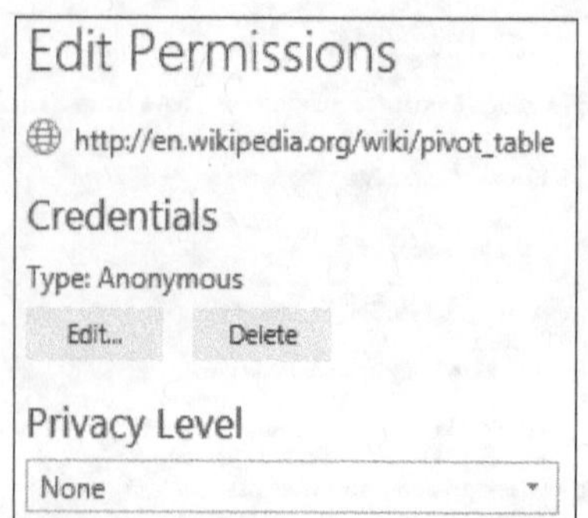

Figure 1-31 Settings for a web data source

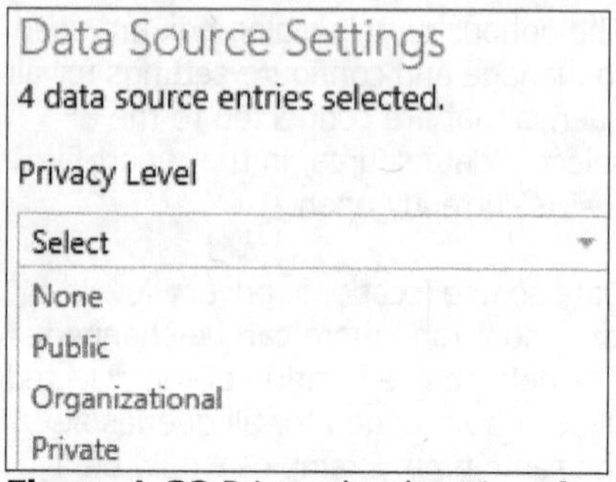

Data Source Settings
4 data source entries selected.
Privacy Level
Select
None
Public
Organizational
Private

Figure 1-32 Privacy level settings for multiple data sources

When selecting these privacy options, keep the following in mind: The privacy options shown earlier in Figure 1-26, are used to protect company data, when it is merged or combined with non company or external data. By default, when you attempt to combine company and external data, you will be prompted to select a data privacy level, from the options shown above in Figure 1-30. If you only use company data, selecting the **IGNORE THE PRIVACY LEVELS AND POTENTIALLY IMPROVE PERFORMANCE** option, shown earlier in Figure 1-26, will let you ignore the privacy functionality in Power BI Desktop. I have read posts on a forum that stated that when the privacy options are disabled, queries run faster.

Clicking the Edit button shown above in Figure 1-31, displays the options shown in Figure 1-33.

Select the **USE MY CURRENT CREDENTIALS** option if you want to use your Windows credentials, to connect to the data source.

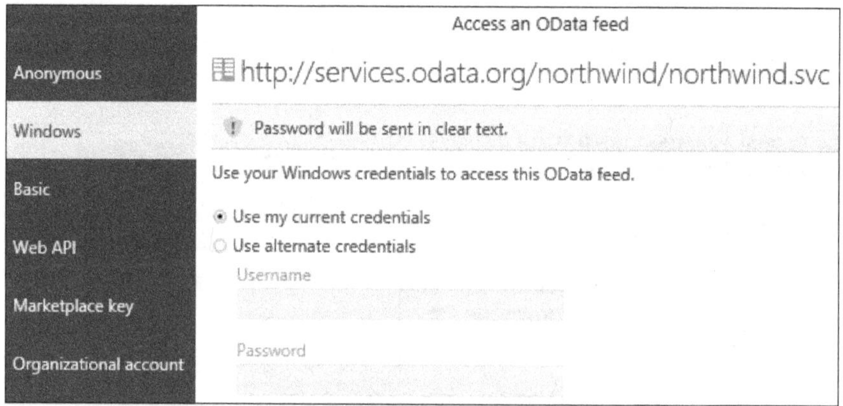

Figure 1-33 Current credential options

Managing Your Credentials

Maybe it's just me, but I think that how credentials work is a well kept secret. I figured it out the hard way. Some of the data source options require you to login. You will see this later in this book, if you log into the Azure Marketplace to download a data file. Once you enter your login information for a data source, it is saved, so that you do not have to log into the data source again.

This login information (which some refer to as authentication) is saved in an encrypted file on your computers hard drive, not in the report file, as I originally thought. This is great if your file will be used by someone else, because your personal information is not saved in the file. Not so great if you use the file on another computer. PS and by the way, that is how I found out <smile>.

When the report file is opened on another computer, Power BI Desktop searches for the encrypted file, when you select a data source that requires a user name and/or password. If this file is found, it is used. If the encrypted file is not found, you or the person using the report file, will be prompted to login.

The encrypted file is for all of the files that you create in Power BI Desktop on the computer. Each user has their own encrypted file on the computer. If you get a new computer, you can copy the file to the new computer.

The location of this file (in Windows 8.1) is: C:\users\username\AppData\Local\Microsoft\Power BI Desktop\user.zip. If you do not see the user.zip file in this location, search for it on the hard drive that Power BI Desktop is installed on.

Customize The Quick Access Toolbar

Throughout this book you will create a lot of report files and save existing report files with a new name. You may find it easier and faster to have options for these "File saving" tasks on the Quick Access Toolbar. The steps below show you how to add the Save options to the toolbar, shown earlier in Figure 1-2. Customizing the Quick Access Toolbar in Power BI Desktop is not required to complete the exercises in this book.

The Undo and Redo buttons on the Quick Access Toolbar work from the Report view. You can also use CTRL+Z (undo) and CTRL+Y (redo).

Quick Access Toolbar
Currently, there is no way to change the order of the buttons on this toolbar.

1. Open Power BI Desktop ⇒ File tab.
2. Right-click on the Save As option ⇒ On the shortcut menu shown in Figure 1-34, select the Add to Quick Access Toolbar option.

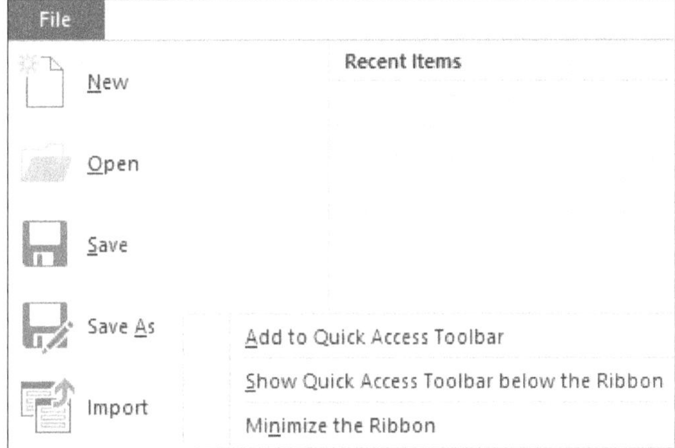

Figure 1-34 Quick Access Toolbar option

Add A Toolbar Button To The Quick Access Toolbar

If you want to add a button on the menu to the Quick Access Toolbar, right-click on the button ⇒ Select the Add to Quick Access Toolbar option.

Summary

This chapter provided a high level overview of the Power BI Desktop. Specific features of the software were covered, in preparation for the rest of the book. The next chapter covers loading data. The goal is to get you familiar with where options are and to demonstrate how to get data from a variety of data sources and load it into Power BI Desktop.

Concepts and terminology that will help you become familiar with Power BI Desktop were also covered in this chapter. Hopefully, you downloaded the practice files, so that you can dive right in to the next chapter. I think that once you start using this software, you will start to see the potential of what it has to offer.

LOADING DATA INTO POWER BI DESKTOP

In this chapter you will learn about the following:

- ☑ Data sources that Power BI Desktop supports
- ☑ Many of the options in the External Data section of the Home tab
- ☑ Loading (Getting) data from a variety of file types

CHAPTER 2

Importing Data

Without data, Power BI Desktop is useless. The most used way to get data into Power BI Desktop is to import it. Small amounts of data can be pasted in. The options on the **GET DATA BUTTON** are used to import data that will be used to perform data analysis, usually for some type of decision making.

You can search for (which is referred to as **DATA DISCOVERY**) the data that you need. This tool can import data (which Power BI Desktop refers to as **LOADING DATA**) from a variety of sources and locations, including the web, text files and databases. Data from various sources can be added to one Power BI Desktop file. Data can also be imported from corporate data sources, including big data (like Hadoop) and even social media data sources.

Once you have the data in Power BI Desktop, you can query it to reduce the number of rows and columns (also known as **CLEANSING THE DATA**). The columns of data can be rearranged to best meet your needs. Being able to **MASH UP DATA** in this manner is helpful when you need to query, slice and dice data to create charts and other types of visualizations. Cleaning data is not a requirement to loading data into Power BI Desktop. If the data that you will use, is already clean, you can start creating reports and dashboards as soon as the data is loaded.

Additionally, once you have the data the way that you want it, you can load it to the data model. Loading the data into the data model allows the data to also be used by other software like Power BI and Excel. If you have used options in the **GET EXTERNAL DATA, CONNECTIONS** and **RELATIONSHIPS** sections on the Data tab in Excel or Power Query, you will be familiar with some of the Get Data button functionality in Power BI Desktop.

External Data Options

The options shown in Figure 2-1 are on the Home tab. They are used to bring data into Power BI Desktop and manage it. The options are explained in Table 2-1.

The other options on the Home tab are covered in Chapter 9, because they are mainly used to create reports.

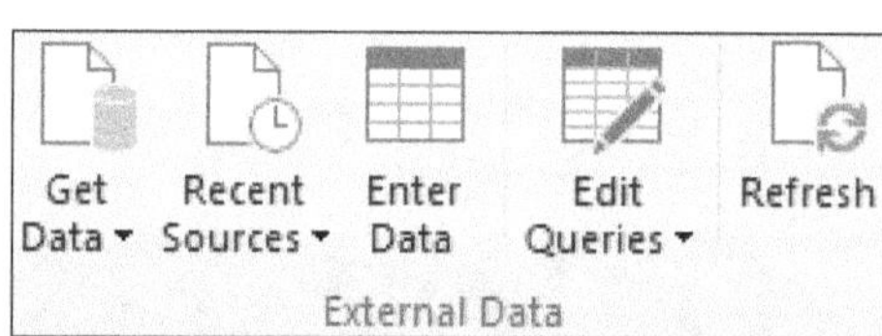

Figure 2-1 External Data options

Button	Description
Get Data	[See Get Data Button Options]
Recent Sources	[See Recent Sources Option]
Enter Data	[See Chapter 8, Create A Table]
Edit Queries	Clicking on the arrow displays a shortcut menu with the following options: The **EDIT QUERIES OPTION** opens the Query Editor. The **DATA SOURCE SETTINGS OPTION** opens a dialog box with the same name, that was covered in the previous chapter. The **EDIT PARAMETERS OPTION** is used to view the current parameter values or modify them. This option is only enabled if a parameter has already been created in the file.
Refresh	Reloads the data from the data source for each table in the file.

Table 2-1 External Data options explained

Clicking on the top half of a button (where the icon is, above the words on the button) with an arrow, automatically selects the first option on the drop-down list. For example, look at the Get Data button, shown in Figure 2-2. If you click on the top half of the Get Data button, the Excel option would be displayed and selected on the Get Data dialog box, because it is the first option on the drop-down list.

Get Data Button Options

Data from multiple sources can be imported into the database (called the **DATA MODEL**) that is part of and stored in the Power BI Desktop (.pbix) file. You may see the terms "internal data model" and "data model" used interchangeably. They are one in the same.

Figure 2-2 shows the options on the Get Data button. They are the most common data sources. The options on the Get Data button are used to select the type of data that you want to import. Each of these options has what is known as a **CONNECTOR**, which contains instructions on how to import data from that specific data source. Table 2-2 explains the data source categories.

The **MORE OPTION** displays the dialog box shown in Figure 2-3. The **ALL OPTION** displays all of the data source options.

The word **(BETA)** after an option (as shown on the right side of Figure 2-3), means that the data source is in the testing phase, but you can use it now.

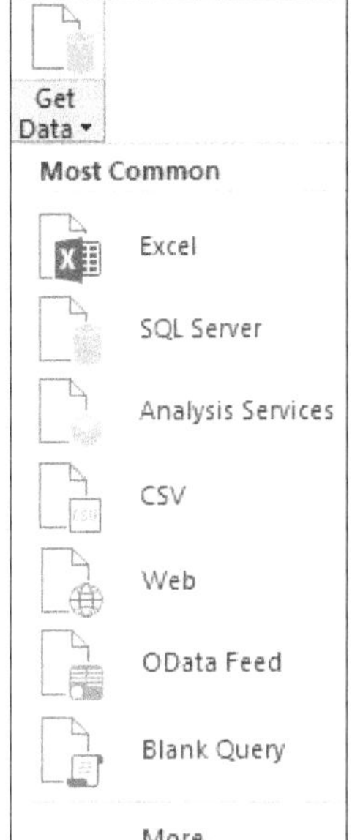

Figure 2-2 Get Data button options

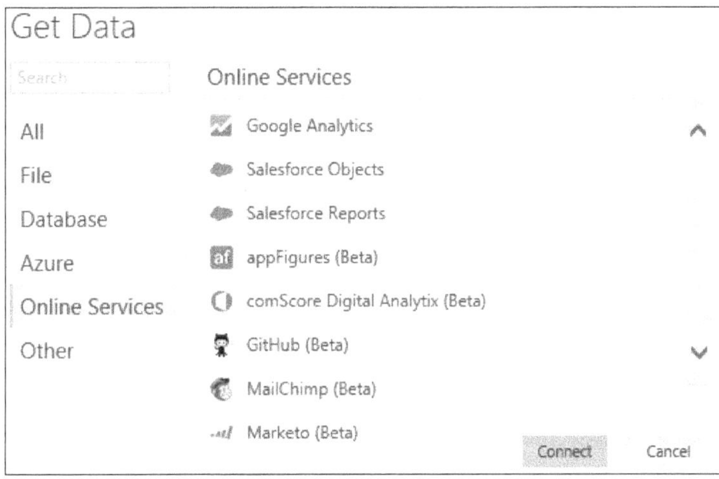

Figure 2-3 Get Data dialog box

Category	Is Used To Import . . .
File	Excel, CSV, XML, JSON and Text files. Metadata can also be imported.
Database	Relational databases.
Azure	An Azure data source.
Online Services	Databases that are stored online.
Other	Data from a variety of sources, including data feeds, a web page, Hadoop and R Script.

Table 2-2 Data source categories explained

My Data Source Is Not Listed. What Should I Do?
If the data source that you want to use is not listed, you can try the following. Select the ODBC option if your data source has an ODBC or OLE DB driver. The latter comes pre-installed with Windows. If this does not work, search the Power BI Desktop forum to see if a solution has been posted for your data source. If not, post a question.

Recent Sources Option

This option displays a list of files that you have imported data from. The **MORE OPTION** (is at the bottom of the list, but not shown in the figure) displays the dialog box shown in Figure 2-4. You can select a file from this list to load data from into the current file.

When connected, Text file data sources will open a dialog box, like the one shown later in Figure 2-18. Database and spreadsheet data sources are displayed in the Navigator window (shown later in Figure 2-9), so that you can select the tables, in the database, that you want to import.

Right-clicking on a file in the list, displays the shortcut menu shown in Figure 2-4. The options on the shortcut menu are explained in Table 2-3.

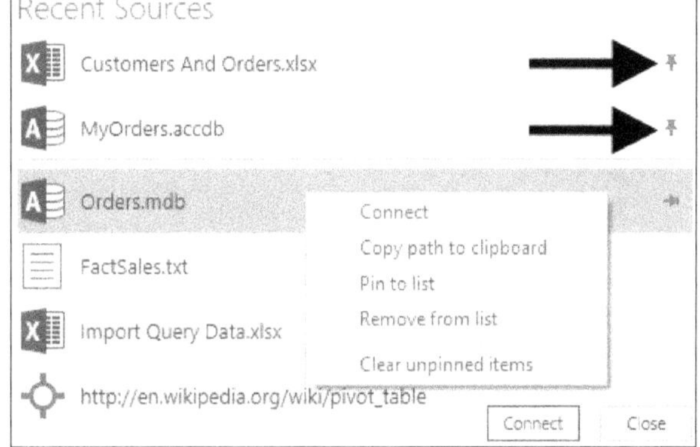

Figure 2-4 Recent Sources list with pinned files

In addition to storing a list of at least the last 30 data sources (it is probably more, but that is how many data sources are in my Recent Sources list right now, while I am writing this <smile>), your login information for the data sources in the Recent Sources list is also maintained.

Option	Is Used To . . .
Connect	Add the selected data source to the current file.
Copy path to clipboard	Copy the path (location) of the data source so that it can be pasted some place else.
Pin to list	Attach the selected data source to the top of the Recent Sources list, as illustrated by the push pins at the top of Figure 2-4 above.
Remove from list	Remove the selected data source from the Recent Sources list.
Clear unpinned items	Remove the items on the Recent Sources list that are not pinned. I personally do not see the point in removing an item unless you have no plans to use it anytime soon. Also, keep in mind that removing an item from this list, removes it from all files created in Power BI Desktop, not just the current file.

Table 2-3 Recent Sources list right-click shortcut menu options explained

Getting Data

DATA DISCOVERY, as it's called, is a component of business intelligence. It focuses on finding the data needed for both graphical and visual analysis, instead of text based reports (like reports that are created using tools like Microsoft SQL Server Reporting Services and SAP Crystal Reports). The rest of this chapter covers how to connect to and get data from some of the data sources supported by Power BI Desktop.

What Happens To The Data Now?

This chapter through Chapter 6 covers discovering data, then transforming it by using sorting and filtering techniques, as well as, creating calculated columns and applying aggregations in the Query Editor. You also have to decide whether to keep (load) the data or discard it and any changes that you may have made to the data.

Import Exercise Tips

① Unless specified otherwise, at the beginning of each exercise in this chapter, open a new report file.

② The options to select a data source are on the Get Data button, shown earlier in Figure 2-2. If the file type that you need is not shown in Figure 2-2, select the More option, at the bottom of the list, to view all of the file types.

③ After you select the type of file that you want to import, click the **CONNECT BUTTON**, shown earlier at the bottom of Figure 2-3. Then select the file that you want to import data from.

④ When you see the instruction "Close and Apply the changes", it means to click the **CLOSE & APPLY** button ⇒ Close & Apply option, in the Query Editor, unless stated otherwise.

Web Option

This option is used to retrieve data from a web site. This option requires you to type in the web site address of a page that has data formatted in an HTML table or to select or create a parameter that will retrieve the web address.

Figure 2-5 shows the advanced options that are available to import data from a web page. If you are going to type or paste the URL in, you can use the **BASIC OPTIONS**.

Holding the mouse pointer at the end of the URL parts field will display the ellipsis button shown on the right side of the figure. Click on this button to display the shortcut menu shown.

Select **DELETE** to remove the option as part of the URL.

Select **MOVE UP/MOVE DOWN** to change the order of the parts of the URL.

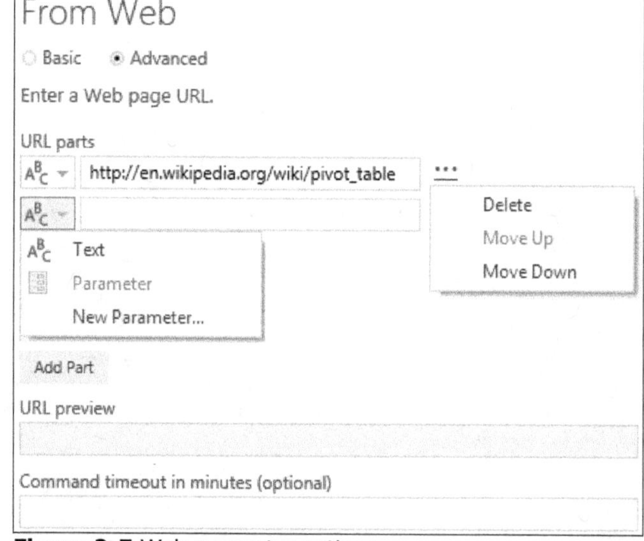

Figure 2-5 Web connector options

The **ADD PART BUTTON** adds another field that is used to select another part of the URL.

The **URL PREVIEW FIELD** displays all of the values from the URL parts that were used.

The **COMMAND TIMEOUT IN MINUTES OPTION** is used to enter the amount of time to wait for the web page to be displayed, before the connection times out.

The **URL OPTIONS** drop-down list (the button with ABC on it) is used to select where the URL is. The options are explained below.

- ☑ Select **TEXT** if you want to type in the web page. This is the default option.
- ☑ Select **PARAMETER** if you want to use an existing parameter field to select the web site to use. (1)
- ☑ Select **NEW PARAMETER** if you need to create a new parameter, that will be used to select the website from. (1)

(1) A parameter field would be useful if there are several web pages that you could select data from to get the data that you need. For example, you need to be able to import statistics for three basketball teams. The web page for each team would be listed in the parameter.

Exercise 2.1: Import Data From A Web Site

The URL in step 2 is in the Vol 5 links.txt file in the zip file that you downloaded in Chapter 1, in case you do not want to type it in.

1. Get Data button ⇒ **WEB** option.

2. On the Basic or Advanced screen, type `http://en.wikipedia.org/wiki/pivot_table` in the URL field, as shown above in Figure 2-5 ⇒ Click OK. The Navigator window shown below in Figure 2-6, will open.

Navigator Window

The window shown in Figure 2-6 displays the tables in the data source. This window is only displayed when the data source has more than one table. In Excel, each sheet counts as at least one table. Sheets can have more than one table defined.

Power BI Desktop displays data sets that it recognizes and believes that can be imported. One feature that I think is cool about the Navigator window is that regardless of the format that the data is saved in, it looks the same on the right side of this window.

The **REFRESH** button (the sheet of paper icon, illustrated in Figure 2-6) is used to update the data from the data source.

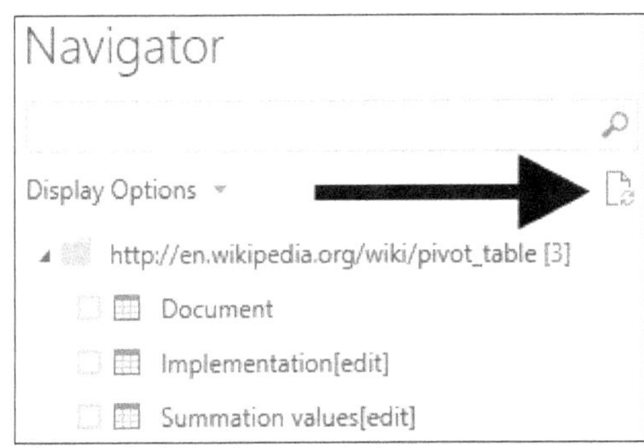

Figure 2-6 Navigator window

This window can be used as a **DATA DISCOVERY TOOL** because it displays some of the data before it is loaded into Power BI Desktop. Keep in mind that the tables retrieved can change, especially when getting data from a web site. This window appears for most data sources. It does not appear when the following data source file types are used: CSV, TXT, XML and **METADATA FILES**.

Click on a table name in the list on the left side of the Navigator window to display the data. The check boxes are used to select the tables that you want to import. A query is created for each table that you select.

The exercises in this book do not connect to corporate databases. On your own, if you need to connect to corporate databases, you will often see a list of databases on the Navigator window first. When that is the case, select the database that you need, then select the tables. You will probably need authorization to connect to and view corporate databases.

Display Options

The options shown in Figure 2-7 are used to select whether or not preview data is displayed on the right side of the Navigator window.

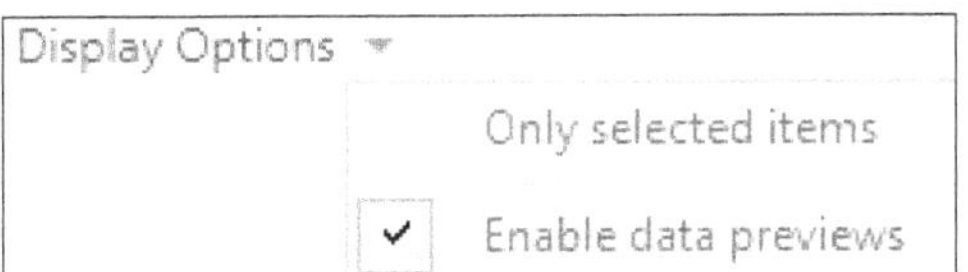

Figure 2-7 Display Options on the Navigator window

Check the **ONLY SELECTED ITEMS OPTION** to display tables that you have checked. The tables that are not checked in the list on the left, are hidden.

If checked, the **ENABLE DATA PREVIEWS OPTION** allows data from the selected table to be displayed on the right side of the Navigator window, as shown below in Figure 2-9.

Column Name Conflicts
If you have a table that has columns with the same name except for the case (for example, Orders and orders), you do not have to rename one of them before importing the table, unless you want to. That is because the import process will add ".1" after one of the column names, as illustrated in Figure 2-8.

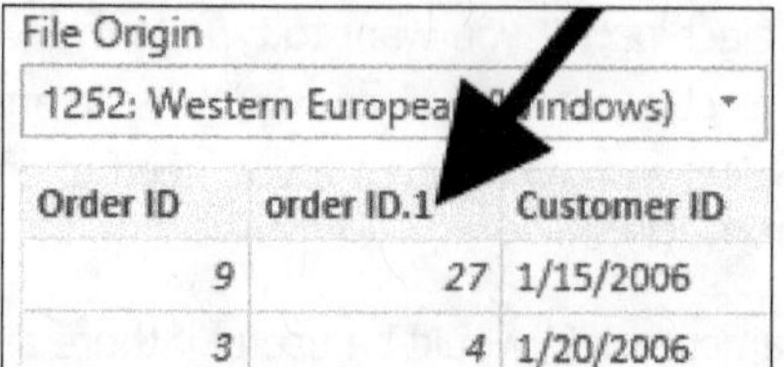

Figure 2-8 Column name conflict resolution

Resizing The Navigator Window
What may not be obvious is that this window can be resized. Dragging the line, illustrated below in Figure 2-9, changes the size of the left and right panels of the window. Dragging the lower right corner of the window is used to make the window smaller or larger.

Navigator Window Table Shortcut Menu

Right-click on a table to display the shortcut menu shown in Figure 2-9. The Load and Edit buttons at the bottom of the window are enabled when a table is selected (has a check mark next to it).

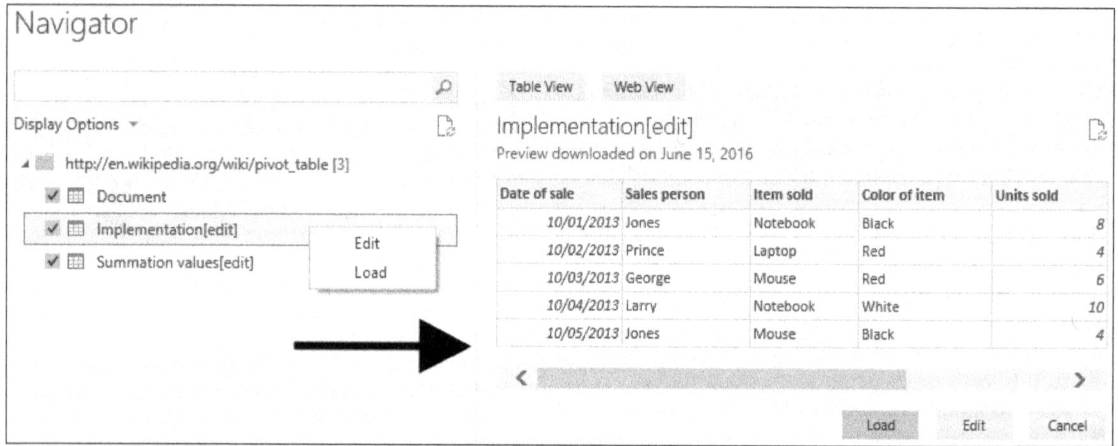

Figure 2-9 Navigator window

The **EDIT OPTION** (on the shortcut menu on the left of the figure) and **EDIT BUTTON** (in the lower right corner of the figure) creates a query for the data, then displays the data in the Query Editor. This gives you the opportunity to view more of the data and transform it before it is loaded to the data model. This can be helpful if you are not familiar with the data or if the dataset has millions of rows of data.

The **LOAD OPTION** and the **LOAD BUTTON** automatically bypasses the editing option and places the data in the data model.

The **TABLE VIEW BUTTON** displays the data, as shown above in Figure 2-9. This is the default view. (2)

The **WEB VIEW BUTTON** displays the selected table, as shown in Figure 2-10. Tables have an orange background. In the figure, you can see the data in the table in a format that is easy to understand. (2)

This button is helpful because when you see tables that do not have a descriptive name, you don't know what type of data they contain.

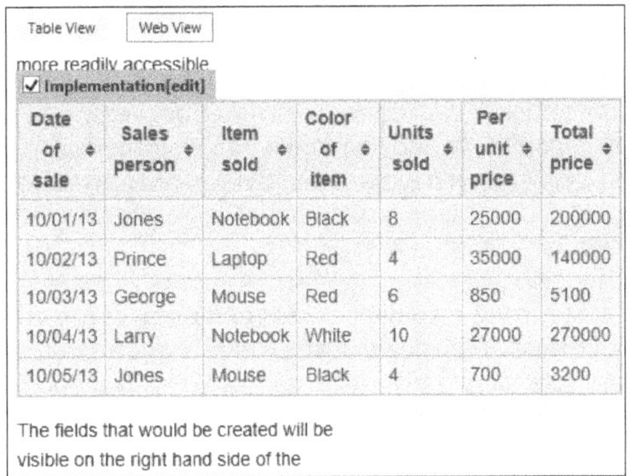

Date of sale	Sales person	Item sold	Color of item	Units sold	Per unit price	Total price
10/01/13	Jones	Notebook	Black	8	25000	200000
10/02/13	Prince	Laptop	Red	4	35000	140000
10/03/13	George	Mouse	Red	6	850	5100
10/04/13	Larry	Notebook	White	10	27000	270000
10/05/13	Jones	Mouse	Black	4	700	3200

Figure 2-10 Web view of the data in a table on a web page

(2) This button is only available when the data is on a web page.

3. Check all three tables, shown earlier in Figure 2-9 ⇒ Click the Edit button. You should see three queries in the Query Editor.

4. On the Query Editor, click the Save button on the Quick Access Toolbar ⇒
On the dialog box shown in Figure 2-11, click the **APPLY LATER BUTTON.**

   The Apply and Apply Later buttons are explained in Chapter 3. [See tip box above Figure 3-2]

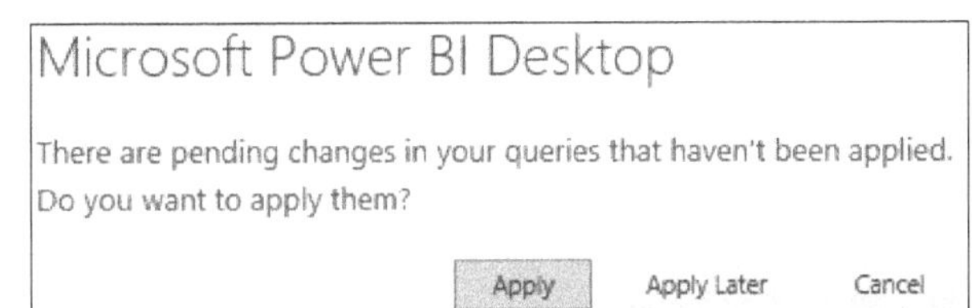

Figure 2-11 Query pending changes options

5. On the Save As dialog box, navigate to your folder ⇒ Save the file as `E2.1 Web and Excel data` ⇒ Minimize the Query Editor window.

Navigator Window Data Source Shortcut Menu

Right-clicking on the file name displays the shortcut menu shown in Figure 2-12.

The **EDIT OPTION** displays information about each table (in the data source) in the Query Editor, as shown in Figure 2-13. This is used to view more of the data and perform transformations, if needed, to help decide if the data is what you need.

The **LOAD OPTION** loads information about each table, in the data source, into the data model.

The **REFRESH OPTION** re-imports the data from the data source.

If you want to view the data in a table shown in Figure 2-13, that has not been loaded, click on the word "Table", in the Data column, for the table that you want to see.

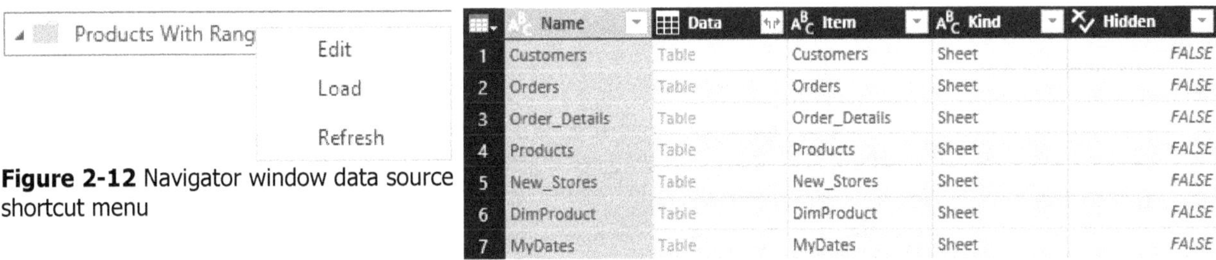

Figure 2-12 Navigator window data source shortcut menu

	Name	Data	Item	Kind	Hidden
1	Customers	Table	Customers	Sheet	FALSE
2	Orders	Table	Orders	Sheet	FALSE
3	Order_Details	Table	Order_Details	Sheet	FALSE
4	Products	Table	Products	Sheet	FALSE
5	New_Stores	Table	New_Stores	Sheet	FALSE
6	DimProduct	Table	DimProduct	Sheet	FALSE
7	MyDates	Table	MyDates	Sheet	FALSE

Figure 2-13 Information about each table

File Import Options

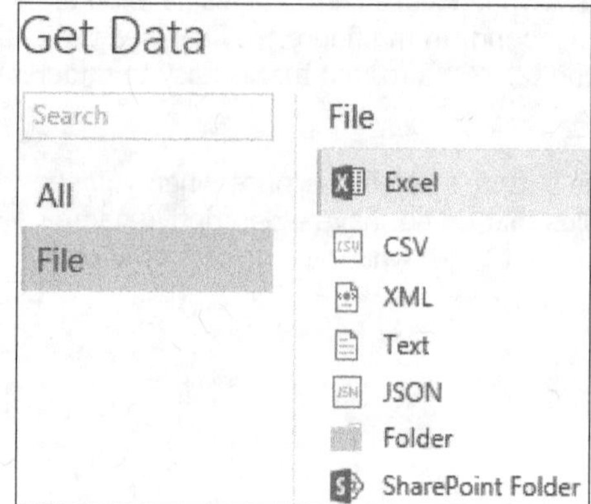

Figure 2-14 File options

The **EXCEL OPTION** is used to get data (that is not in the data model of the workbook) from an Excel workbook. Excel files from version 97 and higher can be imported. In addition to data on worksheets in the workbook, Named tables, **NAMED RANGES** and **DYNAMIC NAMED RANGES**, can also be imported. They will be displayed on the Navigator window, just like worksheets (tabs of data) are.

.xls and .xlsx Excel files have automatic **COLUMN TYPE DETECTION** enabled during the import process. This means that Excel files are treated more like tables in a database, during the import process. This is a good thing because more of the data types that are automatically selected, will be correct.

Data filters that are applied in Excel are ignored when the data is imported. The filter criteria is not imported, so it will have to be set up in the Query Editor, if it is still needed.

The CSV, XML, Text and JSON options, shown above in Figure 2-14, are used to import data from different types of text files. These options are explained in this chapter, in the exercise that they are covered in.

The **FOLDER OPTION** is used to import several files (that are in the same folder) at one time and then they are combined (appended) into one file.

Import Data From Excel

In this part of the exercise, you will import data that is on a worksheet, that has not been converted to an Excel table. The data will be loaded to the data model.

1. Select the Excel option shown above in Figure 2-14 ⇒ Click the Connect button ⇒ Select the More Data Files workbook.

   You should see the worksheets shown in Figure 2-15.

   Check the 02 Products table.

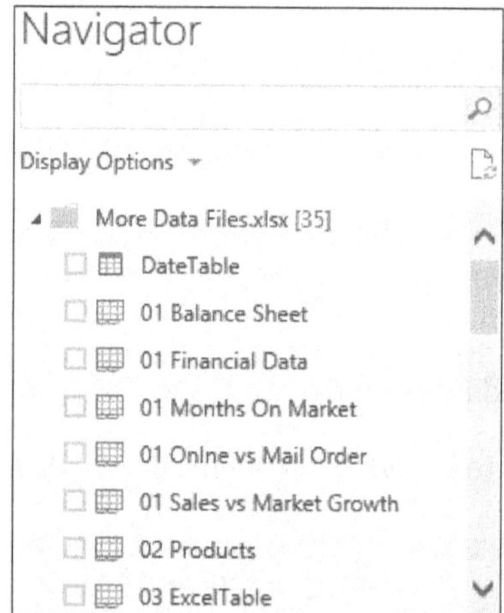

Figure 2-15 Worksheets in the workbook

Empty Worksheets
If you scroll down the list of tables shown above in Figure 2-15, you will see is a worksheet named "Sheet 1". If you click on a worksheet in the Navigator window that does not have any data, you will see a message indicating that the table is empty. Clear the check mark for empty sheets before importing the data. There is no value in importing empty worksheets. It would be helpful if the number of rows was displayed next to each table or sheet, to help make it easier to know whether or not it contains data.

2. Click the Load button. The Products table will be loaded to the data model ⇒ Save the changes to the report file.

Importing Data Using Named Ranges

This option is also known as a **NAMED SET**. A named range is a pre-selected section of a worksheet. Named ranges are often created when there is a need to only print or import part of the data on a worksheet. An example would be only needing to import data for two years, but the spreadsheet has six years of data. You would create a named range or two, for the two years of data that you need to import.

Figure 2-16 shows the named ranges in the workbook that will be used in the next exercise.

As you will see, each named range will be displayed as a table in the Navigator window.

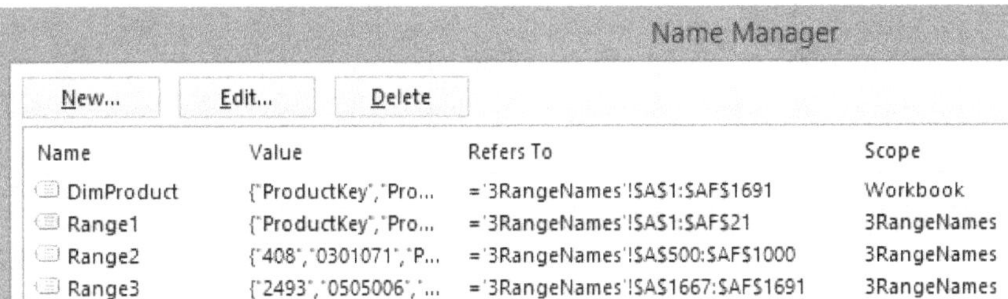

Figure 2-16 Range name information in Excel

Named Range Tips
① Make sure that the named ranges that you plan to import include column headings, otherwise, no headings will be imported.
② When using a named range to import data, the query name will be the name of the named range.

Exercise 2.2: Import Data From Multiple Sources Into One Workbook

The way spreadsheets can be set up varies. Some have multiple tables on one worksheet, while others have ranges set up. In this exercise you will see a variety of worksheet layouts that can be imported.

Import Data Using Named Ranges

In this part of the exercise you will import data that will be accessed by a named range.

1. Get Data button ⇒ Excel ⇒ Products With Range Names workbook.
2. You should see the tables shown in Figure 2-17.

   Notice that the icon next to the range name tables is different from the 3 Range Names table. The different icons let you know that they are not a true table, or in the case of a workbook file, they are not worksheets, like the 3 Range Name option is.

   Check all of the tables ⇒ Edit button ⇒
   Close and apply the changes ⇒
   Save the file as `E2.2 Import from multiple workbooks`.

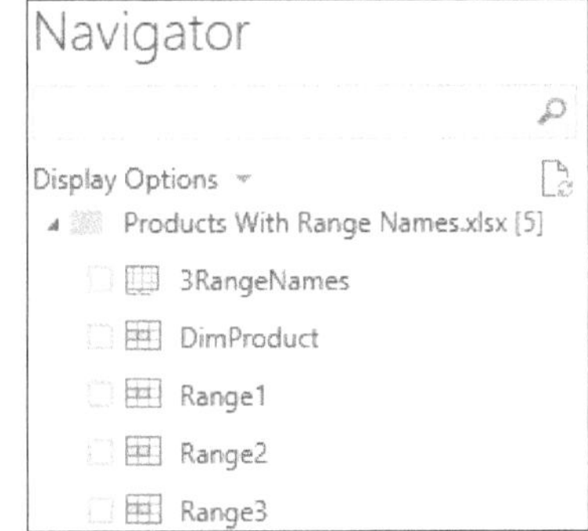

Figure 2-17 Named Range tables

Import Multiple Sets Of Data

In this part of the exercise you will import data from a different workbook.

1. Get Data button ⇒ Excel ⇒ More Data Files workbook ⇒ Check the 03 Excel table ⇒ Edit button. Notice that only one table was loaded. As you will see in the Query Editor, there are actually three tables on one worksheet, in the workbook.
2. Apply the changes and save the file.

Text And CSV File Connector Import Options

The dialog box shown in Figure 2-18 is displayed (instead of the Navigator window) when a Text or CSV file is being imported. The three drop-down lists are used to select import options, as needed. A custom delimiter can be created.

The **DELIMITER FIXED WIDTH OPTION** shown in Figure 2-19, is used to list the positions to split the data into columns. Replace the default fixed widths, with the length of the fields in the file that you are using.

The **DATA TYPE DETECTION FIELD OPTION** is used to select how many rows of data are used to determine the data type. The default is the first 200 rows, but the entire data set can be used to determine the data type.

The **DO NOT DETECT DATA TYPES OPTION** turns off data type detection. Select this option when you want to select the data types yourself on the Data view or Query Editor.

The preview data displayed in Figure 2-18, can change based on the options that you select, in the Delimiter drop-down list.

This will let you see what the data will look like before it is loaded.

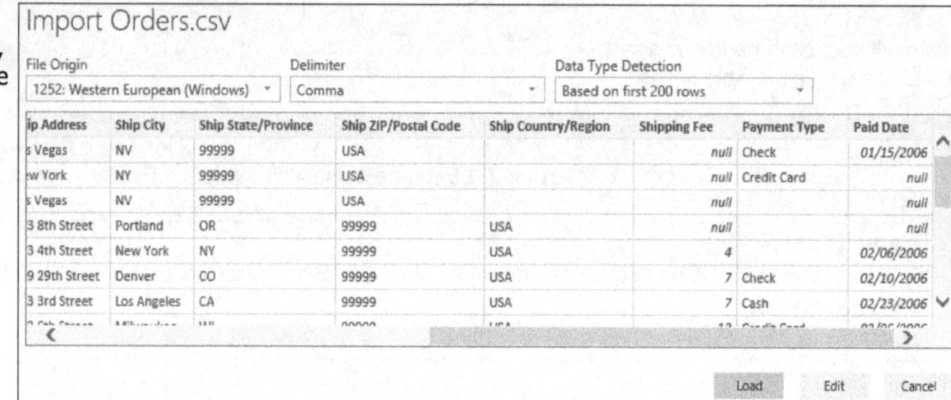

Figurer 2-18 Text and CSV file connector options

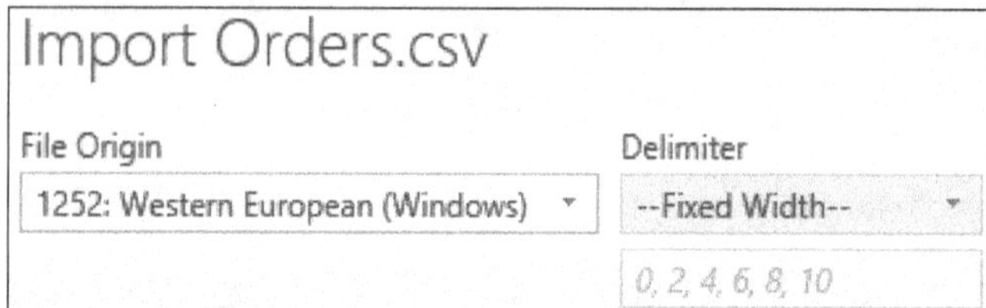

Figure 2-19 Connector fixed width delimiter options

CSV File Tips

To use a CSV file, it must meet certain criteria, in addition to having the CSV file extension. On your own, if you are having trouble loading a CSV file, open the file in Note Pad or another text editor and confirm the following:

① The file does not have anything other than a header row and the rows of data. If used, the header row has to be the first row in the file.

② If column headings are used, the first row must contain a heading for every field. The remaining rows can have fewer fields then the first row, but not more fields. For example, most addresses have a zip code field, but there are a few records that do not. The first row must have a zip code field heading.

③ Commas or double quotes need to separate each field.

④ Each row must end with a line feed or carriage return (the equivalent of pressing Enter).

Exercise 2.3: Import Data From Different Text File Types

CSV, XML, TXT and JSON files are different types of text files. CSV and TXT files should only contain data for one table. XML files can contain data for more than one table. In this exercise you will import data from all of these data types into one file.

Import Data From A CSV File

CSV files are text files because they do not contain any formatting, even though they are usually saved in Excel. This file type is most often created as an export file from a database or a spreadsheet, especially when moving data between systems or applications.

Having the ability to import data into Power BI Desktop from CSV files opens up a lot of possibilities, especially if you do not have direct access to data that is stored in an enterprise system. You can get the IT department to export the data from an enterprise system and save it in a CSV file for you.

1. Get Data button ⇒ CSV ⇒ Import Orders.csv file ⇒ On the dialog box shown earlier in Figure 2-18, click the Edit button.

2. On the right side of the Query Editor, change the Name from Import Orders to `Orders`.

3. Close and apply the changes.

4. Save the file as `E2.3 Text file data sources`. Leave the file open to complete the rest of this exercise.

Using CSV Files That Have Different Numbers Of Columns

The concept of a csv file that has rows of data with a different number of columns is also known as a **JAGGED CSV FILE.**

Most of the time, the CSV files that you use have the same number of columns of data for each row. As shown earlier in Figure 2-18, some of the cells do not have data. Figure 2-20 shows the last three columns from the CSV files that you just imported.

The **CSV CONNECTOR** also supports files, where each row does not have data in the same number of columns, as shown in Figure 2-21. You do not have to do anything different for csv files that fall into this category. The null values and empty cells indicate that there is no data in the cell. The columns data type determines whether null values or empty cells are displayed when the field does not have any data.

Shipping Fee	Payment Type	Paid Date
200	Check	01/15/2006
5	Credit Card	01/20/2006
5	Credit Card	01/22/2006
50	Credit Card	01/30/2006
4	Check	02/06/2006
7	Check	02/10/2006
7	Cash	02/23/2006

Figure 2-20 Imported data with each row having the same number of columns

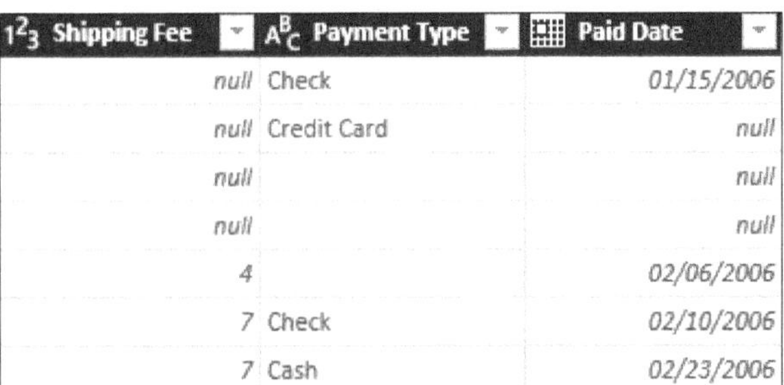

Shipping Fee	Payment Type	Paid Date
null	Check	01/15/2006
null	Credit Card	null
null		null
null		null
4		02/06/2006
7	Check	02/10/2006
7	Cash	02/23/2006

Figure 2-21 CSV file with different number of columns

Import Data From An XML File

XML stands for **EXTENSIBLE MARKUP LANGUAGE**.

XML produces a text file, as shown in Figure 2-22. It is used to send formatted data between systems or applications.

In this type of text file, the data is enclosed (wrapped) in tags. These tags are what allows the data in XML files to be displayed on the web. Keep in mind that there are different types of XML files.

Some XML files can have more than one table. When that is the case, each table (dataset) will be displayed in the Navigator window.

```
<?xml version="1.0" encoding="utf-8"?>
<xml>
  <Months>
    <MonthID>1</MonthID>
    <MonthName>January</MonthName>
  </Months>
  <Months>
    <MonthID>2</MonthID>
    <MonthName>February</MonthName>
  </Months>
  <Months>
    <MonthID>3</MonthID>
```

Figure 2-22 XML file

Check the table(s) that you need from the XML file to load them. In this respect, an XML file acts like an Excel workbook that has more than one table of data.

1. Get Data button ⇒ More ⇒ XML ⇒ MonthsXMLTable.xml file.

2. Add the Months table to the report file.

Text File Tips

One way to know that there is a problem with a text file is that all of the fields have been imported into one column, when displayed in the Query Editor. To use a text file in Power BI Desktop, the file must meet certain criteria in addition to having the TXT file extension. On your own, if you are having trouble importing the data in a text file, open the file in Note Pad and confirm the following:

① The file does not have anything other than a header row and the rows of data. If used, the header row has to be the first row in the file.

② The separator between fields is valid.

③ When each row does not have the same number of fields the data will not line up properly, as shown in Figure 2-23. Notice in the first three rows that the Customer ID field has dates. This lets you know that these rows are missing either the Order ID or Employee ID field. The data should be modified before it is imported.

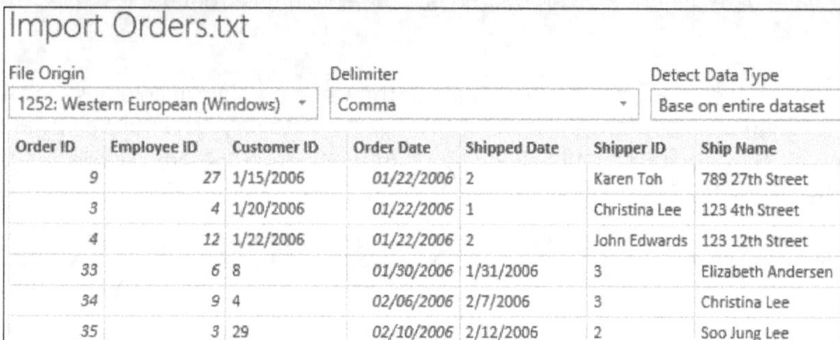

Order ID	Employee ID	Customer ID	Order Date	Shipped Date	Shipper ID	Ship Name
9	27	1/15/2006	01/22/2006	2	Karen Toh	789 27th Street
3	4	1/20/2006	01/22/2006	1	Christina Lee	123 4th Street
4	12	1/22/2006	01/22/2006	2	John Edwards	123 12th Street
33	6	8	01/30/2006	1/31/2006	3	Elizabeth Andersen
34	9	4	02/06/2006	2/7/2006	3	Christina Lee
35	3	29	02/10/2006	2/12/2006	2	Soo Jung Lee

Figure 2-23 Rows of data with a different number of fields

Import Data From A Text File

Text (TXT) files do not have any formatting like bold, italic or font size. To be used in Power BI Desktop, this file type has to have rows of data, as shown in Figure 2-24. Each row of data has fields (columns). An advantage of text files is that they can handle millions of rows of data. The fields are usually separated by commas. While the comma is the most used separator for text files, other separators like **QUOTES**, can also be used as a separator. Another type of file that can be imported using the Text import option, is text files with the **.TAB EXTENSION**.

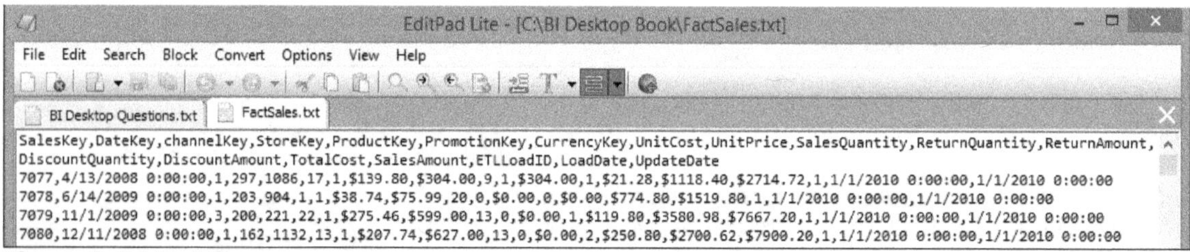

Figure 2-24 Text file

1. Get Data button ⇒ More ⇒ Text ⇒ FactSales.txt file (This file has over 2 million rows of data) ⇒ Click the Edit button.

2. Change the Query Name to `FactSalesTxt` ⇒ Close and apply the changes ⇒ Save the changes.

Import Data From A JSON File

JSON stands for **JAVASCRIPT OBJECT NOTATION.**

This is a programming language used for simple data structures. It is often used instead of XML because it requires fewer tags. Figure 2-25 shows the JSON file that you will import in this part of the exercise.

```
{
    "firstName": "Jane",
    "lastName": "Smith",
    "age": 25,
    "address":
    {
        "StreetAddress": "21 3rd Avenue",
        "City": "New York",
        "State": "NY",
        "ZipCode": "10021"
    },
    "PhoneNumber":
    [
        {
          "type": "home",
          "number": "212 555-1234"
        },
        {
          "type": "fax",
          "number": "646 555-2345"
```

Figure 2-25 JSON file

1. Get Data button ⇒ More ⇒ JSON ⇒ Select the CustomerForm.json file.

2. On the Query Editor, type `JSON` in front of the query name. You should see the contents of the file, as shown in Figure 2-26 ⇒ Save the changes to the file. You will also see a new tab. The Record Tools Convert tab and the **RECORD** and **LIST DATA TYPES** are covered in Chapter 5.

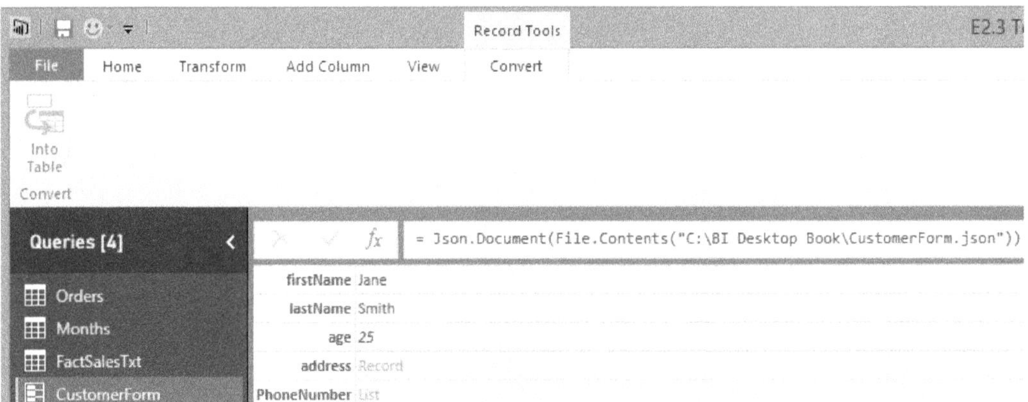

Figure 2-26 Record Tools Convert tab and the imported JSON file

Database Import Options

Figure 2-27 shows some of the database types that can be used to import data into Power BI Desktop. This section explains some of the relational database options shown in the figure.

SQL Server Database is a scalable data warehouse solution that is capable of storing hundreds of terabytes of data. Oracle, IBM DB2, and Sybase are all enterprise level relational database management systems, owned by different companies.

Many data sources require that connectors (also known as drivers or providers) be installed. You will see a message like the one shown below in Figure 2-28, when that is the case.

The Learn More link will let you know what needs to be installed. If you need to connect to one of these types of databases, you have to get and install the drivers from the company.

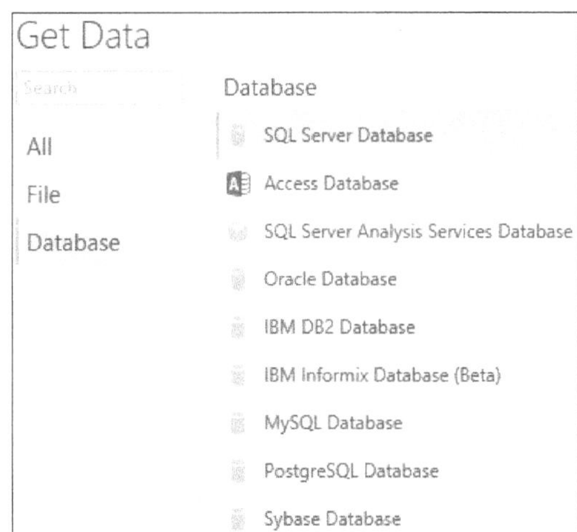

Figure 2-27 Database options

Keep in mind that many of the databases shown in the figure, will require you to get permission from someone in IT, just to get a logon account.

Many of these databases use the connection options shown in Figure 2-29. In addition to using an **SQL STATEMENT** to get the data that will be imported, a call to a **STORED PROCEDURE** can be used in the SQL Statement field.

To connect to OLAP (Online Analytical Processing) cubes, select the SQL Server Analysis Services database option.

The **DIRECT QUERY OPTION**, shown in Figure 2-29, is used to connect to a live data source. This option does not load data to the data model. While using a Direct Query connection means reports will display the most current data, without having to refresh, keep the following in mind:

① This connection type is slower then using data in the data model because the data is not stored on your computer. The data is constantly being updated at the source.
② If you need to publish the data to Power BI, you will have to install one of the Gateway tools.

The **NAVIGATE USING FULL HIERARCHY OPTION** shown in Figure 2-29, is used to see schema information with the Navigation hierarchy.

Relationships
Power BI Desktop does not automatically recognize or use relationships that are created between tables in a database. The relationships can be loaded to the data model, if the **IMPORT RELATIONSHIPS OPTION** is selected on the Options dialog box.

Sybase Database

This connector is not configured correctly.

This connector requires one or more additional components to be installed before it can be used.

Learn More

Figure 2-28 Message indicating additional software needs to be installed

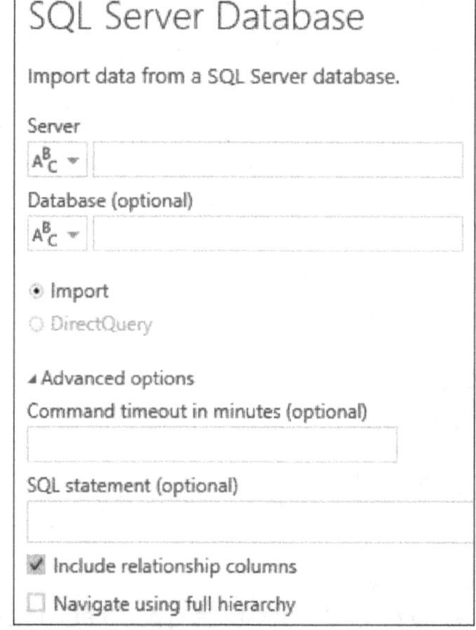

Figure 2-29 Database connector options

Exercise 2.4: Use An Access Database As The Data Source

1. Get Data button ⇒ More ⇒ Access Database ⇒ My Orders database.

2. In the Navigator window, check the following tables: Customers, Customers Extended, Order Details, Order Price Totals, Orders and Products ⇒ Click the Load button.

3. Save the file as `E2.4 My Orders database`.

Microsoft Access Import Tip
Access views can also be imported. Currently, there is no way to distinguish a table from a view on the Navigator window for Access databases, unless the table name indicates that it is a view. It is best to use a view, if one exists, for the data that you need. The reason is because views have fewer columns of data and often, the data in a view has been cleaned.

Load Data From Another Source

If you need data from other sources, you can load the data now.

1. Import all of the 04 tables and the Products table in the More Data Files workbook.

Both of the data sources that you loaded data from in this exercise, have a table named Products. While Power BI Desktop can handle this, it will be confusing for us, so we will rename one of the Product queries.

2. In the Query Editor, rename the Products (2) query to `New Products`.

3. Click on the Monthly Sales Pivot Table query ⇒ Home tab ⇒ Use First Row As Headers button ⇒ Use First Row As Headers ⇒ Home tab ⇒ Close & Apply button ⇒ Close & Apply.

How To Pin A File To The Recent Items List

The file that you just created in this exercise will be the starting point for many of the exercises in this book. You may want to pin it on the Recent Items list (on the File tab), shown in Figure 2-30, so that you can get to it quickly.

To pin a file, click on the icon illustrated in the figure.

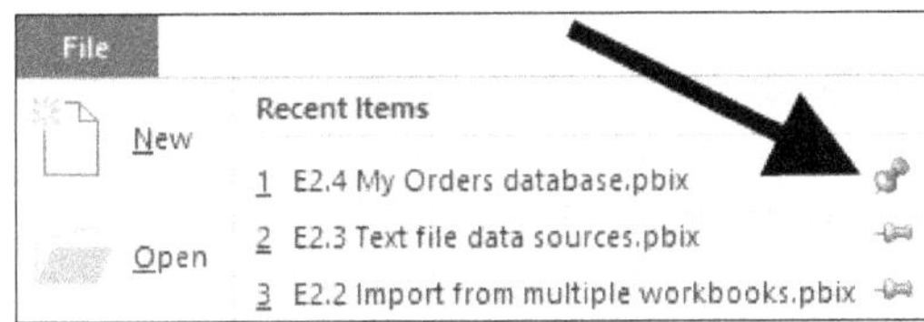

Figure 2-30 E2.4 File pinned to the Recent Items list

Selecting Related Tables

You will see the **SELECT RELATED TABLES BUTTON** shown at the bottom of Figure 2-31, when a database is selected as the data source and at least one table has been checked to be imported.

Clicking this button will search the relationships in the database to see if there are any tables that have a relationship created for the selected table. If so, the related tables will automatically be checked. If you are not familiar with the selected tables or do not need them, you can view the data and decided whether or not you want to import any of the related tables.

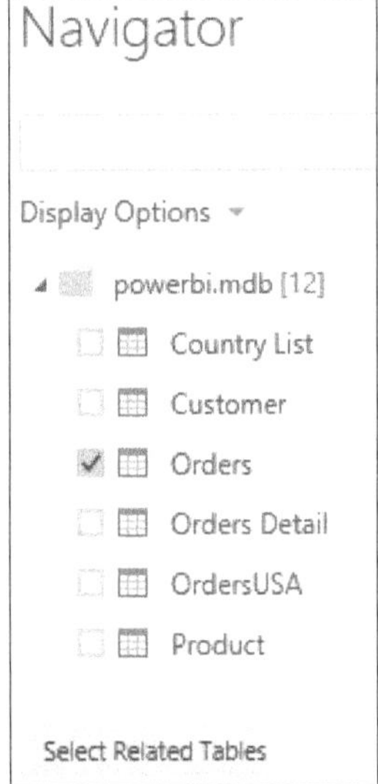

Figure 2-31 Select Related Tables button

Azure Options

Figure 2-32 shows some of the Azure data source options. "Azure" is Microsoft's cloud. The **AZURE MARKETPLACE** is a web site that has third-party data that can be used for analysis or testing purposes. Some of the data sets are free and others are not.

This data resource is helpful when you need historical data, like stock prices. Another popular resource on this web site is historical weather data.

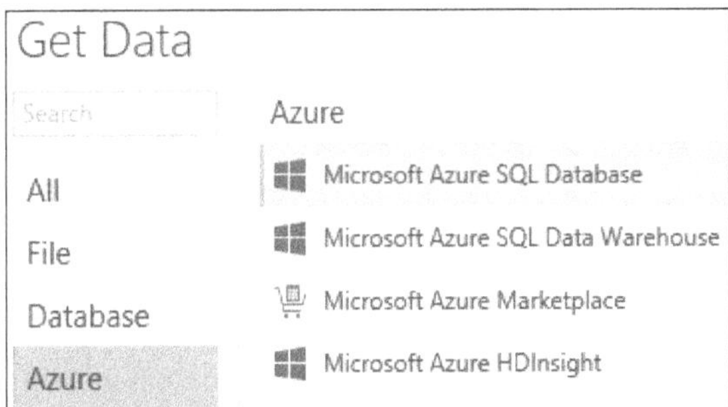

Figure 2-32 Azure data source options

To download and use data from the marketplace, you need to create an account (it's free), then subscribe to the data set(s) that you want to use. If you have a Microsoft account (formerly known as a Windows Live ID account) or an Azure Marketplace account key, you can use either of these accounts to log into the Azure Marketplace.

> **Azure Marketplace**
> In March, 2016, I checked the Azure.com web site and saw a message saying that they are working on a new marketplace web site. I wanted to let you know, in case the process covered below to create an account or download data changes. Hopefully, after the web site changes, you will still be able to get to the data to download it, using the instructions below.

How To Get Data From The Azure Marketplace

This section will show you how to connect to and download data from the Azure Marketplace. If you already have one of the accounts discussed above, go to the "Connect To The Azure Marketplace" section.

Create An Account

If you do not have one of the accounts discussed above, follow the steps in this section to create an account.

1. In your web browser, go to `https://datamarket.azure.com/partner/excel.`
2. At the top of the page, click on the **SIGN IN** link. Near the bottom of the page, you should see a **SIGN UP NOW** link ⇒ Click on it.
3. Fill out the Create an account form.

Connect To The Azure Marketplace

If you have already used the Azure Marketplace, you will see slightly different options then the ones shown in some of the figures.

1. Get Data button ⇒ More ⇒ Azure ⇒ Microsoft Azure Marketplace ⇒ Connect button ⇒ Sign in button. You should see the web page shown in Figure 2-33.

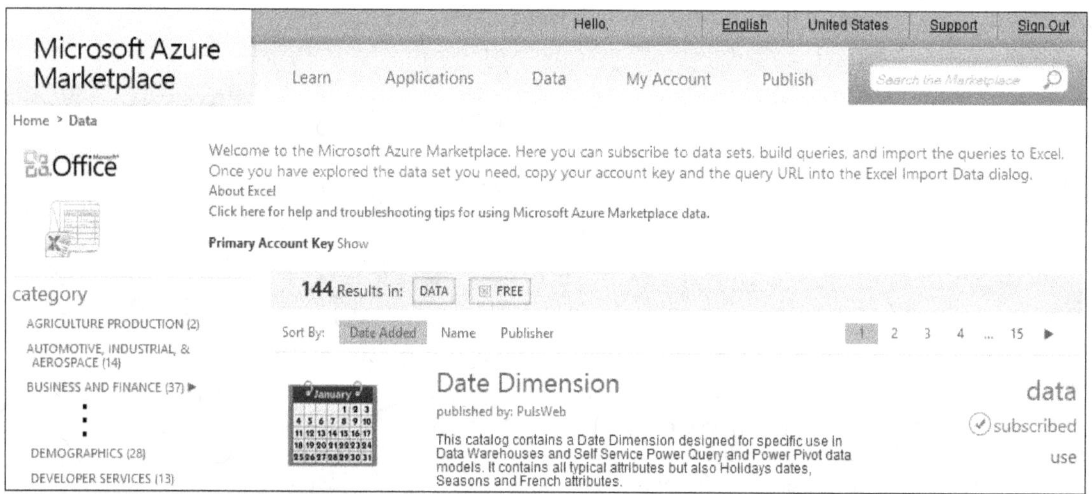

Figure 2-33 Azure Marketplace web site

2. Click on the Data tab at the top of the web page ⇒ In the Category list on the left, click on the **DEVELOPER SERVICES** link ⇒ Click on the Date Dimension option.
3. Click on the Sign Up link, illustrated in Figure 2-34 to subscribe ⇒ On the Sign Up screen, check the Terms and Privacy policy option ⇒ Click the Sign Up button.

If you need a date table and do not want to create one, you can download this one for free.

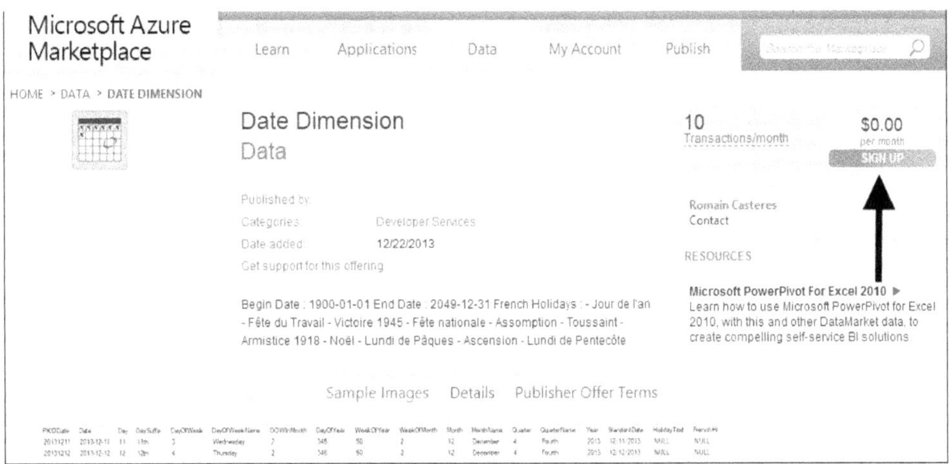

Figure 2-34 Date Dimension data feed page

4. On the Thank you page shown in Figure 2-35, click on the **EXPLORE THIS DATASET** link.

   Once your Azure Marketplace account is set up and you select Azure ⇒ Microsoft Azure Marketplace ⇒ Connect, you will automatically be logged in.

   The **NAVIGATOR WINDOW** (shown in Figure 2-36) will automatically open and will display a list of all of the datasets that you are subscribed to.

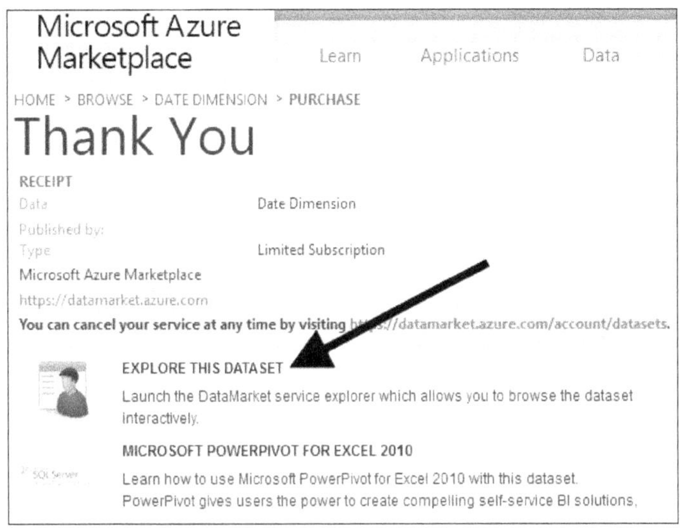

Figure 2-35 Thank you page

View The Data

1. Get Data button ⇒ Azure ⇒ Microsoft Azure Marketplace.

   You should see the Date Dimension dataset in the Navigator window, as shown in Figure 2-36 ⇒ Add the DimDate table.

   The **ADD DATA FEEDS LINK**, illustrated in the figure, will open the Azure Marketplace, so that you can subscribe to more datasets.

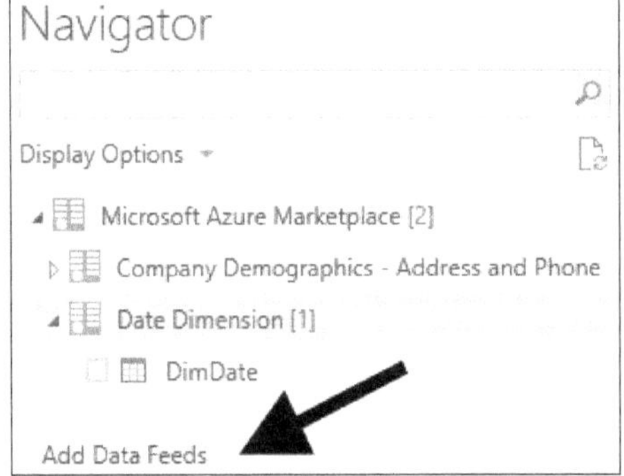

Figure 2-36 Date Dimension dataset

2. Close and apply the changes ⇒ Save the file as `Chapter 2 Azure Marketplace data`.

Other (Data Sources) Options

In addition to the data sources that have been covered so far, the data source options shown in Figure 2-37 are also available.

The **BLANK QUERY OPTION** is used to write a script using the **M LANGUAGE** to import the data.

The **ODBC OPTION** is used to select a Data Source Name (DSN) from the ones already set up on your computer, as shown in Figure 2-38. The options in the drop-down list can vary from computer to computer. Select (None) in the Data Source Name drop-down list to create a connection string that does not rely on an existing DSN. This dialog box can also be used to create or add connection string information, as well as, connect to database types that are not listed in the Database or Azure sections on the Get Data dialog box.

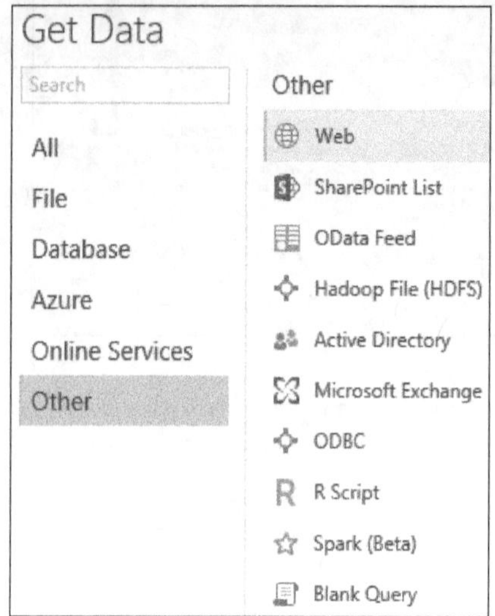

Figure 2-37 Other data source options

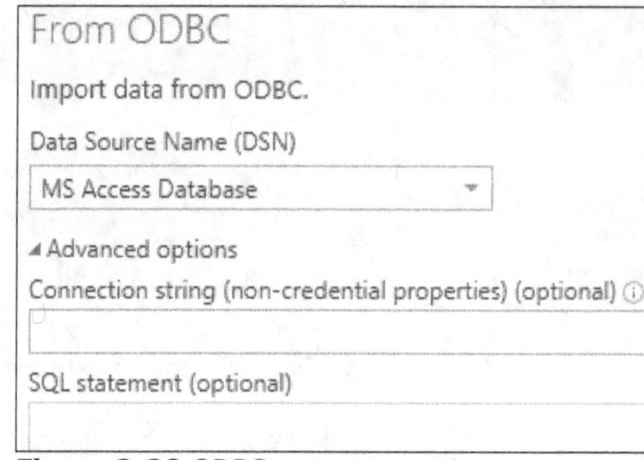

Figure 2-38 ODBC connector options

What Is A Data Feed?

Earlier in this chapter you read that data feeds can be used as a data source. If you have seen the icon shown in Figure 2-39 on a web site and clicked on it, you were subscribing to a data feed.

Figure 2-39 Data Feed icon

A data feed is a way to exchange data. They provide the data via web services. To connect to a web service, type in the web site address of the web service. Data feeds allow people to receive updates when the data on the web site changes.

Using Data Feeds As The Data Source

Select this option when the data that you need to import is on a web site or corporate intranet. A data feed is an **XML DATA STREAM** that is created from an online source. This data stream is sent to a document or application.

Figure 2-40 shows the OData Feed connector options.

The **INCLUDE OPEN TYPE COLUMNS OPTION** is used to indicate that there are columns of data that have dynamic properties (that were created using the Open Type) that you want to import.

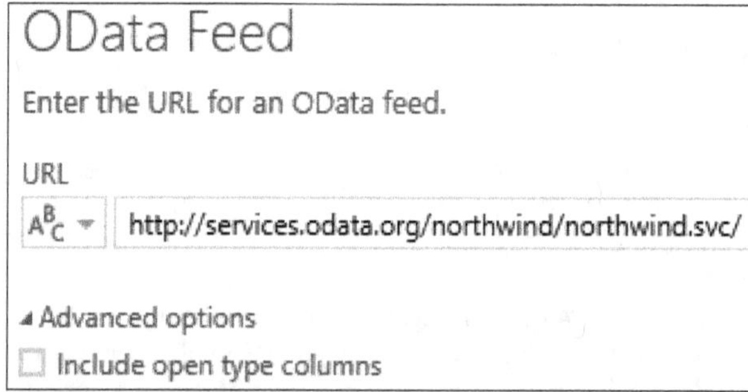

Figure 2-40 OData Feed connector options

Importing Reporting Services Reports
If you have used Power Pivot, you know that SSRS (SQL Server Reporting Services) reports could be imported as a data feed. The OData import option in Power BI Desktop does not support the **ATOM DATA FEED** import format, which is what SSRS reports generate. Instead, the reports URL has to be used to export the report data to a .csv file and then import the CSV file into Power BI Desktop.

Exercise 2.5: Import Data From An OData Data Feed

In this exercise you will learn how to import data from a public data feed.

1. Get Data button ⇒ More ⇒ Other ⇒ OData Feed.

2. In the **URL** field, type `http://services.odata.org/northwind/northwind.svc/`, as shown above in Figure 2-40 ⇒ Click OK. You should see the tables shown in Figure 2-41. You will see more tables then those shown in the figure.

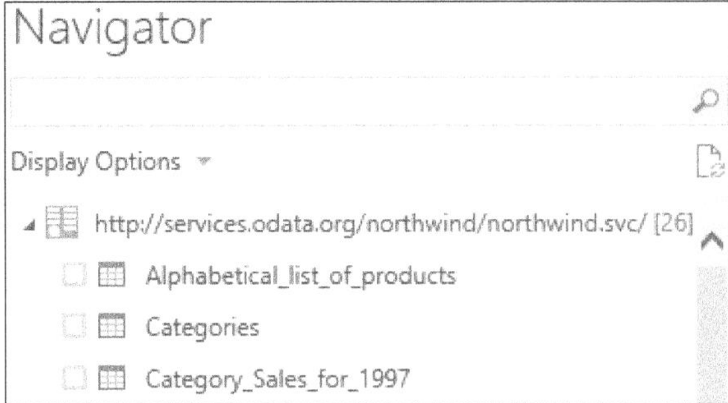

Figure 2-41 Tables from the data feed

3. Select some of the tables ⇒ Click the Load button ⇒ Save the file as `E2.5 Import from an OData feed`.

How To Copy Data To An External File

While this chapter focused on loading data into Power BI Desktop, the options listed below are used to copy data in a query in Power BI Desktop to an external file, like a spreadsheet.

① Copy entire table option [See Chapter 3, Table 3-1]
② Copy entire list option [See Chapter 3, Table 3-7]
③ Copy table option [See Chapter 8, Table 8-1]

Summary

This chapter covered finding (discovering) and loading data from a variety of data source types, including data from the web. As you saw, some data source types allow you to preview the data in the Navigator window, and other data sources automatically bypass viewing data in the Navigator window and immediately display the data in the Query Editor.

While the import exercises in this book work as expected, out in the real world, this may not always be the case, with some of the data that you need to import. Take your time to work through the issue.

Regardless of how the data can be viewed, it does not have to be loaded to the data model first. The goal of this chapter is to get you acquainted with the external data options on the Home tab, especially the options on the Get Data button, because they are how you import data.

Yes, I know that there wasn't a lot of exciting topics in this chapter. The next chapter will formally introduce the Query Editor and show you some techniques for cleaning data and getting the data ready to create reports.

GETTING STARTED WITH THE QUERY EDITOR

In this chapter you will learn about the Query Editor. This includes learning about the types of data shaping options that are available.

CHAPTER 3

Query Editor Overview

In the previous chapter, you learned how to connect to and import data from a variety of data sources. Once you have found the data that you need to create reports, you will probably realize that the data needs to be cleaned or modified. This is what the Query Editor was designed to handle.

As you will see, the Query Editor does not have any formatting options like bold or selecting a font. That type of formatting is done when the report is created in the Report view. You will also see that many of the options on the toolbars are also on more than one shortcut menu. The Query Editors role is to get the data ready to be used to create reports.

Power BI Desktop refers to this process as **TRANSFORMING DATA** or **TRANSFORMATIONS**. Examples of transformations are excluding and removing rows or columns of data, merging and creating new columns of data. This is usually done before the data is loaded to the data model, but transforming the data can be done after the data is in the data model. The Query Editor is the tool that is used to accomplish the tasks listed below, plus a whole lot more.

☑ Filter records
☑ Merge and append data from different tables
☑ Rename, reorder or delete columns

If all of the data that you will use on your own, comes from databases and you will not have a need to clean the data or the data cleaning is the DBA's responsibility, you may not have as much of a need to use the Query Editor. On the other hand, if you have data that comes from CSV, text, web pages or multiple spreadsheets, the Query Editor will quickly become your friend <smile>.

If any of the following tasks even vaguely resembles how you currently get data ready to create reports, the Query Editor will make your life easier.

① Copy and paste data between sheets or workbooks.
② Use data on hidden sheets in an Excel workbook and use VLOOKUP to combine data.
③ Spend hours cleaning data in Excel.
④ The data is in columns, but you need it in rows.
⑤ Create macros to try and automate the tasks listed above.

The reason that the Query Editor will make your life easier is because you can accomplish each of the tasks listed above, usually with a few mouse clicks and you do not have to write code to do it. As you will see, the Query Editor has a lot of options that you can use to modify data. I realize that the number of options can be overwhelming, especially if you are just getting stared. This is why I devoted four chapters, in this book, to the Query Editor. I tried to structure the exercises to cover options that I think people will use the most. Most of the options are probably not as complicated to use, as you may be thinking.

What Is The Query Editor Designed To Do?

It is used to discover (find), search, connect to, filter, view, append and merge data sets, without being forced to load the data into the data model first. The Query Editor makes it easy to get data into the right format and clean it. The selected data can be loaded to the data model so that it can be analyzed using several tools including the other Power BI tools and Excel. In some respects, the Query Editor is like Print Preview, because you can see the data before making the decision to use it to create a visualization. [See What Is ETL?]

The section below discusses what the Query Editor brings to the table. It is designed to do all of the following:

☑ **DATA DISCOVERY** This is the process of finding the data sources that possibly have the data needed to create visualizations. The data can be a public or private data source.
☑ **DATA MODIFICATION** In Power BI Desktop, this is referred to as **TRANSFORMING** the data. This is the process of filtering, cleaning (changing the formatting from all lower case to all upper case, for example) and changing the structure of the table. When needed, data from one table can be added to another table, even if the tables come from different file types. For example, you have a list of all basketball games for the season on a spreadsheet and the stats for each game are on different web pages. You could download each web page to a query in Power BI Desktop, then add the stats for each game to your table of games.
☑ **DATA LOADING** This feature loads the data into the data model. This process copies the data from where it is, to the data model.

Another reason to take a look at the Query Editor is if you currently use or know that you are just around the corner from having to use or learn to use (but don't want to), Excel formulas or functions, like **VLOOKUP** or **VISUAL BASIC FOR APPLICATIONS (VBA)**, to transform your data. The Query Editor takes nothing away from these tools, as in some instances, they are more powerful. Being powerful though, does come with a higher and longer learning curve. And if you already know SQL, you can use SQL queries in the Query Editor.

If you have had or are currently having difficulty getting data from a data source or are having to write SQL formulas to get data, also give the Query Editor a try, because it does make "getting" the data easy. For the most part, writing SQL or M code is optional because they extend what the Query Editor offers. Hopefully, you will be pleasantly surprised with what can be achieved in the Query Editor alone.

What probably is not obvious is that the Query Editor works like a macro. Behind the scenes (of the Query Editor interface), options that you select to get data, as well as, the steps that are created in the Query Editor to transform the data, are recorded and saved in what the Query Editor calls a query. This "query" will remind you of an Excel table. This query is created in the M language. Like a macro that you can create in Excel, the steps created and saved in the query can be used over and over. The steps can also be reordered or changed easily.

What Is ETL?

The process of selecting data, loading data, rearranging or deleting columns, joining columns from different tables and creating calculated fields are all part of getting the data ready to be analyzed. The IT world refers to this process as **EXTRACT TRANSFORM LOAD** (ETL for short). Yes, the Query Editor is an ETL tool. Many Excel users have been completing these tasks manually for years, without knowing what its called.

It is very possible that you will need to repeat many of the ETL steps several times to get the data the way that you need it. It took me hours and hours to create the practice files for this book. I remember spending six hours creating and loading data into a database, then realized that I had some fields in the wrong table. ETL tools provide the functionality discussed below.

Extract

This is the process of selecting a data source (or as many data sources as needed) and extracting a subset of the data in each data source. Power BI Desktop supports many data sources and new connectors are currently created on a regular basis. For example, the Power BI Desktop team has already created connectors for SalesForce and Facebook. Connectors provide access to data sources that Power BI Desktop can connect to and import data from.

Transform

Transformation shapes and cleans the extracted data. This is the process of changing the data by using one, some or all of the following data enhancement techniques:

① **DATA INTEGRATION** Appending, joining and grouping data are examples of integration.

② **DATA CLEANSING** Deleting rows or columns of data that are not needed. Other examples of data cleansing include formatting, which includes changing the data type, or filtering data.

③ **DATA ENRICHMENT** Usually refers to adding new data. Adding a new column by combining data from other columns or creating a calculated field, are examples of data enrichment. If the data will be loaded to the data model, data enrichment tasks, are best accomplished using the Data view.

Load

Load takes the dataset from the transform process and adds it to the data model.

Understanding The "Query" In Power BI Desktop

This may be the most important concept or component of the Query Editor to understand. Queries, like the data model, are stored in the report .pbix file. Unlike the data model, which is one per file, in theory, there can be an unlimited number of queries in the report file. Just like tables can be joined, so can queries. A query in Power BI Desktop, is the equivalent of a table in a database.

What Is A Query?

In Power BI Desktop, in addition to storing the data, a query contains a list of instructions (called **STEPS**), in a specific order, that get (imports the data) and transform data. Usually, this data will be used to create a report. Think of a query like a macro (because it has the same functionality), where the instructions (steps) are processed in the order that you specify. Queries have at least one step (importing the data into Power BI Desktop), usually more.

Each step generates code using the **M LANGUAGE**, which is a language that is used to create queries that **MASHUP DATA**. It is case sensitive. In addition to using it in the Query Editor in Power BI Desktop, it can also be used in Power Query for Excel. Behind the scenes, the Query Editor generates M code for the steps that you add to the query. Learning the M language, in detail, is beyond the scope of this book.

The data source always creates the first step of a query. The options that you select and save in the Query Editor are added to the query. The query contains instructions for how the data needs to be manipulated. A Power BI Desktop report file can have more than one query, because each table or file that is imported, has its own query, as well as, tables that you create using the **ENTER DATA BUTTON.**

M Language Reference Guide
If you are interested in learning more about the M language, this web page is a good starting point.
https://msdn.microsoft.com/en-us/library/mt211003.aspx

Opening The Query Editor

There are several ways to open the Query Editor, as listed below.

① Home tab ⇒ Edit Queries button ⇒ Edit Queries
② Navigator window ⇒ Select a table ⇒ Click the Edit button
③ Navigator window ⇒ Right-click on a table ⇒ Select Edit
④ Data view ⇒ Right-click on a column heading ⇒ Edit Query
⑤ Data view ⇒ Right-click on a table in the Fields panel ⇒ Edit Query
⑥ Report view ⇒ Right-click on a table in the Fields panel ⇒ Edit Query

The Query Editor

The window shown in Figure 3-1 is used to transform the data. I guess you could say that this is where the magic happens in Power BI Desktop <smile>. In addition to the numbered sections, there are four more tabs (Home, Transform, Add Column and View), that have options to complete the ETL tasks. The options on the tabs are explained in different Query Editor chapters. The numbered sections are explained below.

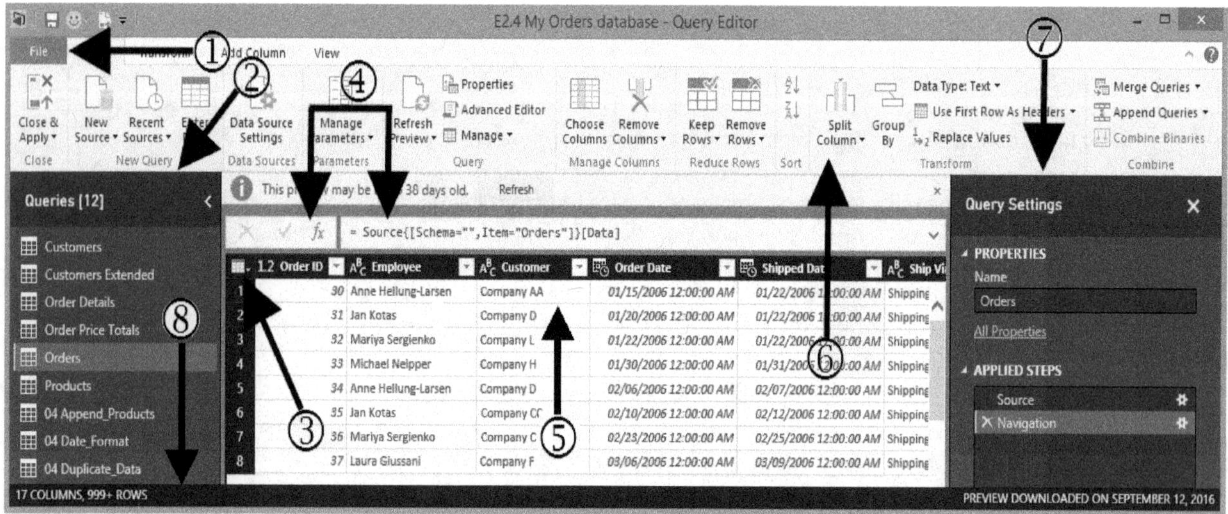

Figure 3-1 Query Editor

① **FILE TAB** [See File Tab Options]

② The **QUERIES PANEL** is similar to the Navigator window, because it displays the queries (tables) that are connected to the report file. The difference is that in the Query Editor, the panel is collapsible, by clicking the arrow to the right of the number of queries. This panel is used to switch between queries without having to close and reopen the Query Editor.

③ The **TABLE BUTTON** displays the shortcut menu shown later in Figure 3-5. The options are used to customize the data and are applied to the entire table. These options are also on the Home tab, except for the Add Custom Column, Add Conditional Column and Add Index Column options, which are on the Add Column tab.

④ The **FORMULA BAR** is used to create and edit **M FORMULAS** for each step in the query. The **FX BUTTON** adds a custom step, that is used to create an M formula.

⑤ The **RESULTS SECTION** (which is also called the **GRID** or **DATA WINDOW**) displays the data up to and including the selected step in the Query Settings panel. Selecting different steps, displays the data differently.

⑥ The **QUERY EDITOR TOOLBAR** contains the options to get the data in the right format. Making changes to the data is what creates the steps and formulas in the query.

⑦ The **QUERY SETTINGS PANEL** [See Query Settings Panel]

⑧ The **STATUS BAR** displays the number of columns and rows in the selected query. The far right side of the status bar displays the date that the data was imported into Power BI Desktop. If you enabled the option to be notified when a new version of Power BI Desktop is available, you will see a message here, letting you know.

Saving Changes In The Query Editor
There are two ways that **PENDING CHANGES** can be saved: Now or Later. If you want to apply the pending changes and save the report file, at the same time, click the Save button on the Query Editors Quick Access toolbar. If there are pending changes when the Save button is clicked, you will see the dialog box shown in Figure 3-2. Click the **APPLY BUTTON**, to apply the pending changes and save the file now. Click the **APPLY LATER** button to keep the pending changes, but not save them now.

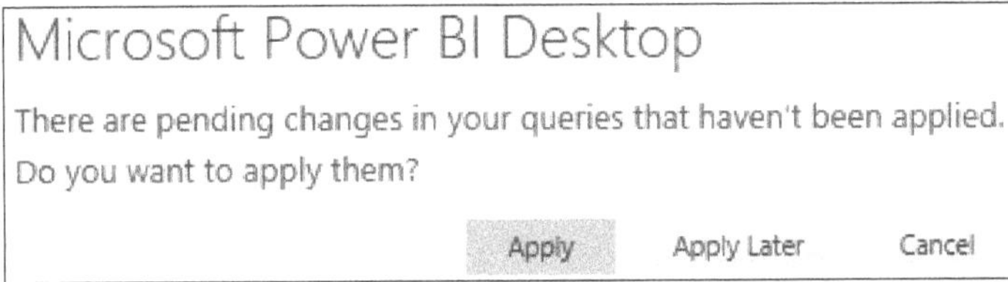

Figure 3-2 When to apply pending changes message

Queries Panel Icons

The queries can have different icons, as shown in Figure 3-3.

Imported data has an icon that looks like a spreadsheet.

Parameters and queries created using the **BLANK QUERY OPTION**, has the icon shown next to Query 3 in the figure.

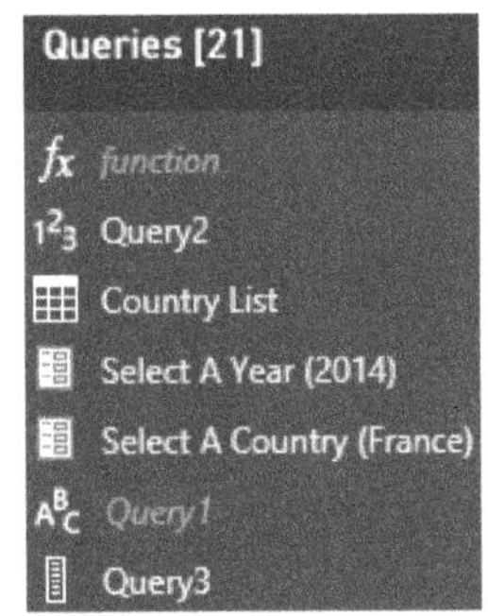

Figure 3-3 Queries panel

Query Editor Row Limit
The Query Editor will only display a maximum of 1,000 rows per table. When this is the case, "999+ Rows" will be displayed in the lower left corner of the status bar, as shown earlier in Figure 3-1. Keep this in mind if you need to copy data to another source, like a spreadsheet, because you will only be copying 1,000 rows maximum. If you need to copy more than 1,000 rows, use the Data view to copy the data.

Save As Button On The File Menu
For a reason that I do not understand, the Save As button was renamed to **THIS PC**, as shown in Figure 3-4.

File Tab Options

Figure 3-4 shows the options on the File tab. The options unique to the Query Editor, are explained below.

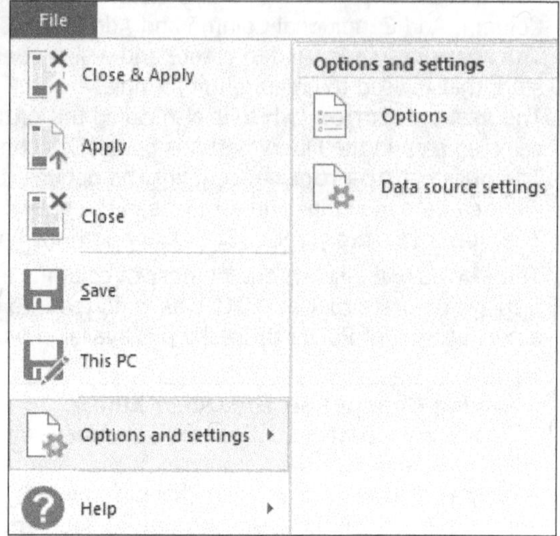

Figure 3-4 File tab

CLOSE & APPLY [See Close & Apply Options]

CLOSE Closes the Query Editor without applying the pending changes to the query.

OPTIONS AND SETTINGS Displays the options on the right side of the figure. It is helpful having these options on the Query Editor, so that you do not have to switch between the Power BI Desktop window and the Query Editor, to change options on these dialog boxes. An example is changing the location of a data source.

OPTIONS Opens the Options dialog box. [See Chapter 1, Figure 1-12]

DATA SOURCE SETTINGS Opens the Data Source Settings dialog box. [See Chapter 1, Figure 1-28]

Table (Button) Shortcut Menu

Copy Entire Table
Use First Row As Headers
Add Custom Column...
Add Conditional Column
Add Index Column
Choose Columns...
Keep Top Rows...
Keep Bottom Rows...
Keep Range of Rows...
Keep Duplicates
Keep Errors
Remove Top Rows...
Remove Bottom Rows...
Remove Alternate Rows...
Remove Duplicates
Remove Errors
Merge Queries...
Append Queries...

Figure 3-5 Table (button) shortcut menu

Option	Description
Copy Entire Table	Is used to copy the data in the query to a file, like a worksheet in Excel or a text file.
Use First Row As Headers	[See Use First Row As Headers Options]
Add Custom Column	[See Chapter 4, Add Custom Column Options]
Add Conditional Column	[See Chapter 5, Conditional Columns]
Add Index Column	[See Chapter 4, Add Index Column Options]
Choose Columns	(1)
Keep Top Rows	(2)
Keep Bottom Rows	(2)
Keep Range of Rows	(2)
Keep Duplicates	(2)
Remove Top Rows	(2)
Remove Bottom Rows	(2)
Remove Alternate Rows	(2)
Remove Duplicates	(2)
Remove Errors	Removes rows that have an error in any cell in the row.
Merge Queries	(1)
Append Queries	(1)

Table 3-1 Table (button) shortcut menu options explained

(1) [See Merge Queries And Append Queries Buttons]
(2) [See Keep And Remove Rows Options]

Queries Shortcut Menu

Right-clicking on a query in the Queries panel displays the shortcut menu shown in Figure 3-6. The options are explained in Table 3-2.

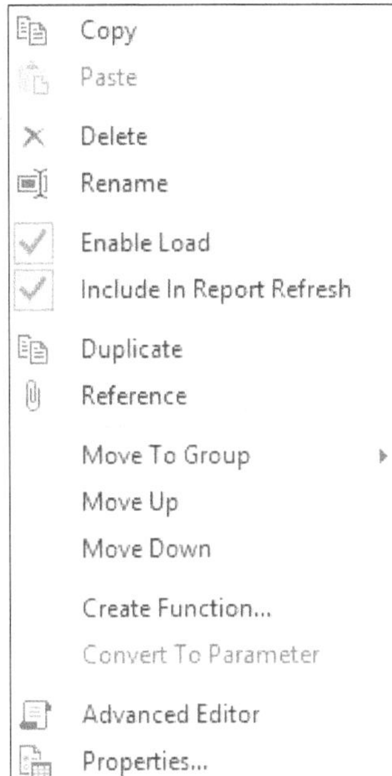

Figure 3-6 Queries shortcut menu

Option	Description
Copy	Copies the code for the query, so that it can be used for another query. Once selected, the Paste option is enabled.
Paste	Adds a copy of the query to the current file or another file.
Delete	Deletes the selected query.
Rename	Is used the change the name of the query. Double-clicking on the query name or clicking on the query name and pressing F2, is also used to rename a query.
Enable Load	Loads the data in the query into the data model. (3)
Include in Report Refresh	If checked, the data in the query will be refreshed when the Refresh All option is selected. [See Figure 3-44] (3)
Duplicate	(4)
Reference	(4)
Move To Group	[See Move To Group Option]
Move Up	Moves the selected query up one row in the group. (5)
Move Down	Moves the selected query down one row in the group. (5)
Create Function	Is used to create a function from the selected query, whether or not it references a parameter.
Convert To Parameter	This option is only enabled when a query is selected that does not reference a parameter. When selected, the query will be converted to a parameter.
Convert To Query	This option is only enabled when a parameter query is selected. This option will change the parameter query to a regular query.
Advanced Editor	[See Chapter 5, Advanced Editor]
Properties	Is used to add a description or note to the query.

Table 3-2 Queries shortcut menu options explained

(3) Clicking on this option also enables/disables the corresponding option on the Query Properties dialog box. [See Figure 3-25]
(4) [See Using A Query As A Data Source]
(5) This option cannot be used to move queries to another group.

Queries Panel (Blank Space) Shortcut Menu

Right-clicking on a blank space on the Queries panel displays the shortcut menu shown in Figure 3-7. The options are explained in Table 3-3.

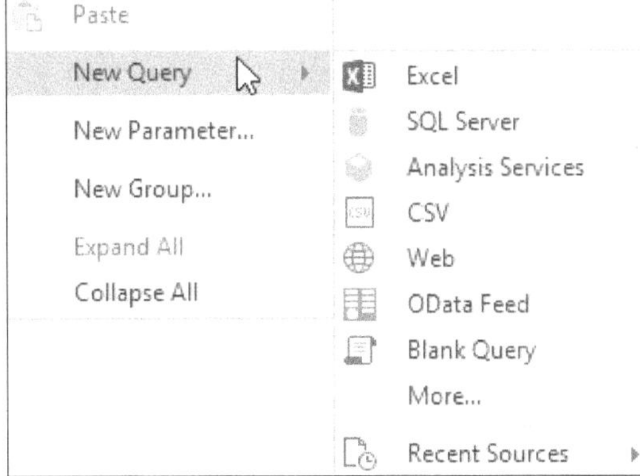

Figure 3-7 Queries panel (blank space) shortcut menu

Option	Description
Paste	Places a copy of the query (that is in the clipboard) into the Queries panel.
New Query	Is used to import data by creating a new query. The import options are the same as the Get Data options covered in Chapter 2.
New Parameter	[See Chapter 8, Query Parameters]
New Group	[See Table 3-4]
Expand All	[See Table 3-4]
Collapse All	[See Table 3-4]

Table 3-3 Queries panel (blank space) shortcut menu options explained

Query Naming Convention
Function names (like DATE and UPPERCASE) should not be used as a query name. Doing so will generate an error.

Renaming A Column
While you have the option to rename a column to whatever you want, within reason, there should be some consideration for the people that will use the reports and dashboards that you create. They need to understand the column name.

Another consideration is if you are going to use the **Q&A NATURAL LANGUAGE OPTION** in PowerBI.com, with the reports and dashboards that you create in Power BI Desktop. This option works best when the column names can be recognized as Synonyms.

Using A Query As A Data Source

There are two ways to use a query as a data source, as explained below. Both options can be accessed from the shortcut menu on the Queries panel and the **MANAGE BUTTON** on the Home tab.

DUPLICATE Creates a copy of the selected query, then displays the data in the Query Editor. The copy can be used to make changes to the data and leave the existing query unchanged. There is no link if you will, between the original query and the duplicated query. Changes made in the original query do not affect the duplicated query.

REFERENCE This option also creates a copy of the query. The difference is that this option uses the output (the structure of the data, as it is, on the last applied step) of the original query. This is often done with a query that has a lot of data and needs to be divided into smaller queries. Doing this can make the data easier to maintain. The other difference between this option and the Duplicate option is that this query is linked to the original query. This means that changes made to the original query can cause queries that reference it, to no longer work as intended.

Move To Group Option

This option is used to create groups (folders) for the queries and move the queries to a folder, to organize them. It provides a way to display selected queries together. Figure 3-8 shows 12 queries that are in one of three groups.

This technique is useful if several queries have something in common, like a group for each department that needs reports or a group of queries that have the same data source. For example, the queries in Group A, could use tables in database A and the queries in Group B use data from the Azure Marketplace.

The **OTHER QUERIES** group, shown in the figure, is automatically created, after you create the first group in the file. By default, this group contains all of the queries, until you move them to another group.

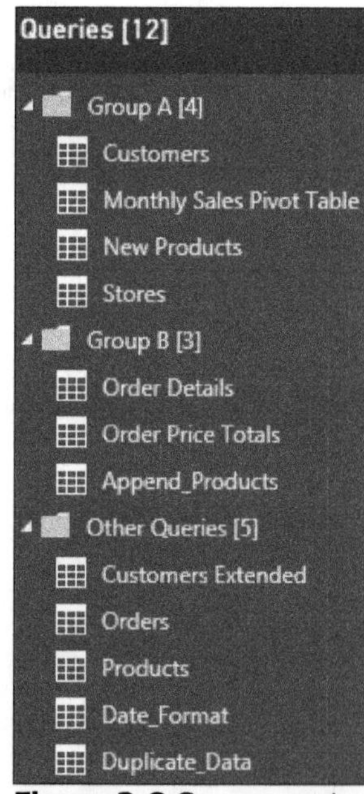

Figure 3-8 Groups created for the queries

Queries Panel Tip
In addition to creating groups to place queries in, you can also rearrange the order that the queries are displayed in, on the Queries panel shown above in Figure 3-8, by using drop and drag to move the query to where you want it.

Group Name Shortcut Menu

Groups have their own shortcut menu, as shown in Figure 3-9. The options are explained in Table 3-4.

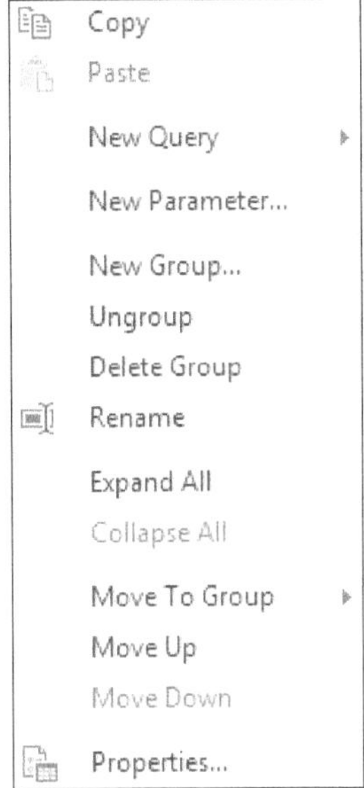

Figure 3-9 Group name shortcut menu

Option	Description
Copy	Places a copy of the group and all items in it, in the clipboard. (6)
Paste	Pastes the copied group in the clipboard and all queries in it, into another location on the Queries panel. (6)
New Query	[See Table 3-3] (6)
New Parameter	[See Chapter 8, Query Parameters] (6)
New Group	Displays the dialog box shown in Figure 3-10. The options are used to create a subgroup for the group that this option was selected from.
Ungroup	Deletes the selected group and moves the queries in the group to the Other Queries group, unless the group being deleted has a sub group. If there is a subgroup, the sub group is promoted to a group and the queries that were in the original group are moved to the promoted group.
Delete Group	Deletes the selected group and queries in the group. (6)
Rename	Is used to rename the group. (6)
Expand All	Displays all of the queries in the Queries panel. (6)
Collapse All	Hides all of the queries in the Queries panel. (6)
Move To Group	Moves the group to another group and becomes a sub group. The **NEW GROUP OPTION** creates a group, a level above the selected group.
Move Up	Moves the selected group up, above the previous group. (7)
Move Down	Moves the selected group down, below the next group. (7)
Properties	Displays the Group Properties options, which are the same as the New Group options, shown in Figure 3-10. You can change the name of the group.

Table 3-4 Group name shortcut menu options explained

(6) This option is also on the "Other Queries" group shortcut menu.
(7) The queries in the group are also moved.

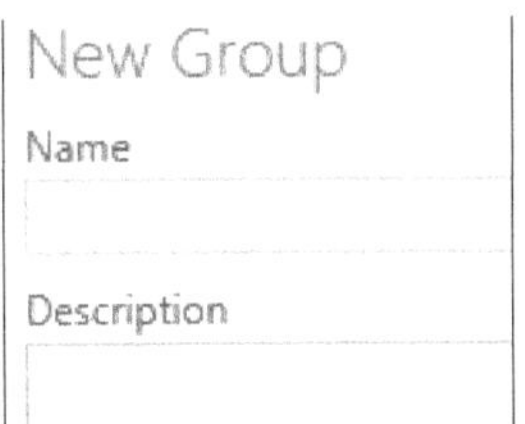

Figure 3-10 New Group dialog box

Column Shortcut Menu

The options shown in Figure 3-11 are used to transform (change) the data.

This shortcut menu is available when you right-click on one column header. Keep in mind that these options are applied to all of the data in the column, not just a specific cell.

These options are also available on the Query Editor toolbar.

If you need to transform a single cell of data, use the cell shortcut menu options covered later in this chapter.

If multiple columns are selected, you will only see options on the shortcut menu that can be applied to all of the selected columns, as shown in Figure 3-12.

The options that are available on either shortcut menu, depend on the data type of the selected columns.

The options shown on both shortcut menus are explained in Table 3-5.

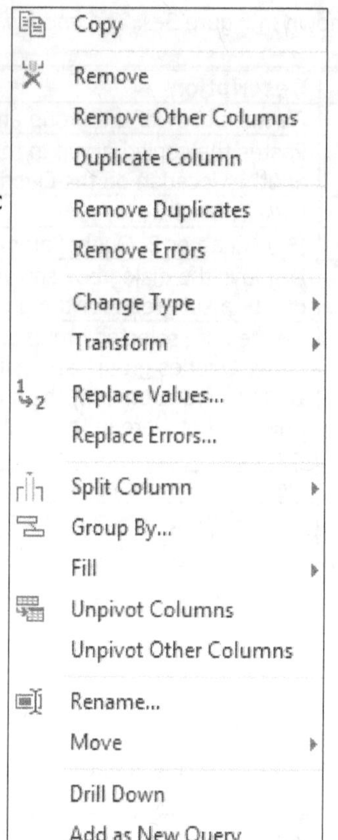

Figure 3-11 Column shortcut menu

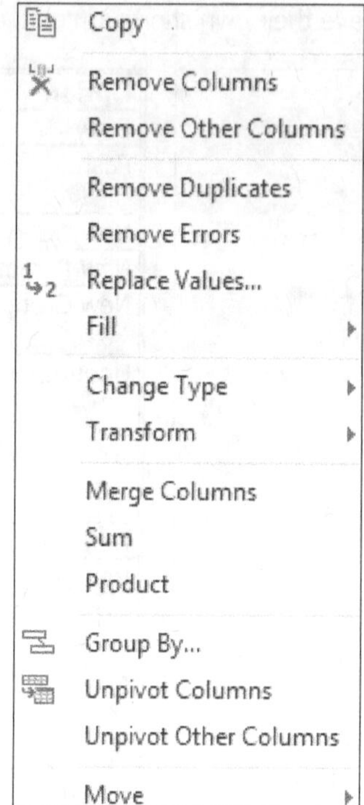

Figure 3-12 Column shortcut menu when multiple columns are selected

Option	Description
Copy	Is used to copy the data in the selected column to a file, like a worksheet in Excel.
Remove	[See Remove Columns Options] (8)
Remove Columns	[See Remove Columns Options] (8)
Remove Other Columns	[See Remove Columns Options] (8)
Duplicate Column	Creates a copy of the column of data and places the new column at the end of the table, on the right.
Remove Duplicates	[See Keep And Remove Rows Options] (8)
Remove Errors	Deletes rows that have a data error in the column, that this option is applied to. (8)
Change Type	[See Change Type Option] (8)
Transform	[See Transform Option] (8)
Replace Values	[See Replace Values] (8)
Replace Errors	[See Chapter 5, Table 5-1]
Split Column	This option is only available for a text data field. [See Split Column Options]
Group By	[See Group By Options] (8)
Fill	[See Chapter 5, Using The Fill Option] (8)
Unpivot Columns	[See Chapter 6, Unpivoting Data] (8)
Unpivot Other Columns	[See Chapter 6, Unpivoting Data] (8)
Rename	Is used to change the column heading name. Keep in mind that the column name is what is displayed on the visuals that you create, as well as formulas that use the column. Currently, there is no way to display a different name for the column displayed on a visual.
Move	[See Chapter 5, Move Options] (8)
Drill Down	Adds a step to the query that changes the view to only display the data in the selected column. This option is mostly used with columns that have metadata that has embedded information.

Table 3-5 Column shortcut menu options explained

Option	Description
Add as New Query	[See Add As New Query Option]
Merge Columns	[See Chapter 5, Table 5-1] (8)
Sum	Adds the values in the selected columns and places the result in a new column named **SUM**. This option works the same as the **ADD FUNCTION**. (9)
Product	Multiples the values in the selected columns and places the result in a new column named **MULTIPLY**. This option works the same as the **MULTIPLY FUNCTION** with two columns selected. (9)

Table 3-5 Column shortcut menu options explained (Continued)

(8) This option can be applied to multiple columns at the same time.
(9) This option is only available when two or more columns with a numeric data type are selected. There is a corresponding option on the Add Column tab ⇒ Standard button.

Change Type Option

This option works the same as the Data Type option on the Home tab. It is used to change the data type of the selected column.

The difference is that the Change Type option, also has the **USING LOCALE OPTION**, shown at the bottom of Figure 3-13. This option opens the dialog box shown in Figure 3-14.

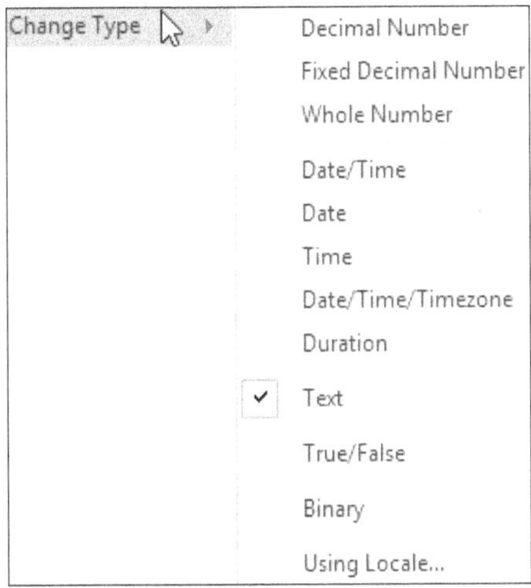

Figure 3-13 Change Type options

Change Type With Locale Options

The options shown in Figure 3-14 are used to override the Current File Locale options on the Options dialog box, for the selected column.

This is helpful when the other Change Type options shown above in Figure 3-13, do not display the data, the way that you need it displayed.

When you select a data type other then the one currently applied to the column, **SAMPLE INPUT VALUES** will be displayed, as shown a the bottom of the figure. This allows you to see formats that the data in the column will be changed to.

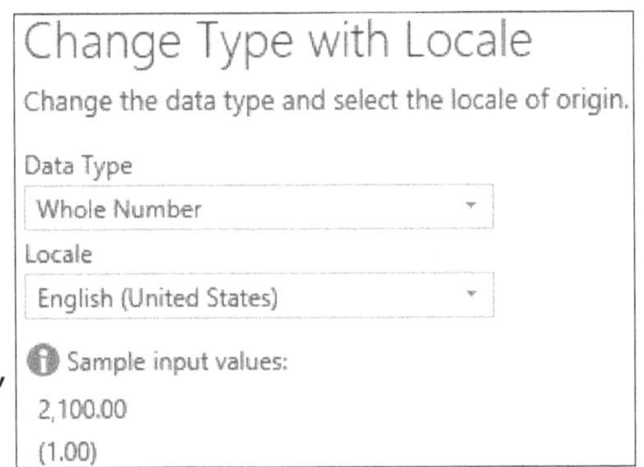

Figure 3-14 Change Type with Locale options

The locale options can be applied to one column or all columns in the query at the same time, by selecting the columns that you want to apply the option to, before opening this dialog box.

The **DATA TYPE** drop-down list contains all of the data types that Power BI Desktop supports.

The **LOCALE** drop-down list contains a list of world-wide regional formatting settings.

You may have the need to change how dates are displayed. As shown earlier in Figure 3-13, there are several date formats that can be selected. If the imported date field is not in the format that you need, select the format that you need from this list.

The Locale option is also important if you use data from countries other then you own, because date and numeric data is often formatted differently. For example, if the imported date field has time zone information and you do not need to display it, select the Date or Date/Time data type. Before applying the Change Type with Locale options, I check to see if the column already has a Changed Type step (in the Query Settings panel). If it does, I remove it.

One reason that importing dates is problematic is because not all software that we use, uses the same standard. Dates are a good example. Dates in the US are formatted as MM/DD/YYYY and in Europe, dates are formatted as DD/MM/YYYY. The Locale option is only applied when importing and transforming data in Power BI Desktop.

Transform Option

This option provides shortcuts to some of the most popular transform formatting options. The options are used to change the appearance of the value.

Figure 3-15 shows the text field transform options. Applying the Uppercase option to the Ship Name field in the Orders table, formats and displays the values, as shown in Figure 3-16.

Figure 3-17 shows the date/time field transform options. Figure 3-18 shows the **DAY OF WEEK FUNCTION** applied to the Order Date field. Zero equals Sunday.

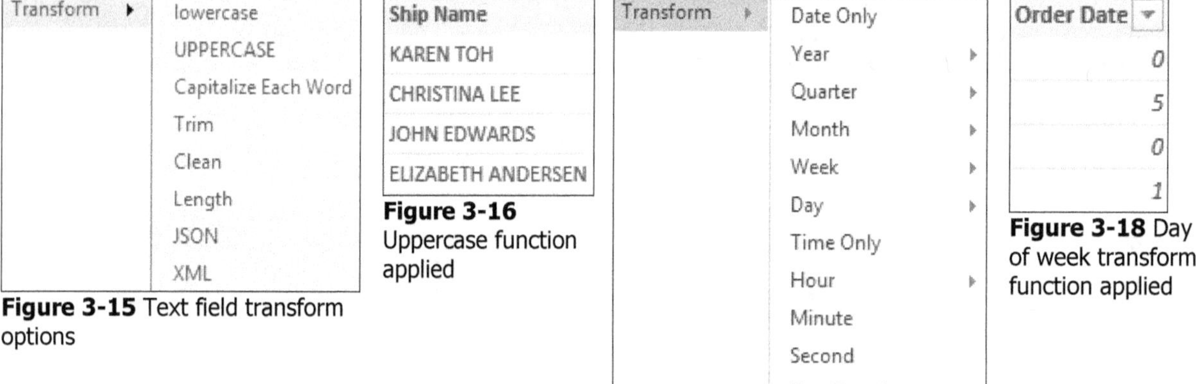

Figure 3-15 Text field transform options

Figure 3-16 Uppercase function applied

Figure 3-17 Date field transform options

Figure 3-18 Day of week transform function applied

Add As New Query Option

This option is used to create a new query. The query is created from the selected column or a single cell.

The contents of the new query contains the values in the column or cell. Figure 3-19 shows a new query created from the Product Name column.

The name of the new query is the column header name used to create the query. All of the steps, up to and including the one selected when the Add As New Query option is applied, is also copied to the new query. There is no dependency on the original query.

If the new query is created from a column, you will see the **LIST TOOLS TRANSFORM TAB**, at the top of the Query Editor.

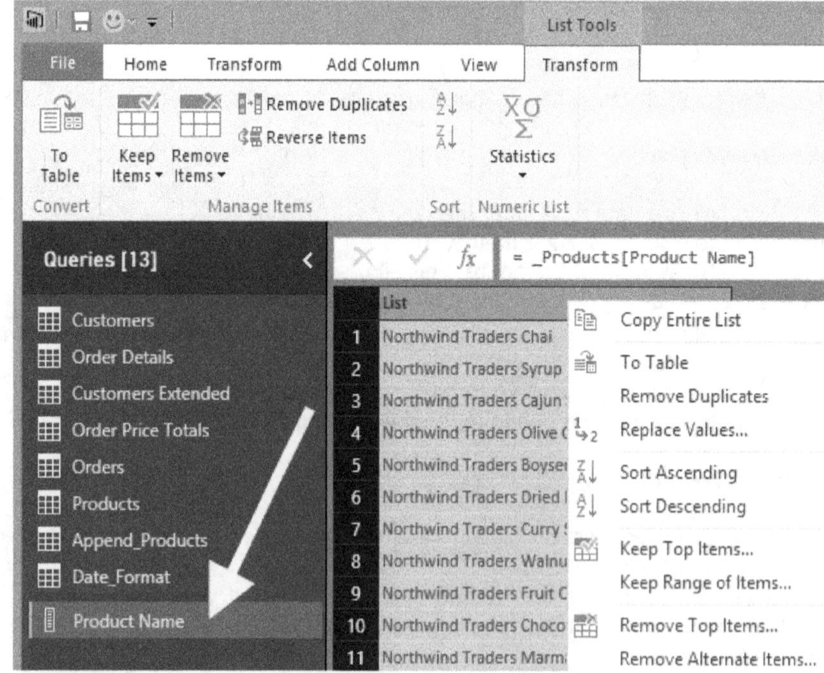

Figure 3-19 New (list) query options

Right-clicking on the **LIST** column heading displays the shortcut menu, shown in the lower right corner of Figure 3-19.

List Tools Transform Tab Options

The List Tools Transform tab options are explained in Table 3-6.

Option	Description
To Table	[See To Table Options]
Keep Items	(10)
Remove Items	(10)
Remove Duplicates	(10)
Reverse Items	[See Chapter 5, Table 5-1 Reverse Rows]
Sort	[See Table 3-11]
Statistics	[See Chapter 5, Table 5-1]

Table 3-6 List Tools Transform tab options explained

(10) [See Keep And Remove Rows Options]

To Table Options

The **TO TABLE** button, shown earlier at the top of Figure 3-19, is used to convert the list (the column) of data, to a table (query), by using the options shown in Figure 3-20.

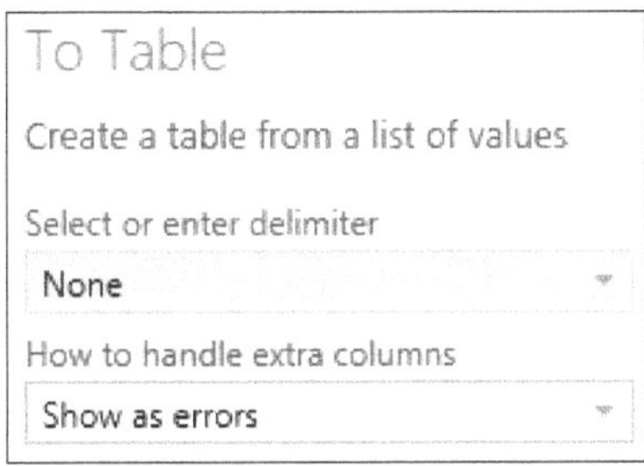

Figure 3-20 To Table options

List Column Shortcut Menu Options

The options on the shortcut menu shown earlier in Figure 3-19, are explained below in Table 3-7.

Option	Description
Copy Entire List	Copies the data in the List column to the clipboard, so that it can be pasted someplace else, like in a spreadsheet.
To Table	[See To Table Options]
Remove Duplicates	(11)
Replace Values	[See Replace Values]
Sort Ascending	Sorts the values in the list in low to high order.
Sort Descending	Sorts the values in the list in high to low order.
Keep Top Items	(11)
Keep Range of Items	(11)
Remove Top Items	(11)
Remove Alternate Items	(11)

Table 3-7 List column shortcut menu options explained

(11) [See Keep And Remove Rows Options]

Cell Shortcut Menu (From Using The Add As New Query Option)

Figure 3-21 shows the shortcut menu for a cell, in a query, created from using the Add As New Query option, like the query shown earlier in Figure 3-19. The options are explained in Table 3-8.

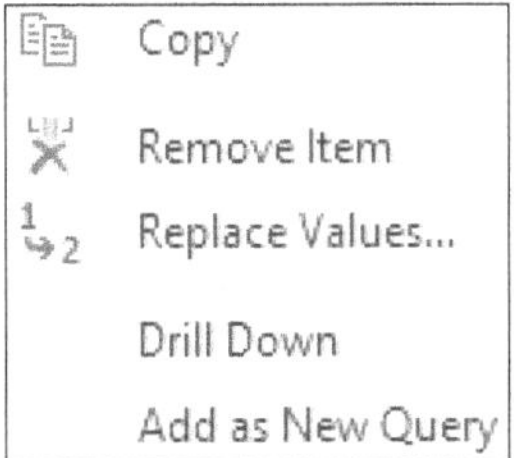

Figure 3-21 Cell shortcut menu

Option	Description
Copy	Is used to copy the value in the cell, then paste the value into a field on the Replace Values dialog box or to a file, like a spreadsheet.
Remove Item	Deletes the row from the list.
Replace Values	[See Replace Values]
Drill Down	Adds a step to the query that changes the view to only display the data in the selected cell.
Add as New Query	Creates a new query from the selected cell.

Table 3-8 Cell shortcut menu options explained (from using the Add As New Query option to create the query)

Cell Shortcut Menu

Right-clicking on a cell in the grid displays the shortcut menu shown in Figure 3-22, for a text field. The name of the Filters option at the top of the menu, changes to match the type of data in the cell.

These options are only applied to the selected cell. They are explained in Table 3-9.

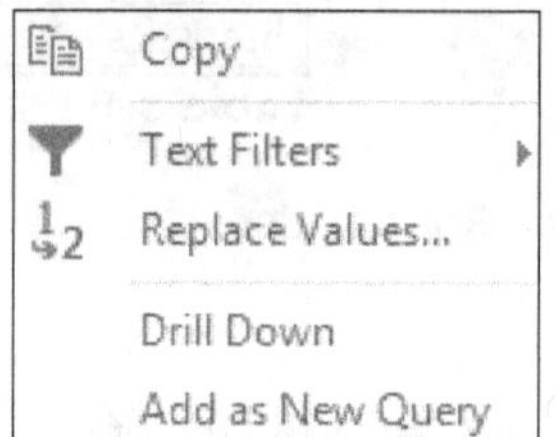

Figure 3-22 Cell shortcut menu

Option	Description
Copy	[See Table 3-8]
Filters	This option displays the filter options. The difference between the filter options on the column shortcut menu and the options on this shortcut menu, is that the options for the cell do not open the Filter Rows dialog box. Instead, the filter options for the cell are automatically created and applied to the data in the grid, based on the value in the cell that was right-clicked on, to open the cell shortcut menu. Once created, you can open the Filter Rows dialog box by clicking on the cog wheel button for the Filtered Rows step on the Query Settings panel. [See Chapter 4, Tables 4-1, 4-2 and 4-3]
Replace Values	[See Replace Values]
Drill Down	[See Table 3-8]
Add as New Query	[See Add As New Query Option]

Table 3-9 Cell shortcut menu options explained

Column Data Type Shortcut Menu

The icon to the left of the column heading indicates the **DATA TYPE** of the column, as illustrated in Figure 3-23. Clicking the icon displays the shortcut menu shown in the figure. The options are used to change the data type for the column. Notice that the icons next to the column headings are also on the shortcut menu. The options are explained in Chapter 5, Table 5-2.

Figure 3-23 Column data type shortcut menu

Query Settings Panel

The panel shown in Figure 3-24 displays information about the selected query, including the name and steps.

Each table displayed in the Queries panel has its own set of query settings. They are used to modify the selected query.

Clicking on the X before the step name, will delete the step.

NAME This is the name of the query. The default name is the table name, but it can be changed. Usually, it is changed to something descriptive. I find it easier to change the query name here, then renaming the query on the Queries panel or on the Query Properties dialog box.

ALL PROPERTIES Clicking on this link displays the dialog box shown in Figure 3-25.

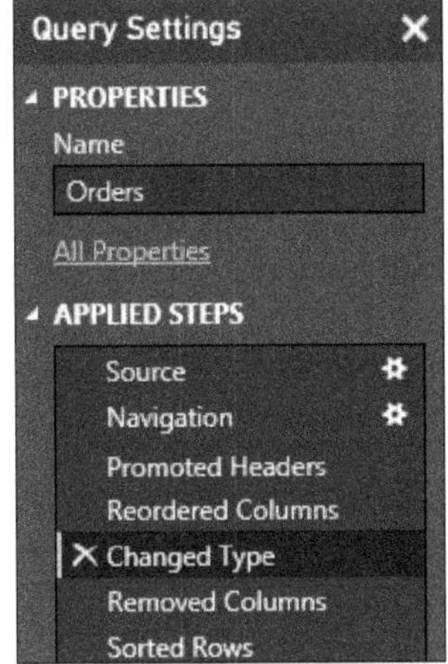

Figure 3-24 Query Settings panel

Query Properties Dialog Box

The **NAME** field is used to rename the query.

The **DESCRIPTION** field can be used to explain what the query does, especially the applied steps.

The **ENABLE LOAD TO REPORT OPTION** is used to select whether or not the data in the query is loaded to the data model.

If a query is only used because some columns will be merged into another query, you may not want to keep loading that query to the data model. Not loading a query prevents it from being displayed in the Fields panel, in the Report view. This may be a good thing if the report file has a lot of tables.

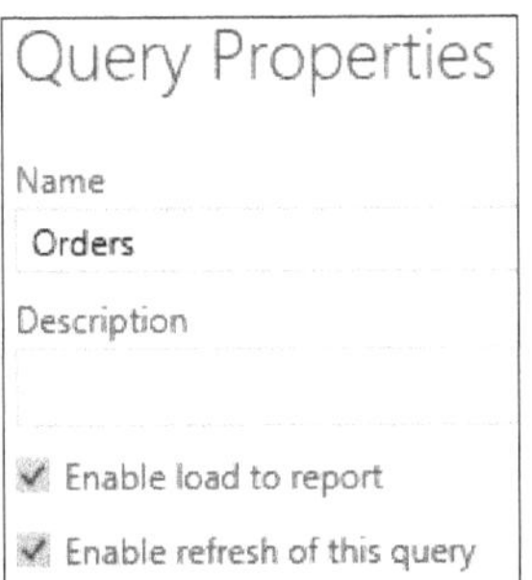

Figure 3-25 Query Properties dialog box

Keep in mind that doing this will remove the table from the data model, but not from the Query Editor.

When the Enable load to report option is not enabled, the query will be displayed in italic text on the Queries panel. This makes it easier to know which queries are loaded and which ones are not. Query 1 shown earlier in Figure 3-3, is an example of a query that does not have this option enabled.

The **ENABLE REFRESH OF THIS QUERY OPTION** is used to select whether or not the data in the query should be refreshed when the Refresh button is clicked in the Power BI Desktop workspace. This option is only enabled if the Enable load to report option is checked. This means that only data in the data model can be refreshed.

If the enable options are checked here, they will also be checked on the Queries shortcut menu [See Figure 3-6].

Loading Data

If either of the following is true, the data is not loaded into the data model.

① The **EDIT BUTTON** on the Navigator window is clicked.

② The Enable load to report option shown above, is not checked.

If the data has not been loaded to the data model, it is still able to be used and saved in the report file. This functionality is the same as the **CREATE CONNECTION OPTION** in Power Query for Excel. Not loading the data, but having access to it, allows for more "discovery" because you can use all of the Query Editor features, as if the data was loaded into the data model.

Often, tables that will be used as lookup tables, to add data to a different table are not loaded, because only specific fields are needed. Tables that fall into this scenario can be deleted, once the data has been added to another table.

Queries that are not loaded to the data model cannot be used to create a visual (table, chart, etc). Queries that have not been loaded are not displayed in the Report, Data or Relationships view.

Applied Steps

This section on the Query Settings panel, contains an entry (a step) for each action (modification) applied to the query.

What Is A Step?

A step is an action that helps get the data ready to be analyzed. During the import, other steps in addition to the Source and Navigation steps can be created. More steps will be created when you clean the data or add columns of data to a query.

Each option on the toolbar and shortcut menus, creates a step that is also displayed in the **APPLIED STEPS** section of the Query Settings panel. A step is created for each action that you take. This includes deleting a column and rearranging the column order. Keep in mind that the data will change in each step, based on the instructions for the step. Each step will display the data slightly differently, which is what should happen.

What you will come to appreciate about the steps (the M code) is that they are run automatically, each time the data is refreshed. This means that you do not have to reapply the steps manually.

Each step is one instruction, like load the data or format a column of data. Change the format of a date field, would be another step. Sorting the data would be another step. By default, these steps are displayed in the **APPLIED STEPS** section of the Query Settings panel, shown earlier in Figure 3-24, in the order that they are created in. The order of the steps can be changed. Make sure that the last step displays the data that will be used to create visualizations. The data displayed in the last step is also what will be loaded into the data model.

By default, new steps are added to the end of the Applied Steps section. If a step other then the last one is selected and a new step is created, it is placed after the selected step and not at the end of the steps.

There are two categories of instructions (steps), as explained below:

① **SHAPING THE DATA** Instructions in this category remove data (rows and columns) that are not needed, filter data and rename columns. Creating calculated columns and splitting data in existing columns, is also classified as shaping the data.

② **DATA TRANSFORMATION** Instructions in this category are used to change the appearance of the data, including rounding numbers, changing the case of text and extracting part of the data in a field. These tasks are also known as "modifying data".

Applied Steps Shortcut Menu

The options shown in Figure 3-26 are available when you right-click on a step.

The options are used to edit the selected step. They are explained in Table 3-10.

Changing The Order Of The Applied Steps
In addition to using the Move Up/Move Down options shown in Figure 3-26, to change the order of the query steps, you can change the order of the steps by using drop and drag.

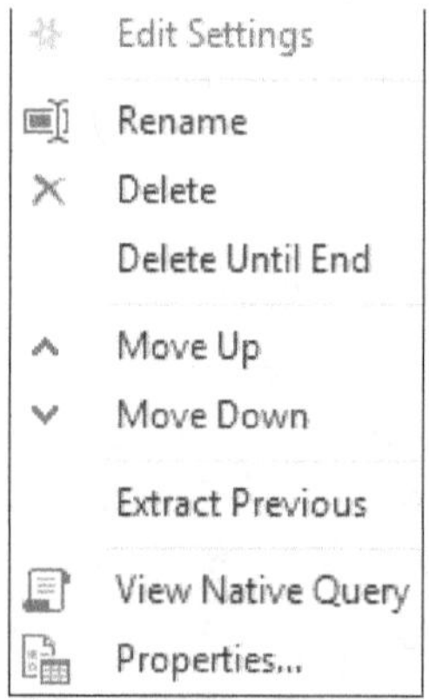

Figure 3-26 Applied Steps shortcut menu

Option	Description
Edit Settings	This option is only enabled for steps that have the icon. [See Applied Steps Options]
Rename	Is used to rename the step. Renaming a step is optional, but it is helpful because you can provide a better description of what the step does. I only rename a step that I think that I will have the need to modify at some point in the future. Doing this makes it easier for me to find the right step.
Delete	(12)
Delete Until End	(12) Also deletes all steps below it, in the Applied Steps list.
Move Up	Moves the selected step up once. (13)
Move Down	Moves the selected step down once. (13)
Extract Previous	[See Extract Previous Option]
View Native Query	[See View New Native Query Option]
Properties	Opens the **STEP PROPERTIES DIALOG BOX**, which has the same options as the New Group dialog box. [See Figure 3-10] This is helpful if you want to document what the step does or why you created the step. The information entered on the dialog box will be displayed as a tooltip when the mouse pointer is held over the step, as shown in Figure 3-27.

Table 3-10 Applied Steps shortcut menu options explained

(12) Deletes the selected step. The data is put back to the way it was before this step changed the data. Selecting this option displays the message shown in Figure 3-28. Click the Delete button if you want to remove the step.

(13) Using this option changes the order that the steps in the query will be processed in. Changing the order means that it is possible that the data can change in a way that you are not expecting it to change. This option can be used more than once, to move the same step.

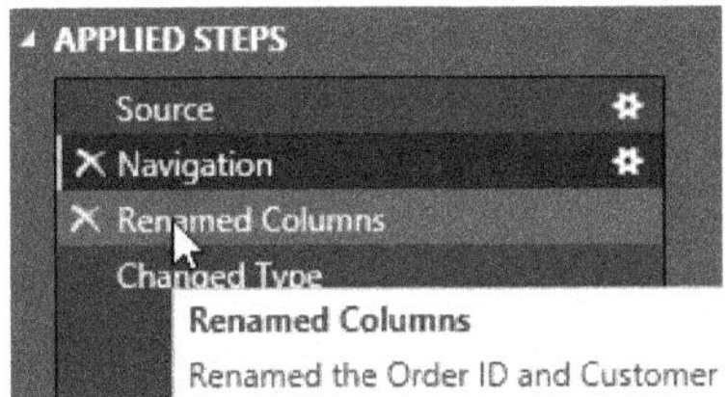

Figure 3-27 Step properties description displayed as a tooltip

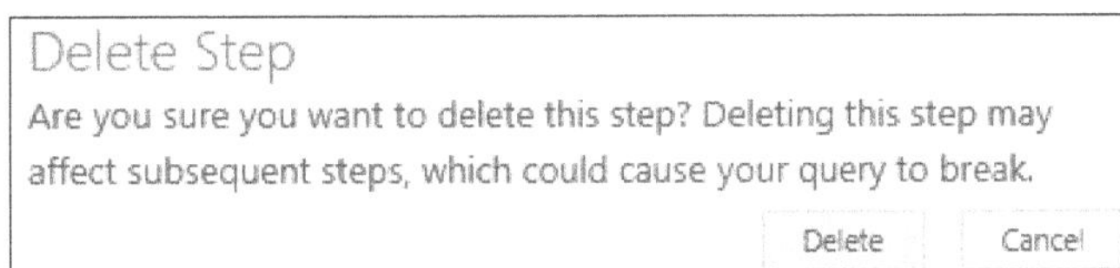

Figure 3-28 Delete Step message

Extract Previous Option

The Extract Previous option, shown earlier in Figure 3-26, displays the dialog box shown in Figure 3-29. This option is used to create a new query using the steps above the one selected, when this dialog box was opened. The steps above are deleted from the current query and placed in the new query. The Source step is copied to the new query, but not deleted from the current query.

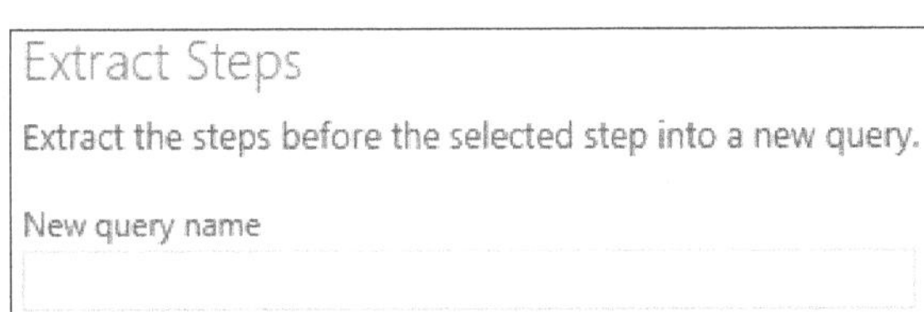

Figure 3-29 Extract Steps dialog box

View Native Query Option

Figure 3-30 shows the code used to select the fields from the data source and any filters that were created in the Query Editor.

The **WHERE CLAUSE** (the last line) contains the options that were selected to filter the data that is displayed in the query. The code cannot be edited on this dialog box.

Native Query

```
select [_].[ID],
    [_].[Company],
    [_].[Last Name],
    [_].[First Name],
    [_].[Job Title],
    [_].[Address],
    [_].[City],
    [_].[State],
    [_].[Zip Code],
    [_].[Country]
from [Customers] as [_]
where ((([_].[State] = 'CA' and [_].[State] is not null or [_].[State] = 'FL' and [_].[State]
```

Figure 3-30 Native Query dialog box

Applied Steps Options

As shown earlier in Figure 3-24, some of the steps have an icon to the right of the step name (often referred to as a **COG WHEEL ICON**). Steps that have this icon have a dialog box. This is also how you will change the import options for the step, if needed. The icon means that the values in the step can be changed in one of the following ways:

① Selecting the Edit Settings option, shown earlier in Figure 3-26.

② Clicking on the cog wheel icon.

③ Double-clicking on the step. The corresponding dialog box opens and displays the options that were selected to create the step.

Applied Steps Tips

① Most of the time, each action that you do, adds a step to the Applied Steps list. The exception that I noticed is when you perform the same action (remove or change the data type for example) two or more times consecutively (on the same or a different column), the actions are all added to the same step. The way that you know this, is to click on the step and view the formula, in the formula bar.

② At the end of some step names, you may see a number. The number is a counter of how many times the action has been used in the query. If you rename a step, the counter number is no longer applied.

③ What I think is cool about the Applied Steps list is that you can click on any step to display the data as it was after the selected step was applied.

The Source, Navigation and Promoted Headers steps are ones that you will see often. They are explained below.

Source Step

Queries always have a step named **SOURCE**. This step contains the import information about the data source for the query. Figure 3-31 shows the import options for an Excel file. The options displayed vary, depending on the data source type. For example, Figure 3-32 shows the import options for a CSV file.

The options on a source step dialog box are used to change the data source options. This is helpful if the path or data source name changes. You can make the change here and not have to close the Query Editor to use the Power BI Desktop window to make the changes.

If the query has a database as the data source, clicking on the Source step displays a list of tables and views in the query, as shown in Figure 3-33. Notice that the formula bar displays the data source, path and file name. You can change the information in the formula, as needed. Figure 3-34 shows the import options for an Access database.

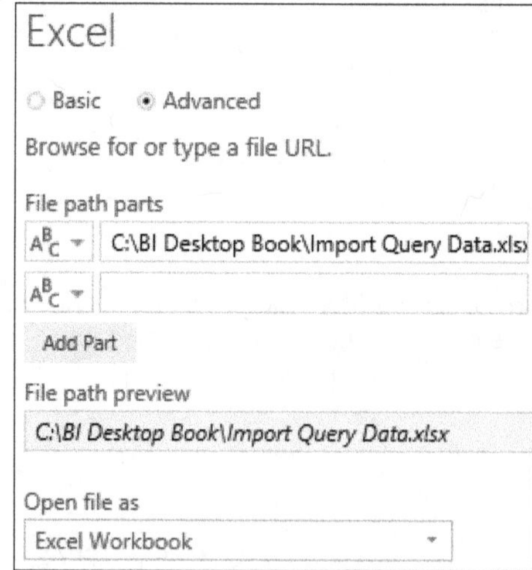

Figure 3-31 Source step import options for an Excel file (in Advanced mode)

Source Step
This step is always the first step. It cannot be renamed or moved, like the other steps can.

Comma-Separated Values Connector

The options shown in Figure 3-32 are for importing a CSV file.

By default, the delimiter character is automatically detected. If necessary, you can change or customize the delimiter on this dialog box.

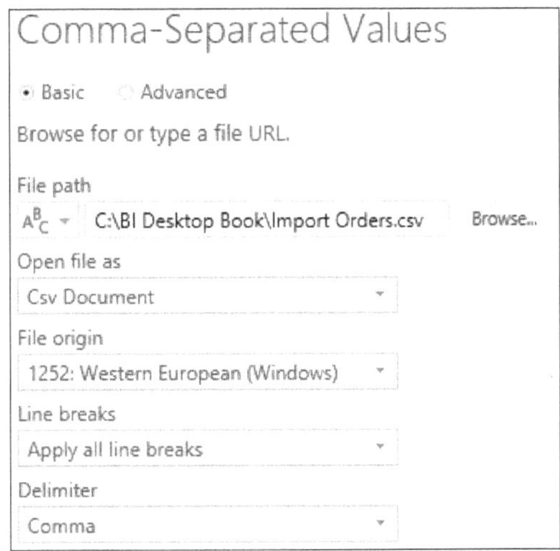

Figure 3-32 Source step import options for a CSV file

Access Database Connector

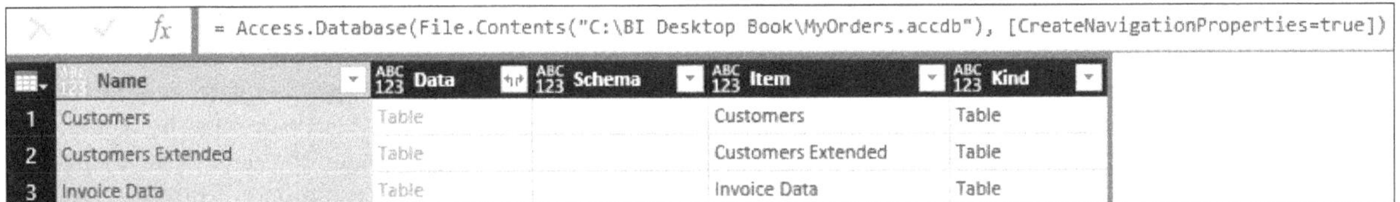

Figure 3-33 Source step table data for a database

Check the **INCLUDE RELATIONSHIP COLUMNS OPTION** when you need to have related tables automatically selected to be imported.

I don't see where this option adds any value for Access databases because you can use the Selected Tables button on the Navigator window, when you first import the data. This option may be useful for other types of databases, but I haven't tested that.

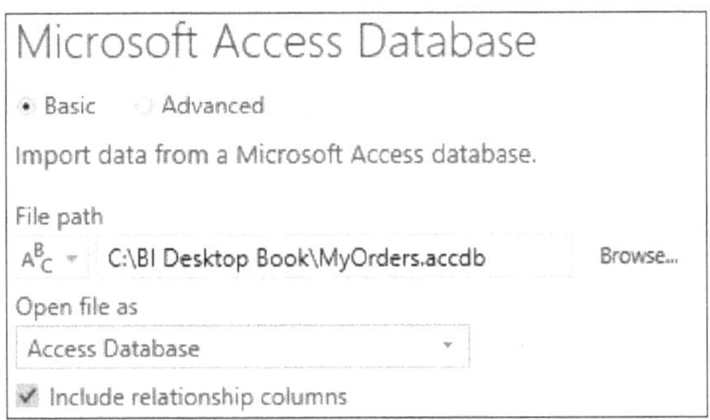

Figure 3-34 Source step import options for an Access database

Changing The Locale In The Query Editor

Chapter 1 covered the Locale option, on the Options dialog box, and it was also covered earlier in this chapter. For CSV files, there is another way to change the Locale. On the Source step, open the **FILE ORIGIN** drop-down list, shown earlier in Figure 3-32 and select the Locale that you want the data interpreted as.

Navigation Step

The Navigation step is only available for data sources that use the Navigator window during the import process.

When available, this is the second step in the Applied Steps list. Right-clicking on the **NAVIGATION** step and selecting Edit Settings, displays the options shown in Figure 3-35. This option displays all of the tables and views (called **RESOURCES**) in the data source, for the selected query. This window is used to select a different table to view.

Keep in mind that all of the resources shown in the Navigation window, may not have been imported (meaning that there is no query for it). Even if the resource that you select to view has not been imported, you will still be able to view the data. Having this option on the Query Editor, just allows all of the tables and views in the data source to be viewed.

For example, the Date Table shown in Figure 3-35 was not imported in Exercise 2.4. Selecting the table here, will allow you to view the data in it.

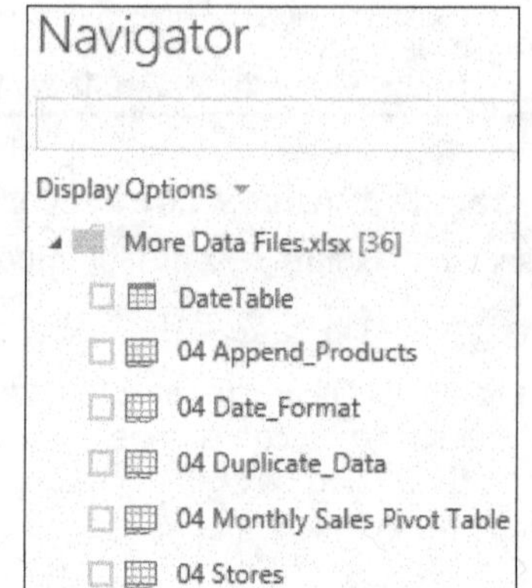

Figure 3-35 Navigation step options

Viewing Other Tables From The Navigation Step
The paragraph above worked until I installed the July 2016 update. Now, following those steps, overwrites the query that you selected, so I do not advise using it. If you want to view data from a table that has not been loaded, click on the Source step ⇒ Click on the word "Table", next to the table that has the data that you want to view ⇒ You will see the Navigation step message ⇒ Click Cancel ⇒ At the bottom of the window, you will see the data.

Promoted Headers Step

You may see the Promoted Headers step, shown earlier in Figure 3-26, when a file type in the Get Data button ⇒ File section, is used as the data source.

When you first display a query and see this step, it means that during the import, the first row had data that was not consistent with the rest of the data in the table and the import process concluded that the first row must be header information. When that is the case, the first row of data is changed (promoted). This changes the data in the first row to the column headings for the table. This saves you from having to do this manually, once the data is displayed in the Query Editor. You will also see this step, when you manually select to have the first row used as the headers for the query.

The **TYPE DETECTION** option on the Options dialog box (Current File Data Load screen), determines whether or not you see the Promoted Headers step, when data is first imported. If this option is checked, you probably will not see the Promoted Headers step, unless you apply it manually.

Modifying Steps

How you modify a step depends on how it was created. If the step that you want to modify has the **EDIT SETTINGS** option enabled on the Applied Steps shortcut menu, you can modify the step from there. If the Edit Settings option is not enabled, you have to use the corresponding option on a tab in the Query Editor or modify the formula for the step.

Modify A Step
What may not be obvious is that if you click on an existing step, for example, the Renamed Columns step and rename another column, even though you see the Insert Step message, the column will be renamed and the change will be added to the existing Renamed Columns step, instead of a new step being created.

To me, adding to an existing step makes it much easier to know, all of the same type of changes that were made to the query. If there is only one Changed Type step and one Renamed Columns step, you know where to look for that type of change. This is also helpful if you need to change the order of the steps.

Deleting Steps

Deleting steps can produce unexpected outcomes for the steps below the step that you are deleting. When an error occurs, the icon for the query changes, in the Queries panel, and the data is replaced by an error message, as shown on the right side of Figure 3-36.

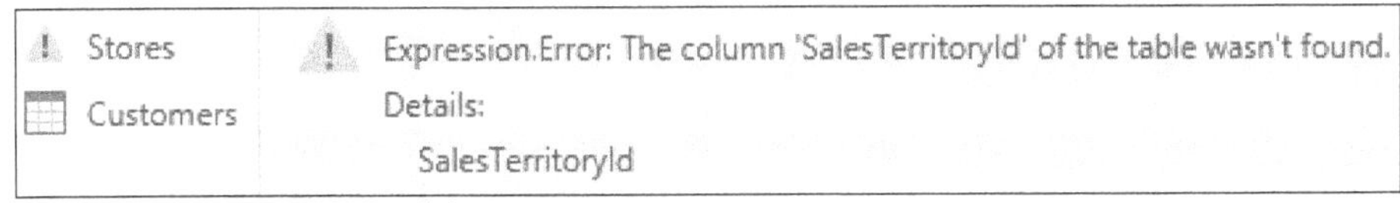

Figure 3-36 Error from deleting a step

Try To Avoid Deletion Errors

Often, the steps that cause an error when deleted, are dependent on a prior step. While there is no rule on the order that steps should be created in, I have fewer problems when I complete tasks in the order listed below.

① Use the Close & Apply option a few times during the data modification process, as this option applies the query changes up to that point.
② Delete columns that are not needed.
③ Promote and/or rename column headers.
④ Filter out records that are not needed.
⑤ Change the data type, as needed.

After these tasks are completed, I apply and close again, especially before creating new columns and cleaning the data. Then, I save the changes. Think about it. If you create formulas, then insert a step to delete a column (above the formula step), used in the formula, the formula would stop working and the word "Error" would be displayed in the column.

Home Tab

Figure 3-37 shows the options on the Home tab in the Query Editor. The options are explained in Table 3-11.

Figure 3-37 Home tab

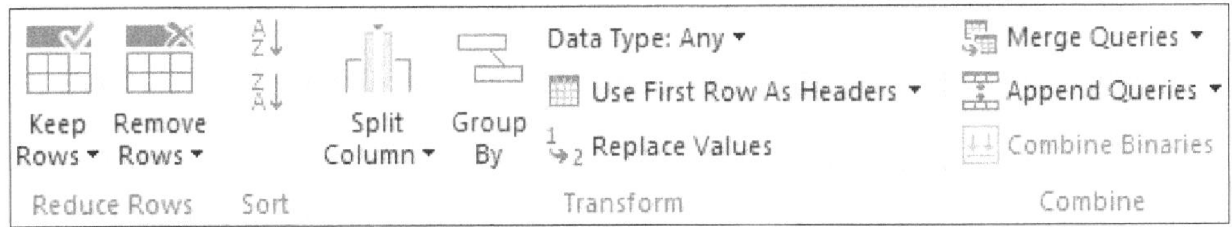

Figure 3-37 Home tab (Continued)

Option	Description
Close & Apply	[See Close & Apply Options]
New Source	[See New Source Options]
Recent Sources	[See Chapter 2, Recent Sources Option]
Enter Data	[See Chapter 8, Create A Table]
Data Source Settings	[See Chapter 1, Data Source Settings]
Manage Parameters	[See Chapter 8, Manage Parameters]
Refresh Preview	[See Refresh Preview Options]
Properties	[See Figure 3-25]
Advanced Editor	[See Chapter 5, Advanced Editor]
Manage	[See Manage Options]
Choose Columns	Displays all of the columns in the query, as shown in Figure 3-38. Remove the check mark for the column(s) that you want removed from the query.
Remove Columns	[See Remove Columns Options]
Keep Rows	[See Keep And Remove Rows Options]

Table 3-11 Home tab options explained

Option	Description
Remove Rows	[See Keep And Remove Rows Options]
Sort	The buttons sort in ascending, descending, low to high or high to low order, based on the values in the column that is selected, prior to selecting this option.
Split Column	[See Split Column Options]
Group By	[See Group By Options]
Data Type	Is used to change the data type for the selected column.
Use First Row As Headers	[See Use First Row As Headers Options]
Replace Values	[See Replace Values]
Merge Queries	[See Merge Queries And Append Queries Buttons]
Append Queries	[See Merge Queries And Append Queries Buttons]
Combine Binaries	[See Combine Binaries Button]

Table 3-11 Home tab options explained (Continued)

The **SORT BY** options are used to change the order that the columns are displayed in, on the Choose Columns dialog box.

NATURAL ORDER is the default sort option and displays the columns in the order that they are in the table.

The **NAME** option displays the column names in alphabetical order.

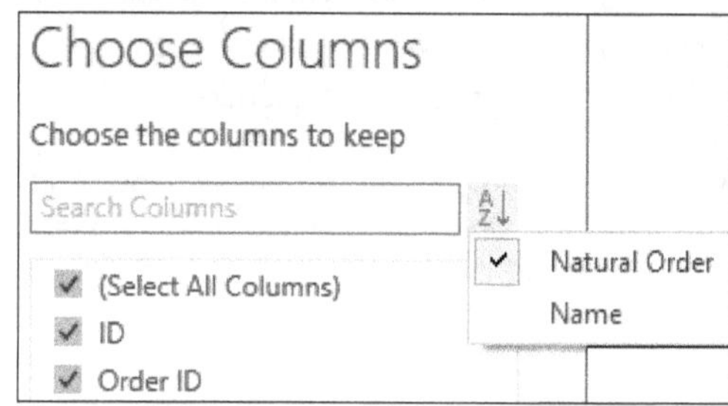

Figure 3-38 Choose Columns options

Close & Apply Options

The options shown in Figure 3-39 are used to select how to save the pending changes made in the Query Editor.

The **CLOSE & APPLY** option saves the pending changes to the query, then closes the Query Editor and loads the data, based on the changes.

The **APPLY** option applies the pending changes and leaves the Query Editor open. If there are any problems applying the changes, you will see a message similar to the one shown in Figure 3-40. To load the data, the problems need to be fixed.

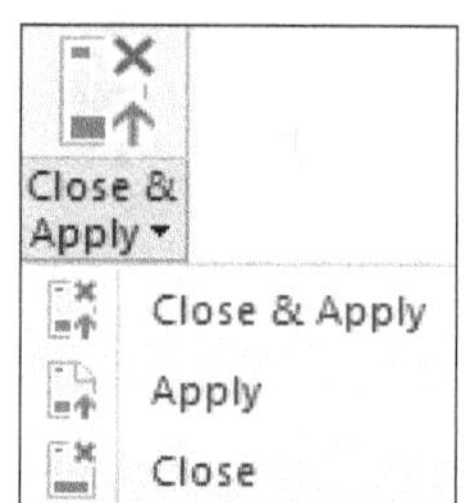

Figure 3-39 Close & Apply button options

Select the **CLOSE** option when you do not want to apply the pending changes to the data model now. The Query Editor window will close. The changes are not removed. You will see the message shown in Figure 3-41 in the Power BI Desktop workspace as a reminder, that there are **PENDING CHANGES**. I use the Close option when I am not sure that I have the data the way that I need it to be. When you save the report file, you will see the message shown in Figure 3-42. You can apply the changes now or later. Selecting Apply Later, saves the pending changes when the file is saved, but does not apply them. This means that when you reopen the report file later, the changes that have not been applied are still there and the message shown in Figure 3-41, is still displayed.

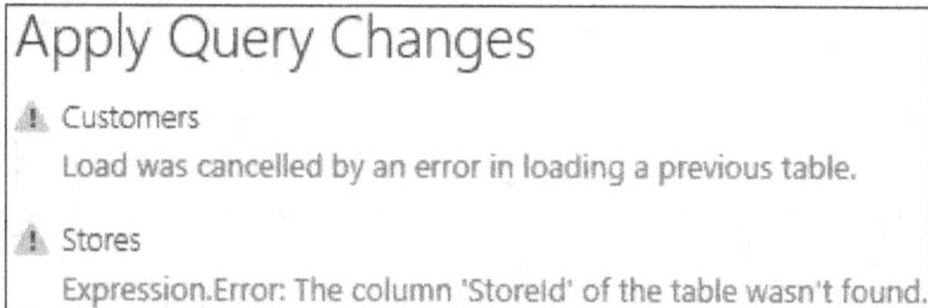

Figure 3-40 Apply Query Changes message

There are pending changes in your queries that haven't been applied. Apply Changes

Figure 3-41 Pending changes message

How To Get Rid Of The Pending Changes
When you close the Query Editor without applying the pending changes, you will see the message shown above in Figure 3-41. You also see this message when you save the report file. If you do not want to save the pending changes, click the X in the upper right corner of the Power BI Desktop window, instead of using any Close, Apply or Save options on the Query Editor. You will see the message shown in Figure 3-42. Click the **DON'T SAVE** button. The file will close and all pending changes (made after the last time pending changes were applied) will be removed from the file. The next time that you open the report file you will not see the message shown above in Figure 3-41, letting you know that there are pending changes.

Just be sure when clicking the Don't Save button that you haven't made changes that you want to keep. After I have made a few changes that I want to keep, I apply them and save the file. That way when I make a change that I do not want, using this solution is not a problem.

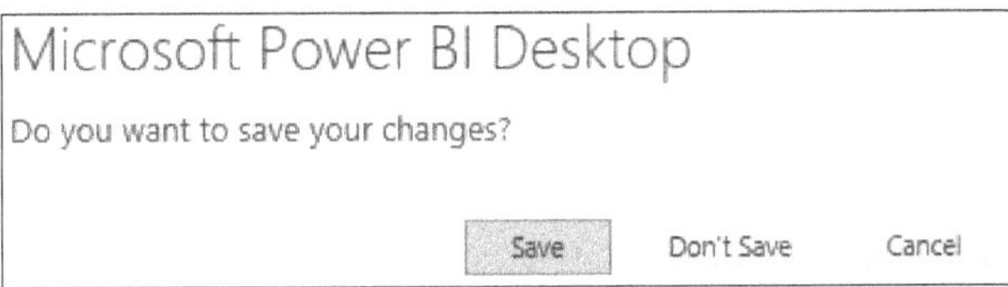

Figure 3-42 Save changes message

New Source Options

The options shown in Figure 3-43 are used to select the data source type for a file that you want to import data from.

These options work the same as the options on the Get Data button.

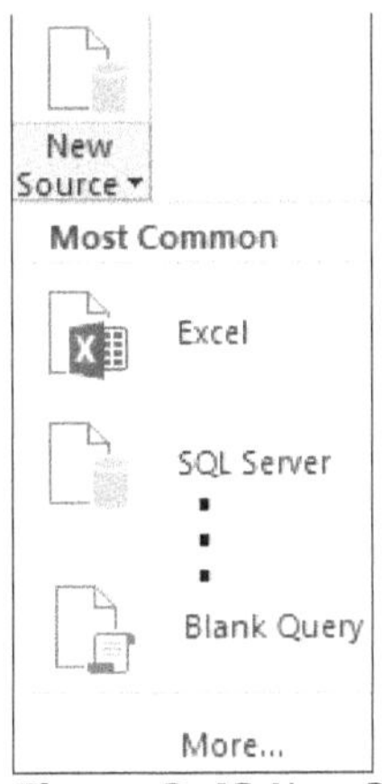

Figure 3-43 New Source button options

Refresh Preview Options

The options shown in Figure 3-44 are used to select which queries are refreshed.

REFRESH PREVIEW Refreshes the selected query.

REFRESH ALL Refreshes all of the queries on the Queries panel, that have the Enable refresh query option selected.

CANCEL REFRESH Is used to stop the refresh that is in progress.

Figure 3-44 Refresh Preview button options

Manage Options

The options shown in Figure 3-45 are used to modify the selected query.

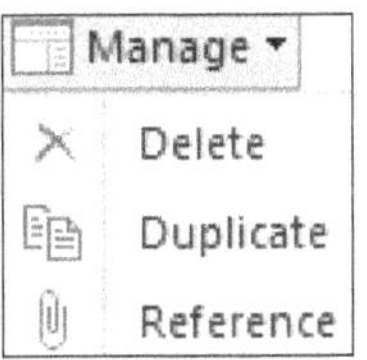

Figure 3-45 Manage button options

Remove Columns Options

The remove options are shown in Figure 3-46.

REMOVE COLUMNS Deletes the selected columns.

REMOVE OTHER COLUMNS Deletes all of the columns, except the ones that are selected.

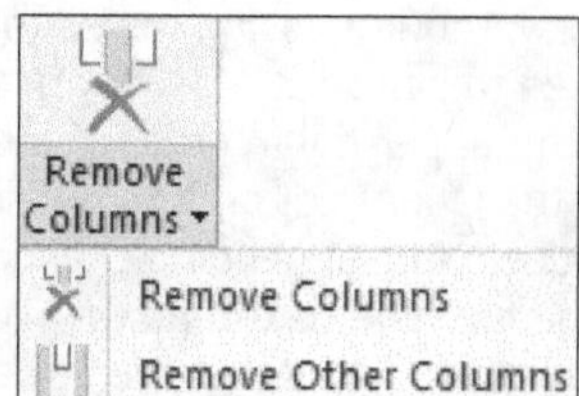

Figure 3-46 Remove Columns button options

Keep And Remove Rows Options

The **KEEP ROWS** options shown in Figure 3-47, are used to select which rows to keep in the query.

The **KEEP DUPLICATES** option shown in Figure 3-47, will only keep, sort and display records that have duplicate values. This option is helpful when you need to clean the source data because you can work from the records that this query creates.

The **KEEP ERRORS** option will only display rows of data that have an error. (14)

The **REMOVE ROWS** options shown in Figure 3-48, are used to remove rows from the query. These options are used to keep or delete records, based on the value of **N**. The rows that are selected to be removed are removed from the query. They are not deleted from the data source. The next time data is refreshed, removed rows will not be re-imported. If you are already familiar with **TOP N REPORTS**, you will be familiar with these options.

The **TOP ROWS** and **BOTTOM ROWS** options, display the window shown in Figure 3-49. The option is used to select the number of rows (from the top or bottom of the data displayed in the query) to keep.

Use the **KEEP TOP ROWS** option if you need to display the rows that have one of the top N values in the selected column. To do this, sort the column that has the data that will determine which rows to keep, in ascending or descending order, then use the Keep Top Rows option and type the number of rows to keep, in the field.

The **KEEP RANGE OF ROWS** options shown in Figure 3-50, are used to select the range of rows of data to keep. The number entered in the First row field equals the first row in the table to keep. The number entered in the Number of rows field equals how many rows, in total, you want to keep.

The **REMOVE ALTERNATE ROWS** options shown in Figure 3-51, are used to select the starting point and pattern for how rows will be removed from the query. The values shown in the figure will remove rows as follows: Rows 5 to 15 will be deleted. The next two rows will be saved. This process is repeated until the end of the table is reached.

The **REMOVE BLANK ROWS** option deletes any blank rows in the table.

The **REMOVE ERRORS** option deletes rows that have an error. Use this option with caution because you can remove rows of data that should be kept. (14)

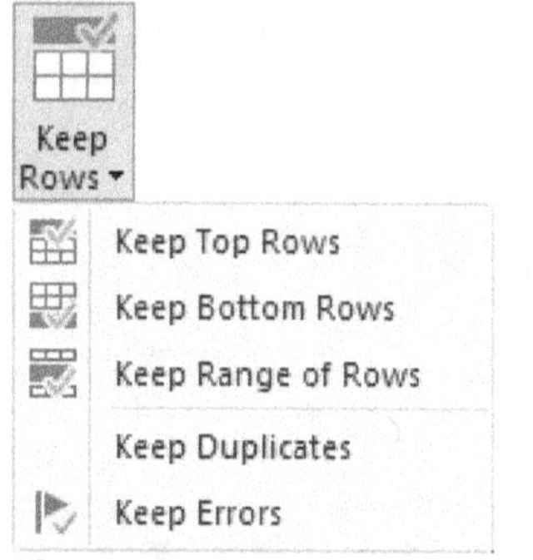

Figure 3-47 Keep Rows button options

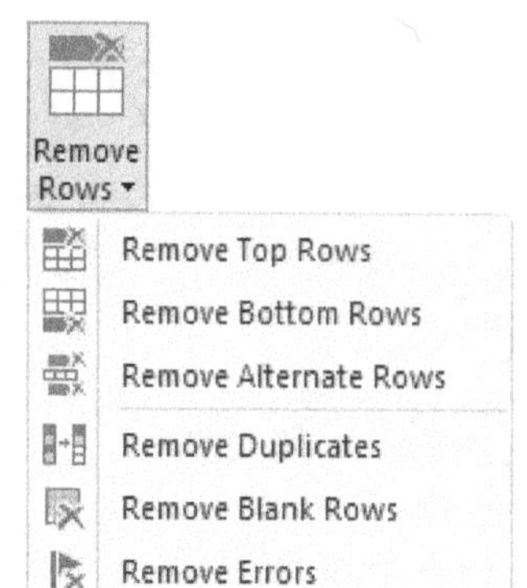

Figure 3-48 Remove Rows button options

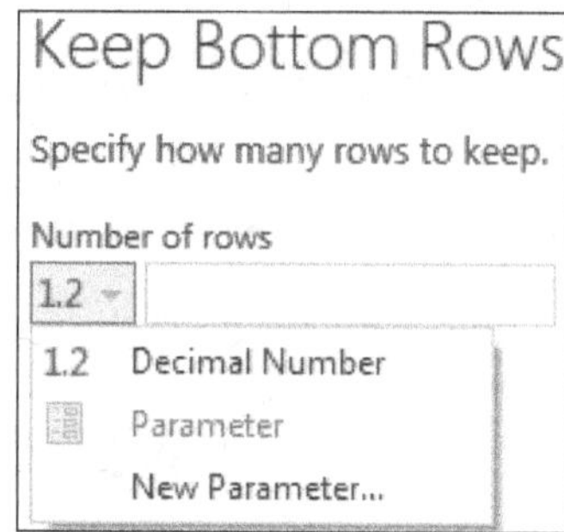

Figure 3-49 Keep Bottom Rows option

Keep Range of Rows

Specify the range of rows to keep.

First row

1.2 ▾

Number of rows

1.2 ▾

Figure 3-50 Keep Range of Rows options

Remove Alternate Rows

Specify the pattern of rows to remove and keep.

First row to remove

1.2 ▾ 5

Number of rows to remove

1.2 ▾ 10

Number of rows to keep

1.2 ▾ 2

Figure 3-51 Remove Alternate Rows options

The **REMOVE DUPLICATES** option is used to delete duplicate records. If you want to remove duplicate rows of data, you have to select enough columns in the table to make the rows that you want to delete, duplicate. Often, in addition to selecting criteria to use to determine what makes records duplicate, looking at some of the data will help you select the correct criteria. Most of the time, at least two columns should be used as criteria to select duplicate records. For example, Figure 3-52 shows a table that will have duplicate rows deleted, based on the values in two columns. (14)

If multiple columns are selected (like the Order ID and Quantity) and the Remove Duplicates option is applied, rows 3, 5, 9 and 10 would be deleted because each of these rows have the same value as the record above it, in those columns. Row 13 would not be deleted because the Quantity column does not have the same value as row 12.

The Query Editor is also case sensitive when checking for duplicate values. In this scenario, only rows with matching values in both columns will be deleted.

I don't know if I can stress enough, how important it is to remove duplicate records. Having duplicate records, distorts the totals that are created, which can cause the wrong conclusion or decisions to be made.

	ID	Order ID	Quantity	Unit Price
1	1	1	1	41.9
2	2	1002	3	33.9
3	3	1002	3	1652.8599
4	4	1003	3	48.51
5	5	1003	3	13.78
6	6	1004	3	274.35
7	7	1005	2	14.5
8	8	1006	1	16.5
9	9	1006	1	33.9
10	10	1006	1	14.5
11	11	1007	3	16.5
12	12	1008	2	726.61
13	13	1008	1	431.87

Figure 3-52 Query that has duplicate rows of data

(14) This option is based on the columns that are selected, before this option is applied.

Sorting On Multiple Columns

It is possible to sort on multiple columns. The thing to remember is that the columns have to be sorted on, back to back. This will combine the sorts into one step. The steps below show you how to sort on multiple columns.

1. Click on the first column that you want to sort on ⇒ Home tab ⇒ Click the Sort Ascending or Sort Descending button.

2. Click on the next column that you want to sort on ⇒ Home tab ⇒ Click the Sort Ascending or Sort Descending button.

3. Repeat step 2 for each column that you want to sort on.

When finished, each column will have a number after the column header, as illustrated in Figure 3-53. The formula for the **SORTED ROWS** step should have all of the columns that you sorted on, as shown in Figure 3-54. If not, clear the sort and start over.

The sort numbers and buttons only appear when the Sorted Rows step is selected on the Query Settings panel.

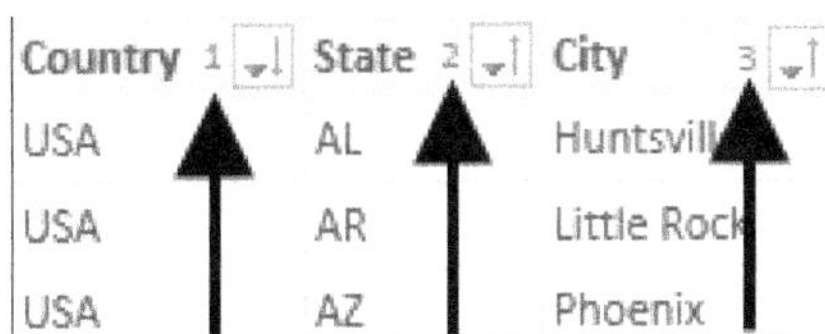

Figure 3-53 Multiple columns sorted on

```
= Table.Sort(#"Renamed Columns",{{"Country", Order.Descending}, {"State", Order.Ascending}, {"City", Order.Ascending}})
```

Figure 3-54 Sorted Rows step formula

Split Column Options

The options shown in Figure 3-55 are used to split the data in a column, into two or more columns.

The options are explained below.

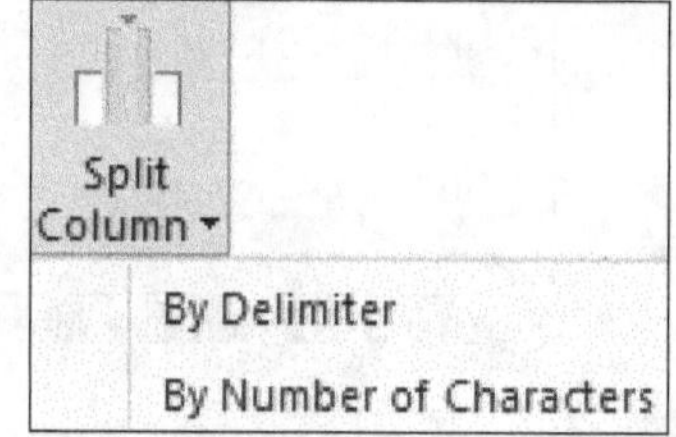

Figure 3-55 Split Column button options

By Delimiter Options

Figure 3-56 shows the **BY DELIMITER** options. These options change, depending on the delimiter character that is selected. Figure 3-57 shows the delimiter options that you can select.

The **CUSTOM DELIMITER OPTION** is used to enter something other then the options shown in Figure 3-57 to select what should be used to separate the columns. The option that comes to mind of when to use the Custom option is the pipe | character (The pipe character is to the right of the right bracket key, on my keyboard).

Select the **AT THE LEFT-MOST DELIMITER OPTION** when the column should only be split once, at the first occurrence of the delimiter.

Select the **AT THE RIGHT-MOST DELIMITER OPTION** when the column should only be split once, at the last occurrence of the delimiter.

Select the **AT THE EACH OCCURRENCE OF THE DELIMITER OPTION** when the column should be split every time the delimiter occurs.

The **ADVANCED OPTIONS** change, based on the Split option that is selected.

The **QUOTE STYLE OPTION** is used to select whether or not you want to use the CSV quote style (" ") or not. Comma delimited is also supported.

Selecting the **SPLIT USING SPECIAL CHARACTERS OPTION** enables the **INSERT SPECIAL CHARACTERS** drop-down list (shown at the bottom of Figure 3-56). It has additional special characters that can be used, as the character to determine where to split the data.

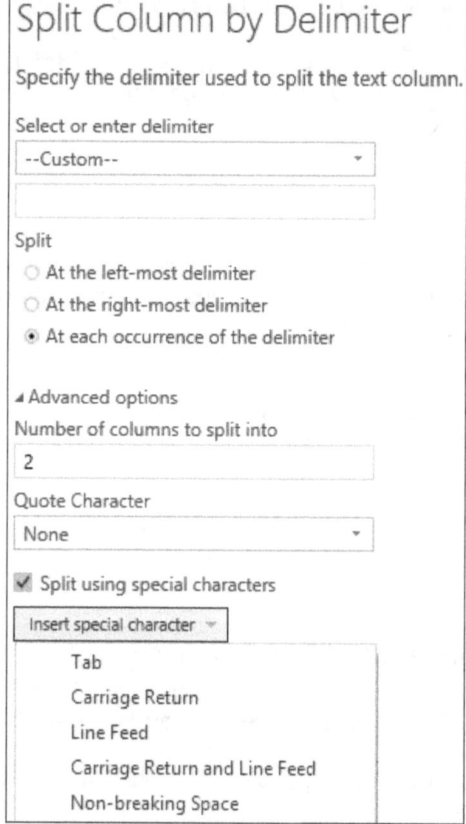

Figure 3-56 By Delimiter options

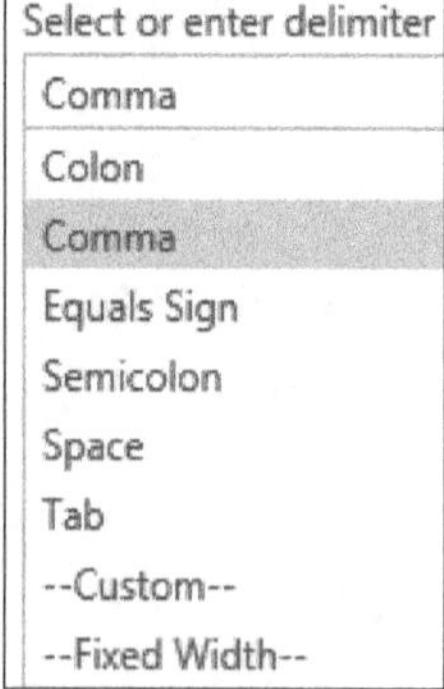

Figure 3-57 Split Column delimiter options

The options selected in Figure 3-58, change the data in the Ship Name column, to the columns shown in Figure 3-59.

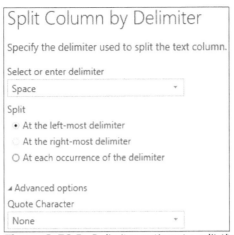

Split Column by Delimiter

Specify the delimiter used to split the text column.

Select or enter delimiter

Space

Split

At the left-most delimiter

At the right-most delimiter

At each occurrence of the delimiter

Advanced options

Quote Character

None

Figure 3-58 By Delimiter options to split the Ship Name column

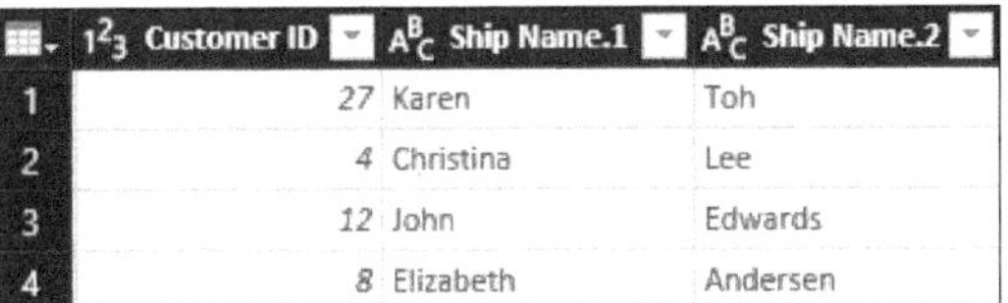

	Customer ID	Ship Name.1	Ship Name.2
1	27	Karen	Toh
2	4	Christina	Lee
3	12	John	Edwards
4	8	Elizabeth	Andersen

Figure 3-59 Split column by delimiter option applied

By Number Of Characters Options

Figure 3-60 shows the **BY NUMBER OF CHARACTERS OPTIONS**. I think the intended use of these options is to only to split columns that have a text data type, even though they can be used to split columns with other data types.

This option is designed to split a column into at least two columns where the data is the same length. The options in the Split section work the same as the options in the By Delimiter Split section.

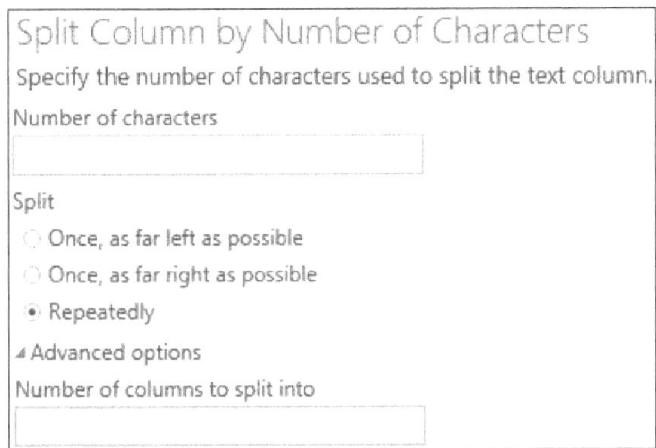

Figure 3-60 By Number of Characters options

Group By Options

The options shown in Figure 3-61 are used, for lack of a better word, to create a pivot table to aggregate (summarize) the data in a table. This is also known as an **AGGREGATE VIEW.**

The **GROUP BY OPTION** changes the structure of the query because it puts the rows of data into groups.

The rows in the query are rolled up into one of the Group by categories (fields), at the top of the dialog box, so that the aggregations at the bottom of the dialog box, can be applied.

For example, the options shown in Figure 3-61 summarize the data shown in Figure 3-62, to display the data in the layout shown in Figure 3-63.

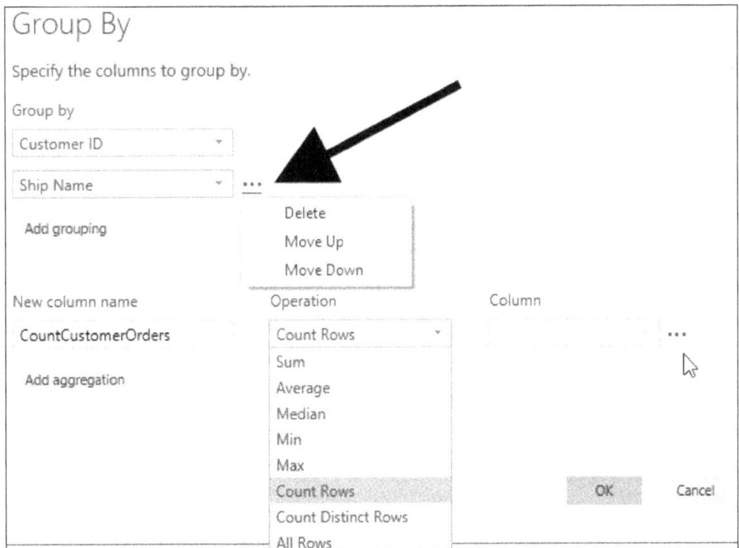

Figure 3-61 Group By dialog box

The options shown in Figure 3-61 group the data in the query, by customer (Customer ID field). A count of the orders shipped to each customer is also calculated.

The top section of the Group By dialog box is used to select columns that you want to create groups for. The columns not used in the Group By section are not initially displayed in the query.

You can select the columns to group by before you open this dialog box. The order that you select them in does not matter. When selecting columns before opening the dialog box, they will be displayed in the order that they appear in the query, from left to right.

When clicked, the **... ELLIPSIS BUTTON** to the right of a Group By or Column field, displays options to delete or move the selected field up or down, as illustrated above in Figure 3-61.

The **ADD GROUPING BUTTON** is used to add another field to the Group by section.

The bottom section of the dialog box is used to create the aggregate columns. These new columns will appear to the right of the group by fields in the query.

The **NEW COLUMN NAME FIELD** is used to type in the name for the aggregate column that will be created, to display a total (summary) for the group(s) at the top of the dialog box.

The **ADD AGGREGATION BUTTON** is used to add another row to create a calculation.

The **OPERATION** drop-down list contains the types of summary totals (**AGGREGATE FUNCTIONS**) that can be created, as shown above in Figure 3-62. This drop-down list also has a **ROW OPERATION**. The options in this drop-down list are explained in Table 3-12.

The **COLUMN** drop-down list contains all of the fields in the query. Select the field that the calculation should be based on.

```
= Table.PromoteHeaders(Source)
```

	Order ID	Employee ID	Customer ID	Order Date	Shipped Date	Shipper ID	Ship Name
1	30	9	27	1/15/2006	1/22/2006	2	Karen Toh
2	31	3	4	1/20/2006	1/22/2006	1	Christina Lee
3	32	4	12	1/22/2006	1/22/2006	2	John Edwards
4	33	6	8	1/30/2006	1/31/2006	3	Elizabeth Andersen
5	34	9	4	2/6/2006	2/7/2006	3	Christina Lee
6	35	3	29	2/10/2006	2/12/2006	2	Soo Jung Lee
7	36	4	3	2/23/2006	2/25/2006	2	Thomas Axen

Figure 3-62 Data without the group by options applied

```
= Table.Sort(#"Grouped Rows",{{"Customer ID", Order.Ascending}})
```

	Customer ID	Ship Name	CountCustomerOrders
1	1	Anna Bedecs	2
2	3	Thomas Axen	3
3	4	Christina Lee	5
4	6	Francisco P,rez-Olaeta	6
5	7	Ming-Yang Xie	2
6	8	Elizabeth Andersen	6

Figure 3-63 Data with the group by options shown earlier in Figure 3-61 applied

Group By Functions

Function	Description
Sum	Adds the values in the column to get a total. (15)
Average	Calculates the average of the values. (15)
Median	Returns the middle value. (15)
Min	Returns the lowest value. (15)
Max	Returns the highest value. (15)
Count Rows	This operation is always displayed by default, when the dialog box is first opened. It can be changed or removed. It returns the number of rows in the query. (16)
Count Distinct Rows	Returns the number of rows that have a unique value in the selected column. (16)

Table 3-12 Group By functions explained

Function	Description
All Rows	Creates a new column in the current query that has the **TABLE DATA TYPE**. The table displays the columns from the query. It is used to select additional columns that can be displayed in the query. This is how you can add columns that would not be displayed in the query, because they were not used on the Group By dialog box. (16)

Table 3-12 Group By functions explained (Continued)

(15) This operation is an **AGGREGATE FUNCTION**. The values come from the Column field in the same row on the Group By dialog box.
(16) This option is known as a **ROW OPERATION**. It does not use the Column field on the Group by dialog box.

The options shown in Figure 3-64 display the data shown in Figure 3-65.

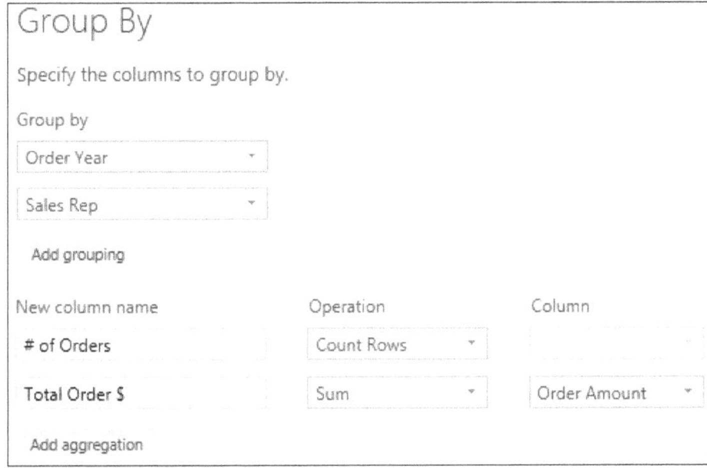

Figure 3-64 Group By options

	Order Year	Sales Rep	# of Sales	Total $ Sales
1	2013	Justin Brid	14	12821.37
2	2013	Xavier Martin	10	13386.07
3	2013	Margaret Peacock	18	23878.33
4	2013	Albert Hellstern	15	41820.13
5	2013	Steven Buchanan	7	9932.2

Figure 3-65 Query based on the options shown above in Figure 3-64

Use First Row As Headers Options

When the data being imported is from a database, this option is automatically applied to the data. The Use First Row As Headers button displays the options shown in Figure 3-66. If the data in the query looks like the data shown in Figure 3-67, selecting the **USE FIRST ROW AS HEADERS** option replaces the current column headings with the values in the first row of data, as shown in Figure 3-68. This works the same as the Promote Headers function. Selecting the **USE HEADERS AS FIRST ROW** option, moves the header row down, so that it becomes the first row of data.

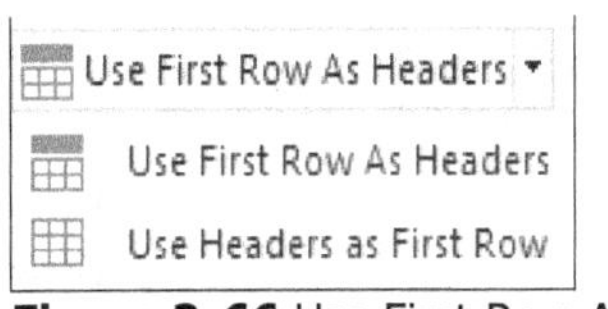

Figure 3-66 Use First Row As Headers options

	Column1	Column2	Column3	Column4
1	ProductID	ProductName	CategoryID	QuantityPerUnit
2	1	Chai	1	10 boxes x 20 bags
3	2	Chang	1	24 - 12 oz bottles
4	3	Aniseed Syrup	2	12 - 550 ml bottles

Figure 3-67 Data without column headings

	ProductID	ProductName	CategoryID	QuantityPerUnit
1	1	Chai	1	10 boxes x 20 bags
2	2	Chang	1	24 - 12 oz bottles
3	3	Aniseed Syrup	2	12 - 550 ml bottles
4	4	Chef Anton's Cajun Seasoning	2	48 - 6 oz jars

Figure 3-68 Data with the Use First Row As Headers option applied

Replace Values

This option will remind you of the search and replace functionality that is available in other software, because it works the same way. It is used to replace the value in the selected column(s), using the options shown in Figure 3-69.

Clicking in the Value To Find field or the Replace With field first and then selecting a special character, adds the character to the field. This allows special characters to be searched for or used to replace the value in the cell.

These options can also be used to fill in fields that do not have data. The two types of blank fields are empty fields (which usually have the Text data type) and **NULL VALUES** (which have a numeric data type).

While it is not a requirement that all cells have data, it can present problems if there are too many empty cells. This is particularly true for numeric fields that are used in calculations.

Allowing null values in numeric fields means that you will have to test for null values before each calculation, because formulas can fail if a numeric field is empty. It is better to replace null values in numeric fields that will be used in a calculation, with a zero.

The Advanced options shown in the figure are used to customize the value in the Replace With field.

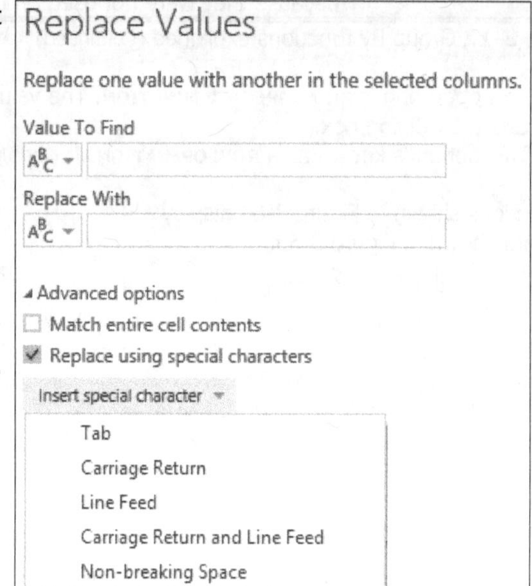

Figure 3-69 Replace Values options

If checked, the **MATCH ENTIRE CELL CONTENTS OPTION** will only replace the current value, if the current value is all that is in the cell.

Selecting the **REPLACE USING SPECIAL CHARACTERS OPTION** enables the **INSERT SPECIAL CHARACTER BUTTON**. This button has the additional special characters shown in the figure, that can be searched for. These options can be used as replacement characters.

To select a special character to use in the Value To Find or Replace With field with, click in the field, then click on the special character that you want to use.

Replace Values Tips

① This option only works with columns that have the Text data type. If you need to use it with date or numeric data type columns, you can try changing the data type to text, use the Replace Values options, then change the data type back to what it was.

② The **COPY OPTION FOR CELLS** [See Figure 3-22] can be used with this dialog box.

③ If you want to delete a value in a column and not replace it with anything (meaning you want the cell to be blank), leave the Replace With field empty.

④ The Replace Values option searches for every occurrence of the text entered in the Values To Find field. By default, it does not check to see if the value being searched for is all that is in the cell, unless the Match entire cell contents option is checked.

⑤ If you want to replace empty cells with a null value, leave the Value To Find field empty and type `null` in the Replace With field.

Merge Queries And Append Queries Buttons

These buttons have two options, as shown in Figure 3-70. The options are explained below.

The **MERGE QUERIES OPTION** adds columns from one query to the selected query. A column to link the queries on is required.

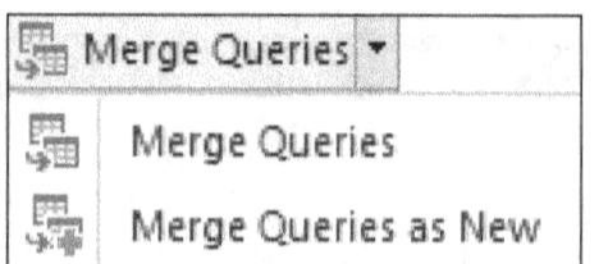

Figure 3-70 Merge Queries options

The **MERGE QUERIES AS NEW OPTION** creates a new query (table) by combining the data in the two queries that you select. Once the tables are merged, you can delete the columns from either table, that you do not need. (17)

The **APPEND QUERIES OPTION** adds all of the rows in one query to the bottom of the selected query.

The **APPEND QUERIES AS NEW OPTION** creates a new query (table) by appending the data in the two queries that you select. (17)

(17) This option leaves both of the original queries (tables) intact.

Combine Binaries Button

This button is enabled for columns that have the word **BINARY** in the cells. Columns set to binary that have a null value will not work. This option is used to merge binary data, in the selected column, into one binary file. For example, this feature will combine several CSV files (in the same folder) into one file. This button is used in Chapter 6, Exercise 6.7.

Customize The Quick Access Toolbar

Just like the Power BI Desktop workspace has a Quick Access Toolbar, so does the Query Editor. If there are options on any of the tabs in the Query Editor that you know that you will use a lot, you can add them to the Quick Access toolbar, by following the steps below.

1. Right-click on the button (on one of the tabs) that you want to add to the Quick Access Toolbar.
2. Select the Add to Quick Access Toolbar option, illustrated in Figure 3-71.

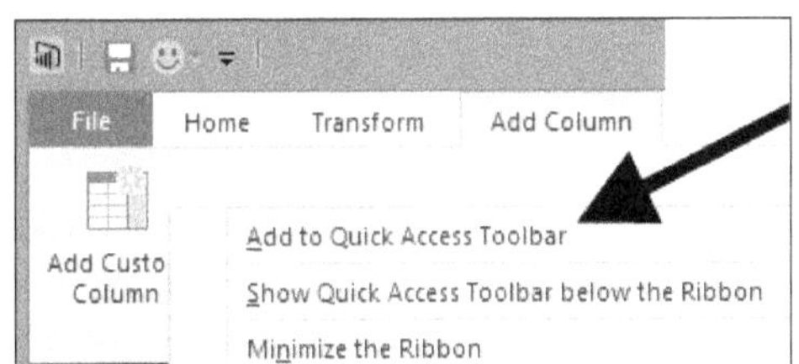

Figure 3-71 Option to add a button to the Quick Access Toolbar illustrated

How Old Is The Data Displayed In The Query Editor?

The Query Editor will display a message, like the one illustrated in Figure 3-72, once the data is more than 24 hours old.

The message lets you know approximately how old the data is, based on when it was imported.

Click the **REFRESH** button if you want to refresh the data.

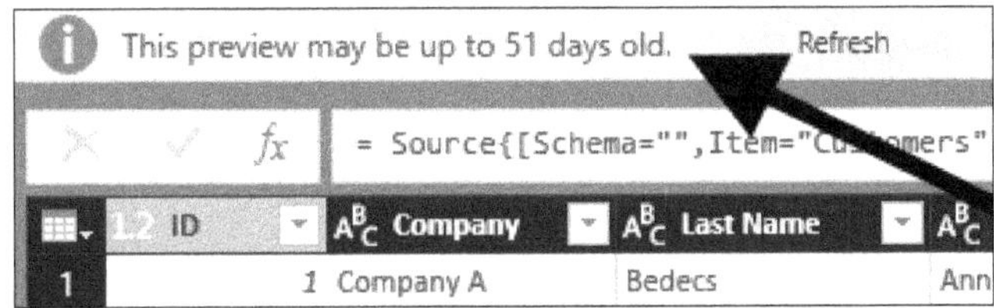

Figure 3-72 Age of data message

Exercise Tips For This Chapter

① Unless stated otherwise, you do not have to apply the pending changes. Saving the file without appending changes is fine.

② After I select a Close & Apply button option, I tend to save the file. Doing this is optional. You can save the file whenever you want.

Exercise 3.1: Use The Remove Columns And Rows Options

In this exercise you will learn how to use options that reduce the amount of data that is loaded into the data model.

1. Import all of the 05 tables in the More Data Files workbook.
2. Query Editor ⇒ Click on the Products query ⇒ Change the query name to `ModifyRowsAndColumns`. The next three parts of the exercise use this query.

Use The Choose Columns Option

1. Home tab ⇒ Choose Columns button.

2. On the Choose Columns dialog box, clear the check mark for the Discontinued column ⇒ Click OK.

Use The Remove Columns Option

1. Click on the Reorder Level column, in the query.

2. Home tab ⇒ Remove Columns button ⇒ Remove Columns.
   As you see, the Choose Columns and Remove Columns options can be used to remove columns from the query.

Use The Remove Errors Option

1. Home tab ⇒ Remove Rows button ⇒ Remove Errors.

   You should have the Applied Steps shown in Figure 3-73.

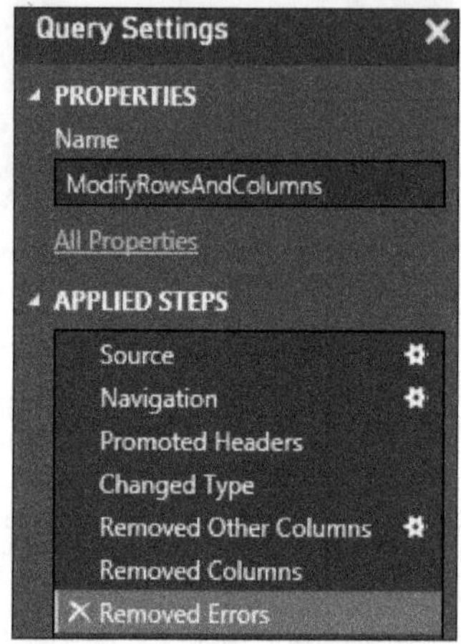

Figure 3-73 Properties and Applied Steps options

2. Save the file as `E3.1 Remove Columns And Rows`. Leave the file open to complete the rest of the exercise.

Use The Remove Bottom Rows Option

In this part of the exercise you will learn how to remove the last 50 rows of data in a table.

1. Display the Modify Rows and Columns query ⇒ Click on the Removed Columns step in the **APPLIED STEPS** section on the Query Settings panel.

2. Remove Rows button ⇒ Remove Bottom Rows ⇒

   On the window shown in Figure 3-74, click Insert.

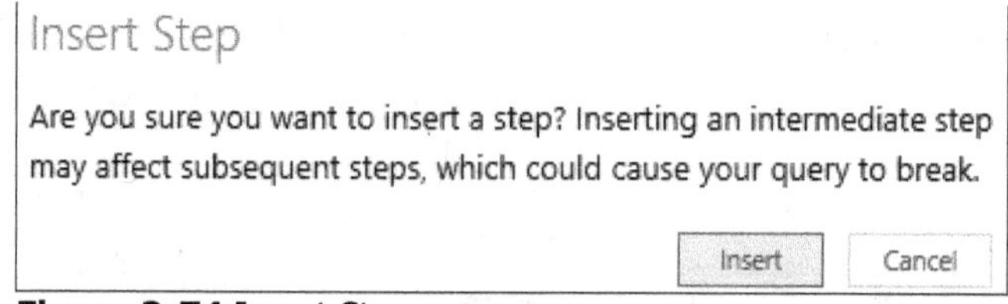

Figure 3-74 Insert Step message

The message wants to confirm that you really want to add a step between existing steps and to let you know that inserting a step can change the how the steps below it, are applied. Prior to starting this part of the exercise, you would not see this message. If you wanted to move this step, you could use the Move Up and Move Down options in the Applied Steps shortcut menu.

3. On the Remove Bottom Rows dialog box, type `50`. There should now be 27 rows in the query ⇒ Close the Query Editor without applying the changes.

Exercise 3.2: Remove Duplicate Records

1. Save the E2.4 file as `E3.2 Remove duplicate records.`

2. Select the Duplicate_Data query in the Query Editor. Notice that there are 26 records.

3. Home tab ⇒ Remove Rows button ⇒ Remove Duplicates. There should only be 20 records now. Do you have any idea what rows were deleted and if they are truly duplicates?

By default, the first column in the query is used to determine whether or not there are duplicate rows of data. Most of the time, you will probably want to use more than one column to determine if the rows are duplicate.

At this point, I would like to be able to view the records that were are selected to be deleted, to make sure that they are duplicate. You can make a copy of the query and try the **KEEP DUPLICATES OPTION**, to see if you can display duplicate rows of data. If not, you can create a formula to display duplicate records. The formula is covered in Chapter 8.

Exercise 3.3: Loading A List Of Tables

In Chapter 2, you imported a few tables from an Access database. Databases can have a lot of tables and views, sometimes hundreds. I don't know about you, but I can't remember that many table names. The good news is that you do not have to remember the table names. A list of tables and views can be imported. Even better, once the list of tables and views is imported or a connection is created, you can view the data in the tables and views. This process (storing a list of tables and/or views) is known as storing **METADATA** about the database.

1. Open a new file ⇒ Get Data button ⇒ More ⇒ Access Database ⇒ Select the My Orders database.

2. Right-click on the database name, in the Navigator window and select Edit, as shown in Figure 3-75.

   The Query Editor will open and display a query that has the metadata for all of the tables and views in the database, as shown in Figure 3-76.

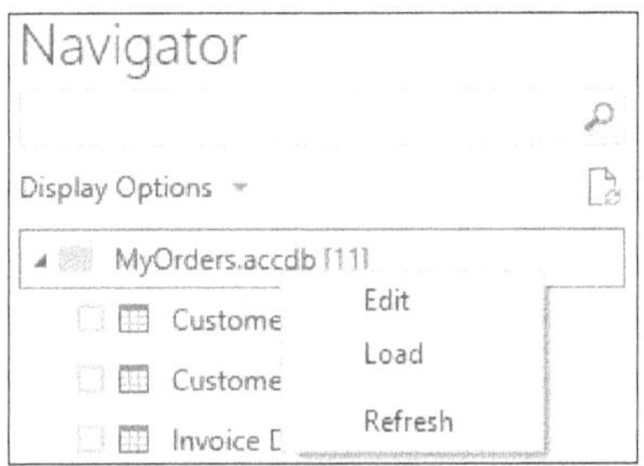

Figure 3-75 Data source shortcut menu

Use The Metadata Query To View Data

1. Rename the My Orders accdb query to `My Orders database tables.`

2. Right-click on a Table link, in the **DATA COLUMN**. You will see the shortcut menu shown in Figure 3-76.

   The options on the shortcut menu are explained in Table 3-13, at the end of this exercise.

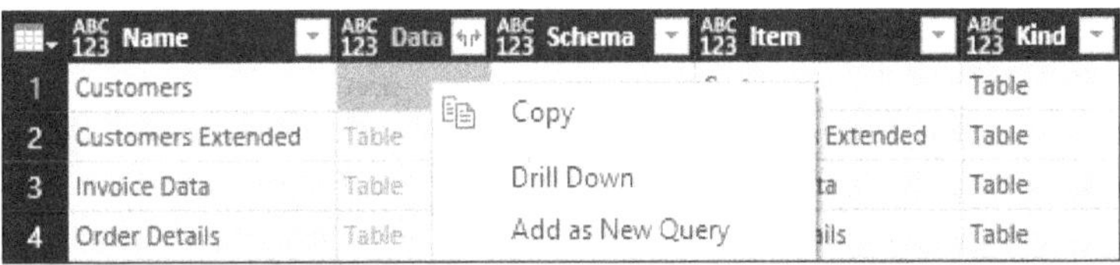

Figure 3-76 Database metadata in the Query Editor

3. In the Data column, click to the right of the "Table" link, of the table or view that you want to see the data of.

   In the grid below the table, you will be able to view some of the data, as shown at the bottom of Figure 3-77.

   To make the grid larger, place the mouse pointer above the grid, as illustrated in the figure, and drag the bar up.

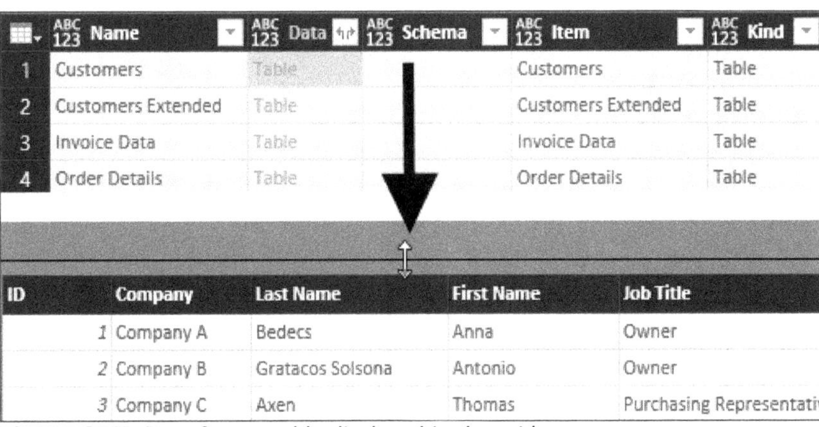

Figure 3-77 Data from a table displayed in the grid

To close the grid, click on a blank space in the query.

4. Save the file as `E3.3 List of tables.`

Data Column Shortcut Menu Options

Option	Description
Copy	Nothing is copied because the Table link displays the data in the table.
Drill Down	Displays the data for the table or view.
Add as New Query	Creates a query for the selected table or view.

Table 3-13 Data column shortcut menu options explained

Excel Workbook Contents Import Option

This import option is used to import the data model in an Excel workbook and other objects, including queries created in the Query Editor, in Power Query for Excel, linked tables, measures and calculated columns. Objects that are created from the data in the data model are also imported using this option. This includes reports created in Power View. Connections to external data sources that were created in Power Pivot are also imported.

Import Limitations
There are some features of an Excel workbook that can't be imported, including the following:
☑ Power View Scatter charts that have a Play Axis, Themes or drill-down functionality.
☑ Named Ranges that were created using the From Table option in Power Query.
For more information, see
https://powerbi.microsoft.com/en-us/documentation/powerbi-desktop-import-excel-workbooks/
Over time, I suspect that some, if not all of these limitations will be removed.

Exercise 3.4: Import Data From The Data Model In Excel

So far, all of the exercises that demonstrated importing Excel data, have used data on worksheets in the workbook. Data can also be imported from the data model in an Excel workbook. It does not matter if the data that was loaded into Excels data model was done using Power Query, Power Pivot or Excel.

In this exercise, you will import data from the data model in an Excel workbook.

1. Open a new file ⇒ File tab ⇒ Import ⇒ **EXCEL WORKBOOK CONTENTS**.

2. Select the dm_orders workbook ⇒ On the Import Excel Workbook Contents dialog box, click Start. The data in the data model will be imported.

3. When finished, you will see the dialog box shown in Figure 3-78. You have to scroll down to see all of the content categories shown in the figure ⇒ Click Close.

   If you open the Query Editor, you will see that the tables from the data model in Excel were imported and converted to queries.

Figure 3-78 Import Excel Workbook Contents results

4. Apply the changes ⇒ Save the file as `E3.4 Imported from an Excel data model.`

Summary

This chapter introduced you to the Query Editor and explained the options on the Home tab. The exercises showed you how to use many of the most popular options on the Home tab. Hopefully, you are thinking about how to use the options with your own data.

My Views On The Query Editor

① I think the Query Editor should be used with the Data view, not instead of.

② As much as possible, keep the Query Editor formulas to a minimum. Formulas that you create in the Query Editor should be to transform data, opposed to creating calculated columns of data.

③ It is better to create a measure or calculated column in the Data view because measures automatically adjust to accommodate filter and slicer selections. This makes measures dynamic.

④ It has been reported that the Query Editor calculations (custom columns) can run slow or increase the data model size significantly. I tested this by recreating DAX formulas using the M language in the Query Editor and the query took a long time to process the data.

⑤ Merged queries in the Query Editor (aka a **FLATTENED TABLE**), that are loaded into the data model are not the best option, because the data model was designed to use data from multiple tables, to create a chart or table, meaning that the lookup data should not be in the same table, as the main data.

⑥ **M FORMULAS** are only recalculated when the data is refreshed.

Don't Be Overwhelmed I understand that the concept of data cleansing can be a bit much to grasp at first. After viewing your data, make a short list by table/query of the changes that need to be made. If you break down the process into smaller groups of tasks, it will be easier to accomplish all of the tasks. Below is an example of how to group the list of changes that you wrote down. Start with the changes in your list that fit into Task 1 below, then move to your changes that fit into Task 2 and so on. While the topics listed in the tasks below do not cover every change that may be on your list, you will be well on your way.

Think of it in terms of remodeling a house. Task 1 is cleaning the house, by getting rid of what you don't want or need. Tasks 2 and 3 is fixing each room in the house. Task 4 is adding new rooms, if needed.

Task 1: Delete rows and columns that are not needed, delete duplicate records.

Task 2: Rename columns, filter data if necessary, reorder the columns.

Task 3: Change the data type, modify the data by filling in empty cells if possible, remove or add formatting of numeric values, confirm date fields have the data type that you need.

Task 4: Merge or append data, add calculated columns, group data.

CREATING FILTERS, CUSTOM COLUMNS AND FORMULAS

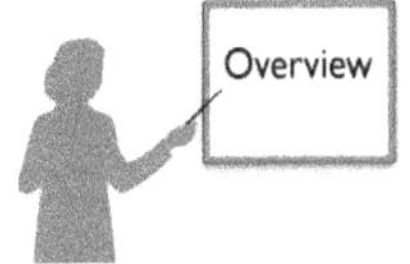

In this chapter you will learn how to complete the following tasks, using the Query Editor:

☑ Create different types of filters
☑ Create custom columns
☑ Create calculations
☑ Use the IF function

CHAPTER 4

Using Filters

Filters have several uses, including the following:

① To select which records are displayed on a report.

② To select records that have incorrect data, records that need to be updated or records that need to be deleted.

Filter Options

In the previous chapter you saw some of the filter options that are available in the Query Editor.

The filter options in the Query Editor are like the filter options in Excel and Power Pivot.

Clicking the arrow button at the end of a column header in the Query Editor, displays filter options like the ones shown in Figure 4-1.

These options are used to change the order that records are displayed in or reduce the number of records that are displayed in the query.

The **REMOVE EMPTY OPTION**, deletes rows that have an empty or null value in the column.

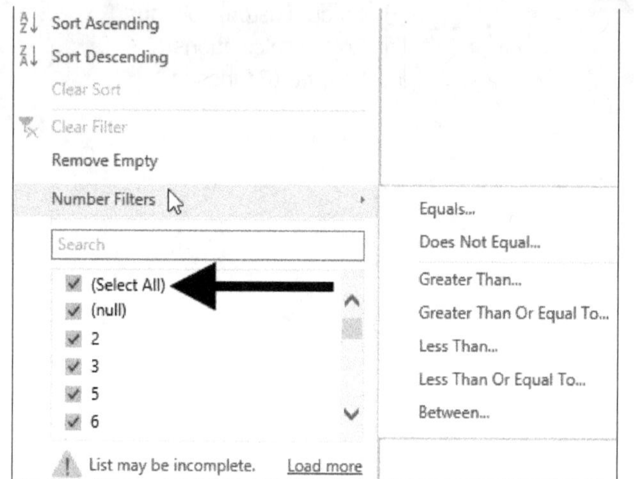

Figure 4-1 Numeric filter options and List incomplete message

What you will find is that there are two ways to filter data in the Query Editor, as explained below.

① By selecting one or more values at the bottom of a filter shortcut menu, like the one shown above, on the left side of Figure 4-1.

② By creating filter criteria, as shown in Figure 4-3.

The **LIST MAY BE INCOMPLETE** message, shown above in Figure 4-1, indicates that all of the values in the column are not displayed in the list. By default, the Query Editor displays the first 1,000 unique values in the column.

Clicking the **LOAD MORE LINK** loads the next 1,000 unique values in the column.

Using The (Select All), (Null) And (Blank) Filter Options
By default, the (Select All) and (Null) options are checked, as illustrated above in Figure 4-1.
When checked, the **(SELECT ALL)** option causes all of the options below it to also be checked. If you clear this option, the check mark for all of the options below it are also cleared. This is helpful when you only want to use a few of the options to filter the data because you can select them one by one.
The **(NULL)** option indicates that there are null values in the column. Clear this option when you do not want rows with a null value, in the selected column, to be displayed. Null values are in numeric fields.
The **(BLANK)** option shown in Figure 4-2, indicates that there are rows of data that do not have a value in the selected field. You will see this option for text fields.

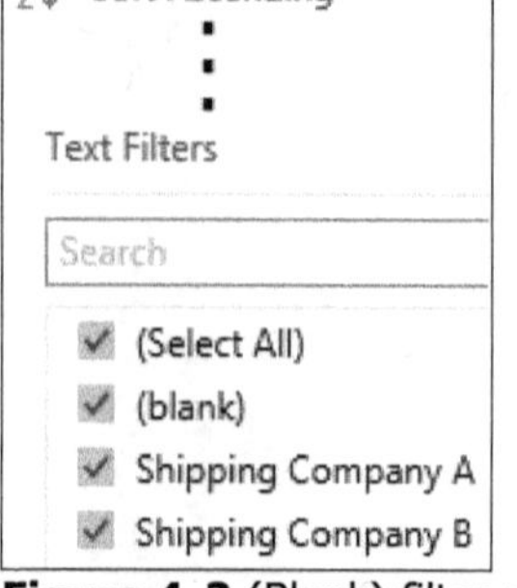

Figure 4-2 (Blank) filter option

Basic Filter Criteria

Selecting one of the filter options on the right side of Figure 4-1, opens the dialog box shown in Figure 4-3. The filter option that you select, is displayed in the first drop-down list. Select the filter options that will display the data that you need.

The AND & OR operators are used to create two or more conditions to filter on. Basic filter criteria (as shown in Figure 4-3), only allows one of these operators to be used. If you need to use both, select the Advanced option.

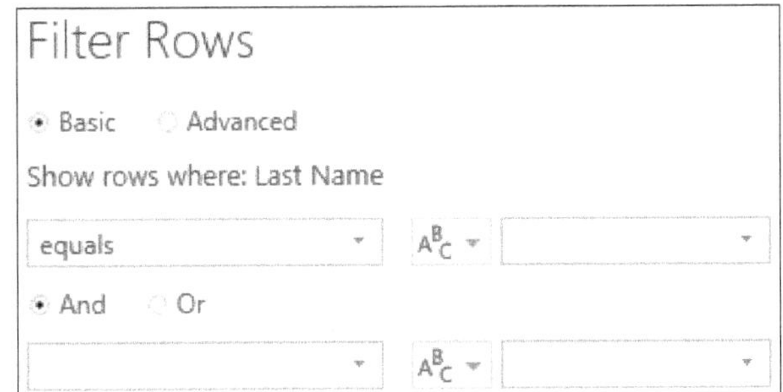

Figure 4-3 Basic Filter Rows options

Select **AND** when the data must meet both filter conditions. This reduces the rows of data that will be displayed. Select **OR** when the data only needs to meet one of the filter conditions to be displayed. This increases the number of rows of data that will be displayed, because the data only needs to meet one of the filter conditions. The Advanced Filter Rows options are covered later in this chapter.

Using The Filter Rows Options
Use these options when selecting values from the field, shown earlier, on the left side of Figure 4-1, will not handle your needs. All of the options (on the right side of Figure 4-1) open the Filter Rows dialog box, just like selecting the Custom Filter option, on the cell shortcut menu, does. The difference is that if an operator is selected before opening the Filter Rows dialog box, the operator is displayed on the dialog box. You can select a different operator once the dialog box is open.

Filter Data In The Query Editor

In addition to reducing the number of rows of data that are added to the data model, filtering data is also helpful when you want to analyze the data before adding it to the data model.

Figure 4-4 shows the filter functions for date fields.

The date and time functions use the computers current date and time, as part of the formula. If the formula evaluates to True, meaning the date in the field meets the criteria, the record is selected.

CUSTOM FILTER Select this option when the filter options on the shortcut menu are not sufficient enough to create the filter that you need. Selecting this option also opens the Filter Rows dialog box shown above in Figure 4-3.

The options shown in Figure 4-5 are the **MONTH FILTER OPTIONS** that can be selected.

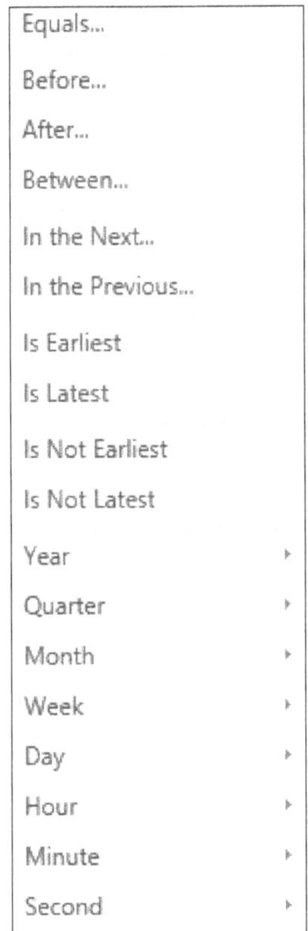

Figure 4-4 Query Editor date and time functions

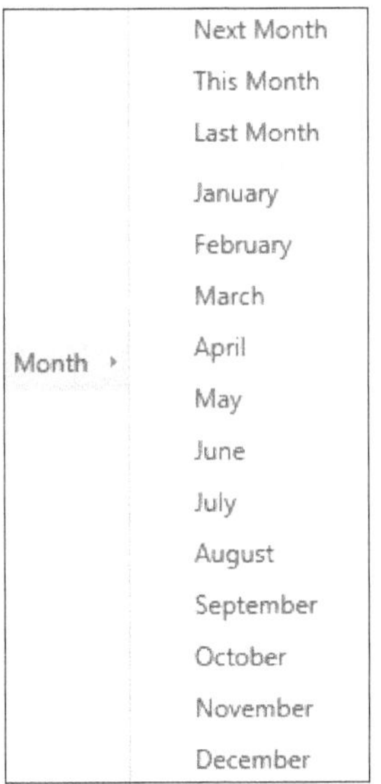

Figure 4-5 Month submenu filter options

Using The Search Field To Filter Data

Scrolling through the list of values at the bottom of the filter list can be exhausting.

If you do not want to scroll, type the first few characters of the value that you are looking for in the **SEARCH** field illustrated in Figure 4-6. This will reduce the number of values in the list.

As shown in the figure, the search returns all entries that have the characters in the order that you typed them in, anywhere in the field. It does not matter whether or not the Select All option is checked.

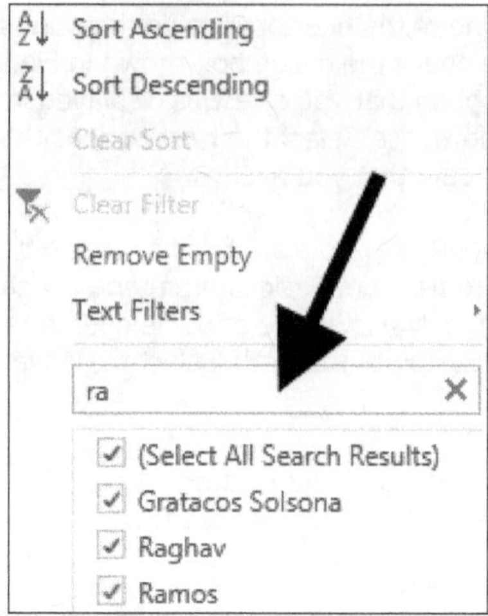

Figure 4-6 Search field filter results

Text Functions

The functions explained in Table 4-1 are used to create filter criteria for text data.

Function	Selects Records That . . .
Equals	Match the text entered.
Does Not Equal	Do not match the text entered.
Begins With	Have the text entered, at the beginning of the field.
Does Not Begin With	Do not have the text entered, at the beginning of the field.
Ends With	Have the text entered at the end of the field.
Does Not End With	Do not have the text entered, at the end of the field.
Contains	Have the text some place in the field.
Does Not Contain	Do not have the text some place in the field.

Table 4-1 Text functions explained

Numeric Functions

The functions explained in Table 4-2 are used to create filter criteria for numeric data.

Function	Selects Records That . . .
Equals	Match the value entered.
Does Not Equal	Do not match the value entered.
Greater Than	Have a value larger than the value entered.
Greater Than Or Equal To	Have the same value entered or a value larger than the value entered.
Less Than	Have a value smaller than the value entered.
Less Than Or Equal To	Have the same value entered or a value smaller than the value entered.
Between	Have a value that is in the range selected.

Table 4-2 Numeric functions explained

Date And Time Functions

The functions explained in Table 4-3 are used to create filter criteria for date and time data.

Function	Selects Records That . . .
Equals	Have the date entered.
Before	Have a date earlier than the date entered.
After	Have a date later than the date entered.
Between	Have a date in the range selected.
In the Next	Have a date in the future range selected. (1)
In the Previous	Have a date in the past range selected. (1)

Table 4-3 Date and Time functions explained

Function	Selects Records That . . .
Is Earliest	Have the oldest date in the column. (2)
Is Latest	Have the most recent date in the column. (2)
Is Not Earliest	Do not have the oldest dates in the column.
Is Not Latest	Do not have the most current dates in the column.
Next Year	Have a date in the next year. (3)
This Year	Have a date in the current year. (3)
Last Year	Have a date in the previous year. (3)
Year To Date	Have a date from January 1 of the current year through today. (3)
Next Quarter	Have a date in the next calendar quarter. (4)
This Quarter	Have a date in the current calendar quarter. (4)
Last Quarter	Have a date in the previous calendar quarter. (4)
Specific Quarter	Have a date in the quarter selected, based on the options shown in Figure 4-8. (4)
Next Month	Have a date in the next calendar month. (5)
This Month	Have a date in the current calendar month. (5)
Last Month	Have a date in the previous calendar month. (5)
Specific Month	Have a date in the month selected from the list shown earlier in Figure 4-5. The year does not matter. (5)
Next Week	Have a date in the next calendar week. (6)
This Week	Have a date in the current calendar week. (6)
Last Week	Have a date in the previous calendar week. (6)
Tomorrow	Have the next days date. (7)
Today	Have the current date. (7)
Yesterday	Have the previous days date. (7)
Next Hour	Have a time within the next hour. (8)
This Hour	Have a time within the current hour. (8)
Last Hour	Have a time within the previous hour. (8)
Next Minute	Have a time within the next minute. (9)
This Minute	Have a time within the current minute. (9)
Last Minute	Have a time within the previous minute. (9)
Next Second	Have a time within the next second. (10)
This Second	Have a time within the current second. (10)
Last Second	Have a time within the previous second. (10)
Custom Filter	Have a date that meets the criteria that you create on the Filter Rows dialog box.

Table 4-3 Date and Time functions explained (Continued)

(1) The **IN THE NEXT** and **IN THE PREVIOUS** functions are used to filter dates in seconds, minutes, hours, days, weeks, months, quarters or years. Both functions have the filter options shown in Figure 4-7.
(2) This function is dynamic, which means that different rows can be retrieved each time the data is refreshed.
(3) This function is on the **YEAR** sub menu and is used as a date range.
(4) This function is on the **QUARTER** sub menu and is used as a date range.
(5) This function is on the **MONTH** sub menu and is used as a date range.
(6) This function is on the **WEEK** sub menu and is used as a date range.
(7) This function is on the **DAY** sub menu and is used as a date range.
(8) This function is on the **HOUR** submenu.
(9) This function is on the **MINUTE** submenu.
(10) This function is on the **SECOND** submenu.

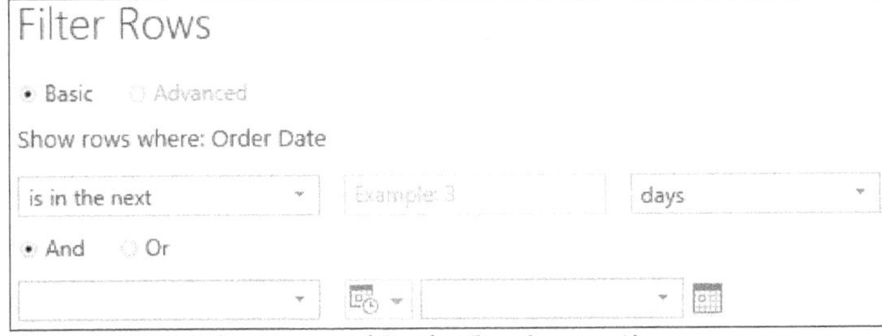

Figure 4-7 In the Next and In the Previous options

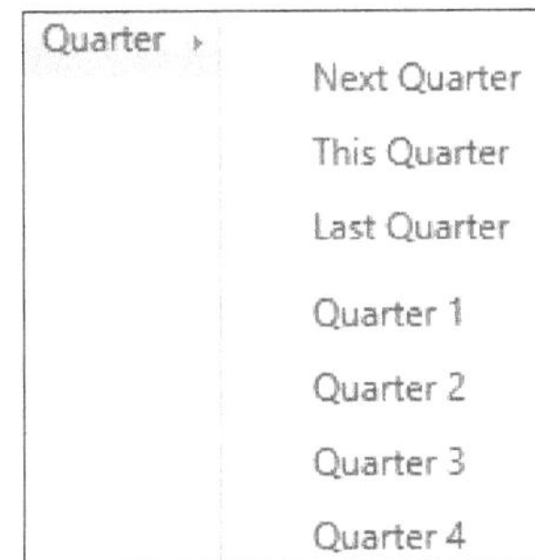

Figure 4-8 Quarter submenu options

Shaping The Data

Depending on the amount of data and the condition of the data, it could take some time to get the data ready to be analyzed or used to create reports. To accomplish this task, in addition to figuring out which fields have data that needs to be cleaned, you need a game plan (a process) to get everything done. As you will see, these tasks need to be done in a somewhat specific order. Yes, there is some wiggle room to change the order, without putting the data in more of a disarray then it already is in.

While cleaning the data, make note of items that fall into the categories of consistent missing data and incorrect data entry. The first steps that I take to clean data are listed below. These steps are often referred to as **SHAPING THE DATA.**

① Filter out the columns and rows that are not needed. Filtering data is a popular option for reducing the number of rows.
② Bring in any other data that is needed by using the merge and append options. I keep this task to a minimum because I prefer to use the **RELATIONSHIPS VIEW** to join tables.
③ Create calculated columns as needed (only if the data is not going to be loaded into the data model).
④ Give the list of missing and/or incorrect data issues to the appropriate departments, so that they can fix the recurring data problems.

Exercise 4.1: Use The Filter Options In The Query Editor

In this exercise you will learn how to filter data by filtering the Stores table to only display stores in the United States that have less than 30 employees, that are still open.

1. Save the E2.4 file as `E4.1 Filter data`.

2. Duplicate the Stores query ⇒ Rename the query to `1 Filter Stores`.

3. Display the filter list for the Region Country Name column ⇒

   Clear the (Select All) option ⇒

   Scroll down the list and check the United States option, shown in Figure 4-9 ⇒

   Click OK.
   The number of rows displayed, has been reduced.

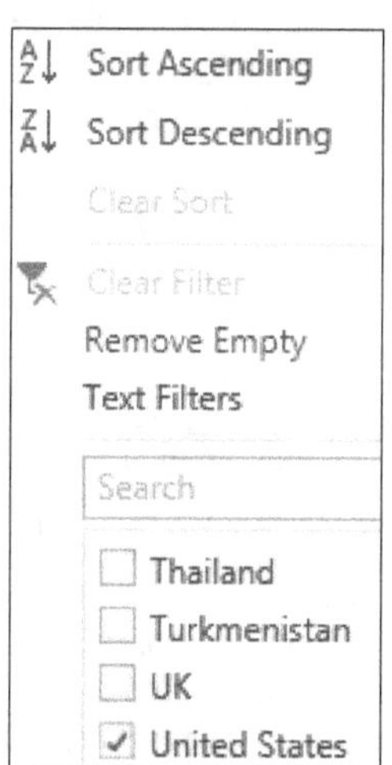

Figure 4-9 Country Name filter options

4. Open the filter for the Employee Count column ⇒ Select the Number Filters option ⇒ Select Less Than.

5. Type `30` in the field, as shown in Figure 4-10 ⇒ Click OK.

   Notice that the table now displays 147 rows of data.

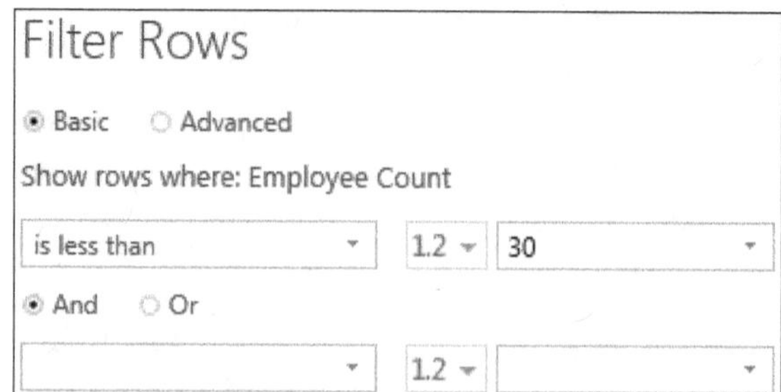

Figure 4-10 Employee Count column custom filter options

6. Open the filter for the Close Date column ⇒ Clear the (Select All) option ⇒ Check the **(NULL)** option.
   In this exercise, null means that the store is still open.

Based on all of the filters that you created in this query, out of the 306 stores in the table, there are 137 stores in the United States that are open and have less than 30 employees.

Create Date And Text Filters

In this part of the exercise you will learn how to create a filter that selects dates that fall within a range and a text filter that selects multiple values.

1. Display the Orders query ⇒ Order Date field filter ⇒ Date/Time Filters ⇒ Between.

2. On the first row type `03/01/2006`.

   On the second row type `12/31/2006`, as shown in Figure 4-11.

   All of the rows displayed in the query, will have an order date in the range shown in the figure.

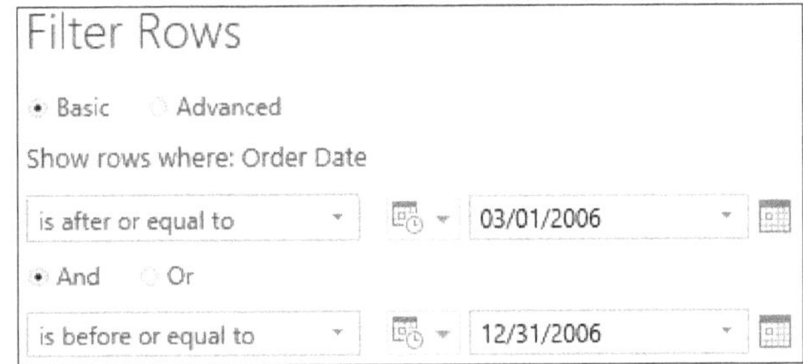

Figure 4-11 Filter options for a date field

Create Filters For More Than One Column

In this part of the exercise you will create filters, for two columns in the same query.

1. Display the Stores query ⇒ Create a filter for the Open Date field, that the date has to be before 12/31/2005.

2. Create a filter for the State Province Name field. The value has to be Florida, Texas or Virginia. There should be 54 rows in the query.

3. Apply and save the changes to the file.

Exercise 4.2: Create A Custom Filter

This exercise will show you how to create custom filters to only display records with a Unit Cost between $1 and $100 and a Discount Quantity between 3 and 4 percent.

1. Save the E2.3 file as `E4.2 Custom filters`.

2. Delete all of the queries except the Fact Sales Txt query ⇒ Display the Fact Sales Txt query.

3. Open the Unit Cost filter drop-down list ⇒ Select the **BETWEEN** function.

4. Type `1` in the field across from the Greater than or equal to function.

   Type `100` in the field across from the Less than or equal to function. You should have the options shown in Figure 4-12.

   The values that you just typed in do not have to be in the table, because this criteria is creating a range of values that are acceptable.

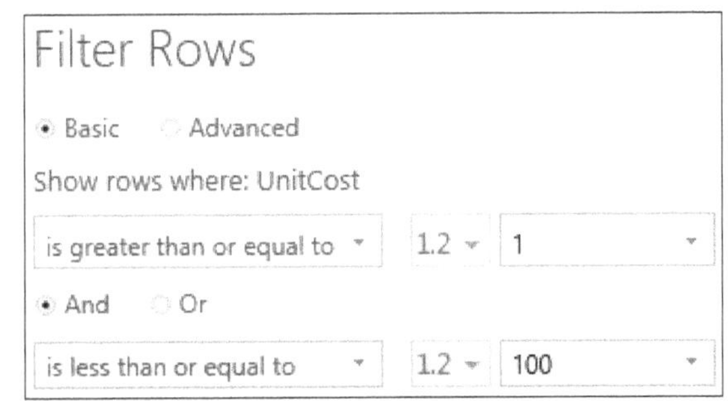

Figure 4-12 Unit Cost custom filter options

   Even though you can't see the exact number of how many rows are displayed, the number of rows has been reduced to 1.2 million from over 2.2 million.

Create Another Custom Filter

In this part of the exercise you will add another filter to only display records that have a Discount Quantity between 3 and 4 percent.

1. Open the Discount Quantity filter drop-down list ⇒ Select the Between function.

2. Type `3` in the field across from the Greater than or equal to function ⇒ Type `4` in the field across from the Less than or equal to function.

3. Apply the changes.

Advanced Filter Criteria

If the basic filter options shown above in Figure 4-12 do not let you create the filter criteria that you need, select the **ADVANCED OPTION** at the top of the Filter Rows dialog box.

This will display the options shown in Figure 4-13.

The options are used to create more than two sets of criteria for the same field or criteria for multiple fields.

Dates can be selected by clicking the Calendar button. When clicked, the current month and year are displayed.

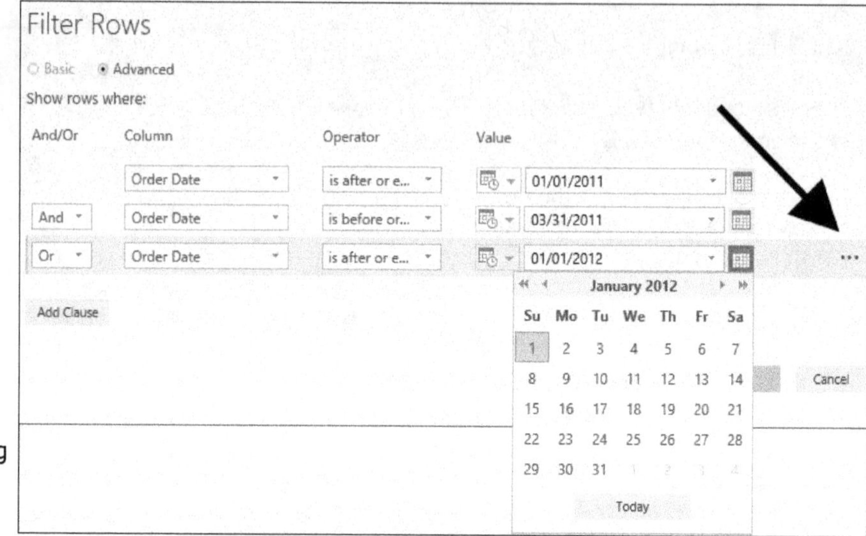

Figure 4-13 Advanced Filter Rows options

Click the arrow to the left of the month to select a date in the past. Click the arrow to the right of the year to select a date in the future.

The **ELLIPSIS BUTTON**, illustrated above in Figure 4-13, is used to move or delete the selected filter criteria.

The **ADD CLAUSE BUTTON** adds another row, so that more filter criteria can be created.

The criteria shown in the figure will select records that have an order date between 1/1/2011 and 3/31/2011 **OR** an order date greater than or equal to 1/1/2012.

Exercise 4.3: Create Advanced Filter Criteria

In this exercise you will learn how to use the Advanced filter options.

Create Advanced Date Filters

In this part of the exercise you will create multiple date filters. The filters that you will create will select records that fall into one of two date ranges.

1. Save the E3.4 file as `E4.3 Advanced filter options`.

2. Select the Orders table ⇒ Display the filter options for the Order Date column ⇒ Select the Between option.

3. Next to the Is after or equal to option, type `1/1/2011` ⇒ In the next field type `3/31/2011`. Don't click OK. This criteria will select records with an Order date in the first quarter of 2011.

4. Select the Advanced option ⇒ Click the **ADD CLAUSE BUTTON.**

5. Open the Operator drop-down list for the last Order Date field ⇒ Select **IS AFTER OR EQUAL TO** ⇒ Type `1/1/2012` in the Value field.

6. Because the goal of the filter is to select records that fall into either criteria range, the second And/Or operator needs to be changed. Change the last And operator to **OR**. You should have the options shown earlier in Figure 4-13 ⇒ Click OK.

7. Sort the Order Date column in ascending order ⇒ If you scroll through the records, you will see that all of the order dates are within one of the ranges that you created.

Create Advanced Text And Numeric Filters

In this part of the exercise you will learn how to create a filter that selects customers in the USA that have a last years sales amount greater than $20,000 or less than $5,000.

1. Display the filter options for the Country column in the Customer table ⇒ Select the Equals filter option ⇒ Select USA in the second drop-down list on the first row.

2. Select the Advanced option ⇒ Click the Add Clause button.

3. Open the second column drop-down list ⇒ Select the Last Years Sales field ⇒ Change the Operator to **IS GREATER THAN OR EQUAL TO** ⇒ In the Value field type `20000`.

4. On the last row, change the And/Or operator to Or ⇒ Select the Last Years Sales field ⇒ Change the operator to **IS LESS THAN OR EQUAL TO** ⇒ In the Value field type `5000`.

   You should have the options shown in Figure 4-14.

   128 records should be displayed in the Customer query.

Figure 4-14 Text and numeric advanced filter options

Custom Columns

Custom columns are used to add more data to a table. A custom column in the Query Editor is the same as a **CALCULATED COLUMN** in the Data view. It is not a requirement to create custom columns in the Query Editor.
I personally prefer to create all calculations in the Data view, instead of some in the Query Editor and some in the Data view, if for no other reason then I only have to look in one place to view all of the calculations. Custom columns are used to:

① Extract part of an existing column
② Create new data
③ Join or combine data from existing columns

Formulas created in the Query Editor look similar to formulas created in Excel. The biggest difference is that in Power BI Desktop and the Query Editor, column names are used in the formulas, instead of cell references.
The column names must be enclosed in brackets. Other differences between Excel formulas and Custom columns include the following:

① The data type is a factor in creating a custom column. If there is a data type mismatch, you have to use what is known as a **CONVERSION FUNCTION**, like **NUMBER.TOTEXT** to create the formula.
② A formula created in the Query Editor is case sensitive.
③ There are no tool tips or auto complete options to help you create a formula, using the Custom Column dialog box.

Add Custom Column Options

This dialog box is used to create expressions (a custom column). These expressions can be based on constant values and values from other data in the same row. The fields in the **AVAILABLE COLUMNS** list are from the query displayed on the Query Editor. To add a field to the formula, select it in the list, then click the Insert button or double-click on the field in the list. The new column is automatically added to the end of the query in the Query Editor.

A feature that I think is really cool is that if you add a column to a table that is only needed to create a calculation, (using the Merge feature) after the calculation is created, the column that was only added to the query to be used in the calculation can be deleted. Once deleted, the calculation still works because the calculation is saved as a step. And the deleted column action is in a step below the calculation step. This cannot be done in Excel because it saves the formula.

Exercise 4.4: Add Columns To A Table

In this exercise you will learn how to create different types of expressions to create data that is not usually stored in a table.

Create A Total Calculated Column

In this part of the exercise you will create a custom column to calculate the line item total for each row in the Order Details query.

1. Save the E2.4 file as `E4.4 Add columns and use the IF function.`

2. Display the Order Details query.

3. Add Column tab ⇒ Add Custom Column button ⇒ In the New column name field, type `LineTotal.`

4. In the Available columns list, double-click on the Quantity field ⇒ Type a `*` after the Quantity field in the formula.

Custom Column Error Messages
While you are creating the formula for a custom column, you will often see one of the error messages shown in Figure 4-15. You can ignore the error messages until you have finished creating the formula, and the OK button is enabled, on the Add Custom Column dialog box. If you have finished creating the formula and there is an error message, there is a problem with the formula that you need to fix.

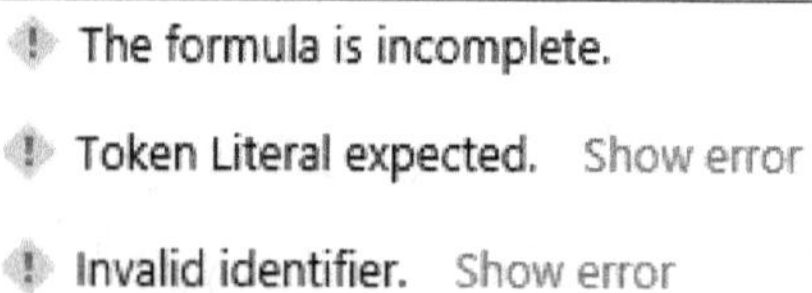

Figure 4-15 Custom column error messages

5. Double-click on the Unit Price field, in the Available columns list.

   You should have the formula shown in Figure 4-16.

   The **LEARN ABOUT POWER BI DESKTOP FORMULAS LINK**, opens a web page that has links for the formula categories functions and syntax.

   These documents are helpful if you want to learn about the **M LANGUAGE** functions available in Power BI Desktop.

   Click OK.

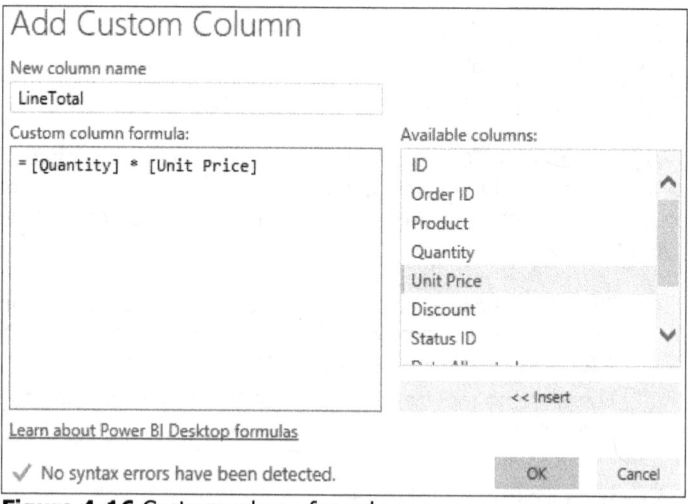

Figure 4-16 Custom column formula

6. Scroll to the far right of the Order Details query. You should see the Line Total column shown in Figure 4-17.

   Click in the column. The M formula that you created is in the formula bar.

1.2 Inventory ID	ABC 123 LineTotal
83	1400
63	105
64	300
65	530

Figure 4-17 Line Total custom column

Congratulations! You just created new data for the query and your first **M FORMULA**, from scratch. As you see, you can create basic M formulas without knowing a lot about the M language.

Combine Columns Of Data

There may be times when you need to display data from two or more fields together, as one field. A common use of this type of formula is to combine the first and last name fields into one column, so that the full name can be displayed together. That is the formula that you will create in this part of the exercise.

1. Display the Customers query.

2. Open the Add Custom Column dialog box ⇒ In the New column name field, type `FullName`.

3. Click after the equal sign in the formula field and type `[First Name] & " " & [Last Name]`, as shown in Figure 4-18.

   Make sure that there is a space between the quotes. The quotes with a space will place a space between the first and last name fields when they are combined into one field.

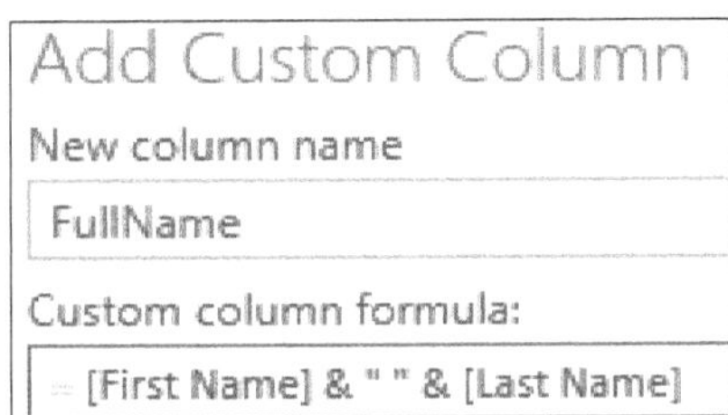

Figure 4-18 Concatenation formula

Figure 4-19 shows the data from the combined fields in one column in the table.

While part of the exercise showed you how to create a formula to combine the data in two columns to create a new column, the Add Column tab ⇒ Merge Columns option can create the same new field.

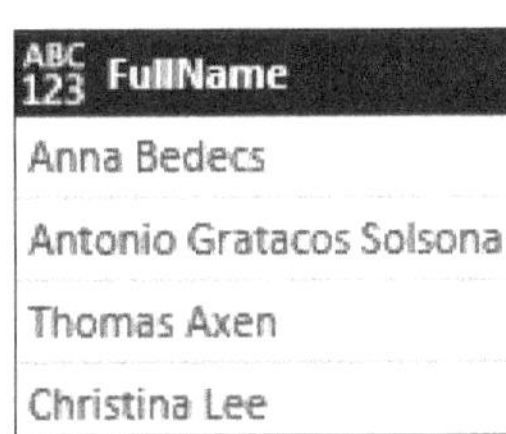

ABC 123 FullName
Anna Bedecs
Antonio Gratacos Solsona
Thomas Axen
Christina Lee

Figure 4-19 Full Name custom column

What Is A Function?

Functions are prewritten, built-in formulas or procedures. The functions that Power BI Desktop supports have been thoroughly tested and from what I can tell, they are error free. However, this does not mean that if there is bad data in a table that you won't have a problem with the function. If you do not follow the syntax rules or fill in the arguments correctly when using the function, an error will be generated. Power BI Desktop has a few hundred functions that you can use. Sum, Average, Count and Distinct Count are some of the functions that are covered in this book.

Combine The First Initial And Last Name

The previous part of this exercise showed you how to combine the data from two columns. This part of the exercise will show you how to select the first character from the First Name field and combine it with the Last Name field.

The **TEXT.START FUNCTION** starts at the beginning of the data in the field and extracts a specific number of characters.

1. Display the Customers query.

2. Open the Add Custom Column dialog box ⇒ Create the formula shown in Figure 4-20. The new column should look like the one shown in Figure 4-21.

Add Custom Column

New column name

First Initial

Custom column formula:

```
= Text.Start([First Name],1) & " " & [Last Name]
```

Figure 4-20 Formula to display the first name initial and last name

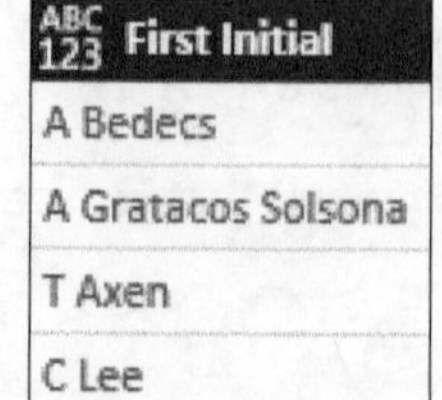

First Initial
A Bedecs
A Gratacos Solsona
T Axen
C Lee

Figure 4-21 Data combined from two columns

Use The IF Function To Create A Formula With Conditional Logic

The **IF FUNCTION** is used to create a conditional formula. It tests to see if the condition that you specify is true or not. Based on the result of the test, different actions are taken.

This function checks the value in a field to see if it meets the criteria in the formula. If the value meets the criteria, the first argument after the criteria in the formula is performed. If the value does not meet the criteria, the second argument after the criteria is performed. If you have used the **IF . . . THEN . . . ELSE STATEMENT** in other software, you will see that the IF function in Power BI Desktop works the same way.

The formula that you will create in this part of the exercise will check to see if the shipped date is greater than the order date plus two days. If it is, display "Shipped Late" in the cell, otherwise, display "On Time" in the cell.

1. Display the Orders query.

2. Open the Add Custom Column dialog box ⇒ Type `Order Shipped On Time`, as the column name.

3. After the equal sign, type the formula shown in Figure 4-22. You can add the fields in brackets, by double-clicking on them in the Available columns list. The column should look like the one shown in Figure 4-23.

```
if [Shipped Date] >[Order Date] + #duration (2, 0, 0, 0) then "Shipped Late" else "On Time"
```

Figure 4-22 IF formula

The cells in the column that have the word "Error", represent rows where one of the fields used in the formula has no value or a null value.

In reality, a formula should be created to verify that both of the fields used in the formula that you just created have data. If either is null, the calculated column should display something like "missing data", so that the person analyzing the data will be alerted to the fact that there is a problem with the data.

Hopefully, when some one sees a message like that, they will fix the data.

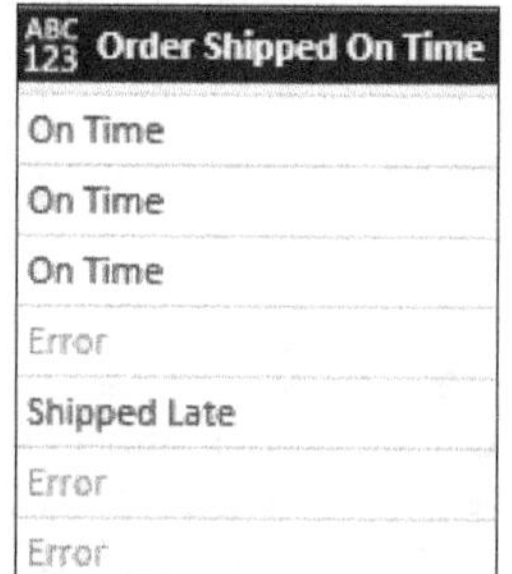

Order Shipped On Time
On Time
On Time
On Time
Error
Shipped Late
Error
Error

Figure 4-23 Order shipped on time calculated column

The #duration(2, code in the formula, adds two days to the Order Date. You can use any duration number. 2 days, is just what I selected to demonstrate the concept with.

The formula (in Figure 4-22) translates to: If the Order Date is 9/6/14 and if the Shipped Date is 9/19/14, "Shipped Late" will be added to the cell for the row because the Order Date +2 returns a date of 9/8/14, which is the expected ship date. Any date that is greater than 9/8/14, in this example, is considered to be shipped late.

Because the formula field on the Add Custom Column dialog box ignores spaces, you can type a formula on multiple lines, as shown in Figure 4-24, instead of typing the formula on one line.

I find formulas that use multiple lines easier to read. Doing this is optional.

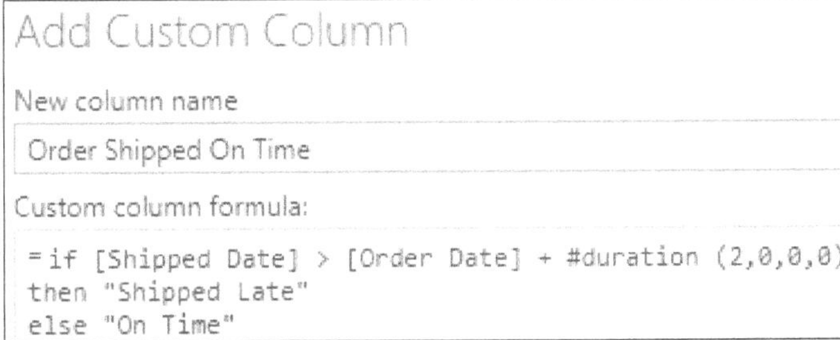

Figure 4-24 Formula using multiple lines

Add Index Column Options

The first two options shown in Figure 4-25 are used to create a column in the table named "Index", that starts with a zero or 1. These options create an incremental counter that would be useful for tables that need a field with a unique value, because it numbers each row sequentially.

The **CUSTOM** option displays the dialog box shown in Figure 4-26. The options are used to create an index that does not use sequential values or the index needs to start with a specific number other then zero or one. Like the From 0 and From 1 options, custom indexes must also use numeric values.

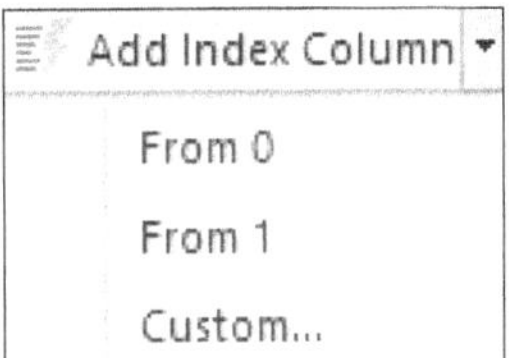

Figure 4-25 Add Index Column button options

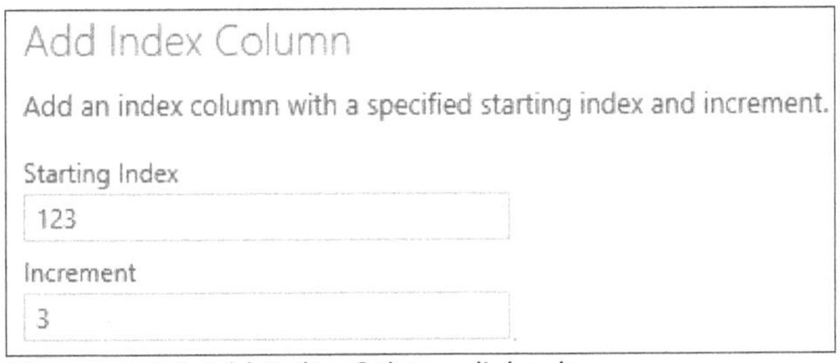

Figure 4-26 Add Index Column dialog box

Summary

The text, numeric, date and time filter functions were covered in this chapter. The exercises showed you how to create each of these filter types. If you have created filters in Excel, you probably recognized and are familiar with the filter options in the Query Editor.

When you think of transforming data, you also usually think about ways to reduce the number of rows or columns. There are times when columns have to be created because some data that is needed does not exist, in the data source. An example of data that fits into this category is a sales tax field because it is the calculation of at least two other fields. The options used to add new columns are Split Column, Add Custom Column, Add Index Column and Duplicate Column.

Creating formulas was also covered. These topics introduced you to "writing code", the M language and combining data from different columns. While the exercises only demonstrated combining data from two columns, data can be combined from as many columns as needed. Hopefully, the exercises in this chapter have you wanting to see what else you can do in the Query Editor.

USING THE QUERY EDITOR TO TRANSFORM DATA

In this chapter you will learn about more features in the Query Editor, including the following:

- ☑ How the "Any" data type works
- ☑ Splitting data in a column
- ☑ Grouping data
- ☑ Merging data

CHAPTER 5

Transforming The Data

Chapter 2 covered how to discover data. Chapter 4 covered how to filter the data and add new columns of data to a query. By this point in the process, you should have all or almost all of the data needed for the analysis process.

This chapter shows you techniques on how to clean the data. The Transform tab has options that are used to clean the data. Not surprisingly, this is known as **TRANSFORMING THE DATA** and is the "T" in ETL. Splitting data in a column, replacing values and grouping data is also covered, because they transform data.

Transform Tab vs Add Column Tab Options

As you have probably seen, these tabs have many of the same options. For the most part, the options work the same. The **BIGGEST DIFFERENCE** is that the options on the Transform tab replace the data in the selected column when the option is applied. The options on the Add Column tab create a new column and place the result in the new column, leaving the data in the original column unchanged. On your own, you need to decide whether or not you need or want to keep the original data.

How Transformation Options Are Applied
Keep in mind that transformation options are applied, based on the data type. This means that you cannot apply a text transformation to a column that has a numeric data type. Also note that many transformations that are available in the Query Editor, can be created in the Data view, by creating DAX formulas.

Transform Tab

The options shown in Figure 5-1 are used to change the appearance of the data in the selected column. The options are explained in Table 5-1.

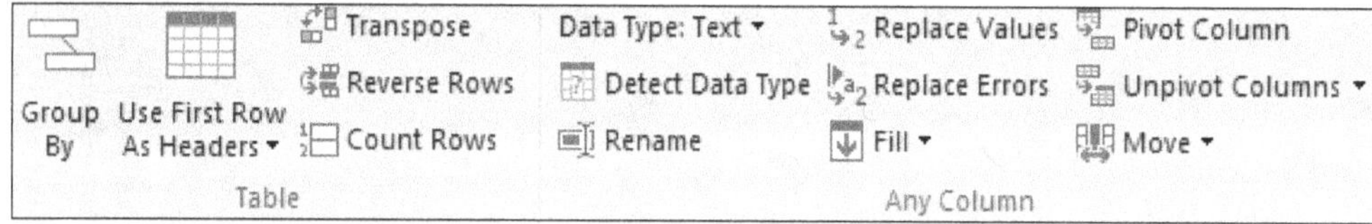

Figure 5-1 Transform tab

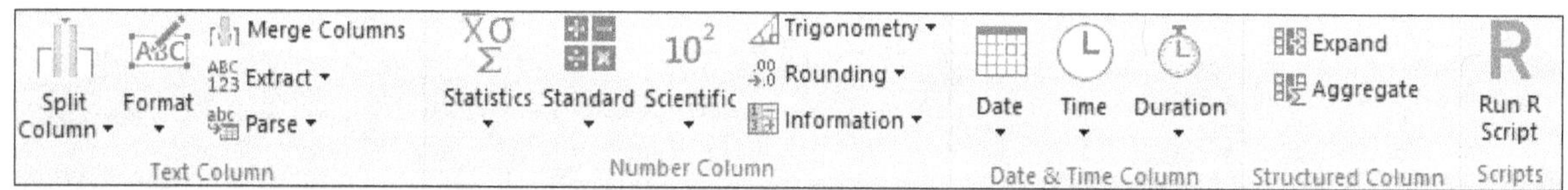

Figure 5-1 Transform tab (Continued)

Option	Description
Group By	[See Chapter 3, Group By Options] (1)
Use First Row As Headers	[See Chapter 3, Use First Row As Headers Options]
Transpose	Switch the rows to columns and the columns to rows.
Reverse Rows	Displays the last rows first. This option will remind you of the Sort descending option.
Count Rows	Displays the number of rows in the table, as illustrated in Figure 5-2.
Data Type	[See Data Types]
Detect Data Type	[See Detect Data Type]
Rename	Rename the selected column.
Replace Values	[See Chapter 3, Replace Values]
Replace Errors	The option shown in Figure 5-3 is used to enter the value that will replace the errors (the values that are not correct) in the selected column(s).
Fill	[See Using The Fill Option]
Pivot Column	[See Chapter 6, Pivot Column Options] (1)
Unpivot Columns	[See Chapter 6, Unpivoting Data] (1)
Move	[See Move Options]
Split Column	[See Chapter 3, Split Column Options]

Table 5-1 Transform tab options explained

Option	Description
Format	The functions shown in Figure 5-4 are used to change the case of characters, as well as, remove spaces from the beginning and end of a cell. The **CLEAN FUNCTION** removes non-printable characters. The **ADD PREFIX** and **ADD SUFFIX FUNCTIONS** are used to add text to the beginning or end of the data in the column.
Merge Columns	This option is only enabled when two or more columns are selected. It combines the data from the selected columns into one new column. The original columns are removed from the table after this process is completed. If you want to keep the existing columns, use the Merge Columns option on the Add Column tab.
Extract	[See Extract Options]
Parse	Coverts the selected column(s) or cells to **XML** or **JSON** format. This option is only enabled for columns with a Text data type.
Statistics	Applies the statistical functions shown in Figure 5-5, to the values in the selected column and displays the result.
Standard	The functions shown in Figure 5-6 are used to create basic formulas. (2)
Scientific	The functions shown in Figure 5-7 are used to create scientific calculations. (2)
Trigonometry	These functions are used to create formulas that use trigonometry functions. (2)
Rounding	The functions are used to round the values up, down or to a specific number of decimal places. (2)
Information	These functions are used to determine if each value in the column is even, odd, positive or negative. The column on the left of Figure 5-8 shows numeric data. The column on the right, shows the same column of data, after the **IS EVEN FUNCTION** is applied. True means the number is even. False means that the number is not even. (2)
Date	The functions shown in Figure 5-9 are used to extract or return part of the date. The **EARLIEST FUNCTION** retrieves the oldest date in the selected column. The data in the query is replaced with the oldest date. (3)
Time	The functions shown in Figure 5-10 are used to extract or return part of the time. (3)
Duration	The majority of functions shown in Figure 5-12 are used to calculate the duration (the length of time) and display the value in the format that the function represents. The functions in this category are only available for the Duration data type.
Expand	[See Chapter 6, Expand Button Options] (4)
Aggregate	[See Chapter 6, Aggregate Button Options] (4)
Run R Script	Is used to run an R script that will transform the data.

Table 5-1 Transform tab options explained (Continued)

(1) This option changes the data structure.
(2) The functions in this category are only available for columns with a numeric data type.
(3) The functions in this category are only available for columns that have any of the Date or Time data types. The functions are used to replace the date or time in the selected column. For example, if the Date button ⇒ Month ⇒ Start of month function is selected, all of the dates in the column will be changed, from the dates shown in the column on the left of Figure 5-11, to the dates in the column on the right of the figure. What you will see is that all of the dates have been changed to the first of the month, which is based on the original month.
(4) If the Query Editor window is not wide enough, this option will collapse and the Structured Column button shown in Figure 5-13, will be displayed instead.

To redisplay the rows of data, delete the **COUNTED ROWS** applied step.

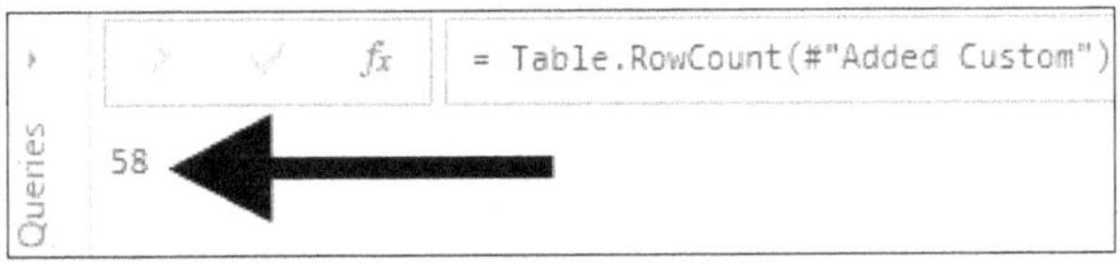

Figure 5-2 Count rows option applied

Replace Errors

Enter the value which will replace errors in the selected columns.

Value

Figure 5-3 Replace Errors option

Transform Tab Options

Figures 5-4 to 5-13 are options on the Transform tab and examples of some of the functions.

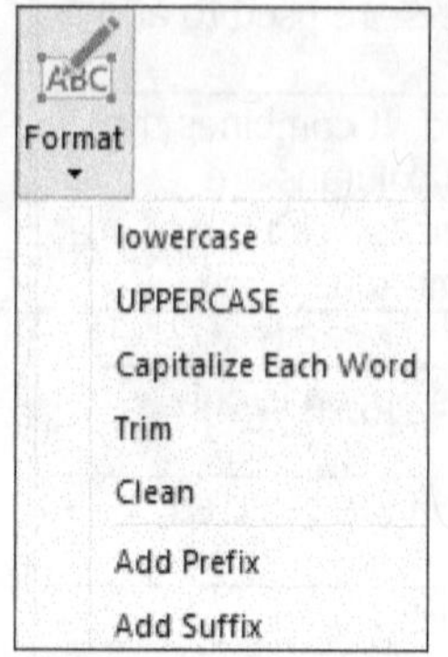

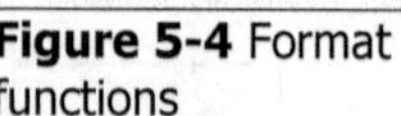

Figure 5-4 Format functions

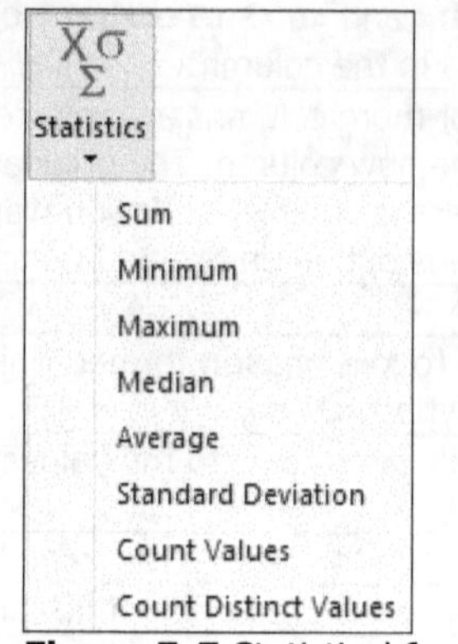

Figure 5-5 Statistical functions

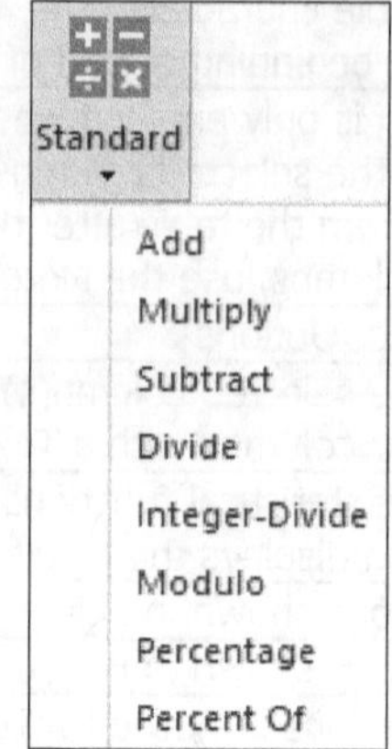

Figure 5-6 Standard functions

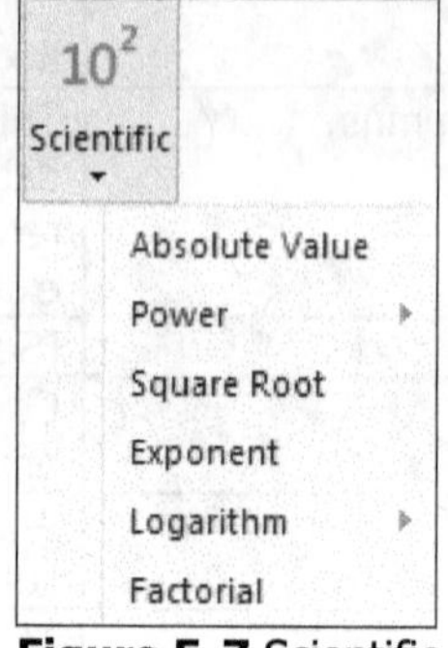

Figure 5-7 Scientific functions

$ Price Total	Price Total
1505	FALSE
865	FALSE
1190	TRUE
276	TRUE

Figure 5-8 Is EVEN information function applied

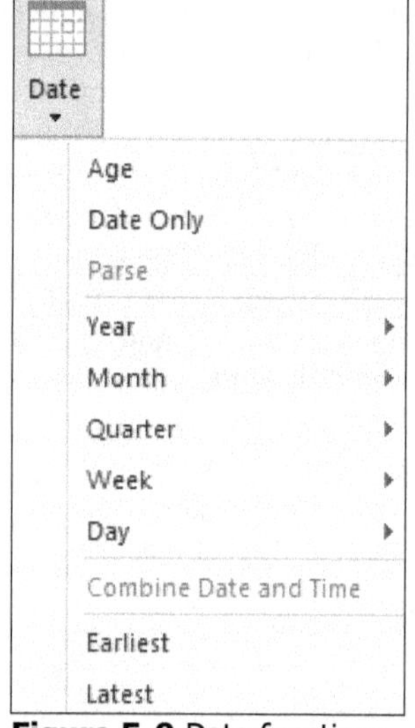

Figure 5-9 Date functions

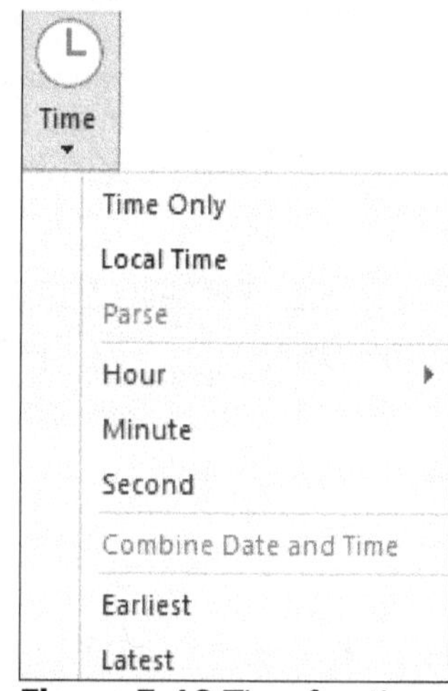

Figure 5-10 Time functions

Required Date	Required Date
02/25/2011	02/01/2011
03/03/2010	03/01/2010
12/26/2011	12/01/2011
01/04/2012	01/01/2012

Figure 5-11 Start of month function applied to a date column

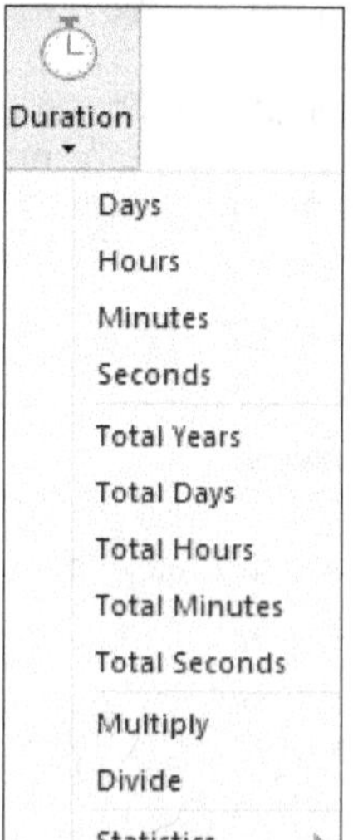

Figure 5-12 Duration functions

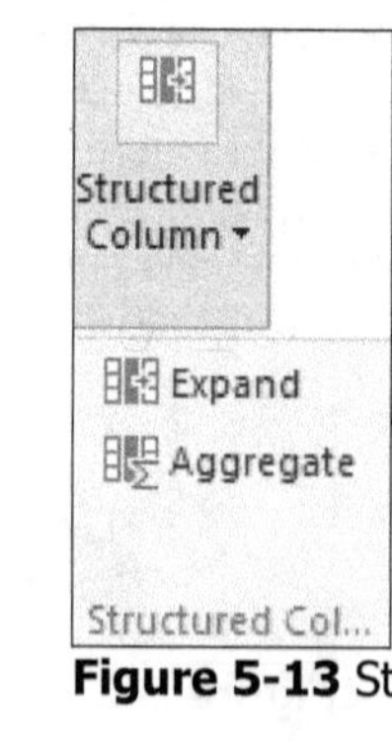

Figure 5-13 Structured Column options

Data Type Options

The options shown in Figure 5-14 are used to change the data type of the selected column. The options are explained in Table 5-2.

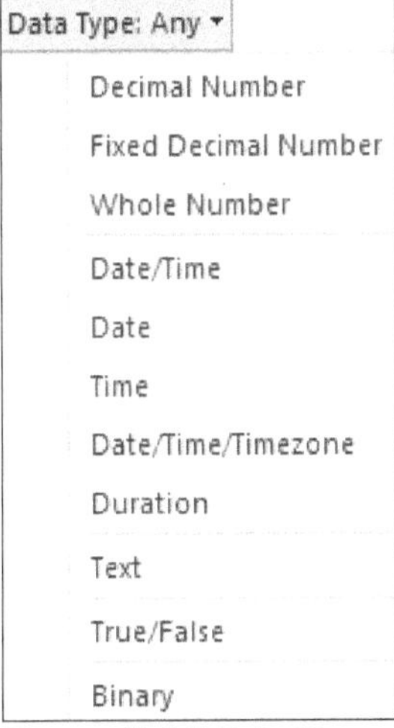

Figure 5-14 Data Type options

Data Type	Select This Data Type When The Data . . .
Decimal Number	Is numeric and needs to display cents or a decimal point.
Fixed Decimal Number	Is numeric and needs to display cents, like currency formatting.
Whole Number	Is numeric and does not need to display a decimal point.
Date/Time	Needs to display a date and time. (5)
Date	Should be displayed in date format.
Time	Should be displayed in time format. (5)
Date/Time/Timezone	Should be displayed in date, time and time zone format. The time zone comes from the system settings on your computer. (5)
Duration	[See Table 5-1, Duration]
Text	Should be displayed as alpha numeric. Zip code fields are usually assigned the Text data type, as they are not used in calculations that require numeric data types. At best, they are used with Count and Count (Distinct) functions, which do not require numeric values.
True/False	Should be displayed in Boolean format (on/off).
Binary	Is an object, like a file. This is the data type used when the Query Editor imports files. The binary data type can also be used to store the location of image files.

Table 5-2 Data Type options explained

(5) If the date does not have a time, this option adds the default time of 12:00:00 AM (midnight), to the column.

What Is The Any Data Type?

The "Any" data type option, shown above at the top of Figure 5-14, is the data type that the Query Editor gives a column when it cannot figure out what type of data is in the column. This data type can store any value. The easiest way to know if the **ANY DATA TYPE** was applied during the import, is to look at the code for the **CHANGED TYPE STEP**, as shown in Figure 5-15.

```
= Table.TransformColumnTypes(#"Promoted Headers",{{"Order ID", Int64.Type}, {"Employee ID",
Int64.Type}, {"Customer ID", Int64.Type}, {"Order Date", type any}, {"Shipped Date", type date},
{"Shipper ID", Int64.Type}, {"Ship Name", type text}, {"Ship Address", type text}, {"Ship City",
type text}, {"Ship State/Province", type text}, {"Ship ZIP/Postal Code", Int64.Type}, {"Ship
```

Figure 5-15 Changed Type step code

On the second line of code, you will see that the Order Date column has been assigned the Any Data type and the Shipped Date column has been assigned the Date data type. If you looked at the data, both columns have dates in this format MM/DD/YYYY. I notice inconsistencies like this more, when the data source is not a database.

It is important to ensure that columns that will be used in a calculation have the correct data type. It is best to fix the data types at the end of performing a lot of other steps. This is especially true of columns that have the Any data type. One place where I noticed that changing the data types early in the transformation process does not help is when the

APPEND QUERIES option is used. The data type will be changed to **ANY**, for matching columns (in the queries that will be appended) that do not have the same data type before the queries are appended.

If you see that there are rows or columns that are missing data, see if the people that created the data can clean up the data. They should know the data the best. If they can't or will not fill in the blanks <pun intended>, you need to figure out what to do with the incomplete data. I personally, do not modify empty fields because if something goes wrong with the analysis, it is not my fault. And because I notified the user group of the empty fields, the ball is in their court.

Structured Data Types

In addition to the data types shown earlier in Figure 5-14, there are three more data types: **TABLES, RECORDS** and **LISTS**. Columns with these data types cannot be changed. These data types are objects that have a lot of values that are bound together. They are explained below. If you want to see these data types, up close and in person, you can use the E2.3 file. It contains the examples that I use in this section.

Tables

As its name suggests, this data type contains a table. The Months table (query), shown in Figure 5-16, was created from an XML file.

The formula bar for the Source step shows the Table data type, as shown at the top of Figure 5-16.

When clicked, the button to the right of the Table column heading, displays a list of the columns in the table, as shown in Figure 5-17.

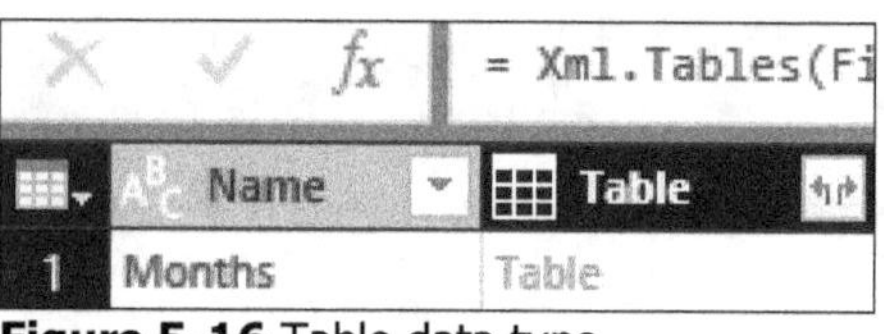

Figure 5-16 Table data type

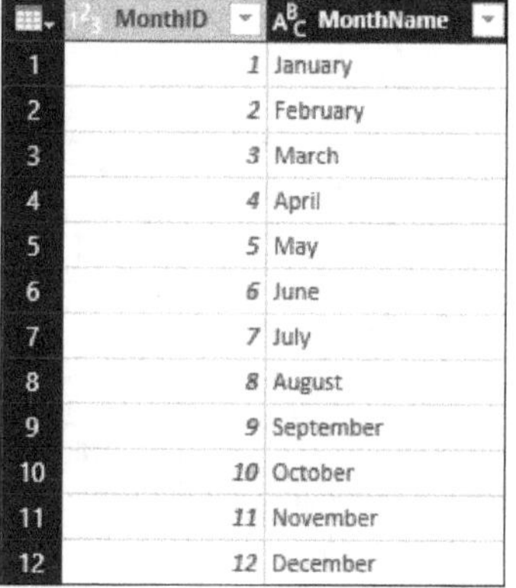

	MonthID	MonthName
1	1	January
2	2	February
3	3	March
4	4	April
5	5	May
6	6	June
7	7	July
8	8	August
9	9	September
10	10	October
11	11	November
12	12	December

Figure 5-17 Data from an XML file

What may not be obvious is that each row in the query contains a pointer to a different table. If you click on the Table link, all of the columns in the table are displayed in the query, as shown above in Figure 5-17.

Records

This data type indicates that the column has more than one field. Figure 5-18 shows the Record and List data types.

To view this figure, click on the JSON Customer Form query ⇒ Click on the Source step.

As you read the discussion below, it may be helpful to refer back to Chapter 2, Figure 2-25, to see where the data is coming from in Figures 5-18 and 5-19.

Clicking on the links explained below will add steps to the query that are not needed and cannot be deleted without modifying the code for the query.

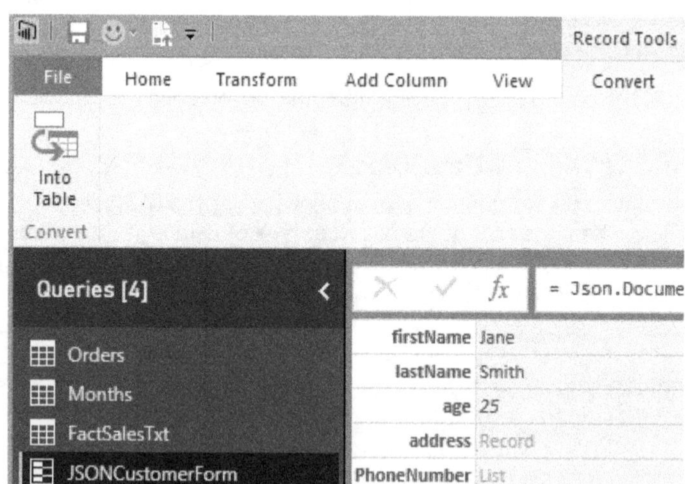

Figure 5-18 Record data type and tools

If you do click on any of these links now, the steps in the next section will prompt you to insert a step. It is ok, because you can close the Query Editor and select the Discard changes option.

The **RECORD** data type (in the Address field, shown above in Figure 5-18) means that there are multiple fields for the address. Clicking on this link displays all of the address fields, shown in Figure 5-19. Notice that a Navigation step was added.

Figure 5-19 Address fields

Lists

This data type means that the element has more than one entry (row of data).

The **LIST** data type (in the Phone Number field, shown earlier in Figure 5-18) means that there are multiple phone numbers (detail records) for the customer. Clicking on this link displays the table shown in Figure 5-20. (To return to the layout shown earlier in Figure 5-18, click on the Source step.) The table lets you know that there are two phone numbers for the record. This would be the "many" table, in a one-to-many relationship.

Each **RECORD LINK**, shown in Figure 5-20, will display one of the phone numbers for the customer, as shown in Figure 5-21.

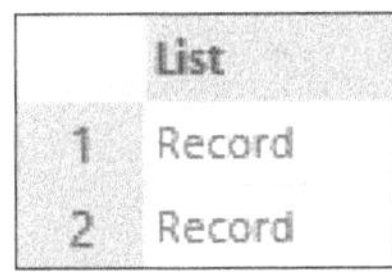

Figure 5-20 Phone number table

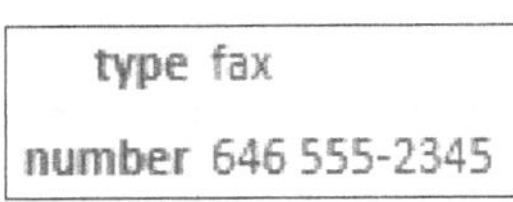

Figure 5-21 Phone number record

Record Tools Convert Tab

This tab was shown earlier in Figure 5-18. The **INTO TABLE BUTTON** converts the record (data type) into a table.

1. In the Query Settings panel, click on the **SOURCE STEP**.
2. Click the Into Table button.

   You should see the table shown in Figure 5-22.

Figure 5-22 Record converted to a table

3. Transform tab ⇒ Transpose button ⇒ Home tab ⇒ Use First Row As Headers button. You will see a table with one row of data.

If you are shaking your head and asking "Why?", don't worry. Unless you will be working with a lot of data that is in XML or JSON format, you probably will not see the Record and List data types. You will see the Table data type in some databases that you may use. And yes, there are exercises that show you how to work with the Table data type.

Detect Data Type

Click this button to let the Query Editor select the data type for the selected column(s). If you want the data type to be detected for the entire table at one time, you have to select all of the columns in the table before clicking this button. Keep in mind that this function does not always select the correct data type. Therefore, it is a good idea to review the code created for the **CHANGED TYPE STEP**. You can view the code by clicking on the Changed Type step, then looking at the code, in the formula bar.

For example, Figure 5-23 shows the code for the Changed Type step and some of the data in the query. Notice that the Revenue column was changed to the text data type, even though the column has numeric data.

```
= Table.TransformColumnTypes(#"Removed Duplicates",{{"Revenue", type text}})
```

	Product	Region	Revenue
1	Prod A	North America	14.22
2	Prod B	North America	20.12
3	Prod C	North America	12.18

Figure 5-23 Result of using the Detect Data Type option

Using The Fill Option

This option copies the data from the selected cell to the empty cells, (in the same column), above or below the selected cell. Usually, this feature is best suited for data that is grouped on the column that you want to apply the Fill option to.

The Fill option will be useful if you have to import a spreadsheet that looks like the one shown in Figure 5-24.

To fill in the Store column, you would follow the steps below.

1. Click on the column heading of the column that you want to fill. In this example, you would click on the Store column.

2. Transform tab ⇒ Fill ⇒ Down. The query will look like the one shown in Figure 5-25.

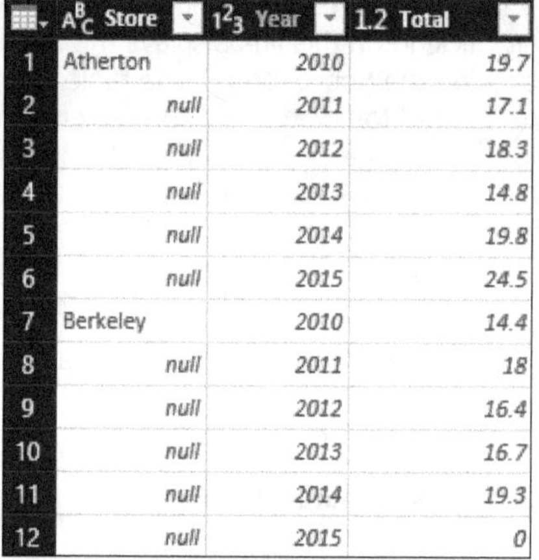

	Store	Year	Total
1	Atherton	2010	19.7
2	null	2011	17.1
3	null	2012	18.3
4	null	2013	14.8
5	null	2014	19.8
6	null	2015	24.5
7	Berkeley	2010	14.4
8	null	2011	18
9	null	2012	16.4
10	null	2013	16.7
11	null	2014	19.3
12	null	2015	0

Figure 5-24 Query missing data

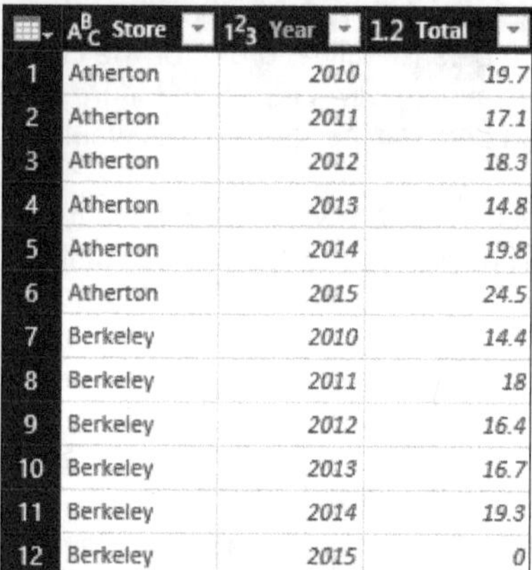

	Store	Year	Total
1	Atherton	2010	19.7
2	Atherton	2011	17.1
3	Atherton	2012	18.3
4	Atherton	2013	14.8
5	Atherton	2014	19.8
6	Atherton	2015	24.5
7	Berkeley	2010	14.4
8	Berkeley	2011	18
9	Berkeley	2012	16.4
10	Berkeley	2013	16.7
11	Berkeley	2014	19.3
12	Berkeley	2015	0

Figure 5-25 Query data filled in

Move Options

The options shown in Figure 5-26, are used to move the selected column(s) left, right, or to the beginning or end of the table.

By default, the columns are loaded in the same order that they are in the data source, which you can view in the Navigator window. When I know which columns I will use the most, I tend to move them to the beginning of the query, so that I do not have to keep scrolling to the right to find what I need. Keep in mind that columns cannot be moved in the Data view.

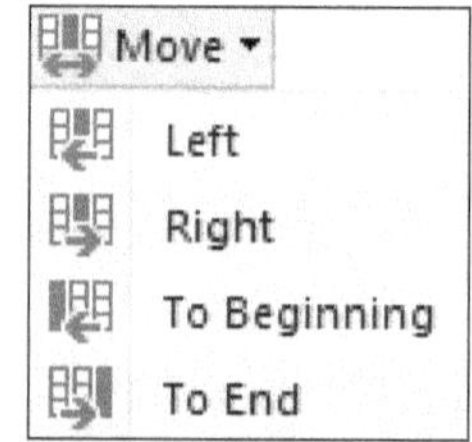

Figure 5-26 Move options

Extract Options

The options shown in Figure 5-27 are used to select how the data will be transformed. The options explained in Table 5-3 are used to select how many characters to extract (pull out) from the column.

The Extract option on the Transform tab replaces the values in the column currently selected, with values already in the cell. A new column is created when this option is selected on the Add Column tab.

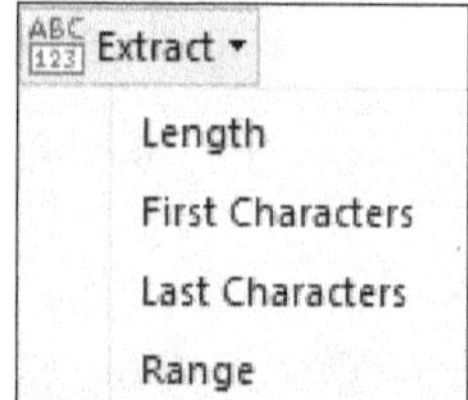

Figure 5-27 Extract options

Option	Description
Length	Replaces the data in each cell with a count of the length of the data in the cell. Doing this changes the columns data type to Decimal Number.
First Characters	Is used to select a specific number of characters from the beginning of the field to keep, as shown in Figure 5-28.
Last Characters	Is used to select a specific number of characters from the end of the field to keep.

Table 5-3 Extract options explained

Option	Description
Range	Displays the options shown in Figure 5-29. The options are used to select the first position in the field to keep and the number of characters in total to keep. The entries shown in the figure will start at the second character in the field and select three characters to keep. This means that a total of three characters will be kept in the field and the other characters in the field will be removed.

Table 5-3 Extract options explained (Continued)

Extract First Characters

Enter how many starting characters to keep.

Count

Figure 5-28 Extract First Characters option

Extract Text Range

Enter the index of the first character, and the number of characters to keep.

Starting Index

2

Number of Characters

3

Figure 5-29 Extract Text Range options

Exercise Tip
To make it easier for you to know which queries you modified, the queries will be duplicated and renamed to indicate what was done. The duplicated queries will start with a number to make it easier to recognize the modified queries.

Exercise 5.1: Use The Transform Tab Options

The options covered in this exercise are used to change the appearance of data.

Use The Split Column By Delimiter Option

In this part of the exercise, you will use the Split Column option to place the first and last name, which are currently in one column (the Contact Name column), in separate columns.

1. Save the E2.4 file as `E5.1 Transform tab options`.
2. Duplicate the Customers Extended query ⇒ Rename it to `1 Split Column`.
3. Click on the Contact Name column ⇒ Transform tab ⇒ **SPLIT COLUMN BUTTON** ⇒ By Delimiter ⇒ Open the Delimiter drop-down list and select Space.

If you display the Advanced options, you will see that the suggested number of columns to split the data into, is three. That is because the **AT EACH OCCURRENCE** split option is selected. Some of the contact names have two spaces, indicating that the name has three words. In this scenario, you do not know if records with three words are middle names or a last name followed by a suffix, like Jr.

4. Select the **AT THE LEFT MOST DELIMITER** option ⇒ Click OK. You will see two columns labeled Contact Name.1 and Contact Name.2, in place of the original Contact Name field, as shown in Figure 5-30.

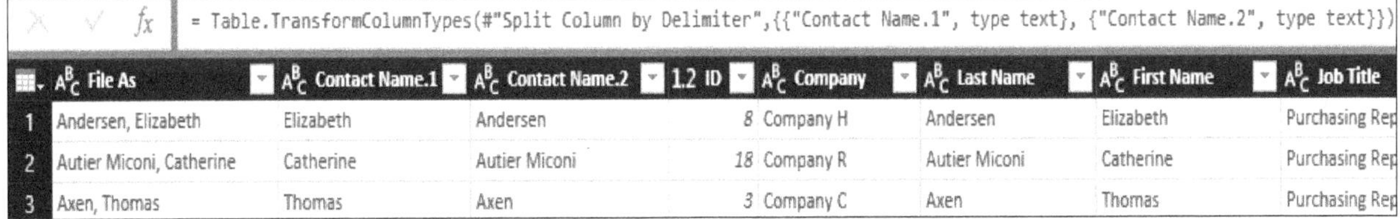

```
= Table.TransformColumnTypes(#"Split Column by Delimiter",{{"Contact Name.1", type text}, {"Contact Name.2", type text}})
```

	File As	Contact Name.1	Contact Name.2	ID	Company	Last Name	First Name	Job Title
1	Andersen, Elizabeth	Elizabeth	Andersen	8	Company H	Andersen	Elizabeth	Purchasing Rep
2	Autier Miconi, Catherine	Catherine	Autier Miconi	18	Company R	Autier Miconi	Catherine	Purchasing Rep
3	Axen, Thomas	Thomas	Axen	3	Company C	Axen	Thomas	Purchasing Rep

Figure 5-30 Result of the By Delimiter split column option

The dot notation at the end of a column name indicates that the data in the column came from another column.

The **M FORMULA** to create this data split is shown in the formula bar, at the top of the figure.

Use The Split Column By Number Of Characters Option

One way that I find this option useful, is to get the first letter of a first name. What I wish would not happen is that the original field is not changed by default. I would rather have the option to decide if it is ok to change the field. If this becomes a problem for you in the Query Editor, you could duplicate the column before using this option or create a custom column. In the Data view you could create a formula.

1. Duplicate the 1 Split column query ⇒ Rename it to `2 Number of characters`.

2. Click on the First Name column ⇒ Transform tab ⇒ Split Column button ⇒ By Number of Characters ⇒ Type `1` in the **NUMBER OF CHARACTERS** field.

3. Select the Once, as far left as possible option. The table should have the two new columns, shown in Figure 5-31.

   More than likely, the First Name.2 column would be deleted, because it is not needed.

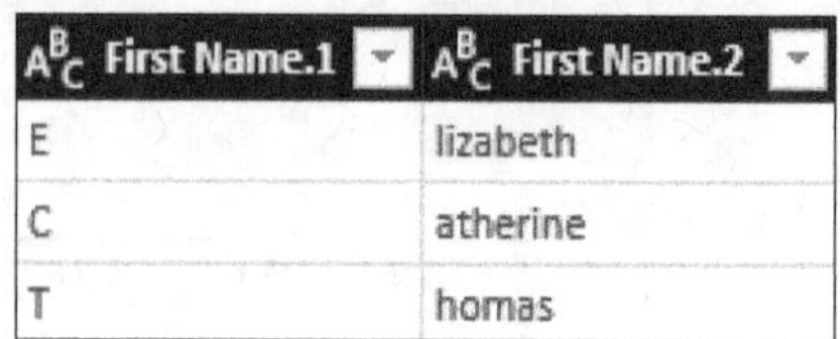

First Name.1	First Name.2
E	lizabeth
C	atherine
T	homas

Figure 5-31 Result of the Number of characters split column option

Use The Group By Option

In this part of the exercise, you will use the Group By option to group the data in the Order Details table, by the Order ID field.

1. Duplicate the Order Details query ⇒ Rename it to `3 Group By`.

2. Click on the Order ID column ⇒ Transform tab ⇒ Group By button.

3. Change the New column name field to `Item count per order`. The options shown in Figure 5-32 will display a count of items per order. Figure 5-33 shows the top of the Group By query.

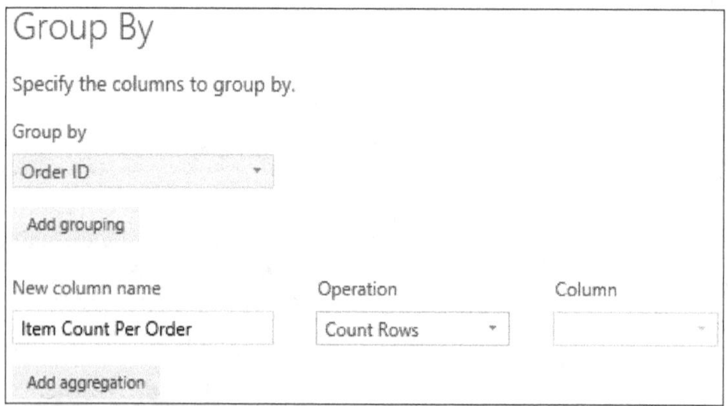

Figure 5-32 Group By options

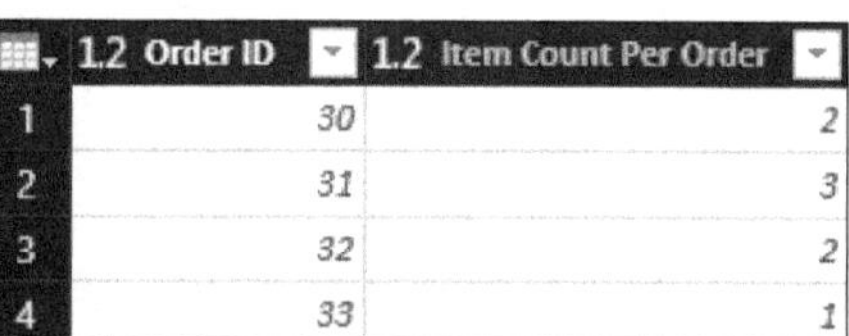

	Order ID	Item Count Per Order
1	30	2
2	31	3
3	32	2
4	33	1

Figure 5-33 Group By query

On its own, the Item count per order column is not very useful. It would be more useful if it was merged into the Orders table, because that table contains the majority of information for each order.

Use The Replace Values Option

If a field does not have data, it has a **NULL VALUE**. When displayed in a visual format, it can be difficult to tell that there are null or missing values. There are times when you need to bring this to someone's attention. One way to do this is to display content in the cell, instead of leaving it blank.

In this part of the exercise, you will replace null values with text.

1. Duplicate the Products query ⇒ Rename it to `4 Replace Values`. Notice that there are no values in the Description column.

2. Click on the Description column ⇒ Transform tab ⇒ Replace Values button.

3. Leave the Value To Find field blank.

   In the Replace With field, type `*missing data*`, as shown in Figure 5-34.

   If you wanted to replace cells that have the word "null" in the cell, type `null` in the Value To Find field.

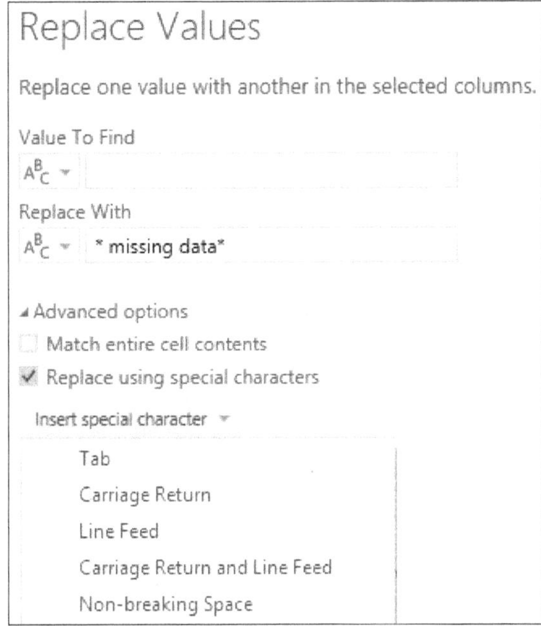

Figure 5-34 Replace Values options

4. Check the **MATCH ENTIRE CELL CONTENTS** option. The Description column in the table should look like the one shown in Figure 5-35.

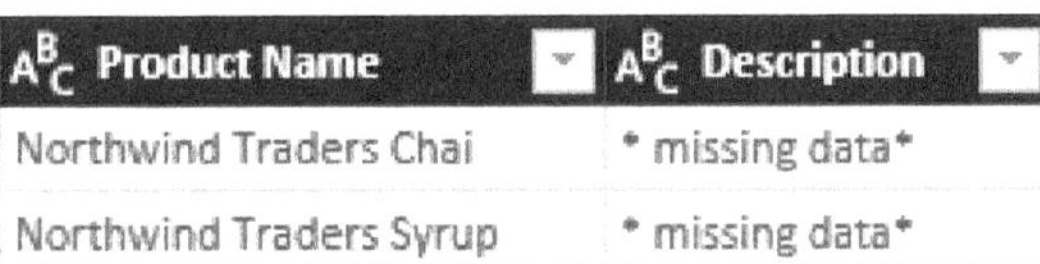

Figure 5-35 Description column value replaced, based on a condition

Add Column Tab

The options shown in Figure 5-36 are used to create new columns in the table. They work the same as the options on the Transform tab. The difference is where the output is placed. The options are explained in Table 5-4.

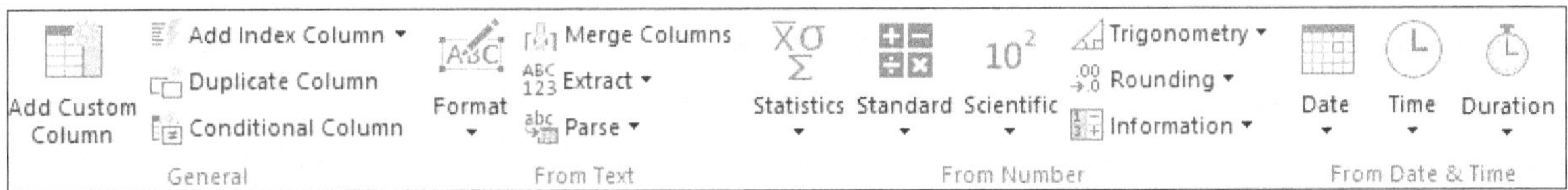

Figure 5-36 Add Column tab

Option	Description
Add Custom Column	Is used to create a column in the table, based on a formula. [See Chapter 4, Custom Columns]
Add Index Column	[See Chapter 4, Add Index Column Options]
Duplicate Column	[See Chapter 3, Table 3-5]
Conditional Column	[See Conditional Columns]
Format	[See Table 5-1]
Merge Columns	[See Table 5-1] (6)
Extract	[See Extract Options, earlier in this chapter]
Parse	[See Table 5-1]
Statistics	[See Table 5-1] (6)
Standard	[See Table 5-1]
Scientific	[See Table 5-1]
Trigonometry	[See Table 5-1]
Rounding	[See Table 5-1]
Information	[See Table 5-1]
Date	[See Date Functions]

Table 5-4 Add Column tab options explained

Option	Description
Time	[See Time Functions]
Duration	[See Table 5-1]

Table 5-4 Add Column tab options explained (Continued)

(6) Two columns must be selected to enable this option.

Merge Columns Options

There are two merge columns options. One in the Transform tab and the other on the Add Column tab. While the merge columns options have the same name, they worked differently.

When creating a merge column using either option, the order that you click on the columns, is the order that the fields will be merged in.

In both scenarios below, the order that the columns are clicked on is the First Name, then Last Name. Both Merge Columns buttons, display the dialog box shown in Figure 5-37.

The **SEPARATOR** drop-down list has a **CUSTOM** option, which is free form. It is used to type in what character(s) you want displayed between the columns that will be merged into one column.

An example would be combining the city and state fields. The custom option would be used to display a comma and space between the fields, as shown in Figure 5-38.

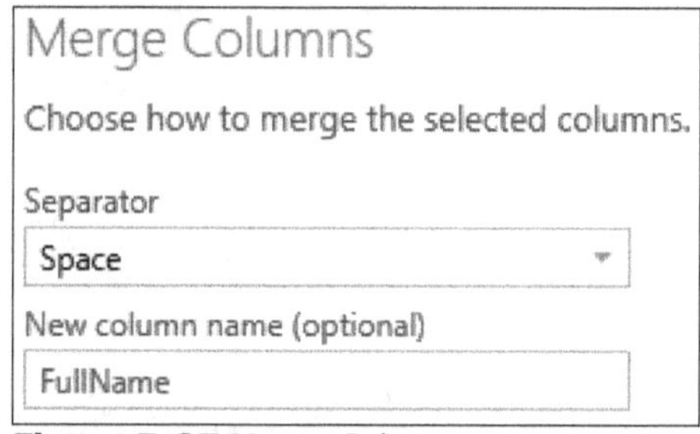

Figure 5-37 Merge Columns options

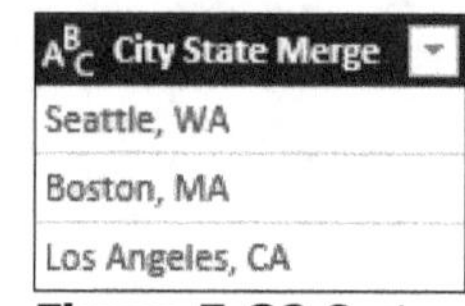

Figure 5-38 Custom separator option used

Transform Tab Merge Columns Option

Clicking on the name columns, then clicking the **MERGE COLUMNS** button, replaces both name columns with the Full Name column shown in Figure 5-39.

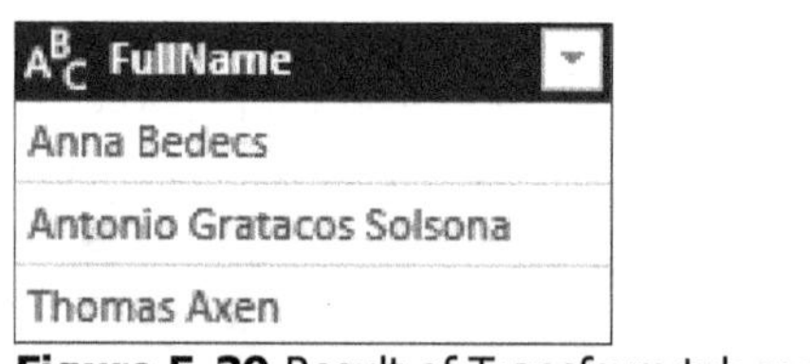

Figure 5-39 Result of Transform tab merge

Add Column Merge Columns Option

When this merge columns option is used, a new field is created and the two original fields stay intact.

Exercise 5.2: Create Calculations Using Options On The Add Column Tab

This exercise will show you how to use the Merge Columns option and how to create calculated columns using columns in the query. In previous chapters you learned how to create calculated columns by writing code. There are options on the Add Column tab that can be used to produce the same result.

1. Open a new file ⇒ Import the 06 Invoices Shipping table in the More Data Files workbook.

2. Save the file as `E5.2 Add Column Calculations`.

Merge Columns

Chapter 4, Exercise 4.4, covered how to create a formula that combined the data in the first and last name columns and placed the result in a new column. This part of the exercise will show you another way to combine columns of data and place the result in a new column.

1. Duplicate the Invoices Shipping query ⇒ Rename it to `1 Merge First & Last Name`.

2. Select the First Name and Last Name columns ⇒ Add Column tab ⇒ Merge Columns button.

3. Select the options shown earlier in Figure 5-37. The new column should have the first and last name, as shown earlier in Figure 5-39. The original name columns are still there.

Calculate A Total Using Two Columns Of Data

In this part of the exercise you will use a function to calculate the invoice total.

1. Duplicate the Invoices Shipping query ⇒ Rename it to `2 Create the invoice total.`

2. Select the Amount and Shipping columns ⇒ Add Column tab ⇒ Standard button ⇒ Add.

3. Rename the **INSERTED ADDITION** column to `Invoice Total`, as shown in Figure 5-40.

1.2 Amount	1.2 Shipping	1.2 Invoice Total
45	1.8	46.8
479.85	19.19	499.04
107.8	4.31	112.11

Figure 5-40 Invoice total calculation

Calculate The Line Item Total

Chapter 4, Exercise 4.4, covered how to create a formula to calculate the Line total of each item ordered. The formula multiplied the values in two columns. In this part of the exercise you will recreate the Line Total formula, using the **MULTIPLY FUNCTION WITH 2 COLUMNS**.

1. Home tab ⇒ Recent Sources button ⇒ More Data Files workbook ⇒ Import the 06 Invoices Detail table.

2. Duplicate the Invoices Detail query ⇒ Rename it to `3 Create Line Total.`

3. Select the Quantity and Unit Price columns ⇒ Add Column tab ⇒ Standard button ⇒ Multiply.

4. Rename the **INSERTED MULTIPLICATION** column to `New Line Total`. As you can see, the values are the same as the result of the formula that you created in Chapter 4. [See Chapter 4, Figure 4-17]

Calculate The Sales Tax Amount

In the previous part of this exercise you used the Multiply function with two columns to create a calculated column. If the **MULTIPLY FUNCTION** is used with one column, you can enter a number that each value in the column will be multiplied by. One way to use this function with one column is to calculate the sales tax.

1. Duplicate the Invoices Shipping query ⇒ Rename it to `4 Sales Tax.`

2. Click on the Amount column ⇒ Add Column tab ⇒ Standard button ⇒ Multiply.

3. On the dialog box shown in Figure 5-41, type `.045` in the field next to the Value field.

   This is the sales tax rate of 4.5%.

   Click OK.

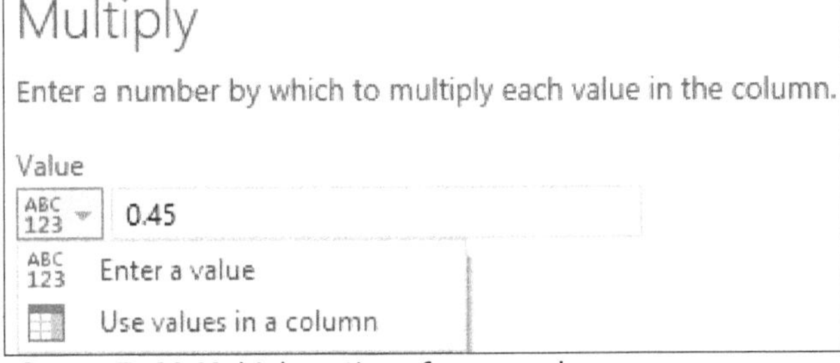

Figure 5-41 Multiply options for one column

The options in the Value field drop-down list, shown above in Figure 5-41, are explained below.

Select the **ENTER A VALUE OPTION** if you want to type in a value, like you did in this step.

Select the **USE VALUES IN A COLUMN OPTION** to select the column that has the data that you want to use, as shown in Figure 5-42.

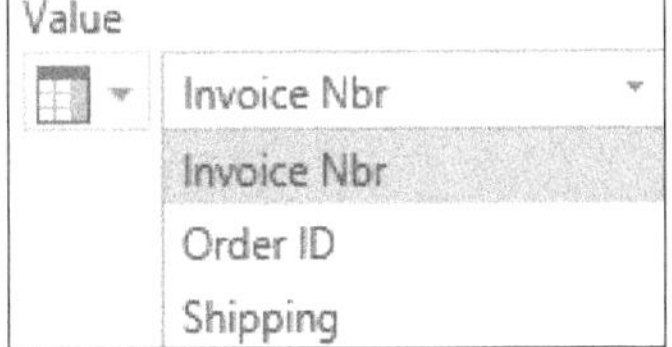

Figure 5-42 Multiply values in column option

4. Rename the **INSERTED MULTIPLICATION** column to `Sales Tax`.

Rename Column Tip
Double-clicking on the column heading allows it to be renamed.

Use More Than Two Columns To Create A Calculated Column

More than two columns can be used to create a calculated column. To create an Invoice total, the Amount, Shipping and Sales Tax columns are needed to create the calculation. This part of the exercise will show you how to use multiple columns in a calculation.

1. Duplicate the Sales tax query ⇒ Rename it to `5 Three columns`.
2. Select the Amount, Shipping and Sales Tax columns ⇒ Add Column tab ⇒ Statistics button ⇒ Sum.
3. Rename the Sum column to `Invoice Total`.

Date Functions

Figure 5-43 shows the date functions on the **ADD COLUMN TAB**.

The **AGE FUNCTION** creates a new column that calculates the difference between the local current time and the time in the selected column. This function returns the difference in days and hours.

Figure 5-44 shows the Age function applied to the Date column in the Invoices shipping query. I applied the **DURATION ⇒ DAYS FUNCTION** to the Age From Date column, to display the age in days, as shown in the last column in the figure.

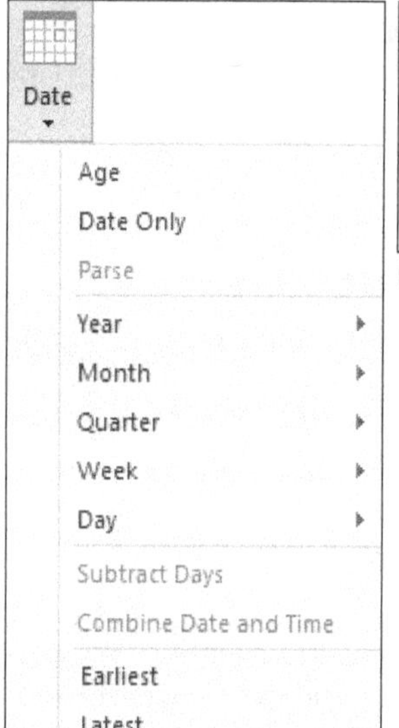

Figure 5-43 Date functions

Date	AgeFromDate	DurationDays
06/28/2014	722.00:00:00	722
06/29/2014	721.00:00:00	721
06/29/2014	721.00:00:00	721
06/30/2014	720.00:00:00	720

Figure 5-44 Age and duration in days functions

The **DATE ONLY FUNCTION** converts the data to a date.

The **PARSE FUNCTION** returns the date portion of the data in the cell. This option is only enabled for Text data type columns.

The **SUBTRACT DAYS FUNCTION** is only enabled when two date columns, with the same date type are selected. This function creates a new column and calculates the difference between the two dates. Select the columns in the order that you want the calculation to use. For example, if the Order Date and Ship Date are the columns that you will use, select the Ship Date column first.

The **COMBINE DATE AND TIME FUNCTION** is only enabled when a date data type column and a time data type column are both selected. The data in both columns will be combined (merged) into one new column. This option is also on the Time button.

The **EARLIEST FUNCTION** is used to create a new column that contains the earliest date from the columns selected for each row. (7)

The **LATEST FUNCTION** is used to create a new column that contains the most recent date from the columns selected for each row. (7)

(7) This function is only enabled when two or more date columns are selected.

Popular Date Functions

Chapter 8 covers creating a date table, which is used to display parts of a date in different ways. Some of the most popular fields in a date table include, the year portion of a date, the quarter that the date is in, the month name of the date spelled out and the month number.

If these are fields that you need, you are in luck, as there are functions built into the Query Editor for them. As you will probably want to add these columns to a table, so that you can keep the date field intact, select the options listed in Table 5-5 from the Date button on the Add Column tab.

Figure 5-45 illustrates the two month options that I just mentioned. Just select the one(s) you need and a new column will be created and populated with the values.

The only downside to using these functions, in my opinion, is that they increase the size of each table that they are added to. If you need to add these fields to more than one table, it is better to create a date table, because the date table does not increase the size of each table that is linked to it.

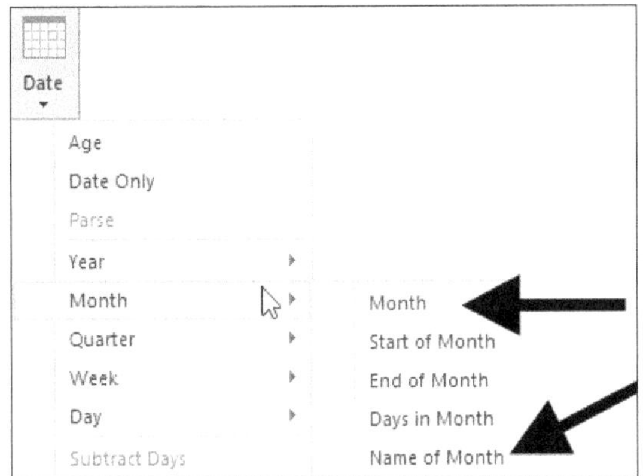

Figure 5-45 Month functions illustrated

This Function . . .	Displays This Portion Of The Date Field
Year ⇒ Year	The four digit year.
Quarter ⇒ Quarter of Year	The quarter of the year that the date is in (1-4).
Month ⇒ Month	The month number (1-12).
Month ⇒ Name of Month	The month name spelled out (January, February)

Table 5-5 Date functions explained

Time Functions

Figure 5-10 shown earlier, displays the time functions on the Transform tab. Figure 5-46 shows the time functions on the Add Column tab.

The **LOCAL TIME FUNCTION** is only enabled for columns that have the **DATE/TIME/TIME ZONE** data type. It converts the time zone of the date to the local time zone.

The **PARSE FUNCTION** returns the time portion of the data in the cell. This option is only enabled for Text data type columns.

The **SUBTRACT FUNCTION** works the same as the Subtract Days function, that was explained above.

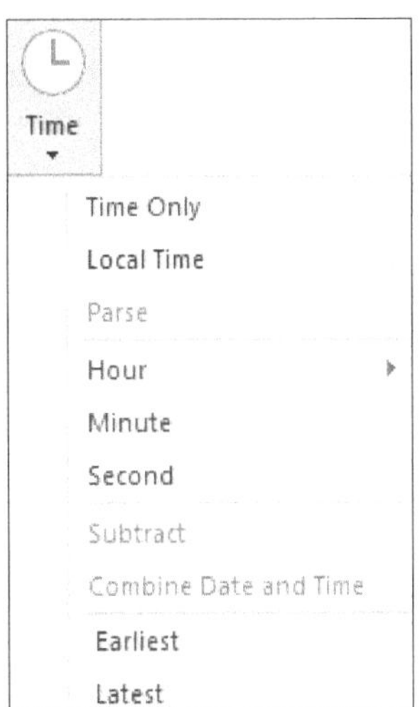

Figure 5-46 Time functions

Duration Functions

Figure 5-47 shows the Duration functions on the Add Column tab. These options are only available for columns that have the Duration data type.

The **TOTAL YEARS FUNCTION** divides the total number of days by 365. This function is demonstrated and shown below, in the third column in Figure 5-48.

The **SUBTRACT FUNCTION** is only enabled when two columns with the Duration data type are selected. This function calculates the difference between the two columns.

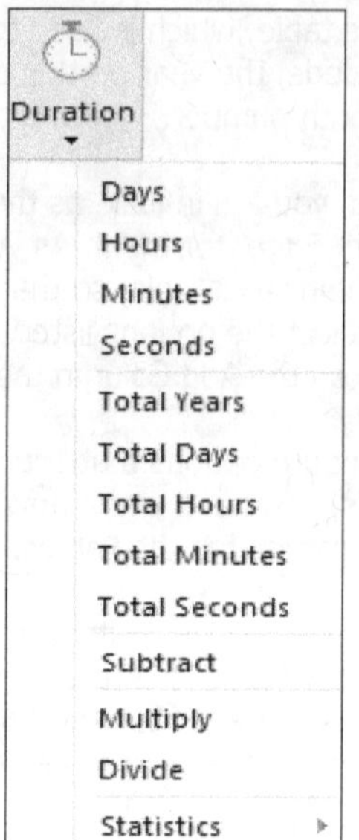

Figure 5-47 Duration functions

How To Calculate The Age In Years

If you have the need to calculate peoples age or calculate something like the number of years someone has been a customer, the steps below show you how, as long as you have a date field. The number of years calculated, is the difference between the date in the query and today's date.

1. Open the query that has the date field that you want to convert to years ⇒ Click on the date column to use in the calculation.

2. Add Column tab ⇒ Date button ⇒ Age function ⇒ Click on the new column (the Age From Date column, shown below in Figure 5-48) ⇒ Add Column tab ⇒ Duration button ⇒ **TOTAL YEARS FUNCTION.**

3. Click on the Duration Total Years column ⇒ Add Column tab ⇒ Rounding ⇒ Round ⇒ Type 0 (zero) in the Decimal Places field on the Round dialog box.

4. Rename the Inserted Rounding column as needed.

   Figure 5-48 shows the original date (the Birth Date column) and each column that was created in the steps above. The last column in this figure is the age.

Birth Date	AgeFromDate	1.2 DurationTotalYears	1.2 Inserted Rounding
12/08/1972	15899.00:00:00	43.55890411	44
02/19/1969	17287.00:00:00	47.36164384	47
08/30/1971	16365.00:00:00	44.83561644	45
09/19/1973	15614.00:00:00	42.77808219	43
03/04/1975	15083.00:00:00	41.32328767	41

Figure 5-48 Calculated age in years columns

How The Trim And Clean Functions Work

Have you had or seen data in a text file that looked like the file shown in Figure 5-49, that you needed to import and clean?

If so, you know that the data probably has spaces in places where they are not needed.

It is also possible that the data has non-printable characters. This is often the case with **NON-DELIMITED FILES.**

```
Page 1                                                     January 2016

                                                             Invoices

Invoice Nbr     Order ID        Date     Amount  Customer
181      1121   01/01/2016      $851.77          City Cyclists
182      1122   01/01/2016      $1,025.40        Pathfinders
183      1123   01/02/2016      $5,219.55        Bike - A - Holics Anonymous
184      1124   01/02/2016      $59.70  Psycho - Cycle
185      1125   01/02/2016      $75.42  Sporting Wheels Inc.
186      1126   01/02/2016      $3,842.55        Rockshocks for Jocks
187      1127   01/02/2016      $520.35          Poser  &  Cycles
```

Figure 5-49 Non-delimited data

Based on my experiences, when this type of file is imported into the Query Editor, often, all of the data shown above in Figure 5-49 is imported into one column. The functions explained below can help you get non-delimited data ready to be analyzed, after it has been imported into Power BI Desktop.

The **TRIM FUNCTION** removes leading and trailing spaces in cells. This option does not replace duplicate spaces in the middle of the data, like the Trim function does in Excel.

The **CLEAN FUNCTION** removes invisible characters, like non printable characters and carriage returns.

If you import a text file and it looks like the one shown in Figure 5-50, the next few sections demonstrate how to get the data into separate columns.

This figure shows the imported data from the text file shown above in Figure 5-49.

As you can see, all of the data is in one column.

As shown in the Applied Steps, notice that none of the data was converted.

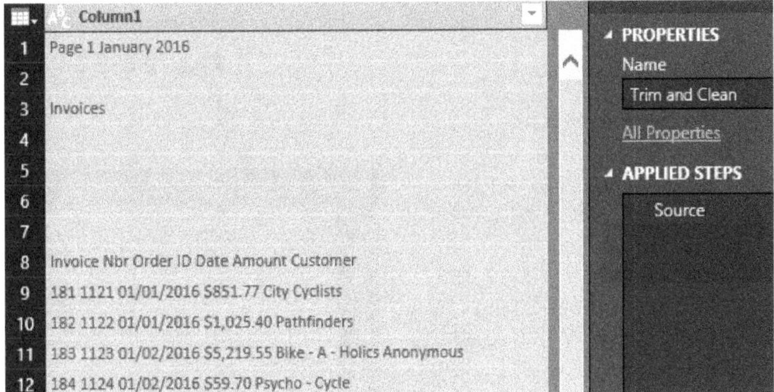

Figure 5-50 Imported non-delimited data

Clean The Data

The first task that needs to be completed is to remove rows of data that are not needed and remove the empty rows at the top of the column. As shown above in Figure 5-50, the first seven rows need to be removed.

In this example, if you kept the column headings row, it would be impossible to create columns of data because the length of some of the column headings is longer then the length of the data in the column. Plus, you can add the column headings back, once the single column of data, shown above in Figure 5-50, has been split into several columns. If you need to remove the row of column headings on your own, either write them down, take a screen shot of them or something that will let you see what they were, so that you can recreate them later. The steps below and in the next section, demonstrate how to use the Trim and Clean functions.

1. Home tab ⇒ Remove Rows button ⇒ Remove Top Rows ⇒ Enter the number of rows that need to be deleted.
2. Add Column tab ⇒ Format button ⇒ Trim. Notice the new columns name.
3. Add Column tab ⇒ Format button ⇒ Clean.

   Notice that all of the spaces between the columns have been removed.

   You should have steps similar to those shown in Figure 5-51.

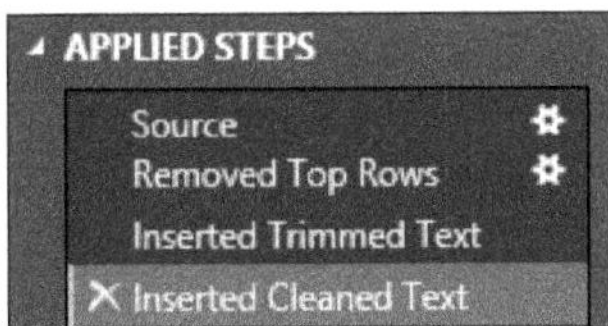

Figure 5-51 Steps to trim and clean the data

Create The Columns

Even though the data is clean, it is still in one column. This section will show you how to separate the data to create the columns. Because the data does not have delimiter characters, most of the columns have to be split by a number of characters, which can take several steps to accomplish.

1. Home tab ⇒ Split Column button ⇒
   By Number of Characters ⇒ Type 3 in the field.
   That is the length of the Invoice number field.

   Select **ONCE, AS FAR LEFT AS POSSIBLE**, as shown in Figure 5-52.

   I prefer to create one column at a time, so that I do not have to split a column that I already split, to put two columns together.

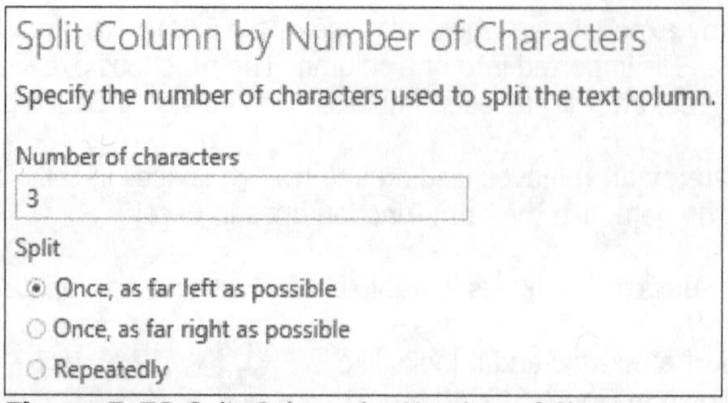

Split Column by Number of Characters

Specify the number of characters used to split the text column.

Number of characters

3

Split

◉ Once, as far left as possible

○ Once, as far right as possible

○ Repeatedly

Figure 5-52 Split Column by Number of Characters options

2. Rename the new column.

3. Repeat this process for each column that needs to be created.

   It is possible that you may also have to use the Split Column by Delimiter options. When finished, Figure 5-53 shows what the query would look like.

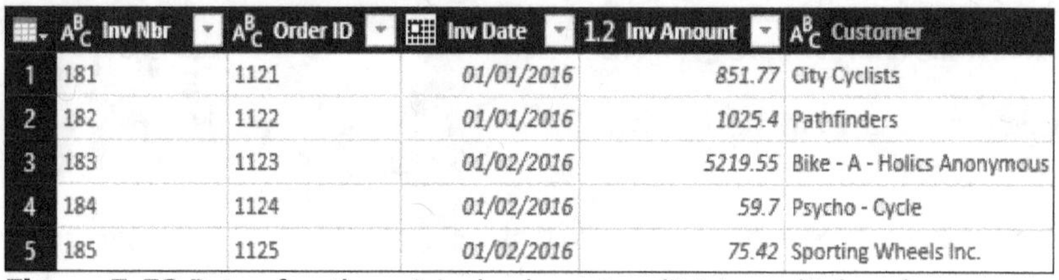

	Inv Nbr	Order ID	Inv Date	Inv Amount	Customer
1	181	1121	01/01/2016	851.77	City Cyclists
2	182	1122	01/01/2016	1025.4	Pathfinders
3	183	1123	01/02/2016	5219.55	Bike - A - Holics Anonymous
4	184	1124	01/02/2016	59.7	Psycho - Cycle
5	185	1125	01/02/2016	75.42	Sporting Wheels Inc.

Figure 5-53 Data after the original column is split into multiple columns

Exercise 5.3: Use Functions On The Transform And Add Column Tabs

This exercise will show you how to use more functions that are available on the Query Editor.

Use The Count Distinct Values Function

If you have the need to display a count of values, text or numeric, the Count Distinct Values function is the solution. This part of the exercise will show you how to display a distinct count of states that have customers.

1. Save the E2.4 file as `E5.3 Using Functions.`

2. Duplicate the Customers query ⇒ Rename it to `1 Count Distinct States.`

3. Select the State column ⇒ Transform tab ⇒ Statistics button ⇒ **COUNT DISTINCT VALUES.**
   You should see the value shown on the left side of Figure 5-54.

   I displayed the query name next to it in the figure, so that when you look at this figure, a month from now, you will know what the number represents.

15 | 1 Count Distinct States

Figure 5-54 Distinct count value

Use The Round Up Function

The Round functions are used to make numbers, especially long numbers, easier to read, while keeping the rounded value close to the original value.

This part of the exercise will show you how to round values up to the next whole number.

This **ROUND UP FUNCTION** removes the decimal places and adds "1" to the value, regardless of the cents portion of the value. This may be different then the rounding up function that you may be use to.

1. Duplicate the Monthly Sales Pivot Table query ⇒ Rename it to `2 Round Up function.`

2. Click on the 2012 column ⇒ Add Column tab ⇒ Rounding button ⇒ Round Up.

3. Rename the new column to `2012 Rounded Up` ⇒ Move this column next to the 2012 column, as shown in Figure 5-55.

   Moving the column makes it easier to see how the Round Up function works.

1.2 2012	1²3 2012 Rounded Up
2233575.113	2233576
3705635.498	3705636
2611621.26	2611622
3041865.441	3041866

Figure 5-55 Rounding up function applied

Use The Quarter Of Year Function

Many reports need to display or group the data by the quarter of the year (which is based on a date field). This part of this exercise will show you how to add a column that displays the quarter for the order date.

1. Duplicate the Orders query ⇒ Rename it to `3 Quarter of Year function.`

2. Select the Order Date column ⇒ Add Column tab ⇒ Date button ⇒ Quarter ⇒ Quarter of Year.

3. Rename the Quarter column to `Order Date Quarter` ⇒

   Move the column left, next to the Order Date column, as shown in Figure 5-56.

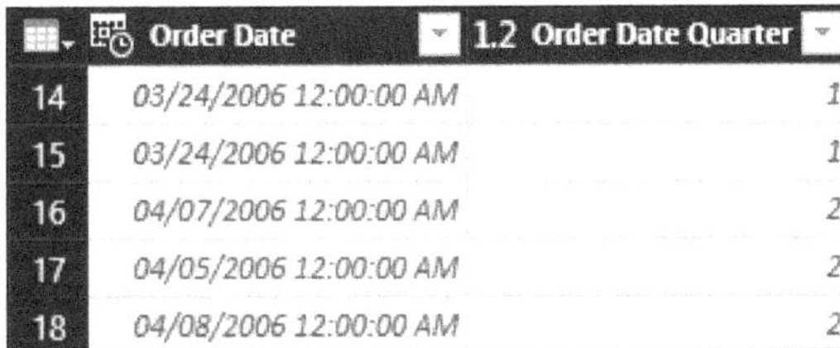

	Order Date	1.2 Order Date Quarter
14	03/24/2006 12:00:00 AM	1
15	03/24/2006 12:00:00 AM	1
16	04/07/2006 12:00:00 AM	2
17	04/05/2006 12:00:00 AM	2
18	04/08/2006 12:00:00 AM	2

Figure 5-56 Order date quarter column

Use The Subtract Days Function

This part of the exercise will show you how to calculate the number of days between two dates.

1. Duplicate the Orders query ⇒ Rename it to `4 Subtract Days function.`

2. Change the data type of the Order Date and Shipped Date columns to Date.

3. Select the Shipped Date column ⇒ Hold down the CTRL key ⇒ Select the Order Date column.

4. Add Column tab ⇒ Date button ⇒ Subtract Days ⇒ Move the Date Difference column to the left, after the Shipped Date column.

You should see the values shown in Figure 5-57. In this exercise, the Date Difference column displays how many days are between the date the order was placed and the date the order was shipped.

Null values mean that at least one of the cells used to create the calculation for the row, does not have a date.

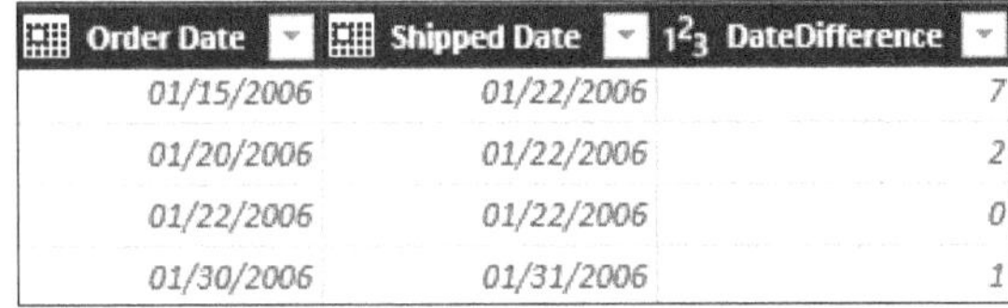

Order Date	Shipped Date	1²3 DateDifference
01/15/2006	01/22/2006	7
01/20/2006	01/22/2006	2
01/22/2006	01/22/2006	0
01/30/2006	01/31/2006	1

Figure 5-57 Subtract Days calculation

A zero in the Date Difference column means that the order was shipped in less than 24 hours after it was placed. This is true, even if the order and shipped dates are a date apart. That is because the Subtract Days function actually uses the time portion of a date field, whether or not the date has a time value. In order for the Subtract Days function to really be accurate, the date fields used, need to also have the time portion of the date field being used.

Creating Percents

The Standard button on the Transform and Add Column tabs have the following **PERCENT FUNCTIONS**.

① **PERCENTAGE** Use this function to calculate a percent of the values in the selected column. For example, you need to know what 25% of the monthly sales is, for a specific year. On the dialog box shown in Figure 5-58, you would type in 25. A column would be created that displayed what 25% of each months sales is.

② **PERCENT OF** Use this function to display the values in the column as a percent of a value that you select.

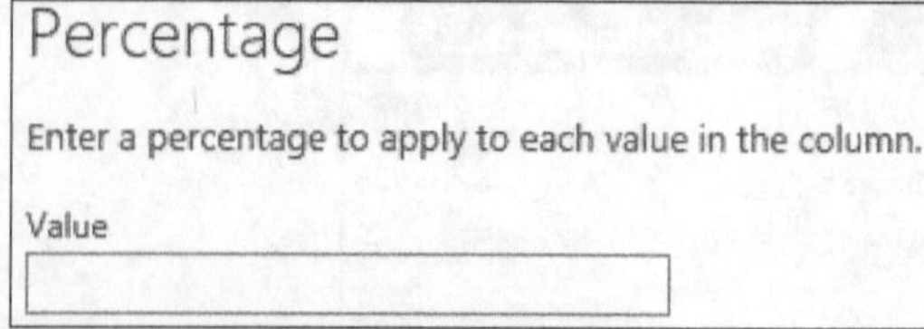

Figure 5-58 Percentage dialog box

Conditional Columns

The Add Conditional Column dialog box is used to create criteria that selects the value to be added to the new column that is created. This dialog box is used to create an IF Then Else statement without writing code. In Chapter 4, Exercise 4.4, you typed in code to create an IF statement [See Chapter 4, Figure 4-24]. Instead of typing in all of the code, you can use this dialog box to create it, as you will see in the next exercise.

The Add Conditional Column dialog box has the options shown in Figure 5-59 for selecting a **VALUE** (the data used for the comparison), the **OUTPUT** (what you want to happen if the value meets the criteria rule) and **OTHERWISE** (what to do if the data does not meet any of the rules created for the column. Using the Otherwise condition is optional. If it is not used, rows that do not meet any of the rules will not have any data in this column.

Select the **ENTER A VALUE OPTION** to type in a value.

The **SELECT A COLUMN OPTION** is used to select a column from the query as the data to use for the value.

The **PARAMETER OPTION** is used to select an existing parameter, to get the data to use for the value.

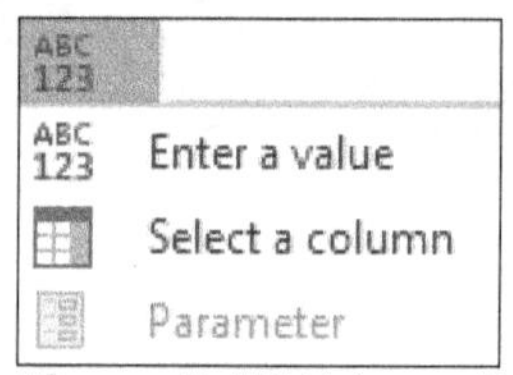

Figure 5-59 Value options

Exercise 5.4: Create A Conditional Column

In this exercise you will duplicate the IF Then Else statement that you created in Exercise 4.4. The Add Conditional Column dialog box does not support the "duration" part of the formula, so you will create a custom column for that portion of the formula and use it in place of the Order Date field.

Create The Duration Custom Column

In this part of the exercise you will create a column that replaces the duration portion of the formula in Chapter 4, Figure 4-24.

1. Save the E2.4 file as `E5.4 Conditional column.`
2. Duplicate the Orders query ⇒ Rename it to `1 Conditional column.`
3. Create the custom column shown in Figure 5-60 ⇒ Apply and save the changes.

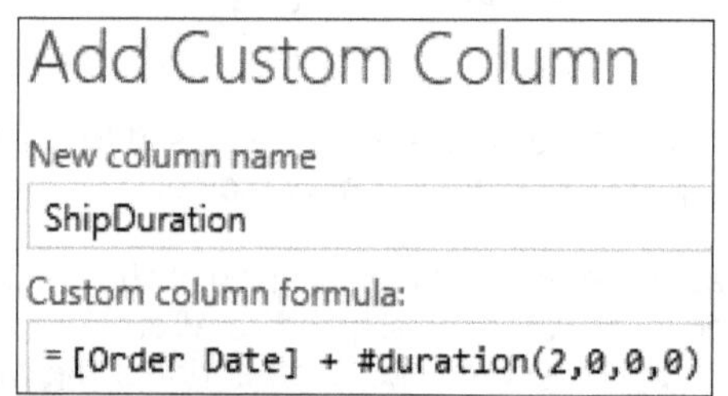

Figure 5-60 Duration custom column formula

Create The Shipped On Time Conditional Column

1. In the 1 Conditional column query ⇒ Add Column tab ⇒ **CONDITIONAL COLUMN BUTTON**.
2. In the New column name field type `Shipped On Time.`
3. In the Column Name field drop-down list, select the Shipped Date field ⇒ Select the **IS AFTER OR EQUAL TO** operator.

4. In the Value field drop-down list, select the **SELECT A COLUMN** option ⇒ Select the Ship Duration field in the next drop-down list.

5. In the Output field drop-down list, select Enter a Value ⇒ Type `Shipped Late` in the next field.

Create The Else If Portion Of The Condition

1. Click the **ADD RULE BUTTON**.

2. Open the Column Name field drop-down list and select the Shipped Date field ⇒ Select the **IS BEFORE** operator.

3. In the Value field drop-down list, select the **SELECT A COLUMN** option ⇒ Select the Ship Duration field in the next drop-down list.

4. In the Output field drop-down list, select Enter a Value ⇒ Type `On Time` in the next field.

Create The Otherwise Portion Of The Condition

1. Open the Otherwise drop-down list and select Enter a Value.

2. Type `Problem with Order or Shipped Date field`. You should have the options shown in Figure 5-61 ⇒ Click OK.

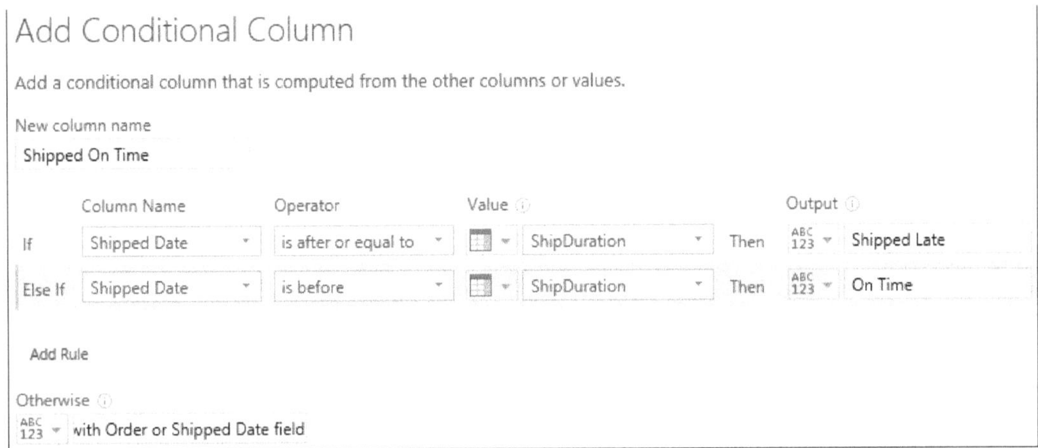

Figure 5-61 Add Conditional Column criteria

If you scroll down the Shipped On Time column, you will see some cells have the word error, as shown in Figure 5-62. That is because the Shipped Date field does not have a date for some rows of data. I was expecting to see the text entered in the "Otherwise" field, shown above in Figure 5-61.

I then created the criteria shown in Figure 5-63. I left the "Otherwise" field blank. Initially, the condition to check for a null value was the last condition, but that did not work. As shown in Figure 5-64, the check for null values works. Compare this to Figure 5-62. No, I do not understand why! <smile>

Figure 5-65 shows the conditions to check for a null value. Notice in Figure 5-66, that the "Otherwise" condition works. Hopefully, these inconsistencies will eventually be fixed.

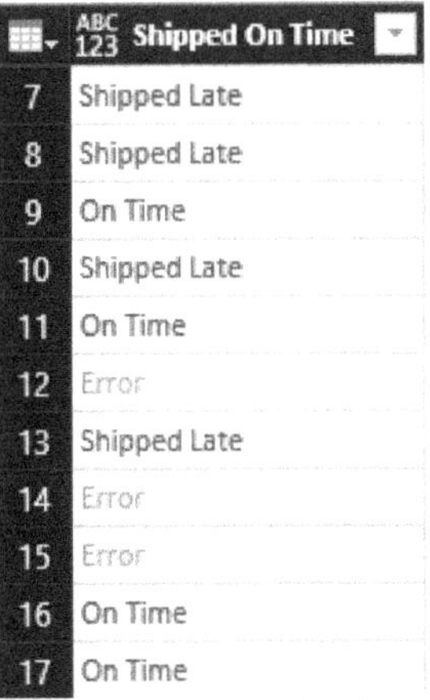

Figure 5-62 Result of conditional column criteria

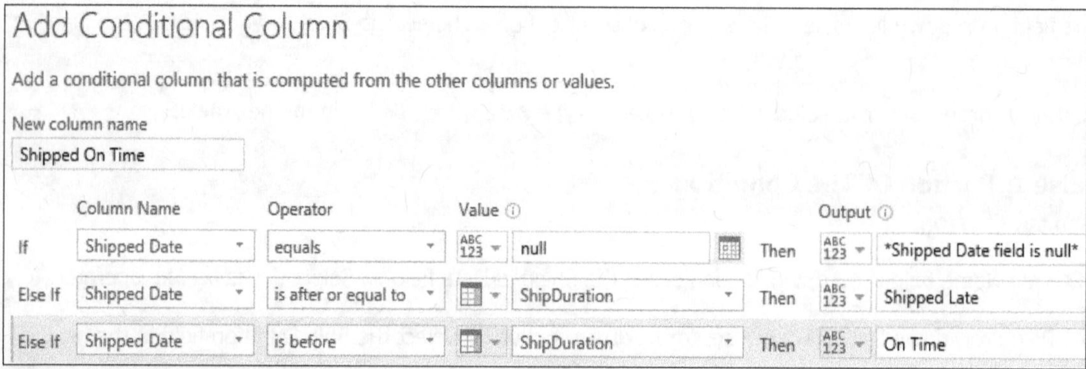

Figure 5-63 Criteria to check for null values with other criteria

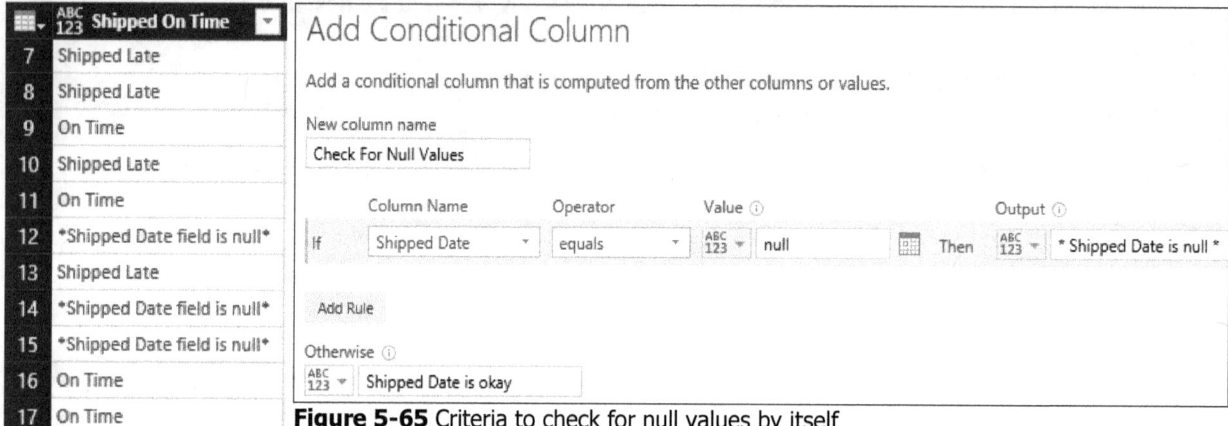

	Shipped On Time
7	Shipped Late
8	Shipped Late
9	On Time
10	Shipped Late
11	On Time
12	*Shipped Date field is null*
13	Shipped Late
14	*Shipped Date field is null*
15	*Shipped Date field is null*
16	On Time
17	On Time

Figure 5-65 Criteria to check for null values by itself

Figure 5-64 Result of the null value condition in Figure 5-63

	Check For Null Values
13	Shipped Date is okay
14	* Shipped Date is null *
15	* Shipped Date is null *
16	Shipped Date is okay
17	Shipped Date is okay

Figure 5-66 Result of the null value conditional checking by itself, in Figure 5-65

Add Conditional Column Dialog Box Issues

Even though multiple requests were submitted to have the following issues resolved, at the time this book went to print, the bugs had not been fixed.

① **ISSUE #1** The Add Conditional Column dialog box does not display the operators that are selected, when you re-open the dialog box, even though the pending changes are saved and applied. The operators are not saved with the rest of the options that are selected on this dialog box. This seems like the Operators fields are missing the code to save the values, like the other fields have.

② **ISSUE #2** The criteria created for the **OTHERWISE OPTION** on this dialog box does not work, if there is more than one condition created at the top of the dialog box. I was expecting the text that I entered to be displayed for records that do not meet the criteria that I created at the top of the dialog box, but that doesn't happen. Instead, cells that do not meet the criteria, have the word "error" in them.

③ **ISSUE #3** When checking for null values, the criteria only works if the null value criteria is first on the Add Conditional Column dialog box.

View Tab

The options shown in Figure 5-67 are used to display or hide parts of the Query Editor. They are explained in Table 5-6.

All of the options on this tab, except the Advanced Editor, can be set as a default for all report files, on the Options dialog box. [See Chapter 1, Figure 1-13]

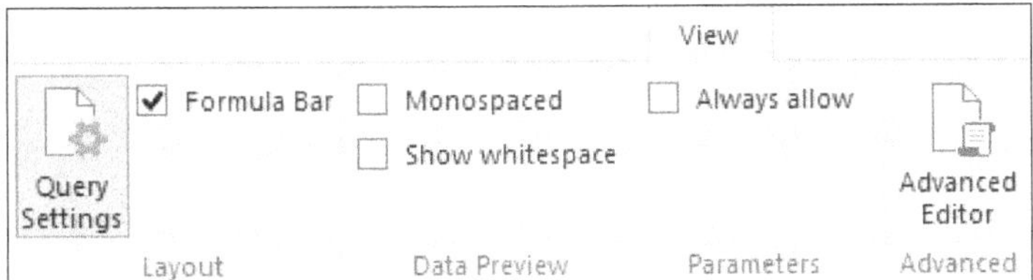

Figure 5-67 View tab

Option	Description
Query Settings	Displays or hides the Query Settings panel.
Formula Bar	Displays or hides the formula bar.
Monospaced	Displays the data in the query with a monspaced font. The font used resembles the `Courier font.`
Show white space	Displays or hides white space characters like line feeds (pressing the Enter key), in the data displayed in the query.
Always allow	If checked, many dialog boxes will have the parameter options enabled, as shown earlier in Figure 5-59.
Advanced Editor	[See Advanced Editor]

Table 5-6 View tab options explained

Advanced Editor

The dialog box shown in Figure 5-68 displays the M code for a query. Each step in the Query Editor creates its own line of code. The lines of code that start with #, do not wrap on this dialog box. This dialog box is also used to write code from scratch. You can also modify the code on this dialog box, if necessary. In depth coverage of the M language is beyond the scope of this book.

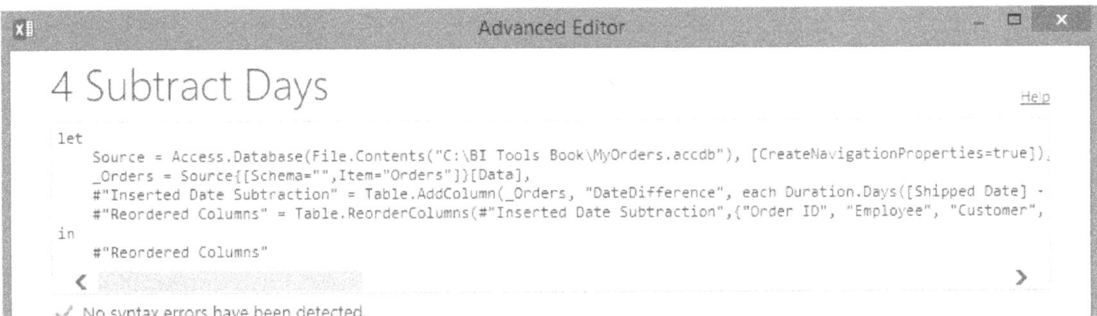

Figure 5-68 Advanced Editor

Summary

This chapter took transforming data up a notch or two. This was accomplished by showing another way to extract data from a column and merge columns in one query into another query.

The Add Conditional Column dialog box was covered. It is used to add a column to a table to display whether or not each row of data meets the criteria. Exercise 5.4 demonstrated using this tool to determine if the data in a field is valid. A report could be created using this data checking feature to let users know which records they need to fix.

USING THE QUERY EDITOR TO MASHUP DATA

After completing this chapter you will be able to perform the following tasks:

- ☑ Merge data
- ☑ Append data
- ☑ Group data
- ☑ Pivot and Unpivot columns of data
- ☑ Import all files (with the same file type) in a folder, at one time

CHAPTER 6

What Does Mashup Mean?

The terms **MASHUP** and **DATA MASHUP** often refer to the process of pivoting and unpivoting data, adding columns and rows to tables and joining tables or datasets. Usually, these are some of the last tasks that are applied to the data. Some of these topics were covered in previous chapters, but the bulk are covered in this chapter. You can use the features in the order that works best for the data that you are working with.

Why Would I Need To Combine Data From Different Tables?

While some of the terminology used in this chapter is only used when discussing databases, the concepts also apply to the data not stored in a database. The ability to join tables and use the data from multiple tables to create one report, may be the number one reason that many people will use Power BI Desktop.

A relationship is a link between two tables. Relationships are created between a column of data that the two tables have in common. Relationships between tables allow for a higher level of analysis, because columns of data from different tables can be reported on, as if they were one table. Data in one table can be filtered by data in another table, which provides even more flexibility and control over the data that is displayed on a visualization. Relationships are covered in detail in Chapter 7.

Merging Data

Merging data in Power BI Desktop is the process of adding columns from one table to another table. This is also known as **COMBINING DATA**. The reason data is merged is because there is a need to create a report or perform analysis that needs to display data from two or more tables. If you have used the **VLOOKUP FUNCTION** in Excel to combine data from different tables, those days are over. Some, or all of the columns in the second table can be added to the first table. Having said that, even though it is better to create relationships between tables then to merge data from one table to another, the merge functionality is covered.

Merge Queries Option

Home tab ⇒ **MERGE QUERIES**, displays the dialog box shown in Figure 6-1. The options are used to add columns in one table to another table. You select the columns that will be added after the queries are merged. The columns that you select to join on, have to have similar data types.

Display the table that you want the columns to be added to, before opening this dialog box.

While Power BI Desktop has the ability to link tables, queries only support one table. That is why you have to add columns from one table to another, while using the Merge Queries option.

The icons illustrated in the figure are used to refresh the data.

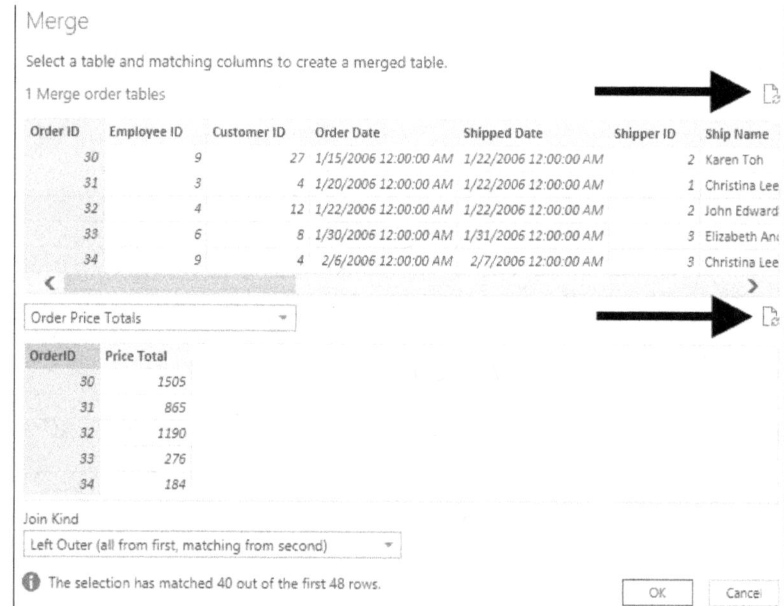

Figure 6-1 Merge options

The first drop-down list contains all of the queries in the file.

If you do not want to alter either table, use the **MERGE QUERIES AS NEW OPTION**, to create a new table.

Selecting Columns To Match On
What may not be obvious is that more than one column in each query, on the Merge dialog box, can be selected to create the matching criteria. The order that multiple columns are selected in, in each query matters.

Join Kind Options

The Join Kind drop-down list, at the bottom of the Merge dialog box, contains options for selecting how the tables will be joined. The options also decide what happens to records in a table that do not have matching records in the other table, in the join. The options are explained in Table 6-1.

Option	This Join Option Selects . . .
Left Outer	All records in the first query and the matching records in the second query. This is the default join option. This option will retrieve/display all records in the first table. This option is useful if you are trying to ensure that each record, in the first table, has at least one matching record in the second table. This provides another way to clean the data.
Right Outer	All records in the second query and the matching records in the first query.
Full Outer	All records from both queries, without using any matching criteria.
Inner	Records from both queries that have an exact match on the column that is selected for the join. Unlike the Left Outer join option, which selects all records in the first table, regardless of whether or not there is a matching record in the second table, the Inner join option only retrieves records when there is a match.
Left Anti	Records in the first query that do not have a matching record in the second query.
Right Anti	Records in the second query that do not have a matching record in the first query.

Table 6-1 Join Kind options explained

Appending Data

Appending data is the process of combining the data in two or more queries. The data in one query is added to the bottom of another query. The Query Editor provides several ways to append data, as explained below.

① Append data in one query to another query. This option adds data to the first query that is selected. To create this type of query, use the **APPEND QUERIES OPTION** on the Append Queries button. This option adds the data from one query to the query selected before the Append Queries option is selected. This query option does not keep the original query intact.

② Append data from two queries to create a new query. This option keeps both of the original queries intact. To create this type of query, use the **APPEND QUERIES AS NEW OPTION** on the Append Queries button.

③ Append data from three or more queries at the same time.

How Appending Data Works

The new query is created by adding the data from existing queries to it. Columns that have the same name in both queries are usually appended. All columns in the first query selected, are added to the new query, as is. Columns in the second query that do not have a matching column name in the first query, create new columns in the first or new query. When this happens, rows from the first query are filled in with null values for these new columns. If you need to append more than one query, select the Append Queries as New option.

If the column names are identical between the data sources and you want to rename a column or if you want to change something else, it is best to make this type of change after all of the queries have been appended, so that you only have to make the change (like rename a column) once, instead of multiple times before the append.

As long as the structure (the columns have the same name, are in the same order and have the same number of columns) is the same, the tables can be from different source types (for example, one table could be imported from a text file and another table from a database).

Append Queries Option

Home tab ⇒ **APPEND QUERIES BUTTON** ⇒ Append Queries, displays the dialog box shown in Figure 6-2. The options are used to select one or more queries (tables) that have data that you want to add to the table, currently displayed in the Query Editor.

What I found interesting about the Append Queries option is that the data being appended does not have to have the same structure as the table that it is being appended to.

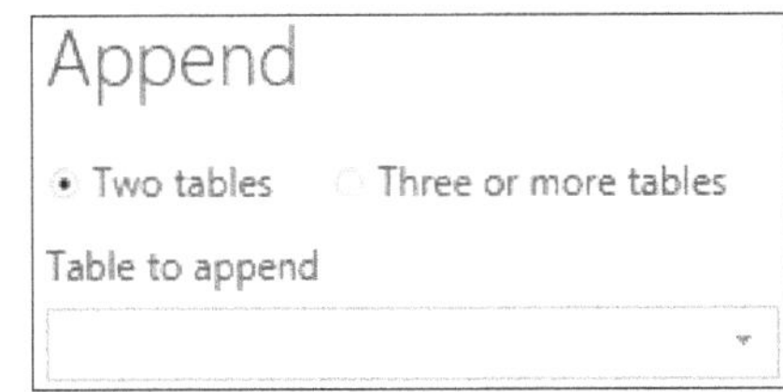

Figure 6-2 Append options

By that I mean, if the structures and/or data types are not the same for each column, no error is generated and the data is not appended. Null values are appended instead.

Structured Column Options

The two options in this section are on the Transform tab. They are used to add columns of data from one query to another query. The options in this section are only enabled when a column, like the New column shown on the left of Figure 6-3, is selected that contains a link to a related table.

An example is a field in one table that is merged from a different table, like you will see in Exercise 6.1. You should see the word "Table" in each cell in the column, as shown in Figure 6-3.

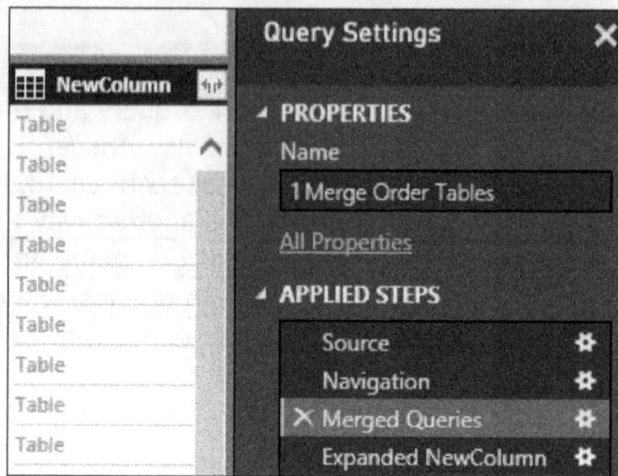

Figure 6-3 Merge column created

Expand Button Options

Clicking this button displays the dialog box shown in Figure 6-4. The options are used to add fields from the linked table to the current table.

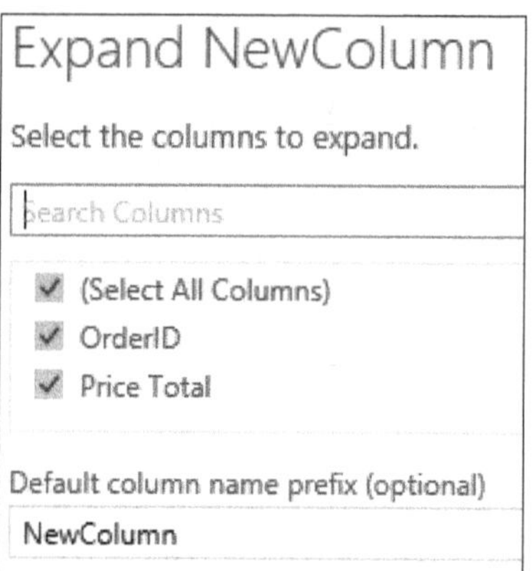

Figure 6-4 Expand New Column dialog box

The **DEFAULT COLUMN NAME PREFIX** option is used to enter what you want added to the beginning of column names for the columns that are selected to be added to the current table. The prefix default is "New Column".

One option is to use the table name or an abbreviated table name that the merge columns are from. Doing this will visually let you know what table the column is from. Using this field is optional. If you delete the default prefix and leave the field empty, no prefix will be added to the column headings.

Aggregate Button Options

Clicking this button displays the dialog box shown in Figure 6-5. If you hold the mouse pointer over a field on the dialog box, you will see a button at the end of the field. Clicking the button will display the aggregate options, shown in the figure. Check the options for how you want the column to be summarized.

The default aggregate type is **SUM**. You can change the aggregation type.

If checked, the **USE ORIGINAL COLUMN NAME AS PREFIX** option adds the words "New Column" to the beginning of the column header name, as shown in Figure 6-6.

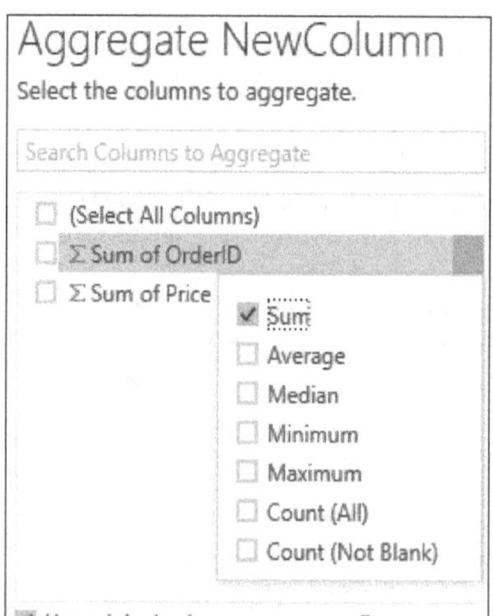

Figure 6-5 Aggregate New Column dialog box

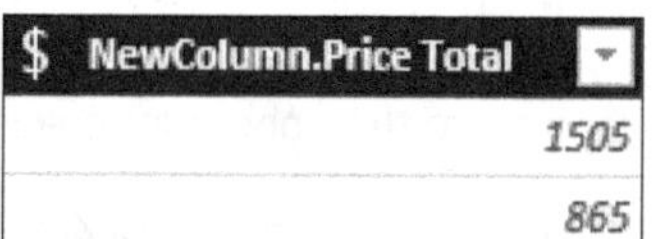

Figure 6-6 Result of applying the Use original column name as prefix option

The product of a numeric column in another query can also be calculated. [See Table 3-5, Product option]

The options on the Aggregate New Column dialog box add a step to the query.

The functions are the same as the **PIVOT COLUMN AGGREGATE** value functions that are covered later in Table 6-3.

The **USE ORIGINAL COLUMN NAME AS PREFIX OPTION**, shown earlier in Figure 6-5, does not work as expected on the Aggregate New Column dialog box. When checked, neither the query source name or the column name is added to the column name. The words "New Column" are added instead. In my opinion, the query name should be added. The words "New Column" do not provide any value to the column name. Hopefully, the development team will fix this in the future, so that this option is useful. When merging columns, it is possible that the same column name exists in both tables. Being able to use this option in a meaningful way, would be helpful.

Exercise 6.1: Use The Merge And Append Queries Options

This exercise will show you how to merge columns of data and how to create aggregate columns of data.

Use The Merge Queries Option

This part of the exercise will show you how to add columns from one table to another table.

1. Save the E2.4 file as `E6.1 Add Columns options`.

2. Duplicate the Orders query ⇒ Rename it to `1 Merge Order Tables`.

3. Home tab ⇒ Click the **MERGE QUERIES** button ⇒ Merge Queries option.

4. Open the drop-down list below the table and select the Order Price Totals table.

5. In the top table, click on the Order ID column ⇒ Hold the CTRL key down ⇒ Click on the Order ID column in the second table. Your dialog box should look like the one shown earlier in Figure 6-1. Notice the message at the bottom of the dialog box. It displays how many matching rows between the tables were found ⇒ Click OK.

6. Scroll to the end of the table. You should see a column named New Column ⇒

   Click the Expand button to the right of the column heading. You should see the options shown in Figure 6-7.

   The options are used to select which field(s) from the second table will be copied (merged) into the first table.

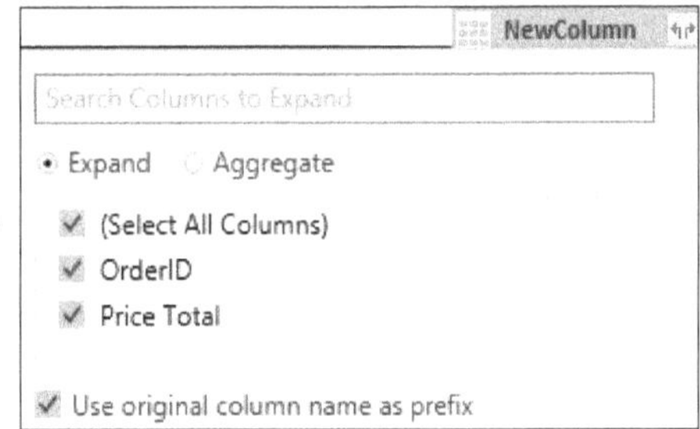

Figure 6-7 Available fields list for the merged query

7. Clear the check mark for the (Select All Columns) option ⇒ Check the Price Total field. There is no reason to add the Order ID field because it is already in the first table.

8. Clear the check mark for the Use original column name option ⇒ Click OK. Clearing this option keeps you from having to rename the column after it is created. The Price Total field will be added to the 1 Merge Order Tables query and the New Column, shown above in Figure 6-7, will be replaced with the Price Total column, which can be renamed.

9. Right-click on the Price Total column heading ⇒ Move ⇒ To Beginning ⇒
   Move the column to the right, so that it is after the Order ID column, as shown in Figure 6-8.

	1.2 Order ID	$ Price Total
1	30	1505
2	31	865
3	32	1190

Figure 6-8 Merged column from another query (table)

Aggregate The Data, Then Merge It

Aggregating data means to create a total, for a column of data. Figure 6-5 shown earlier, displays the list of aggregate functions that are available, when merging data. In this part of the exercise, you will learn how to change the default aggregate function and add aggregated columns of data to a table.

1. Duplicate the Orders query ⇒ Rename it to `2 Aggregate data`.

2. Click the Merge Queries button ⇒ Merge Queries ⇒ Open the first drop-down list on the Merge dialog box and select the Order Details table.

3. Select the Order ID column in both tables ⇒ Click OK.

4. Click the button at the end of the New Column ⇒
   Select the **AGGREGATE** option. You will see the options shown in Figure 6-9.

   If you want to create or change the calculation, click the button illustrated at the end of the field. You will see the aggregate options, shown earlier in Figure 6-5. Select the option that you want to use.

   Check the Sum of Unit Price option ⇒
   Check the Sum of Quantity option ⇒ Click the button at the end of the column ⇒
   Check the **COUNT (NOT BLANK)** aggregate option on the drop-down list.

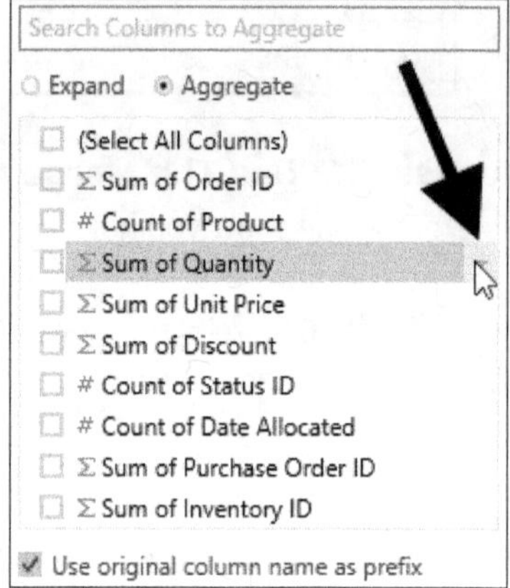

Figure 6-9 Aggregate options

Keep in mind that more than one aggregate value can be added at the same time for the same column, to create additional columns.

5. You should have the options checked, as illustrated in Figure 6-10 ⇒ Clear the check mark for the **USE ORIGINAL COLUMN NAME AS PREFIX OPTION** ⇒ Click OK. You will see the three new columns shown in Figure 6-11, at the end of the table.

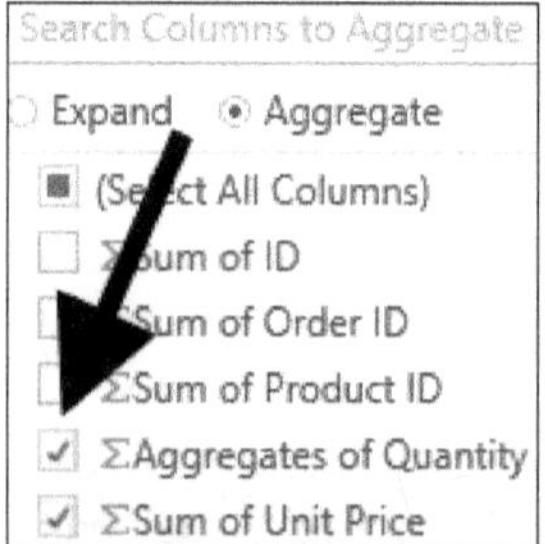

Figure 6-10 Aggregate options selected

Sum of Quantity	Count (Not Blank) of Quantity	Sum of Unit Price
130	2	17.5
30	3	86.5
35	2	64
30	1	9.2

Figure 6-11 Aggregate columns added to the table

Use The Append Queries Option

In this part of the exercise, you will learn how to append data in one query to another query.

1. Duplicate the New Products query. Rename it to `3 Append queries`. Notice that there are 20 records in the query.

2. Home tab ⇒ Append Queries button ⇒ Append Queries ⇒ Open the drop-down list and select the Append_Products table. The records in the Append_Products table will be added to the bottom of the 3 Append queries table ⇒ Click OK. The table should now have 27 rows of data.

The (Current) Option
As shown in Figure 6-12, the 3 Append Queries query has the word (**CURRENT**) next to it. This indicates the query that data will be appended to.

There is nothing stopping you from selecting the current query, as the one to append. If the current query is selected as the table to append, the data in it will be appended to itself. Doing so will cause the current query to have duplicate records. The probably is not what you want to happen. Merging queries has the same (Current) option.

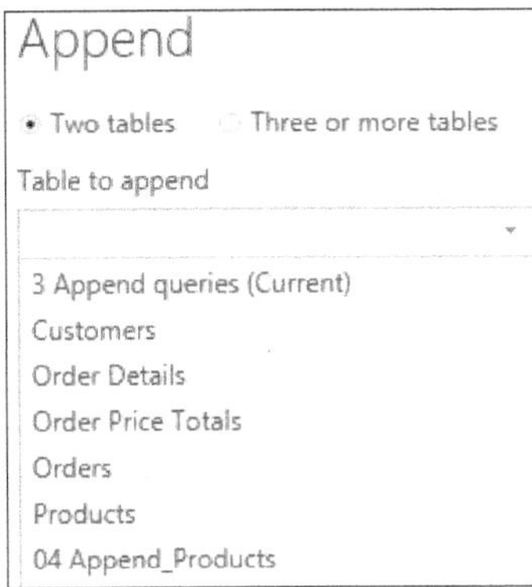

Figure 6-12 Append options

Viewing A Row Of Data

As you saw earlier when you merged two tables of data, you have to scroll to the right to see the new columns of data. You can make the grid shorter and display all of the columns for one record. Follow the steps below to view one record. (You can use the 1 Merge Order Tables query to follow along.)

1. Display the query that you want to view ⇒ Click on the row number that you want to view.
2. To **RESIZE THE GRID**, place the mouse pointer a little below the scroll bar at the bottom of the grid, as illustrated in Figure 6-13, then drag the grid up.

   As shown at the bottom of the figure, you can see the data for one record.

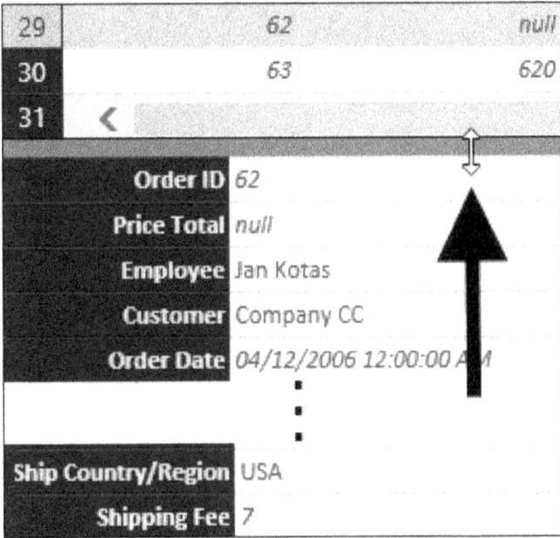

Figure 6-13 Mouse pointer in position to make the grid shorter

Grouping Data

Grouping data is a way to sort data. This forces the data to be displayed in a particular order, based on the fields selected to create the group(s). Grouping is used when you need to create a total or subtotal for all of the rows that have the same value in a column. For example, you need to create an order total amount for each sales rep. You would create a group using the sales rep field and a calculated field (a total) to sum the order totals for each sales rep.

These totals are known as **SUMMARIZING** the data. Each time the value in the field being grouped on changes, a subtotal is created. If you do not need to display totals, the data can be sorted.

Exercises in this chapter take grouping up a notch, from what was covered in previous chapters, by creating what is known as **NESTED GROUPS**. (A group within a group. It is a way to create subtotals.)

Exercise 6.2: Merging Data To Group By

This exercise will show you how to combine the merge and group by features, plus a few others, to prepare data to be used to create reports. Not to scare you, but this exercise is long. Keep in mind that all of the merging parts of the exercise can be handled by creating relationships between the tables and that it is far less steps to create relationships <smile>.

Transform The Data

This part of the exercise will show you how to create new columns, bring in columns from another table and create calculations. These tasks are needed to be able to group data in different ways.

Using The Query Editor To Mashup Data

1. Open a new file ⇒ Import the 07 tables in the More Data Files workbook.

2. Save the file as `E6.2 Transform and group data.`

Add A Year Field To The Orders Table

There is often a need to display data by a portion of a date field, like by year, quarter or month. Usually, these fields are not stored in non date tables, by themselves. The Query Editor has some functionality to help. Creating a year column will let the data be grouped by year.

3. Display the Orders table ⇒ Duplicate the Order Date column ⇒ Rename the duplicate column to `Order Year.`

Insert A Step Between Existing Steps

This part of the exercise will show you how to add a step between steps in the Applied Steps section of the Query Settings panel. To do this, click on the step right above where you want to add a step.

1. In the Applied Steps list, click on the Changed Type step ⇒ Delete (Remove) the Required Date column. You should see the Insert Step message ⇒ Click the **INSERT** button. The column will be deleted.

2. Click on the Renamed Columns step ⇒ Right-click on the Order Year column ⇒ Transform ⇒ Year ⇒ Year ⇒ Move the Order Year column next to the Order Date column.

Merge The Sales Rep Name Column

The Orders table contains the Sales Rep ID column. Displaying that column on a report will not be helpful unless the person viewing the report has memorized all of the sales reps ID numbers <smile>. A better solution is to display the sales reps name. This part of the exercise will add the Sales Rep name field (in the Sales Reps table) to the Orders query.

1. Select the Orders query ⇒ Click on the last step in the Applied Steps list ⇒ Home tab ⇒ Merge Queries button ⇒ Merge Queries.

2. Open the drop-down list and select the Sales Reps table ⇒
Select the Sales Rep ID column in both tables.

   Notice at the bottom of the dialog box, that all of the rows in the Orders table have a matching value (in this exercise, a sales rep) in the Sales Reps table.

   This is known as a **ONE-TO-ONE RELATIONSHIP.**

   There does not have to be a 100 percent match for the merge to be valid. In my experience, it is rare that there is a 100 percent match of rows.

   Figure 6-14 shows the options that should be selected ⇒ Click OK.

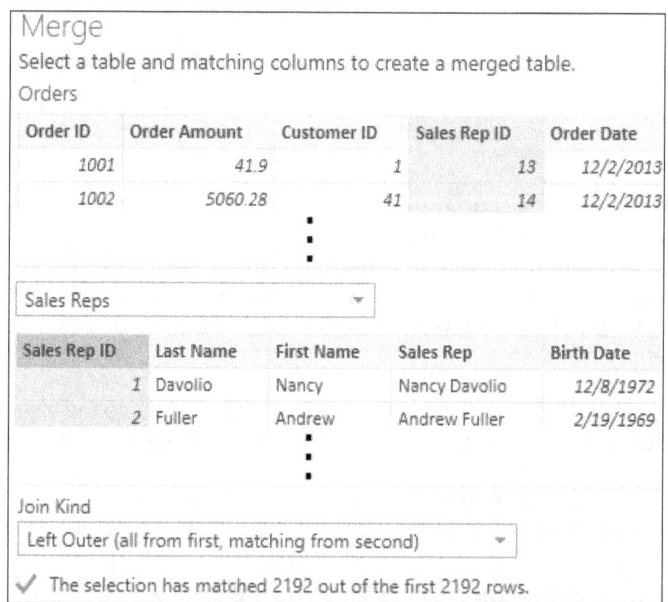

Figure 6-14 Merge options for the Orders and Sales Reps tables

3. Click the button at the end of the New Column heading ⇒ Clear the **(SELECT ALL COLUMNS)** option ⇒ Check the Sales Rep field ⇒ Clear the Use original column option ⇒ Click OK. Now, each order displays the sales reps name.

4. Rename the Merged Queries step to `Merge Sales Rep table.`

Merge The Customer Name Column

Just like the Orders table needs the Sales Reps name, having the Customer Name in the Orders table would also be helpful. In this part of the exercise, you will add the Customer Name column (that you will create) to the Orders table. The goal is to **COMBINE** (merge) the first and last name columns into one new column. If you view the Customers table, you will see that the name is in two fields, which is the norm.

1. Display the Customers query ⇒ Select the First Name and Last Name columns.
2. Add Column tab ⇒ Merge Columns button.
3. Open the Separator drop-down list and select Space.
4. In the New column name field, type `Customer Name`. You should see the first and last name in a new column, at the end of the table.
5. Display the Orders query ⇒ Merge Queries button ⇒ Merge Queries ⇒ Select the Customers table ⇒ Use the Customer ID column to join the tables.
6. Using the New Column, add the Customer Name column that you just created to the Orders table ⇒ Also add the State and Country columns to the Orders table ⇒ Clear the Use original column name as prefix option.

Merge Columns From A Date Table

Earlier in this chapter, you used the Year Transform function. The Transform shortcut menu has a month option. If you select that option, the date will be converted to the number value for the month of the date field.

I exported a portion of a custom date table that I created, to use in this book. Part of the My Date Table is shown in Figure 6-15. This table can be created in Power BI Desktop by creating DAX formulas. In this part of the exercise, you will add columns in the date table to another table. In Chapter 8, you will learn how to create a basic date table.

	DateKey	Year	MonthFull	MonthAbbr	QuarterAbbr	WeekDay	WeekDayAbbr
1	01/01/2012	2012	January	Jan	Q1	Sunday	Sun
2	01/02/2012	2012	January	Jan	Q1	Monday	Mon
3	01/03/2012	2012	January	Jan	Q1	Tuesday	Tue
4	01/04/2012	2012	January	Jan	Q1	Wednesday	Wed
5	01/05/2012	2012	January	Jan	Q1	Thursday	Thu

Figure 6-15 A portion of the My Date Table

1. Add the Month Abbr and Quarter Abbr columns in the My Date table to the Orders table ⇒ Use the Date Key column in the My Date Table to link to the Order Date column in the Orders table.
2. Rename the Quarter Abbr column to `QTR`. You have just merged data from three tables into another table!

Modify The Merge Query Formula

Oops! You just realized that you would rather use the Month Full Name column instead of the Month Abbr column, to display the month name. You could delete the column that you do not want and merge the column that you need. Another option is to modify the formula for the column that you want to replace.

1. Display the Orders query ⇒ Click on the last **EXPANDED NEW COLUMN** step, in the Applied Steps list.
2. Look at the formula. You should see "Month Abbr" in the formula, twice ⇒ Change the first occurrence to `MonthFull`. This is the column name.
3. The second occurrence of Month Abbr, is the column heading name that will be displayed ⇒ Change Month Abbr to `Month`, as illustrated in Figure 6-16 ⇒ Press Enter. Yes, you just modified the M formula.

```
= Table.ExpandTableColumn(#"Merged Queries2", "NewColumn", {"MonthFull", "QuarterAbbr"},
{"Month", "QuarterAbbr"})
```

Figure 6-16 Modified M formula

Group The Order Records By Year

This part of the exercise will show you how to display orders by year and display a count of orders per year and quarter.

1. Duplicate the Orders query ⇒
   Rename it to `1 Orders Grouped By Year` ⇒
   In the Description field, on the Query Properties dialog box, type `Based on the Orders table`,
   as shown in Figure 6-17.

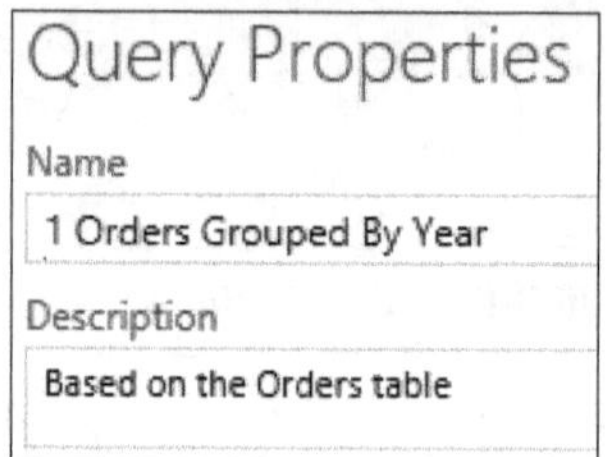

Figure 6-17 Query Properties dialog box

2. Home tab ⇒ Group By button ⇒ Create these three groups: Order Year, QTR, Sales Rep.
3. Change the New column name to `# Of Orders`.
4. Add another row to create an aggregation ⇒

   In the New column name field, type `Total Order $` ⇒

   Select the Sum operation ⇒

   Select the Order Amount field.

   You should have the options shown in Figure 6-18.

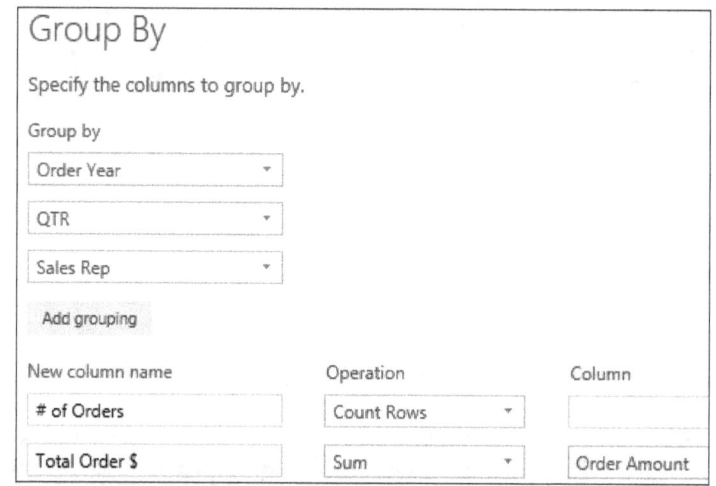

Figure 6-18 Group By options

5. Sort the data in ascending order, by the Order Year column, then in ascending order by the QTR column.

   The groups should look like the ones shown in Figure 6-19.

   Each row displays the sales reps order totals for each year and quarter.

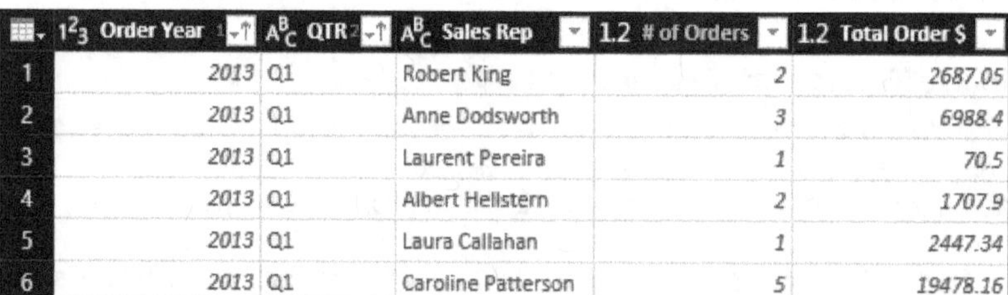

	Order Year	QTR	Sales Rep	# of Orders	Total Order $
1	2013	Q1	Robert King	2	2687.05
2	2013	Q1	Anne Dodsworth	3	6988.4
3	2013	Q1	Laurent Pereira	1	70.5
4	2013	Q1	Albert Hellstern	2	1707.9
5	2013	Q1	Laura Callahan	1	2447.34
6	2013	Q1	Caroline Patterson	5	19478.16

Figure 6-19 Order amount grouped by year, quarter and sales rep

Modified Sort Order

If the sales rep column, shown above in Figure 6-19, was moved to the beginning of the table, the data would be displayed, as shown in Figure 6-20. The sort order was changed to sort on the Order Year, Sales Rep and QTR columns.

	Sales Rep	Order Year	QTR	# of Orders	Total Order $
43	Caroline Patterson	2014	Q1	25	34914.9
44	Caroline Patterson	2014	Q2	30	22468.66
45	Caroline Patterson	2014	Q3	4	1019.2
46	Caroline Patterson	2014	Q4	13	10208.75
47	Janet Leverling	2014	Q1	35	78940.46
48	Janet Leverling	2014	Q2	61	115418.43

Figure 6-20 Modified sort order

Group The Order Records By Sales Rep

This part of the exercise will show you how to create a group that will display one row for each sales rep. The total number of orders and total order amount will also be displayed.

1. Duplicate the Orders grouped by year query ⇒ Rename it to `2 Orders grouped by sales rep.`
2. Delete the Sorted Rows step.
3. Open the Group By dialog box by clicking the * button at the end of the Grouped Rows step ⇒ Delete the Order Year and QTR group options, by clicking the ellipsis button next to them.

   The query should look like the one shown in Figure 6-21. This query would be considered a top level query because there are no sub groups.

   On a chart, users would want to drill-down on a sales rep to see the order detail records.

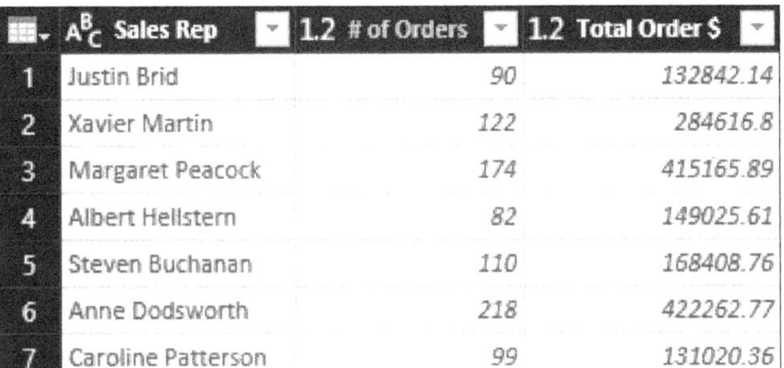

	Sales Rep	# of Orders	Total Order $
1	Justin Brid	90	132842.14
2	Xavier Martin	122	284616.8
3	Margaret Peacock	174	415165.89
4	Albert Hellstern	82	149025.61
5	Steven Buchanan	110	168408.76
6	Anne Dodsworth	218	422262.77
7	Caroline Patterson	99	131020.36

Figure 6-21 Orders grouped by sales rep

Display The Orders Grouped By Customer

If you wanted to display the orders grouped by customer, instead of by sales rep, change the Group By option to Customer Name, as shown in Figure 6-22.

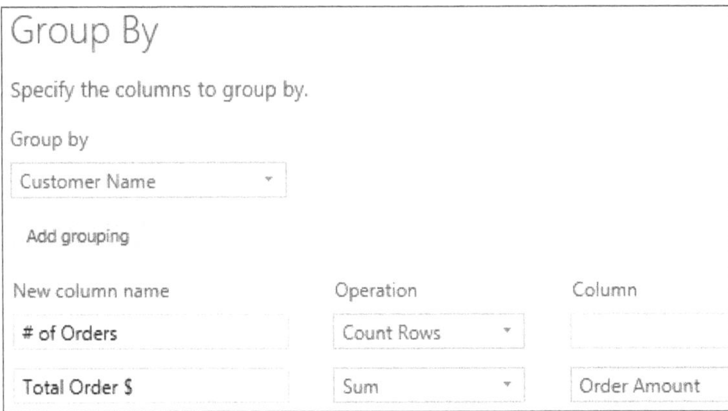

Figure 6-22 Group by options to display orders by customer

Change The Sort Options

The data is grouped by sales rep, but there is a problem with the Sort step. That happened because some of the columns that were sorted on, are no longer displayed in the query. In this part of the exercise, you will add the Last Name column from the Sales Rep query, so that the data can be sorted by the sales reps last name. If you sorted the data by the Sales Rep column, it would not be sorted by the last name, because the Sales Rep column starts with the first name.

1. Duplicate the Orders grouped by sales rep query ⇒ Rename it to `3 Grouped & sorted by sales rep.`
2. Add the Last Name column from the Sales Reps query. Use the Sales Rep column to join the tables.

3. Sort the Last Name column in ascending order.

   The table should look like the one shown in Figure 6-23.

	Sales Rep	# of Orders	Total Order $	Last Name
1	Justin Brid	90	132842.14	Brid
2	Steven Buchanan	110	168408.76	Buchanan
3	Laura Callahan	98	149768.8	Callahan
4	Nancy Davolio	224	423904.36	Davolio

Figure 6-23 Data sorted by the last name

It would be better if the Last Name column could be hidden, but there is no option to hide a column. However, the order that the steps are currently in, provides the following solution. Each time the data is refreshed, the Last Name column would be added to the query. The data will be sorted on the Last Name column, then the Last Name column could be deleted. As long as these steps, in particular, the step to delete a column are done as the last or one of the last steps, you should not run into any problems.

Group The Order Records By State

The group options needed to display orders by state are similar to the options used to display orders by sales rep.

1. Duplicate the Orders grouped by sales rep query ⇒ Rename it to `4 Orders grouped by state`.

2. Double-click on the Grouped Rows step ⇒ Change the Group By field to State.

3. Change the # of Orders column name to `# of Sales` ⇒

   Change the Total Order $ column name to `Total Sales Amount`.

   The table should look like the one shown in Figure 6-24.

	State	# of Sales	Total Sales Amount
1	MI	81	124970.6
2	IL	199	389455.97
3	Warsaw	35	41055.83
4	MN	98	207211.94

Figure 6-24 Orders grouped by state

Modify The Data Displayed In The Group

As you can see, there are some international customers in the data displayed above in Figure 6-24. For this part of the exercise, the goal is to only display orders shipped to a USA address. Because the country is not displayed in the group, the filter has to be created before the group is created.

1. Click on the step above the **GROUPED ROWS** step. You should see all of the columns in the table.

2. Open the Country column filter ⇒ Clear all options ⇒ Select USA.

3. Click on the Grouped Rows step. You should only see rows for the states in the USA.

4. Sort the Total Sales Amount column in descending order.

   The table should look like the one shown in Figure 6-25.

	State	# of Sales	Total Sales Amount
1	IL	199	389455.97
2	CA	148	275657.93
3	PA	102	232311.69
4	AL	83	223506.47
5	MN	98	207211.94

Figure 6-25 Orders grouped by state

Add Currency Formatting To Numeric Data

If the Fixed Decimal Number (currency) data type was applied to the Total Sales Amount column shown above in Figure 6-25, the values would not be displayed with currency formatting that you are probably expecting to see.

The formula that I use to display a dollar sign and commas, to emulate currency formatting is shown in Figure 6-26.

It displays the values shown in the last column shown in Figure 6-27.

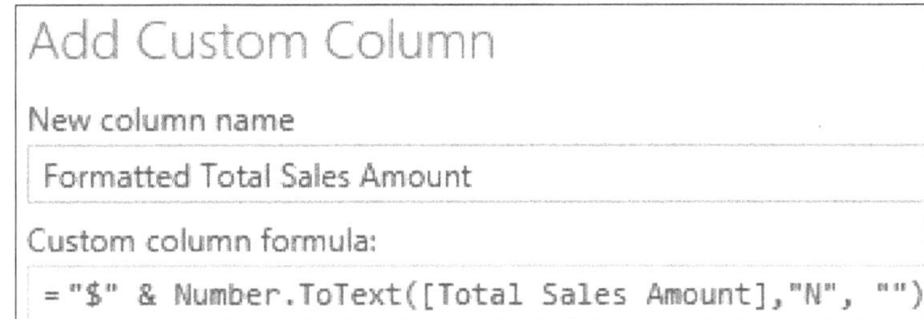

Figure 6-26 Formula to display data in currency format

	State	# of Sales	Total Sales Amount	Formatted Total Sales Amount
1	IL	199	389455.97	$389,455.97
2	CA	148	275657.93	$275,657.93
3	PA	102	232311.69	$232,311.69

Figure 6-27 Result of currency formatting

Keep in mind that the new column is created using the **NUMBER.TOTEXT FUNCTION**, which converts numeric values to text. This means that the new column, that displays currency formatting, cannot be used in a calculation. A better solution is to apply the currency formatting in the Data view because the data type is not changed.

Conversion Functions

Table 6-2 lists some other conversion functions that you may find useful.

Function	This Function Converts . . .
Date.From	Numeric dates to a date format.
Date.FromText	A text field date to a date format.
Date.ToText	A date to text.
Number.FromText	Text to a number.
Time.ToText	Time date to text.

Table 6-2 Conversion functions explained

Use The Merged Queries Step To View The Matching Rows Of Data

Clicking on this step will display the matching record(s) from the second table. These are the columns of data that could be merged into the query currently selected. To follow the steps below, use Exercise 6.2.

1. Display the Orders query.

2. Click on the first Merged Queries step. You should see the New Column at the end of the query.

3. Click to the right of the word "Table" in a cell, in the column. At the bottom of the window, you will see the matching row(s) of data from the second table that the data will be merged from, as illustrated in Figure 6-28. These are the columns that can be merged into the query displayed at the top of the figure.

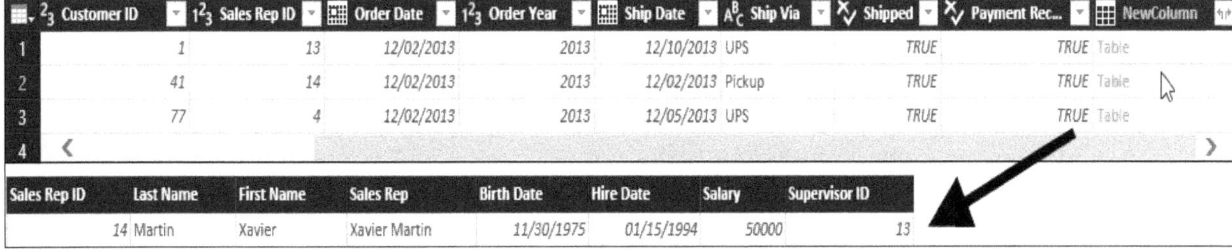

	Customer ID	Sales Rep ID	Order Date	Order Year	Ship Date	Ship Via	Shipped	Payment Rec...	NewColumn
1	1	13	12/02/2013	2013	12/10/2013	UPS	TRUE	TRUE	Table
2	41	14	12/02/2013	2013	12/02/2013	Pickup	TRUE	TRUE	Table
3	77	4	12/02/2013	2013	12/05/2013	UPS	TRUE	TRUE	Table
4									

Sales Rep ID	Last Name	First Name	Sales Rep	Birth Date	Hire Date	Salary	Supervisor ID
14	Martin	Xavier	Xavier Martin	11/30/1975	01/15/1994	50000	13

Figure 6-28 Matching row of data illustrated for row 2 in the query

Clicking on the word "Table" will add a step to the query. This step will replace the source data, with the linked data. More than likely, when creating a merge, this is not what you want to have happen.

Create An Aggregated Column To Merge

In the previous parts of this exercise, one-to-one relationships were used to add columns to the Orders table. One way to tell what type of relationship you are creating is if the number of matching records between the tables is the same on the Merge dialog box.

The Order Details table can have multiple rows of data for each order. It is very common to have the need to get an aggregation of a column in the "many" table (the Order Details table, in this exercise) and add the aggregation to the "one" table (the Orders table).

The next few sections of this exercise will show you how to:

☑ Create a formula in the Order Details table to calculate the line total for each row in the table.
☑ Add the Line Total column to the Orders table to get a sub total for each order. It is a subtotal versus a grand total because shipping and taxes are calculated at run time.
☑ Create a count of items per order, that will also be added as a column in the Orders table.

Create A Calculated Column

In this part of the exercise, you will create a formula that calculates the total for each item that was ordered. Keep in mind that each order can have more than one item. If you looked at the data in the Order Details table, you will see multiple rows with the same Order ID number. All of the rows with the same Order ID number belong to one record (in this case, one order) in the Orders table.

Aggregate data must have a numeric data type to be used in a calculation.

1. Display the Order Details table ⇒

   Add Column tab ⇒ Add Custom Column button ⇒ Create the formula shown in Figure 6-29.

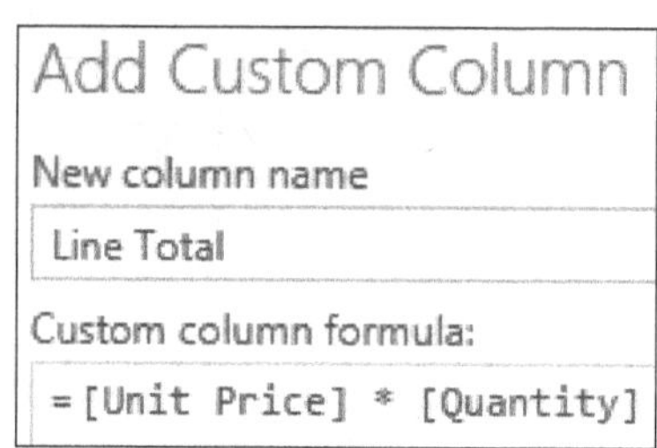

Figure 6-29 Line Total formula

2. Change the data type of the Line Total column to Fixed Decimal Number.

Create And Merge Aggregations

In this part of the exercise, you will merge the Line Total column into the Orders table and create a column that displays a count of items for each order.

Before creating this type of calculation, it is a good idea to make all other changes to the table first, as calculations that use data in another table can take longer to run.

1. Duplicate the Orders query ⇒ Rename it to `5 Orders with detail sub total.`

2. Filter the table to only display orders in the USA.

3. Home tab ⇒ Merge Queries button ⇒ Merge Queries ⇒ Select the Order Details table ⇒ Select the Order ID column in both tables.

4. With the New Column selected ⇒ Transform tab ⇒ Aggregate button ⇒ Check the Sum of Order ID field ⇒ Change the aggregation type to Count (All) ⇒ Clear the Sum option.

5. Check the Sum of Line Total field ⇒ Clear the Use original column name as prefix option ⇒ Click OK. You may see circles moving above the formula bar. This indicates that the data is being generated to display the new columns of data that you created.

6. Rename the Count of Order ID column to `Count of items on order` ⇒ Rename the Sum of Line Total column to `Order Subtotal Amount`.

7. Move both columns to the beginning of the table, right after the Order ID column, so that your table looks like the one shown in Figure 6-30.

	Order ID	Count of items on order	Order Subtotal Amount
1	1001	1	41.9
2	1002	2	260.28
3	1004	1	823.05
4	1033	3	146.32

Figure 6-30 Calculated columns from data in different tables

If you look in the Order Details table, you will see two rows of data that have Order ID 1002. If you add up the Line Total column values for these two rows, it will equal $260.28, which is what is displayed as the Order Subtotal Amount in the Orders table, shown above in Figure 6-30. The reason that you see Order ID's in the Order Details table that are not in the Orders table, is because the Orders table has a filter to only display Orders in the USA. Filtered records are not displayed.

Merge Queries To Create A New Table

This chapter has covered merging columns from one table into another table. There is one more merge option. This option is used to create a new table by selecting columns from two queries. This leaves both of the original queries intact.

Exercise 6.3: Create A New Table By Merging Queries

This exercise will show you how to create a new table by merging columns from two queries. The **MERGE QUERIES AS NEW OPTION** on the Merge Queries button is used to start from scratch, to create a query with just the columns that you need. As you will see, the options are similar to the **MERGE QUERIES** options. The difference is that you select both tables. This option works the same as duplicating an existing query and then using it as the first table on the Merge dialog box.

This option could be used to create a table that will be used as the basis for a lot of reports. It is a great tool to use when you have tables like Products, Products Category and Product Subcategory and need a few fields from each of these tables. It will allow you to create a table that only has the fields that you need, then either unload tables from the data model or delete the tables from the report file.

1. Open a new file ⇒ Load the 07 Customers and 07 Orders tables in the More Data Files workbook.

2. Save the file as `E6.3 My New Table`.

3. Merge Queries button ⇒ Merge Queries as New.

4. In the first drop-down list, select the Orders table ⇒ In the second drop-down list, select the Customers table.

5. Select the Customer ID column in both tables.

   You should have the options shown in Figure 6-31.

   Click OK.

   From here, the process is the same as using the Merge Queries option.

Figure 6-31 Options to create a new table

6. Rename the query to `1 My Custom Orders`.

At this point, you would display the options on the New Column at the end of the query and select the columns from the Customers table that you want to add to the new query, just like you have done in previous exercises. After that, you would delete the columns in the Orders table that are not needed.

Many-To-Many Merge Criteria

So far, all of the merge exercises have used the one-to-many relationship criteria. There are times when you need to create a many-to-many merge. Sometimes, it is possible to create a many-to-many merge and not even know it. When you do, additional rows will be added to the query. A one-to-one merge has the same or fewer rows (then the first table selected for the merge) that have a match. Many-to-many merges produce more rows then the first table has.

For example, Figure 6-32 shows two tables that can be used to create a merge. Notice that the table on the left has more rows of data then the table on the right side of the figure. Figure 6-33 shows the result of a one-to-many merge. In the lower left corner of the figure, you can see the number of rows after the merge.

3	Order ID	Product ID	Unit Price	Quantity	Vendor
4	1001	1001	$18.88	1	Roadster
5	1002	1101	$14.50	4	Active Outdoors
6	1002	1102	$14.50	2	Active Outdoors
7	1003	2161	$9.85	3	Wheeler
8	1003	1150	$4.85	3	SlickRock
9	1004	1151	$39.85	3	Descent
10	1005	2002	$24.35	2	Changing Gears
11	1006	2151	$19.29	1	Mozzie
12	1006	2161	$9.85	1	Wheeler
		⋮			
25	1012	1151	$39.85	3	Descent
26	1013	2002	$24.35	2	Changing Gears
27	1013	2151	$19.29	3	Mozzie
28	1014	2161	$9.85	2	Wheeler

Product ID	Vendor	Show Room	Color	Price (SRP
1001	Roadster	Online	blue	$18.88
1101	Active Outdoors	Retail Location	red	$14.50
1102	Active Outdoors	Online	green	$14.50
1150	SlickRock	Kiosk	champagne	$4.85
1151	Descent	Retail Location	steel satin	$39.85
2002	Changing Gears	Expo	purple	$24.35
2151	Mozzie	Expo	green	$19.29
2161	Wheeler	Expo	purple	$9.85
2162	Rapel	Online	silver	$9.85
2206	Triumph Pro Helmet	Online	white	$11.90

Figure 6-32 Tables for a merge

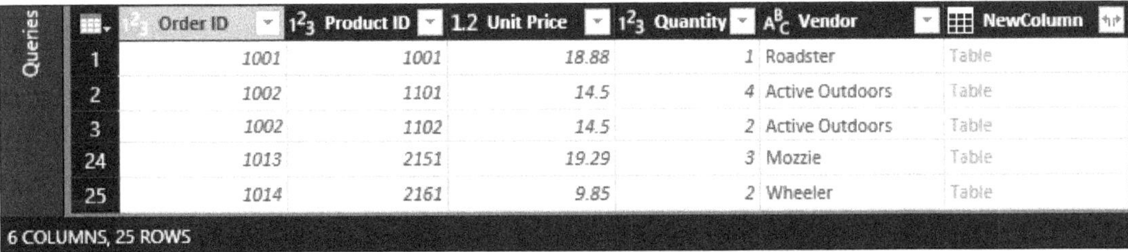

	Order ID	Product ID	Unit Price	Quantity	Vendor	NewColumn
1	1001	1001	18.88	1	Roadster	Table
2	1002	1101	14.5	4	Active Outdoors	Table
3	1002	1102	14.5	2	Active Outdoors	Table
24	1013	2151	19.29	3	Mozzie	Table
25	1014	2161	9.85	2	Wheeler	Table

6 COLUMNS, 25 ROWS

Figure 6-33 One-to-many merge result

Exercise 6.4: Use The Merge And Append Options

This exercise will show you other ways to use the merge and append options.

1. Import the following tables from the Store Sales workbook: June_invoices, Nov_invoices, Order Details, Products, Sept_invoices and Sales.
2. Save the file as `E6.4 Merge And Append New Table Options`.
3. Import the two CSV files in the 2016 invoices folder.

Create A Many-To-Many Merge

In this part of the exercise you will learn how to create a many-to-many merge.

1. Duplicate the Order Details query ⇒ Rename the query to `1 Merged On Vendor`.
2. Home tab ⇒ Merge Queries button ⇒ Merge Queries ⇒ Select the Products table in the drop-down list.
3. Select the Vendor column in both tables. Notice that the message at the bottom of the dialog box says that 25 of 25 rows were matched ⇒ Click OK.
4. As shown at the top of Figure 6-34, the two rows with the Order ID 1002 have different Product ID's, which is what is expected ⇒ Click next to the word "Table", in the new column, in row 2. You will see that there are two matching records in the Products table.

This probably is not what you were expecting. The reason that two matches were found for row 2 is because the Vendor column was used to link the tables for the merge. Both products are from the same vendor, which is fine. Row 3 will also display two rows. This means that two rows will be created in the query that are not needed (one for the current row 2 and one for the current row 3).

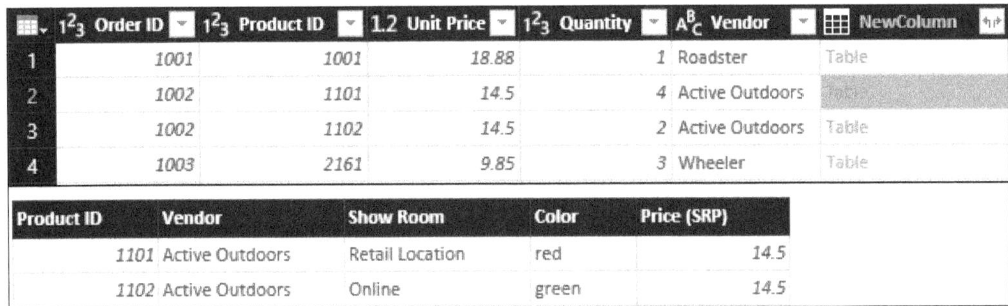

	Order ID	Product ID	Unit Price	Quantity	Vendor	NewColumn
1	1001	1001	18.88	1	Roadster	Table
2	1002	1101	14.5	4	Active Outdoors	Table
3	1002	1102	14.5	2	Active Outdoors	Table
4	1003	2161	9.85	3	Wheeler	Table

Product ID	Vendor	Show Room	Color	Price (SRP)
1101	Active Outdoors	Retail Location	red	14.5
1102	Active Outdoors	Online	green	14.5

Figure 6-34 Result of a many-to-many merge

5. Use the New Column button to add the Show Room column from the Products table.

Notice that there are now 27 rows in the query. Figure 6-35 illustrates the duplicate rows. Most of the time, this is not the result that you want.

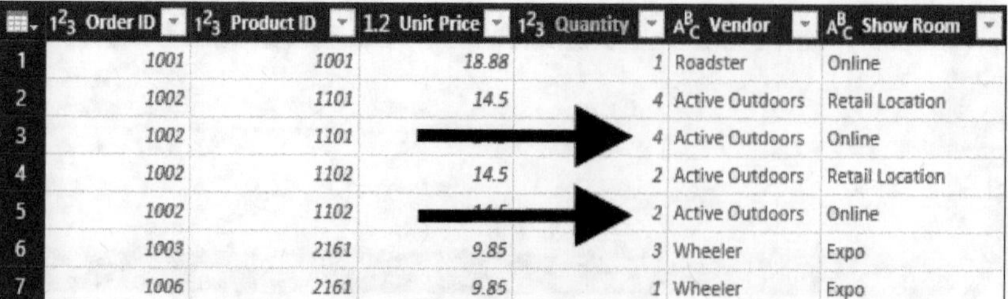

	Order ID	Product ID	Unit Price	Quantity	Vendor	Show Room
1	1001	1001	18.88	1	Roadster	Online
2	1002	1101	14.5	4	Active Outdoors	Retail Location
3	1002	1101	[illegible]	4	Active Outdoors	Online
4	1002	1102	14.5	2	Active Outdoors	Retail Location
5	1002	1102	[illegible]	2	Active Outdoors	Online
6	1003	2161	9.85	3	Wheeler	Expo
7	1006	2161	9.85	1	Wheeler	Expo

Figure 6-35 Duplicate rows of data illustrated

This is also an example of why many IT people cringe when end users want to link tables on a text field. This is why tables in a database use automatic sequential numeric values, as the Primary key field to link on.

If you have data that is part of a many-to-many relationship and want to use it in Power BI Desktop, unpivoting it will be helpful. An example of this type of data is orders that have different bill to and ship to addresses. Another example would be a customer that has multiple ship to addresses.

Adding More Data To A New Table
If you wanted to merge (or append) more data to the new merge table after initially creating it, use the Merge Queries option with the new table. Using the Merge (or Append) Queries as New option will create another new table, which would not hurt anything, but it is probably not what you want.

Append Queries To Create A New Table

Earlier in Exercise 6.1, the Append Queries option was used to append data in one table to an existing table. In Exercise 6.3, the Merge Queries as New option on the Merge Queries button was used to create a new table. The Append Queries as New option on the Append Queries button is also used to create a new table.

Create A New Table From Appended Queries

This part of the exercise will show you another way to create a new table and how to append data with different column names.

1. Append Queries button ⇒ Append Queries as New ⇒

   Select the June Invoices file ⇒

   Select the Sept Invoices file, in the last drop-down list, as shown in Figure 6-36.

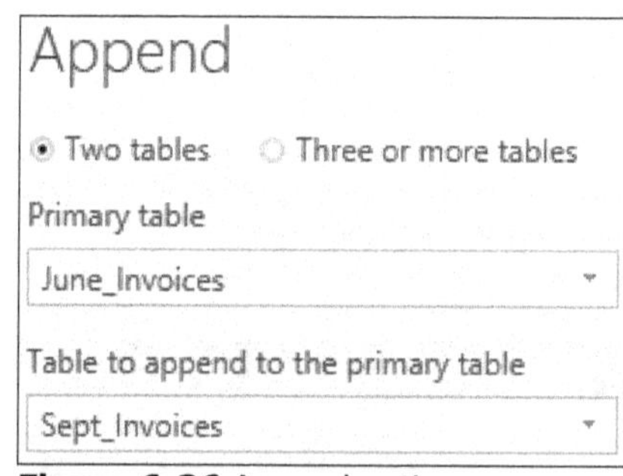

Figure 6-36 Append options

2. Click OK ⇒ The new query will be created. Rename the query to `2 Append Invoices`. The query should have 368 rows.

Appending Queries With Different Column Names

The append exercise that you just completed, went off without a problem. That is because during the append process, the column headings from the first table were loaded into memory and the data in the query was added to the new table. When the second table was scanned, the column headings were compared to the ones from the first table, so that columns can be appended to the new table. As hard as you try to get people to follow naming conventions, at some point, you will get data that does not follow the rules.

Column Order For Appending Queries
As long as the column headings are the same, the data will be appended, even if the columns are not in the same order, as the table that the data will be appended to. The columns will be matched and appended to the correct column.

This part of the exercise will show you what happens when the column names are not the same.

1. Duplicate the Append Invoices query ⇒ Rename it to `3 Append with different headings.`

2. Append Queries button ⇒ Append Queries ⇒ Select the Nov Invoices query ⇒ Click OK.

As illustrated in Figure 6-37, there is a new column named Order Nbr. The existing records in the table have "null" in this column because the table that they are from, does not have a column with this name.

	Invoice Nbr	Order ID	Date	Amount	Order Nbr
366	1360	2169	09/30/2014	1751.02	null
367	1361	2170	09/30/2014	[illegible]	null
368	1362	2171	09/30/2014	33.9	null
369	1493	null	11/01/2014	135.35	2302
370	1494	null	11/01/2014	41.9	2303

Figure 6-37 Result of append with different column names

If you scroll down the table and view the data for November, you will see values in the Order Nbr column.

Also notice that there are null values in the Order ID column for the Nov Invoice rows. That is because the Nov Invoices table does not have this column.

If the Nov Invoices table had three columns of data that the current table did not have, three new columns would be added to the new query. When Power BI Desktop cannot find a match for the column heading, a new column is created. This is easy to fix. The Order Nbr column heading needs to be renamed to Order ID.

3. Click on the Nov Invoices query ⇒ Rename the Order Nbr column to `Order ID.`

4. Display the Append with different headings query. You will not see the last column shown above in Figure 6-37, that was created when the Nov Invoices query was initially appended.

Append Three Or More Tables At One Time

The previous part of this exercise demonstrated appending two queries. As shown below in Figure 6-38, there is an option to append three or more tables, which is what this part of the exercise covers.

1. Duplicate the Append with different headings query ⇒ Rename it to `4 Append five tables.`

2. Home tab ⇒ Append Queries button ⇒ Append Queries ⇒ Select the **THREE OR MORE TABLES** option.

3. Add the following tables to the Tables to Append column: Jan 2016, Feb 2016, June Invoices, Sept Invoices and 2 Append Invoices, as shown in Figure 6-38 ⇒ Click OK.

   The new query will be created.

   The append order of the tables can be changed before the query is created, by clicking the up and down buttons.

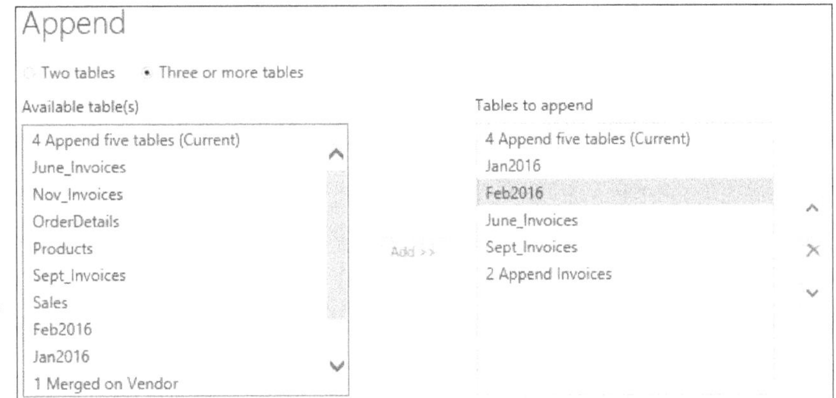

Figure 6-38 Append three or more table options

Discover The Top Selling Product By Year

There seems to always be a need to find the top this or top that. At the time this book went to print, Power BI Desktop does not have what is known as Top 10 functionality built in. I remember reading a request that said that this was being worked on.

This part of the exercise will show you how to find each sales reps top selling product per year, based on the largest line total amount.

Create The Group

The group that you will create in this part of the exercise, will display the orders by order year and sales rep.

1. Duplicate the Sales query ⇒ Rename it to `5 Sales Reps Orders.`

2. Home tab ⇒ Group By button ⇒ Create the group shown in Figure 6-39.

   The **ALL ROWS OPERATION** creates a new column of tables. The table contains the detail rows that are used to create the calculation for the row above it on the Group by dialog box.

   In this exercise, the Sales Detail table will display the rows needed to create the values in the Total Sales column.

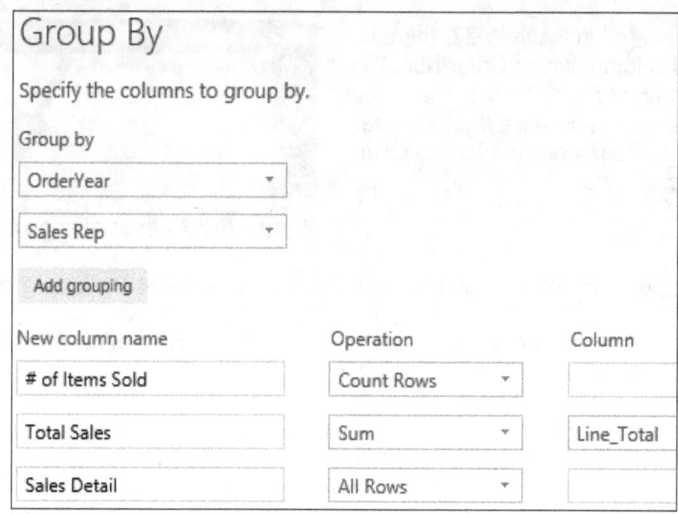

Figure 6-39 Group By options

The top of Figure 6-40 shows some of the grouped data. Clicking next to the word "Table", displays the rows (shown at the bottom of the figure) that are used to create the Total Sales calculation for the selected row in the table at the top of the figure. Remember that when the data is grouped, columns not used to create the groups are not displayed, once the Group By options are applied.

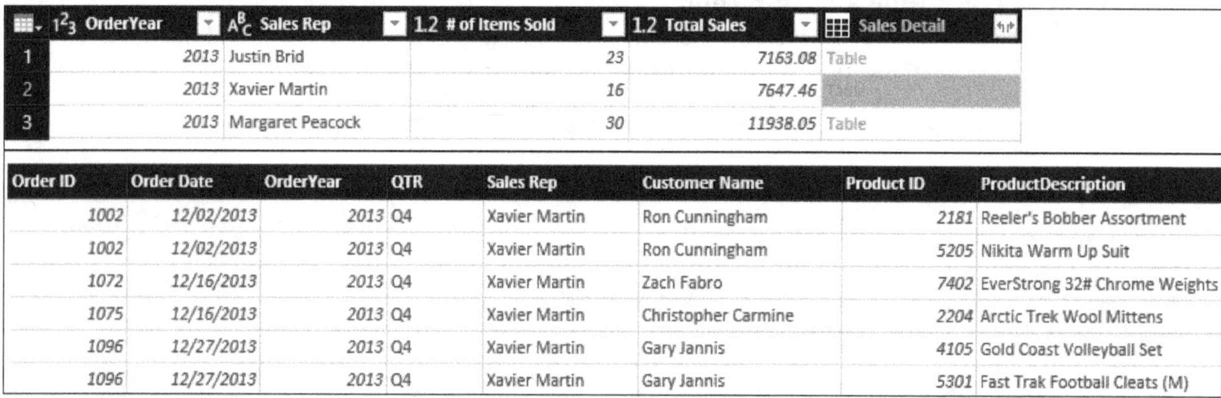

	OrderYear	Sales Rep	# of Items Sold	Total Sales	Sales Detail
1	2013	Justin Brid	23	7163.08	Table
2	2013	Xavier Martin	16	7647.46	
3	2013	Margaret Peacock	30	11938.05	Table

Order ID	Order Date	OrderYear	QTR	Sales Rep	Customer Name	Product ID	ProductDescription
1002	12/02/2013	2013	Q4	Xavier Martin	Ron Cunningham	2181	Reeler's Bobber Assortment
1002	12/02/2013	2013	Q4	Xavier Martin	Ron Cunningham	5205	Nikita Warm Up Suit
1072	12/16/2013	2013	Q4	Xavier Martin	Zach Fabro	7402	EverStrong 32# Chrome Weights
1075	12/16/2013	2013	Q4	Xavier Martin	Christopher Carmine	2204	Arctic Trek Wool Mittens
1096	12/27/2013	2013	Q4	Xavier Martin	Gary Jannis	4105	Gold Coast Volleyball Set
1096	12/27/2013	2013	Q4	Xavier Martin	Gary Jannis	5301	Fast Trak Football Cleats (M)

Figure 6-40 Result of the group by options shown above in Figure 6-39

3. Change the data type of the # of Items Sold column to Whole Number.

Discover The Top Selling Products By Dollar Amount

This part of the exercise will show you how to create a formula to find each sales reps highest selling product for each year, based on the Line Total value. This value will be displayed in the query.

1. Click on the last Changed Type step.

2. Add Column tab ⇒ Add Custom Column button ⇒ Create the column using the formula shown in Figure 6-41.

   In this formula, the **TABLE.MAX FUNCTION** looks in the Sales Detail records for each row (shown above, at the bottom of Figure 6-40) and pulls out the row that has the largest value for each sales rep.

Add Custom Column

New column name

Largest Line Total

Custom column formula:

```
= Table.Max([SalesDetail], "Line_Total")
```

Available columns:

OrderYear
Sales Rep
# of Items Sold
Total Sales
SalesDetail

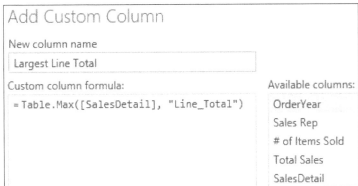

Figure 6-41 Formula to find each sales reps largest selling product

You should see a column with the word "Record", as shown in the upper right corner of Figure 6-42.

Clicking next to the word "Record", displays the row (from the rows retrieved in the table in the Sales Detail column) with the largest Line Total value, as shown at the bottom of the figure.

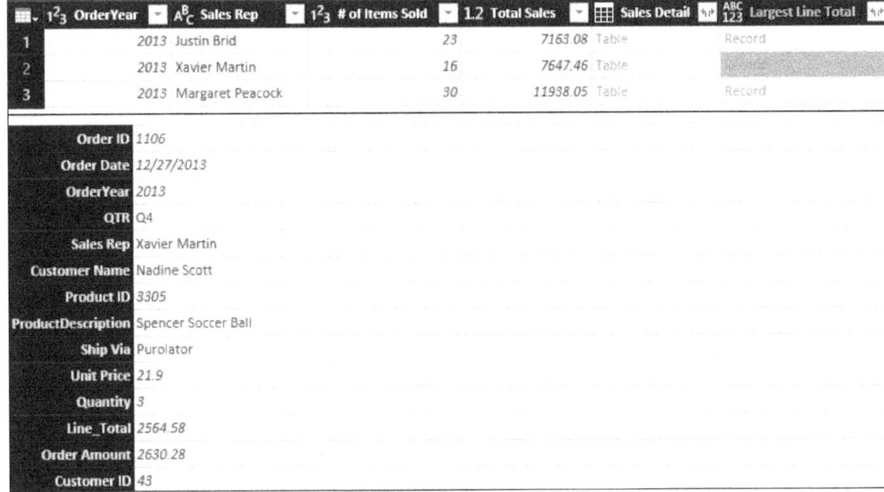

OrderYear
Sales Rep
# of Items Sold
Total Sales
Sales Detail
Largest Line Total
2013 Justin Brid 23 7163.08 Table Record
2013 Xavier Martin 16 7647.46 Table
2013 Margaret Peacock 30 11938.05 Table Record
Order ID 1106
Order Date 12/27/2013
OrderYear 2013
QTR Q4
Sales Rep Xavier Martin
Customer Name Nadine Scott
Product ID 3305
ProductDescription Spencer Soccer Ball
Ship Via Purolator
Unit Price 21.9
Quantity 3
Line_Total 2564.58
Order Amount 2630.28
Customer ID 43

Figure 6-42 Record with the largest Line Total amount

Add Columns From The Record With The Largest Value

The steps below are used to add columns to the query.

1. Click the button to the right of the Largest Line Total column heading.

2. Check the fields shown in Figure 6-43 ⇒ Clear the Use original column option.

   When selecting columns, if you are not 100% sure, if you need to display a column, it is best to select it now. If you find that you do not need it, you can always delete it later. This is a step that I would rename, in case I needed to change the columns.

   If you need to add more columns later, repeat this step. You will see an error message. Delete the old Expanded Column name step.

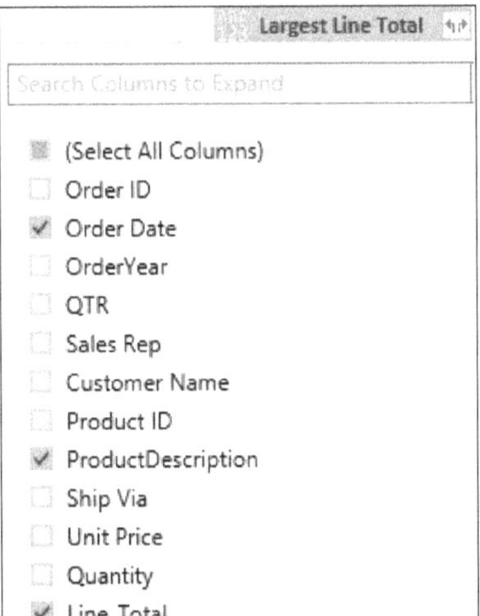

Figure 6-43 Columns selected to be added to the table

Clean Up The Table

1. Rename the Product Description column to `Best Seller`.

2. Rename the Line_Total column to `$Best Seller` ⇒ Change the $Best Seller column data type to Fixed Decimal Number.

3. Delete the Sales Detail column.

4. Change the Order Date column data type to Date.

Calculate The Best Seller Percent

The steps below show you how to create a formula that will display what percent of the yearly total, each best selling product represents. Keep in mind that the percent may not be displayed as you expect in the Query Editor, but in the Data view, you can format the column to display as a percent. You can also create a formula in the Query Editor, to display the values with a percent symbol.

1. Add Column tab ⇒ Add Custom Column button ⇒ Create the formula shown in Figure 6-44.

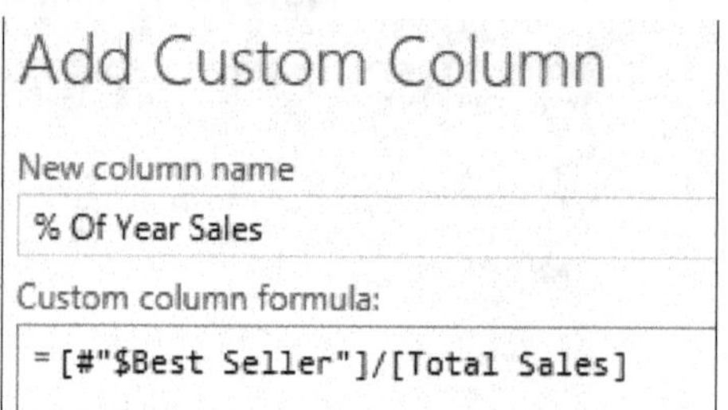

Figure 6-44 Formula to calculate the percent

2. Click on the % of Year Sales column ⇒ Transform tab ⇒ Rounding button ⇒ Round ⇒ Type 2 in the Decimal Places field. The query should look like the one shown in Figure 6-45. The % of Year Sales values are actually whole numbers.

	OrderYear	Sales Rep	# of Items Sold	Total Sales	Order Date	Best Seller	$Best Seller	% Of Year Sales
1	2013	Justin Brid	23	7163.08	12/19/2013	ProTech Bike Helmet	1079.7	0.15
2	2013	Xavier Martin	16	7647.46	12/27/2013	Spencer Soccer Ball	2564.58	0.34
3	2013	Margaret Peacock	30	11938.05	02/27/2013	Gold Coast Volleyball Set	2497.05	0.21
4	2013	Anne Dodsworth	32	8778.38	12/17/2013	Johnson Bowling Ball	2372.19	0.27
5	2013	Albert Hellstern	25	8473.76	12/13/2013	Flexall Dual Stack Gym Mach...	2497.05	0.29

Figure 6-45 Table showing each sales reps best selling item for each year

Add Percent Formatting To Numeric Data

Earlier in this chapter you saw how to use the **NUMBER.TOTEXT FUNCTION** to display values with currency formatting. The same function can also be used to display values with percent formatting. Figure 6-46 shows the formula used to display the % of Year Sales values with percent formatting, as shown in Figure 6-47. The "P" in the formula is what displays the percent sign.

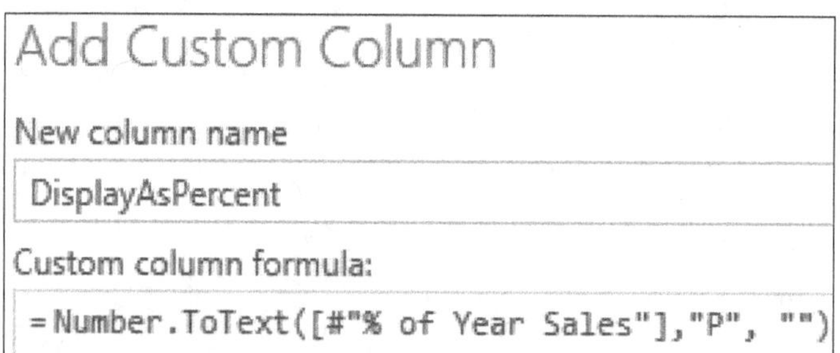

Figure 6-46 Formula to display values with percent formatting

% Of Year Sales	DisplayAsPercent
0.15073125	15.07 %
0.335350561	33.54 %
0.209167326	20.92 %

Figure 6-47 Result of percent formatting

Pivot And Unpivot Data

These options are used to change the structure of the data after it has been imported. Data that has been imported in multiple columns (like data in a pivot table layout), but really needs to be in one column is an example of when you would use these options.

Pivot Column Options

The options selected in Figure 6-48 take the data shown later in Figure 6-56 and pivots it so that it is in the layout shown in Figure 6-60. These options are used to create a table that has an aggregate value for each unique value in the selected column. This is another way to group raw data. An example would be providing a count of customers per state. The Pivot Column option creates a column in the table for each unique value in the column that you select, before opening the Pivot Column dialog box. Figure 6-49 shows part of a Products table.

The **AGGREGATE VALUE FUNCTION** options shown in Figure 6-48, are used to create a calculated field for the column selected in the **VALUES COLUMN** field. The functions are explained in Table 6-3. For example, if the query needed to have quarterly totals for each store, for each year, you would use the Sum function to get a total per store, per year. These functions are also available on the Aggregate New Column dialog box that was covered earlier in this chapter.

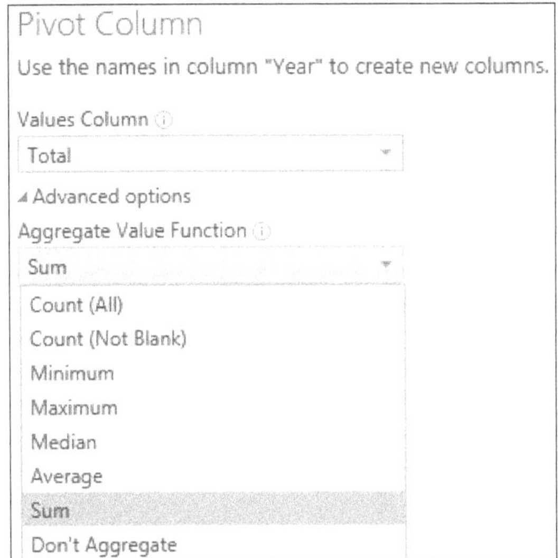

Figure 6-48 Pivot Column options

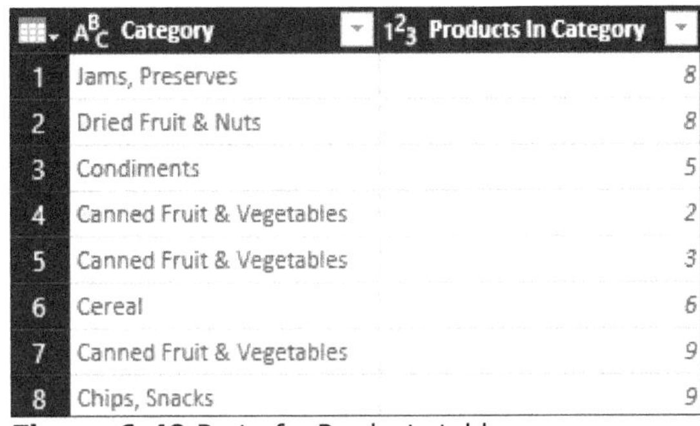

	Category	Products In Category
1	Jams, Preserves	8
2	Dried Fruit & Nuts	8
3	Condiments	5
4	Canned Fruit & Vegetables	2
5	Canned Fruit & Vegetables	3
6	Cereal	6
7	Canned Fruit & Vegetables	9
8	Chips, Snacks	9

Figure 6-49 Part of a Products table

Function	Description
Count (All)	Creates a count per category.
Count (Not Blank)	Only counts the number of rows that have a value in the column.
Minimum	Creates columns that display the smallest value in each category.
Maximum	Creates columns that display the largest value in each category.
Median	Creates columns that display the middle value for each category.
Average	Creates columns that display the average value for each category.
Sum	Creates columns for each unique category and adds the values for all rows that have the same category to calculate the total.
Don't Aggregate	Does not create a calculation for the categories.

Table 6-3 Aggregate functions explained

DISPLAY A COUNT PER CATEGORY The options selected in Figure 6-50 create the columns shown in Figure 6-51.

If the table was sorted by the Category column before selecting the pivot column options, the new columns will be displayed in alphabetical order.

Pivot Column
Use the names in column "Category" to create new columns.
Values Column
Products In Category
Advanced options
Aggregate Value Function
Count (All)
Learn more about Pivot Column

Figure 6-50 Count (All) function options

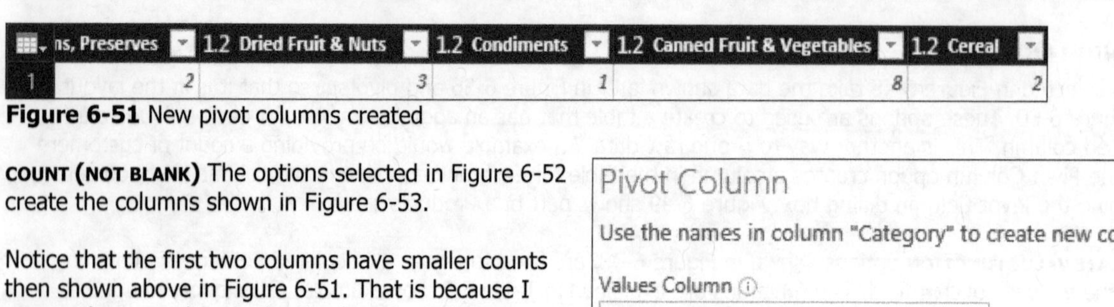

ns, Preserves	1.2 Dried Fruit & Nuts	1.2 Condiments	1.2 Canned Fruit & Vegetables	1.2 Cereal
2	3	1	8	2

Figure 6-51 New pivot columns created

COUNT (NOT BLANK) The options selected in Figure 6-52 create the columns shown in Figure 6-53.

Notice that the first two columns have smaller counts then shown above in Figure 6-51. That is because I removed some values in the Products in Category column.

Figure 6-52 Count (Non Blank) function options

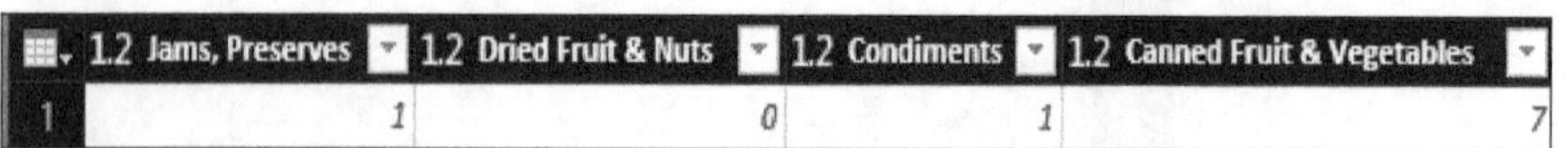

1.2 Jams, Preserves	1.2 Dried Fruit & Nuts	1.2 Condiments	1.2 Canned Fruit & Vegetables
1	0	1	7

Figure 6-53 New pivot columns created

Exercise 6.5: Use The Pivot Column And Reverse Rows Options

This exercise will show you how to use the Pivot Column dialog box and Reverse Rows options.

Create A Pivot Table

In this part of the exercise, you will learn how to create a table that displays a yearly total per store, in a column layout, like a pivot table.

1. Import the Yearly Sales table in the More Data Files workbook ⇒ Save the file as `E6.5 Yearly sales data`.

2. Duplicate the Yearly Sales query ⇒ Rename it to `1 Pivot table`.

3. Click on the Year column ⇒ Transform tab ⇒ Pivot Column button.

4. Select Total from the Values Column drop-down list.

   In this exercise, the values in the Total column have already been aggregated.

   Selecting Sum or Don't Aggregate will produce the same results in this exercise, because each store only has one total per year.

   Click OK. The pivot table should look like the one shown in Figure 6-54.

	Store	1.2 2010	1.2 2011	1.2 2012	1.2 2013	1.2 2014	1.2 2015
1	Atherton	19.7	17.1	18.3	14.8	19.8	24.5
2	Berkeley	14.4	18	16.4	16.7	19.3	0
3	Carmel-by-the-Sea	18.8	13.5	18.7	13.9	15.7	17.2
4	Cupertino	12	16.2	17.5	17.8	13.8	15.55
5	Fresno	19.2	15.6	19.6	15.9	14.4	14.3
6	Laguna Beach	18.9	14.6	16.7	12.1	13.9	16.2
7	Los Angeles	0	12.75	0	0	0	130
8	Mailbu	18.7	17.8	14	18.5	13.7	19.1
9	Palm Springs	0	0	0	0	0	6.55
10	Pasadena	17	19.4	17.1	17.3	17.3	18.88
11	San Francisco	14.4	14	13.9	15.4	18.3	0
12	Santa Barbara	0	0	0	0	8.2	9.19

Figure 6-54 Pivot table

Use The Reverse Rows Option

This option works similar to sorting in descending order. The difference is that there is no ranking involved. The Reverse Rows option moves the physical last row in the query to the first row and vice versa.

1. Duplicate the Pivot table query ⇒ Rename it to `2 Reverse Rows`.

2. Transform tab ⇒ Reverse Rows button. The table should look like the one shown in Figure 6-55.

This transform option does not seem to add any value to a pivoted data layout. What can I say? <smile>

	Store	2010	2011	2012	2013	2014	2015
1	Santa Barbara	0	0	0	0	8.2	9.19
2	San Francisco	14.4	14	13.9	15.4	18.3	0
3	Pasadena	17	19.4	17.1	17.3	17.3	18.88
4	Palm Springs	0	0	0	0	0	6.55

Figure 6-55 Reverse Rows option applied to a pivot table

Unpivoting Data

This option works the opposite of the Pivot Column option, that was covered in the previous exercise.

This option takes data in a pivot table layout, as shown in Figure 6-56 or data that is in a non tabular format and changes it to a flat file (unpivoted layout), as shown later in Figure 6-58. This process is known as changing the **DATA STRUCTURE**.

A	B	C	D	E	F	G
(In Millions)						
Store	**FY 2010**	**FY 2011**	**FY 2012**	**FY 2013**	**FY 2014**	**Total**
Atherton	$19.70	$17.10	$18.30	$14.80	$19.80	$89.70
Berkeley	$14.40	$18.00	$16.40	$16.70	$19.30	$84.80
Carmel-by-the-Sea	$18.80	$13.50	$18.70	$13.90	$15.70	$80.60
Cupertino	$12.00	$16.20	$17.50	$17.80	$13.80	$77.30
Fresno	$19.20	$15.60	$19.60	$15.90	$14.40	$84.70
Laguna Beach	$18.90	$14.60	$16.70	$12.10	$13.90	$76.20
Mailbu	$18.70	$17.80	$14.00	$18.50	$13.70	$82.70
Pasadena	$17.00	$19.40	$17.10	$17.30	$17.30	$88.10
San Francisco	$14.40	$14.00	$13.90	$15.40	$18.30	$76.00
Total	**$153.10**	**$146.20**	**$152.20**	**$142.40**	**$146.20**	**$740.10**

Figure 6-56 Data in a pivot table layout

If you have a spreadsheet that looks like the one shown above in Figure 6-56, you will appreciate how the Unpivot Column option can help you import this non table data into Power BI Desktop. This option is used to change the layout into one that Power BI Desktop supports. By support, I mean that the data will be changed to a layout that can be used to create a table or chart visualization. This data layout is often referred to as a **PIVOTED LAYOUT**. It does not lend itself to be used to create reports because the data is already pivoted (not in **TABULAR FORMAT**).

The unpivot options rearrange the layout of the data. The columns selected before either of these unpivot options are selected, are placed in the left most columns of the query. The other data is placed in the columns explained below. The **UNPIVOT COLUMNS** options create the following columns:

① The **ATTRIBUTE COLUMN** contains the data for each column heading in the data source.

② The **VALUE COLUMN** contains the data for each cell in the data source. The columns in the data source become rows, once the unpivot option is applied.

Unpivot Columns vs Unpivot Other Columns Options

Both options switch data from columns to rows. The difference between these options is that the Unpivot Other Columns option will also unpivot columns that are added to the query after the initial query is created.

For example, a spreadsheet currently has columns for January, February and March when you first import it. In the Query Editor, you would apply the Unpivot Other Columns option to the non month columns. When the query is refreshed, it has two more month columns, April and May. These new columns will automatically be unpivoted.

Exercise 6.6: Use Data In Non Tabular Format

This exercise will show you how to transform the data shown above in Figure 6-56 into a layout that Power BI Desktop supports.

Import The Data

1. Import the Stores table in the More Data Files workbook.
2. Delete the first two rows of data.
3. Click the Use First Rows as Headers button.

4. Delete the Total Column and Total Row. They are not needed for this exercise.

   The table should look like the one shown in Figure 6-57.

   Hold on, you are just a few clicks away from having the data in the correct layout to create visuals.

	Store	FY 2010	FY 2011	FY 2012	FY 2013	FY 2014
1	Atherton	19.7	17.1	18.3	14.8	19.8
2	Berkeley	14.4	18	16.4	16.7	19.3
3	Carmel-by-the-Sea	18.8	13.5	18.7	13.9	15.7
4	Cupertino	12	16.2	17.5	17.8	13.8
5	Fresno	19.2	15.6	19.6	15.9	14.4
6	Laguna Beach	18.9	14.6	16.7	12.1	13.9
7	Mailbu	18.7	17.8	14	18.5	13.7
8	Pasadena	17	19.4	17.1	17.3	17.3
9	San Francisco	14.4	14	13.9	15.4	18.3

Figure 6-57 Data in a pivoted layout

5. Save the file as `E6.6 Unpivot columns.`

Unpivot The Other Columns And Transform The Data

1. Duplicate the Stores query ⇒ Rename the query to `1 Yearly Sales.`

2. Right-click on the Store column and select **UNPIVOT OTHER COLUMNS.**

   Figure 6-58 shows some of the data.

   Now you can applaud <smile>.

	Store	Attribute	Value
1	Atherton	FY 2010	19.7
2	Atherton	FY 2011	17.1
3	Atherton	FY 2012	18.3
4	Atherton	FY 2013	14.8
5	Atherton	FY 2014	19.8
6	Berkeley	FY 2010	14.4

Figure 6-58 Data in an unpivoted layout

3. Rename the Attribute column to `Year` ⇒ Rename the Value column to `Year Total.`

Remove Part Of The Data In A Column

To make the Year column easier to work with, the letters FY and the space after it, need to be removed.

1. Right-click on the Year column header ⇒ Replace Values.

2. In the Value To Find field, type `FY`, then press the space bar, as shown in Figure 6-59 ⇒ Click OK. While you may have been tempted to rename the column heading in Excel, it would work the first time the data was imported. When the data is refreshed, the changes would not be there, if for no other reason then the person using the worksheet will probably change the heading back to the way it was. The table should look like the one shown in Figure 6-60.

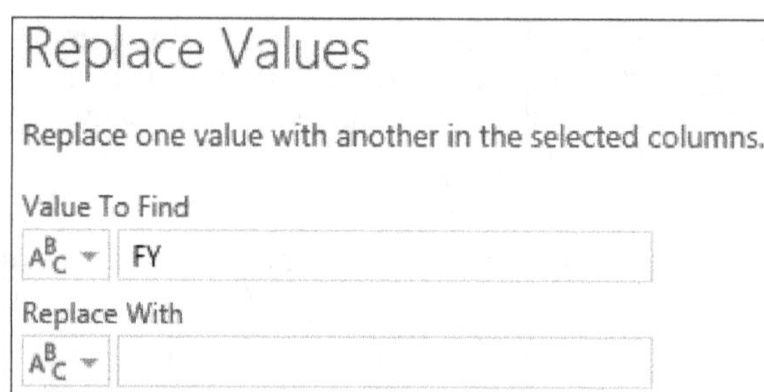

Figure 6-59 Replace Values criteria

	Store	Year	Year Total
1	Atherton	2010	19.7
2	Atherton	2011	17.1
3	Atherton	2012	18.3
4	Atherton	2013	14.8
5	Atherton	2014	19.8
6	Berkeley	2010	14.4

Figure 6-60 Data in the Year column modified

Create Averages In A Pivot Table Layout

Figure 6-57 shown earlier, displays data in a pivot table layout. If you have the need to display an average per row, in this case, an average per store, the steps below will show you how. The **LIST.AVERAGE FUNCTION** is used to calculate the average of the selected values in a row. If you are using your own data, start with step 3.

1. Duplicate the Yearly Sales query ⇒ Rename it to `2 Display Averages.`

2. Delete the Unpivoted Other Columns step and all steps after it.

3. Add Column tab ⇒ Add Custom Column button.

4. Create the formula shown in Figure 6-61. Don't forget to add the ({ }) brackets around the first and last column names. Figure 6-62 shows the average sales amount for each store.

It is not a requirement to use all of the columns in the formula.

You can pick and choose the columns that you want to create the average for.

Add Custom Column

New column name

StoreAverage

Custom column formula:

```
= List.Average({[FY 2010],[FY 2011],[FY 2012],[FY 2013],[FY
2014]})
```

Figure 6-61 Average formula

	Store	FY 2010	FY 2011	FY 2012	FY 2013	FY 2014	Store Average
1	Atherton	19.7	17.1	18.3	14.8	19.8	17.94
2	Berkeley	14.4	18	16.4	16.7	19.3	16.96
3	Carmel-by-the-Sea	18.8	13.5	18.7	13.9	15.7	16.12
4	Cupertino	12	16.2	17.5	17.8	13.8	15.46
5	Fresno	19.2	15.6	19.6	15.9	14.4	16.94
6	Laguna Beach	18.9	14.6	16.7	12.1	13.9	15.24
7	Mailbu	18.7	17.8	14	18.5	13.7	16.54
8	Pasadena	17	19.4	17.1	17.3	17.3	17.62
9	San Francisco	14.4	14	13.9	15.4	18.3	15.2

Figure 6-62 Average yearly sales amount per store

Refreshing The Data

Once the raw data has been changed to a table in Excel, the user should not remove the table characteristics, if the data needs to be refreshed in Power BI Desktop. More rows or columns can be added (to the table in Excel), as long as they are adjoining to the current table. If they add any data outside of the table in Excel, that needs to be refreshed, Power BI Desktop will not automatically include that data as part of the refresh process.

What happens if the spreadsheet shown earlier in Figure 6-56, now looks like the one shown in Figure 6-63.

The following changes were made to the spreadsheet.

	A	B	C	D	E	F	G	H
3	Store	FY 2010	FY 2011	FY 2012	FY 2013	FY 2014	FY 2015	Total
4	Atherton	$19.70	$17.10	$18.30	$14.80	$19.80	$24.50	$89.70
5	Berkeley	$14.40	$18.00	$16.40	$16.70	$19.30		$84.80
6	Carmel-by-the-Sea	$18.80	$13.50	$18.70	$13.90	$15.70	$17.20	$80.60
7	Cupertino	$12.00	$16.20	$17.50	$17.80	$13.80	$15.55	$77.30
8	Fresno	$19.20	$15.60	$19.60	$15.90	$14.40	$14.30	$84.70
9	Laguna Beach	$18.90	$14.60	$16.70	$12.10	$13.90	$16.20	$76.20
10	Los Angeles		$12.75				$130.00	
11	Mailbu	$18.70	$17.80	$14.00	$18.50	$13.70	$19.10	$82.70
12	Pasadena	$17.00	$19.40	$17.10	$17.30	$17.30	$18.8[illegible]	$88.10
13	Palm Springs						$[illegible].55	
14	San Francisco	$14.40	$14.00	$13.90	$15.40	$18.30		$76.00
15	Santa Barbara					$8.20	$9.19	
16	Total	$153.10	$158.95	$152.20	$142.40	$146.20		$740.10

Figure 6-63 Modified table in Excel

① Rows for the following cities are new: Los Angeles, Palm Springs and Santa Barbara.

② The column FY 2015 has been added to the worksheet, but it is not part of the table.

③ Some cells do not have a total.

How To Tell What Data Is Not Part Of The Table

The last cell in the table frame is cell F15, as illustrated above in Figure 6-63. The column does not have a Filter button.

Empty Cell Considerations

When the data is refreshed in Power BI Desktop, rows will not be created for cells that do not have data, when the data is unpivoted. For example, a row would not be created for Los Angeles 2010 or Berkeley 2015.

Figure 6-64 shows the data that was unpivoted for Los Angeles. This could make the reports created based on this data skewed. Also, people reading the reports may not notice that data is missing, which would be a problem. If you need rows to be created for every cell in the table, a zero needs to be added to the cells, that currently do not have data. The Total cells (column and rows) can remain empty in this scenario because they are not used in the Query Editor.

	Store	Attribute	1.2 Value
33	Laguna Beach	FY 2013	12.1
34	Laguna Beach	FY 2014	13.9
35	Laguna Beach	FY 2015	16.2
36	Los Angeles	FY 2011	12.75
37	Los Angeles	FY 2015	130

Figure 6-64 Unpivoted data for Los Angeles

What Is Metadata?

Metadata is data about other data. In the context of Power BI Desktop, this would be data that describes files in a folder.

For example, Windows Explorer can display any of the data shown in Figure 6-65 about files on the hard drive. Each field shown in the Details list, is a piece of metadata.

Metadata is often used with the Folder import option on the Get Data button in Power BI Desktop.

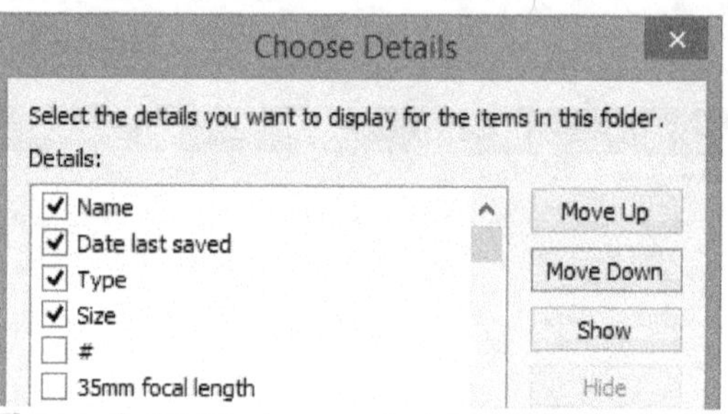

Figure 6-65 Windows metadata fields

Exercise 6.7: Import An Unlimited Number Of CSV Files From A Folder At One Time

If you have several files with the same file type and data structure, in a folder or folder/subfolder structure, Power BI Desktop can import and refresh all of them at the same time.

If you are of a particular age <smile>, you may have used the DOS command prompt to combine the contents of files that are in the same folder, by typing something like copy * .csv Newfilename.csv.

This exercise will show you how to complete the same task of appending data from several CSV files into one file, in Power BI Desktop. You may find this exercise helpful if you have data that is sent to you on a regular basis, like daily sales or monthly invoice data. Instead of manually appending them one by one, using the Append Queries as New option, never mind formatting each files columns, you can set up a query to import each file, filter out file types in the folder that you do not want to import, format columns and much more.

Once the initial query is set up and works the way that you need it to, with the click of a button, new files can be imported, transformed and appended to the main table. As you will see, the end result of importing several files from a folder is another way to append data. There are five main steps to setting up a query that will import CSV files from a folder or subfolder, to create one large table.

This exercise uses CSV files. The same steps can be used with .txt files. While this exercise uses CSV files that are on your hard drive, you can use CSV files that are on the web or a server, as long as they are in the same folder.

Just a word of caution, the steps in this exercise will not work with Excel files. The next exercise covers importing multiple Excel files. I did not test this exercise on any other file type.

Step 1: Select The Folder With The Data

The goal of this step is to select the folder that will be used by the query to get the files from. This folder should already be in the location that you need and have the name that you want. If the folder name or location needs to be changed later, the query will have to be modified. If you need to import files from different folders, you should create a parameter that has a list of folders that has files that you need to import.

1. Open a new file ⇒ Get Data button ⇒ More ⇒ Select the Folder option.

2. Click the Browse button ⇒ Select the invoice import files folder, in your folder.

   You should have the options shown in Figure 6-66 ⇒ Click OK ⇒ Click Edit.

Figure 6-66 Folder that has the files to import

3. Save the file as `E6.7 Import csv files from a folder.`

Understanding The Folder Query Results

You should see the files shown in Figure 6-67. As you can see, there are files in the folder that are not CSV files. That is okay, because the other file types can be filtered out. I purposely added non CSV files to the folder, to demonstrate how to filter out other file types.

As hard as you try, if other people are suppose to place files in the import folder, at some point, someone will place a file in the folder that has a different file type. That would cause the query to fail, if you do not set up a filter to exclude other file types.

Each row shown in Figure 6-67 represents a table. The **CONTENT COLUMN** stores a link to the data for the file in the Name column. In the Content column, clicking on the word **BINARY**, will import the data in the associated table into the query.

The button next to the Content column heading is called the **COMBINE BUTTON**. When this button is clicked, the Query Editor will try to combine all of the data in all of the binary files displayed in this query, into one table. This is done by importing and appending the data, hopefully, error free <smile>.

For this to work, the files must be the same type and the fields should be in the same order. If the fields are not in the same order, the data can still be combined, but it can be difficult to clean up the data.

The **COMBINE BINARIES BUTTON** on the Home tab in the Query Editor, works the same as the Combine button on the Content column, shown in Figure 6-67.

The **EXTENSION COLUMN** displays the extension for the file.

The **DATE MODIFIED** column will be helpful if you need to know when the file (in the Name column) was last saved.

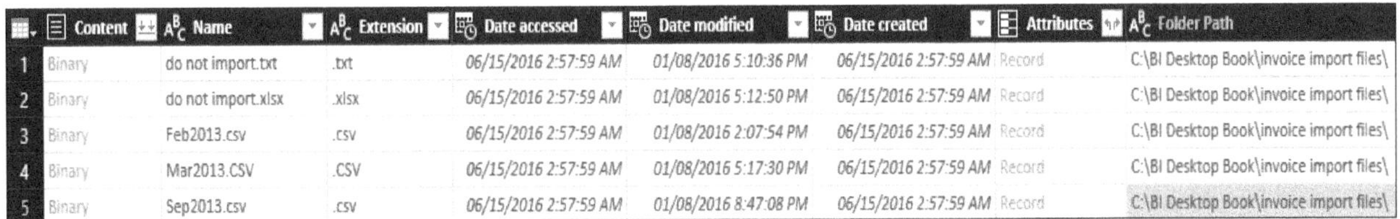

	Content	Name	Extension	Date accessed	Date modified	Date created	Attributes	Folder Path
1	Binary	do not import.txt	.txt	06/15/2016 2:57:59 AM	01/08/2016 5:10:36 PM	06/15/2016 2:57:59 AM	Record	C:\BI Desktop Book\invoice import files\
2	Binary	do not import.xlsx	.xlsx	06/15/2016 2:57:59 AM	01/08/2016 5:12:50 PM	06/15/2016 2:57:59 AM	Record	C:\BI Desktop Book\invoice import files\
3	Binary	Feb2013.csv	.csv	06/15/2016 2:57:59 AM	01/08/2016 2:07:54 PM	06/15/2016 2:57:59 AM	Record	C:\BI Desktop Book\invoice import files\
4	Binary	Mar2013.CSV	.CSV	06/15/2016 2:57:59 AM	01/08/2016 5:17:30 PM	06/15/2016 2:57:59 AM	Record	C:\BI Desktop Book\invoice import files\
5	Binary	Sep2013.csv	.csv	06/15/2016 2:57:59 AM	01/08/2016 8:47:08 PM	06/15/2016 2:57:59 AM	Record	C:\BI Desktop Book\invoice import files\

Figure 6-67 List of files in the folder

Step 2: Prepare The Files To Be Combined

This step will show you have to create a filter that only selects a specific file type.

The query name cannot be the same as any table name or folder name used in the query.

1. Display the Extension column filter options ⇒ Select both CSV extensions, as shown in Figure 6-68.

   As shown above in Figure 6-67, one file has the CSV extension in all caps, which really is not correct.

   I would force all extensions to be lower case, but I am trying not to bog you down with too many steps. <smile>

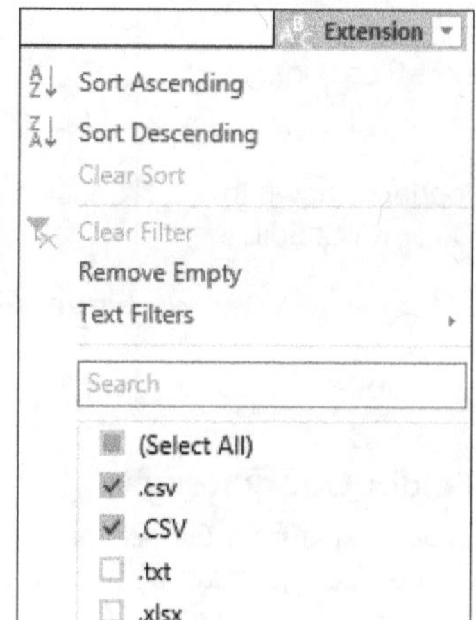

Figure 6-68 Filter options for the file type

2. Rename the query to `Import Invoices.`

If your folder initially only had files with the file type that you wanted to import, using the Extension column filter option would not work. The reason is because when the filter only has one item to filter on, the **(SELECT ALL)** option stays enabled by default. With the (Select All) option being selected, all file types would be acceptable and would appear in the list of tables, just like what was shown above in Figure 6-68. On your own, if this is the case, follow the steps below to force the filter to only select the file type that you want. You would do this after completing step one above.

1. Right-click on the Extension column header ⇒ Transform ⇒ Lowercase. This step is optional, if it does not apply to your data files. It changes the extension to be lowercase. Remember, **TEXT FILTERS ARE CASE SENSITIVE.**
2. Open the Extension column filter ⇒ Text Filters ⇒ Equals ⇒ On the dialog box shown in Figure 6-69, type the extension, including the period before the letters in the field, as illustrated ⇒ Click OK.

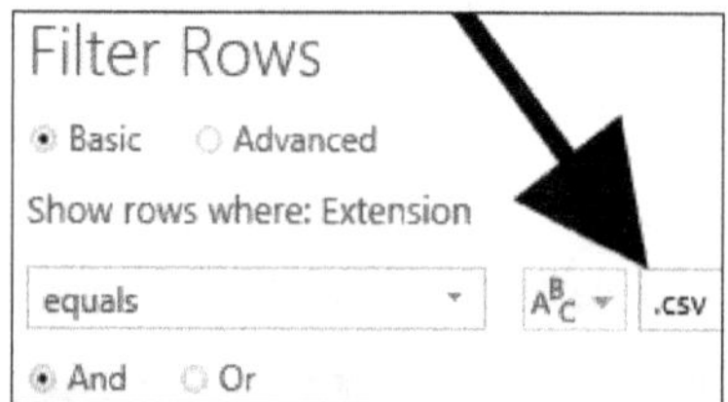

Figure 6-69 Options to force the filter to use a specific file extension

Step 3: Import And Transform The Data

The transformations that are applied, depend on the data. Sometimes you will need to rename columns, change the data or add columns.

1. Click the Content column **COMBINE BUTTON** ⇒ 356 rows of data will be imported. The first few rows are shown in Figure 6-70. This is the data in the three CSV files in the folder. You should have the steps shown in Figure 6-71. Pretty good for not writing code, huh? Yes, I know what you are thinking, because I am thinking the same thing: "Why can't this work the same way for all file types?" All I can say is, maybe one day.

	Column1	Column2	Column3	Column4
1	Invoice Nbr	Order ID	Date	Amount
2	1	1303	02/18/2013	$1,505.10
3	2	1312	02/19/2013	$789.51
4	3	1313	02/19/2013	$3,479.70

Figure 6-70 First few rows of the imported data

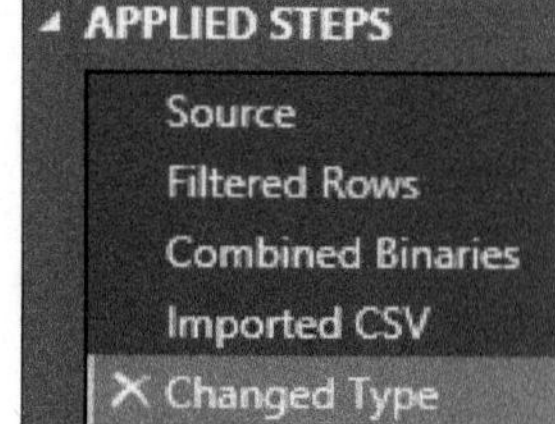

Figure 6-71 Applied steps after the import

Notice the formula for the Changed Type step. It contains what Power BI Desktop thinks the data type is for each column of data that was imported. I prefer to select the data types manually, as the actual data on future imports is based on this criteria and may also need to be converted. I have noticed that when the first row of data is not used as the column headings, like what is shown above in Figure 6-70, that at least some of the data types that were selected are not correct.

Before you boo me for adding a step, remember that the data type only has to be changed now. Going forward, the same data types that are applied now, override what Power BI Desktop thinks the data type is, when more data is imported.

2. Delete the Changed Type step.

3. Home tab ⇒ Click the Use First Row As Headers button.

4. Home tab ⇒ Remove Rows ⇒ Remove Blank Rows.

5. Rename the Date column to `Inv Date` ⇒ Rename the Amount column to `Inv Amount`.

6. Right-click on the Invoice Nbr column ⇒ Change Type ⇒ Whole Number.

7. Change the data types for the columns in Table 6-4.

Column	Change The Data Type To . . .
Order ID	Whole Number
Inv Date	[See Figure 6-72]

Table 6-4 Columns to change the data type of

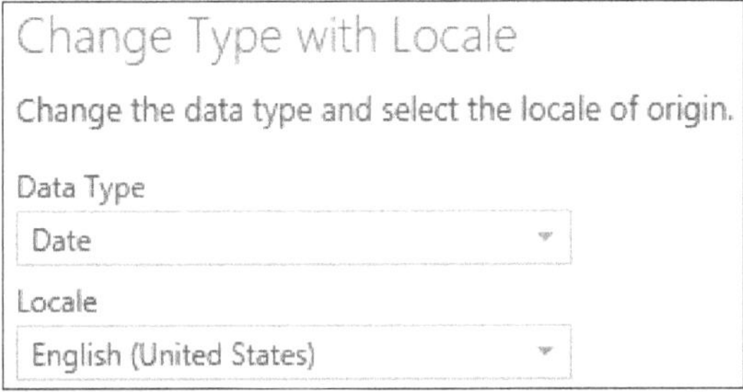

Figure 6-72 Inv Date column change type options

8. Apply the pending changes.

Keep in mind that if more files are added to the folder and the Refresh button is clicked, the files that were added to the folder will automatically be imported also. This is why creating a filter for the file type to be imported is important. If someone adds files that have a different file type, like .pdf for example, to the folder, the import would fail.

Step 4: If Necessary, Fix The Errors

This step is only needed if the imported data generates errors. Most of the time, so much data is imported that the rows with errors are not displayed in the Query Editor. I don't know about you, but I prefer to see the rows that have errors, before trying to resolve the problem. Seeing them first, I can decide if the data can or should be fixed in the data source and re-imported or if the rows should be deleted in the data source. That will prevent them from being imported the next time the data is refreshed. The other option is to determine if the data can be cleaned in the Query Editor. This is one instance when the **KEEP ERRORS OPTION** will be helpful.

Ideally, when trying to automate a data import, it is better to have the errors fixed in the data source. Otherwise, every time the data is imported, you will have to check for errors, which defeats automating the data import process. A query could be created to display rows that have the word "Error" in any column. If the query does not display any data, no errors were generated during the import. That does not mean that the data does not have to be cleaned. If you scroll down the query to row 49, you will see that the row has errors. In this exercise, row 49 is column headings from a file that was imported.

1. Home tab ⇒ Keep Rows button ⇒ Keep Errors. You will see the data shown in Figure 6-73.

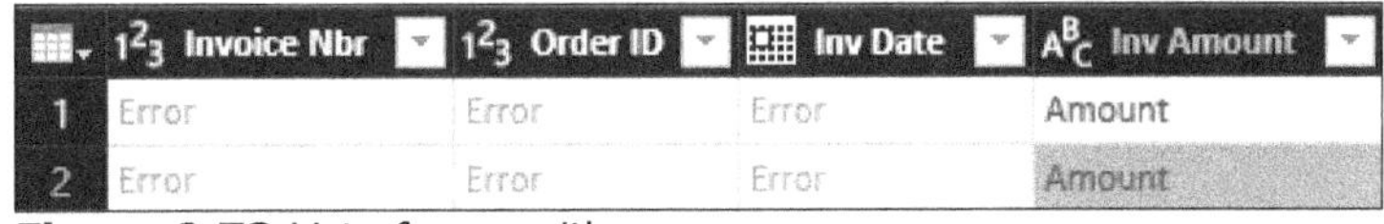

	Invoice Nbr	Order ID	Inv Date	Inv Amount
1	Error	Error	Error	Amount
2	Error	Error	Error	Amount

Figure 6-73 List of rows with errors

Clicking on an Error link shown in Figure 6-73, will display what the error is, as shown in Figure 6-74. Every Error link that you click on in Figure 6-73, will add a step, which you will need to delete, once you figure out what to do with each row of data that has an error. For this exercise, the rows with errors can be deleted.

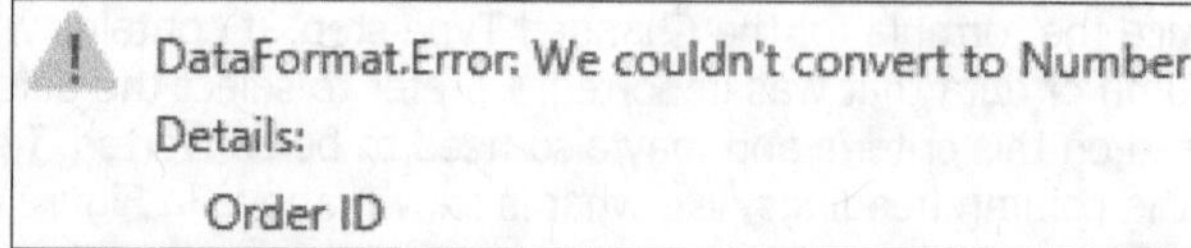

Figure 6-74 Error message

On my own, I add a column to each table that is imported. The column contains the table name. I do this to make it easier to know which table the error is in. When the import is done and there are no errors, I delete the file name column, right before I load the data to the data model. On your own, you will find what works best for you.

2. Delete all steps after the Changed Type with Locale step.

3. Click on the last step ⇒ Home tab ⇒ Remove Rows button ⇒ Remove Errors.

Step 5: Import Data From Other Folders

The files that were imported so far in this exercise were in the Invoice import files folder. I am sure by now, that you have seen the four folders that have a year in their name. If you moved those folders under the Invoice import files folder, guess what? The query that you created in this exercise would import the files in those folders, the next time the query is refreshed.

Yes, if you were doing this on your own, those four folders may have been moved into the Invoice import files folder before you started creating the query. I left them out on purpose so that you could see how the **FOLDER OPTION** works. It is also possible that you may have the need to set up sub folders also, and this part of the exercise would serve as the template, if you will, of what to do. On your own, this step is optional.

1. In Windows Explorer, display your folder ⇒ Drag/move the four (year) Invoices folders into the invoice import files folder, as shown in Figure 6-75.

Figure 6-75 Structure to have files in multiple folders imported at the same time

2. Open the Query Editor ⇒ Refresh the Import Invoices query. The lower left corner of the window should display that there are more than 999 rows. To be exact, there are 1,734 rows. The reason that I know the exact number of rows is because I created all of the files that were imported <smile>.

Group The Data From The Tables

It would be great to be able to see the data from all of the tables. In this part of the exercise you will group the data.

1. Duplicate the Import Invoices query ⇒ Rename the duplicated query to `1 Invoices grouped by year`.

2. Duplicate the Inv Date column ⇒ Rename it to `Inv Year` ⇒ Right-click on the column ⇒ Transform ⇒ Year ⇒ Year.

3. Change the Inv Amount column data type, to Fixed Decimal Number.

4. Home tab ⇒ Group By button ⇒ Change the Group By field to Inv Year.

5. Rename the Count column name to `Nbr of Invoices`.

6. Add a column named `Total $ For Year` ⇒ Select the Sum operation ⇒ Select the Inv Amount column.

   The table should look like the one shown in Figure 6-76.

	Inv Y...	Number of Invoices	Total $ For Year
1	2013	484	748402.13
2	2014	712	1295045.44
3	2015	228	385715.57
4	2016	310	483600.83

Figure 6-76 Invoices grouped by year

View How The Steps Change The Data

There will probably be things about the data that you import that are not easily seen. Changing the data type can cause errors. The steps below show you how to spot an error and show you how you can prevent it from being an error. This is especially helpful if there are a lot of tables that will be imported.

1. Duplicate the Import Invoices query ⇒ Rename the query to `2 Fix potential errors.`

2. Click on the Renamed Columns step ⇒ Scroll down to view row 49.

As shown in Figure 6-77, the row has column headings. Unless you can get the people that add files to the import folder to be consistent, things like this will happen. It is better for you to be proactive.

	Invoice Nbr	Order ID	Inv Date	Inv Amount
48	48	1375	02/28/2013	$1,529.70
49	Invoice Nbr	Order ID	Date	Amount
50	6418	1122	03/03/2013	$1,025.40

Figure 6-77 Rename Columns step data

Row 49 contains the column headings for one of the files that was imported and appended. Each file that was imported could have its own header row. It is also possible that some files that are imported from the folder do not have headings.

The best solution that I can think of is to add a step to remove rows that are headings from files that are imported. It is probably a good idea to do this so that if there are other errors, you do not delete them by mistake. When new tables are added or the data is refreshed, rows that have column headings will be filtered out.

Using the **REMOVE ERRORS OPTION**, deletes rows regardless of what the error is and it is possible that none of the steps that you create, will generate an error for the additional header rows. Using the Remove Errors option should be your last resort. Also remember that the Query Editor does not display all of the data, meaning you cannot see all of the data. And even if all of the data was displayed, do you really want to view thousands of rows of data?

3. Click on the Changed Type step. As you see, after the data type was changed for the Invoice Nbr and Order ID columns (look in the formula bar), errors were generated for these columns. Based on the data changes, the best place to insert a step is after the Renamed Columns step.

4. Click on the Renamed Columns step ⇒ In row 49, right-click on the Invoice Nbr cell ⇒ Text Filters ⇒ Does Not Contain ⇒ Click the Insert button to create the step. Now, when the data is refreshed and more tables are added, if they have "Invoice Nbr" in the column, the row will be filtered out.

5. Rename the Filtered Rows 1 step to `Remove column heading rows`. This will help in the future if there is another problem, because I look at the renamed steps first.

Exercise 6.8: Import An Unlimited Number Of Excel Files From A Folder At One Time

The previous exercise showed you how to import CSV files that are in the same folder. This exercise will do the same for Excel files. The difference is that a function needs to be created. The good news is that most of the function can be created by using the macro (M language) functionality that is built-in Power BI Desktop.

To import multiple Excel files successfully, **THE TAB (WORKSHEET) IN EACH WORKBOOK THAT WILL BE IMPORTED, HAS TO HAVE THE SAME NAME.** If you need to know which workbook each row of data comes from, you can create a new column on each worksheet, that includes the name of the workbook that the data comes from.

Load An Excel File

1. Open a new file ⇒ Get Data button ⇒ Excel ⇒ Select any Excel file in the Import_Excel folder.

2. On the Navigator window, check the Load File table ⇒ Click the Edit button. (Load File is the name of the tab that all workbooks have, that will be imported.) On your own, you can name the tab what you want in Excel, before you import the worksheet.

On your own, at this point, you should do any or all of the following, as needed:

☑ Rename the query ☑ Create calculations
☑ Transform the data ☑ Any task that you want to be applied to all tables that will be imported

3. Rename the query to `fn_loadfiles`.

Function Naming Conventions
fn is a prefix that is often used to indicate that the query is a function. Using a prefix is optional. (And yes, fn is suppose to be all lower case <smile>)

Create The Function That Will Select The Files To Load

In this part of the exercise, you will modify the M code (macro) to change it to a function.

1. Home or View tab ⇒ Advanced Editor. You will see the dialog box shown in Figure 6-78. On your own, you will see more lines of code if you performed any of the tasks listed above step 3 in the previous section.

fn_loadfiles

```
let
    Source = Excel.Workbook(File.Contents("C:\BI Desktop Book\import_excel\Jun2014.xlsx"), null, true),
    LoadFile_Sheet = Source{[Item="LoadFile",Kind="Sheet"]}[Data],
    #"Promoted Headers" = Table.PromoteHeaders(LoadFile_Sheet),
    #"Changed Type" = Table.TransformColumnTypes(#"Promoted Headers",{{"Invoice Nbr", Int64.Type}, {"Order ID", Int64.Type}, {"Date",
in
    #"Changed Type"
```

Figure 6-78 Code before the changes

2. Add a blank line at the top of the window ⇒ Type the line of code shown in Figure 6-79.

   The => is a tag that indicates that you are creating a function.

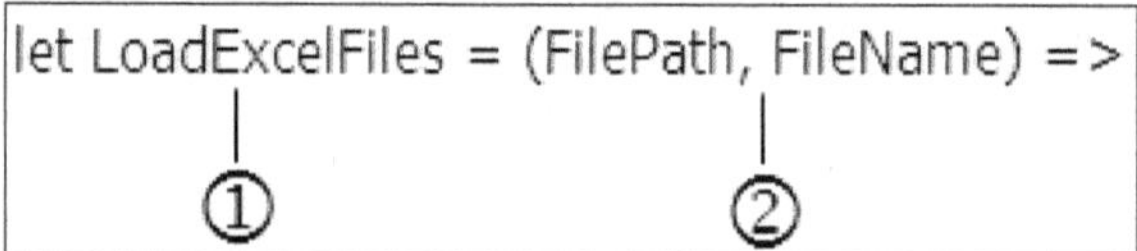

Figure 6-79 First line of M code to create the function

The illustrated parts of the code are explained below.

① This is the function name, which can be whatever you want.

② The **FILEPATH ARGUMENT** will be passed the folder name that the Excel files are in, that you want to import. The **FILENAME ARGUMENT** is a place holder for the name of the Excel files that have the data that will be imported.

3. On the Source line, replace "C:\BI Desktop . . . with `FilePath&FileName`, as illustrated below in Figure 6-80.

4. After the last line of code, type `in LoadExcelFiles`.

   This tag (line of code) indicates that this is the end of the function.

   Figure 6-80 illustrates the changes that you should have made to the code.

fn_loadfiles

```
let LoadExcelFiles = (FilePath, FileName) =>
let
    Source = Excel.Workbook(File.Contents(FilePath&FileName), null, true),
    LoadFile_Sheet = Source{[Item="LoadFile",Kind="Sheet"]}[Data],
    #"Promoted Headers" = Table.PromoteHeaders(LoadFile_Sheet),
    #"Changed Type" = Table.TransformColumnTypes(#"Promoted Headers",{{"In
in
    #"Changed Type"

in LoadExcelFiles
```

Figure 6-80 Modified M code for the function

5. Click Done ⇒ Apply the pending changes.

   You should see the parameters shown in Figure 6-81, for the function that you just created.

   Because the function will pass the data to the parameters, you will not actually see the parameters during the process of importing the files in this exercise. On your own, you could run the function and use the parameters to get the path to the files that you want to import.

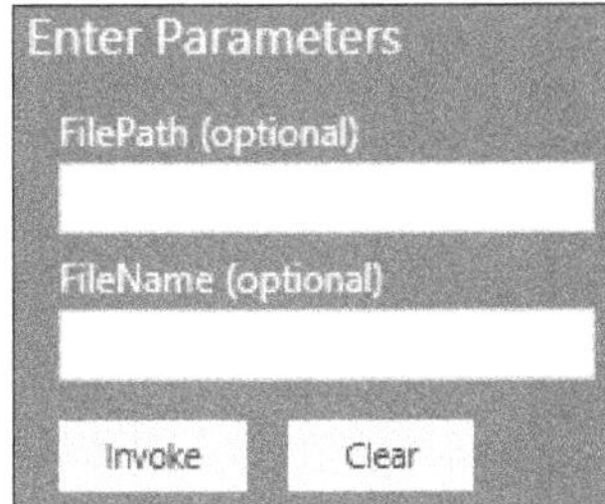

Figure 6-81 Parameters for the function

This type of query is known as a **QUERY FUNCTION**. If you have used a programming language like Visual Basic, the concept of one query calling/using another query will be familiar.

6. Save the file as `E6.8 Function to load Excel files`.

Create The Query To Import The Workbook Files

In this part of the exercise you will create a query that will use the function that you just created. You will create a formula that will pass the folder path and file name fields to the function.

This is the query that you will run to the import the Excel files. If you find that you need to import workbooks that have the same tab as the one used in the function, but are in a different folder (location), duplicate the query in this part of the exercise, open the Advanced Editor and change the path. If you can copy or move the workbooks to the folder used in the current function, you do not have to duplicate the query. The other option is to create a parameter that has a list of folders that have the Excel files to import.

1. Get Data button ⇒ More ⇒ Folder ⇒ On the Folder dialog box, select the import_excel folder ⇒ Click Edit. You will see the query shown in Figure 6-82.

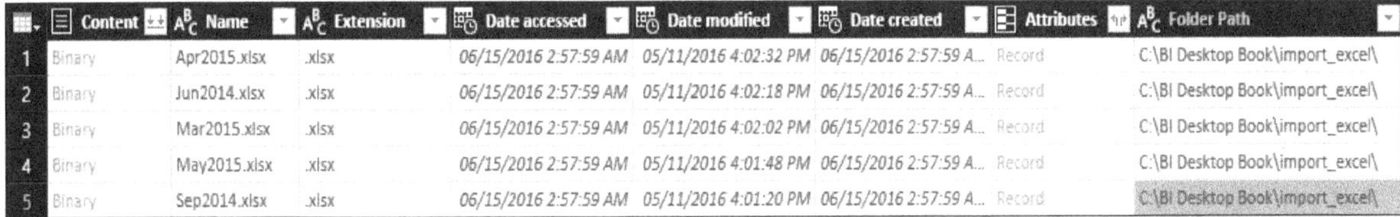

	Content	Name	Extension	Date accessed	Date modified	Date created	Attributes	Folder Path
1	Binary	Apr2015.xlsx	.xlsx	06/15/2016 2:57:59 AM	05/11/2016 4:02:32 PM	06/15/2016 2:57:59 A...	Record	C:\BI Desktop Book\import_excel\
2	Binary	Jun2014.xlsx	.xlsx	06/15/2016 2:57:59 AM	05/11/2016 4:02:18 PM	06/15/2016 2:57:59 A...	Record	C:\BI Desktop Book\import_excel\
3	Binary	Mar2015.xlsx	.xlsx	06/15/2016 2:57:59 AM	05/11/2016 4:02:02 PM	06/15/2016 2:57:59 A...	Record	C:\BI Desktop Book\import_excel\
4	Binary	May2015.xlsx	.xlsx	06/15/2016 2:57:59 AM	05/11/2016 4:01:48 PM	06/15/2016 2:57:59 A...	Record	C:\BI Desktop Book\import_excel\
5	Binary	Sep2014.xlsx	.xlsx	06/15/2016 2:57:59 AM	05/11/2016 4:01:20 PM	06/15/2016 2:57:59 A...	Record	C:\BI Desktop Book\import_excel\

Figure 6-82 Query with all of the files in the folder to import

   The previous exercise demonstrated how to make sure that the only files imported are ones that have a specific file extension. On your own, you may want to incorporate that functionality into any Folder query that you set up. As Excel supports two file extensions, the filter should include the .xls and .xlsx options.

2. Add Column tab ⇒ Add Custom Column button ⇒ Create the formula shown in Figure 6-83 ⇒ Click OK.

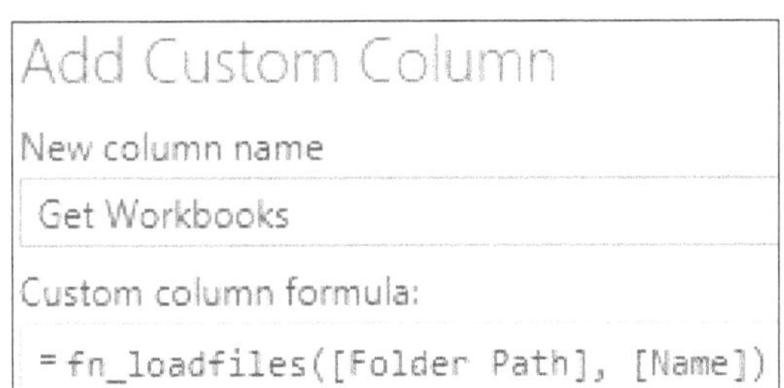

Figure 6-83 Formula that calls the function to get the files in the folder

3. In the Import_Excel query, click the button at the end of the Get Workbooks column header ⇒ Clear the check mark for the Use original column option on the Expand window ⇒ Click OK. You will see that the columns of data from the tab in the Excel workbooks have been added to the query. On your own, you do not have to import all of the columns.

4. Perform any tasks that are needed to get the data ready for analysis. Below are some examples.

   ☑ Delete the columns of data that are not needed, like the ones shown earlier in Figure 6-82.
   ☑ Rearrange the remaining columns as needed.
   ☑ Rename the query.

Summary

This chapter covered using the merge and append options, to help get the data ready to be analyzed. The Group By dialog box was used to create calculations that are often needed for analysis purposes. Knowing how to unpivot data is important when working with data that does not come from a database.

One reason some exercises contained multiple queries is to emulate what would be needed for different analysis and reporting requests for the same dataset.

As the last chapter in this book dedicated specifically to the Query Editor, I wanted to include more real life scenarios of the types of transformations that you could encounter. Hopefully, you have a good understanding of the Query Editor and how it can be used to import data and get the data ready for the analysis step of the process. I hope that you have enjoyed learning about the Query Editor and are ready to learn about the views in the Power BI Desktop workspace.

USING THE RELATIONSHIPS VIEW

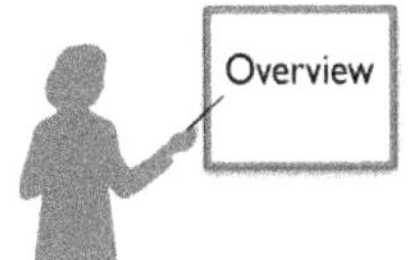

After completing this chapter you will:

- ☑ Understand relationships and how to create them
- ☑ Know how to use the Relationships view
- ☑ Know what the data model is and it's role in Power BI Desktop

CHAPTER 7

What Is A Data Model?

This topic was briefly covered in Chapter 1, but it needs further discussion, because it is a key component of using Power BI Desktop. A data model is a way to create a relational database, if you will, inside a Power BI Desktop report file. When using Power BI Desktop, imported tables can be added to the data model. So yes, you have already created a data model.

A data model is a group of tables and their relationships. Relationships allow data from different tables to be used to create one chart. This is possible without having to use the **VLOOKUP FUNCTION** in Excel or the Merge options in the Query Editor. Figure 7-1 shows tables in a data model.

While the data in a data model can come from queries created in the Query Editor, it is not a requirement, because the data can also be added to the model by creating tables, using the **ENTER DATA OPTION**. Data can also be imported from the data model in Excel workbooks. Keep in mind, that each report file can only have one data model.

In my opinion, the biggest benefit of putting data in the data model is that the data model can support millions of rows of data, which is often needed for analysis, while an Excel worksheet has a maximum of 1,048,576 rows. Another benefit of the data model is that calculations are processed faster because the data in a data model is loaded into the computers memory (RAM).

Other benefits of using a data model include:

① Saves disk space because an efficient data compression algorithm is used to store data.
② Supports complex calculations.
③ Data models support KPI's and hierarchies.

When viewed, a data model contains tables with lines between them that point to the field (in the table) that they have in common. These lines represent the relationships between the tables. Figure 7-1, displays a data model that includes the Orders, Orders Detail, Customer, Order Subtotals and Employee tables and their relationships.

Data modeling is an important concept to understand because even though the relationships that are imported with tables from a database are saved in the data model, relationships are not automatically created from data that is imported from other file types, like spreadsheets and text files.

What Is The Star Schema?

Hopefully, now that you have a better understanding of data models, it is time to clearly define what the data model will be used for. Data models are used for storing, analyzing and reporting on data. The three **SCHEMA TYPES** for data models are:

① **STAR** Has one level of **CHILD TABLES**.
② **SNOWFLAKE** Can have multiple levels of child tables. Some people say that this schema can cause performance issues because of the increased number of relationships. My advice is to try it and see for yourself.
③ **CONSTELLATION** Is used when there is more than one fact table.

The Star schema has what is called a **FACT TABLE** (the **PARENT** or **PRIMARY TABLE** in the data model). My personal preference is the Star schema, because it handles large datasets. That, and it is easy to understand.

The primary table is surrounded by the other tables in the data model, forming, you guessed it, a star, as shown in Figure 7-1. This is also known as **DIMENSIONAL MODELING** because it describes the logical way that data should be structured to obtain the best performance.

The arrows on the link line between tables, point in the direction of the relationship. The number "1", on the link line, indicates that the field used to create the link, has unique values. The asterisk * on the link line, indicates the "many" table in the relationship.

The Orders table is the fact table in this figure. It is not a requirement to arrange the tables in this layout in the Relationships view. On your own, if you are not sure which table is the fact table, create the relationships for the tables and see which table has the most relationships. More than likely, the table with the most relationships with other tables is the fact table.

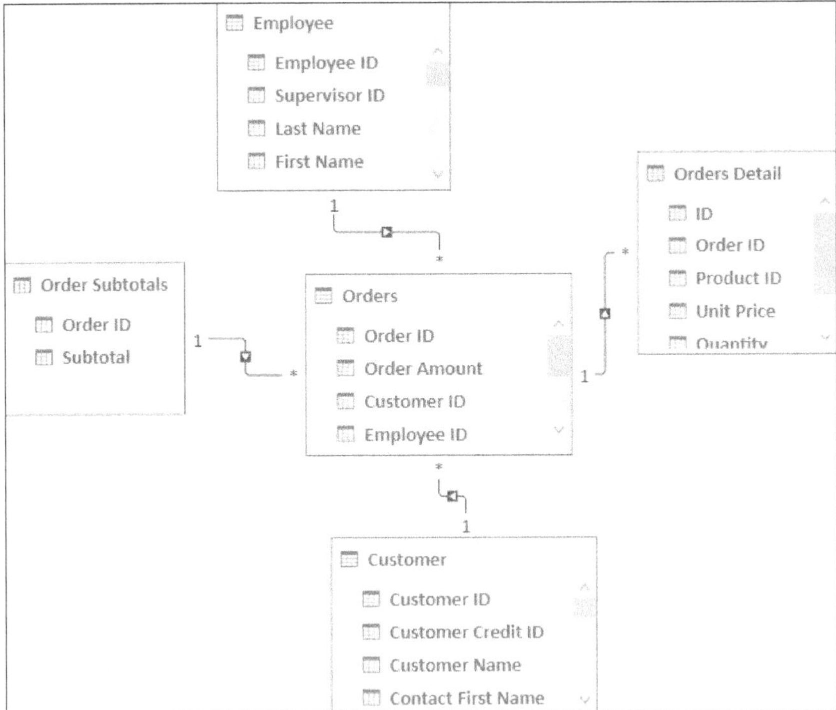

Figure 7-1 Star schema

The fact table usually has some or all of the following characteristics:

① It has measurable data, meaning that it will answer a question. For example, the Orders table has an order amount. This field could be used to answer which five states have the most sales.
② Other tables are linked to it.
③ It has one or more date fields, which confirm when something happened, like when the order was placed or the date of each basketball game.
④ Fact tables usually have more of rows of data, then any other table in the data model. (Date tables are not included when determining the fact table, because they do not contain data that will be analyzed).

The other tables (known as the **DIMENSION** or **CHILD TABLE**) in the schema contain supporting data, if you will, that provide additional information about a field in the fact table. For example, in Figure 7-1 above, the Customer table contains information on who placed each order. The Order Details table contains the items for each order. Notice that each dimension table is linked to the fact table and none of the dimension tables are linked to each other.

Dimension tables can be linked to each other. An example would be adding a Products table to the schema in Figure 7-1. It would be linked to the Orders Detail table, using the Product ID field. That would allow the product name to be displayed on the report. If the schema rules were strictly followed, adding the Product table would make the star schema shown above in Figure 7-1, a Snowflake schema, because the Product table does not have a direct relationship with the fact table (the Orders table).

Supported Data Types In The Data Model

Chapter 5 explained the supported data types in Power BI Desktop. This section provides more detail about the data types and how they are mapped to the data types that DAX supports. The data model supports the data types listed in the first column in Table 7-1. The first column in the table is how the data is "classified". The second column in the table is how DAX classifies data.

The data model does not support all of the data types that some databases use. This means that some columns of data may not be displayed in the Navigator window and that they may not be imported. While some databases support more than one variation of a data type listed in the first column, the data model does not. If the original data type for the field is similar to one in the table, it will be mapped to a data type in the first column in Table 7-1.

Data Type	DAX Data Type	Description
Text	String	Usually contains text. Dates and numbers are displayed as text in this data type.
Decimal Number	64-bit real number	Positive and negative numbers with or without a decimal point. Zero is also a decimal number.
Whole Number	64-bit integer	Positive and negative numbers without a decimal point.
Date	Date/Time	DAX only supports dates and times on or after January 1, 1900.
Fixed Decimal Number	Currency	Currency values are imported into the currency format that the computer is set to use. This could produce different or unexpected results from one computer to the next.
True/False	Boolean	A true or false value.
(Not available)	Blank	In DAX, this data type replaces SQL null values.

Table 7-1 Data model supported data types explained

Importing Comment And Note Fields
At some point, you will come across a table or file that has a comment or note field. As these fields are not normally used to create a visualization, you should not import them because this type of field will take up unnecessary space in the data model. This field type also prohibits the engine behind the data model from doing the job that it was intended to do.

Data Type Tips
① If all of the data in a column cannot be converted to any of the other data types in Table 7-1, the column defaults to the **ANY DATA TYPE**, that was covered in Chapter 5.
② It is a good idea to check the data type of the fields after the import, especially fields that will be used in a formula. Data that "looks" like it is a certain data type, may not actually be defined with the data type needed for calculations.

Importing Data From A Database

Importing data from a database is a popular way to add data to the data model. In addition to tables, databases can use queries to add data to a table. Views and stored procedures are other ways to import data from a database. Views and stored procedures retrieve a subset of the data that is in the tables in the database, instead of retrieving all of the records, in all of the tables in the database.

For example, there could be a view that only retrieves orders from specific states. **UNLIKE TABLES, VIEWS AND STORED PROCEDURES DO NOT STORE DATA.** They contain code that specifies which records should be retrieved or in the case of Power BI Desktop, which records should be imported. If you find that you are using the same criteria over and over to remove data from the same dataset in the Query Editor, each time you import the data, you can create a view or stored procedure in the database. This will save you time when importing data from the database because you do not have to manually create criteria in the Query Editor, to filter out data that you do not need. Views and stored procedures are discussed in more detail in the next two sections.

Views

Views are usually created by a Database Administrator, report designer or someone that has administrator rights to the database. Views are used to get data from a variety of tables and combine the data into a "view". This makes it easier to only access the data that you need.

A view is a **RECORDSET** (the result) of a query and usually retrieves a subset of the data in a data source. Views are stored in the database and are like tables, but they do not have the physical characteristics of a table. For example, records cannot be added to or deleted from a view. Fields cannot be added to a view unless the query that creates the view is modified to include more fields. The field length cannot be changed in a view, like it can in a table.

Views are useful if you use the sorting, grouping and data selection (filter) options in the Query Editor. Views are created when the same recordset, calculation or query needs to be used in several reports or in the case of Power BI Desktop, several charts or dashboards. Using a view means that you would not have to select the same options over and over again, in the Query Editor, each time that you import data. Instead of selecting all of the tables, fields and options in Power BI Desktop, select the view in the database, instead of the individual tables, when importing the data.

Tables vs Views

When possible, using views is preferred over using tables. There are some differences between importing tables and views, as described below.

① Tables already have relationships that Power BI Desktop recognizes, when the tables are imported.
② In views, the tables have already been joined for you, so you may not need to create relationships, unless you need to use a date table.
③ Once a view is imported, you can see how the tables are linked (or not linked), as well as, the actual data, if you have the rights to open a view in design mode.
④ Imported views usually have cleaner data because they only include the fields that are needed, the data is usually filtered when the view is created.

Stored Procedures

Stored Procedures contain queries that are more complex then views, but less complex than commands.

The majority of the time, stored procedures are created by a DBA or programmer. Figure 7-2 shows the views and stored procedures in a database.

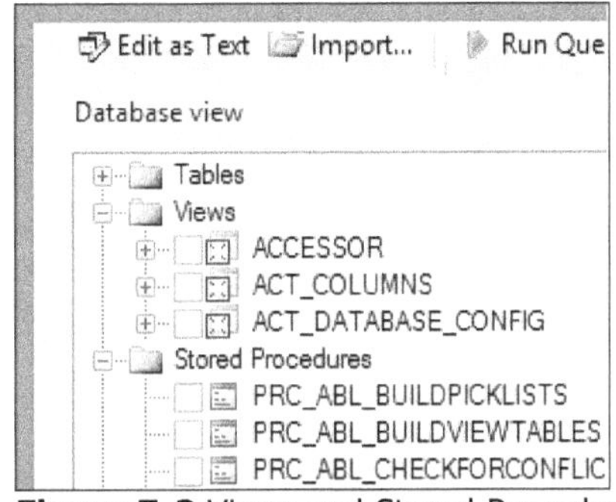

Figure 7-2 Views and Stored Procedures in a database

What Is A Relationship?

In order to be able to use the tables (in a report file) together, to create a report, there has to be a connection between the tables. The actual connection is called a **LINK**. The result of a link between tables is called a **RELATIONSHIP**. The ability to create relationships between tables and use the data from multiple tables to create one visualization, may be the number one reason that many people will use Power BI Desktop.

Relationships are created between a column of data that two tables have in common. Relationships between tables also allow for a higher level of analysis. Data in one table can be filtered by data in another table, which provides even more flexibility and control over the data that is displayed on a report.

Relational Databases

The reason that tables can have relationships created between them is because there is at least one column of data in each table that has related data, thus the term "Relational Databases". Yes, this is a complicated topic and there are a lot of books on the concepts associated with relational databases and how to create them, so I won't bore you with all of the details, but please hear me out and don't skip this section. Creating relationships in Power BI Desktop and creating relationships in a database have a lot in common.

While databases are not the primary focus of this chapter, it is important that you understand a little more than the fundamentals. My goal is to explain, as painless as possible, how all of the components fit together <smile>. The reason that you need to understand this database concept is because it will probably be the foundation of the reports that you create and modify. If you have never created a database, or have very little experience creating them, the next few sections in this chapter will be your crash course in databases and relationships. Figures 7-3 and 7-4 illustrate the layout of two tables.

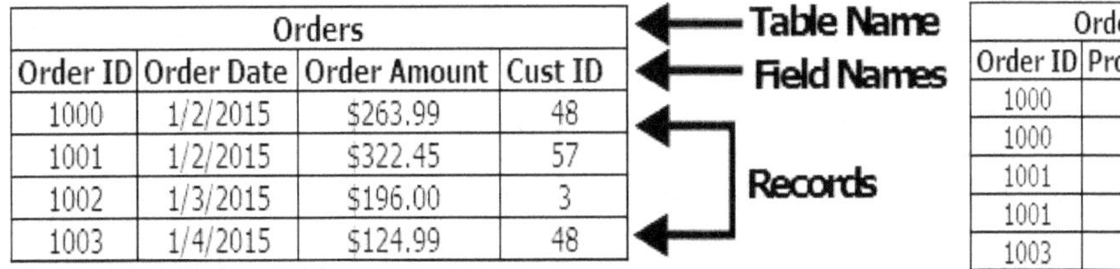

Orders			
Order ID	Order Date	Order Amount	Cust ID
1000	1/2/2015	$263.99	48
1001	1/2/2015	$322.45	57
1002	1/3/2015	$196.00	3
1003	1/4/2015	$124.99	48

Figure 7-3 Orders table

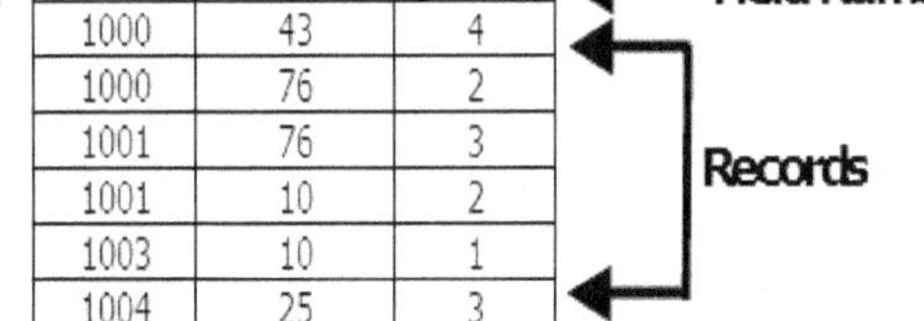

Orders Detail		
Order ID	Product ID	Quantity
1000	43	4
1000	76	2
1001	76	3
1001	10	2
1003	10	1
1004	25	3

Figure 7-4 Orders Detail table

Primary Key Fields

Primary key fields and ID fields are terms that are used interchangeably. I prefer to use the term ID field because primary key fields in databases often have "ID" as part of the field name. Recently, I have seen the word "Key" at the end of a field name to signify that the field is a primary key field.

> ID is short for identification. It is jargon that the computer programming community uses to reference a field that can be used to link one table to another table.

The majority of the tables in the databases that you use in the this book have at least one ID field. Hopefully, you will find that this is also true out in the real world. The reason ID fields are used is because by design they provide a way for each record in the table to have a unique way to be identified. A **FOREIGN KEY** points back to a primary key in a related table.

I have taught several database classes and almost without fail, this topic caused a lot of confusion. For some reason, people want to create links on string (text) fields. Please don't do that. It can cause you problems and should be avoided. It is a bad table design choice. However, creating relationships for tables in the data model on text fields is acceptable, in particular, for data that is not imported from a database.

If you needed to create a report that displays all of the orders and what items were on each order, you would need a way to link the Orders and Orders Detail tables. Think of creating relationships as having the ability to combine two or more tables "virtually" and being able to display the result of this "virtual linking" on a visualization. The result of this virtual linking will remind you of a view.

In Figures 7-3 and 7-4 above, the common ID field is the Order ID field. If you look at the data in the Orders Detail table, you will see that some records have the same Order ID number. That's okay. This means that some orders have more than one item. Each record in the Orders Detail table represents one item that was ordered. If you were to virtually join the data in the tables shown above in Figures 7-3 and 7-4, the virtual table would look like the one shown in Figure 7-5.

This "virtual" join is what happens when tables are **LINKED** (have a relationship). If all of this data was stored in one table instead of two, at the very minimum, all of the fields in the Orders table would be repeated for every record that is in the Orders Detail table, which is exactly what the virtual table, in Figure 7-5, shows.

Orders				Orders Detail		
Order ID	Order Date	Order Amount	Cust ID	Order ID	Product ID	Quantity
1000	1/2/2015	$263.99	48	1000	43	4
1000	1/2/2015	$263.99	48	1000	76	2
1001	1/2/2015	$322.45	57	1001	76	3
1001	1/2/2015	$322.45	57	1001	10	2
1002	1/3/2015	$196.00	3			
1003	1/4/2015	$124.99	48	1003	10	1
				1004	25	3

Figure 7-5 Virtually joined tables

Virtually joined tables represent the concept of merging queries, that was covered in the previous chapter. The difference is that merging queries places a copy of the selected fields into the first table selected on the Merge dialog box or into a new query. The problem with merging is that the same data is stored in multiple tables.

Repetition of data is why this information is stored in two tables in a database, instead of one. In this example, an additional row would be added to the Orders table for each row in the Orders Detail table. It is considered poor table design to have the same information (other than fields that are used to join tables) stored in more than one table.

> Usually if you see a record in the Orders Detail table, like Order ID 1004 shown above in Figure 7-5, or any **CHILD TABLE** that is in a **PARENT-CHILD RELATIONSHIP**, there is a problem with the data in at least one of the tables because all of the records in the child table should have a matching record in the parent table. Parent tables are used to get data from a **CHILD TABLE.** In this scenario, the record for Order ID 1004, in the Orders Detail table, would not be retrieved or shown on a report.

An ID field in the Orders table is how you find the matching record (known as a **ONE-TO-ONE RELATIONSHIP**) or matching records (known as a **ONE-TO-MANY RELATIONSHIP**, which is the most popular type of relationship) in another table. These are the two most common types of relationships. The **MANY-TO-MANY RELATIONSHIP** is a third type of relationship. It is not used as much as the other two relationship types. The data model currently does not support this type of relationship, but there is a way to imitate a many-to-many relationship.

Understanding Relationships In Power BI Desktop

A relationship between tables may appear to work in the reverse of what you may be use to. They work in a **MANY-TO-ONE RELATIONSHIP** because the table at the top of the Create Relationship dialog box, is the "many" table and the second table, is the "one" table. The good thing though, is that you can create relationships traditionally, with the "one" table at the top and the "many" table at the bottom. Fortunately, if you create a relationship between tables that Power BI Desktop wants in the opposite direction, you will see a warning message.

Lookup tables usually have values in the primary field that are repeated. This type of table is the "Many" side of a relationship. The primary table usually has values that are not repeated in the primary field. This type of table is the "One" side of a relationship. This concept of primary and lookup tables is also known as the **CARDINALITY** of a relationship.

How Relationships Work

More than likely, many of the reports that you create will require data from more than one table in the data model. Reports that display the equivalent of a Product List report will probably only use one table, so there is no linking involved.

When you need to view or modify existing relationships, you can do so by opening the Manage Relationships dialog box. Even though some of the time the relationships that you need are automatically created, if you select the relationship options on the Options dialog box, it is important to understand what is going on behind the scenes, as they say. The best way to understand the basic concept of creating relationships between tables, especially if you are not familiar with the data, is to take the time to view at least some of the data in the tables that need to have a relationship created.

Depending on the table structure, tables can have more than one field that they can be linked on. An example of this would be the Orders Detail table. This table has an ID field that would be used to link it to the Orders table. There is a Product ID field in the Orders Detail table that would be used to retrieve the Product Name from another table (the Product table) to display on the report, instead of displaying the Product ID number. Displaying the product name is more meaningful then displaying the Product ID field, which contains a number. If you are asking why the Product Name is not stored in the Orders Detail table, there are three reasons that I can think of, as explained below.

① The ID field takes up less space then the Product Name field, thereby keeping the size of the Orders Detail table (and any other table that would potentially store the Product Name field instead of the Product ID field) smaller.

② If a Product Name has to be changed for any reason, it only has to be changed, on one record, in the Product table. Every report that the Product Name field is displayed on, would automatically be updated with the revised product name, the next time the report is run or in the case of Power BI Desktop, the next time the data is refreshed. If the product name was stored in the Orders Detail table, every record in the Orders Detail table that had that product name would have to be changed, as well as, any other table that stored the product name. That would be a lot of extra work (for you) and increase the chance for inaccurate data.

③ Without a Product table, there would be no place to add new products.

Relationship Requirements

Having the ability to create relationships between tables provides a lot more flexibility. The requirements (the do's and don'ts) are explained below.

① **MANY-TO-MANY RELATIONSHIP** DAX functions can be used to imitate this type of relationship. (1)

② **COMPATIBLE DATA TYPES** The column in each table that will be used to create a relationship must have the same or compatible data type. For example, the primary key column in the primary table can have a whole number data type and the lookup column in the second table can have a text data type. In this example, the lookup column could not be a date, currency or True/False data type.

③ **COMPOSITE KEYS** Are a unique value that is created by combining the values in two or more fields. To emulate this type of key, you have to combine the values in the fields before creating the relationship. There are two options for combining values: 1) Import the columns and create a calculated column using DAX or 2) Combine the values in the data source and import the new column. (1)

④ **SELF JOINS** In many types of databases, this is also known as a **RECURSIVE JOIN**. This type of join uses one column in the table to reference data in another column in the same table. A recursive join example would be using the Supervisor ID field (shown in Figure 7-6) to create a report that displays a list of supervisors and the people in their department. (1) (2)

⑤ **ONLY ONE RELATIONSHIP PER COLUMN** A primary key column cannot be used to create multiple relationships. This is a problem if you need to use the same column in a table to create a relationship with two or more other tables. (2)

⑥ **UNIQUE COLUMN OF DATA FOR EACH TABLE** A table used as the primary or fact table, to create a relationship must have one column that has a unique value that can be used to identify each row of data. This means that no two rows of data can have the same value in this column. At most, there can only be one empty cell in this column. This is because empty cells are the same as a blank cell, which is a data type. [See Supported Data Types In The Data Model, earlier in this chapter]

(1) Power BI Desktop does not technically support this type of relationship, but I have provided a work around.
(2) The work around is to import the table, then duplicate and rename the duplicate table, and create the second link that you need between the duplicate table and the other table.

Employee

	Employee ID	Supervisor ID	Last Name	First Name	Position	Birth Date	Hire Date
+	1	5	Davolio	Nancy	Sales Representative	12/8/1972	3/29/1991
+	2		Fuller	Andrew	Vice President, Sales	2/19/1969	7/12/1991
+	3	5	Leverling	Janet	Sales Representative	8/30/1971	2/27/1991
+	4	5	Peacock	Margaret	Sales Representative	9/19/1973	3/30/1992
+	5	2	Buchanan	Steven	Sales Manager	3/4/1975	9/13/1992
+	6	5	Suyama	Michael	Sales Representative	7/2/1963	9/13/1992

Figure 7-6 Employee table

Keep in mind that if the relationships are incorrect, the data displayed on visualizations that are created from the tables with incorrect relationships, will not display the correct data or may not display any data.

Relationships View

Figure 7-7 shows the Relationships view. It displays the tables, the columns and relationships in the data model. (This data model is from Exercise 2.4.) As you can see, not all tables have a relationship. That may not be a problem if the tables that do not have a relationship are either going to be used to create a list report, not going to be used to create a report or that a field in the table was merged into a table that will be used to create a report.

When data is imported from a database, some, if not all of the relationships are created, as long as you have the correct relationship options selected on the Options dialog box.

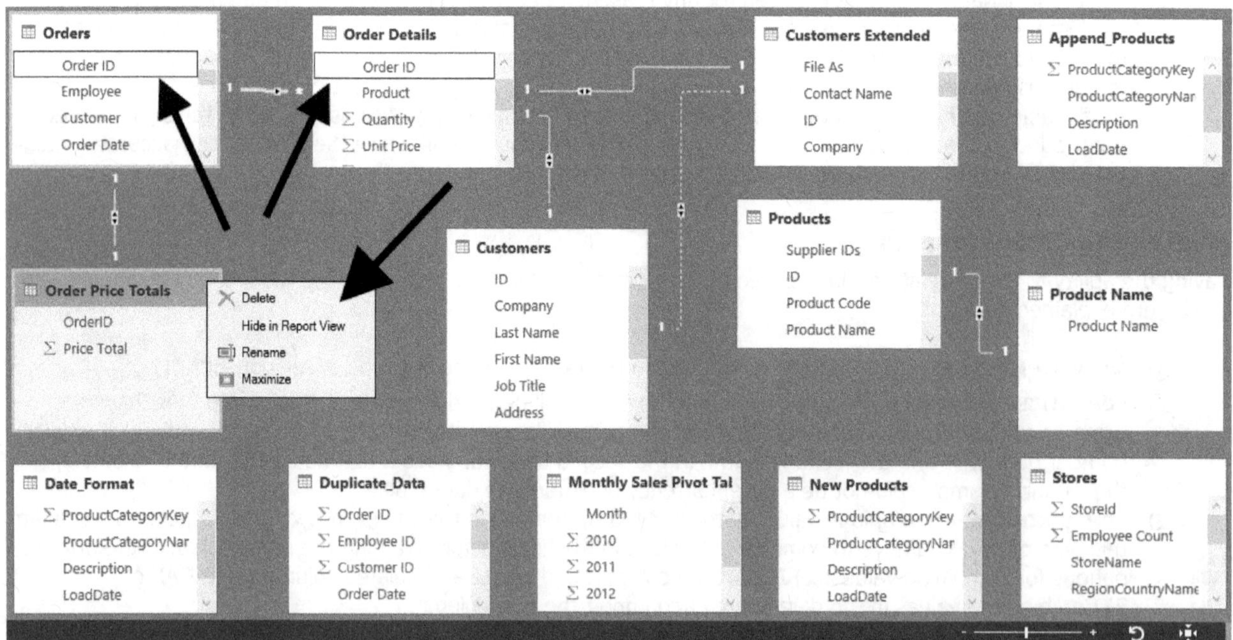

Figure 7-7 Relationships view

The **MAXIMIZE OPTION** shown above in Figure 7-7, on the shortcut menu, is used to display all of the fields in the table.

The option is also available when you hold the mouse pointer to the right of the table name. When a table is maximized, this option changes to **RESTORE**.

If you want to see the details of a relationship or edit a relationship, double-click on the line between the tables. You will see the Edit Relationship dialog box. This dialog box looks like and has the same options as the Create Relationship dialog box. [See Figure 7-14]

It can be difficult to tell which fields are used to link the tables. The easy way to tell is to click on the line between the tables. The field in each table that is used as the link, will have a border around it, as illustrated in the upper left corner of Figure 7-7. The other option is to click the **MANAGE RELATIONSHIPS BUTTON** on the Home tab.

Status Bar Options

In the lower right corner of Figure 7-7 are three options that are used to change the appearance of the Relationships view. The options are explained below.

The **ZOOM SLIDER** is used to increase or decrease the size of the tables displayed in the window. In addition to this option, you can use drag and drop to rearrange where the tables are displayed.

The **RESET LAYOUT BUTTON** restores the previous layout of the view.

The **FIT TO SCREEN BUTTON** resizes the tables so that they are all displayed in the current window size.

Rearranging The Tables
If you rearrange the tables on this view, the new layout is saved when you save the report file.

Table Shortcut Menu

The Order Price Totals table in Figure 7-7, shows the shortcut menu. To display this menu, right-click near the table name. The options are explained in Table 7-2.

Option	Description
Delete	Deletes the table from the data model. There is no Undo option for this feature. If you make a mistake and need the table, you can import it again or if it is not too late, close the report file and not save the changes to it, then reopen it. (3)
Hide in Report View	Prevents the table from being displayed in the Report view. This means that the table cannot be used to create a report. The table is grayed out in the Relationships view. The table is also grayed out on the Data view, but has all of the functionality that tables have on that view. (3)
Rename	Renames the table. This change is made throughout the data model automatically. (3)
Maximize	Displays the table longer and hides the other tables. Press the ESC key to return to the Relationships view. If you hold the mouse pointer to the right of the table name, there is a button that will also maximize the table.

Table 7-2 Table shortcut menu options explained

(3) This option is also available for each field.

Hiding vs Deleting Columns Tips
Below are some tips and guidelines that you may find helpful in deciding whether to hide or delete a column.
① If a column is deleted from a table, the data in the column is no longer available in Power BI Desktop.
② Before deleting a column, make sure that it is not a column that is needed to create a relationship with another table. When in doubt about deleting a column, hide it instead.
③ Hiding a column prevents it from being displayed in the Report view.
④ Hide columns that are used to create a relationship. The reason to consider doing this is because these fields are rarely used to create a report because the end user probably will not understand the numeric values in the field.
⑤ As you have seen, many tables that you imported have a lot of fields. On the Report view, having to sift through all of the fields in the Fields panel can take a lot of time. If you know that some fields will not be used, hide them if you do not want to delete them.

Modeling Tab

The **SYNONYMS BUTTON** shown in Figure 7-8, displays the panel shown in Figure 7-9. This panel is used to enter words or phrases for a table that have the same or similar meaning. Click the Synonyms button again, to close the panel.

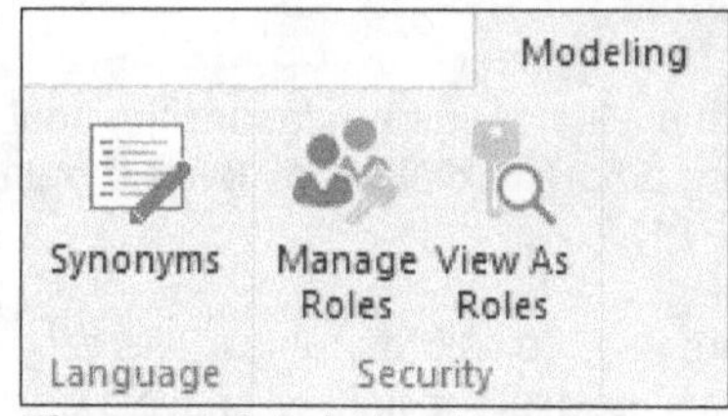

Figure 7-8 Relationships view Modeling tab

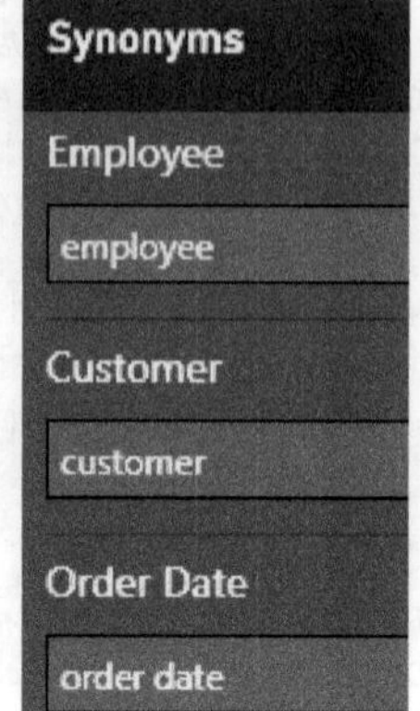

Figure 7-9 Synonyms panel

This option is used with Power BI's **Q&A NATURAL LANGUAGE.**

The **MANAGE ROLES BUTTON** displays the dialog box shown in Figure 7-10. This tool is used to create and edit security options for the report file.

The **VIEW AS ROLES BUTTON** is used to view the data that each user or security role (group) has access to.

ROW LEVEL SECURITY can be created on this dialog box by:

① Creating a DAX expression to filter the data that can be viewed in Power BI Desktop.
② Creating a role.
③ Assign an expression to the role.

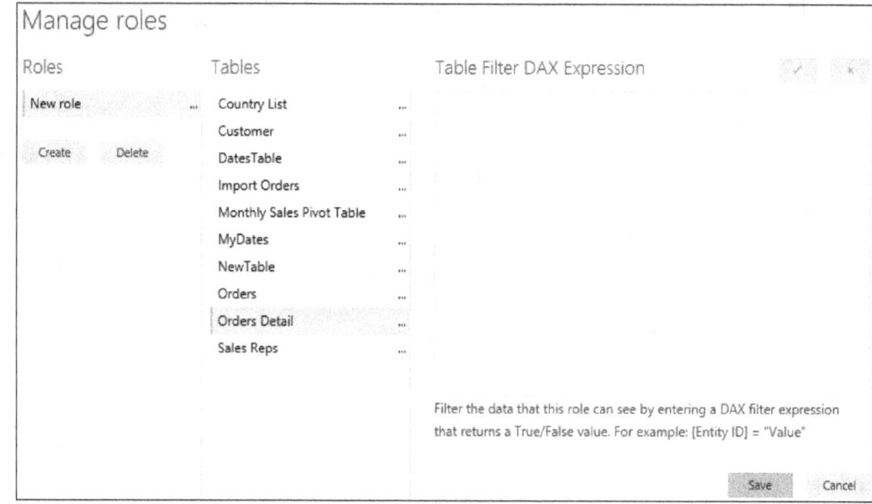

Figure 7-10 Manage Roles dialog box

Manually Creating Relationships

To create a relationship on the Relationships view, click on the Key field in the primary table of the relationship, that you want to create, and drag the mouse pointer to the matching field in the child table, then release the mouse button. The field names do not have to be the same to create a relationship.

While you can create relationships starting with the secondary table, it is possible that you will not retrieve all of the records from the primary table. For example, in Figure 7-3 shown earlier, Order ID 1002 would not be displayed because the Orders Detail table does not have any matching records. Granted, that is a data problem (often because referential integrity was not enforced), but I prefer to display bad data like this on a report, so that hopefully someone, that uses the report, will see the bad data and fix it.

Exercise 7.1: Create Relationships

In this exercise you will learn how to create relationships in a data model.

1. Save the E2.4 file as `E7.1 Create relationships.`

2. Display the Relationships view.

3. Right-click on each of the lines between the tables and select Delete. You may have to scroll to the right to see all of the tables. You are doing this, so that you can recreate them.

4. Drag the Order ID field in the Orders table to the Order ID field in the Order Price Totals table.

5. Drag the Order ID field in the Order Details table to the Order ID field in the Orders table. This will create a Many-To-One relationship, which you will edit and change to a One-To-Many relationship, later in this exercise. The next section shows you another way to create relationships.

Using The Same Field In A Table To Create More Than One Relationship
Currently, Power BI Desktop only supports using each field in each table to create one relationship. Most of the time, this is sufficient. If you need to use the same field in a table to create a relationship with a second table, the work around is to import the table a second time, rename it, then create the second relationship. An example of when this would be needed, is when you need to create a **RECURSIVE JOIN**, as discussed earlier in this chapter. If you use the same field twice, the second relationship will be created. The link line will have dashes instead of a straight line. When you view the relationship on the Manage Relationships dialog box, you will see that the second relationship is not active. That is how you know that if you need this second relationship, you have two choices:
① De-activate the other relationship that uses the same field, then activate the second relationship.
② Import the table again and rename it to use to create the second relationship for the field.

Manage Relationships

The dialog box shown in Figure 7-11 is used to create, edit and delete relationships. I tend to create relationships manually, then view them on this dialog box and make any changes that are needed.

The **ACTIVE OPTION** indicates whether or not the relationship is currently being used.

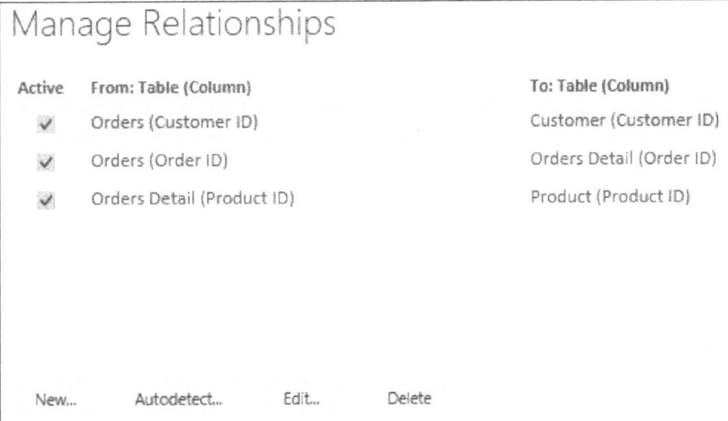

Figure 7-11 Manage Relationships dialog box

Use The Auto Detect Option

The **AUTODETECT BUTTON**, shown above in Figure 7-11, will check to see if there are any relationships that can be created. If relationships are found, they are created. Keep in mind that just because a relationship is automatically created when using this button, doesn't mean that the Active box for the relationship is automatically checked.

1. Home tab ⇒ Manage Relationships button. You should see the two relationships that you created in the previous part of this exercise.

2. Click the Auto detect button. You should see the message shown in Figure 7-12.

   This feature lets you know how many relationships were found ⇒ Click the Close button.

Figure 7-12 Auto detect relationship results

Delete Relationships

The previous part of this exercise automatically created relationships. In this part of the exercise, the relationships created by the Auto Detect feature will be deleted. The **DELETE BUTTON** deletes all of the selected relationships.

1. Click on the first Customers table relationship ⇒ Press and hold down the CTRL key.

2. Click on the each of the relationships below it ⇒ Click the Delete button ⇒ Click the Delete button again to confirm that you want to delete the relationships ⇒ Leave the dialog box open to complete the next part of this exercise.

Create A New Relationship

In this part of the exercise you will create a One-To-Many relationship. The **NEW BUTTON** is used to create a relationship.

1. Click the New button.

2. Open the first drop-down list and select the Orders table.

3. Open the next drop-down list and select the Order Details table. You should see the message shown in Figure 7-13. It lets you know that you are creating a relationship that has already been created.

Figure 7-13 Duplicate relationships message

4. Open the first table drop-down list and select the Customers table ⇒ Select the Orders table in the next drop-down list.

5. As you can see, a relationship was not automatically detected. The good news is that like creating a merge, you can click on the column in each table to use, to create a relationship.

   In the Customers table, click on the Company column ⇒

   In the Orders table, click on the Customer column. You should have the options shown in Figure 7-14 ⇒

   Click OK.

   The options at the bottom of the dialog box are explained below.

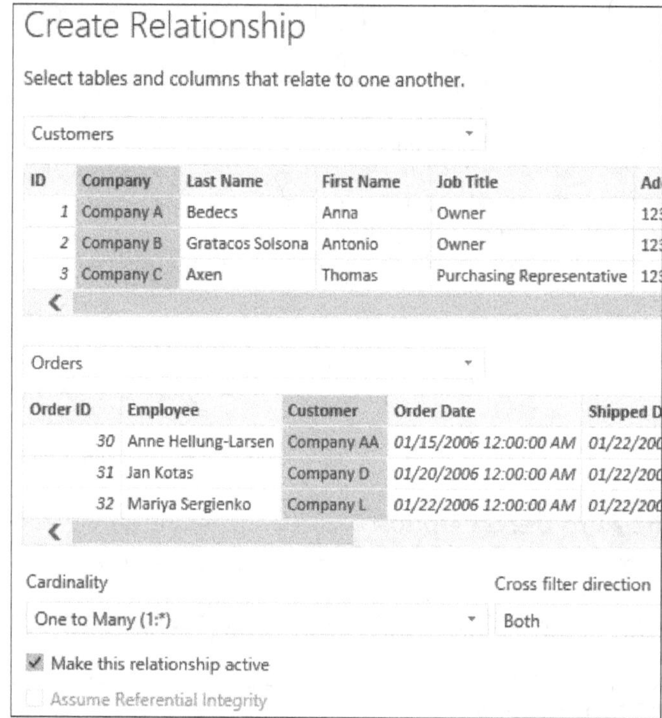

Figure 7-14 Relationship options

Create Relationship Dialog Box Options

The options discussed in this section also apply to the **EDIT RELATIONSHIP DIALOG BOX**.

The **CARDINALITY OPTIONS**, shown in Figure 7-15, are used to select the type of relationship to create between the tables. These are the same relationship options that were covered earlier in this chapter. If you select an option that is not appropriate for the tables and columns selected to create the relationship, you will see the message shown in Figure 7-16.

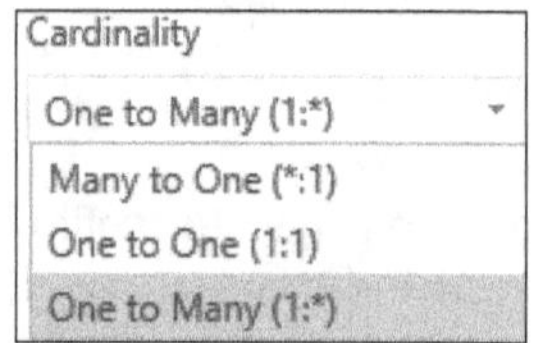

Figure 7-15 Cardinality options

The cardinality you selected isn't valid for this relationship.

Figure 7-16 Cardinality warning message

The **CROSS FILTER DIRECTION OPTIONS**, shown in Figure 7-17, are used to select which table the relationship (filter) should be applied to.

SINGLE OPTION This option means that the fact table can be filtered by the lookup table, but not the other way around. For example, the Order table can be filtered by the Dates table, but the Dates table cannot be filtered by the Order table.

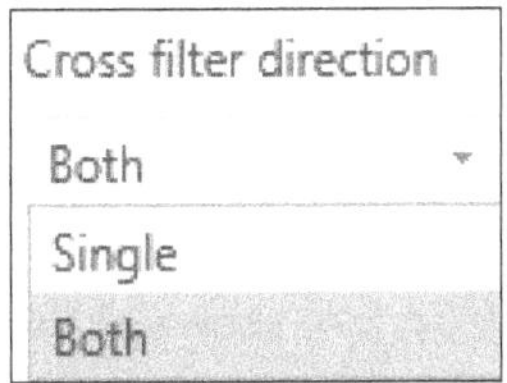

Figure 7-17 Cross filter direction options

The **BOTH OPTION** applies the filter to either table, which filters the data in the other table. This option is referred to as a **MANY-TO-MANY RELATIONSHIP**. An example of when to select this option is when you need a count of an item by date. In the Orders table, you would use the Order Date field. In the Item table (maybe a products table) you would use the Item number. In the example just explained, there are many items sold on the same date and the same item is sold on many dates.

The **MAKE THIS RELATIONSHIP ACTIVE OPTION** is used to select whether or not the relationship should be applied to the tables. There may be times when you do not need to have tables in the data model related.

The **ASSUME REFERENTIAL INTEGRITY OPTION** is enabled for certain types of databases. Referential integrity is a concept used to ensure that relationships between tables are consistent. This means that both tables must have the same keys. This prevents records from being added to the child table using a key field that does not already exist in the primary table.

For example, Figure 7-4 shown earlier, shows a foreign key of 1004. If referential integrity had been applied to these tables in the data source, this record could not have been created. If at some point, there was a corresponding record in the Orders table, shown in Figure 7-3 and it was deleted, any corresponding records in the Orders Detail table would have been deleted at the same time, if referential integrity was enabled.

Edit An Existing Relationship

The **EDIT BUTTON** is used to view or change an existing relationship. Earlier in this exercise you created a Many-To-One relationship between the Orders and Order Details table. In this part of the exercise, you will change the relationship to a One-To-Many relationship.

1. On the Manage Relationships dialog box, click on the relationship that has the Orders Detail table in the From table column.
2. Click the Edit button to open the Edit Relationship dialog box.
3. Change the Order Details table to the Orders table in the first drop-down list ⇒ Select the Order Details table in the next drop-down list. The Cardinality field should have the One-To-Many option selected ⇒ Click OK ⇒ Click Close.

Summary

Using relationships to link data instead of merging data from one table to another is the most important topic to understand in this chapter, in my opinion. Not only are relationships easier and faster to create, they are also easier to maintain. Other then needing to create a recursive join, relationships do not add redundant data to the data model, like merging data does. On your own, if you have trouble creating relationships between tables, it is usually for one of the following reasons:

① At least one table is missing a primary or foreign key.
② Another table needs to be imported.

The Relationship view was also covered. You learned how to create, edit and auto detect relationships. The data model was covered in detail to provide a better understanding of the data and what is required to be able to create the reports that you need.

The data model schema options were covered. The **STAR SCHEMA** was discussed as being the easiest schema to understand, in terms of the data model. As you saw, there are two types of tables, as discussed below.

① The **PRIMARY TABLE** is also known as the "fact", "parent" or "transaction table". Usually, primary tables have a lot of rows, when compared to child tables. Primary tables also tend to have less columns then child tables. Primary tables have the data that needs to be analyzed. This table type has a key field for each table that it needs to get additional data from, to create the report. These key fields are the ones used to link to the child tables.

② The **CHILD TABLE** is also known as the "dimension" or "lookup table". This table type is used to look up an item that is being reported on. For example, when displaying orders, it is helpful to display customer information for the order. The customer information has to be looked up, as it is not stored in the Order table. Child tables have at least one row for each unique value in the parent table. Usually, only one field is used to make each row of data unique.

One exception that comes to mind is an order or sales detail table. This table contains one row for each item on each order. This means that if one order contains five items, the detail table has five rows for the order. Each of the five rows, in the detail table, has the same Order ID number. The table also often has another field that has a unique value for each row in the detail table. This field (with the unique value) is not the field that is linked on, in the scenario just described.

USING THE DATA VIEW

After completing this chapter, you will have a better understanding of the following:

- ☑ Options on the Data view
- ☑ Data view Modeling tab options
- ☑ Formatting data
- ☑ Creating a new table
- ☑ Measures

CHAPTER 8

Data View Overview

As it's name suggests, this view is used to see the data (similar to viewing data in the Query Editor). One difference is that the Data view is used to view data after it has been loaded into the data model. The other difference is that the Data view displays all of the rows of data. If you recall, in Chapter 2, Exercise 2.3, you imported a text file that had over 2 million rows of data.

In the Query Editor, you could not see all of the rows in this table. In the Data view, you can view all 2 plus million rows if you want to, as shown in Figure 8-1.

TABLE: FactSalesTxt (2,282,482 rows)

Figure 8-1 Total number of rows in the Fact Sales table

In addition to viewing the data, this view is primarily used to manage the data model, which includes formatting data and adding new columns of data to tables. Some of the other features are the same as ones in the Query Editor.

In addition to being able to analyze millions of rows of data and create relationships, hierarchies and calculated columns, calculations (also known as **MEASURES**) can also be created and used to analyze data. This view is an additional way to get the data ready to create reports. Figure 8-2 shows the Data view and its Modeling tab. The options are explained below.

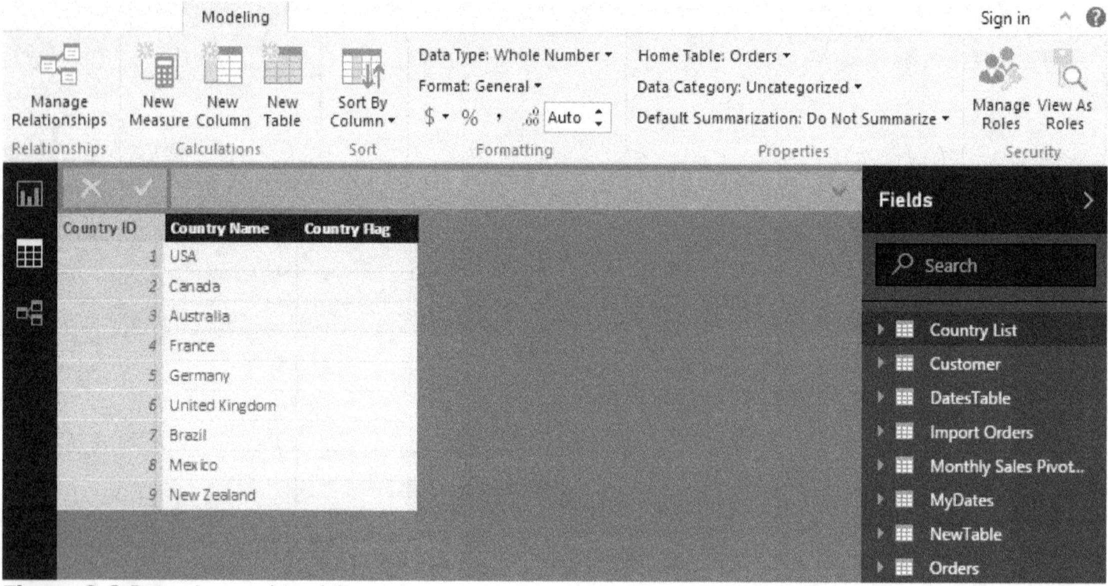

Figure 8-2 Data view and Modeling tab

Data View Options

Column Shortcut Menu

The shortcut menu shown in Figure 8-3 is available for each column of data, like the ones shown above in Figure 8-1. The options are explained in Table 8-1.

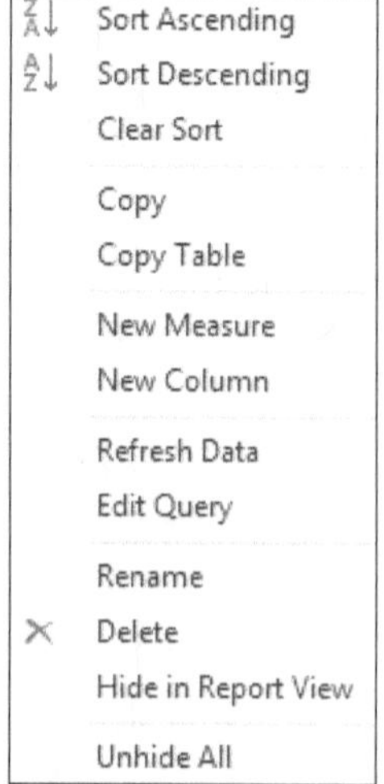

Figure 8-3 Column shortcut menu

Option	Is Used To . . .
Sort Ascending	Sort the data in the table in ascending (A to Z or 1 to 9) order, based on the values in the field. (1)
Sort Descending	Sort the data in the table in descending (Z to A or 9 to 1) order, based on the values in the field. (1)
Clear Sort	Remove the sort that was applied.
Copy	Copy the column of data. (2)
Copy Table	Copy the entire table. (2)
New Measure	[See What Is A Measure?] (3)
New Column	[See Table 8-2] (3)
Refresh Data	Update the data in the table.
Edit Query	Open the Query Editor and display the data in the table.
Rename	Change the name of the column. (4)
Delete	Delete the column from the table. (4)
Hide in Report View	Keep the selected column from being displayed in the Report view. When this option is applied, the column is grayed out and a check mark is added to the shortcut menu for the column.
Unhide All	Displays all columns that have the Hide in Report View option applied.

Table 8-1 Column shortcut menu options explained

(1) Only one column in the table can be sorted on at a time.
(2) The column or table that is copied can be pasted in an external file, like a spreadsheet.
(3) This option enables the formula bar above the table of data.
(4) There is no Undo option, but this change creates a step in the Query Editor to undo the change.

Resizing Columns In A Table
The columns in a table can be resized the same way that they are resized in Excel. Drag the vertical line after the column name in the direction that you want to resize the column to.

Fields Panel

This panel is on the right side of the Data view. It contains all of the queries (tables) and fields like the Query Editor has. The table name and column name shortcut menus have a subset of options that the Column shortcut menu, shown earlier in Figure 8-3 has.

To access the shortcut menu for a table, right-click on the table name or hold the mouse pointer to the right of the table name and click on the ellipsis button after the table or field name.

The symbol shown in Figure 8-4 indicates that the field is numeric.

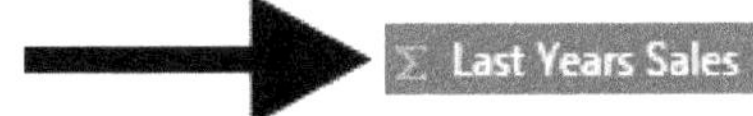

Figure 8-4 Numeric symbol (sigma) illustrated

In addition to many of the options shown earlier in Figure 8-3, the field shortcut menu also has the **NEW HIERARCHY OPTION**. [See Understanding Hierarchies]

Modeling Tab

This tab was shown earlier at the top of Figure 8-2. The options are explained in Table 8-2.

Option	Description
Manage Relationships	[See Chapter 7, Figure 7-11]
New Measure	[See What Is A Measure?] (5)
New Column	Is used to create a calculated column in the current table. (5)
New Table	[See Create A Table]
Sort By Column	[See Sort By Column Button]
Data Type	Is used to change the data type of the selected column. The data type options are the same as the ones in the Query Editor.

Table 8-2 Data view Modeling tab options explained

Option	Description
Format	The options vary, depending on the data type. The options are used to change how the data in the column is displayed. Figure 8-5 shows some of the date/time format options.
Apply Currency Format	Displays the options shown in Figure 8-6.
Apply Percentage Format	Displays the data in percent format.
Thousands Separator	Adds commas to the data value.
Decimal Places	Increases or decreases the number of decimal places. The **AUTO OPTION** defaults to the number of decimal places that the data in the column currently has.
Home Table	This option is enabled when a Measure column is selected. It is used to select a table to move the measure to.
Data Category	[See Data Category Options]
Default Summarization	[See Default Summarization Options]

Table 8-2 Data view Modeling tab options explained (Continued)

(5) This option uses DAX to create the formula.

Common Date Formats
*03/14/2001 1:30:55 PM (G)
*03/14/2001 (MM/dd/yyyy)
March 14, 2001 (MMMM dd, yyyy)
Wednesday, March 14, 2001 (dddd, MMMM d, yyyy)
03/14/2001 (MM/dd/yyyy)

Figure 8-5 Date and Time format options

Figure 8-6 Currency format options

Sort By Column Button

This option is used to select the column to sort another column by. The options in the drop-down list are the columns that are not selected in the table. Select a column that has the values that you want to sort the selected column(s) by. This is a useful feature because there are times when the column that you want displayed on the visual, cannot be sorted in the order that you need it displayed in.

Data Category Options

The options shown in Figure 8-7 are used to select a category for the selected column. As needed, these category options are used to better define the data in a table.

This option is especially helpful for fields that have a URL, because URL's are normally stored in a text field.

Applying the **WEB URL OPTION** to a field will cause the web site address to be displayed as a link instead of plain text. The supported links are HTTP and HTTPS. [See Chapter 11, Figure 11-13]

Data categories are also used to categorize geographical fields that will be displayed on a map.

Power BI Desktop also uses these options to help select a visualization type when a field is added directly to a page to start a new visualization, opposed to selecting a visualization type and then adding fields to the Field Well.

Figure 8-7 Data Category options

Default Summarization Options

The options shown in Figure 8-8 are used to select how the column should be aggregated (summarized), by default, when creating a visualization. Selecting a default option is helpful because it will reduce the number of times that you have to select what type of summary should be applied to the column when it is added to a visualization.

The Count and Count (Distinct) summarization options can be applied to any column. The other options can only be applied to numeric data.

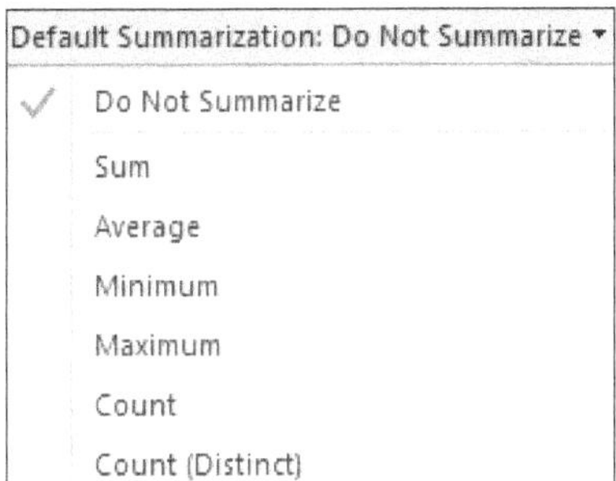

Figure 8-8 Default Summarization options

The options are used to change the aggregate option that is automatically selected. If you know that a field will not need to be summarized, select the Do Not Summarize option.

Use these options when you want a total of the values displayed in the column to be used as the default option. For example, if you know that most of the time, you need to calculate sum values for the tables that you will create, you would select the Sum function in this drop-down list. Then, when you add the field to the table, a sum total for the column would be calculated and added to the table. If you select a default summarization option, you can override it when creating a report. The options are explained in Table 8-3.

Option	Description
Do Not Summarize	No aggregation is applied to the field.
Sum	The values are added together to get a total for the field.
Average	Calculates the average of the values in the field.
Minimum	Displays the smallest value in the field.
Maximum	Displays the largest value in the field.
Count	Displays a count of the number of records that have data in the field. Null values are not included in the count.
Count (Distinct)	Displays a count of the number of records that have a unique value in the field. Null values are included in the count, as if it was a value. The null values are what make up the (Blank) group, that you will see in a visualization, filter criteria or on a slicer.

Table 8-3 Default Summarization options explained

Data Type Icons

Each field in a table has a data type. Data types determine what type of data (numeric, text etc.) the field can contain. Most of the data types that the data model supports has its own icon, as shown in the first column in Table 8-4. You will see these icons next to fields in the Fields panel in the Data and Report views.

Icon	Data Type	This Data Type . . .
Σ	Aggregate	Is a numeric field. The aggregation type can be changed. Aggregations are not just for numeric fields. Earlier, the **COUNT** function was covered. If this option is applied to a non numeric field, a count is displayed, instead of the data in the field.
None	Attribute	Is for non numeric fields. It can be counted, but not averaged or summed.
None	Binary data	Is used for fields that contain images.
	Calculated Column	Uses a formula to create a new column of data.
	Calculation	Cannot be aggregated because it is based on a DAX formula. Measures contain numeric values like counts or percents.
	Geography	Is most often used to display data on a map, as a geographical reference. The data in the field contains an address, city, state or some entity, like longitude or latitude coordinates, that point to a location on a map.
	Hierarchy	Contains two or more fields that are used to drill down, in the data displayed on the visualization. A popular hierarchy is Country/State/City.

Table 8-4 Data types explained

Icon	Data Type	This Data Type . . .
	KPI	Uses a KPI as the data source. (KPI stands for **KEY PERFORMANCE INDICATOR**) KPI's are a way to measure the performance of a process. The goal is to uncover performance that is not in the normal, acceptable range. Many dashboards are created around this concept.

Table 8-4 Data types explained (Continued)

Data View vs Query Editor

While it may not seem like these tools have any significant differences, this section explains the biggest differences that I have observed.

① The Data view only displays data in the data model. The Query Editor displays tables in the data model and tables that have been imported, but not loaded into the data model.
② DAX formulas can be created in the Data view. The Query Editor uses the M language.
③ The Data view displays all of the data in each table. The Query Editor only displays the first few hundred rows per table.
④ Relationships can be created and modified in the Data view. This can eliminate the need to merge columns of data in one table into another table or eliminate the need to create a new table that adds data from two or more existing tables. Both of these duplicate data, which makes the report file larger than it has to be.

When a table or column is renamed in the Data view, it is also renamed throughout the report file, which includes the Query Editor.

Report Data File

The majority of report exercises in this book will use the Report Data file, that will be created in the exercise below. This file has seven tables in the data model and the relationships for the tables have already been created. The relationships allow you to use all of the fields, in all of the tables, as if all of the fields are in one table. This makes creating reports much easier. There are two reports in the file, that will be used as the basis for many of the chart exercises.

Exercise 8.1: Import The Data And Reports

In this exercise, you will import a data model that was created in Power Pivot for Excel. The workbook also has two reports that were created in Power View for Excel, to use as the basis for many of the reports that you will create.

1. Open a new file ⇒ File tab ⇒ Import ⇒ **EXCEL WORKBOOK CONTENTS**.

2. Select the Report Data workbook ⇒ Click Start. When the import is finished, you will see that seven tables (queries) and two Power View sheets were imported ⇒ Click Close.

3. Save the file as `Report Data`. You should see two pages (tabs), one named Customer List and one name Order List.

Modify Some Of The Table Options

In this part of the exercise, you will change some options for the tables that were just imported, so that you do not have to keep switching back to the Data view while you are creating reports, to make these changes. Making the changes to the Report Data file will make them available to all reports that are based on this file.

Modify The Customer Table

1. Display the Data view ⇒ Display the Customer table.

2. In the table, right-click on the Customer ID column and select Sort Ascending.

3. Modeling tab ⇒ Change the Default Summarization option to Do Not Summarize.

4. Click on the Region column ⇒ Change the Data category to State or Province.

5. In the Fields panel, right-click on the Country_Drill Down (hierarchy) and select Delete ⇒ Click Delete, on the Delete Hierarchy dialog box.

Modify The Dates Table

1. Display the Dates Table.

2. Change the Default Summarization option to Do Not Summarize for the following fields: Year, Month Num and Quarter Num.

3. Click on the Year field ⇒ Change the Data type and Format to Whole Number.

Modify The Orders Table

1. Display the Orders table.

2. Make the changes below for the following fields: Order ID, Customer ID and Sales Rep ID.

   ☑ Change the Data type to Whole Number
   ☑ Change the Default Summarization option to Do Not Summarize

3. Click on the Month Full column ⇒ Modeling tab ⇒ Sort By Column button ⇒ Select the Month Num column.

4. Change the Format to $English (United States) for the following fields: Discount Amount, Shipping Amount, Sales Cost and Sales Net.

Modify The Orders Detail Table

1. Change the Default Summarization option to Do Not Summarize for the following fields: Order ID and Product ID.

Modify The Sales Rep Table

1. Click on the Sales Rep ID column ⇒ Change the Default Summarization option to Do Not Summarize.

Report Data.pbix File
This file is used as the starting point for the rest of the chapters in this book. It may be a good idea to pin it to the Recent Items list on the File tab, to make it easy to find. The rest of this chapter covers functionality that at some point, you may have a need to use on your own.

Understanding Hierarchies

A hierarchy is a collection of fields in a table, usually arranged from the highest level to the lowest level, as shown later in Figure 8-10. Think of the levels as a way to drill down on the data. The top level field is the one that all other levels are a part of. The next level down is a subset of the level above. All of the fields in the hierarchy, can be added to the report at the same time. Hierarchies are usually used to add drill down functionality to charts. Hierarchies can be created in Data or Report view.

Hierarchies create relationships. Creating a hierarchy is easy. All you have to do is select the dimension (column) that will be used as the parent level. If the dimension selected does not have a value for each level in the hierarchy, a level without a value will not be created. A popular hierarchy to create is Country ⇒ State ⇒ City. The first field added to the hierarchy is used as the default hierarchy name, but you can rename it.

Exercise 8.2: Create A Hierarchy

In this exercise, you will create a hierarchy for the Country, State and City fields.

1. On the Fields panel, display the fields in the Customer table.

2. Right-click on the Country field and select New Hierarchy. You will see an entry called Country Hierarchy. This is the default name for the hierarchy, that you just started to create.

3. Right-click on the Region field in the Customer table and select Add to Country Hierarchy, as illustrated in Figure 8-9.

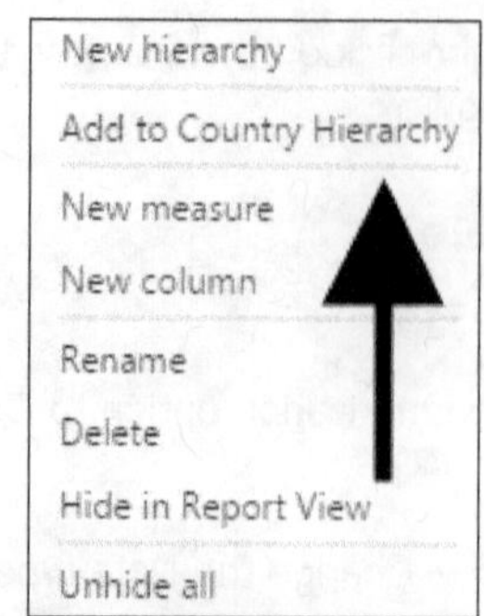

Figure 8-9 Field shortcut menu

Another Way To Add A Field To An Existing Hierarchy
You can also add a field to an existing hierarchy by dragging it to the hierarchy in the Fields panel.

4. Add the City field to the hierarchy, below the Region field. The hierarchy should look like the one shown in Figure 8-10.

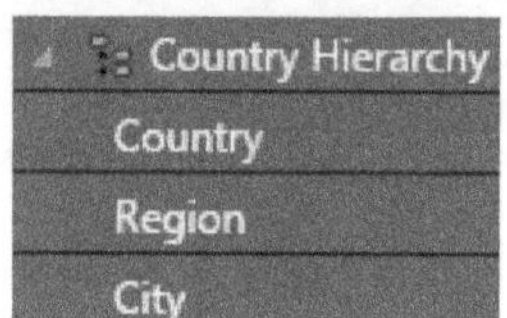

Figure 8-10 Country Hierarchy

M vs DAX
M is the programming language used in the Query Editor to create columns of data. This language cannot reference fields in the data model. DAX is the programming language used in the Data and Report views to create calculated columns. DAX can reference fields in the same table that the formula is created in, as well as, reference other tables in the data model.

Calculated Column vs Measure
Create a calculated column when the formula should be applied to every row of data in the table. Create a measure when the formula can be applied to some or all of the records in a table or dataset.

DAX Reference Guide
In depth coverage of DAX is beyond the scope of this book. It you want to learn more about DAX, this link provides a good starting point. https://msdn.microsoft.com/en-us/library/gg413422.aspx

Exercise 8.3: Create Calculated Columns

In this exercise you will learn how to create calculated columns. Some of them will be used in reports, later in this book.

The formula bar has **INTELLISENSE** functionality built-in, that displays suggestions as you type in the formula, as shown later in Figure 8-22.

Create A Formula To Check For Duplicate Records

Chapter 3 introduced the Keep Duplicates option. If that option does not handle your needs, this part of the exercise will show you how to create a formula that uses two columns (the Address and City columns) to determine if there are duplicate rows of data. The formula can easily be modified to use more columns as criteria, to check for duplicate rows of data.

1. Load the More Duplicate Data table from the More Data Files workbook.

2. Data view ⇒ Display the More Duplicate Data table.

3. Modeling tab ⇒ New Column button.

4. In the formula bar, delete what's there and type the formula shown in Figure 8-11, all on one line, then press Enter.

```
#OfDups = CALCULATE (COUNTROWS('MoreDuplicateData'),
FILTER ('MoreDuplicateData',
'MoreDuplicateData'[City] = EARLIER
('MoreDuplicateData'[City])
&& 'MoreDuplicateData'[Address] = EARLIER
('MoreDuplicateData'[Address])))
```

Figure 8-11 Formula to check for duplicates

You should see the columns shown in Figure 8-12. Any row with a number greater than 1, means that there is a duplicate record. In Chapter 10, you will create a table to only display the duplicate rows of data.

Customer ID	Company Name	First Name	Last Name	Address	City	State	#OfDups
1	Company 19	Anna	Bedecs	123 1st Street	Seattle	WA	3
2	Company 20	Antonio	Gratacos Solsona	123 2nd Street	Boston	MA	2
3	Company 21	Thomas	Axen	123 3rd Street	Los Angeles	CA	2
4	Company 22	Christina	Lee	123 4th Street	New York	NY	2
5	Company 23	Martin	O'Donnell	123 5th Street	Minneapolis	MN	1
6	Company 24	Francisco	Pérez-Olaeta	123 6th Street	Milwaukee	WI	1

Figure 8-12 Duplicate checking result

5. Change the Default Summarization option to Do Not Summarize for the # Of Dups column.

Create A Formula To Calculate The Order Processing Time

In this part of the exercise, you will create a formula to find out how long it is between the date an order is placed and the date the order is shipped. This is known as the order processing time. This field will be used on a Gantt chart that will be created later.

The **DATEDIFF FUNCTION** is used to calculate the difference between two date fields. You can select how the difference will be displayed. In this exercise, the difference will be displayed in days.

1. Display the Orders table ⇒ On the Modeling tab, click the New Column button.

2. Type the formula shown in Figure 8-13. The new column should look like the one shown in Figure 8-14. I moved the column over in the table to make it easier to compare the calculated column to the dates used.

```
Order Processing Time = DATEDIFF([Order Date],[Ship Date],DAY)
```

Figure 8-13 Formula to calculate the order processing time

Order Date	Ship Date	Order Processing Time
12/02/2013	12/10/2013	8
12/02/2013	12/02/2013	0
12/02/2013	12/05/2013	3
12/02/2013	12/02/2013	0
12/03/2013	12/03/2013	0
12/03/2013	12/05/2013	2

Figure 8-14 Order Processing time column

3. Change the Default Summarization option to Do Not Summarize for the Order Processing Time column.

DateDiff Function
The DateDiff function has arguments that are used to determine how to calculate the difference between two date fields. Three of the most used arguments are explained below.
DAY calculates the difference in days.
MONTH calculates the difference in months.
YEAR calculates the difference in years.

What Is A Date Table?

The data contained in this table is a contiguous (no gaps in the series of dates in the table) list of dates that are used to see how data (in other tables) changes over time. Power BI Desktop refers to this as **ADDING TIME INTELLIGENCE** to a data set.

Each row of data in the date table is for a specific date. Each column contains all or part of the date for that row, in a specific format. For example, the first column in Figure 8-15 is the Date Key column. It contains the full date. (This is the column that has the contiguous list of dates.) The Year column contains the year of the date in the Date Key column. The Quarter Full column contains which quarter the date is in.

The table should contain all of the date variations needed to create all of the reports that you need. That way, you only need to create and maintain one table and use it as much as needed. The number of dates to include in the table is up to you. At the very least, the date range should include the earliest date in any table in the data model. That last date in the date table is up to you. At the very least, you should use 12/31/of the current year. I think most people use a date two or three years in the future for the last date, so that they do not have to update the date table yearly.

Over time, you may have the need to add more date variations (columns) to the date table, which is fine. Because I do not want to have to create this table every few years, I created one that included dates until the end of the year 2025. By then, hopefully, I will be retired. <smile>

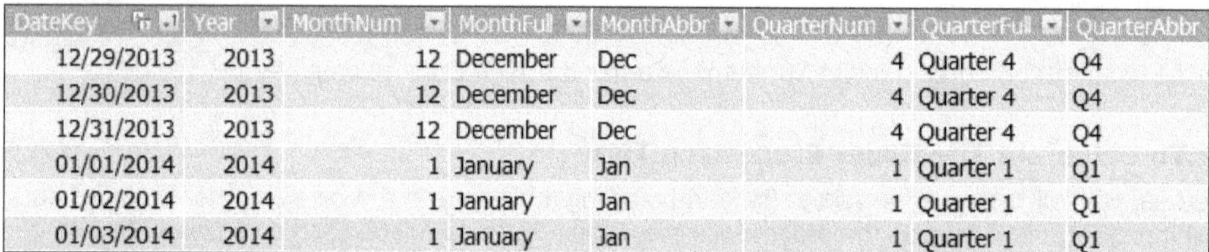

DateKey	Year	MonthNum	MonthFull	MonthAbbr	QuarterNum	QuarterFull	QuarterAbbr
12/29/2013	2013	12	December	Dec	4	Quarter 4	Q4
12/30/2013	2013	12	December	Dec	4	Quarter 4	Q4
12/31/2013	2013	12	December	Dec	4	Quarter 4	Q4
01/01/2014	2014	1	January	Jan	1	Quarter 1	Q1
01/02/2014	2014	1	January	Jan	1	Quarter 1	Q1
01/03/2014	2014	1	January	Jan	1	Quarter 1	Q1

Figure 8-15 Portion of a date table

Date Table Requirements

Date tables have a few requirements that you should be aware of, as explained below.

① The date range must be consecutive, as DAX functions that use the date table rely on it and will produce incorrect results if dates as missing.
② At least one column must have the Date data type.

It is not a requirement that you create a date table from scratch. You can import it, if any of the following are true:

① You have a date table on a worksheet in Excel.
② You have a date table in a Power Pivot workbook.
③ Your company has a date table stored in a database.
④ You can use the date table in the Azure Marketplace. The data source shown earlier in Chapter 2, Figure 2-31 shows a date table, which you can download for free. In the Vol 5 links file, there is a link in the Chapter 2 section, for another free date table.

While you may initially feel that you do not need a date table, one thing to keep in mind is that some DAX functions like **TOTALYTD** (total year to date) require a date table.

Sorting Columns In The Date Table

By default, the data in tables is loaded into the data model in the order that it is in the data source. This means that the data probably is not sorted the way that you may need it to be.

You may have the need to display text columns, like the Month Full column, in calendar month order. Sorting on that column, will display the month names in alphabetical order, which is probably not the result that you want. You probably want the months sorted in calendar month order. Earlier in this chapter, the **SORT BY COLUMN BUTTON** was covered. You used this option in Exercise 8.1.

Sorting the Month Name field by the Month Nbr field, works best when you are only displaying data for one year on a chart. If you are displaying more than one year of data, the months will still be sorted properly, but they will be placed side by side. For example, you will see January 2015, January 2016, February 2015, February 2016, etc.

In non date tables, it may be a good idea to hide the column that is used to sort another column because that will help keep the column from being changed, or worse, deleted <smile>.

What Is Time Intelligence?

Dates are a very important component of analyzing data. Dates are used to quantify other data. Examples include last years sales, year to date sales and sales reps orders this quarter compared to the same time last year.

I don't know why this concept is called "Time" Intelligence. I think it should be called "Date" Intelligence, but I digress <smile>. Whatever you want to call it, a date table is needed because it is used to compare data. The other key component of Time Intelligence in Power BI Desktop is DAX functions.

The next exercise will show you how to create a date table using DAX functions. In addition to the DAX functions covered in the exercise, DAX has a category of Time Intelligence functions. They will remind you of accounting functions, because they allow you to compare today's sales to sales from a year ago, calculate the sales for the last 30 days, calculate sales for the last quarter and more. These functions use a range of dates to get the aggregate and related values. Functions in this category use a date table to calculate an aggregation or return a table of dates.

There are also functions to calculate the closing balance for the month, calculate the previous quarters sales and calculate the year to date expenses, which is a running total. All of these functions have one thing in common, they all work based on values in a date table.

DAX time intelligence functions can be used with the built-in time intelligence functions in Power BI Desktop. These DAX functions can also be used with the field used to display **INLINE HIERARCHY** labels.

Exercise 8.4: Create A Date Table

In this exercise you will learn how to create a date table from scratch. The date range covers the range of dates, in the other tables, in the Report Data file.

1. Open the Report Data file, created earlier in this chapter, if it is not already open ⇒ Display the Data view.

2. Display the Modeling tab ⇒ Click the **NEW TABLE BUTTON**.

3. In the formula bar, you will see Table = ⇒ Replace it with this formula:
   `MyDateTable = CALENDAR("01/01/2010", "12/31/2016")`, as shown in Figure 8-16.

   MyDate Table is the name of the table that will be created. For the most part, you can name the table anything that you want.

   ```
   MyDateTable = CALENDAR("01/01/2010", "12/31/2016")
   ```
   Figure 8-16 Formula to create a date table

4. Press Enter. You will see the table with one column ⇒ In the Fields panel, right-click on the Date field, in the My Date Table, and rename it to `DateKey`. (This is a standard field name that is used, for this field.)

5. Change the Data type to Date ⇒
   Change the Format to 03/14/2001 (MM/dd/yyyy).
   The column should look like the one shown in Figure 8-17 ⇒
   Save the changes.

   This table has one row for each date specified in the date range created in step 3 above. On your own, if you know that you need to use time functionality, leave the Data Type as Date/Time.

DateKey
01/01/2010
01/02/2010
01/03/2010
01/04/2010

Figure 8-17 Date column

As you will see, this column is used to create many of the other date columns. It should not be deleted from the table.

Add More Columns To The Date Table

In this part of the exercise, you will add nine date fields to the date table. If you have looked at the Dates Table that was imported into the Report Data file, you will see that there are a lot more date combinations that can be created.

1. Create new columns using the formulas in Table 8-5.

Column Name	Formula	Displays . . .
FullYear	YEAR([DateKey])	A 4 digit year. 2015, 2016
MonthNbr	MONTH([DateKey])	A number between 1 and 12
MonthFull	FORMAT([DateKey], "MMMM")	Full month name spelled out, January, February
MonthAbbr	Format([DateKey], "MMM")	First 3 characters of the Month name, Jan, Feb
MonthAndYearAbbr	MyDateTable[Month Abbr] & " " & [FullYear]	Month named abbreviated and year Jan 2016, Feb 2016
QuarterNbr	ROUNDUP(MONTH([DateKey])/3,0)	The quarter number (1-4) that the month is in.
QuarterFull	"Quarter " & ROUNDUP(MONTH([DateKey])/3,0)	Quarter 1, Quarter 2
QuarterAbbr	"Q" & ROUNDUP(MONTH([DateKey])/3,0)	Q1, Q2
QuarterAndYearAbbr	"Q" & ROUNDUP(MONTH([DateKey])/3,0) & " " & YEAR([DateKey])	Q1 2016, Q2 2016

Table 8-5 Formulas to create date fields

2. Change the Default Summarization option for all columns in the date table to Do Not Summarize.

3. Click on the Month and Year Abbr column ⇒ Modeling tab ⇒ Sort By Column button ⇒ Full Year.

4. Click on the Quarter and Year Abbr column ⇒ Modeling tab ⇒ Sort By Column button ⇒ Full Year.
   When you are finished, your date table should look like the one shown in Figure 8-18.

DateKey	FullYear	MonthNbr	Month Full	Month Abbr	MonthAndYearAbbr	QuarterNbr	Quarter Full	QuarterAbbr	QuarterAndYearAbbr
01/01/2010	2010	1	January	Jan	Jan 2010	1	Quarter 1	Q1	Q1 2010
01/02/2010	2010	1	January	Jan	Jan 2010	1	Quarter 1	Q1	Q1 2010
01/03/2010	2010	1	January	Jan	Jan 2010	1	Quarter 1	Q1	Q1 2010
01/04/2010	2010	1	January	Jan	Jan 2010	1	Quarter 1	Q1	Q1 2010

Figure 8-18 My Date Table

Calculated Tables

This type of table is like a calculated column. It is created from other columns and tables in the data model. This table stores DAX formulas that you create. Each column in this table has its own data type, default summarization, formatting etc. You can also create relationships using this table. They are also used to create date/calendar tables.

Calculated tables are useful if you create a lot of formulas and want to keep all of the formulas all in one place, instead of spread out in all of the other tables in the data model. Putting all of the formulas in the same table (except for date table formulas) in the data model, makes the formulas easier to find. This table is created like the date table that you created in the previous exercise, by clicking the New Table button on the Modeling tab.

Create A Table

> The Create Table option is best suited for smaller amounts of data. I don't know what the maximum number of rows and columns are, but I tried pasting in 1,000 rows, which I think is a small number of rows and got an error indicating that there were too many rows in the table.

Clicking the **ENTER DATA BUTTON** on the Home tab, in the Power BI Desktop workspace or the Home tab in the Query Editor, displays the dialog box shown in Figure 8-19. This dialog box is used to create a new table by pasting in the data or by typing the data into the table.

The * (asterisk) to the right of the column header will add another column to the table. The asterisk below the row number will add another row to the table. The Name field is used to type in a name for the new table.

The **LOAD BUTTON** creates the table and loads it into the data model.

The **EDIT BUTTON** creates the table and displays it in the Query Editor.

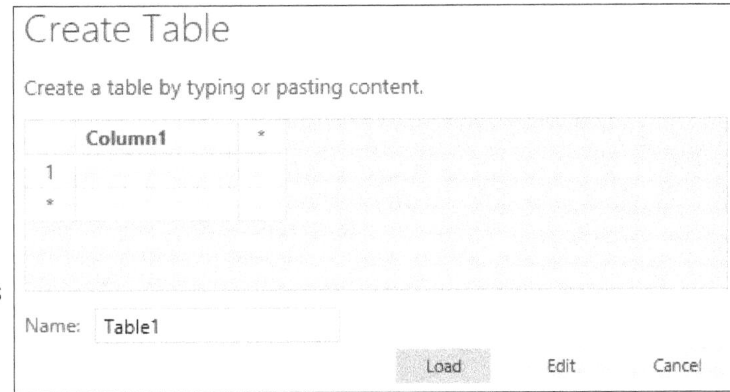

Figure 8-19 Create Table dialog box

This type of table can be useful for data that does not change often or for data that you need to use as a mapping table (an intermediary table used to connect other tables together).

Figure 8-20 shows data pasted into the table from an Excel spreadsheet.

To paste data, follow the steps below.

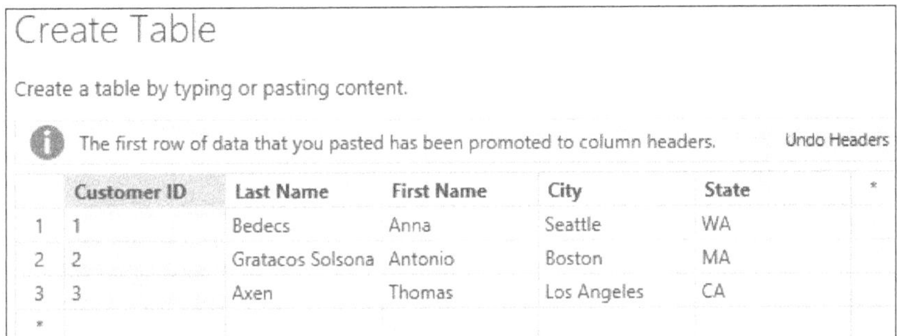

Figure 8-20 Table created from pasted data

1. Select the data in the data source ⇒ Press Ctrl+C.
2. Click the Enter Data button in Power BI Desktop ⇒ Right-click in the cell shown earlier in Figure 8-19 ⇒ Select Paste.
3. Type in a name for the table ⇒ Click the Load or Edit button.

Another Way To Sort By Month Number

Exercise 8.1 showed you how to ensure that the months are sorted in calendar order, when displayed on a chart. That is fine, as long as you have access to a date table. If you do not have a date table, a relatively easy solution is outlined below. The query that you use, needs to have the date column that you want to sort by month number.

1. In the Query Editor, select the query that you need to sort by the month number.
2. Click on the date column that you need to sort on ⇒ Add Column tab ⇒ Date button ⇒ Month ⇒ Month.
3. Click on the date column that you used in step 2 ⇒ Add Column tab ⇒ Date button ⇒ Month ⇒ Name of Month.
4. In the Data view, select the query that you just modified ⇒ Click on the Month Name column ⇒ Modeling tab ⇒ Sort By Column button ⇒ Select the Month field.

Displaying Month Names In Calendar Order

If you will be importing data that is month driven (meaning the data source does not have dates), like the spreadsheets shown in Chapter 13, Figures 13-66 and 13-67, that will be used to create a visual, the months will not be displayed in calendar order.

Exercise 8.4 resolved this issue if you have a date table. The section above resolved this issue by adding fields to a query. There is nothing wrong with that solution, as long as the data source has a date field, other then increasing the query size, by adding more columns. Neither of these solutions work with the data referenced above in Chapter 13. If you find yourself in this situation, the steps below provide a solution.

1. Use the Create Table dialog box covered earlier in this chapter to create the table shown in Figure 8-21.

   You can name the table and columns whatever you want.

Create Table

Create a table by typing or pasting content.

	MonthNbr	Month Name	*
1	1	January	
2	2	February	
3	3	March	
4	4	April	
5	5	May	
6	6	June	
7	7	July	
8	8	August	
9	9	September	
10	10	October	
11	11	November	
12	12	December	
*			

Name: MyMonthTable

Figure 8-21 Month table

2. In the Query Editor, use the Merge Queries option to merge the Month Nbr column shown above in Figure 8-21, into your table that has the months that you want displayed in order.

3. In the Data view, display the table that now has the Month Nbr column ⇒ Click on the column that has the month names.

4. Modeling tab ⇒ Sort By Column button ⇒ Select the Month Nbr field.

Other Uses For This Table
This table is also useful in both of the following scenarios:
① You cannot add a column (that has the month number) of data to the data source.
② If the data source that has a date field that needs to be sorted, is connected to via the Direct Query option or if you cannot add data/content to the data source.

What Is A Measure?

Unlike dimension formulas which are calculated for every row in a table, measures are formulas that are used to aggregate (for example Sum) the values in a column and are only calculated when displayed on the chart. One way to determine whether you need to create a measure or dimension is whether or not the value needs to be calculated for each row of data (create a dimension) or calculated for a group of rows (create a measure).

A **MEASURE** references columns. Measures are also known as **CALCULATED FIELDS**. Measures are usually numbers. Keep in mind that non numeric data in a dimension can be used to create a measure (only a count measure).
If you need to use more than one aggregation (like distinct count and sum), for the same field, you have to create multiple measures for the same field. It is a good idea to name measures something that indicates what the formula creates.

Measures pick up where calculated columns leave off. While calculated columns are applied to each row in the table, measure are applied to some or all of the records in the table. The biggest difference between calculated columns and measures is that measures do not create columns in the table that display data, but the measure names are displayed in a table, in the Fields panel.

Measures are often displayed using the Card visualization, because a measure only contains one value. Like other fields, measure can be filtered. An example of a measure is to count the number of sales.

Exercise 8.5: Create Measures

In this exercise you will learn how to create measures.

Create A Total Order Amount Measure

In this part of the exercise, you will create a measure to calculate the total dollar amount of orders. Yes, I know what you are thinking. Why not just use the Sum aggregation option for the Order Amount field? The main reason is because when you apply an aggregation to a field, the value is tied to the table or chart that it is displayed on. A measure can be displayed on any visual, even if no other fields in the table are used on the table or chart.

1. Click on the Orders table in the Fields panel ⇒ Modeling tab ⇒ Click the New Measure button.

2. Change the word Measure in the formula bar to `Total Order Amount` ⇒ Click after the equal sign.

3. Type `SUM(Orders`.

   You will see a list of tables, measures and columns, as shown on the right side of Figure 8-22. This is known as IntelliSense.

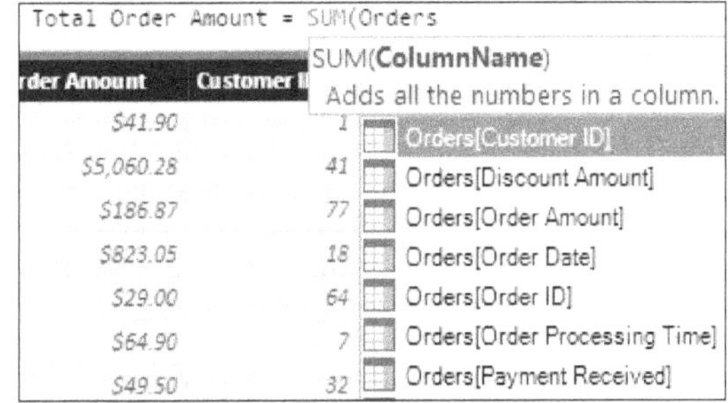

Figure 8-22 IntelliSense functionality

4. Scroll down the list and double-click on the Order Amount field.

Another Way To Select A Table Or Field In The Drop-Down List
Instead of scrolling, you can type some of the first letters of the table or field that you are looking for. Doing this will jump to that section in the list.

5. Type a) at the end of the formula, as shown in Figure 8-23 ⇒ Press Enter.

```
Total Order Amount = Sum(Orders[Order Amount])
```

Figure 8-23 Total Order Amount formula

Create A Count Of Orders Measure

In this part of the exercise, the measure that you will create will calculate the number of orders in a table. Yes, the same reason for creating a formula to calculate the total order amount, applies to this measure also <smile>.

1. Click on the Orders table ⇒ Click the New Measure button.

2. Create the formula shown in Figure 8-24 ⇒ Press Enter.

```
Count of Orders = COUNTROWS(Orders)
```

Figure 8-24 Count of Orders formula

Create A Measure To Rank Sales Reps By Their Total Sales

This part of the exercise will show you how to create a measure that ranks the sales reps, based on their total sales. In the Slicers chapter, you will use this field to create a table and use slicers to filter the data by year. This will show you how each sales rep ranked, for the year selected in the slicer.

1. Click on the Orders table ⇒ Click the New Measure button.

2. Create the formula shown in Figure 8-25.

```
SalesRepRank = RANKX(ALL('Sales Reps'[SalesRep]), SUMX(RELATEDTABLE(Orders), [Order Amount]))
```

Figure 8-25 Formula to rank sales rep by order amount totals

Moving Measures From One Table To Another Table

Earlier in Table 8-2, the Home Table button was discussed one use for this option is if you want to store all of the measures that you create in one table, as discussed earlier in the Calculated Tables section. Having this functionality means that you do not have to recreate the measure again. On your own, if you need to move a measure, the steps below show you how.

1. With a measure selected ⇒ Modeling tab ⇒ **HOME TABLE** drop-down list, displays the list of other tables in the data model, as shown in Figure 8-26.

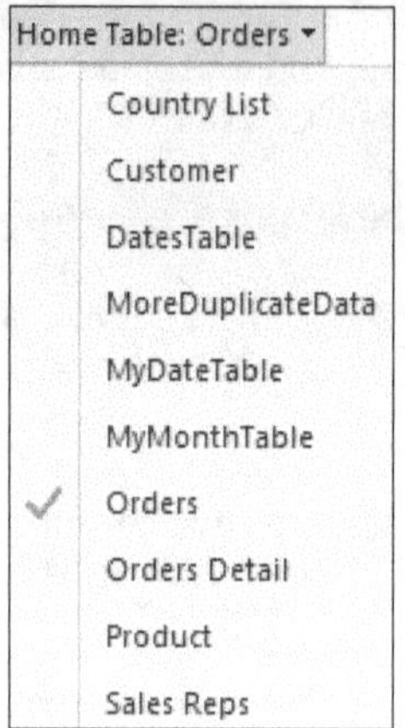

Figure 8-26 Home Table button options

2. Select the table that you want to move the measure to.

3. In the Fields panel, you will see the measure in the table that you selected.

Query Parameters

The last topic in this chapter is on parameters. While it may be out of place being in this chapter, I added it here on purpose, because I wanted the parameter exercises to be included in the Report Data file that will be used in most of the exercises in the rest of this book. That way, adding parameters to reports that are created in the rest of this book is possible. Trust me. There is a method to what appears to be madness <smile>.

Parameters are another way to filter data. They can be used to select a data source to import data from, filter data in the Query Editor, filter data during the import process or filter data on a chart. A parameter can be created or used any place in the Power BI Desktop where you see the last two options shown on the drop-down list, in Figure 8-27.

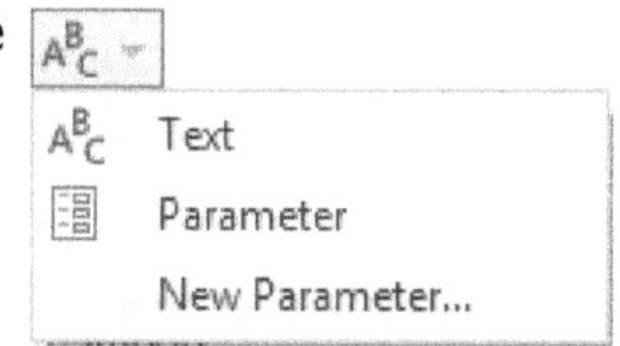

Figure 8-27 Parameter options

Parameters can also used in DAX formulas and referenced from other queries.

If you have used other software like Crystal Reports™, which has parameter fields, you are already familiar with the concept.

At the time this book went to print, the parameter functionality had only been available for a few months. I suspect that the functionality will be enhanced in the future. New features that I think would make parameters much more useful are:

① To have the option of selecting more than one value in the parameter.

② To connect two or more parameters together to create a new parameter (think merge two queries to a new table), so that they appear together. The way parameters currently work is that all of the parameters created in the report file are used on every page. You should be able to select which parameter(s) to use on a particular page. You should also have the option to not use parameters on a page.

Figure 8-28 shows the dialog box used to create and edit a parameter. The options are explained below.

The column on the left is a list of parameters in the report file.

The **NAME FIELD** is used to give the parameter a descriptive name.

The **DESCRIPTION FIELD** is used to explain how the parameter should be used. This text will be displayed next to the parameter name, where the parameter is displayed. Using this field is optional, but can be used as a tool tip.

Check the **REQUIRED OPTION** to force a value to be selected for the parameter.

If a parameter is not required, you are not prevented from only using the other parameter(s) that you want to use. This means that if you only want to use one parameter of four, for report A and two parameters for report B, you can.

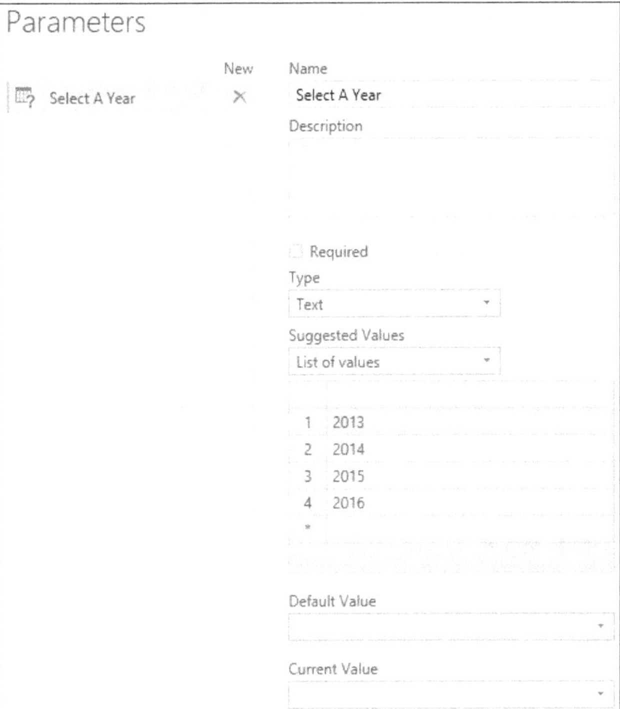

Figure 8-28 Parameters dialog box

The options in the **TYPE FIELD** are the data types that Power BI Desktop supports. Select the one that matches the type of data that will be used in the parameter field. Select **ANY** to make the parameter free form.

The **SUGGESTED VALUES OPTION** is used to select where the values for the parameter come from. Figure 8-29 shows the options currently available. The options are explained below.

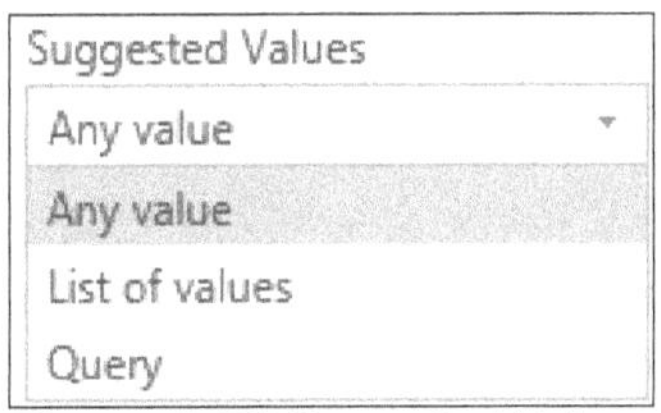

Figure 8-29 Suggested Values options

① Select **ANY VALUE** to allow basically anything to be entered as a value.

② Select **LIST OF VALUES** to provide the values that can be selected. Currently, this option requires you to manually type in the list of values, as the functionality to select a field in a query has not been added, when this book went to print. It is best suited for a short list of values, unless you like to type a lot, until the functionality includes being able to connect the option to a field in a query.

③ **QUERY** This option is used to select what is known as a **LIST QUERY**. It contains a list of values that will be selected from.

The **CURRENT VALUE OPTION** is used to enter a value for the parameter. Once the parameter is used, the value selected is added to this field.

The **DEFAULT VALUE OPTION** is currently only available when the List of values option, shown above in Figure 8-29, is selected. This option is used to enter the value that you think will be used to most for the parameter. This value will automatically be selected when the parameter is first displayed. Entering a value in this field is optional.

Exercise 8.6: Create Parameters

In this exercise, you will learn how to create parameters that use a list of values and query.

Create The Year Parameter

Many reports need to filter the data by year. Having a consistent way to perform this task from page to page, makes it easier for users.

1. Open the Query Editor ⇒ Home Tab ⇒ Manage Parameters button ⇒ New Parameter.

2. In the Name field, type `Select A Year`.

3. Clear the check mark for the Required field.

4. Open the Type drop-down list and select Text.

5. Open the Suggest Values drop-down list and select List of values.

6. Type the following values in the table. `2013`, `2014`, `2015`, `2016`.
   You should have the options shown earlier in Figure 8-28 ⇒ Click OK.
   You will see that a query was created and the parameter input field is displayed, as shown in Figure 8-30.
   (I moved the query up in the Queries panel) By default, no data is displayed because parameters do not store data.

The **CURRENT VALUE FIELD** drop-down list contains the values that you entered for the Value list.

The **MANAGE PARAMETER BUTTON** displays the Parameters dialog box, shown earlier in Figure 8-28.

Parameter queries are like the other queries. They can be loaded to the data model, used in other queries and referenced in DAX formulas.

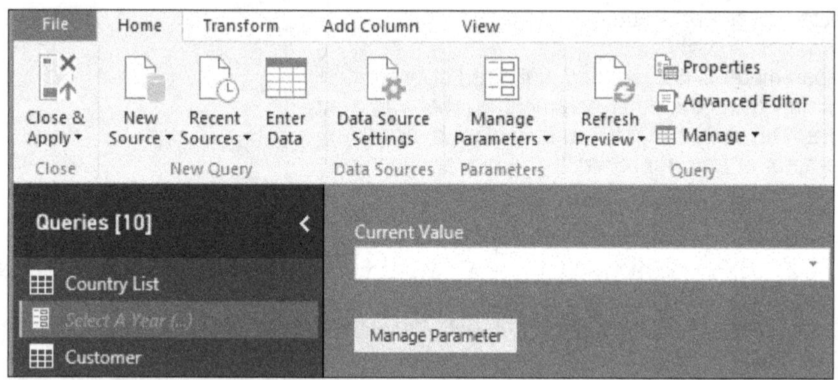

Figure 8-30 Year parameter query

Figure 8-31 shows the M code that was created for the Select A Year parameter.

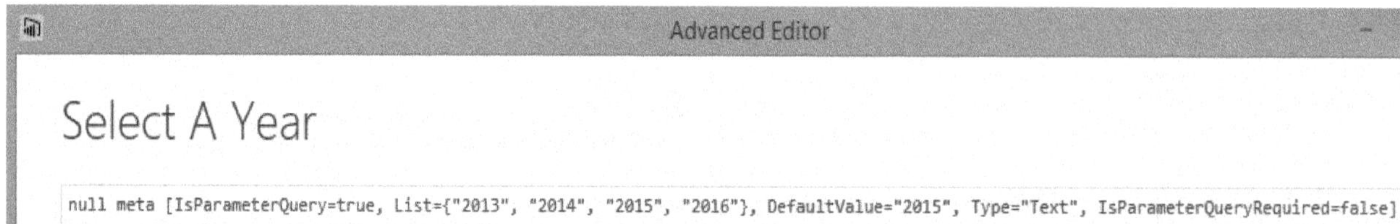

Figure 8-31 M code for the parameter

Creating More Than One Parameter
If you need to create more than one parameter at the same time, click the **NEW LINK**, that is above the list of parameter names, instead of clicking the OK button.

Load A Parameter Query Into The Data Model

By default, parameter queries are not loaded to the data model.

1. Right-click on the parameter query and select Enable Load.

2. Save and apply the changes.

Create The Country Parameter

1. Create a new parameter using the options shown in Figure 8-32.

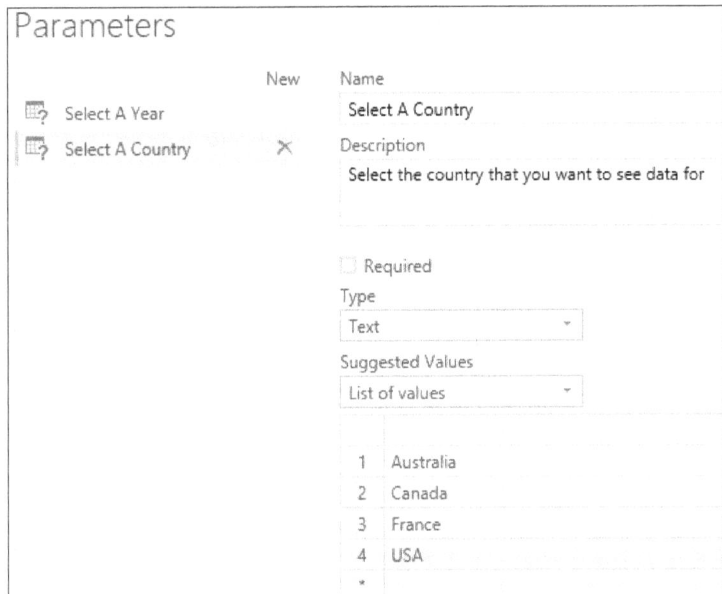

Figure 8-32 Country field parameter options

2. Load the parameter to the data model ⇒ Apply and save the changes. You should see the query options shown in Figure 8-33.

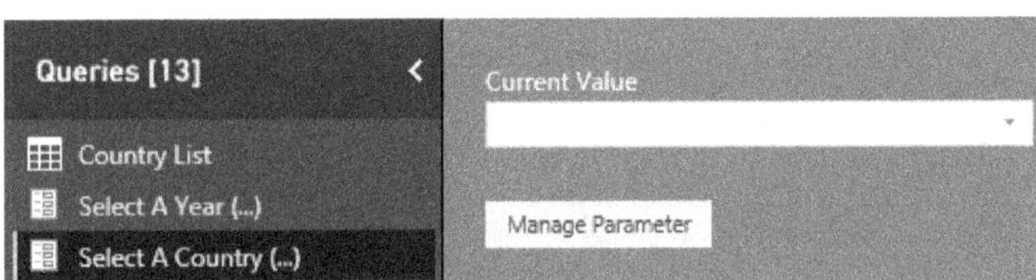

Figure 8-33 Select A Country query

Use The Query Suggested Values Option

This option uses a list of values from a query to populate the parameter, like the List of Values, Suggested Values option that was covered in the previous section of this exercise. While a list may look like a query in the Queries panel, they are not the same.

Chapter 5 covered the Lists data type. One way to create a list query is using the M language. It contains a list of values, which is also known as an **ORDERED LIST**. Don't worry, using the M language to create the list is painless.

Create The List Query

In this part of the exercise, you will learn how to create the list query values.

1. Query Editor ⇒ Home tab ⇒ New Source ⇒ Blank Query option ⇒ Advanced Editor button.

2. Delete all of the code in the Advanced Editor ⇒ Type the expression shown in Figure 8-34.

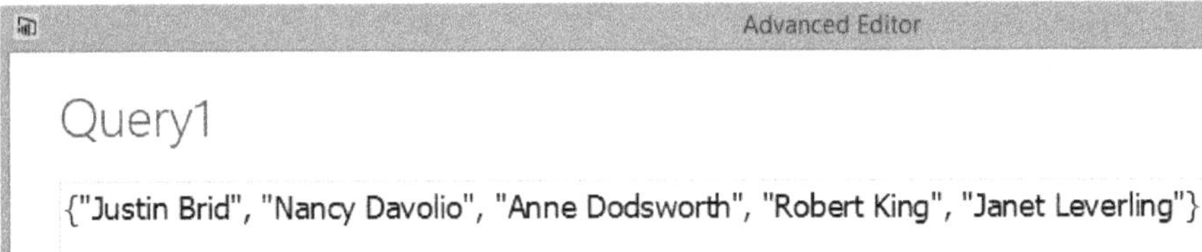

Figure 8-34 Values for the list query

3. Click Done ⇒ Rename the query to `Sales Reps List` ⇒ Save the changes.

Create A Parameter That Uses A List Query

In this part of the exercise you will create the parameter that will use the list query created in the previous part of this exercise.

1. Home tab ⇒ Manage Parameters button ⇒ Manage Parameters option. (Clicking the top half of the Manage Parameters button, will also open the Manage Parameters dialog box.)

2. On the Parameters dialog box, click the New link.

3. Select the options shown in Figure 8-35 ⇒

   Save the changes.

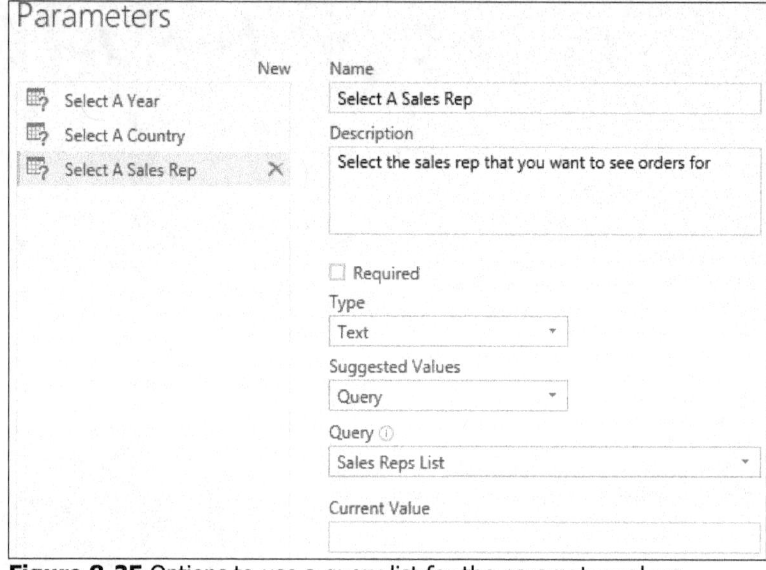

Figure 8-35 Options to use a query list for the parameter values

Manage Parameters

The options on the button shown in Figure 8-36 are explained below.

The **MANAGE PARAMETERS** and **NEW PARAMETER OPTIONS** open the Parameters dialog box. New parameters can be created and existing parameters can be edited.

The **EDIT PARAMETERS OPTION** displays the dialog box shown in Figure 8-37. The options are used to select the values for the parameters.

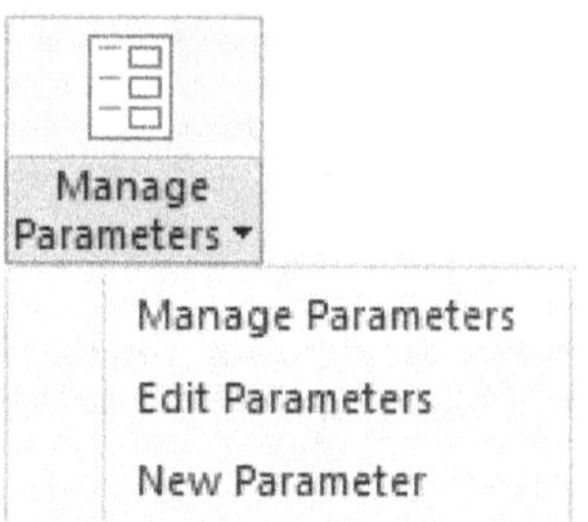

Figure 8-36 Manage Parameters button options

The values that you select here are the ones that will be displayed in the Current Value field, shown earlier in Figure 8-35. They will also be displayed when the query is first run.

Like the Parameters dialog box, all of the parameter fields, for the report file are displayed on the same dialog box.

Notice that the description created for the country parameter is displayed as a tool tip.

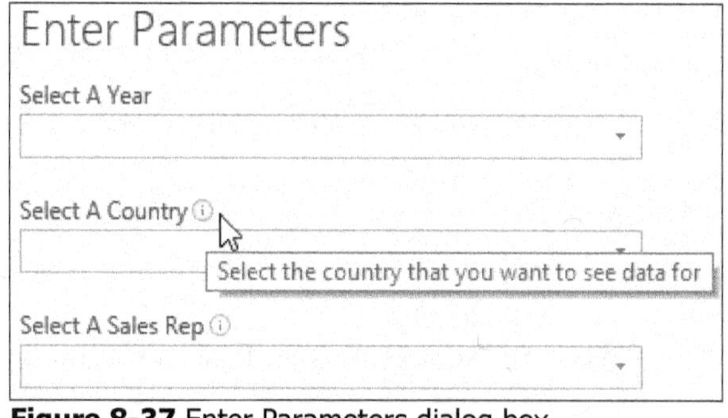

Figure 8-37 Enter Parameters dialog box

Selecting The Parameter Values

Using Parameter Values
As you will see, parameters may not work the way that you think they will. I suspect that in time, the process of using them will become more intuitive.

Before using the parameters to filter or load data, you have to select the value(s) that you want to filter on. You can select the value on the individual query [See Figure 8-33] or you can use the Enter Parameters dialog box. Use this option when you need to select values for more than one parameter.

Exercise 8.7: Use A Parameter With A Query

In this exercise, you will use a parameter to filter data in a query. You will use the country parameter, to filter records in the Customer query.

1. In the Queries panel, click on the Select A Country query ⇒ Open the Current Value drop-down list and select USA.
2. Display the Customer query ⇒ Display the filter options for the Country column ⇒ Select Text Filters ⇒ Equals.
3. On the Filter Rows dialog box, open the first ABC drop-down list and select Parameter, as shown on the right side of Figure 8-38.

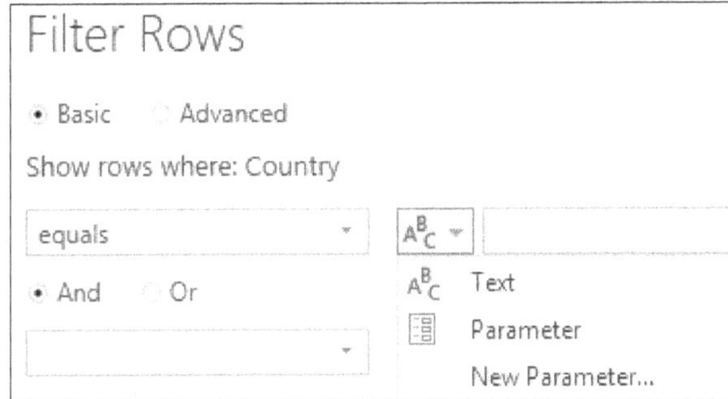

Figure 8-38 Data value options

4. In the next field, select the Select A Country parameter ⇒ Click OK. The query will only display records that have USA in the Country column.
5. Clear the filter options for the Country column in the Customer query ⇒ Apply and save the changes.
6. Display the Select A Country query ⇒ Open the Current Value drop-down list and select the Blank option. This clears the value for the parameter.

Using Parameters
Keep in mind that the parameters that have a value selected, filter the visualizations in the report file. I clear them when creating visualizations, to ensure that all of the data that I am expecting to see is displayed.

Where To Create Parameters
If you are creating a template file and know that the dataset would benefit from parameters, create the parameters in the file that will be used as the template file, so that you do not have to create the same parameters over and over in different files.

Summary

This chapter covered the options on the Data view, including the Modeling tab options. Creating new tables, columns and measures were also covered, as well as, creating and managing parameters. The tasks competed in the Data view are preparation for creating reports.

GETTING STARTED WITH THE REPORT VIEW

After completing this chapter, you will have a better understanding of the Report view workspace and options on the Home tab that are available in this view. You will also learn how to create table visualizations.

CHAPTER 9

Report View

This may be the chapter that you have been most anxious to get to <smile>, because you will start learning how to create reports, based on the data that you have imported and transformed, as well as, any new tables that you create in Power BI Desktop.

The Report view is based on Power View for Excel. It has a lot more features and functionality. Power View originally came from Microsoft's SQL Server Reporting Services (SSRS) environment. Until Power View, SQL Server Reporting Services was Microsoft's primary tool for creating reports. There is nothing wrong with SQL Server Reporting Services. Its use however, is geared more towards the IT department. I say that because SQL Server Reporting Services and many other report creation tools take a while to just learn the interface. Keep in mind the costs associated with having the reports created by the IT department, in addition to any software that may need to be purchased. Power BI Desktop provides the ability to get up and running much faster. I have read articles that discussed some type of integration between Power BI Desktop and SQL Server Reporting Services reports, is being worked on.

Figure 9-1 shows the steps and process that most IT departments follow, to create a report.
Figure 9-2 shows the steps and process needed to have a non IT person create a report in the Report view.

As you can see, there are fewer steps using Power BI Desktop.

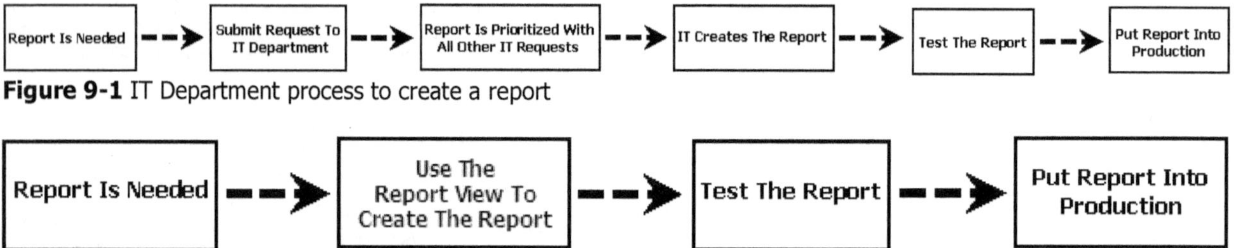

Figure 9-1 IT Department process to create a report

Figure 9-2 Process to create a report in Power BI Desktop

The Report view was not designed to replace SQL Server Reporting Services. To me, the Report view is an easier tool to use, to create reports. What makes it easier is that **VISUALIZATIONS** can be created with a few mouse clicks. The Report view also has options to add interactive functionality to reports. This functionality is well suited for "What If" analysis and being able to answer data related questions quickly.

What Type Of Reports Do You Need To Create?

As covered in Chapter 1, a large goal of Business Intelligence is to get a better understanding of the data needed to aid in the decision making process. The most popular way to do that is by presenting the data in a report format.

Data Analytics

This is the process of collecting and analyzing data to see if there are or are not any correlations, patterns or other insights of the data that can be used in the decision making process.

There are three categories of analytical reports that can be created, as explained below.

① **DESCRIPTIVE** This type of report uses historical data as the basis for the analysis. Using historical data allows reports to be created that can answer questions like what are last years sales by quarter and region and which sales reps sold the most of products a, b, and c?

② **PREDICTIVE** This type of report is used to answer what I call "What If" questions, like which sales reps will have the most sales in the west and what current products will sell the best in the south west? Predictive reports are used to display future forecasted data. Currently, Power BI Desktop does not have a lot of data mining functionality or built-in tools to discover this type of data. But tools like R Script, can be used to create a forecasted dataset and then import the data into Power BI Desktop, so that reports can be created, using the forecasted data. The forecasting feature was introduced right before this book went to print. It can be used with a line chart, to detect seasonality and to step into the data.

③ **PRESCRIPTIVE** This type of report picks up where predictive reports leave off because in addition to trying to predict future data, this type of report can include goal seek results and any implications for the results that are discovered. Like predictive reports, Power BI Desktop does not have built-in tools to create this type of dataset. Azure Machine Learning, is one analytic tool that can be used to build predictive and prescriptive data models, which can be imported into Power BI Desktop.

What Is A Visualization?

A visualization is a graphical representation, like a table or chart, that is used to display data on a report. One way reports created in Power BI Desktop are different from traditional reports is that they do not have report headers, footers or page numbers displayed, probably because visualizations are usually not printed, like traditional paper based reports are. The Report view, like many other Business Intelligence tools, is used to change the data displayed on the report, by creating filters or by using one chart to filter other visualizations on the same page in the report, without writing a line of code.

Understanding Tables In The Report View

In other software packages, the word "table" usually only refers to data. In the Report view, a table has two meanings: 1) The data used to create a report and 2) A way to display data on a report. When displaying data using the Table visualization, it resembles a spreadsheet in Excel. Displaying data is another way to describe what many people call a "layout".

Report View Workspace

A large portion of this chapter explains the workspace and many of the options that are available and what they can be used for. I realize that many readers want to jump ahead and start creating reports without learning about the Report view workspace. If you fall into that category, that's fine. Skip ahead to Exercise 9.1.

Figure 9-3 shows the Report view workspace. Multiple visualizations can be created (even on the same page, which is how a dashboard is created) and saved in the report file. Like paper based reports, reports created in Power BI Desktop, can have more than one page. As you will see, each Power BI Desktop file (also known as a **REPORT FILE**), can have several pages. To demonstrate this, for the most part, you will create all of the exercises in a chapter, in the same file.

The three main sections of the Report view are the tool bar, Fields panel and Visualizations panel. The white space in the middle of the workspace is where you place the visualization(s). The white space is also known as the **CANVAS**. The Visualizations and Fields panels can be collapsed, if you need more room on the canvas, by clicking the arrow button to the right of the panel name.

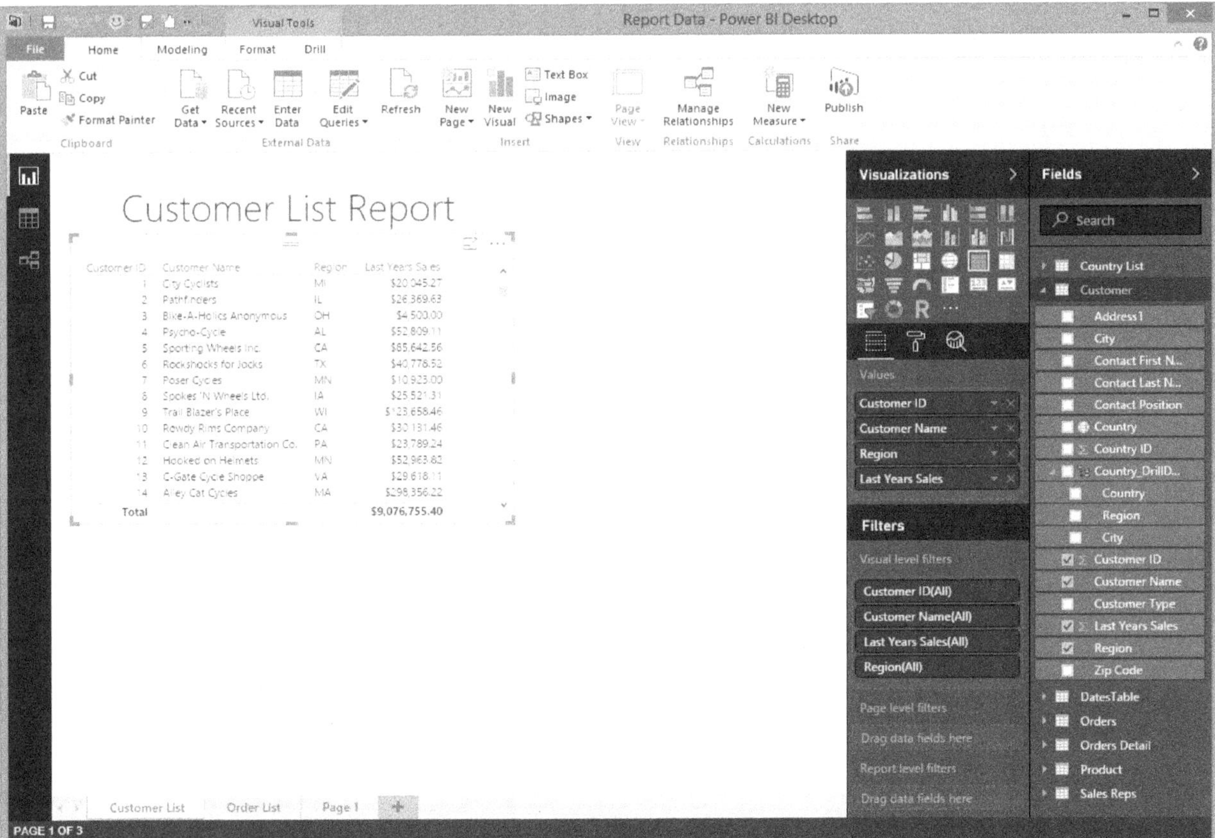

Figure 9-3 Report view workspace

The page in the report file that is displayed before you save the file, will be displayed the next time that you open the file.

Home Tab Options

In Chapter 2, the options in the External Data section of the Home tab were covered. The options in the Clipboard, Insert and View sections are covered below.

Clipboard Options

The options in this section are used to paste data from the Windows clipboard into a table in Power BI Desktop or copy data from a table in the data model to the clipboard. The table-like data that you paste into a table in the data model, can come from another software package like Microsoft Word. The options are explained in Table 9-1.

Option	Description
Paste	Pastes the copied object to the same page or another page in the report file. This option works the same as using **CTRL+V**, which can also be used.
Cut	Removes the selected object from the report page.
Copy	Copies data or an object, like a visualization, to the clipboard, so that it can be pasted into another application. This option works the same as using **CTRL+C**, which can also be used. The object can also be copied from one page to another in the same report file.
Format Painter	It is used to copy the formatting from one object to another object, with a mouse click. Options like data labels, the legend, data colors and background formatting are some of the properties that can be copied.

Table 9-1 Clipboard options explained

Insert Options

The options in this section are used to customize the report. They are explained in Table 9-2.

Option	Description
New Page	The **BLANK PAGE OPTION** on this button, adds a new page to the report file. The **DUPLICATE PAGE OPTION** creates a copy of the selected page.
New Visual	This option adds a blank visualization layout to the current page.
Text Box	This option adds a text box to the page and displays the Text Box toolbar. This is used to add a title to the page or visualization. A URL link can also be added to a Text Box.
Image	This option is used to add an image (graphic) to the page.
Shapes	This option is used to add a shape to the page.

Table 9-2 Insert options explained

View Option

The options on the **PAGE VIEW BUTTON** shown in Figure 9-4, are used to select how the page should be displayed. This option has to be set on a page by page basis.

To save time, you could add a page to the report file and select the Page View option that you need, then duplicate that page to create new pages.

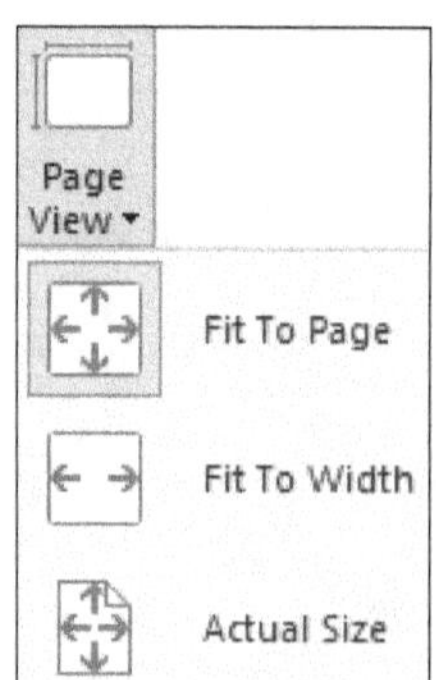

Figure 9-4 Page View options

Relationships Option

MANAGE RELATIONSHIPS BUTTON Opens the Manage Relationships dialog box. [See Chapter 7, Figure 7-11]

Calculations Option

NEW MEASURE BUTTON Displays options to create a measure and column. The formula bar is displayed right below the toolbar, once an option is selected.

Share Option

PUBLISH BUTTON [See Chapter 1, Publish To Power BI]

Status Bar

Figure 9-5 shows the Report view workspace status bar. The options are explained in Table 9-3. Right-clicking on a page (tab) displays the shortcut menu shown in Figure 9-6.

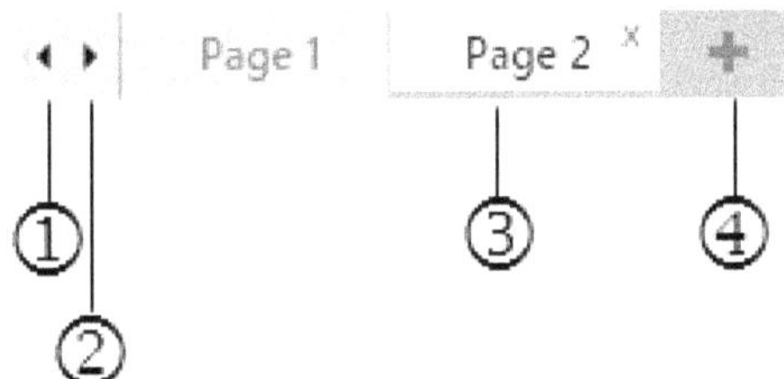

Figure 9-5 Status bar

Button	Description
1	Displays the page to the left of the selected page.
2	Displays the page to the right of the selected page.
3	Holding the mouse pointer over a page, displays an X in the upper right corner of the tab. Click on the X to delete the page.
4	The plus sign button adds a new page to the report file.

Table 9-3 Status bar buttons explained

Reorder (Move) The Pages In A Report File
If you want to change the order of the pages in a report file, click on the tab that you want to move, then drag the tab to the right or left.

Report Pages
Technically, there is no limit to the number of pages that can be created in a report file. It is possible that if the reports require a lot of DAX calculated fields, the report file will take a performance hit when the data model is refreshed or when the report file is first opened.

Tab Shortcut Menu

Select **DUPLICATE PAGE** when you want to create a new page that has everything on the current page.

Select **RENAME PAGE** to change the name of the current page (tab).

Select **DELETE PAGE** to remove the current page from the report file.

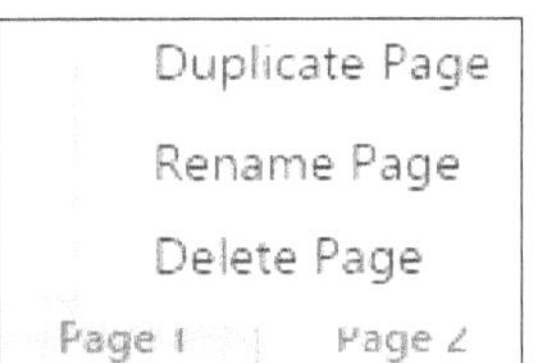

Figure 9-6 Tab shortcut menu

Visualizations Panel

The options on this panel are used to select how the data is displayed on the page. The top section of the panel contains the visualization types (sometimes referred to as templates) and interactive features, like slicers, that can be added to the page. They are explained in Chapter 12.

Visualizations

I think the most important thing to understand about creating reports in Power BI Desktop is that they are not the traditional paper based reports that you may be use to. Reports created in Power BI Desktop are meant to be viewed on a screen. This may be why reports created in Power BI Desktop are referred to as visualizations.

I think the second most important thing to know about reports created in Power BI Desktop is to understand as much about table visualizations as possible. Often, you will see the terms **VISUALIZATION, REPORTS** and **INTERACTIVE VIEWS** used interchangeably. More than one visualization can be displayed on a page. Displaying more than one visualization on a page is how you create a **DASHBOARD** (also referred to as an interactive view).

Different types of visualizations can be created. The **TABLE VISUALIZATION** is one of the most popular. **MATRIX, CARD** and **MULTI-ROW CARD** are the other types of table visualizations that Power BI Desktop supports.

Below the visualization types are three buttons, as explained below:

① The **FIELDS BUTTON OPTIONS** are used to select the fields to display on a visualization. Fields added to the Filters section are used to create filters that are applied to one of the following: The selected visual, the page or all visuals in the report.
② The **FORMAT BUTTON OPTIONS** are used to customize the page or the selected visualization. The options displayed are based on the visualization type or object that is selected on the page.
③ The **ANALYTICS BUTTON OPTIONS** are used to add reference lines to charts that support this functionality.

Field Well, Format And Analytics Panels

Each button discussed in the previous section displays a panel. The panels are explained below.

The **FIELD WELL PANEL** shown in Figure 9-7, is used to add the fields needed to create the visual and to create filters that may be needed. [See Field Well Panel]

The **FORMAT PANEL** is used to format the selected visual or customize the page. [See Chapter 11, Figure 11-1]

ANALYTICS PANEL [See Chapter 13, Analytics Panel]

Field Well Panel

Figure 9-7 shows the Field Well for the Table visualization. As you will see in Chapter 12, most charts have more than one field on the Field Well. Some or all of the options on the shortcut menu shown in the figure are available for fields added to the Field Well. The options available on the shortcut menu depend on the data type of the field.

The **VALUES SECTION** is where the fields are added. The order that the fields are added, is the order that they will appear in the table, from left to right.

Clicking the triangle icon after the field name in the Values section displays the shortcut menu shown on the right side of the figure.

The **REMOVE FIELD** option removes the field from the table.

The **QUICK CALC OPTIONS** and **AGGREGATE FUNCTIONS** are covered later in this chapter.

If checked, the **SHOW ITEMS WITH NO DATA** option displays a row of data, even if the row does not have data in the field(s) used to create the table.

The **FILTERS SECTION** is used to create filters for the visual, page and report.

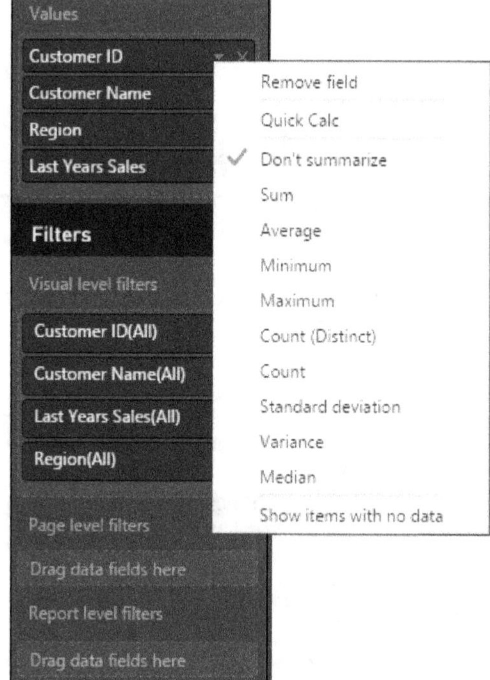

Figure 9-7 Table Field Well

Field Well Tip
If you need to replace a field in a section of the Field Well that only allows one field, you can drag the new field over the one that you want to replace and the original field will be removed automatically.

How To Rearrange The Field Order In The Field Well

From time to time, you may need to change the order that the fields are listed in, on the Field Well.

For example, if you need the Customer ID field shown above in Figure 9-7 to be the last field displayed in the Values section, drag the Customer ID field down below the Last Years Sales field.

As you drag the field, you will see a yellow line indicating where the field will be placed, when you release the mouse button, as illustrated in Figure 9-8.

Figure 9-8 Line illustrated where the field will be moved to

Fields Panel

This panel is similar to the one on the Data view. Notice the icons next to some of the fields. The icons represent the data type. The **SEARCH FIELD**, at the top of the Fields panel, is used to search all of the tables for a field.

Clicking on a check box in front of a field, adds it to the Field Well. The fields that you check are automatically added to the Visual levels filters section, in addition to a section on the Field Well. You can also drag fields to the Field Well or to the canvas on the workspace to create a visualization. When a field is added to the Field Well, the corresponding table name in the Fields panel changes to a yellow/gold color. This lets you know visually, that at least one field in the table is used on the selected visual. In addition to right-clicking, the shortcut menus discussed below, can also be accessed by clicking the ... (ellipsis) button after the table or field name.

Fields Panel Tips
① If you need to add the same field to the same visualization a second time (and the field is already checked), drag the field to the Field Well where you want the field placed.
② I find it easier to keep all of the fields displayed, instead of having to keep clicking on the table name to display them.

Table Name Shortcut Menu

Figure 9-9 shows the shortcut menu for a table. Options that are specifically for tables are explained in Table 9-4. Chapter 8, Table 8-1, explains the other options.

New measure
New column
Refresh data
Edit Query
Rename
Delete
Hide
View hidden
Unhide all
Collapse all
Expand all

Figure 9-9 Table name shortcut menu

Option	Description
Hide	Hides the table in the Report view and grays it out in the Data view.
View hidden	Displays hidden tables, but leaves them grayed out.
Unhide all	Removes the hidden state of the tables.
Collapse all	Hides the fields in all of the tables on the panel.
Expand all	Displays all of the fields, in all of the tables, on the Fields panel.

Table 9-4 Table name shortcut menu options explained

Field Name Shortcut Menu

Figure 9-10 shows the shortcut menu for fields. Options that are specifically for fields are explained in Table 9-5.

Add filter
New hierarchy
New measure
New column
Rename
Delete
Hide
View hidden
Unhide all
Collapse all
Expand all

Figure 9-10 Field name shortcut menu

Option	Description
Add Filter	[See Chapter 10, Filter Levels]
New Hierarchy	[See Chapter 8, Understanding Hierarchies]
Delete	Deletes the field from the table in the data model.

Table 9-5 Field name shortcut menu options explained

If the field is in a table that has a hierarchy, the hierarchy will also be displayed on this shortcut menu. This allows the field to be added to the hierarchy.

Resizing Tables And Charts

To resize a table or chart, hold the mouse pointer over the frame to display the handles. The handles are in the middle and corners of the visualization frame. Place the mouse pointer on one of the handles and drag the mouse in the direction that you want to resize the frame. Place the mouse pointer on one of the corners to resize the table or chart vertically and horizontally at the same time. I use the lower right corner to resize tables and charts.

Resizing charts can change the size of the text displayed on the axis. The text can be truncated and display and ellipsis (dots) to indicate that all of the text is not displayed, when the chart is made smaller.

The other change on charts that I notice when charts are resized, is that numeric markers (the values) will change. Figure 9-11 and 9-12 show the same chart. Figure 9-11 is the default chart size. In Figure 9-12, the chart has been resized. Notice that all of the company name is displayed and that the numeric values are in smaller increments, which provides a more realistic representation of the values.

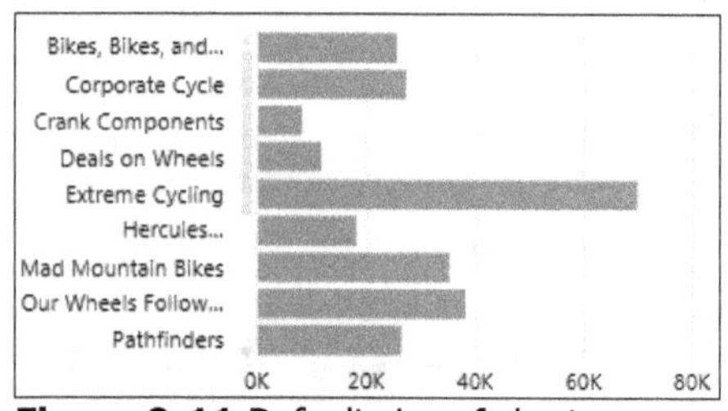

Figure 9-11 Default size of chart

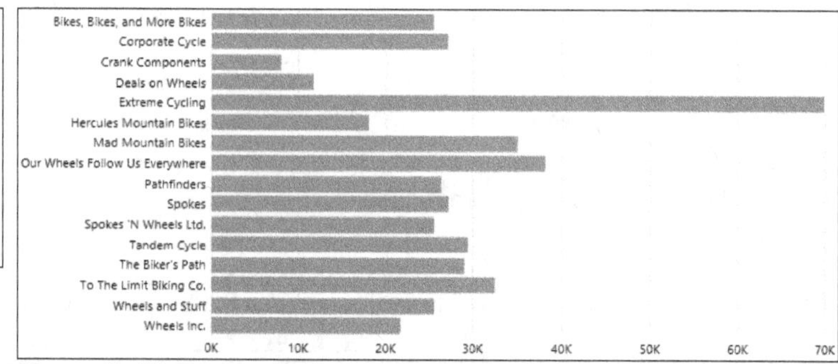

Figure 9-12 Chart resized

Exercise 9.1: Modify The Report Data File

Before creating the report in this chapter, there are some things that need to be changed.

1. Open the Report Data.pbix file.

2. Click on Page 1 ⇒ Click on the table on the page ⇒ Press the Delete key.

3. Move the Order List page left, so that it is next to the Customer List page.

4. Click on the table on the Customer List page ⇒ On the Visualizations panel, click on the **FORMAT BUTTON** (the second button below the visualization types) ⇒ Display the options in the General section ⇒ Change the Text Size to `16`.

As shown earlier in Figure 9-3, the reports that were imported have a title. These pages will be duplicated throughout the rest of this book. There is no point in duplicating the titles each time, just to have to delete them.

5. Click on the title, then press the Delete key.

6. Repeat steps 4 and 5 for the Order List page.

7. Save the changes.

Exercise Tips
Some of the steps are the same for every exercise. Instead of listing these steps in every exercise, they are listed here.
① Some exercises are based on a previous exercise (page). The instruction "Duplicate page Ex.x" means to duplicate the page referenced, then rename the duplicated page to the new exercise number. For example, if you are working on Exercise 9.3, you would rename the duplicated page to E9.3.
② Unless stated otherwise in step 1, each exercise requires a new page. When this is the case, click the plus sign button on the Status bar, then complete the exercise.
③ Unless specified otherwise, when instructed to add a field (to create a visualization) use the fields in Table 9-6. I provided this table so that I do not have to continuously list what table a field is in. The table is sorted by field name. If you do not want to keep flipping back to this page to look up fields, I saved the table in a PDF file named, Report Fields. It is in the zip file. You can leave the PDF file open or print it out.
④ Unless stated otherwise, all exercises in a chapter are to be created in the same report file.
⑤ Save the changes to the report file frequently.
⑥ The **UNDO** and **REDO OPTIONS** on the Quick Access Toolbar work in the Report view.

This Field . . .	Is In This Table
City	Customer
Country_Drill Down hierarchy	Customer table
Country Name	Country List
Customer Name	Customer
Customer Type	Customer
Date Hierarchy	Dates Table
Discount Amount	Orders
Full Name	Sales Reps
Last Years Sales	Customer
Month And Year Abbr	Dates Table
Month Full	Dates Table
Order Amount	Orders
Order Date	Orders
Order ID	Orders
Product Name	Product
Quantity	Orders Detail
Quarter And Year	Dates Table
Quarter Full	Dates Table
Region	Customer
Sales Cost	Orders
Sales Net	Orders
Sales Rep	Employee
Select Month	Dates Table ⇒ Date Hierarchy
Select Quarter	Dates Table ⇒ Date Hierarchy
Select Year	Dates Table ⇒ Date Hierarchy
Ship Date	Orders
Ship Via	Orders
Shipping Amount	Orders
Unit Price	Orders Detail
Year	Dates Table

Table 9-6 Fields used to create visualizations

Table Visualization Options

All of the table visualizations display data in a text format, instead of a graphical format. The look and feel of table and matrix visualizations will remind you of pivot tables in Excel. The table visualization options are explained below.

① **TABLE** displays data in a basic table, which looks like a spreadsheet. It is well suited for non numeric data. This is the default visualization option.
② **MATRIX** is similar to the Table visualization. The difference is that the data is grouped, similar to a pivot table in Excel or a cross tab report.
③ **MULTI-ROW CARD** displays different measures and elements/attributes for each occurrence. The values are displayed on a card.
④ **CARD** displays one numeric value. The Card visual is often used to make a single value stand out on the page or dashboard.

Table visualizations do not have drill down functionality, like charts have. Tables display data in a flat view.

Exercise 9.2: Create A Customer List Report

You will create a list report that displays customer information. A list report is basic and sometimes only uses data from one table.

1. Save the Report Data.pbix file as `Chapter 9 Table reports.`

2. On the Report view, add a page to the report. In the Visualizations panel, click on the **TABLE** visualization button.

3. In the Fields panel, click the check box for the following fields in the Customer table: Customer ID, Customer Name, Region and Last Years Sales. The Field Well should look like the one shown earlier in Figure 9-7.

4. If the Customer ID values are not displayed in numerical order, as shown below in Figure 9-13, click to the right of the Customer ID column heading in the table, to change the sort order.

5. Change the Text Size of the table to 16. [See Exercise 9.1, step 4]

6. Make the table larger ⇒ Rename the page to `E9.2`.

   The table visualization should look like the one shown in Figure 9-13.

   Not bad for a few mouse clicks, huh? <smile>

Customer ID	Customer Name	Region	Last Years Sales
1	City Cyclists	MI	$20,045.27
2	Pathfinders	IL	$26,369.63
3	Bike-A-Holics Anonymous	OH	$4,500.00
4	Psycho-Cycle	AL	$52,809.11
5	Sporting Wheels Inc.	CA	$85,642.56
6	Rockshocks for Jocks	TX	$40,778.52
7	Poser Cycles	MN	$10,923.00
8	Spokes 'N Wheels Ltd.	IA	$25,521.31
9	Trail Blazer's Place	WI	$123,658.46
10	Rowdy Rims Company	CA	$30,131.46
Total			**$9,076,755.40**

Focus mode

Figure 9-13 Customer list report

Using Column Totals

By default, column totals are automatically added to columns that have a numeric data type and a default summarization option, other then Do Not Summarize. The **TOTALS** general formatting option, must be enabled for the totals to appear on the visualization. [See Chapter 11, Figure 11-6]

Displaying More Data In A Table Visualization

When you need to see more of the data in a table, slide the scroll bar illustrated above in Figure 9-13, down or click the down arrow button on the scroll bar, illustrated in the lower right corner of the figure.

Report Options

The **FOCUS MODE** button (in the upper right corner of the visualization), shown above in Figure 9-13, is used to display the report as large as the window, as shown in Figure 9-14.

This lets you view more of the report without having to scroll as much.

< Back to Report

Customer ID	Customer Name	Region	Last Years Sales
1	City Cyclists	MI	$20,045.27
2	Pathfinders	IL	$26,369.63
3	Bike-A-Holics Anonymous	OH	$4,500.00
4	Psycho-Cycle	AL	$52,809.11
5	Sporting Wheels Inc.	CA	$85,642.56

Figure 9-14 Focus mode enabled for the table visualization

Click the **BACK TO REPORT BUTTON**, shown above in the upper left corner of Figure 9-14, to return to the Report view shown earlier in Figure 9-13.

When clicked, the **... ELLIPSIS BUTTON** (in the upper right corner of Figure 9-14), displays the options shown in Figure 9-15.

The **EXPORT DATA** option will save the data displayed in the visualization, as a CSV file.

The **REMOVE** option deletes the selected visualization.

Figure 9-15 Ellipsis button options

How To Delete A Visualization
In addition to using the Remove option shown above in Figure 9-15, a visualization can be deleted by selecting it on the canvas and then pressing the Delete key.

Adding More Fields To A Visualization
If you need to add more fields to an existing visualization, click on the visualization first, then add the field(s). Otherwise, a new visualization will automatically be created for the field that you select. This also means that when you want to add a new visualization to the page, nothing on the page can be selected.

Aggregations

Aggregations are used to group or summarize data. The way that data is displayed in a data table, by default, makes it difficult to see trends in the data or answer "What-If" analysis type questions. For example, if you looked at the data in the table shown in Figure 9-16, can you tell which sales rep had the most sales or what the top five selling products were? Probably not. When added to a visualization, aggregations will group or summarize the data to answer these questions and much more. Table 9-7 explains the aggregate functions shown earlier in Figure 9-7. Many of the aggregations are the same as the Default Summarization options that were covered in Chapter 8, Table 8-3.

SalesOrderID	OrderDate	DueDate	ShipDate	CustomerID	SalesPersonID	SubTotal
71842	6/1/2004	6/13/2004	6/8/2004	460	285	$11.687
71841	6/1/2004	6/13/2004	6/8/2004	10	285	$102,044.1...
71840	6/1/2004	6/13/2004	6/8/2004	571	286	$1,117.094
71839	6/1/2004	6/13/2004	6/8/2004	611	279	$68,030.1615
71838	6/1/2004	6/13/2004	6/8/2004	319	286	$13,724.1893
71837	6/1/2004	6/13/2004	6/8/2004	579	275	$36,189.4664
71836	6/1/2004	6/13/2004	6/8/2004	254	280	$81,644.2102
71835	6/1/2004	6/13/2004	6/8/2004	621	280	$64,801.7394

Figure 9-16 Table of data

Option	Description
Don't Summarize	This option does not create an aggregation for the field. Select this option to remove an aggregation from a field.
Sum	This is the default aggregation. It calculates the total of the values in the field.
Average	Calculates the average of the values in the field.
Minimum	Displays the smallest value in the field.
Maximum	Displays the largest value in the field.
Count (Distinct)	Displays a count of the number of records that have a unique value in the field.
Count	Displays a count of the number of records that have data in the field.
Standard deviation	Calculates how far from the mean, the value is.
Variance	Displays the average of the squared difference from the mean. This function calculates how far a set of numbers are spread out from their mean.
Median	Displays the middle value, from the values in the column.

Table 9-7 Aggregate functions explained

Exercise 9.3: Add A Field To An Existing Table Visualization

In Exercise 9.2 you added fields to the table visualization by checking them on the Fields panel. In this exercise you will duplicate that page, then add a field to the visualization by dragging the field to the Values section of the Field Well.

1. Duplicate page E9.2 ⇒ Rename the new page to `E9.3`.

2. Click on the table visualization ⇒ In the Customer table, drag the Customer Type field to the Values section of the Field Well and place it below the Customer ID field, as shown in Figure 9-17.

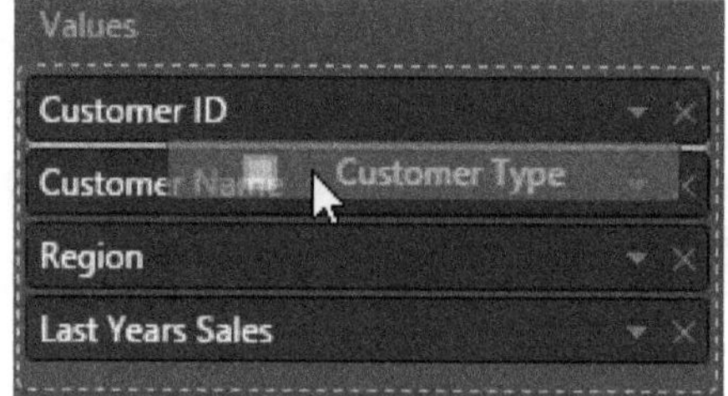

Figure 9-17 Field about to be added between existing fields in the Field Well

3. Make the table wider if necessary, so that all of the fields are visible, as shown in Figure 9-18.

Customer ID	Customer Type	Customer Name	Region	Last Years Sales
1	Retail	City Cyclists	MI	$20,045.27
2	Online	Pathfinders	IL	$26,369.63
3	Retail	Bike-A-Holics Anonymous	OH	$4,500.00
4	Online	Psycho-Cycle	AL	$52,809.11
Total				**$9,076,755.40**

Figure 9-18 Field added to the table

How To Delete A Field From A Table Visualization
Below are two ways to delete a field from a visualization.
① Clicking the X at the end of the field in the Field Well, as shown earlier in Figure 9-17.
② On the Fields panel, remove the check mark for the field.

Default Formatting Options

Be default, Power BI Desktop uses the currency, date and time formats that are set on your computer. If you change these defaults on your computer and a report file is open, you have to close the report file and reopen it for the formatting changes to be recognized in the file. If the report file is used on a different computer, Power BI Desktop will use the default formatting options set on that computer. [See Chapter 1, Figures 1-24 and 1-25]

No Shortcut To Display Rows At The Bottom Of A Table Visualization
Sadly, Power BI Desktop does not have a shortcut key combination that will display the bottom of the table visualization faster then using the scroll bar to display the bottom of the table. As you will see, if a table has hundreds or thousands of records, it can take longer then you would like to scroll to the end of the table.

How To Change The Summary Type

As shown in Figure 9-19, the Order ID field has a total. This is a summary total. This would be indicated by an icon in front of the Order ID field, in the Fields panel. Another way to tell is that the Sum option will be checked, on the shortcut menu, in the Field Well, as shown in Figure 9-20.

There is no value to the visualization, to sum the Order ID numbers. Instead, the Order ID field could be used to count the number of orders or the aggregation can be removed.

Customer Name	Sum of Order ID	Order Date	Order Amount
	3122	06/17/2014	$5,879.70
7 Bikes For 7 Brothers	3054	05/26/2014	$53.90
Against The Wind Bikes	3055	05/26/2014	$479.85
AIC Childrens	3153	06/21/2014	$101.70
Alley Cat Cycles	1322	02/21/2013	$3,479.70
Total	**4594540**		**$4,083,665.34**

Figure 9-19 Table totals

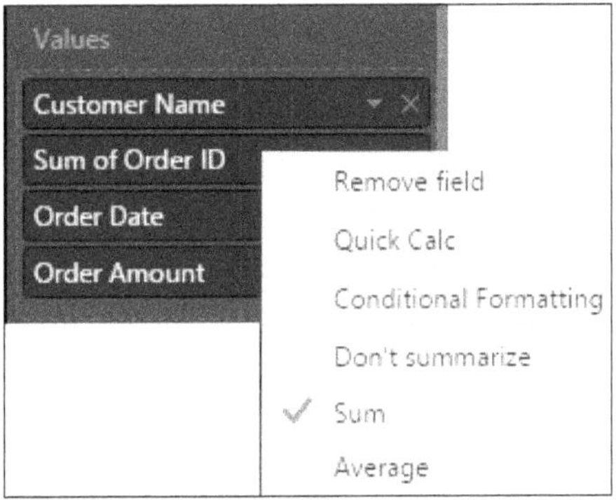

Figure 9-20 Order ID field aggregate options

To change the summary type, open the drop-down list for the Order ID field in the Values section in the Field Well ⇒ Select **COUNT**.

The revised Order ID total is shown in Figure 9-21. The number shown, represents how many orders are displayed on the visualization.

Notice that the Order ID column heading changed to reflect the type of aggregation that has been applied to the field.

Customer Name	Count of Order ID	Order Date	Order Amount
	1	06/17/2014	$5,879.70
7 Bikes For 7 Brothers	1	05/26/2014	$53.90
Against The Wind Bikes	1	05/26/2014	$479.85
AIC Childrens	1	06/21/2014	$101.70
Alley Cat Cycles	1	02/21/2013	$3,479.70
Total	**2192**		**$4,083,665.34**

Figure 9-21 Order ID aggregation changed to Count

Column Heading Titles
Sadly, there is no way to change the text for the column headings.

Quick Calc

The options shown in Figure 9-22 are used to apply a calculation to a field. Currently, the only calculation option available is to replace the existing values in the field, by displaying the values as a percent of the grand total.

I suspect that more options like the Show Value As A Percent of Row Total and Running Total options that are available for pivot tables in Excel will be added to this dialog box over time.

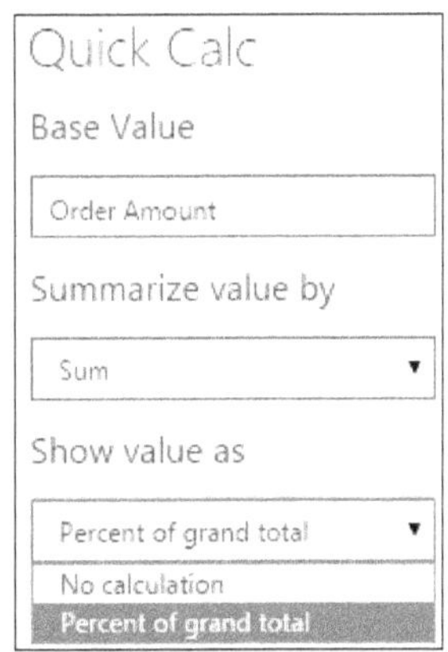

Figure 9-22 Quick Calc options

Exercise 9.4: Use Quick Calc

In this exercise, you will use the Quick Calc options to display the Order Amount (in each row), as a percent of the grand total.

1. Duplicate the Order List page.

2. Click on the table ⇒ In the Values section, display the shortcut menu for the Order Amount field ⇒ Select the Quick Calc option.

3. Change the Show value as option to **PERCENT OF GRAND TOTAL**, as shown above in Figure 9-22 ⇒ Click OK. Notice that the Order Amount values are displayed as a percent of the grand total ($4,083,665.34). The table would look better if the actual order amount is also displayed on the table.

4. Drag the Order Amount field to the Values section and place it after the Order Date field.

   The table should look like the one shown in Figure 9-23.

Customer Name	Order ID	Order Date	Order Amount	%GT Order Amount
	3122	06/17/2014	$5,879.70	0.14%
7 Bikes For 7 Brothers	3054	05/26/2014	$53.90	0.00%
Against The Wind Bikes	3055	05/26/2014	$479.85	0.01%
AIC Childrens	3153	06/21/2014	$101.70	0.00%
Alley Cat Cycles	1151	01/08/2014	$5,879.70	0.14%
Alley Cat Cycles	1204	01/19/2014	$1,583.05	0.04%
Alley Cat Cycles	1239	01/28/2014	$101.70	0.00%
Total			**$4,083,665.34**	**100.00%**

Figure 9-23 Quick Calc Percent of grand total applied to the Order Amount field

Exercise 9.5: Create A Table Using A Hierarchy

In this exercise, you will create a table that uses the Country Hierarchy that you created in Chapter 8, Exercise 8.2.

1. Click the Table button.

2. Add the Sales Rep field ⇒ Add the Country Hierarchy (in the Customer table). You will see the hierarchy and all of the fields in the hierarchy, displayed on the table.

3. Add the Order Amount field.

   The table should look like the one shown in Figure 9-24.

   There is a row in the table for each sales rep order total, per city.

SalesRep	Country	Region	City	Order Amount
Anne Dodsworth	Australia	New South Wales	Sydney	$45.00
Anne Dodsworth	Australia	Western Australia	Perth	$5,879.70
Anne Dodsworth	Austria	Salzkammergut	Salzburg	$33.00
Anne Dodsworth	Bangladesh	Dhaka	Dhaka	$65.70
Anne Dodsworth	Belgium	Brussels	Brussels	$5,027.34
Anne Dodsworth	Bermuda	Pembroke Parish	Hamilton	$5,879.70
Anne Dodsworth	Bolivia	La Paz	La Paz	$97.02
Total				**$4,083,665.34**

Figure 9-24 Table created with a hierarchy

Conditional Formatting

The Conditional Formatting option shown earlier in Figure 9-20, is currently only available for the Table chart type, for fields that have been summarized.

The options shown in Figure 9-25 are used to add a gradient color to the background of every cell in a column, based on the numeric value in the cell.

The **DIVERGING OPTION** is used to select a different background color for cells that are between the range of values in the Minimum and Maximum fields. When this option is enabled, the **CENTER OPTION** is displayed, as shown in Figure 9-26.

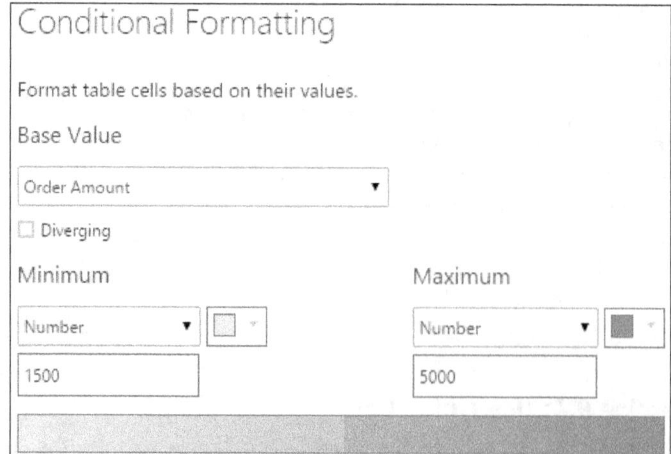

Figure 9-25 Conditional Formatting options

The Lowest and Highest options (in the Minimum and Maximum field drop-down lists), use the entire range of values in the field.

The Number option is used to enter the range of values for the conditional formatting. Values below the Minimum value will have the lightest color. Values above the Maximum value will have the darkest color in the gradient range.

When conditional formatting has been applied, the **REMOVE CONDITIONAL FORMATTING OPTION** is available on the shortcut menu shown earlier in Figure 9-20, in place of the Conditional Formatting option.

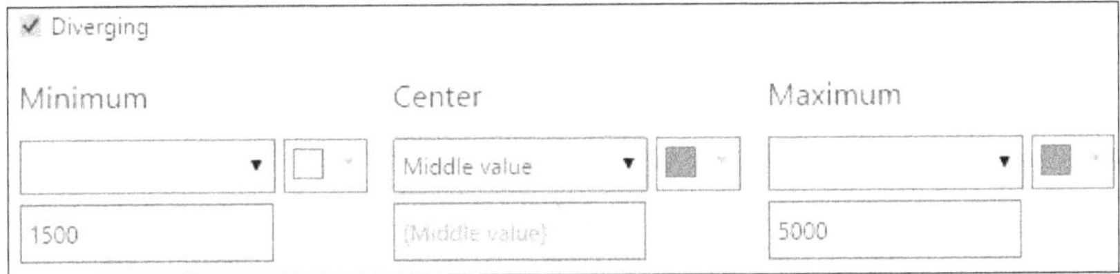

Figure 9-26 Diverging option enabled

Exercise 9.6: Apply Conditional Formatting To Cells

In this exercise you will learn how to create conditional formatting for order amount values in a range of $1,500 and $5,000.

1. Duplicate the Order List page.
2. In the Values section of the Field Well, select the Conditional Formatting option, on the shortcut menu, for the Order Amount field.
3. Select the formatting options shown earlier in Figure 9-25.

   The Order Amount column should be formatted, as shown in Figure 9-27.

   Notice that values below $1,500 have a lighter background color and values over $5,000 have the darkest background color.

Customer Name	Order ID	Order Date	Order Amount
	3122	06/17/2014	$5,879.70
7 Bikes For 7 Brothers	3054	05/26/2014	$53.90
Against The Wind Bikes	3055	05/26/2014	$479.85
AIC Childrens	3153	06/21/2014	$101.70
Alley Cat Cycles	1151	01/08/2014	$5,879.70
Alley Cat Cycles	1204	01/19/2014	$1,583.05
Alley Cat Cycles	1239	01/28/2014	$101.70
Alley Cat Cycles	1260	02/04/2014	$33.90
Alley Cat Cycles	1322	02/21/2013	$3,479.70
Alley Cat Cycles	1656	05/27/2014	$72.90
Total			**$4,083,665.34**

Figure 9-27 Conditional formatting applied to the Order Amount field

Figure 9-28 shows the reports that should have been created in this chapter. You should see these pages in the status bar. This is known as a **MULTI-PAGE REPORT**.

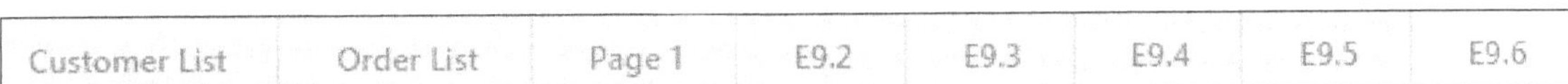

Figure 9-28 Report tabs for Chapter 9 Table reports file

Creating A Visual Using Fields From Tables That Do Not Have A Relationship
While there is initially nothing stopping you from creating a visual (table or chart) with fields from tables that do not have a relationship, you will run into a problem, as shown in Figure 9-29. Clicking the **SEE DETAILS LINK** will display a dialog box letting you know what the problem is, as shown on the right side of the figure.

Clicking the **FIX THIS BUTTON**, displays a dialog box that provides more information about the problem and offers solutions on how to fix the problem, as shown in Figure 9-30.

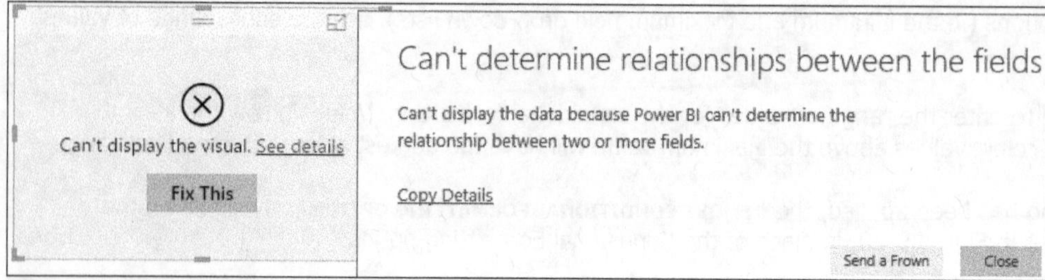

Figure 9-29 Can't display the visual warning message

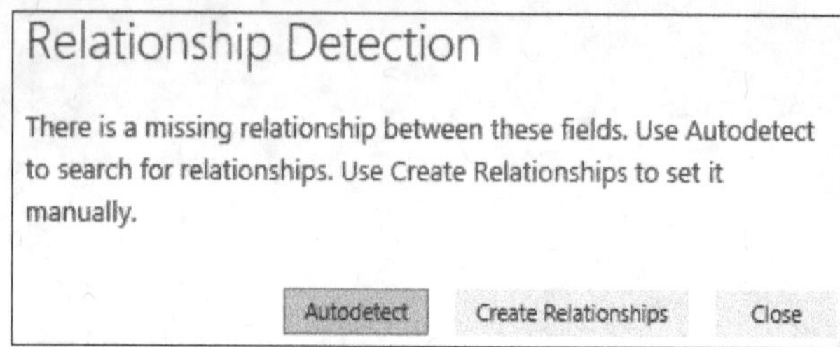

Figure 9-30 Relationship Detection dialog box

Summary

This chapter introduced you to the Report view workspace. The options on the Home tab, that are specifically for the Report view were explained. Data types and aggregations were covered, many of which you are already familiar with if you completed the Query Editor chapters in this book.

The exercises in this chapter showed you how to create basic table visualizations and how to change how some data is displayed. In addition to covering the workspace, a goal was to help you feel comfortable navigating around in the Report view.

FILTER AND SORT DATA IN A REPORT

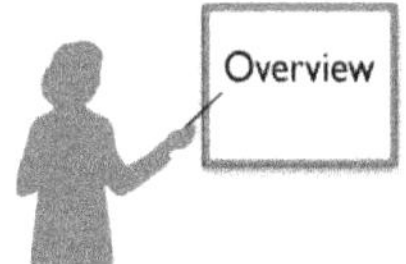

As the title of this chapter indicates, you will learn how to filter and sort the data in a report. The following topics are covered.

- ☑ Visual, report and page level filters
- ☑ Using Text fields as filter fields
- ☑ Wildcard filters
- ☑ Sorting data in a table

In addition to learning how to filter and sort data, using the Power BI template import and export options are also covered.

CHAPTER 10

Overview

Power BI Desktop was designed to handle large amounts of data. By large, I mean millions of rows of data per table. More than likely, you will not have the need to have millions of rows of data displayed on a report, but if you do, Power BI Desktop can handle it. It is also very possible that you will not want to view all of the data in any table.

One way to select the records that will be displayed on a visualization is to create filters. In a way, filters work like queries. The benefit is that filters are easier to create. The types of data that can be filtered are text, dates and numeric. Each data type has its own way of selecting the records that will be included or excluded on the visualization. Filters can be added to a report before, during or after a visualization is created. The data displayed is the same, regardless of when in the process, the filters are created.

Filters Section

The options shown in Figure 10-1 are used to query the data to retrieve the data that you want displayed on the report.

Filter Levels
As shown in Figure 10-1, there are three levels of filters that can be created. The levels are explained below.

① **VISUAL LEVEL FILTER** Is only applied to the visualization that is selected before creating the filter. By default, all of the fields used to create the selected visualization are automatically added to this section. When creating this type of filter, make sure that the corresponding visualization is selected first. If a visualization is not selected, the Visual level filters section is not displayed.
② **PAGE LEVEL FILTER** Is applied to every visualization on the page. To create this type of filter, no visualization can be selected. (1)
③ **REPORT LEVEL FILTER** Is applied to all visuals, on all pages, in the report file. As you will see, Report level filters are displayed in this section on every page in the file, regardless of the page that you create them on. (1)

Filters work the same way, regardless of the level that they are created in. The only difference is which visuals in the report file they are applied to. Each level can have multiple filters.

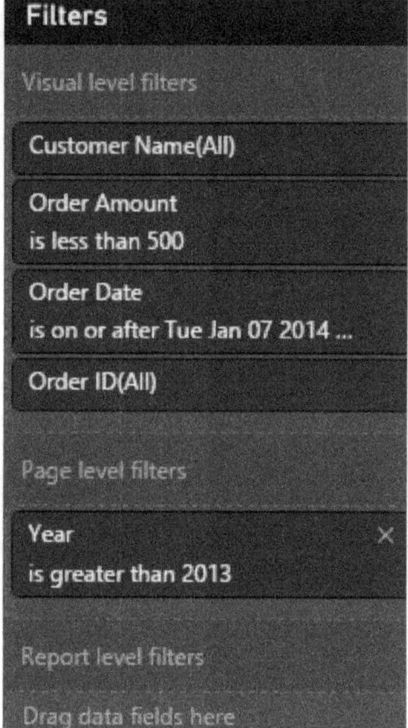

Figure 10-1 Filters section

Filters are applied in this order: Report level, Page level, Visual level, slicers.

(1) Filters in this section are visible, whether or not a visual is selected. This type of filter can be created using fields that already have an active filter.

Filter Options

The options in the Filters section change, depending on the data type of the selected field. Filters can be created for any data type (numeric, dates, text etc).

ACTIVE FILTERS have criteria selected. As shown above in Figure 10-1, there are three active filters: Order Amount, Order Date and Year. **INACTIVE FILTERS** are displayed on the panel, but do not have any criteria selected. Filters that do not have any criteria enabled, have **(ALL)** after their name. In Figure 10-1, examples of inactive filters are the Customer Name and Order ID fields. Most of the time, you may find that fields used to create Page and Report level filters are not displayed on a visualization. An exception would be for testing purposes.

Filter Types

There are two types of filters that can be used to create criteria, as explained below. To switch between the filter types, open the **FILTER TYPE** drop-down list and select the other option.

① **BASIC FILTERING** This filter type displays a list of values from the field. Check the values that you want to filter on, as shown in Figure 10-2. The **REQUIRE SINGLE SELECTION OPTION**, shown in Figure 10-2, is a Page level filter that is used to force a value to be selected if you want the page to be displayed in Q&A or Cortana in Power BI.com.
② **ADVANCED FILTERING** Select this option to create a filter that will include or exclude a range of values, as shown in Figure 10-3. The advanced filter options vary, depending on the fields data type.

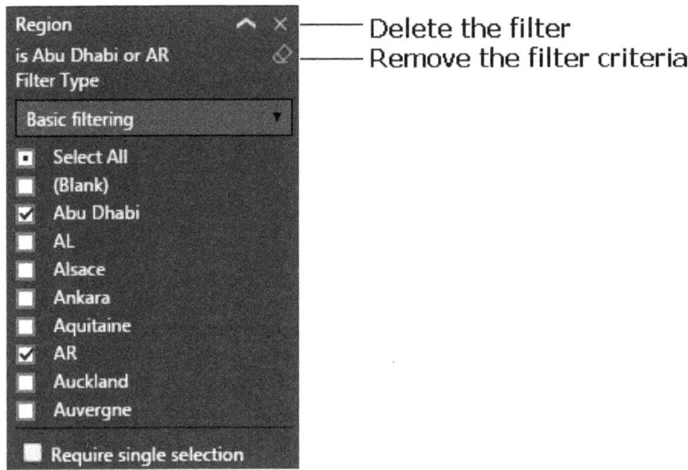

Figure 10-2 Basic filter with criteria selected

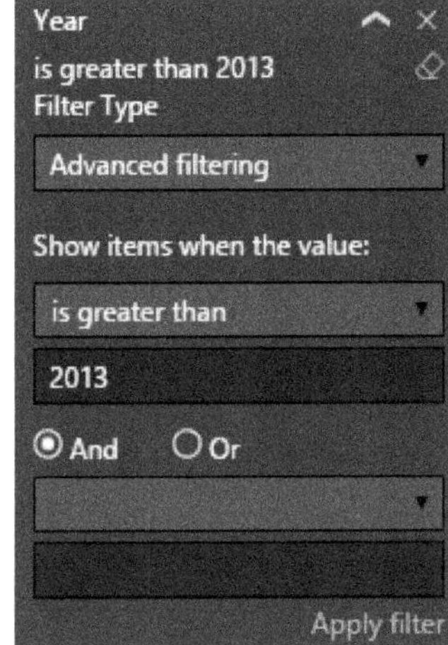

Figure 10-3 Advanced filter options

(Select All) Filter Option

This option is used to control whether or not individual values in the field can be selected to filter the data. This filter has three options, as explained below.

① **CHECKED**, as shown in Figure 10-4, automatically selects all of the values.
② **NOT CHECKED** If the (Select All) option is not checked, none of the values are checked and the filter is not active.
③ **FILLED IN** If you check at least one value, the (Select All) value check box displays a circle in the checkbox, as shown in Figure 10-5. This visually lets you know that at least one value in the field is selected, even if you cannot see the value that is selected, in the list of values.

If a filter is being used, as shown in Figure 10-5, and you clear the (Select All) check box, whatever values that were checked, are unchecked. In this figure, the Online value would be unchecked.

If you click on an **ELEMENT NAME**, like Online or Retail, shown in Figure 10-5, instead of the check box, the element that you click on will be unchecked. All other items rename the same.

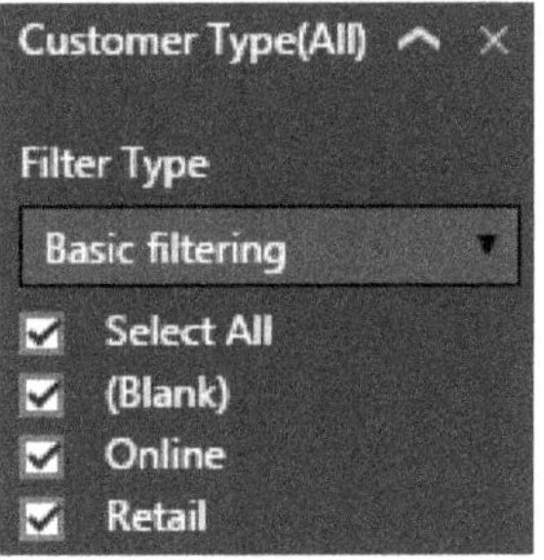

Figure 10-4 (Select All) option checked

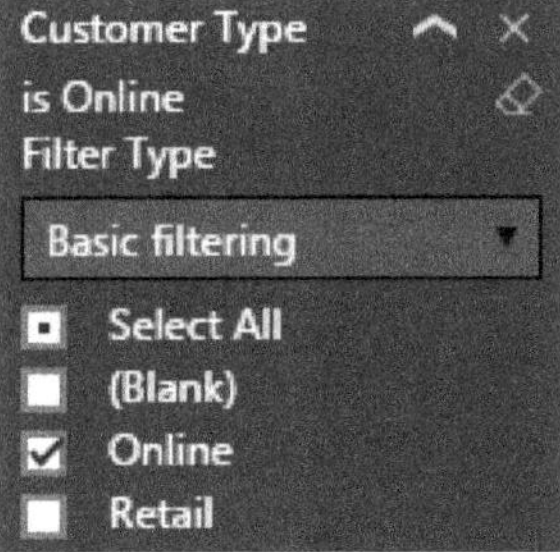

Figure 10-5 (Select All) option when at least one value is selected

Filter Tips

① If a field is displayed on the visual and has an active filter, the filter is not deleted if the field is removed from the visual.

② Keep the following in mind when using multiple filters: Active filters are cumulative. If there are Visual and Page level filters, the filters may not retrieve all of the records that you are expecting to see because each filter reduces the number of records retrieved and the records that are available to be filtered by other filters.

③ The same field can be used more than once to create a filter. You can also use the same field more than once in the same level.

④ Any field available in the report file can be used to create a filter, even if it is not displayed on the visual.

Wildcard Search Characters

Wildcard characters provide another way to filter records. Wildcards are characters that you can use to substitute all or part of the data that you are creating a filter for. Most of the time, using wildcard characters will find values that you are not expecting to see, but I wanted to let you know that the feature is available. Advanced filters support the following wildcard characters. Wildcard characters are most often used with the **CONTAINS** and **DOES NOT CONTAIN** filter criteria options.

① *** ASTERISK** Use this character to replace one or more characters in the criteria. If you entered s*r in the field, the selection criteria would return records that have star, start and sour, or any records that have the letter "s" before the letter "r" in the field that the filter is being created for. This wildcard character is more flexible, but often returns a lot of results, which may not be what you want.

② **? QUESTION MARK** Use this character to replace one character in the filter criteria. If you entered t?n in the field, the selection criteria would return records that have ten, tan, tune and ton in the field, but not toon.

Understanding The Practice Country List Table

In the real world, this table would contain a record for every country in the world and would be used as a lookup table, if you will, because it contains every possible option. The Country List table used in this book, does not have an entry for every country. This was done to keep the data manageable for learning purposes.

Yes, you will see the Country field in another table. You could use that field instead of the one in the Country List table, as long as you know that it has all of the values that you need, to create the report. If you need to create a report that shows countries that do not meet some criteria, you would have to use the Country List table, to ensure that all countries are being checked.

Exercise 10.1: Create Visual Level Filters

In Exercise 9.2, you created a list report that displayed all of the records. Most of the time, all of the records in a data table do not need to be displayed on a report. In this exercise, you will create a filter to select a country that will filter the data that is displayed on the report.

1. Save the Report Data.pbix file as `Chapter 10 Filter and Sort table reports.`

2. Duplicate the Customer List page.

3. Drag the Country Name field to the Visual level filters section.

4. Check the USA option ⇒ To confirm that the only records displayed in the table are in the USA, add the Country field in Customer table, to the visualization. Place it after the Region field.

More than one item in the filter can be selected. Right below the Field name, in the Visual level filters section, you can see the filter criteria that is selected, even when all of the values in the field are not displayed on the panel, as illustrated in Figure 10-6. It shows the filter criteria for the Country Name field. The table should look like the one shown in Figure 10-7.

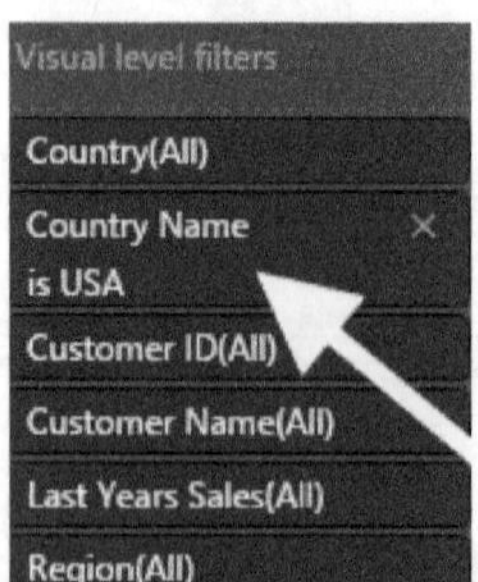

Figure 10-6 Visual level filter criteria illustrated

Customer ID	Customer Name	Region	Country	Last Years Sales
1	City Cyclists	MI	USA	$20,045.27
2	Pathfinders	IL	USA	$26,369.63
3	Bike-A-Holics Anonymous	OH	USA	$4,500.00
4	Psycho-Cycle	AL	USA	$52,809.11
5	Sporting Wheels Inc.	CA	USA	$85,642.56

Figure 10-7 Customers table filtered by country

Advanced Filter Options

Use this filter option to select records that are in a range (that you specify) or for records that need to meet more than one set of criteria. Advanced filters can also be used to select records that have the same value in a field, like the filter created in Exercise 10.1.

Date Field Advanced Filter Options

When using this filter option for date fields, the date and time fields have options to help select the date and time, as shown in Figures 10-8 and 10-9. To display them, click on the icon, illustrated in the figure.

Clicking on AM or PM, next to the time, shown in Figure 10-8, changes it to the other option.

The calendar shown in Figure 10-9 works like ones that you have seen and probably used in other software packages.

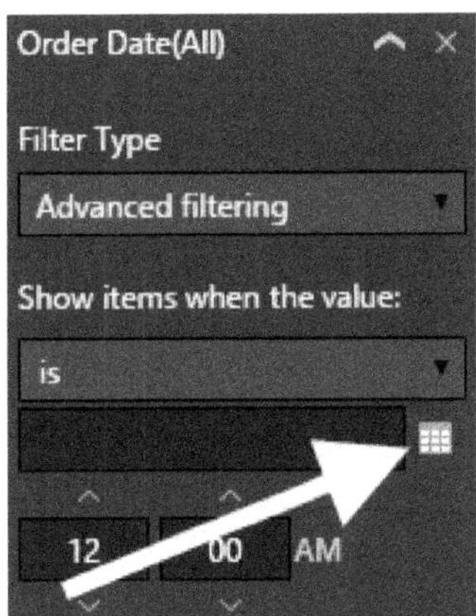

Figure 10-8 Date advanced filter options

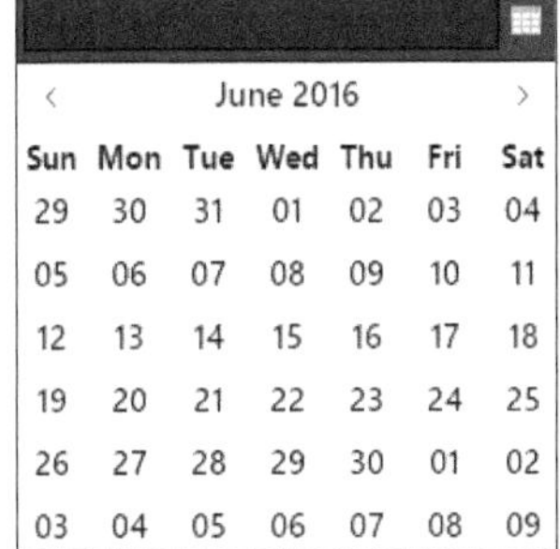

Figure 10-9 Calendar options

How To Use The Calendar Options

① Click on the arrow before the date, shown above in Figure 10-9, to display the previous month.
② Click on the arrow after the date, shown above in Figure 10-9, to display the next month.
③ Click on the month and year, at the top of the calendar, to display the pop up shown in Figure 10-10. This pop up is used to select a different year and month.
④ Clicking on the year, shown in Figure 10-10, displays a range of years that you can select from.

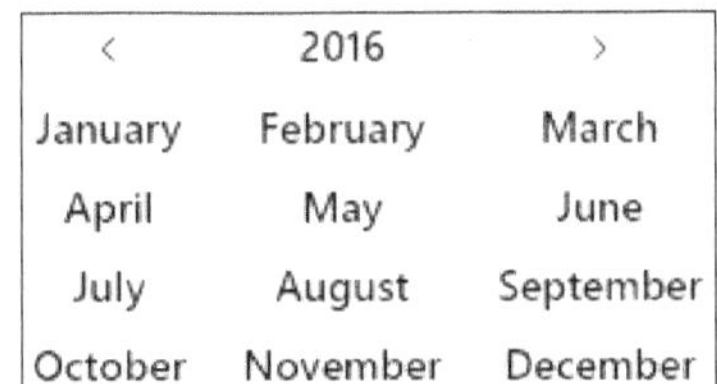

Figure 10-10 Month and year pop up options

It is not a requirement to use the calendar to select a date. You can type in the date, which is faster in my opinion. If you type in a date, it has to be in the same format that the date field uses. You also have to type in a valid date. Typing in 9/31/2016 would not be valid because there are only 30 days in September.

Date Field Advanced Filter Operators

Figure 10-11 shows the date field filter operators. Table 10-1 explains the date field filter operators.

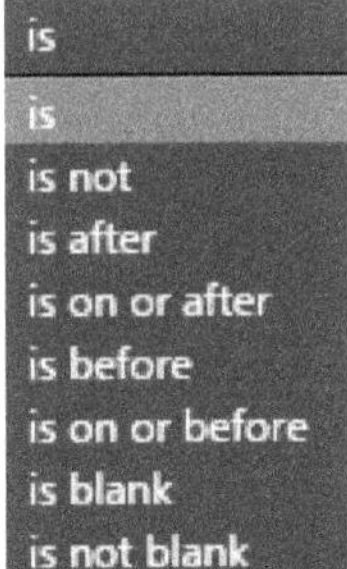

Figure 10-11 Date field filter operators

Operator	Selects Records That . . .
Is	Match the value entered.
Is not	Do not match the value entered.
Is after	Have a date greater than the date entered.
Is on or after	Have the date entered or a date greater than the date entered.
Is before	Have a date earlier then the date entered.
Is on or before	Have a date entered or a date prior to the date entered.
Is blank	Do not have a value in the field.
Is not blank	Have a date in the field.

Table 10-1 Date field filter operators explained

Date Hierarchy Fields

The top of Figure 10-12 shows the Date Hierarchy in the Values section of the Field Well. When a hierarchy (date or otherwise) is added to the Values section, the fields in the hierarchy are automatically added to the Visual level filters section. They are displayed as individual filters. You can select options for each of the fields in the hierarchy, as needed.

To use these fields as filters, you have to select options starting with the field at the top of the hierarchy, because each field in the hierarchy, filters the field in the next level down in the hierarchy.

For example, if you selected the months January and September as filter criteria, the only quarters that would be available to select from to create a filter for the Quarter field, would be Q1 and Q3.

To use these filters correctly, the year(s) need to be selected first, as the year is at the top of the hierarchy. Then select the quarters, then the months. It is not a requirement to create a filter for all of the hierarchy fields.

If you are not sure what order to create the filters in, look at the hierarchy field in the Values section. Most of the time, the physical order that the fields are in the hierarchy, is the order (from top to bottom) that you should create the filters in, for those fields.

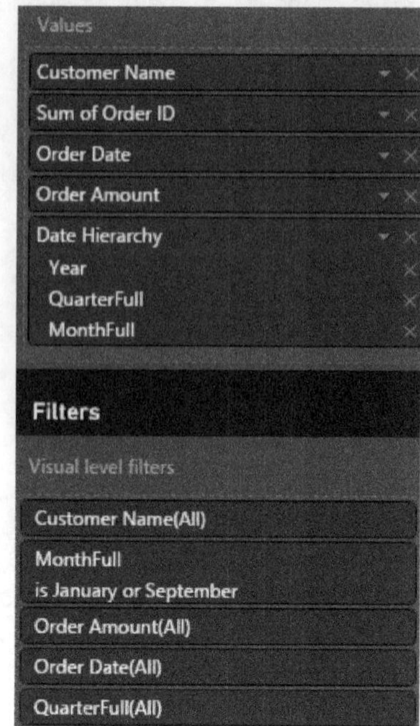

Figure 10-12 Date Hierarchy added to the Values and Filters sections

Exercise 10.2: Create A Date Filter

In this exercise you will learn how to create a filter that selects records after a specific date.

1. Duplicate the Order List page.
2. Display the Visual level filter advanced options for the Order Date field.
3. Open the first drop-down list and select **IS AFTER**.
4. In the field below the operator, type `9/19/2013` ⇒ Click the **APPLY FILTER** button. Your filter should look like the one shown in Figure 10-13.

   You should not see any records (in the visualization) with an Order Date before 9/19/2013.

   To confirm, you can sort the records in the visualization on the Order Date field.

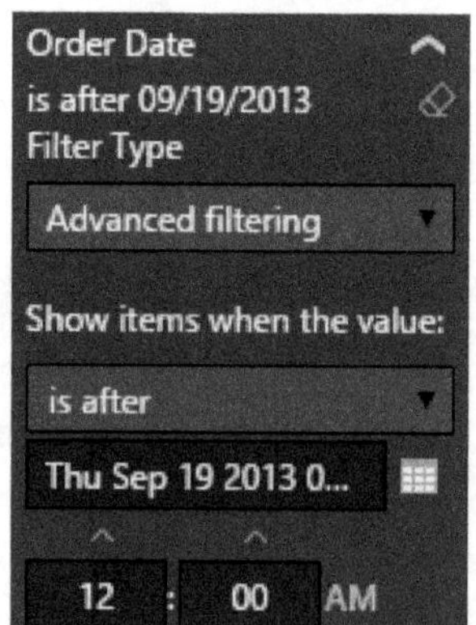

Figure 10-13 Greater than filter criteria

Using The AND & OR Operators

These operators are used to select which of the filter criteria options, the data must meet. These operators work the same as the ones in the Query Editor.

Exercise 10.3: Create A Date Range Filter

In this exercise, you will learn how to create a filter that will select records that have a value in the range of values that you select. Range filters produce the same result as using the **BETWEEN OPERATOR** that you may have used in other software packages. Multiple date range filters can be created for a field, but only one date range filter can be applied (active) for a field, at the same time.

1. Duplicate the Order List page.

2. Display the Visual level filter advanced options for the Order Date field ⇒ Open the first drop-down list and select **IS ON OR AFTER** ⇒ Type `1/1/2014` in the field below.

3. In the field below the word "And", select **IS ON OR BEFORE** ⇒ In the next field type `12/31/2014`.

   Click the Apply Filter button.

   The options shown in Figure 10-14 will display records with an order date in 2014.

   If you scroll through the records in the table, you will see that they all have an order date in 2014.

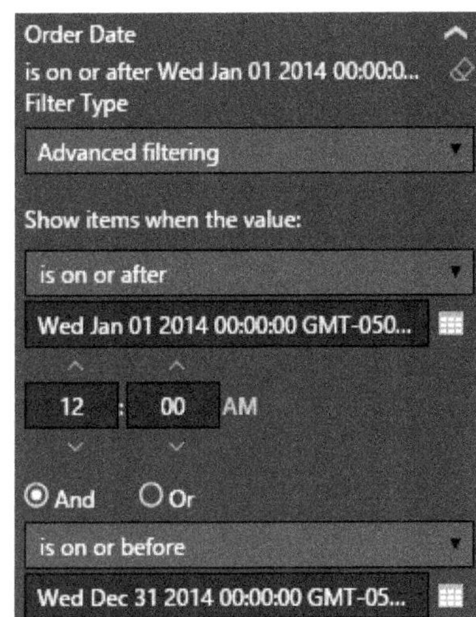

Figure 10-14 Order date range filter criteria

Exercise 10.4: Create A Year Filter

This type of filter is used to select at least one years worth of data to display on the visualization. In the previous exercise, the date filter that you created displayed a year of data. It only allowed one range to be selected. Using the Year field to create the filter criteria will allow multiple years to be selected. The years selected in the filter, do not have to be consecutive.

1. Duplicate the Order List page.

2. In the Dates Table, expand the Date Hierarchy. You will see the fields illustrated in Figure 10-15.

   Drag the Select Year field to the Visual level filters section.

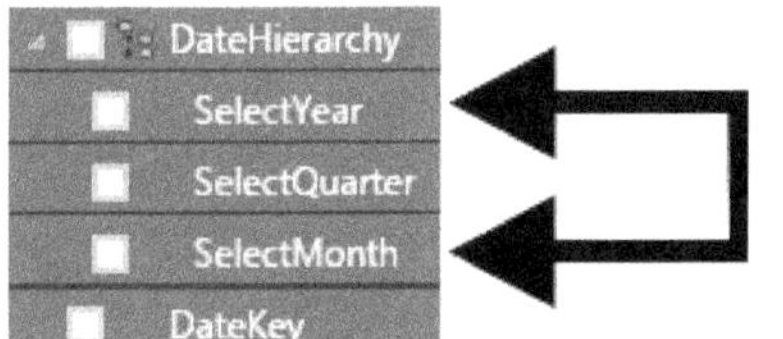

Figure 10-15 Hierarchy fields illustrated

3. Display the Basic filter options ⇒
   Check the year 2014, as shown in Figure 10-16.
   This will display all records with an order date in 2014, in the visualization.

   These options produce the same results as the date range filter that you created in the previous exercise.
   [See Figure 10-14]

   To me, as long as it is appropriate, using the Year field to create the filter is easier to set up and use, when you need to select data by the year, then the range filter options.

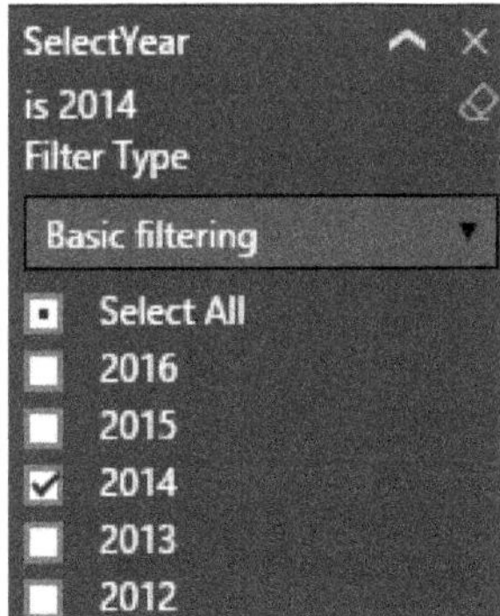

Figure 10-16 Select Year hierarchy field filter

The Dates Table also has a Year field. It has the same data as the Select Year field. The fields in the Date Hierarchy were created to be used with a parameter. On your own, you could use the Year field in the Dates Table.

Sorting The Data Displayed In A Table Visualization

The data in a visualization can only be sorted on one column at a time. The good thing is that the sort order, if any, is saved when the file is saved. On your own, you can follow the steps below to learn how to sort the data in the table.

1. Duplicate the Order List page.

2. Click on the Customer Name column heading in the table. The data should be sorted in ascending order by the customer name. You should see a triangle at the end of the Customer Name column heading, as illustrated in Figure 10-17.

   The triangle indicates that the column is currently being sorted on and the sort order is **ASCENDING** (the triangle points down) or **DESCENDING** (the triangle points up).

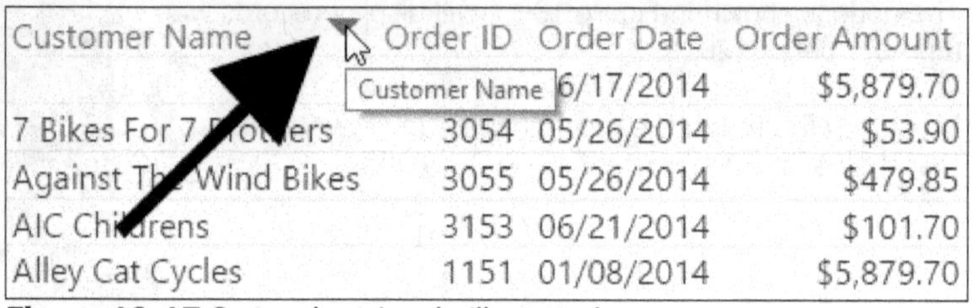
Customer Name
Order ID
Order Date
Order Amount
Customer Name
6/17/2014
$5,879.70
7 Bikes For 7 Brothers
3054
05/26/2014
$53.90
Against The Wind Bikes
3055
05/26/2014
$479.85
AIC Childrens
3153
06/21/2014
$101.70
Alley Cat Cycles
1151
01/08/2014
$5,879.70

Figure 10-17 Sort order triangle illustrated

3. Click on the Order ID column heading. The data should now be sorted in descending order, by the Order ID number.

Using Date Table Fields To Filter Data

What may not be obvious is that fields in a date table can be used to create a filter. For example, in Exercise 10.4, a filter was created to display records with an order date in 2014. If the Quarter Abbr field was used as a filter, you could select a specific quarter to display records for, as shown in Figure 10-18.

If the filter options shown in Figure 10-18 were removed and the Quarter And Year Abbr date field (or the Quarter And Year field) was used as the field to filter on, you could select specific quarters and years at the same time, as shown in Figure 10-19. The options selected in the figure will display orders from the first six months of 2013. To me, this is easier to use then setting up range criteria for 1/1/2013 to 6/30/2013.

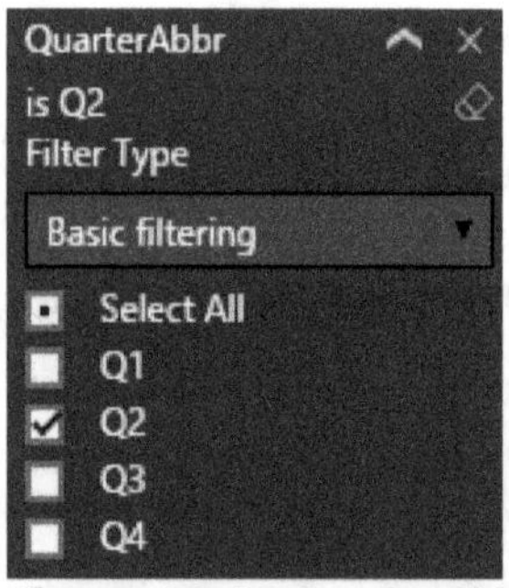
QuarterAbbr
is Q2
Filter Type
Basic filtering
Select All
Q1
Q2
Q3
Q4

Figure 10-18 Quarter Abbr field filter options

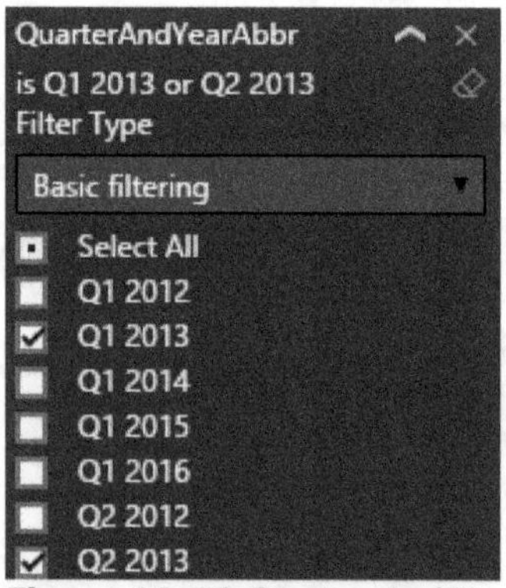
QuarterAndYearAbbr
is Q1 2013 or Q2 2013
Filter Type
Basic filtering
Select All
Q1 2012
Q1 2013
Q1 2014
Q1 2015
Q1 2016
Q2 2012
Q2 2013

Figure 10-19 Quarter And Year Abbr field filter options

Exercise 10.5: Create A Table Visualization Using Fields From Multiple Data Tables

So far, all of the visualizations that you have created, have only used data from one table. That is about to change <smile>. To create or start a new table visualization, you can drag the fields to the canvas, as long as a visualization type is not selected.

1. Add a page ⇒ Rename it to `E10.5`.

2. Add the following fields from the Customer table: Customer Name and Customer Type.

3. Add the following fields from the Orders table: Order ID, Order Date and Ship Date.

4. Right-click on the Ship Date field in the Values section and select Ship Date, as shown in Figure 10-20.

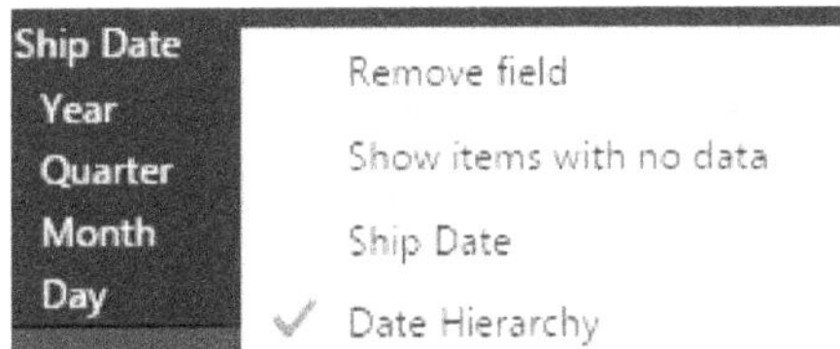

Figure 10-20 Change the value displayed

5. Add the following field from the Dates Table: Quarter Full.

6. Sort the table on the Order Date field in ascending order. The table should look like the one shown in Figure 10-21.

Customer Name	Customer Type	Order ID	Order Date ▲	Ship Date	QuarterFull
On The Edge Cyclery	Retail	1305	02/18/2013	02/24/2013	Quarter 1
Pathfinders	Online	1303	02/18/2013	03/02/2013	Quarter 1
Belgium Bike Co.	Online	1312	02/19/2013	02/27/2013	Quarter 1

Figure 10-21 Report with data from more than one table

Chapter 2 went into detail about loading data to the data model. In my opinion, the exercise that you just completed, demonstrates the power of the data model, because fields from three data tables were added to one visualization.

Exercise 10.6: Use Hierarchy Fields To Filter Data

In this exercise you will use the Country_Drill Down hierarchy fields to filter a table visualization.

1. Duplicate page E10.5.

2. On the Fields panel, in the Customer table, drag the Country_Drill Down hierarchy to the bottom of the Values section.

3. In the Country filter, select Canada and USA.

4. In the Region filter, select AL, BC, CA and ON.

5. In the City filter, select Burnaby, Huntsville, Irvine and Vancouver.

   You should have the filters shown in Figure 10-22.

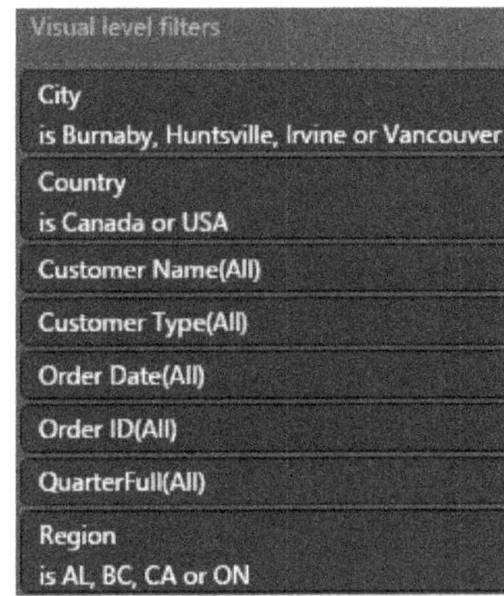

Figure 10-22 Multiple filters

Exercise 10.7: Add Another Visualization To The Page

So far, all of the reports that you created, only have one visualization on the page. Reports can and often do have more than one visualization on a page, especially when creating a dashboard report. In this exercise you will add a visualization to a page that already has a visualization.

1. Duplicate page E10.1.

2. Change the Country Name filter to Australia and USA.

3. Make the table smaller and move it to the upper left corner of the page ⇒ Click on a blank space on the page to deselect the visualization.

4. In the Fields panel, in the Customer table, check the Customer Name, Country and Last Years Sales fields. A new table should have been created.

The reason that I added the Country field is so that when the Country Name filter is changed, you can easily verify that the correct records are being displayed. On your own, you could do this for testing purposes, then delete the Country field from the table visualization before putting the report into production.

5. If necessary, move the new table below the other visualization, by making it smaller, and moving it below the first visualization.

6. Add the following fields to the second visualization: Order ID, Order Date, Order Amount and Ship Via.

Another Way To Add Additional Visualizations To A Page
Steps 3 and 4 above, demonstrated one way to add another visualization to the page. Another way is to drag the fields from the Fields panel to a blank space on the page.

Add An Image To The Page

1. Click on an empty space on the page ⇒ Home tab ⇒ Image button.

2. Select the image6.jpg file in your folder ⇒ Make the image smaller ⇒ Place it to the right of the first table. The page should look like the one shown in Figure 10-23.

Customer ID	Customer Name	Region	Country	Last Years Sales
1	City Cyclists	MI	USA	$20,045.27
2	Pathfinders	IL	USA	$26,369.63
3	Bike-A-Holics Anonymous	OH	USA	$4,500.00
4	Psycho-Cycle	AL	USA	$52,809.11
5	Sporting Wheels Inc.	CA	USA	$85,642.56
Total				**$2,400,847.33**

Customer Name	Country	Last Years Sales	Order ID	Order Date	Order Amount	Ship Via
			3122	06/17/2014	$5,879.70	UPS
7 Bikes For 7 Brothers	USA	$8,819.55	3054	05/26/2014	$53.90	Parcel Post
Against The Wind Bikes	USA	$2,409.46	3055	05/26/2014	$479.85	Purolator
AIC Childrens	China	$5,879.70	3153	06/21/2014	$101.70	UPS
Alley Cat Cycles	USA	$298,356.22	1151	01/08/2014	$5,879.70	Parcel Post
Alley Cat Cycles	USA	$298,356.22	1204	01/19/2014	$1,583.05	UPS
Total		**$9,076,755.40**			**$4,083,665.34**	

Figure 10-23 Page with two table visualizations and an image

Numeric Filter Options

The first thing that you will notice is that numeric fields do not have the Basic filter options. This means that you cannot select specific values from a list, like you can for text fields. If you only need to select one value, use the **IS OPERATOR**, discussed in the next section.

Numeric Field Range Filter Operators

Figure 10-24 shows the numeric field operators.

For the most part, they are used to select more than one value to filter on. The operators are explained in Table 10-2.

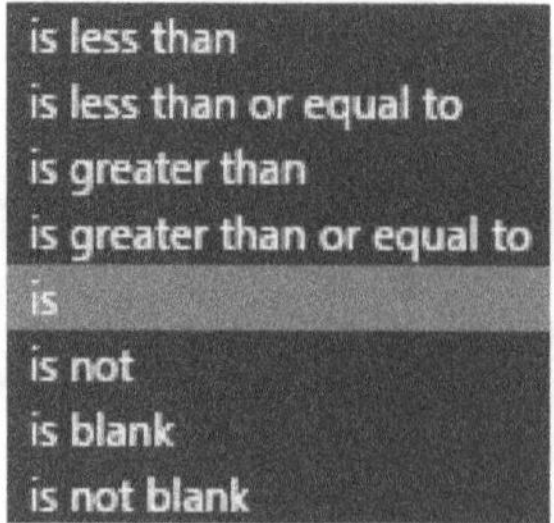

Figure 10-24 Numeric field filter operators

Operator	Selects Records That . . .
Is less than	Have a value smaller than the value entered.
Is less than or equal to	Have the same value entered or a value smaller than the value entered.
Is greater than	Have a value larger than the value entered.
Is greater than or equal to	Have the same value entered or a value larger than the value entered.
Is	Match the value entered. Select this option when you only want records that have a specific value in the field.
Is not	Do not match the value entered.
Is blank	Do not have data in the field. (2)
Is not blank	Have data in the field. (2)

Table 10-2 Numeric field filter operators explained

(2) Selecting this operator disables the field below it, because this operator does not require a value to be entered.

Applying Visual Level Filters To Each Visualization On The Page

So far, all of the filters that you have created have been at the Visual level, which means that they are applied to a specific visualization on the page. Each visualization on a page can also have it's own filters. By default, all fields in the visualization are automatically added to the Visual level filter section, but are not active. The page that you created in Exercise 10.7 has two visualizations. Each visualization has its own filter options.

Exercise 10.8: Create Table Level Filters

In this exercise, you will create a filter for each table on page E10.7.

Create A Filter For The First Table

In this part of the exercise you will create a filter specifically for the first table on the page. The filter will only display customers whose last years sales were greater than or equal to $25,000.

1. Duplicate page E10.7.

2. Delete the image file.

3. Click on the first table ⇒ Display the Last Years Sales field filter options ⇒ Open the first drop-down list and select **IS GREATER THAN OR EQUAL TO** ⇒ Type `25000` in the field below, as shown in Figure 10-25.

   Click the Apply Filter button. Only the records in the first table will be filtered by the Last Years Sales filter criteria, even though the second table has the same field.

   Compare the tables on the page shown in Figure 10-26 to the ones shown earlier in Figure 10-23. Notice that the first table now displays different records. That is because the first table in Figure 10-26 has the filter that you just created.

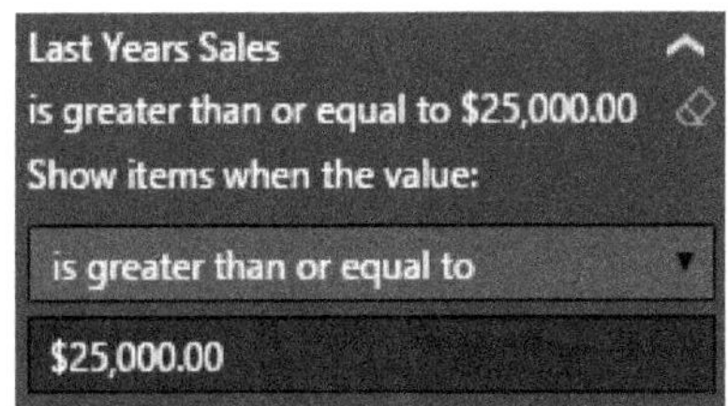

Figure 10-25 Visual level filter options for the Last Years Sales field in the first table

Customer ID	Customer Name	Region	Country	Last Years Sales
2	Pathfinders	IL	USA	$26,369.63
4	Psycho-Cycle	AL	USA	$52,809.11
5	Sporting Wheels Inc.	CA	USA	$85,642.56
6	Rockshocks for Jocks	TX	USA	$40,778.52
8	Spokes 'N Wheels Ltd.	IA	USA	$25,521.31
Total				**$1,998,564.20**

Customer Name	Country	Last Years Sales	Order ID	Order Date	Order Amount	Ship Via
			3122	06/17/2014	$5,879.70	UPS
7 Bikes For 7 Brothers	USA	$8,819.55	3054	05/26/2014	$53.90	Parcel Post
Against The Wind Bikes	USA	$2,409.46	3055	05/26/2014	$479.85	Purolator
AIC Childrens	China	$5,879.70	3153	06/21/2014	$101.70	UPS
Alley Cat Cycles	USA	$298,356.22	1151	01/08/2014	$5,879.70	Parcel Post
Alley Cat Cycles	USA	$298,356.22	1204	01/19/2014	$1,583.05	UPS
Total		**$9,076,755.40**			**$4,083,665.34**	

Figure 10-26 Visual level filter applied to the first table

Create A Filter For The Second Table

In this part of the exercise, you will create a filter for the second table, that only displays records that have Parcel Post or Pickup in the Ship Via field.

1. Click on the second table ⇒
   Display the Ship Via field filter options ⇒
   Select Parcel Post and Pickup, as shown in Figure 10-27.

   All of the records in the second table will have Parcel Post or Pickup in the Ship Via field.

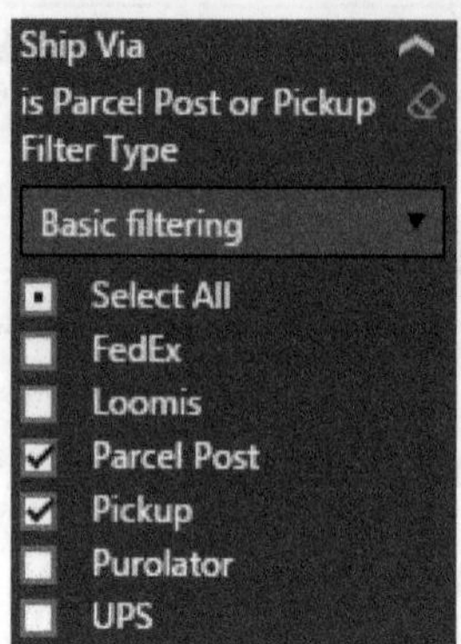

Figure 10-27 Visual level filter options for the Ship Via field in the second table

Advanced Filters For Text Fields

Unlike most numeric and date filters, text filters are a little more free form. The types of filters that can be created for a text field are explained below. The **ADVANCED FILTER** options can be used to search some or all of the contents in a field.

Text Field Advanced Filter Operators

The options shown in Figure 10-28 are used to type in values that will retrieve the records that you are looking for.

The **CONTAINS** filter option is best used when you have a really good idea of the data that you are looking for.

Table 10-3 explains the filter operators for a text field. Advanced filter options for a text field have the following characteristics:

① The values that you type in are not case sensitive.
② If no records match the filter criteria, the visualization will not display any data.
③ Pressing the space bar in the field that you type in, counts as a character and a space will be searched for.

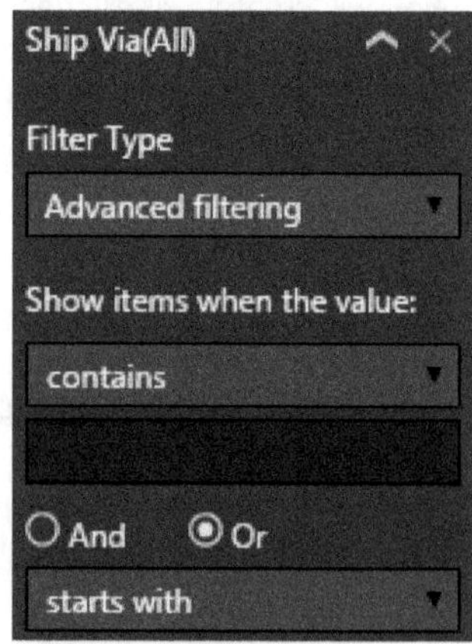

Figure 10-28 Text field advanced filter operators

The result is different from a field that is blank.

Operator	Selects Records That . . .
Contains	Have the value entered some place in the field. This is the default operator.
Does not contain	Do not have the value entered in the field.
Starts with	Have the value entered at the beginning of the field.
Does not start with	Do not have the value entered at the beginning of the field.
Is	Are an exact match to the value entered in the field.
Is not	Are not an exact match to the value entered in the field.
Is blank	Do not have a value in the field.
Is not blank	Have a value in the field.

Table 10-3 Text field advanced filter operators explained

Exercise 10.9: Use The Text Field Advanced Filter Options

In this exercise you will create a filter to find records whose customer name starts with "be".

1. Duplicate the Customer List page.

2. Display the Advanced filter options for the Customer Name field.

3. Select the **STARTS WITH** operator in the first drop-down list ⇒ Type `be` in the field below, as shown in Figure 10-29 ⇒ Click the Apply Filter button. You should see the records shown in Figure 10-30.

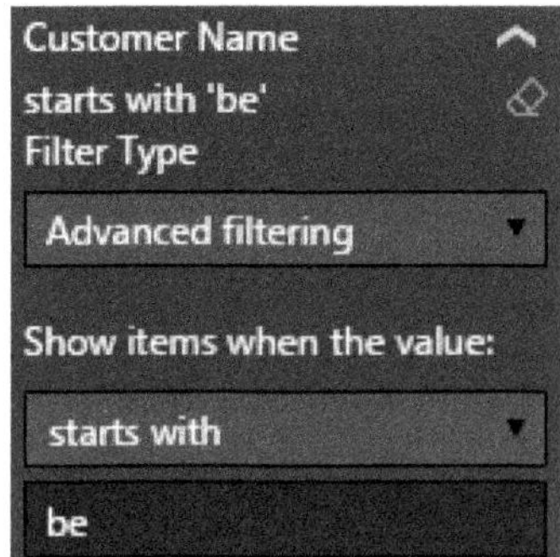

Figure 10-29 Text filter criteria

Customer ID	Customer Name	Region	Last Years Sales
61	Benny - The Spokes Person	AL	$6,091.96
75	Belgium Bike Co.	Brussels	$200,000.00
156	Beach Cycle and Sport	New Providence	$14,463.35
245	Berlin Biking GmBH.	Bayern	$2,989.35
248	Berg auf Trails GmBH.	Nordrhein-Westfalen	$2,939.29
253	Bendai Mountain Bikers	Tokyo To	$14,076.80
261	Beach Trails and Wheels	Waikato	$2,944.00
Total			**$243,504.75**

Figure 10-30 Result of customer names that start with "be" filter

Exercise 10.10: Use A Calculated Column To Filter Records

In Chapter 8, you created a calculated column, using DAX to filter a table and display duplicate records. In this exercise, you will create a table to display the duplicate records.

1. Add the Table visualization to the page ⇒ Add the following fields in the More Duplicate table to the visualization: #OfDups, Customer ID, First Name, Last Name, Address, City and State.

2. Sort the table in ascending order by the Address field.

3. Create and apply the filter shown in Figure 10-31. This filter will only display duplicate records. The table should look like the one shown in Figure 10-32.

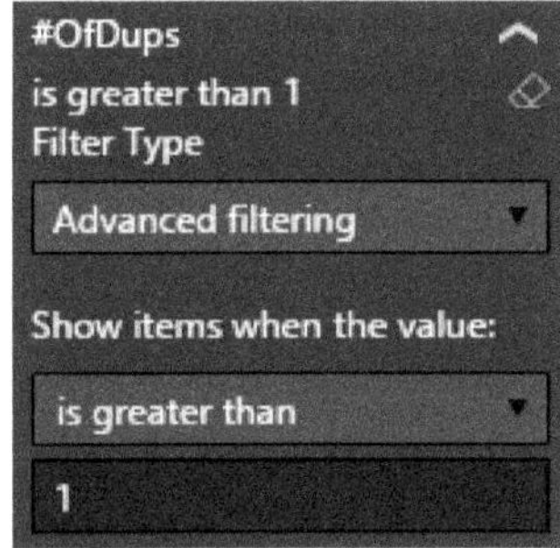

Figure 10-31 Duplicate records filter criteria

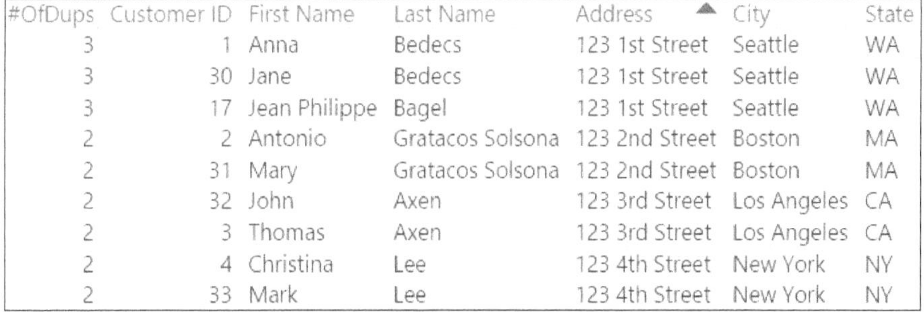

#OfDups	Customer ID	First Name	Last Name	Address	City	State
3	1	Anna	Bedecs	123 1st Street	Seattle	WA
3	30	Jane	Bedecs	123 1st Street	Seattle	WA
3	17	Jean Philippe	Bagel	123 1st Street	Seattle	WA
2	2	Antonio	Gratacos Solsona	123 2nd Street	Boston	MA
2	31	Mary	Gratacos Solsona	123 2nd Street	Boston	MA
2	32	John	Axen	123 3rd Street	Los Angeles	CA
2	3	Thomas	Axen	123 3rd Street	Los Angeles	CA
2	4	Christina	Lee	123 4th Street	New York	NY
2	33	Mark	Lee	123 4th Street	New York	NY

Figure 10-32 Table filtered by a calculated column

The OR Operator

Until now, the filters that you have created that had two sets of criteria used the **AND OPERATOR**, meaning that the data in the field had to meet both arguments (as shown earlier in Figure 10-14) to be displayed in the table. There is another operator available. The **OR OPERATOR** is used when the data only needs to meet one of the arguments, to be displayed in the table. Using this operator increases the number of records that will be displayed on the visualization.

Exercise 10.11: Use The OR Operator To Filter Records

In this exercise you will create a filter that selects records in the region (the state) CA or BC (British Columbia in Canada).

1. Duplicate the Customer List page.

2. Display the Advanced filter options for the Region field.

3. Select **IS** in the first drop-down list ⇒ Type `ca` in the next field.

4. Select the **OR** operator.

5. Select **IS** in the next drop-down list ⇒ Type `bc` in the next field.

6. You should have the filter criteria shown in Figure 10-33. Records that have CA or BC in the Region field, will be displayed in the table.

   You do not have to use the same operator in each drop-down list. For example, the filter options shown in Figure 10-34, will display records where the Customer Name field is empty or the name starts with the letter C.

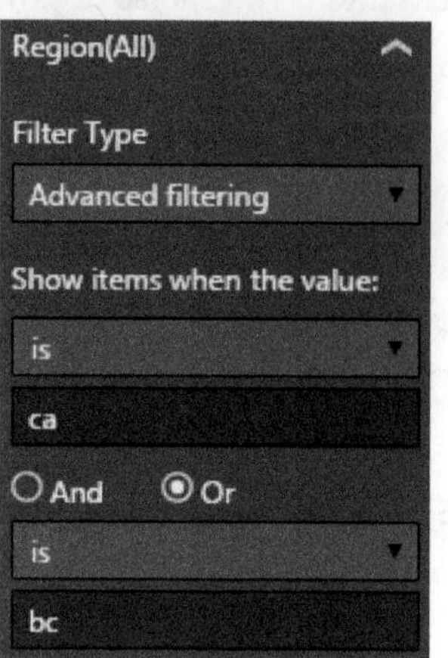

Figure 10-33 OR filter options

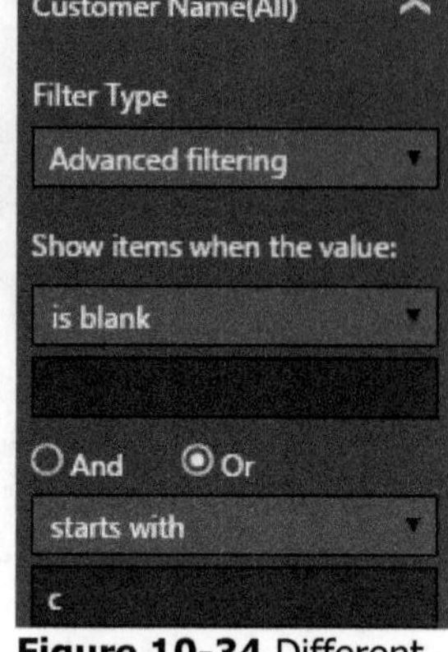

Figure 10-34 Different operators used in the filter

Exercise 10.12: Create A Page Level Filter

This type of filter is applied to all visualizations on the page. In this exercise you will create a Page level filter that will only display records in three countries.

1. Duplicate page E10.8.

2. Delete the Country Name filter for the first table.

3. Add the Country Name field to the Page level filters section ⇒ Select the following countries: Brazil, Canada, USA ⇒ The tables should look like the ones shown in Figure 10-35. Compare the totals to the ones shown earlier in Figure 10-26.

Customer ID	Customer Name	Region	Country	Last Years Sales
2	Pathfinders	IL	USA	$26,369.63
4	Psycho-Cycle	AL	USA	$52,809.11
5	Sporting Wheels Inc.	CA	USA	$85,642.56
6	Rockshocks for Jocks	TX	USA	$40,778.52
8	Spokes 'N Wheels Ltd.	IA	USA	$25,521.31
Total				**$2,278,221.43**

Customer Name	Country	Last Years Sales	Order ID	Order Date	Order Amount	Ship Via
7 Bikes For 7 Brothers	USA	$8,819.55	3054	05/26/2014	$53.90	Parcel Post
Alley Cat Cycles	USA	$298,356.22	1151	01/08/2014	$5,879.70	Parcel Post
Alley Cat Cycles	USA	$298,356.22	1322	02/21/2013	$3,479.70	Pickup
Alley Cat Cycles	USA	$298,356.22	1656	05/27/2014	$72.90	Parcel Post
Alley Cat Cycles	USA	$298,356.22	2081	09/07/2014	$16.50	Parcel Post
Alley Cat Cycles	USA	$298,356.22	2391	11/19/2014	$2,059.05	Pickup
Alley Cat Cycles	USA	$298,356.22	2447	12/02/2014	$161.70	Parcel Post
Total		**$2,701,889.30**			**$1,086,639.81**	

Figure 10-35 Page level filter applied

Exercise 10.13: Create A Report Level Filter

This type of filter is applied to all visualizations in the report file. It can be created on any page in the file. The Report level filter that will be created in this exercise will filter all of the visualizations by sales rep. To not alter all of the other pages in the current report file, this exercise will use a copy of the current report file.

1. Save the Chapter 10 Filter and Sort table reports file as `Chapter 10 Report level filter.`

2. On any page, add the Sales Rep field to the Report level filters section.

3. Check the following Sales Reps: Anne Dodsworth, Janet Leverling, Justin Brid and Robert King. This will filter all tables on all pages in the file, to only display records for these sales reps.

View The Pages In The Report

As you compare the visualizations, you will see that the Report level filter options that you selected are on every page of the report file.

1. Display page E10.4. It should look like the one shown in Figure 10-36.

   Compare it to the one shown earlier in Figure 10-17. Notice that the totals are less.

   Figure 10-37 shows page E10.8.

   Compare it to the page shown earlier in Figure 10-26.

Customer Name	Order ID	Order Date	Order Amount
	3122	06/17/2014	$5,879.70
7 Bikes For 7 Brothers	3054	05/26/2014	$53.90
AIC Childrens	3153	06/21/2014	$101.70
	⋮		
Auvergne Bicross	3023	05/16/2014	$41.90
Backpedal Cycle Shop	1279	02/08/2014	$3,544.20
Total			**$1,473,187.31**

Figure 10-36 Report level filter applied to page E10.4

Customer ID	Customer Name	Region	Country	Last Years Sales
2	Pathfinders	IL	USA	$26,369.63
4	Psycho-Cycle	AL	USA	$52,809.11
5	Sporting Wheels Inc.	CA	USA	$85,642.56
6	Rockshocks for Jocks	TX	USA	$40,778.52
8	Spokes 'N Wheels Ltd.	IA	USA	$25,521.31
Total				**$1,998,564.20**

Customer Name	Country	Last Years Sales	Order ID	Order Date	Order Amount	Ship Via
7 Bikes For 7 Brothers	USA	$8,819.55	3054	05/26/2014	$53.90	Parcel Post
Alley Cat Cycles	USA	$298,356.22	1151	01/08/2014	$5,879.70	Parcel Post
Alley Cat Cycles	USA	$298,356.22	1322	02/21/2013	$3,479.70	Pickup
Alley Cat Cycles	USA	$298,356.22	1656	05/27/2014	$72.90	Parcel Post
Alley Cat Cycles	USA	$298,356.22	2735	02/19/2015	$8,819.55	Parcel Post
Alley Cat Cycles	USA	$298,356.22	2898	04/09/2015	$1,000.96	Parcel Post
Ankara Bicycle Company	Turkey	$43,000.50	3112	06/13/2014	$959.70	Pickup
Total		**$9,076,755.40**			**$642,382.78**	

Figure 10-37 Report level filter applied to page E10.8

Exercise 10.14: Use The Power BI Template Options

In this exercise you will learn how to create a Power BI template file and how to import a Power BI Template file, to use as the basis for a new report file.

Create A Power BI Template File

In this part of the exercise you will create a template that is based on the Report Data.pbix file.

1. Open the Report Data.pbix file.

2. File tab ⇒ Export ⇒ Power BI Template.

3. Type `My Report Template`, as shown in Figure 10-38 ⇒ Click OK.

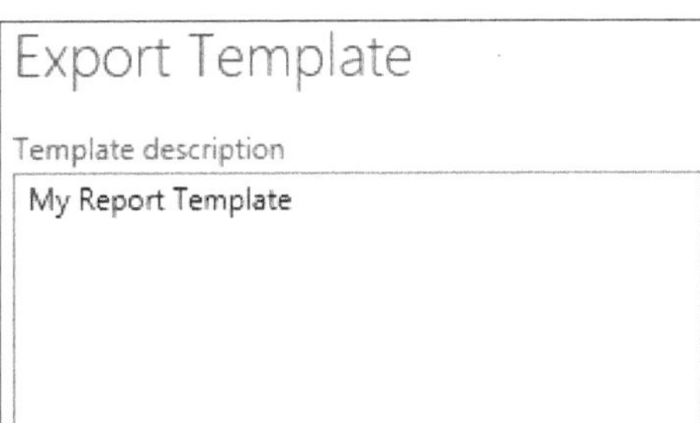

Figure 10-38 Export Template dialog box

4. On the Save As dialog box type `Chapter 10 BI Template`, as the file name. When you open this template, you will see everything that you created in Chapter 8. If you check the file size of this template file and the file size of the Report Data.pbix file, you will see that the template file size is smaller.

Use A Power BI Template File

In this part of the exercise you will import a template file to use as the starting point of a new report file.

1. File tab ⇒ Import ⇒ Power BI Template.

2. Select and open the Chapter 10 BI Template.pbit file ⇒ If the template file has parameters, selecting parameter options before the file is first opened, will filter the data on the report. For now, you can click the Load button and select Load. If none of the parameters are required and you do not select any values for the parameters, before the file is opened, none of the data will be filtered.

3. When the template opens, save it as `Chapter 10 Report file based on a template.`

Summary

This chapter provided in depth coverage of the filter options, including the differences between the three level of filters. You also learned how to create a report that has more than one visualization on a page. Page and Report level filters were also covered.

If you completed the Query Editor chapters, hopefully you are starting to see how important it is to get the data in the best shape possible. On your own, if you find that you are missing fields on the Report view that you need to create a report, you will have to add the data that is needed to create the visualizations.

TABLE VISUALIZATIONS

After completing the exercises in this chapter you will be able to:

☑ Apply formatting options
☑ Create Matrix table visualizations
☑ Create Multi-Row card visualizations
☑ Create Card table visualizations

CHAPTER 11

Overview

As you may have figured out, the table visualization (that you have used up to this point) is not the only table visualization style that is available. This chapter will show you how to use the other table visualizations. Formatting options will also be covered.

Visualization Formatting Options

Power BI Desktop has a lot of options to format the report page and the visualizations. The formatting options are on the Format button on the Visualizations panel.

Page Formatting Options

The options covered in this section are used to change the appearance of the current page in a report file. Currently, there is no functionality to apply the options that you select to all of the pages in the file, at one time. My suggestion is to create a template report file and apply your page formatting options to one page in the template file. Then when you need to start a new report file, use the template file as the starting point, by saving the template file with a new file name. Then, instead of clicking the New Page button, duplicate the page that has the formatting that you created.

As needed, you should add other features, like data tables, queries and logo image files that you know that you will use most of the time to the template file. Don't worry about including everything you need when you first create the template file, as you can add to it over time.

Figure 11-1 shows the Page categories and illustrates the **FORMAT BUTTON**. This button is used to access the options. To use the Page Formatting options, nothing can be selected on the page.

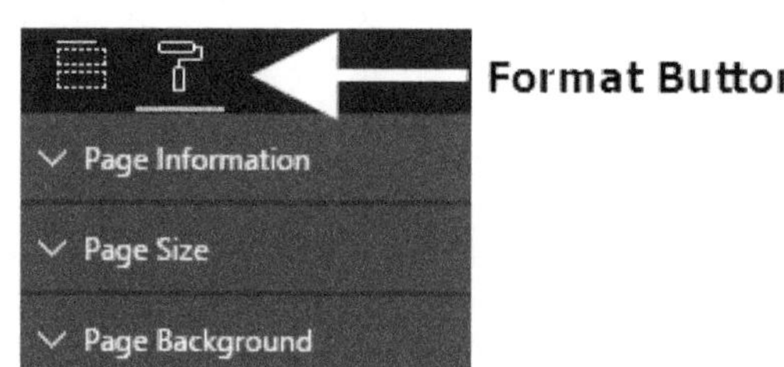

Figure 11-1 Page formatting categories

Page Information Options

The options shown in Figure 11-2 are the general page options.

The **NAME** option is another way to rename the page (the tab).

Enable the **Q&A OPTION** if you are using Power BI (a different tool then Power BI Desktop) and want the page to be searched when using the Q&A natural language feature.

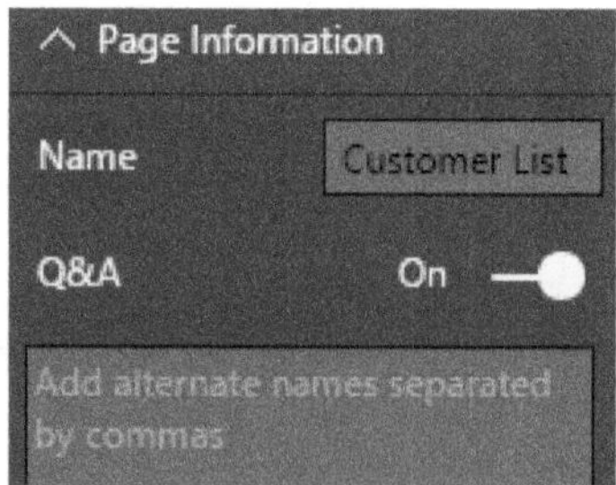

Figure 11-2 Page Information options

Page Size Options

The options shown in Figure 11-3 are used to change how the page is displayed, in terms of its size. Each page in the report can have a different page size, as needed.

The **TYPE OPTIONS** contain pre-configured page sizes for 16:9, 4:3, Cortana, Letter and Custom. Some of the options are explained below.

The **DYNAMIC OPTION** causes the page to automatically expand as needed. This option disables the Width and Height options. At the time this book went to print, this option is no longer available for new pages. The last time I checked, an alternative solution was being worked on.

Figure 11-3 Page Size options

The **CUSTOM OPTION** is free form, meaning you can select the width and height that you want.

Page Background Options

The options shown in Figure 11-4 are used to customize the background of the page by applying color, an image or transparency to the image.

The **REVERT TO DEFAULT OPTION** removes all of the changes that you made in the section. All of the categories shown in Figure 11-5, except the General category, have this option, even though I do not show it in all of the other figures.

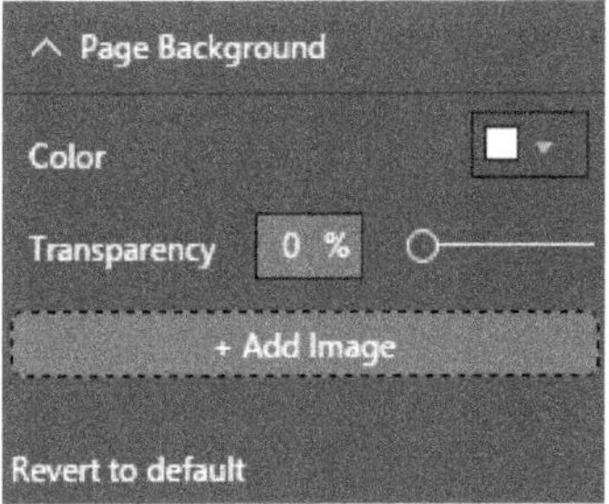

Figure 11-4 Page Background options

Table Formatting Options

The majority of categories shown in Figure 11-5 are also available for Matrix and Card table visualizations that are covered later in this chapter. These options are used to format the visual.

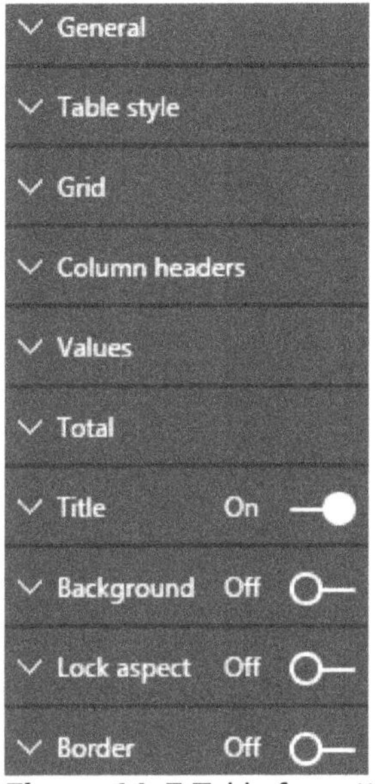

Figure 11-5 Table formatting categories

General Options

The options shown in Figure 11-6 are applied to the table, not a specific part of the table, like the other categories, shown above in Figure 11-5 are.

By default, the **AUTO-SIZE COLUMN WIDTH OPTION** is enabled. When enabled, column widths are automatically resized to accommodate the widest item in each column. Columns cannot be resized in the table. To be honest, I did not see any change with this option enabled, but maybe none of the tables that I have created meet the auto size criteria requirement.

The **TEXT SIZE OPTION** is used to change the font size in the table. You can type in a number in the field or use the slider, to select the font size.

The **TOTALS OPTION** displays or hides all of the totals on the table. Enable this option to display totals on the visualization.

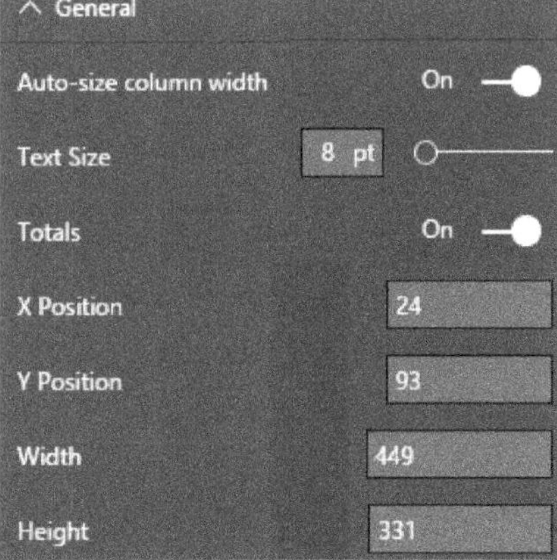

Figure 11-6 General options

The **POSITION**, **WIDTH** and **HEIGHT OPTIONS** change to size and location of the table on the page, all of which are probably easier to do manually, by moving the table to where you want it on the page.

Totals will only be displayed if the table displays two or more rows.

Table Style Options

The options shown in Figure 11-7 are used to format the table.

Figure 11-8 shows the Bold header style applied to a table.

Figure 11-9 shows the Alternating rows style applied to a table.

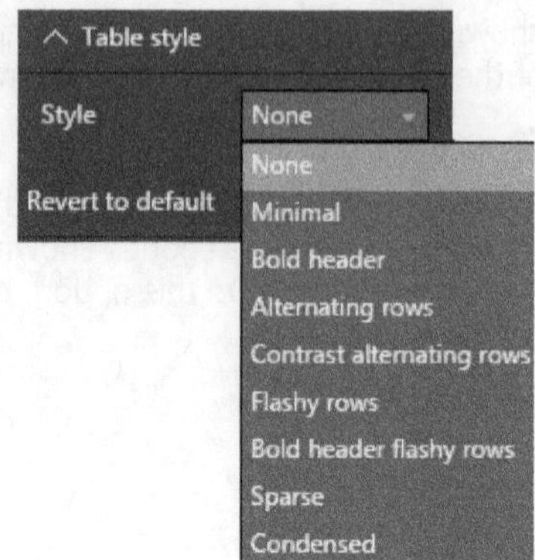

Figure 11-7 Table Style options

Customer ID	Customer Name	Last Years Sales
1	City Cyclists	$20,045.27
2	Pathfinders	$26,369.63
3	Bike-A-Holics Anonymous	$4,500.00
4	Psycho-Cycle	$52,809.11
Total		**$2,360,400.69**

Figure 11-8 Bold header table style

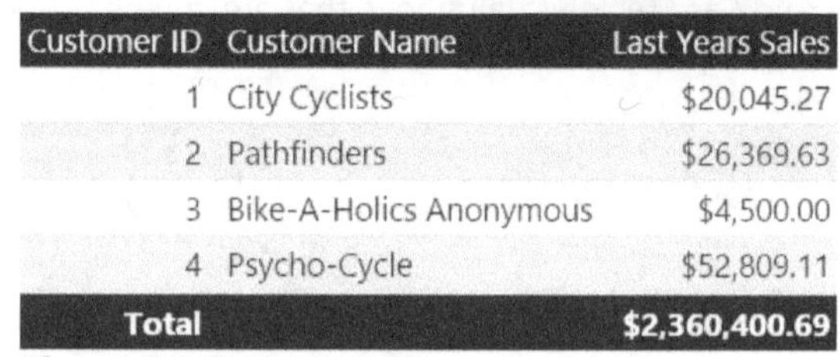

Customer ID	Customer Name	Last Years Sales
1	City Cyclists	$20,045.27
2	Pathfinders	$26,369.63
3	Bike-A-Holics Anonymous	$4,500.00
4	Psycho-Cycle	$52,809.11
Total		**$2,360,400.69**

Figure 11-9 Alternating rows table style

Grid Options

The options shown in Figure 11-10 are used to format the container/grid that the table is in.

The **VERT GRID** and **HORIZ GRID OPTIONS** add lines to the table. When both options are enabled, the table looks like a spreadsheet.

If the Vert grid option is enabled, the Vert grid color and Vert grid thickness options are also enabled, as shown in Figure 11-11.

The **ROW PADDING OPTION** adds space above and below the data in each row in the table.

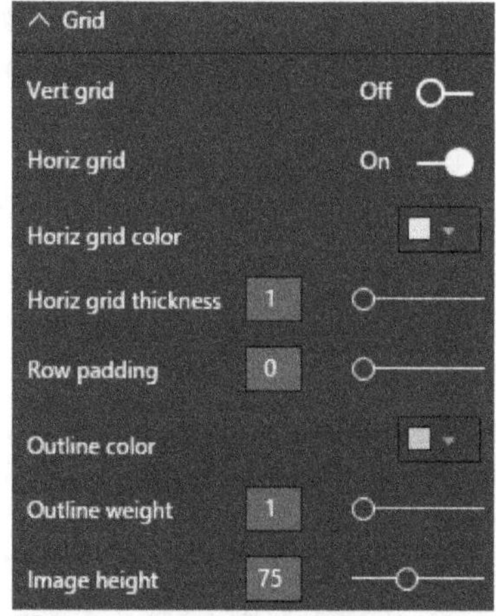

Figure 11-10 Grid options

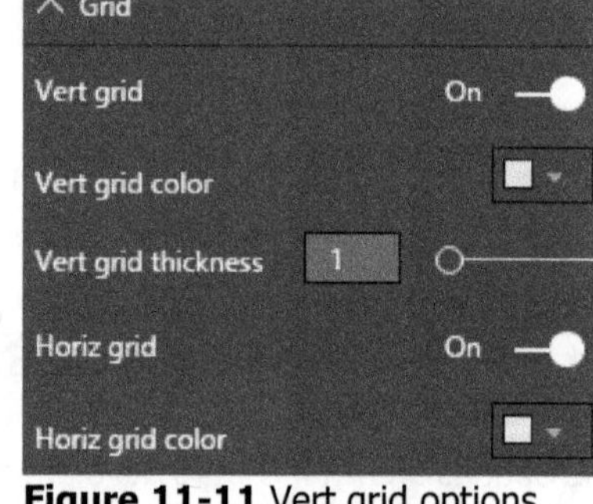

Figure 11-11 Vert grid options

The **OUTLINE COLOR OPTION** changes the color of the line below the column headings and above the totals.

Column And Row Headers Options

The options shown in Figure 11-12 are used to format the column and row headings.

The **OUTLINE OPTIONS** shown in the figure, add a border around all or part of the headings.

The Row header options are only available for **MATRIX TABLES.**

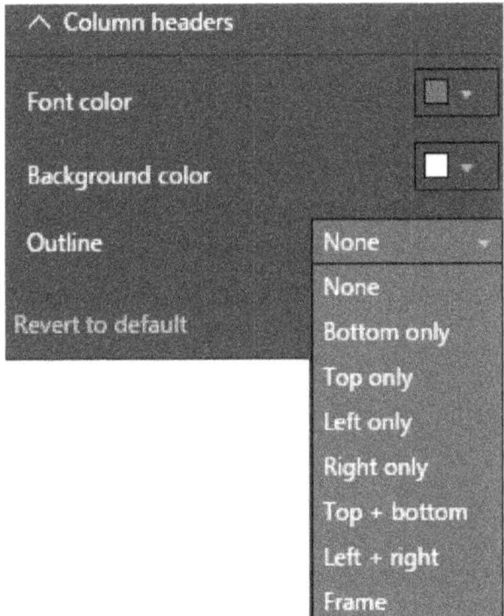

Figure 11-12 Column headers options

Values Options

The options shown in Figure 11-13 are used to format the data in the table.

The **FONT COLOR** and **BACKGROUND COLOR OPTIONS** are applied to the odd number rows in the table.

The **ALTERNATE FONT COLOR** and **ALTERNATE BACKGROUND COLOR OPTIONS** are applied to the even number rows in the table.

The **OUTLINE OPTION** has the same settings as the ones shown above in Figure 11-12.

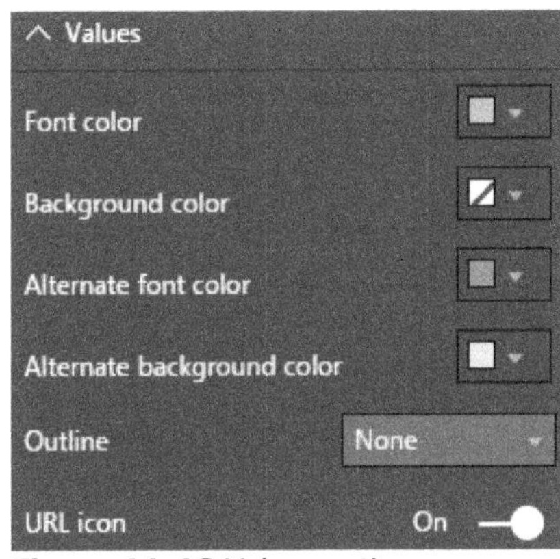

Figure 11-13 Values options

If enabled, the **URL ICON OPTION** will display an icon in the column in the table, as shown in Figure 11-14, instead of the entire URL.

The field with the web site address has to have the Data Category option (in the Data view) set to Web URL.

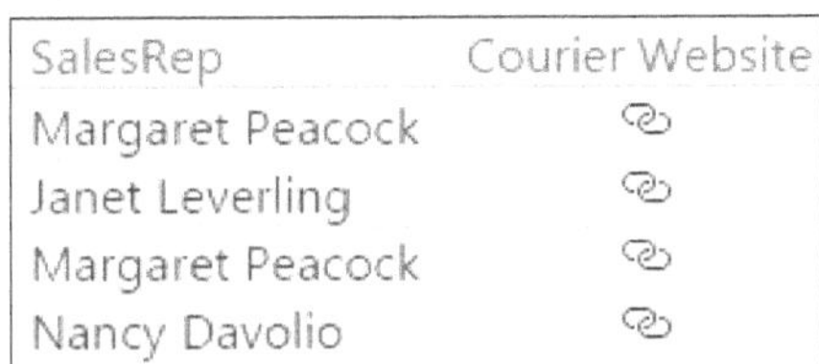

Figure 11-14 URL icon

Total Options

The options shown in Figure 11-15 are used to format the total headings and values.

By default, the **OUTLINE OPTION** is set to Top only. It has the same options, as shown earlier in Figure 11-12.

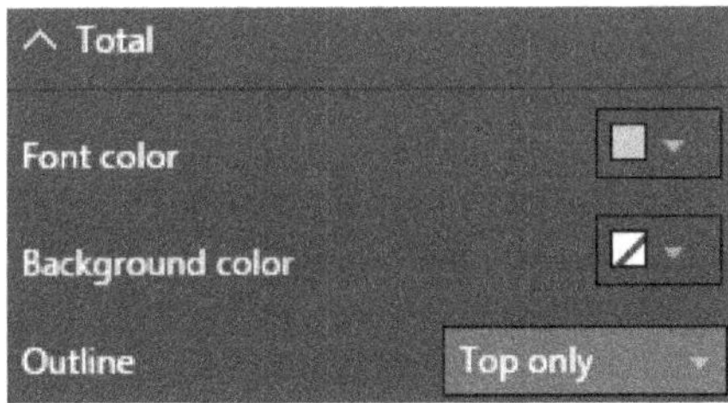

Figure 11-15 Total options

Title Options

The options shown in Figure 11-16 are used to create and format the title for the table. Depending on your needs, you can use this option instead of using a Text Box, especially if the page will only have one visual.

As shown at the top of the figure, the **TITLE CATEGORY** is also an option, and by default, it is enabled, even though initially you cannot see it on the page, until text is added to the **TITLE TEXT** field.

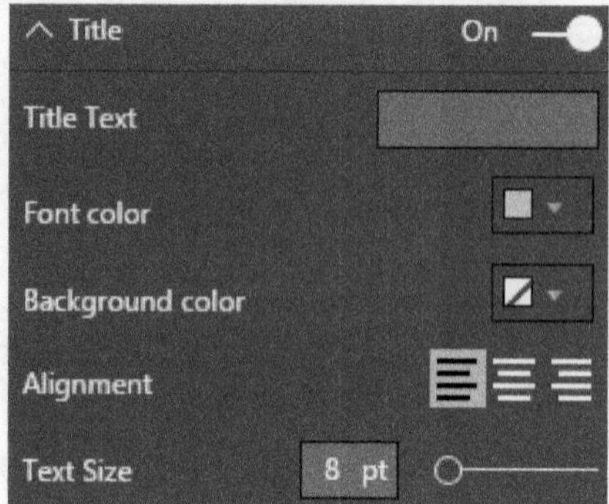

Figure 11-16 Title options

Background Options

The options shown in Figure 11-17 are used to format the background of the table.

By default, the **BACKGROUND OPTION** is not enabled. It has to be enabled to use the options in this section.

The **TRANSPARENCY OPTION** is used to select how light or dark the background color is.

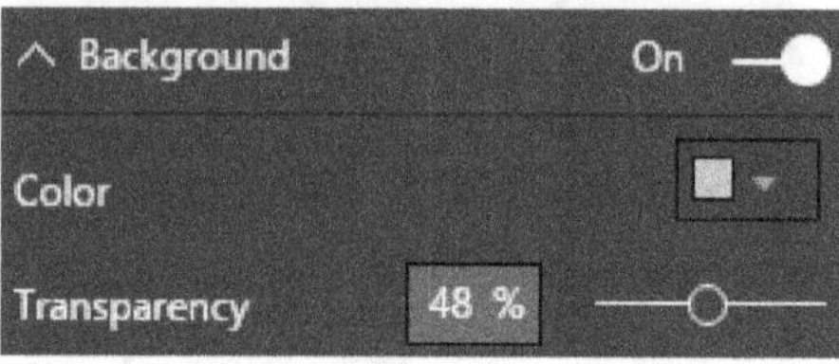

Figure 11-17 Background options

Lock Aspect Option

By default, this category is not enabled. When enabled, as shown in Figure 11-18, there are no other options. Enabling this option forces the height and width of the table, or an object, like a shape to keep its original relative proportions when resized. This option keeps you from distorting an image, if you resize it.

Figure 11-18 Lock Aspect option

Border Options

The options shown in Figure 11-19 are used to add a color border, around the table.

Figure 11-19 Border options

Formatting Options For Other Page Elements

The formatting options covered so far have been for objects that display data or customize the page. The formatting options covered in this section are for objects that can be added to a page. When one of these objects are selected, the Format panel only displays the formatting options for the object.

On your own, you will see that many of the options are the same as ones covered earlier in this chapter. This section only covers the categories of formatting options.

Text Box Formatting Options

Figure 11-20 shows the formatting options for a Text Box. They are the same as the ones explained earlier in this chapter. The Text Box is used to add free form text to the page. It is often used as a page heading. Another use for it is to add helpful information to the page, like explaining how to use a slicer.

Figure 11-21 shows a Text Box added to a page. Most of the options on the toolbar, work the same as they do in other software packages. Clicking on the **INSERT LINK BUTTON**, displays the field to the right of the button, which is used to enter a web site address. After you type in the address, click the Done button and the link will be added to the Text Box.

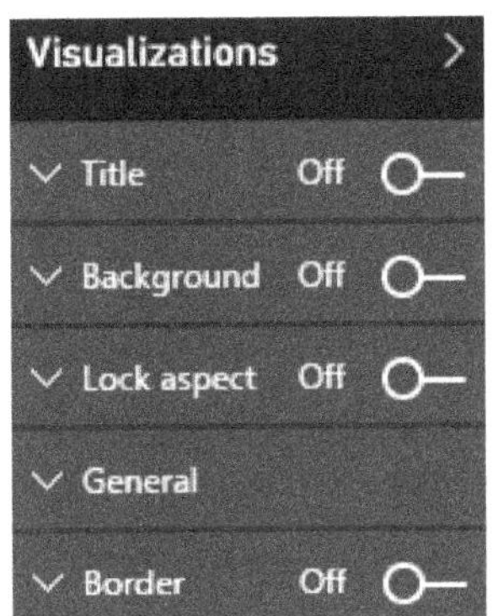

Figure 11-20 Text Box formatting options

Figure 11-21 Text Box and toolbar

Hyperlinks Tips

① You can type the hyperlink in the Text Box, highlight the text, then click the Insert link and Done buttons, on the toolbar to create a hyperlink.

② You can also use text as a hyperlink, as shown above in Figure 11-21. To do this, select the text, click the Insert link button, type the web site address in the field to the right of the Insert link button and click Done.

Image Formatting Options

Once an image is added to the page, the options shown in Figure 11-22 can be used to customize the image. The following image file formats are supported: BMP, GIF, JPEG, PNG and TIFF.

The **SCALING OPTION** is used to select how the image is displayed in its frame. The options are:

- ☑ **NORMAL** Don't scale the image.
- ☑ **FIT** Resize the image so the entire image is in the frame. This option can distort the image.
- ☑ **FILL** Resize the image so that it is the same size as its frame. This option can cut off part of an image.

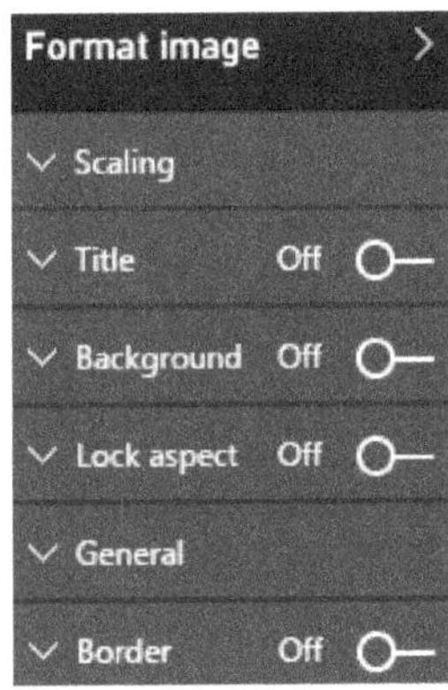

Figure 11-22 Image formatting options

Shape Formatting Options

Figure 11-23 shows the available shapes. They can be resized manually.

The options shown in Figure 11-24 are used to customize the shape.

The categories specifically for shapes are explained below.

The **LINE OPTIONS** are used to customize the border of the shape. The options in this category change, depending on the shape that is selected.

The **FILL OPTIONS** are used to select a color for the interior of the shape. These options are not available for the line shape.

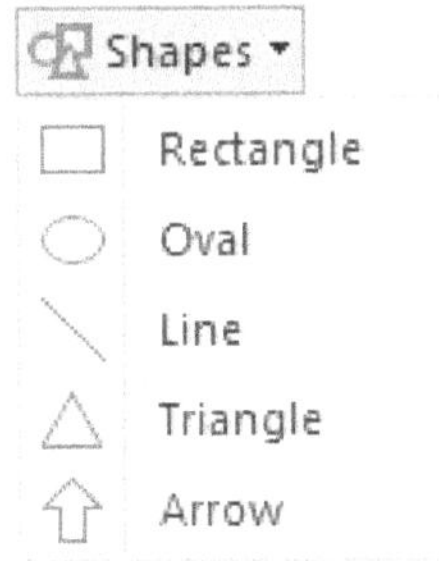

Figure 11-23 Shape options

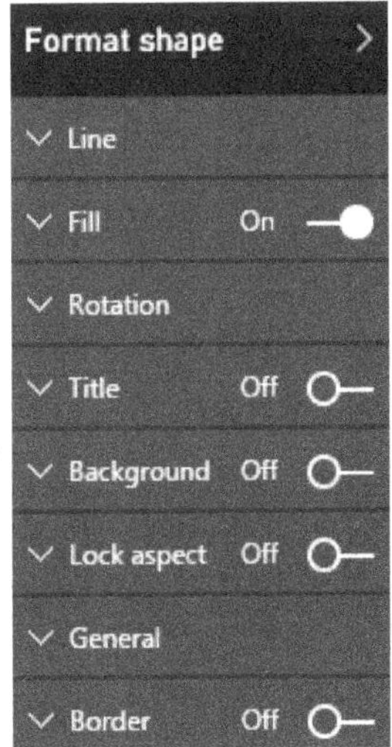

Figure 11-24 Shape formatting options

The **ROTATION OPTIONS** are used to change the direction of the shape in degrees.

Exercise 11.1: Apply Formatting Options To A Table

In this exercise you will use some of the formatting options. After you apply an option, look at the table to see the change. Doing this will help you see where each formatting option is applied.

1. Save the Report Data.pbix file as `Chapter 11 Table reports.`

2. Duplicate the Order List page.

3. In the Grid section, enable the Vert Grid option ⇒ Change the **VERT GRID COLOR** and **HORIZ GRID COLOR** options to black.

4. In the Column headers section, change the Background color option to a light color.

5. In the Total section, change the Background color option to the same color that you used in the previous step.

6. Enable the Title section ⇒
   In the Title Text field, type `Formatted Table` ⇒
   Change the Font color to black ⇒
   Change the **ALIGNMENT OPTION** to Center ⇒
   Change the Text Size to `20`.

   The table should look like the one shown in Figure 11-25.

Formatted Table

Customer Name	Order ID	Order Date	Order Amount
	3122	06/17/2014	$5,879.70
7 Bikes For 7 Brothers	3054	05/26/2014	$53.90
Against The Wind Bikes	3055	05/26/2014	$479.85
AIC Childrens	3153	06/21/2014	$101.70
Alley Cat Cycles	1151	01/08/2014	$5,879.70
Alley Cat Cycles	1204	01/19/2014	$1,583.05
Total			**$4,083,665.34**

Figure 11-25 Formatted table

Other Table Types

The previous chapters covered the Table visualization in detail. As you will see, other table types (matrix, multi-row card and card style) provide different looks for the data that is displayed. One thing that I think is cool, is that you can test each of the table styles by applying one to an existing table visualization. To restore the visualization back to a table, change the visualization style back to Table. Figure 11-26 shows the same data in the different table styles.

Table

Customer Name	Sum of Order ID	Order Date	Order Amount
	3122	06/17/2014	$5,879.70
7 Bikes For 7 Brothers	3054	05/26/2014	$53.90
Against The Wind Bikes	3055	05/26/2014	$479.85
AIC Childrens	3153	06/21/2014	$101.70
Alley Cat Cycles	1322	02/21/2013	$3,479.70
Alley Cat Cycles	1151	01/08/2014	$5,879.70
Alley Cat Cycles	1204	01/19/2014	$1,583.05
Alley Cat Cycles	1239	01/28/2014	$101.70
Alley Cat Cycles	1260	02/04/2014	$33.90
Alley Cat Cycles	1656	05/27/2014	$72.90
Total			**$4,083,665.34**

Matrix

Customer Name	Order Date	Sum of Order ID	Order Amount
	06/17/2014	3122	$5,879.70
	Total	**3122**	**$5,879.70**
7 Bikes For 7 Brothers	05/26/2014	3054	$53.90
	Total	**3054**	**$53.90**
Against The Wind Bikes	05/26/2014	3055	$479.85
	Total	**3055**	**$479.85**
AIC Childrens	06/21/2014	3153	$101.70
	Total	**3153**	**$101.70**
Alley Cat Cycles	02/21/2013	1322	$3,479.70
	01/08/2014	1151	$5,879.70

Multi-Row Card

(Blank)	3122	06/17/2014	$5,879.70
Customer Name	Sum of Order ID	Order Date	Order Amount
7 Bikes For 7 Brothers	3054	05/26/2014	$53.90
Customer Name	Sum of Order ID	Order Date	Order Amount
Against The Wind Bikes	3055	05/26/2014	$479.85
Customer Name	Sum of Order ID	Order Date	Order Amount
AIC Childrens	3153	06/21/2014	$101.70
Customer Name	Sum of Order ID	Order Date	Order Amount

Figure 11-26 Three table styles that display the same data

Matrix Tables

If you were thinking that Power BI Desktop only has functionality to create the list table report style that has been covered so far in this book, things are about to change. As you have seen, the table visualization option displays the data in a list format, with totals. Matrix tables add groups to the table visualization.

Matrix tables display data in a hierarchy layout with groups. When creating this type of table, keep in mind that a hierarchy starts with the top level field. This is the order that the fields need to be in for them to be displayed properly in the matrix table. The data is grouped and totaled by the fields in the hierarchy.

When I use the word hierarchy in this description, I am not saying that only fields in a hierarchy can be used to create a matrix table. Other fields can be used, as long as you add them in a "hierarchy like" order. The fields that you use to create the hierarchy effect, are the ones that the groups will be created for.

Matrix tables also help make the data easier to understand because they add space to the table, as well as, totals for the groups. While similar to a table because it displays data in rows and columns, a matrix table can be expanded and collapsed by the rows or columns. Each level is sorted in ascending order. I find it easier to drag fields to the section on the Field Well, then to click in the check box. Adding a hierarchy, adds drill down functionality to the table. There are two types of Matrix tables (Row and Column) that can be created. Both are covered in this chapter.

Popular matrix tables to create are sales reps total sales by year, as shown in Figure 11-27. Figure 11-28 shows the fields used to create this matrix table.

Another popular matrix table to create is the sales reps total sales by country, as shown in Figure 11-29. Figure 11-30 shows the fields used to create this matrix table.

SalesRep	2013	2014	2015	Total
Anne Dodsworth	$29,049.94	$513,545.52	$140,253.75	**$682,849.21**
Janet Leverling	$44,121.64	$447,235.19	$157,745.16	**$649,101.99**
Margaret Peacock	$38,458.39	$446,150.56	$147,190.82	**$631,799.77**
Michael Suyama	$54,804.22	$496,881.48	$158,715.78	**$710,401.48**
Nancy Davolio	$71,862.70	$450,865.83	$138,028.42	**$660,756.95**
Robert King	$21,093.75	$512,406.60	$215,255.59	**$748,755.94**
Total	**$259,390.64**	**$2,867,085.18**	**$957,189.52**	**$4,083,665.34**

Figure 11-27 Sales reps total sales by year

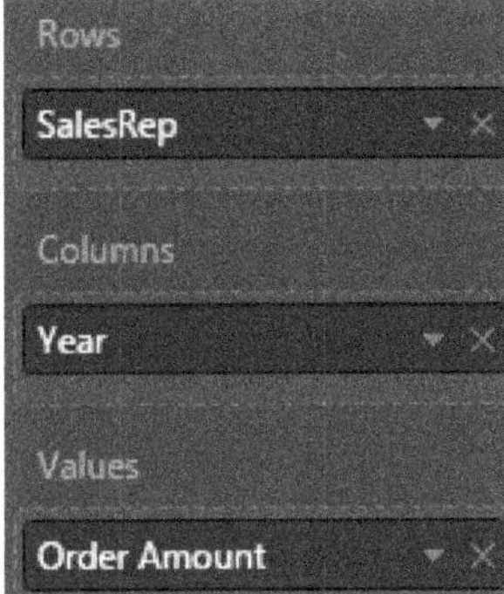

Figure 11-28 Fields used to create the matrix table

SalesRep		Argentina	Aruba	Australia	Austria	Bahamas	Bangladesh	Barbados	Belgium
Anne Dodsworth				$5,924.70	$33.00		$65.70		$5,027.34
Janet Leverling	$5,879.70			$17.50	$606.47			$329.85	$17,168.06
Margaret Peacock				$479.85	$5,911.70	$659.70			$1,875.65
Michael Suyama			$5,879.70		$90.06				$17,141.17
Nancy Davolio					$17,064.63				$1,570.10
Robert King		$1,664.70		$3,477.94	$5,107.55				$12,337.17
Total	**$5,879.70**	**$1,664.70**	**$5,879.70**	**$9,899.99**	**$28,813.41**	**$659.70**	**$65.70**	**$329.85**	**$55,119.49**

Figure 11-29 Sales reps total sales by country

Matrix Table Field Well

Figure 11-30 shows the options used to create a matrix table.

The Field Well shortcut menu is the same as the one for tables.

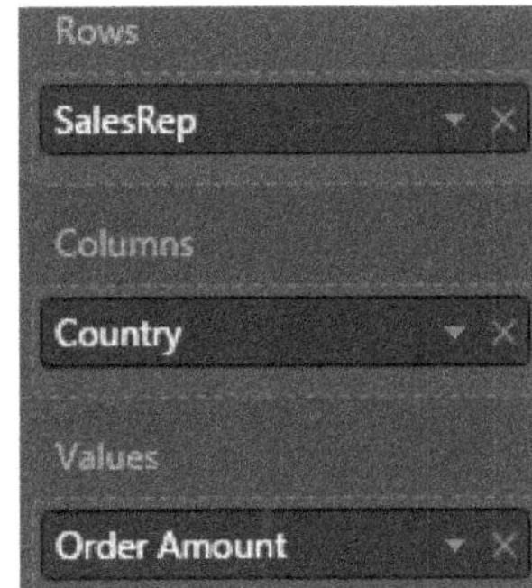

Figure 11-30 Matrix table Field Well

Matrix Table Formatting Options

Matrix tables basically have the same formatting options that tables have. This section covers options specific to Matrix tables. The other options were covered earlier in this chapter. [See Table Formatting Options]

General Options

The options shown in Figure 11-31 can be applied to a Matrix table.

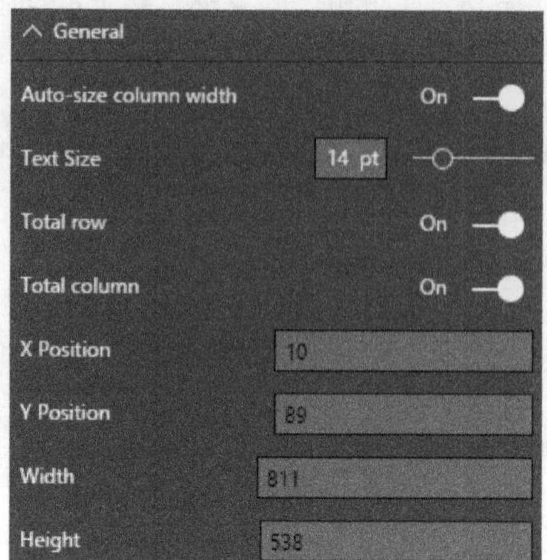

Figure 11-31 Matrix table general options

The **TOTAL ROW OPTION** is used to create a total (per row) for the field(s) in the Values section of the Field Well. This option displays this total as new rows in the table.

The **TOTAL COLUMN OPTION** is used to create a grand total per row. This option creates a new column at the end of the table.

Matrix Style Options

Matrix tables have the same style options as tables. [See Figure 11-7]

Subtotals Options

These options are the same as the Total options shown earlier in Figure 11-15.

Grand Total Options

Figure 11-32 shows the options to customize the grand totals at the bottom of the matrix table.

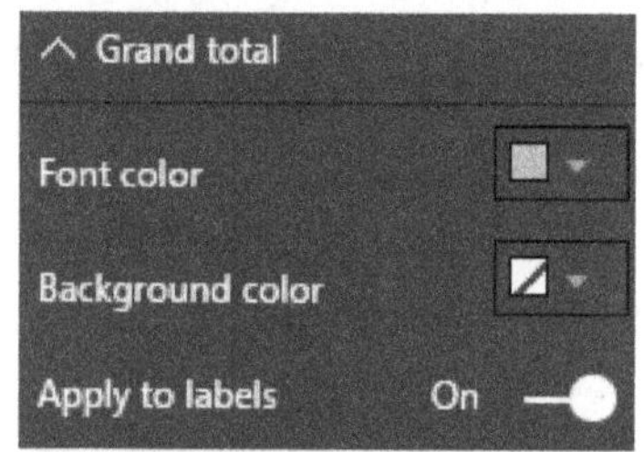

Figure 11-32 Grand total options

The **APPLY TO LABELS OPTION** is used to apply color to the grand total label.

Row Matrix Table

The way that this type of matrix table is created, is based on the hierarchy of the fields that you want the data in the table, grouped on. For example, creating a matrix table using this hierarchy structure is incorrect: Zip Code ⇒ Region ⇒ Country. If these are the fields that you want to use to create a matrix table, the order that the fields should be in, is Country ⇒ Region ⇒ Zip Code. A total is automatically created for each level in the hierarchy or group.

In a Row Matrix table, the fields added to the Values section, in the Field Well, are the fields that you want broken out by (grouped on) the fields in the Rows section. For example, in Exercise 11.2, the total order amount will be broken out by county, sales rep and customer name.

Exercise 11.2: Create A Row Matrix Table

In this exercise you will create a row matrix table that groups the data by country, sales rep and customer name.

1. Click the Matrix visualization button (It's next to the Table visualization button).

2. Add the following fields to the Rows section on the Field Well: Country Name, Sales Rep, Customer Name and Order Amount. The matrix table should look like the one shown in Figure 11-33.

   As shown in the figure, the Row matrix table that you just created, displays records that do not have a country. In this dataset, that is because all of the countries in the Customer table, are not in the Country List table. On your own, your country list table would be fully populated.

The rows in the table that do not display a customer name, are for the customer name above. The matrix table would be easier to understand if it had the Order Date field and a total order amount per customer, per sales rep.

Country Name	SalesRep	Customer Name	Order Amount
	Anne Dodsworth	Belgium Bike Co.	$33.00
			$489.87
			$1,751.02
			$2,753.45
		Bendai Mountain Bikers	$15.00
		Bicicletas de Montaña La Paz	$97.02
		C&C Sports People	$1,529.70
		Canal City Cycle	$47.00

Figure 11-33 Row matrix table

Exercise 11.3: Summarize The Customer Orders By Sales Rep

In this exercise you will modify the E11.2 report to summarize the orders for each customer.

1. Duplicate page E11.2.
2. In the Rows section, drag the Order Amount field down to the Values section.

   Now, each customer has one row with a total order amount, per sales rep, as shown in Figure 11-34.

Country Name	SalesRep	Customer Name	Order Amount
	Anne Dodsworth	Belgium Bike Co.	$5,027.34
		Bendai Mountain Bikers	$15.00
		Bicicletas de Montaña La Paz	$97.02
		C&C Sports People	$1,529.70
		Canal City Cycle	$18,130.70
		Coastal Line Bikes	$101.70

Figure 11-34 Orders summarized by customer

Adding A Count Field

The matrix table shown above in Figure 11-34 looks good. It displays the data in a summary format. By that I mean that each row is a summary of all the orders for each customer, for each sales rep. By looking at each row, you cannot tell if the order amount is for one order or 20 orders.

Adding the Customer ID field (from the Orders table) to the end of the Values section, as shown in Figure 11-35 and changing the aggregation to Count, displays a count of orders by customer, as shown in Figure 11-36.

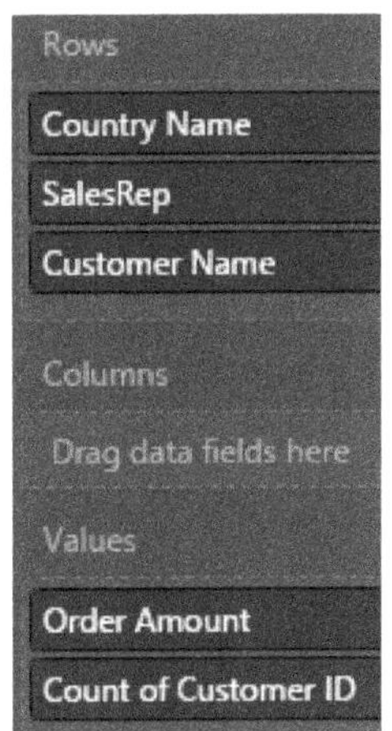

Figure 11-35 Field changes to display a count of orders

Country Name	SalesRep	Customer Name	Order Amount	Count of Customer ID
	Anne Dodsworth	Belgium Bike Co.	$5,027.34	4
		Bendai Mountain Bikers	$15.00	1
		Bicicletas de Montaña La Paz	$97.02	1
		C&C Sports People	$1,529.70	1
		Canal City Cycle	$18,130.70	7
		Coastal Line Bikes	$101.70	1
		Cycle City Rome	$10,665.67	6

Figure 11-36 Matrix table with a count of orders per customer, per sales rep

Exercise 11.4: Add Totals To The Matrix Table

The matrix table, shown earlier in Figure 11-34 may be of more value for people that read it if the order date field was displayed. That would display each customers individual orders on their own row. Adding the Order Date field to the Rows section would accomplish this task.

It would be nice to also display a count of the number of orders, each sales rep had, for each customer, in each country, as shown above in Figure 11-36.

1. Duplicate page E11.3.

2. Add the Order Date field to the Rows section, below the Customer Name field.

   The table should look like the one shown in Figure 11-37.

Country Name	SalesRep	Customer Name	Order Date	Order Amount
	Anne Dodsworth	Belgium Bike Co.	07/02/2014	$489.87
			08/11/2014	$2,753.45
			08/26/2014	$33.00
			09/30/2014	$1,751.02
			Total	**$5,027.34**
		Bendai Mountain Bikers	06/25/2014	$15.00
			Total	**$15.00**
		Bicicletas de Montaña La Paz	06/03/2014	$97.02
			Total	**$97.02**

Figure 11-37 Order Date field added to the matrix table

3. Scroll down the table until you see records for the sales rep Janet Leverling.

   Right above her first row of data, you will see a total for the previous sales rep, as illustrated in Figure 11-38.

Country Name	SalesRep	Customer Name	Order Date	Order Amount
	Anne Dodsworth	Warsaw Sports, Inc.	11/26/2014	$31.00
			12/18/2014	$29.00
			Total	**$1,537.35**
		Total		**$116,695.12**
	Janet Leverling		06/17/2014	$5,879.70
			Total	**$5,879.70**
		Ankara Bicycle Company	06/13/2014	$959.70
			Total	**$959.70**

Figure 11-38 Sales rep total order amount illustrated

Verifying Data

To verify that the total order amount for a company is correct in Figure 11-37, compare the order amount for a company, to the total for the same company, in Figure 11-36. The matrix table in Figure 11-36 displays the data in summary format.

When compared to the matrix table shown earlier in Figure 11-37, in Figure 11-36, you can see that the Belgium Bike Co., has placed has placed four orders with the sales rep, Anne Dodsworth. Figure 11-36 grouped all of each customers orders for the sales rep, into one row. As shown, notice that the total for the company in both tables is the same.

Column Matrix Table

This type of matrix table creates another group, if you will, of the fields in the Rows section on the Field Well. Adding a field to the Columns section on the Field Well, breaks the data into smaller groups with more totals. A column matrix table reminds me of a **CROSS-TAB REPORT**.

Exercise 11.5: Create A Column Matrix Table

In this exercise you will modify the E11.4 row matrix table, to be a column matrix table. Another field will be added, that will provide a more detailed view of the data.

1. Duplicate page E11.4.

2. Remove the Country Name field from the Rows section.

3. Add the Ship Via field to the Columns section, as shown in Figure 11-39.

   The matrix table should look like the one shown in Figure 11-40.

   Notice that you can scroll to the right. When you use the scroll bar at the bottom of the table and scroll to the right, you will see that the first three columns (the ones before the vertical line), stay visible.

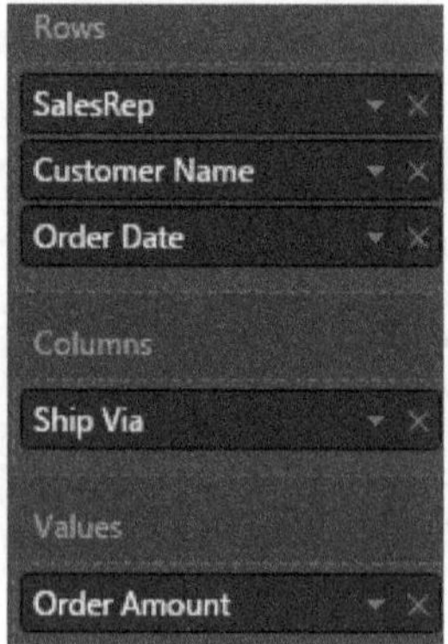

Figure 11-39 Fields for a Column matrix table

SalesRep	Customer Name	Order Date	FedEx	Loomis	Parcel Post	Pickup	Purolator
Anne Dodsworth	Alley Cat Cycles	02/21/2013				$3,479.70	
		01/31/2015	$9,290.30				
		04/09/2015			$1,000.96		
		Total	**$9,290.30**		**$1,000.96**	**$3,479.70**	
	Backpedal Cycle Shop	02/08/2014				$3,544.20	
		06/18/2014			$35.00		
		07/02/2014	$3,479.70				
		07/17/2014					
		10/19/2014				$863.74	
		11/25/2014		$329.85			
		Total	**$3,479.70**	**$329.85**	**$35.00**	**$4,407.94**	

Figure 11-40 Column matrix table

Exercise 11.6: Create A Row And Column Matrix Table

Exercise 11.2 showed you how to create a row matrix table. In this exercise you will modify that table by adding fields to the Columns section, to create a combination row and column matrix table, that has a three level hierarchy. The levels will show the order amount totals by country, sales rep, customer name, year, quarter and month. The table will have row and column totals.

1. Duplicate page E11.2.
2. Delete the Country Name field in the Rows section.
3. Drag the Order Amount field in the Rows section to the Values section.
4. Add the Date Hierarchy field to the Columns section.

   The Field Well should look like the one shown in Figure 11-41.

   The matrix table should look like the one shown in Figure 11-42.

Figure 11-41 Field Well options to create a row and column matrix table

	SelectYear	2013					2014							
	SelectQuarter	Q1		Q4		**Total**	Q1				Q2			
SalesRep	Customer Name	February	**Total**	December	**Total**		January	February	March	**Total**	April	May	June	**Total**
Anne Dodsworth	Alley Cat Cycles	$3,479.70	**$3,479.70**			**$3,479.70**								
	Backpedal Cycle Shop							$3,544.20		**$3,544.20**			$35.00	**$35.00**
	BBS Pty												$8,819.55	**$8,819.55**
	Beach Trails and Wheels			$33.00	**$33.00**	**$33.00**								
	Belgium Bike Co.													
	Bendai Mountain Bikers												$15.00	**$15.00**
	Benny - The Spokes Person													
	Bicicletas de Montaña La Paz												$97.02	**$97.02**
	Bike Shop from Mars						$43.50			**$43.50**				
	Bike-A-Holics Anonymous	$178.20	**$178.20**			**$178.20**		$5,879.70	$659.70	**$6,539.40**	$872.65			**$872.65**
	Bikes and Trikes			$413.65	**$413.65**	**$413.65**								
	Bikes for Tykes												$16.50	**$16.50**
	Bikes, Bikes, and More Bikes							$832.35		**$832.35**			$2,546.12	**$2,546.12**
	Biking's It Industries	$1,391.08	**$1,391.08**			**$1,391.08**					$29.00			**$29.00**

Figure 11-42 Row and Column matrix table

Multi-Row Card Table

This table visualization displays the data in an index card layout. The fields are displayed on the card, in the order they are added to the Fields section of the Field Well. As much as possible, the fields are displayed on one row. It depends on the number of fields used and the size of the card. A table or matrix table can be changed to a multi-row card table. The Multi-Row Card table only scrolls vertically, which is different from the table and matrix visualizations.

Multi-Row Card Table Field Well

Figure 11-43 shows the option used to create a multi-row card table.

The Field Well shortcut menu is the same as the one for tables.

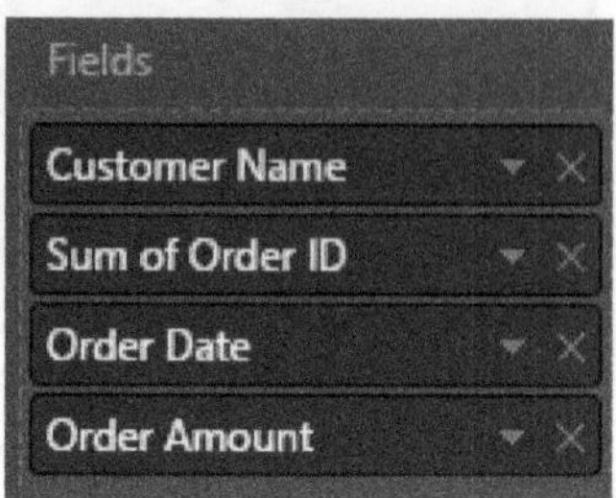

Figure 11-43 Multi-Row Card table Field Well

Multi-Row Card Table Formatting Options

The options covered in this section are specific to multi-row card tables.

Data Labels Options

Figure 11-44 shows the Data Labels formatting options.

The **COLOR OPTION** is used to change the color of the values displayed on the table.

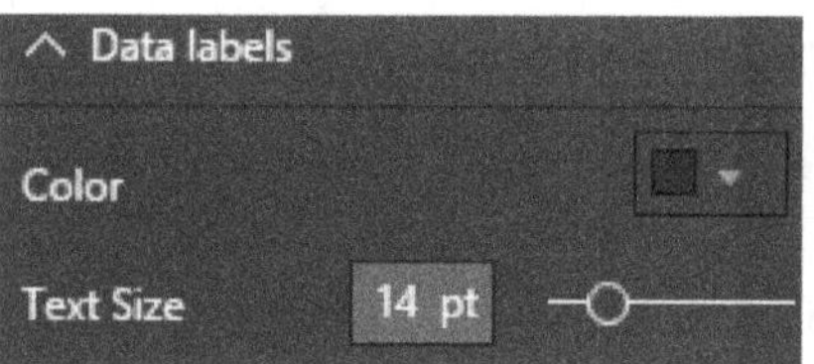

Figure 11-44 Data labels options

Category Labels Options

The options shown in Figure 11-45 work the same as the ones shown above in Figure 11-44.

These options are used to change the color of the headings for the fields in the Fields section.

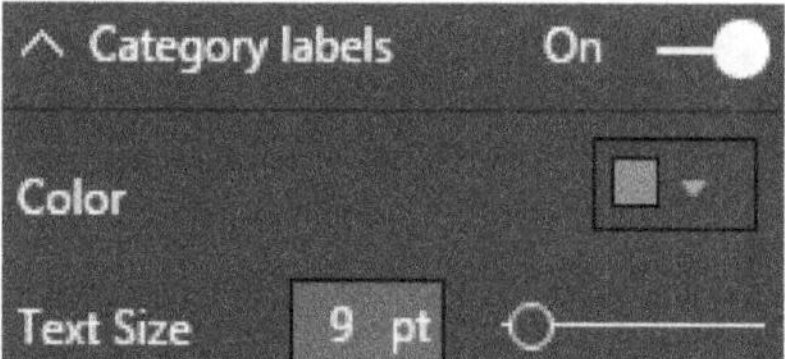

Figure 11-45 Category labels options

Card Options

The options shown in Figure 11-46 are for the bar to the left of each record displayed on the multi-row card. The bar automatically expands to the length of rows for each record.

The **SHOW BAR OPTION** is used to display or hide the bar.

The **BAR COLOR OPTION** is used to select a color for the bar.

The **BAR THICKNESS OPTION** is used to select the width of the bar.

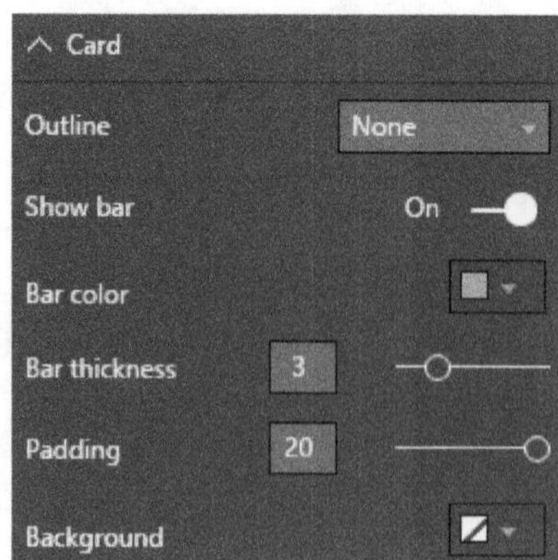

Figure 11-46 Card options

Exercise 11.7: Create A Multi-Row Card Table

In this exercise, you will duplicate a table and change the visualization style.

1. Duplicate page E11.1.
2. Click on the table ⇒ Click the Multi-Row Card button.
3. Turn the Title formatting off ⇒ If necessary, make the frame wider, so that all of the fields are displayed on one row, as shown in Figure 11-47.

(Blank)	3122	06/17/2014	$5,879.70
Customer Name	Order ID	Order Date	Order Amount
7 Bikes For 7 Brothers	3054	05/26/2014	$53.90
Customer Name	Order ID	Order Date	Order Amount
Against The Wind Bikes	3055	05/26/2014	$479.85
Customer Name	Order ID	Order Date	Order Amount

Figure 11-47 Multi-Row Card report

Cards

This visualization displays one value. It displays the total of the selected value (measure). This table type works well in dashboards. The Field Well is the same as the one shown earlier in Figure 11-43.

Card Formatting Options

Data Label Options

Figure 11-48 shows the Data label format options.

The **DISPLAY UNITS OPTION** displays the options shown in Figure 11-49. They are used to select the unit of measurement that the values on the x-axis will be displayed in.

In a way, this is a way of rounding the values, or shorten them, if the chart displays a lot of values.

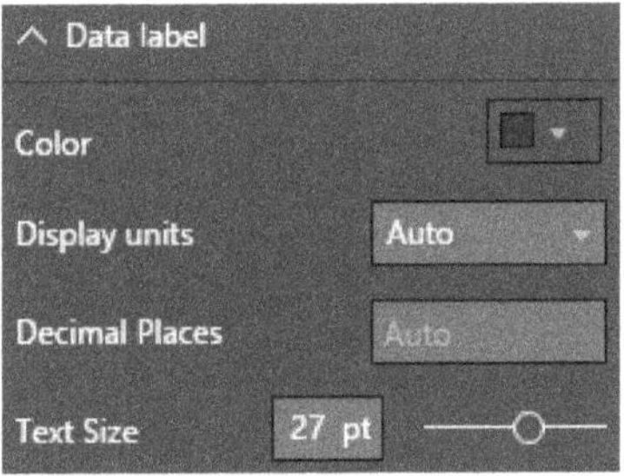

Figure 11-48 Data Label format options

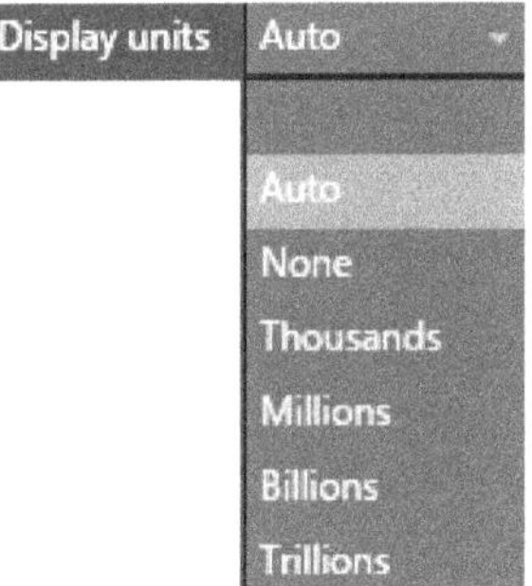

Figure 11-49 Display unit options

The **DECIMAL PLACES OPTION** is used to select how many decimal places you want displayed on the visual. The default is **AUTO**, which displays how many decimal places are in the field. If you do not want to display any decimal places, type a zero in this field.

The actual value displayed in Figure 11-50, is in the format for the Display units option that is selected. Each card is displaying the same value, with different formatting. The options are explained in Table 11-1.

Figure 11-50 Display unit options

Option	Description
Auto	This is the default option. The display unit used is based on the value.
None	Displays the actual value without a display unit.
Thousands	Displays the value with the letter K after it.
Millions	Displays the value with the letter M after it.
Billions	Displays the value with the letters bn after it.
Trillions	Displays the value with the letter T after it.

Table 11-1 Display units options explained

Category Label Options

The options in this section are the same as the options shown earlier in Figure 11-44. The options are used to change the color of the field name displayed below the value on the card.

Word Wrap Option

If enabled, the **WORD WRAP OPTION** shown in Figure 11-51, allows the Data Label (the field name below the value) to wrap, if the card is made smaller.

Figure 11-51 Word Wrap option

Exercise 11.8: Use A Card To Display The Total Order Amount

1. Click the **CARD BUTTON**. It is probably on the last row of visualization buttons.

2. Drag the Order Amount field to the Fields section.

   The value displayed in Figure 11-52 is the total amount of all orders in the Orders table.

Figure 11-52 Total Order Amount card

Create A Card With A Filter

This part of the exercise will show you how to create a filter for a card.

1. Make a copy of the card that you just created and paste it on the same page.

2. Add the Year field to the Visual level filters section ⇒ Create a basic filter to only display the total order amount for orders in 2015.

3. Display and enable the formatting Title options ⇒ In the Title Text field type `Total Order Amount For 2015`.

4. Center the text ⇒ Change the Text Size to `14`.

   The second card should look like the one shown in Figure 11-53.

Figure 11-53 Card value filtered by year

Summary

This chapter covered the Page formatting options. The table formatting options were covered in detail. Many of the table formatting options can be applied to the other table types. Several different matrix table layouts were covered. If you are tired of creating tables, the next chapter covers the basics of creating charts.

INTRODUCTION TO CHARTS

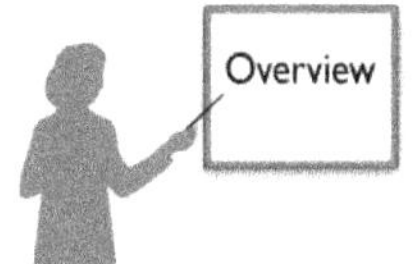

After completing the exercises in this chapter, you will be able to perform the following tasks:

- ☑ Create and modify bar and column charts
- ☑ Change the data displayed on a chart
- ☑ Create chart and page level filters

CHAPTER 12

Creating Charts

In the previous three chapters you created tables and learned about many of the visualization formatting options. Tables are a good way to present data. In addition to being able to format data, charts are used to present data in a graphical format, which often makes the data easier to understand. This is because the relationship between the data elements is visually displayed. Charts also allow data to be presented in formats that text-only visualizations cannot do as well. For example, charts can show trends (in the data) over time, relationships or how one set of data compares to another set of data.

One feature that you may like about creating charts in Power BI Desktop is that it is very easy to change a table to a chart or switch from one chart type to another. You can change the pie chart, shown on the left of Figure 12-1, to the Clustered column chart, shown in the right of the figure, with the click of a button.

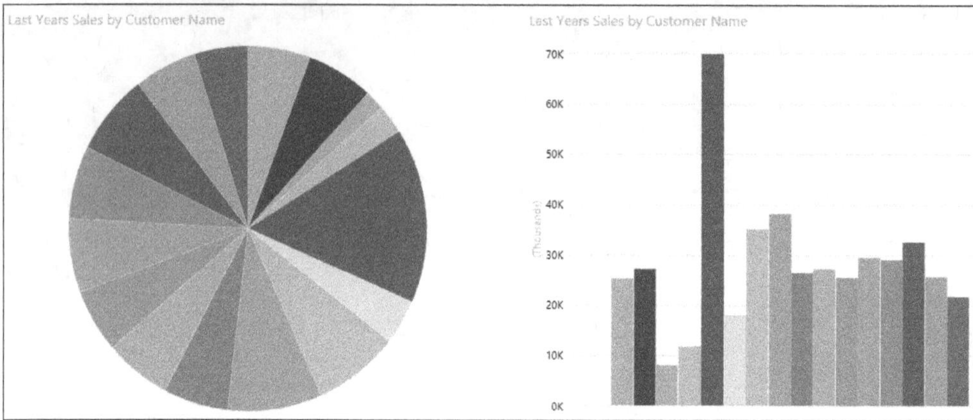

Figure 12-1 Pie chart changed to a column chart

Creating Charts In Power BI Desktop vs Power View
If you have created charts in Power View, you know that you have to add the fields to a table, then select the chart type. In Power BI Desktop, that is not the case. While you can start a chart as a table, it is not a requirement. You can select the chart type without using a table.

Chart Types And Other Visualization Options

Figure 12-2 shows all of the visualization options (including the table options that were already covered in this book), that are available in Power BI Desktop. You may have additional options, because the software is updated monthly.

Table 12-1 explains the types of charts that can be created. The chart types are listed in the table in the order that they are shown in Figure 12-2.

While the column headings in Table 12-1 reference charts, all of the options shown in Figure 12-2 are explained in the table.

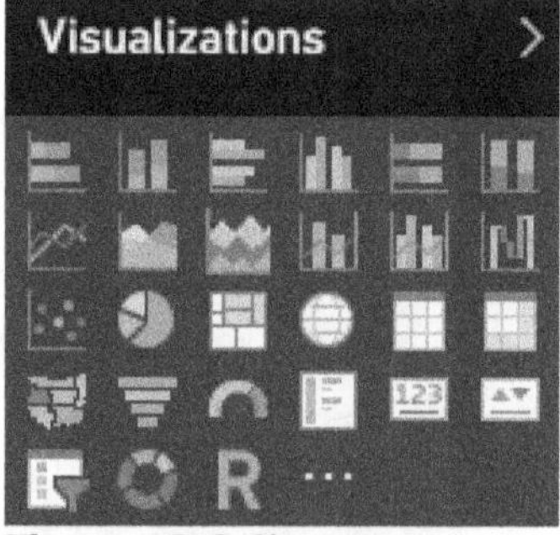

Figure 12-2 Chart types

Chart Type	This Chart Type . . .
Stacked bar	Displays the bars horizontally. (1) (2) (3) (6)
Stacked column	Displays the columns vertically. (1) (2) (3) (6)
Clustered bar	Displays the data in multiple groups. (3) (6) (10)
Clustered column	Displays the data in multiple groups, as shown in Figure 12-3. (3) (6) (10)
100% Stacked bar	Displays each data series as a percent of the total. (9)
100% Stacked column	Displays each data series as a percent of the total. (9)
Line	Show trends and changes for groups of data over a period of time, as shown in Figure 12-4. Most of the time, the range of values on the Y-axis does not include zero. Line charts display the data values as points that are attached to a line. (2)

Table 12-1 Chart types explained

Chart Type	This Chart Type . . .
Area	Is almost identical to line charts. The difference is that area charts are filled in with colors below the trend line, as shown in Figure 12-5. Area charts are probably best suited for a few groups of data. They display cumulative data. This chart type only uses one measure. The Y-axis range of values starts with zero. (4)
Stacked Area	Is similar to an Area chart. The difference is that this chart type compares or shows the data progression over time and how each series adds to the cumulative total. (4)
Line & Stacked column	Uses the first measure to create a column chart and the remaining measures are created with line charts. This is how the "stacked line" chart effect is created. (3) (4) (5) (6) (11)
Line & Clustered column	Works the same as the chart above in this table. The difference is that clustered columns are used, instead of stacked columns. (3) (4) (5) (6) (11)
Waterfall	Displays how each category makes up the total value. This chart type separates and displays each value on a column on the chart. It displays the cumulative effect of sequentially related positive or negative values. The chart shows how the first value is increased or decreased by intermediate values. Overall, this chart type displays data as a running total. A cumulative positive value starts at the top of the previous box on the chart. A cumulative negative value starts at the bottom of the previous box on the chart. The columns are color coded, based on whether the value is greater or less than the previous value. This chart type is also known as a **BRIDGE**, **FLYING BRICKS** or **CASCADE CHART**. (3)
Scatter	Shows how two or more values (measures) are related (like month of year and order amount) and how a change in one value affects the other value. This chart type is used to see if there is a trend between the values or show the correlation between the values, as shown in Figure 12-6. The X and Y axis must display numeric data. If data like dates or months can be converted to numeric data, it can be used with this chart type. This chart type is also known as an **XY SCATTER CHART**. (3) (7)
Bubble	Is similar to Scatter charts because it plots individual points. The difference is that bubble charts use different size plot points (bubbles), based on the data value. The larger the data value, the larger the size of the bubble. (3) (7)
Pie	Shows how the data has changed over a period of time. Figure 12-7 shows how four types of income (mail order, store, kiosk and Internet) make up the total income and how the income changes over the months. Each slice of the pie represents the percent for the item. Pie charts can only display one series of data. This chart type only uses one value because it shows how the whole (100%) is divided. (3) (8) (12)
Tree Map	Displays data by using space. Select this chart type when you need to show how each value relates to the total. It requires multiple measures and only one dimension. This chart type does not display data on a map, like the Map and Filled Map options do. The values are displayed using blocks. The block on the left has the highest value. The block in the lower right corner has the lowest value. This chart type can be used instead of a pie chart. This chart type is similar to a Scatter chart because it can be used to analyze two measures. (3) (12)
Map	Displays geographical data using circles (like bubbles) on a map.
Table	(13)
Matrix	(13)
Filled Map	Displays data using color overlays on a map, instead of bubbles. It is similar to the Map chart.
Funnel	Is similar to stacked bar charts because each bar on the funnel shows each item as a percent of the total. The difference is that the bars are stacked in order, which forms the shape of a funnel. This chart type uses one measure. The rows are placed in order, from high to low, based on the value that they represent. (3)
Gauge	Looks like a gauge in a car. The needle in the chart points to the value that is being represented. This chart type displays one measure against the target goal. It can also be used to compare a measure to a key performance indicator (KPI).
Multi-row card	Displays different attributes and measures for each instance, in a row. (13)
Card	Displays one numeric value of a measure. (13)

Table 12-1 Chart types explained (Continued)

Chart Type	This Chart Type . . .
KPI	Displays one value on a trend line chart in the background. The values are displayed with colors. This chart type allows a KPI value to be viewed over time, in addition to displaying how the KPI value compares to the target value.
Slicer	Is used to filter tables and charts on a report page.
Donut	Is similar to pie charts. The difference is that there is a hole in the center. (3) (8) (12)
R Script Visual	Is used to display charts based on the R language code in the file you select.
Import from file	Is used to import or delete a custom visual chart.

Table 12-1 Chart types explained (Continued)

(1) Stacked bar and column charts are similar to the regular bar and column charts that you are use to seeing. Stacked charts combine two or more data values (bars or columns), in the series, into one bar or column on the chart. Stacked charts show each item as a percent of the total. This chart type is used to compare different measures on the same column or bar. It is a good choice when you need to display different measures that are part of the same whole (category) or different values of the same measure, side by side.

(2) This chart type is often used to create charts that are based on a single set of values (meaning one field in the Values section and one field in the Axis section on the Field Well).

(3) This chart type supports drill down functionality.

(4) This chart type requires at least two sets (series) of data.

(5) This chart type is used to display a second series of data with its own scale or the same scale with a different value of ranges, on the same chart. Sometimes using this chart type instead of stacked charts, makes the data easier to understand. This chart type works the same as a regular Line chart that displays two or more series of data. These charts are useful when you need to display two or more series of data on the same chart. They display changes and the magnitude of the change over time. Two chart types are used to create a combination chart: A line chart and a column chart. A good use of when to use this chart type is when the data lines cross each other often. This makes a line chart easier to read. The major difference between line charts, column charts and combination charts is that a combination chart uses both columns and lines in the same chart and the other two chart types (line and column) do not. This chart type is also known as a **COMBINATION**, **DUAL AXIS**, **TREND LINE** or **VARIANCE** chart.

(6) If the chart will only use one series of data, stacked and clustered charts produce the same results.

(7) This chart type is used for comparison analysis. They plot data as points, instead of values. This can make it easier to see patterns in the data.

(8) This chart type only uses one value because it shows how the whole (100%) is divided.

(9) This chart type is similar to the Stacked chart. The difference is that each data series uses a section of the bar, and the bars always equal 100%. This is done by filling the Plot Area and adding a marker to reference the data points. Figure 12-8 shows the same data used in Figure 12-3, displayed as a 100% Stacked column chart.

(10) This chart type is used to display/compare different measures, side by side. It is similar to Stacked charts.

(11) This chart type is used when measures have different scales (range of values) and need to be displayed on the same chart.

(12) This chart is not well suited to display a lot of values.

(13) Displays data in text format, in rows and columns like a spreadsheet. [See Chapter 9, Table Visualization Options]

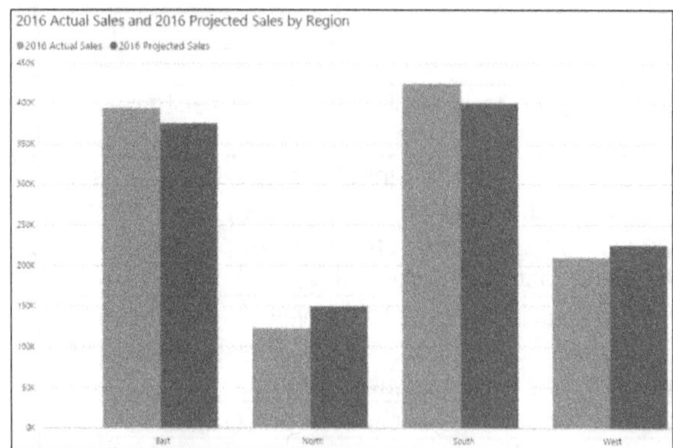

Figure 12-3 Clustered Column chart

Figure 12-4 Line chart

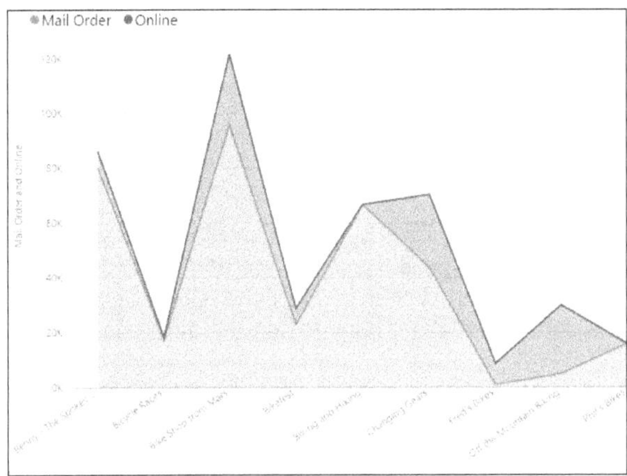

Figure 12-5 Area chart

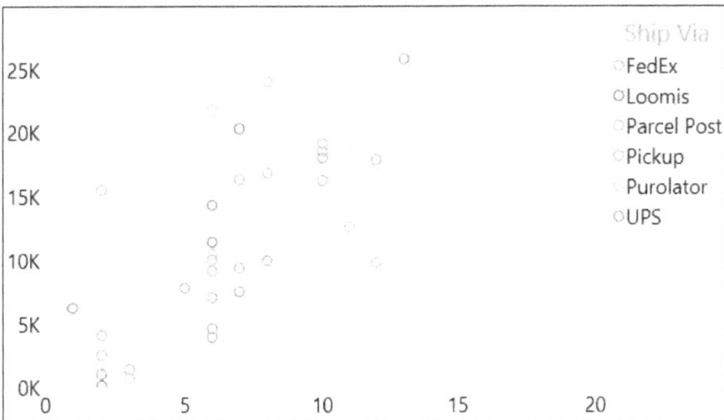

Figure 12-6 Scatter chart

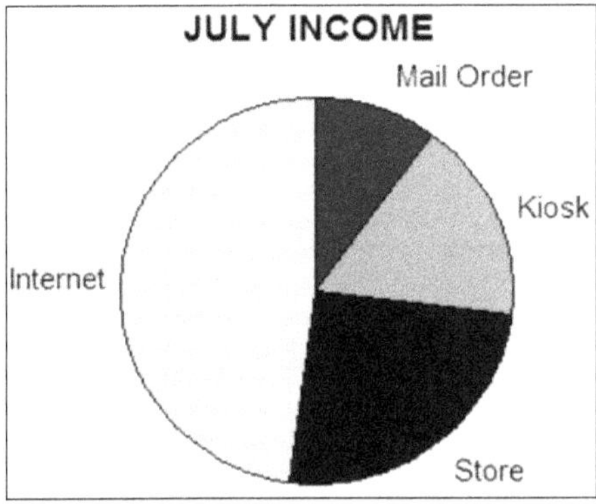

Figure 12-7 Pie chart

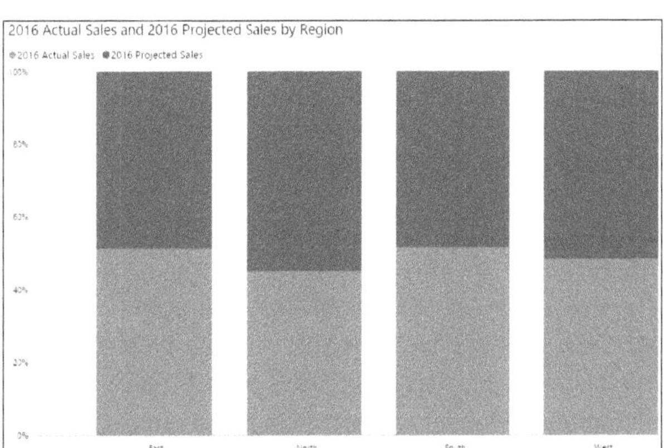

Figure 12-8 100% Stacked column chart

Selecting A Chart Type

The chart type needs to be addressed before you start to create the chart. The chart type can be changed easily, if you feel that the data would be represented better in a different chart type. Having the ability to easily change chart types may help you figure out which chart type is best for the data. Charts should enhance the ability to understand the data and make it easy to see the differences in the data, instead of make it more difficult. The chart types were explained earlier in this chapter and the chart options are explained in the next few chapters.

Starting A Chart As A Table
Sometimes, you may find it easier to create a chart by starting it as a table, because all of the fields are added to the same Fields section. That is fine. When you change the table to a chart, the fields will automatically be moved to a section, based on the chart type and on the order that you added the fields to the table. Each chart type has requirements for which section of the Field Well, fields have to be added to. If needed, you can manually move the fields to the section in the Field Well that best meets the needs of how you want to display the data. Hopefully, after completing the chart exercises in this book, you will not have to rely on this method of creating charts.

Chart Categories

There are several categories of charts. Each category has two or more chart options that can be selected from. While I listed a few chart types for each category, which are based on my experience, it is not a requirement that you have to use them. Charts are used to perform an analysis of the data. The analysis categories are explained below.

① **COMPARISON** Is used to display a comparison (usually of a measure) or display differences between values. Chart types suited for this category include Bar and Column.
② **CORRELATION** Compares more than one measure or displays the relationship between values. This type of analysis is used to find out how the values in one measure effect the values in another measure. Scatter and Tree charts are used to display correlations.
③ **GEOGRAPHICAL** Is used to plot data based on the values that point to a location on a map. The geographic map charts are used for this type of analysis.

④ **PERCENTAGE** This analysis category is used when you need to display data as part of the whole in percents or otherwise. Pie, funnel, donut and stacked column charts are designed to display parts of the whole.
⑤ **TREND** This category is used when the data needs to be displayed to show patterns, progression or how the data changes over time. Line and Waterfall charts allow data to be displayed over time.

Chart Considerations

There are two areas that need to be addressed before you start to create charts: The chart type and the data source for the chart. Changing the chart type is easy. If you are not sure which chart type is the most appropriate, with a few mouse clicks, you can try out a few chart types and variations to see which chart type is best for the data that you need to display. Charts should enhance the ability to understand the data and make it easy to see the differences.

I use to teach a technical writing class and one of the assignments had students create three charts to visually present data. Overall, the students did a good job on the charts. However, I noticed the following on a regular basis.

① Only using bar and column charts, regardless of what the data needed to convey. Newsflash: These chart types are not the best option for all scenarios, especially when the data needs to show trends or needs to show how values have changed over time.
② The values on the X and Y axes were reversed. Dollar amounts, quantity and percents, usually go on the Y axis and time, dates and categories usually go on the X axis. The **X AXIS** is displayed horizontally, across the bottom of the chart. The **Y AXIS** is displayed vertically, on the left side of the chart.
③ Not understanding the data that the chart will use.

Tips For Creating Charts
Below are some tips that will hopefully make creating charts easier.

① When a table visualization is changed to a chart, the options in the Field Well change, based on the chart type. Most, if not all of the fields will automatically be placed in the right chart section.

② Bar and column charts that do not have an axis value cannot be sorted.

③ If the bar or column chart is created from a single data series, the **STACKED** and **CLUSTERED CHART TYPES** will display the same data.

④ Charts that use highlighting, can also use drill down functionality.

⑤ If the size of the legend or axis labels are too large, change the field name or data to something shorter in the data source. For example, instead of displaying a sales reps full name, display the first initial and last name. In some cases, changing the current data in a table is not feasible because it is needed in the format that it is in, for another application. When that is the case, you can create a calculated field that reduces the length of the data. You can see this in the Dates Table. Examples are the Month Abbr and Quarter Abbr fields shown in Figure 12-9. While writing this book, I saw requests for a solution to be able to enter a name or title that would be displayed, instead of the field name, but so far these requests have not been escalated.

⑥ The totals shown on a table visualization are not displayed when the table is changed to a chart.

⑦ Even after a chart has been modified, it can be switched back to a table. If switched back to a table, you will probably see that the changes that you have made to the chart, are still there.

MonthFull	MonthAbbr	QuarterFull	QuarterAbbr
January	Jan	Quarter 1	Q1
February	Feb	Quarter 1	Q1
March	Mar	Quarter 1	Q1
April	Apr	Quarter 2	Q2

Figure 12-9 Shorter data values

Chart Field Well

The options shown in Figure 12-10 are the options that many chart types have.

The options used to create a chart are different from the ones used to create tables. The options are explained in Table 12-2.

Chart types that have additional or different options for creating a chart, are covered in the chapter that the chart type is covered in.

Axis Section Tip
Each field that you add to this section will create another drill down level, on chart types that support drill down functionality.

The Field Well shortcut menu for charts is that same as the one for tables [See Chapter 9, Figure 9-7].

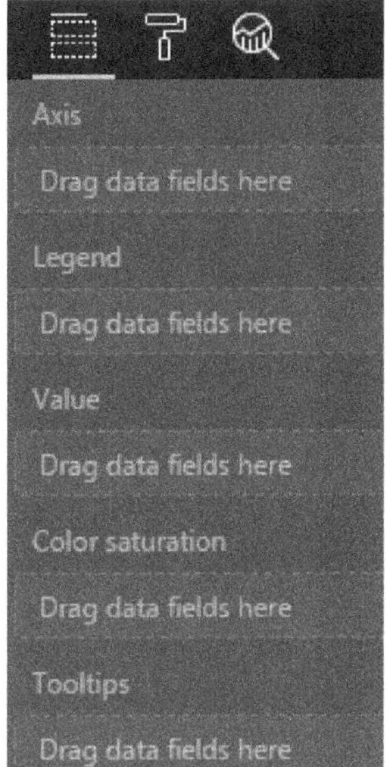

Figure 12-10 Chart Field Well

Section	Adding A Field To This Section . . .
Axis	Creates values along the Y axis.
Legend	Selects the values that will create the legend.
Value	Creates the values for the X axis.
Color Saturation	Determines how much color the data points or bars on the chart have. When a measure is added to this section, the color on each of the bars or data points change, based on the value in the measure.
Tooltips	By default, the tooltips display values that are displayed on the chart when the mouse pointer is held over an element on the chart. Fields added to this section will also be displayed on the tooltip. As far as I can tell, any measure can be added to this section. Adding other field types, changes them to the Count summarization, which probably is not what you want. This happens even if the column is set to Do not summarize.

Table 12-2 Field Well chart sections explained

Chart Formatting Options

Figure 12-11 shows the formatting categories that most chart types have. The options in some of these categories are the same as the ones for tables. The options that are different, are explained in the next few sections.

The options in each category can vary slightly, based on the chart type.

Chart types that have additional or different formatting options, are covered in the chapter that the chart type is covered in.

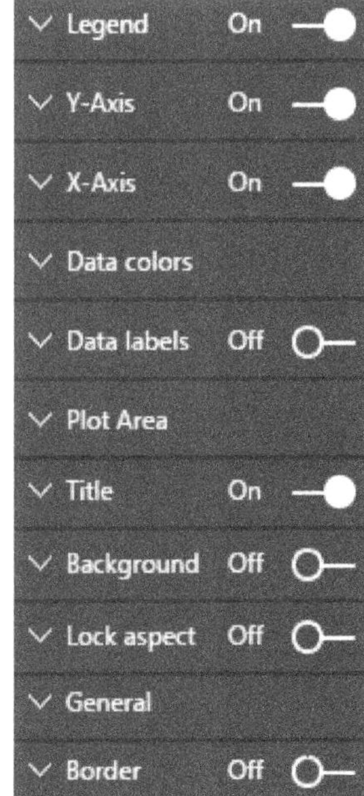

Figure 12-11 Chart categories

Legend Options

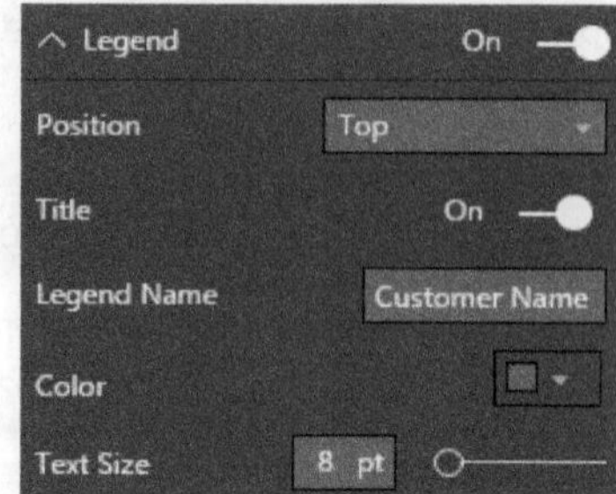

Figure 12-12 Legend options

The options shown in Figure 12-12 are only available when a field is added to the Legend section of the Field Well. The options are used to customize the legend.

The **POSITION OPTION** is used to select where the legend is placed, in respect to the chart location.

The **TITLE OPTION** displays or hides the legend name.

The default value for the **LEGEND NAME OPTION** is the name of the field in the Legend section. If you do not want all of the values in the field displayed in the legend, create a filter to select the values that you want displayed in the legend.

If the field used to create the legend is also displayed on the chart, the data on the chart will also be filtered, which may or may not be what you want. You would have to create a calculated column to use as the field to filter the values displayed in the legend, if you do not want the chart data to be filtered.

The **TEXT SIZE OPTION** is used to change the font size of the text in the legend.

A legend is automatically added to a chart if the chart uses more than one field that displays a value on the chart. A legend is also automatically added to a chart that has two or more series of data.

Y-Axis Options

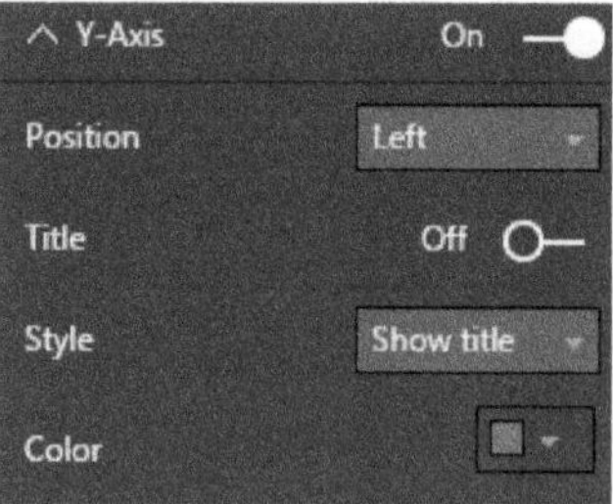

Figure 12-13 Y-Axis options

The options shown in Figure 12-13 are used to customize the values displayed on the Y Axis of the chart.

The **POSITION OPTION** is used to display the values on the Y-Axis, on the right or left side of the chart.

Enable the **TITLE OPTION** if you want to display the field name on the chart, that the values on the Y Axis are from.

Depending on the chart type, the Scale type option explained below, in the X-Axis section, is also available for the Y-Axis.

X-Axis Options

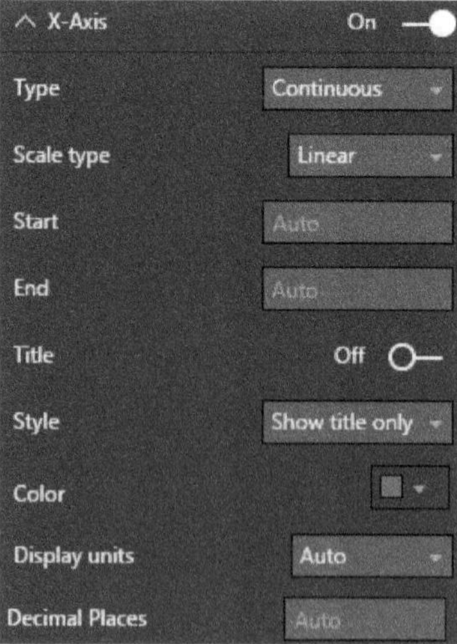

Figure 12-14 X-Axis options

The options shown in Figure 12-14 are used to customize the values displayed on the X Axis of the chart.

TYPE OPTION [See Chapter 13, Figure 13-9]

The **SCALE TYPE OPTION** is used to select one of the following scale types. The options available in this drop-down list depend on the chart type.

① **LINEAR SCALE** is the default scale type for bar, column and line charts. It displays the distance with equal divisions between the values. An example of a linear scale are the tic marks on a ruler.
② **LOG SCALE** (short for Logarithmic scale) Some chart types, like Area charts, have this option. This type of scale skews towards the larger values on the axis. The smaller values are compressed, which can make the smaller values more difficult to evaluate. Figures in Chapter 13, Exercise 13.15, show the differences between these two scale type options.

The **START OPTION** is used to select the lowest value that can be displayed on the chart. (14)

The **END OPTION** is used to select the highest value that can be displayed on the chart. (14)

The **STYLE OPTION** is used to display the field name, display units or both on the axis. The options selected will only be displayed on the chart if the **TITLE OPTION** is enabled.

(14) Selecting a value for this option is another way to filter the data that is displayed on the chart.

Data Colors Options

The options shown in Figures 12-15 and 12-16 are used to change the color of the bars, line, etc, that represent the data. The options in Figure 12-15 are available when one data series is used. The options in Figure 12-16 are available when the chart has two or more series of data.

The **DEFAULT COLOR OPTION** will be applied to values that you do not select a custom color for. As shown at the bottom of the figure, there is an option for each value on the chart.

Enable the **SHOW ALL OPTION** to display a list of each value displayed on the chart, as shown in the last three options, at the bottom of the Figure 12-15. These options are used to select a color for each value displayed on the chart.

Figure 12-17, shows the data colors when the **COLOR SATURATION OPTION** is used on the Field Well.

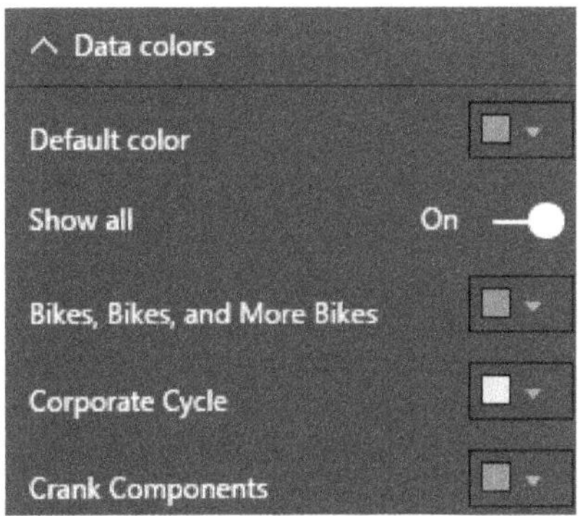

Figure 12-15 Data colors options

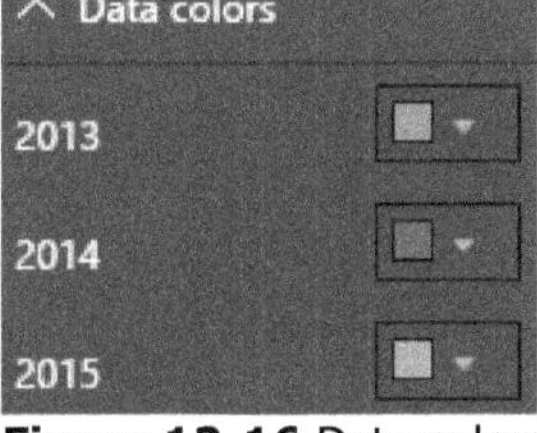

Figure 12-16 Data colors options for multiple series of data

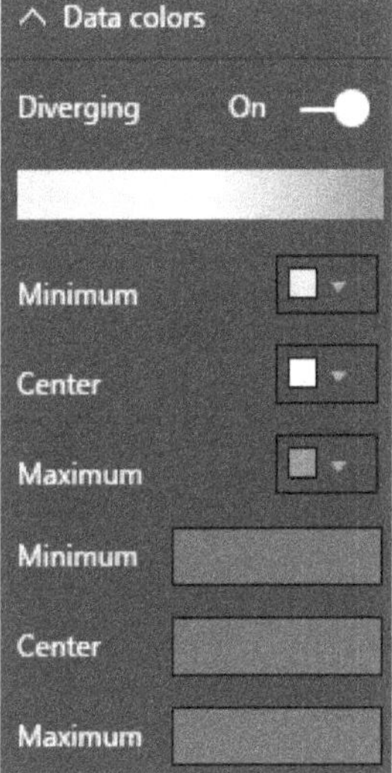

Figure 12-17 Color Saturation data color options

When the **DIVERGING OPTION**, shown above in Figure 12-17 is enabled, the color of the bars will change. The further away from the Color Saturation (field) value, the value that the bar (on the chart) represents is, the darker the color of the bar will be. The other bars on the chart get lighter.

Enabling the Diverging option also displays the Center options shown in the figure. The remaining options are used to select the lightest and darkest colors, as well as, the minimum and maximum values to map to the corresponding colors.

Data Labels Options

The options shown in Figure 12-18 are used to display and customize the values displayed next to each value on the chart.

The **COLOR OPTION** is used to change the color of the data values displayed in the plot area of the chart.

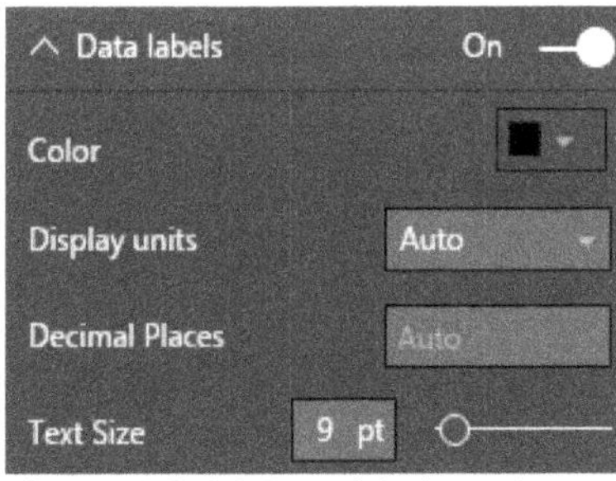

Figure 12-18 Data labels options

Plot Area Options

The options shown in Figure 12-19 are used to set the transparency for the background color of the plot area section (the middle) of the chart and to add an image to the Plot Area section of the chart.

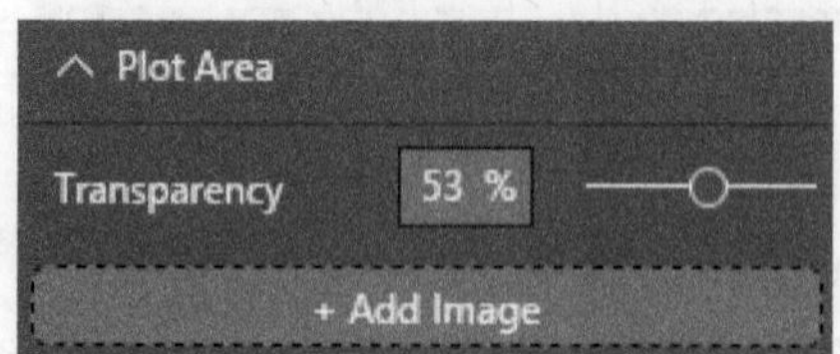

Figure 12-19 Plot Area options

Title Options

The options in this section are the same as the ones for tables. [See Chapter 11, Figure 11-16]

The default value in the **TITLE TEXT FIELD** is the text displayed in the upper left corner of the chart frame, which you can change.

Background Options

The options in this section are used to select a background color for the chart. [See Chapter 11, Figure 11-17]

Lock Aspect

[See Chapter 11, Figure 11-18]

General Options

The **POSITION OPTIONS** shown in Figure 12-20 are used to select specific coordinates, on the page, to place the chart.

The **WIDTH** and **HEIGHT OPTIONS** are used to make the chart a specific size.

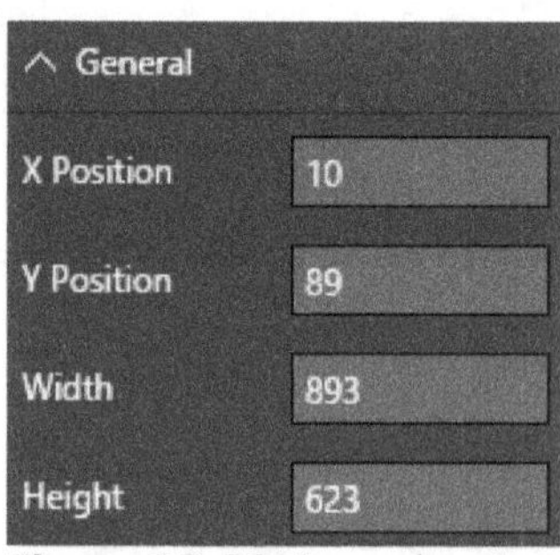

Figure 12-20 General options

Border Options

[See Chapter 11, Figure 11-19]

Adding Fields To The Field Well To Create A Chart

You can drag fields to the sections shown earlier in Figure 12-10. If you check the fields in the Fields panel, to add them to the Field Well, the order that you click them in, is the order that they will be added to the sections. Most of the time, this works. For some chart types, fields are not added where you need them, so you have to drag them from one section to another.

Column And Bar Charts

As you see, there are several variations of these chart types. Following is a description of how these chart types display data. **COLUMN CHARTS** show differences between items and relationships between multiple groups of data, as shown earlier in Figure 12-3. **BAR CHARTS** work the same a column charts. The only difference is the direction of the bars. Technically, Power BI Desktop does not have a button for traditional bar and column charts that you are use to seeing. You can create them though, by using the Clustered chart options.

Column Chart vs Stacked Column Chart

The differences that a Stacked Column chart has from a Column chart are explained below.

① A column chart displays one column per series.

② Each column on a stacked chart is divided into series. Each color represents a different series of data. This prevents additional columns from being added, which saves space on the chart.
③ Stacked column charts can be used to compare totals over a period of time.

Chart Axis Values In The Exercises
Numeric values that you see on the X and Y axis of the charts that you create in the exercises, may have a different interval of values, then the ones shown in the figures. That's ok. The reason that you may not have the same interval values is because most of the time, I enlarged the charts to make them easier to see in this book.

Exercise 12.1: Create A Basic Bar Chart

In this exercise you will learn how to create a bar chart that displays the last years sales total by customer name.

1. Save the Report Data.pbix file as `Chapter 12 Charts.`

2. Add a page ⇒ Click the Clustered bar chart button.

3. Add the following fields to the chart.

   ☑ Add the Customer Name field to the Axis section
   ☑ Add the Last Years Sales field to the Value section

4. Use the Region field to filter the data, by selecting the following states (regions): FL, IA, ID and IL.

5. Make the chart larger. It should look like the one shown in Figure 12-21.

Notice how a description of the data is displayed above the chart. The description also indicates how the data is grouped. The field after the word "by" is the field used to create the groups.

When the chart is not displaying all of the data, a scroll bar is automatically added to the chart, as illustrated in Figure 12-21.

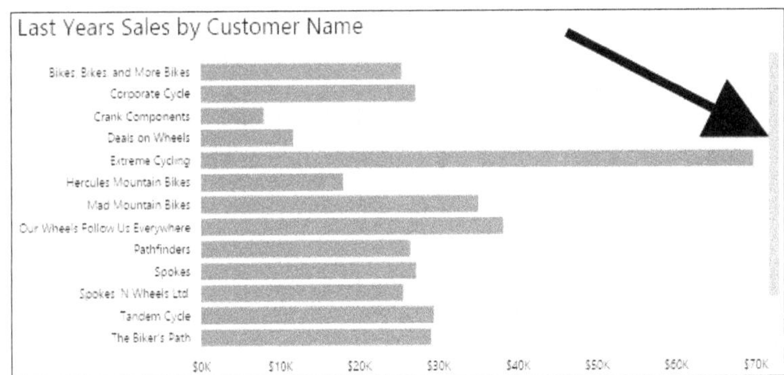

Figure 12-21 Basic bar chart

Selecting the Stacked Column chart option, changes the chart shown in Figure 12-21, to the one shown in Figure 12-22.

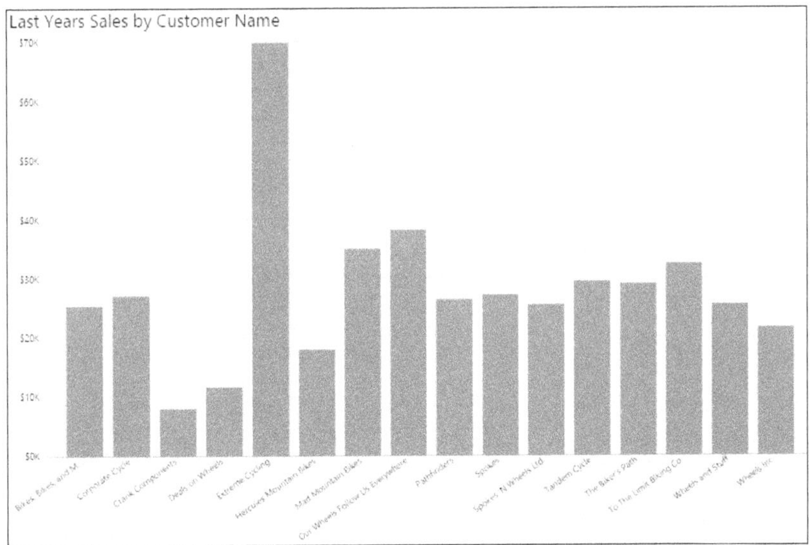

Figure 12-22 Basic column chart

Viewing Chart Data

No matter how large you make the chart, you cannot tell what the exact amount is, unless the bar or line is touching a marker point on the chart or data labels are added.

When you need to see the exact amount, hold the mouse pointer over the marker (the bar, slice, bubble etc.), as shown in Figure 12-23, to see more information.

Figure 12-23 Chart data displayed on the tooltip

Using The Color Saturation Option

This option was explained earlier in Table 12-2. If the Sales Cost measure in the Orders table, was added to this option, the chart shown earlier in Figure 12-21, would look like the one shown in Figure 12-24. The darker color bars, indicate larger values. The Color Saturation option also enables different data color formatting options, as shown earlier in Figure 12-17.

The Extreme Cycling company has a larger sales amount for last year, then the Crank Components company has. The Crank Components company has the highest Sales Cost, even though it had the lowest (number of) sales last year. In addition to the bar for the Crank Components company having the darkest color, you can confirm this by viewing the Sales Cost amount on the tooltip.

I think that most people would not be able to figure this out, by looking at the different color bars. The length of the bar represents the Last Year Sales value and the color of the bar represents the Sales Cost value. The darker the color the bar is, denotes a higher Sales Cost value. Currently, there is no option to explain what the different bar colors mean to the people that view the chart. If you plan to use the Color Saturation option, keep this in mind. A solution would be to use a Text Box to briefly explain what the color range means.

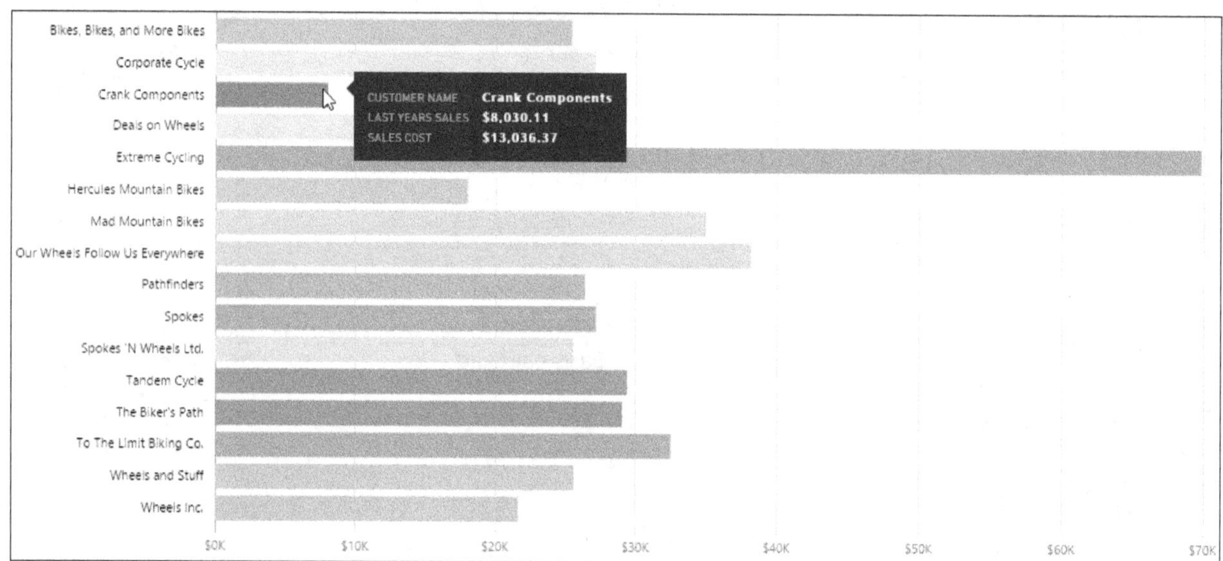

Figure 12-24 Color Saturation applied to a bar chart

Exercise 12.2: Apply Formatting To A Chart

In this exercise you will apply some of the formatting options that were covered earlier in this chapter, to a chart.

1. Duplicate page E12.1.
2. Make the chart the size of the page ⇒ Display the Format chart options.
3. Change the following Y-Axis options.

   ☑ Change the Position to Right
   ☑ Change the Title to On

4. Change the X-Axis Color option to black.

5. Change the following Data Colors options.

   ☑ Default Color = Medium purple
   ☑ Enable the Show All option
   ☑ Change the first three values to colors of your choice. Notice that the remaining bars are the default purple color that you selected.

6. Change the following Data Labels options.

   ☑ Enable the data labels
   ☑ Change the Color to black
   ☑ Change the Text Size to 12

7. Change the following Title options. When finished, the chart should look like the one shown in Figure 12-25. Compare this chart to the one show earlier in Figure 12-21.

   ☑ Change the Title Text to `2015 Sales by Customer`
   ☑ Change the Font color to black
   ☑ Center the text
   ☑ Change the Text Size to 16

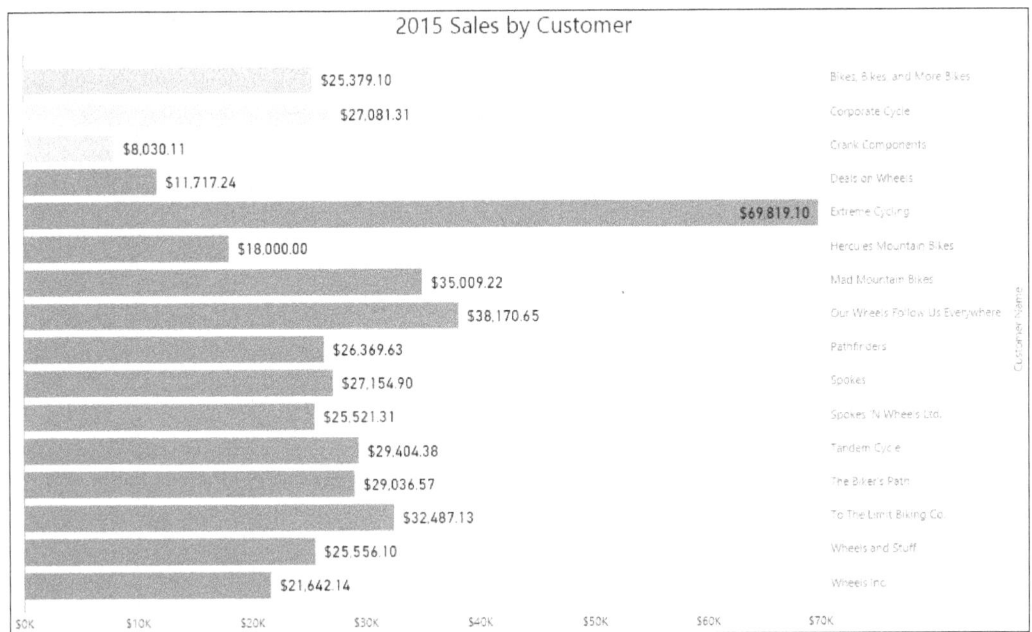

Figure 12-25 Chart with format customization options applied

Chart Resizing Tips
Keep the following in mind when resizing a chart.
① A scroll bar may automatically be added to a bar chart when the height of the chart is reduced, as shown earlier in Figure 12-21, or to a line or column chart, when the width of the chart is reduced. When a scroll bar is added, all of the items on the axis are not displayed.
② Resizing bar or column charts can change the text on an axis by reducing the amount of text displayed and displaying dots (an ellipsis) or placing the text on two or more rows. Text may also be angled to 45 degrees, as shown earlier in Figure 12-22.
③ When resized, the text on a line or column chart can be truncated or displayed on two or more lines.

Scrolling Through The Records On A Chart

To the right of the bars on the chart in Exercise 12.1, you should see the vertical scroll bar, illustrated earlier in Figure 12-21. On my screen, the scroll bar is a very light gray. Sliding the scroll bar or clicking on the up and down buttons on the scroll bar, displays different records.

Sorting Chart Data

By default, the first field in the Axis section is how the data on the chart is sorted. The chart in Exercise 12.1 is sorted on the Customer Name field. By default, the data is displayed in alphabetical order by the text on the axis. This may not be what you want. The chart may make a bigger impact if the data was sorted/displayed by a numeric value, usually in descending order.

Clicking the **... (ELLIPSIS) BUTTON** in the upper right corner of the chart window, displays the shortcut menu shown in Figure 12-26.

The first two options are used to sort the data on the chart.

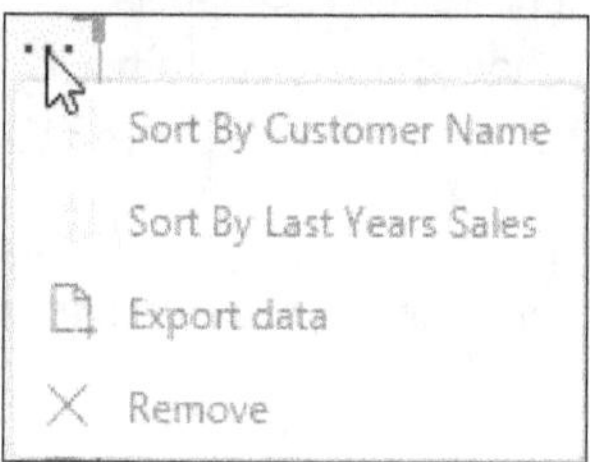

Figure 12-26 Sort options

Exercise 12.3: Sort The Data On A Chart

In this exercise, you will sort the E12.1 chart by the Last Years Sales field, in descending order.

1. Duplicate page E12.1.

2. Click the ellipsis button in the upper right corner of the chart. You should see the options shown above in Figure 12-26 ⇒ Select the Sort By Last Years Sales option. The chart should look like the one shown in Figure 12-27. Often, this chart layout is easier to understand, then the one shown earlier in Figure 12-21.

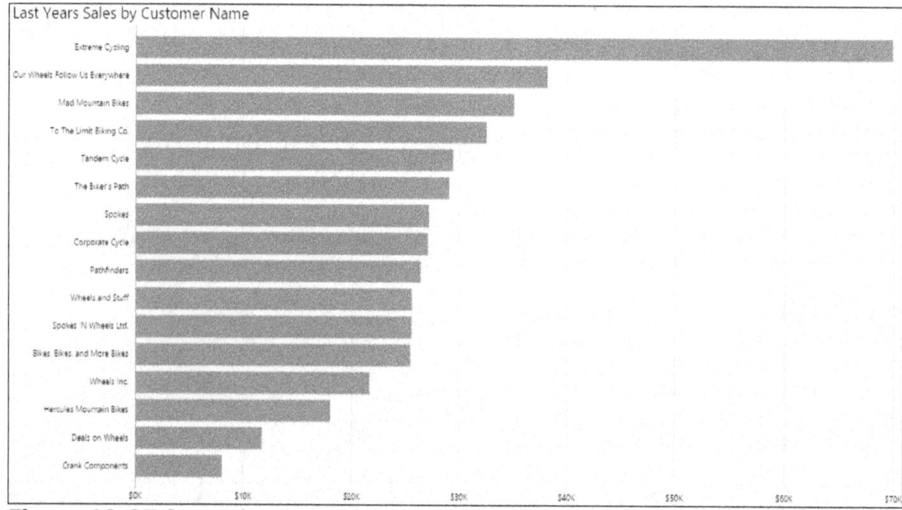

Figure 12-27 Sort order changed

Exercise 12.4: Change The Data Displayed On A Chart

Sometimes, you may have created a chart and then need to see a variation of it. Instead of recreating the chart from scratch, you can duplicate it and then change what's needed. In this exercise you will change the filter on the E12.1 chart.

1. Duplicate page E12.1.

2. Create a Visual level filter for the Country Name field ⇒ Select Canada, France and the USA.

3. Add the Year field to the Legend section. The top of the chart should look like the one shown in Figure 12-28. The Last Years Sales amounts are now grouped by year. This provides another perspective of the data.

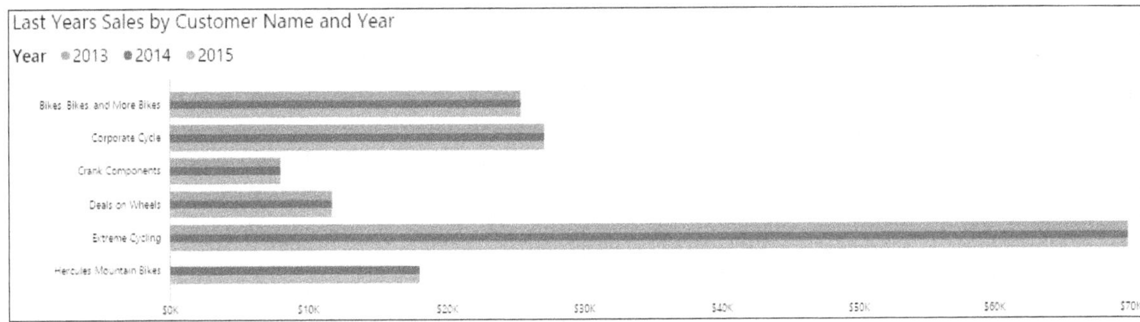

Figure 12-28 Legend added to the chart

Exercise 12.5: Change The Colors On Bar And Column Charts

The colors of the bars on a chart can be changed by dragging a field in the Axis section to the Legend section. And yes, this will also create a color coded legend. How cool is that?

In this exercise you will change the appearance of a bar chart. Currently, all of the bars on the chart are blue.

1. Duplicate page E12.1.

2. Change the chart to a Clustered column chart.

3. Drag the Customer Name field in the Axis section to the Legend section.

4. Display the Legend formatting options ⇒ Change the Position to Right.

   The chart should look like the one shown in Figure 12-29.

   Even in black and white, you can see the "color" difference on the columns.

   Compare this chart to the chart shown earlier in Figure 12-21.

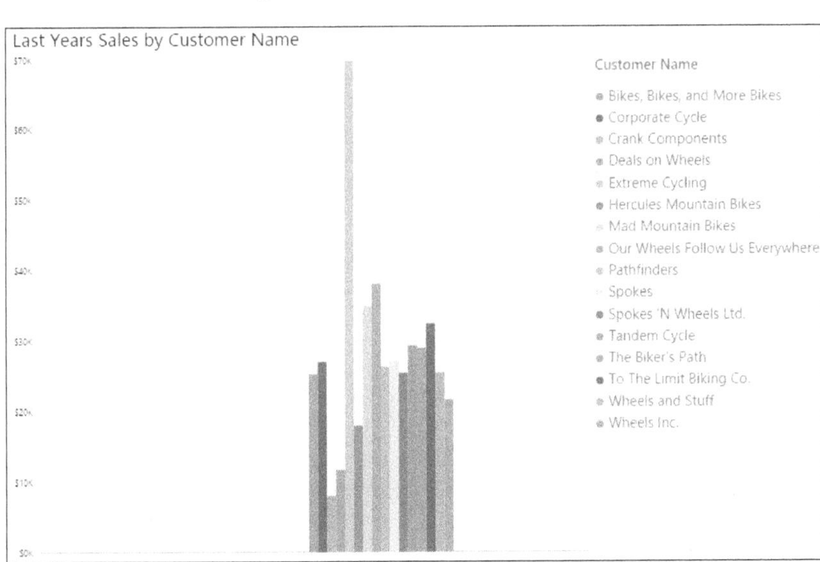

Figure 12-29 Chart columns in color

Exercise 12.6: Create Chart Level Filters

In Chapter 10, Exercise 10.12, you created a Page level filter, which is applied to all visualizations on the page. Like tables, if the page has more than one chart, filters can be created for each chart and for the page. In addition to creating a Page level filter in this exercise, you will also create a filter for each chart.

1. Duplicate page E12.5.

2. Make the chart smaller ⇒ Make a copy of the chart and place it below the current chart.

Create The Last Years Sales Field Filter

In this part of the exercise, you will create a filter that will display customers whose last years sales are greater than or equal to $25,000.

1. Click on the top chart ⇒ Create a filter for the Last Years Sales field to select records with a value that is greater than or equal to $25,000. Figure 12-30 shows the Last Years Sales filter criteria.

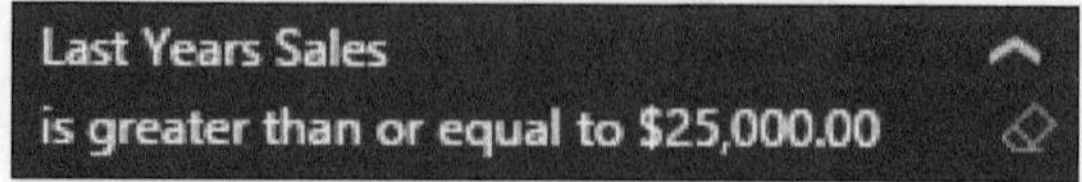

Figure 12-30 Last years sales filter criteria

Create The Customer Type Field Filter

In this part of the exercise you will create a filter that displays customers that have the Online customer type.

1. Click on the bottom chart.

2. Drag the Customer Type field from the Fields panel to the Visual level filters section ⇒
Select the Online option.

   Figure 12-31 shows what both charts should look like.

   Notice the dollar amount range difference in the Last Years Sales values on the left side of both charts.

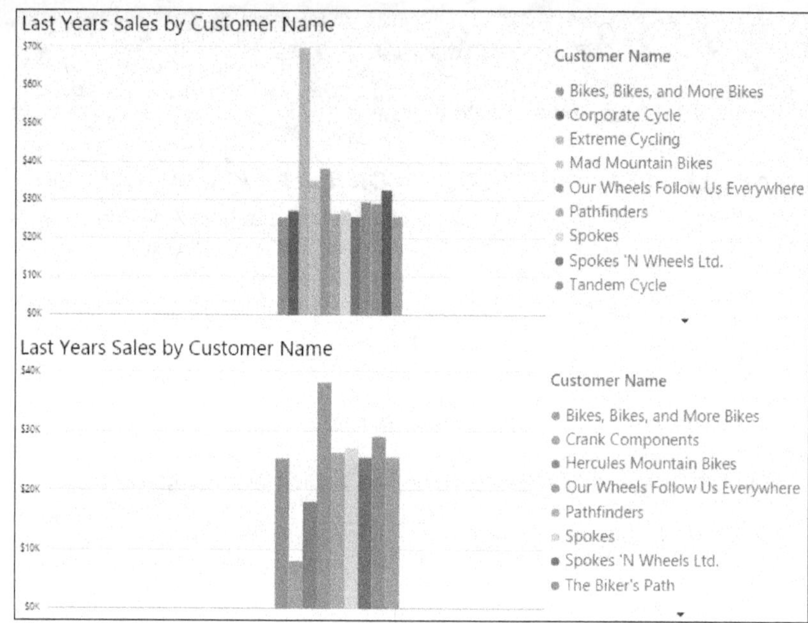

Figure 12-31 Visual level filters applied to both charts

Create The Page Level Filter

1. Click on the second chart ⇒ Delete the Region Visual level filter.

2. Create a Page level filter for the Country Name field to only display customers in Brazil, Canada and the USA.

   Figure 12-32 shows what both charts should look like.

   The arrows at the bottom of the legend, indicate that there are more values in the legend.

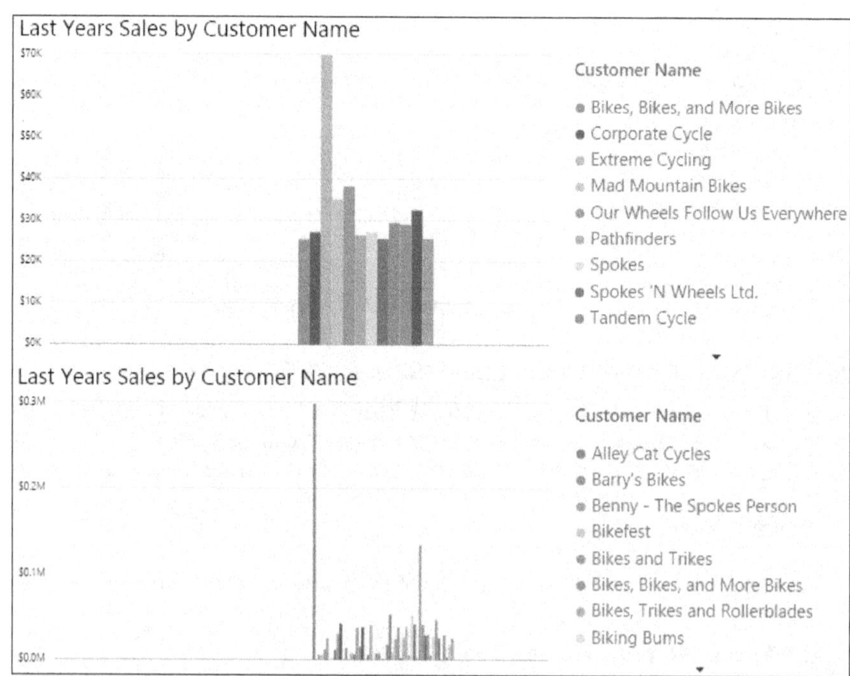

Figure 12-32 Charts with visual and page level filters

Use The Categorical Option To Load More Data

As covered earlier in the X-Axis options section, when enabled, the Categorical option will load more data to a chart. If the chart type X-Axis supports the Categorical format type (like bar and line charts do), the **TYPE OPTION** has to be set to Categorical, to load more data into the chart.

Exercise 12.7: Load Data While Scrolling

This exercise will show you how to load more data in a Cartesian chart.

1. Add the Stacked column chart.

2. Add the Order ID field to the Axis section.

3. Add the Order Amount field to the Value section.

   The chart should look like the one shown in Figure 12-33.

   As you can see, the chart does not display a scroll bar, even if you make the chart really small.

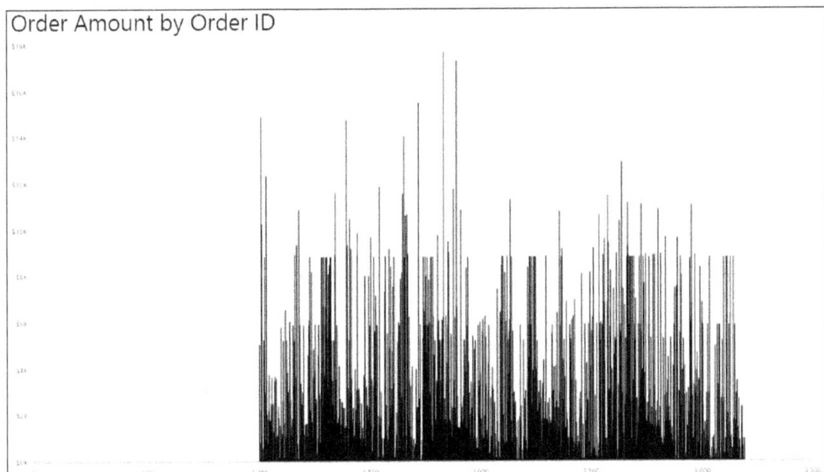

Figure 12-33 Stacked Column chart without scroll bars

4. Format panel ⇒ X-Axis ⇒ Change the Type to Categorical. You should see a scroll bar at the bottom of the chart.

5. Resize the chart so that it is about a quarter of the page size. On your own, this step is not necessary. I am doing it in this exercise to help ensure that the scroll bar is enabled.

6. The chart should look like the one shown in Figure 12-34.

   As you move the scroll bar to the right, you will continue to see more data.

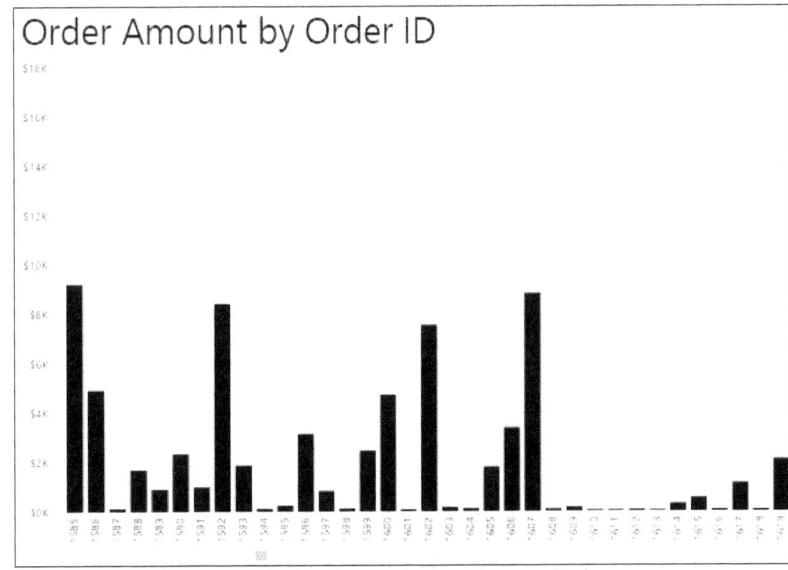

Figure 12-34 Chart with the Categorical option applied

Exercise 12.8: How To Customize Tooltips

In this exercise you will add fields to the Tooltips section of the Field Well, to display a count of orders and the total shipping amount.

1. Duplicate page E12.1.
2. Add the Order ID field to the Tooltips section ⇒ Change the aggregation to Count.
3. Add the Order Amount field to the Tooltips section twice ⇒ Change the aggregation of the second Order Amount field to Average.
4. Add the Shipping Amount field to the Tooltips section twice ⇒ Change the aggregation of the second Shipping Amount field to Average.
5. Hold the mouse pointer over a bar on the chart.

   You should see the fields shown in Figure 12-35, on the tooltip.

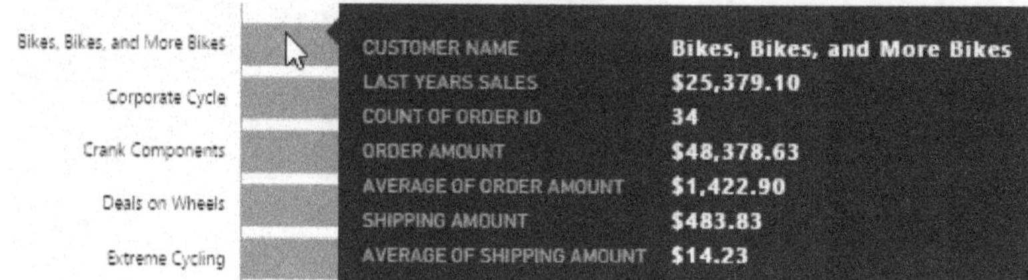

Figure 12-35 Customized tooltip

Exercise 12.9: Export Chart Data

In this exercise you will export the data from the E12.4 page to a .csv file.

1. Display page E12.4.
2. In the upper right corner of the charts frame, display the shortcut menu and select the **EXPORT DATA** option.
3. Type `E12.9` in front of the file name ⇒ Click Save. You can view the file in a text editor like Note Pad or in Excel.

Summary

As promised, this chapter covered creating a variety of chart types. The main reason for using the same data tables for all of the chart exercises in this chapter is to demonstrate the variety of ways that the same data can be displayed. Each chart provides a different interpretation of the same data set.

CHARTS AND INTERACTIVE OPTIONS

After completing this chapter you will be able to perform the following tasks:

- ☑ Create bubble and scatter charts
- ☑ Create a line chart with two series of data
- ☑ Use drill down techniques with charts
- ☑ Use the Play Axis interactive option
- ☑ Use a parameter to filter data on a chart

CHAPTER 13

Overview

This chapter picks up where the previous chapter left off and will show you how to use more chart types and features. The topics covered in this chapter will help make the data displayed, easier to analyze. One goal of this chapter is to introduce features that will make the reports that you create interactive. Keep in mind that all of the interactive features are not available for all table and chart types.

In a way, interactive features provide another way to filter data, that is displayed on a report. This means that these features filter data, in addition to the filters that are set up for the visualization. Interactive features are also very useful if you are creating visualizations for other people to use, even if they do not know how to create or modify visualizations, they will still be able to filter data if they need to. If you use data as part of a presentation and want to use something in addition to or in place of paper reports, this may be your favorite chapter on reports.

Analytics Panel

The options on this panel are shown in Figure 13-1. They are available for the following chart types: Area, Bar, Bubble, Column, Line, Scatter, Stacked Area and Waterfall. The options displayed, depend on the chart type that is selected. This is a relatively new panel, so I suspect that new options will be added from time to time.

The current options on this panel are known as **DYNAMIC REFERENCE LINES** and are based on the minimum, maximum, average, median and percentile of the measure that you select. Each of these options will add a reference line to the chart. More than one reference line can be added to a chart. Options that are chart specific are explained where the chart type is covered.

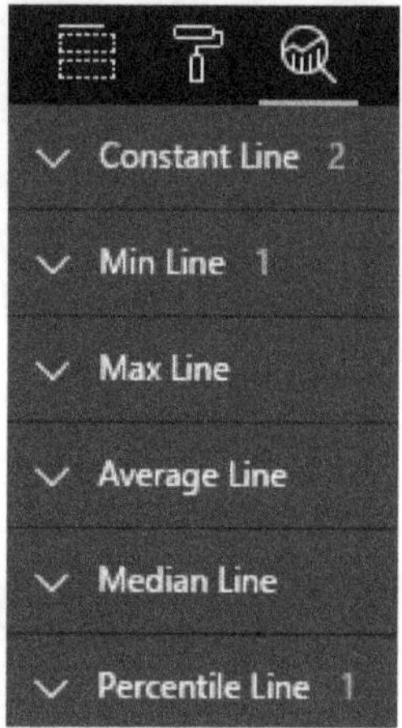

Figure 13-1 Analytics panel

How To Enable The Analytics Options
To enable the options in each section of Figure 13-1, click the **+ADD BUTTON**, shown below in Figure 13-2. If you need to create more of the same type of reference line, click the +Add button again. A counter is displayed next to each section name, on the Analytics panel, to let you know how many of that reference line type have been created.

Constant Line Options

The options shown in Figure 13-2 add a reference line that displays the expected range (lower and upper values) that the data is expected to fall in. This reference line makes it easy to recognize values that are outside of the expected range.

The options selected in Figure 13-2, add the reference line to the line chart shown in Figure 13-3.

To rename the reference line to something meaningful, double-click in the box above the **+ ADD BUTTON** and type in a new name.

The **VALUE OPTION** is used to select the number to use as the static reference value.

The **COLOR OPTION** is used to select the color of the reference line.

The **POSITION OPTION** is used to select if the reference line should be displayed in front or in back of the charts data points.

If enabled, the **DATA LABEL OPTION** will display the number entered in the Value option (see above) on the chart. When enabled, the options below it are displayed.

The **COLOR OPTION** (below the Data label option) is used to change the color of the reference line value.

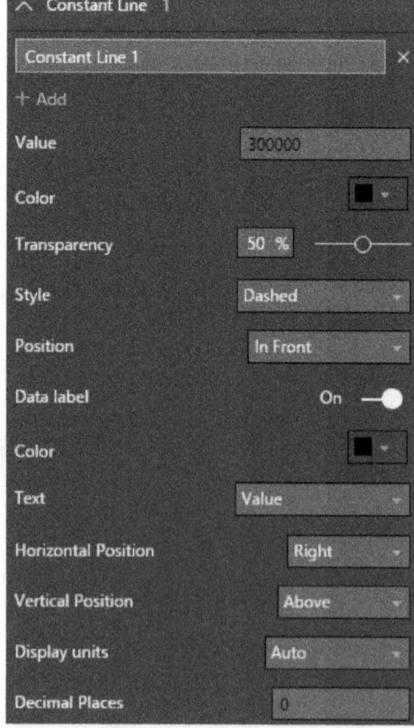

Figure 13-2 Constant Line options

The **HORIZONTAL POSITION OPTION** displays the value before or after of the reference line.

The **VERTICAL POSITION OPTION** displays the value at the top or bottom of the reference line.

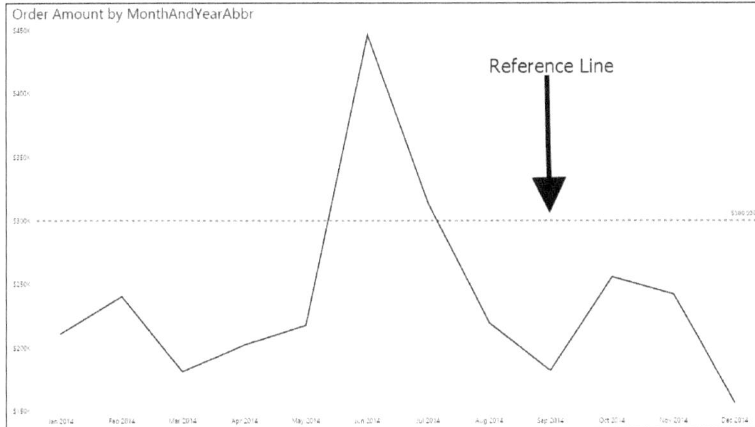

Figure 13-3 Reference line added to a line chart

Min, Max, Average, Median And Percentile Reference Line Options

The options shown in Figure 13-4 are similar to the Constant Line options, covered in the previous section. The difference is that the value for these reference lines are calculated based on the value of the measure that is selected.

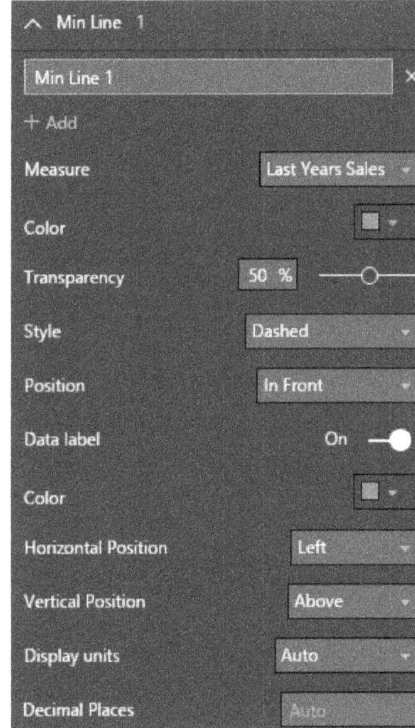

Figure 13-4 Min Line options

Visual Tools

When at least one visual is selected on the page, the Format and Drill tabs are available, as explained below.

Format Tab

Figure 13-5 shows the options on this tab. The options are explained in Table 13-1.

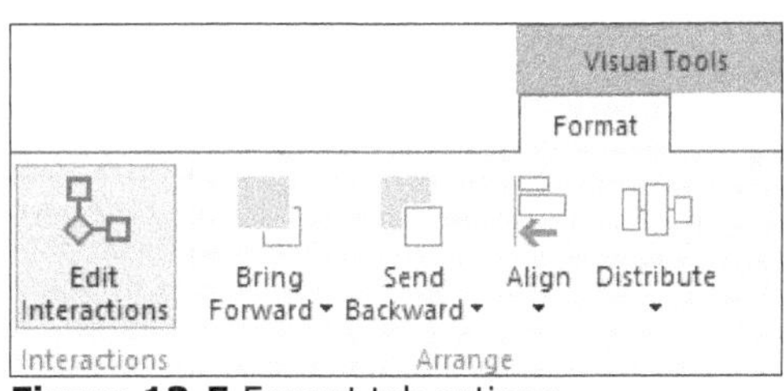

Figure 13-5 Format tab options

Option	Description
Edit Interactions	To be enabled, this option requires at least two visuals on a page, but it works best with three or more visuals on a page. This option is used to select a visual that will not be filtered by a slicer or chart on the page.
Bring Forward	The options on this button are **BRING FORWARD**, which moves the selected object, back one level at a time and **BRING TO FRONT**, which moves the selected object to the top or in front of all other objects on the page. (1)
Send Backward	The options on this button are **SEND FORWARD**, which moves the selected object, up one level at a time and **SEND TO BACK**, which moves the selected object to the bottom or behind all other objects on the page. (1)
Align	[See Align Options]
Distribute	These options are used to ensure that the space between the selected visuals on the page, is the same. The **DISTRIBUTE VERTICALLY OPTION** is used to make the white space above and below the visuals the same. The **DISTRIBUTE HORIZONTALLY OPTION** is used to make the white space on the left and right sides the same.

Table 13-1 Format tab options explained

(1) This option works like the "Layer" feature in image editing software. In Power BI Desktop, you would use these options, when you place one visual on top of another visual on the page.

Align Options

The options shown in Figure 13-6 are used to align the selected objects on the page.

The alignment is based on the first object selected.

The options are explained in Table 13-2.

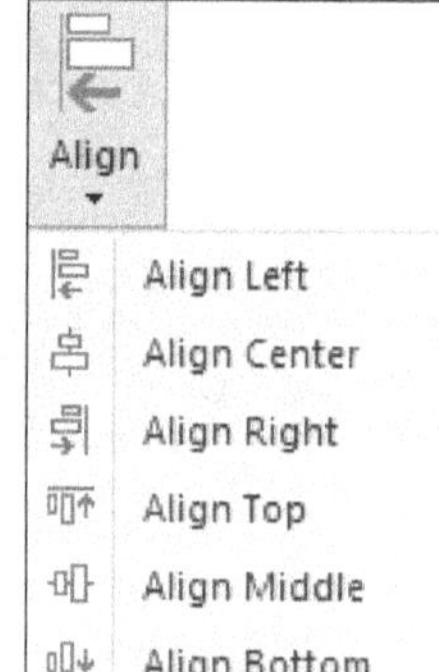

Figure 13-6 Align options

Option	This Option Aligns On The . . .
Align Left	Left side of the selected objects.
Align Center	Center of the selected objects.
Align Right	Right side of the selected objects.
Align Top	Top of the selected objects.
Align Middle	Middle of the selected objects.
Align Bottom	Bottom of the selected objects.

Table 13-2 Align options explained

Drill Down Functionality

This functionality is used to view the aggregated data (the data used to create the chart) behind the chart that is currently displayed.

Drill Tab

Figure 13-7 shows the options on this tab. They are enabled based on what part of a chart is selected. These options are used to drill down to see the data used to create the chart.

Some or all of these options are also available on a shortcut menu when you right-click on a chart element (like a column or bubble), as shown later in Figure 13-12.

The options are explained in Table 13-3.

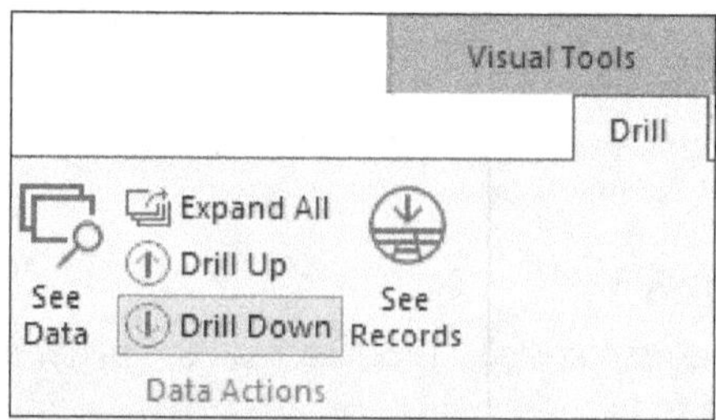

Figure 13-7 Drill tab options

Option	Description
See Data	Displays a panel below the chart, as shown at the bottom of Figure 13-8. The panel shows the data that is displayed on the chart. Notice that the status bar disappears. Click this button again to close the panel. This option does not display data for map charts.

Table 13-3 Drill tab options explained

Option	Description
Expand All	Displays all of the elements (for example, the bars shown in Figure 13-8), combined into one, as shown in Figure 13-10. This flattens the hierarchy and displays all of the items at the lowest level. Hold the mouse pointer over a section of the chart element to see what it represents, if the Data Label format option is not enabled.
Drill Up	This option is enabled after the Expand All option has been applied. Click this button to re-display the chart shown in Figure 13-10, to the one shown in Figure 13-8.
Drill Down	Enables and disables the drill down functionality.
See Records	This option is enabled when a chart (not an element on the chart) is selected. With the chart selected, click this button, then click on a data point on the chart, to display the detail records that were used to create the data point (in this case the bar), as shown in Figure 13-11. If you want to view the data for another section of the chart, click the Back to Report button, then click on another section of the chart. Click the button again to disable the option.

Table 13-3 Drill tab options explained (Continued)

See Data Options

Clicking the switch layout button illustrated in the upper right corner of Figure 13-8, changes the layout to the one shown in Figure 13-9.

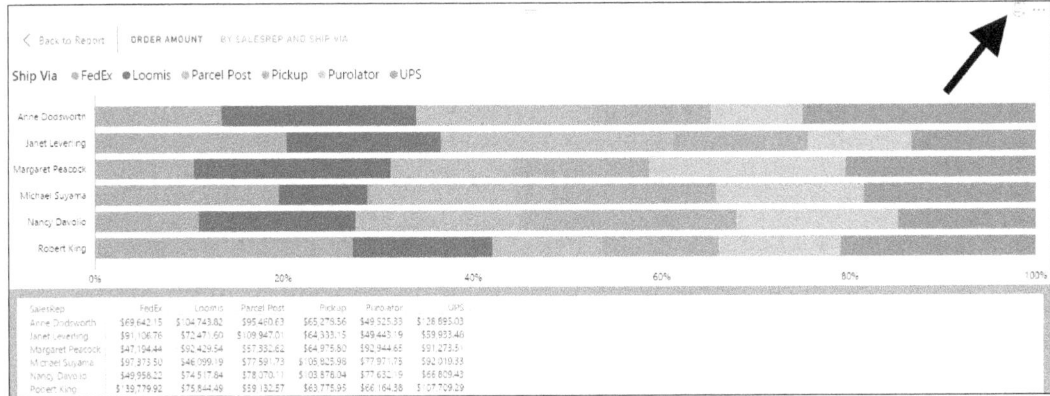

Figure 13-8 See Data panel

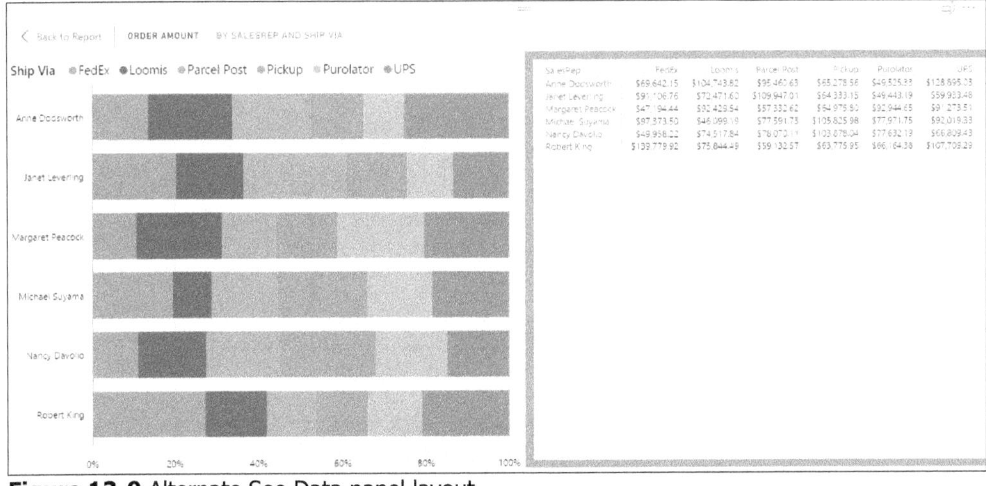

Figure 13-9 Alternate See Data panel layout

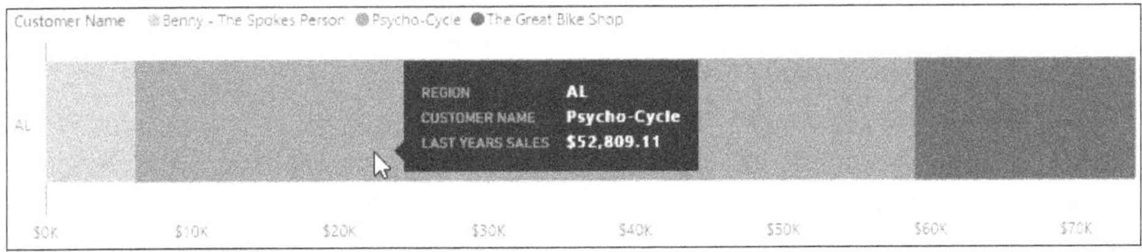

Figure 13-10 Chart with Expand All option applied

See Records Option

< Back to Report

SalesRep	Order Amount ▼	Ship Via	Order Date	Shipped	Payment Received
Anne Dodsworth	$17,658.81	Parcel Post	07/07/2014	True	True
Anne Dodsworth	$9,187.30	Parcel Post	03/12/2014	True	True
Anne Dodsworth	$8,846.55	Parcel Post	09/14/2014	True	True
Anne Dodsworth	$5,879.70	Parcel Post	06/03/2014	True	True

Figure 13-11 See Records option

Drill Down Shortcut Menu

Figure 13-12 shows the Drill Down shortcut menu. The options were explained earlier in Table 13-3. Depending on the level that you have drilled down to, all of the options shown, may not be available.

When the chart is selected, (it is in **DRILL DOWN MODE**) you will see the drill down buttons illustrated in Figure 13-13, above the chart. The options are explained below.

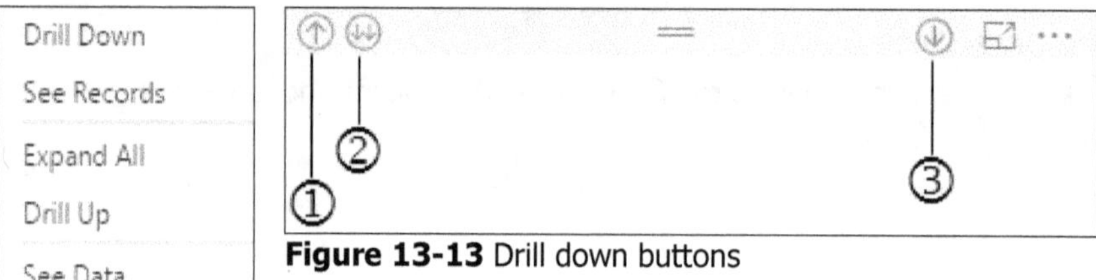

Figure 13-13 Drill down buttons

Figure 13-12 Drill Down shortcut menu

Drill Down Buttons Explained

① **DRILL UP BUTTON** displays the data, one level up.

② **DRILL ALL TO NEXT LEVEL BUTTON** [See Table 13-3, Expand All]

③ **TURN ON DRILL DOWN BUTTON** enables/disables the drill down functionality. The button will be filled in, when the **DRILL DOWN MODE** is enabled.

Inline Hierarchies

This functionality is available when multiple dimensions or categories are added to the same axis. When this is the case, the Expand All drill down option is available. When the Expand All option is selected in this scenario, the data label of the parent category is added to each item (element), so that you can easily tell which parent category the item is for.

Using Drill Down Functionality With Charts

Depending on the chart type, the fields that you want to drill down on, need to be placed in one of the following sections: Axis, Legend or Group. The following chart types support drill down functionality: Bubble, Clustered bar, Clustered column, Donut, Funnel, Line, Line and Clustered column, Line and Stacked column, Pie, Scatter, Stacked bar, Stacked column and Tree Map.

What may not be obvious when drilling down in a chart, is that Visual level filters are automatically created for each level that you drill down to.

When a date/time field is added to the first option on the Field Well, it will display a hierarchy, as shown in Figure 13-14. This also enables drill down functionality.

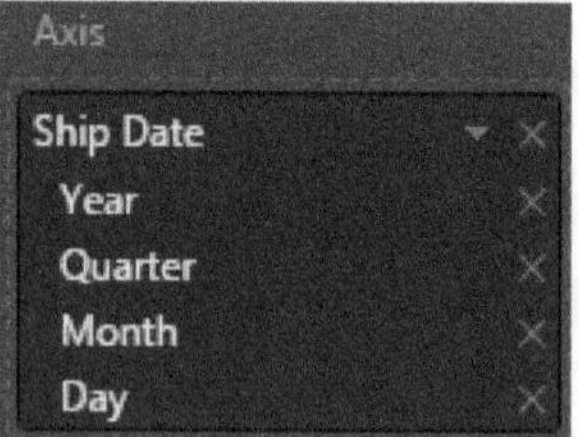

Figure 13-14 Date/Time field added to the Axis section

Exercise 13.1: Add Drill Down Functionality To A Chart

In this exercise you will incorporate drill down functionality in a chart. Keep in mind that each field in the Axis section are the ones that create the drill down levels.

Create The Chart

1. Save the Report Data.pbix file as `Chapter 13 Charts.`

2. Add the Stacked column chart to the page.

3. Add the following fields to the chart.

   ☑ Add the Country field from the Customer table to the Axis section
   ☑ Add the Sales Rep, Ship Via and Customer Name fields to the Axis section
   ☑ Add the Order Amount field to the Value section

4. Create a filter for the Country field to only display records in the following countries: Australia, Canada, France, United Kingdom and USA.

5. Create a filter for the Order Amount field to only display records with an order amount greater than $2,500.

   The chart should look like the one shown in Figure 13-15.

   If you click on a column for a sales rep, you will drill down and see the break down of how their orders were shipped.

   If you click on a column for the shipping method, you will drill down again and see the customers whose orders were shipped via the shipping method that you clicked on.

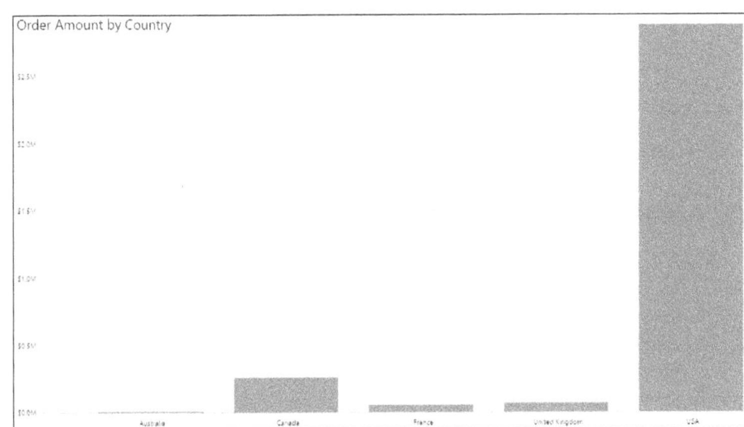

Figure 13-15 Stacked column chart

Use The Drill Down Functionality

The countries are shown across the bottom of the chart. The columns in the chart display the total amount by country.

1. Enable the drill down functionality for the chart.

2. Click on a column in the chart.

   You will see a chart similar to the one shown in Figure 13-16. You will see the sales reps total order amount.

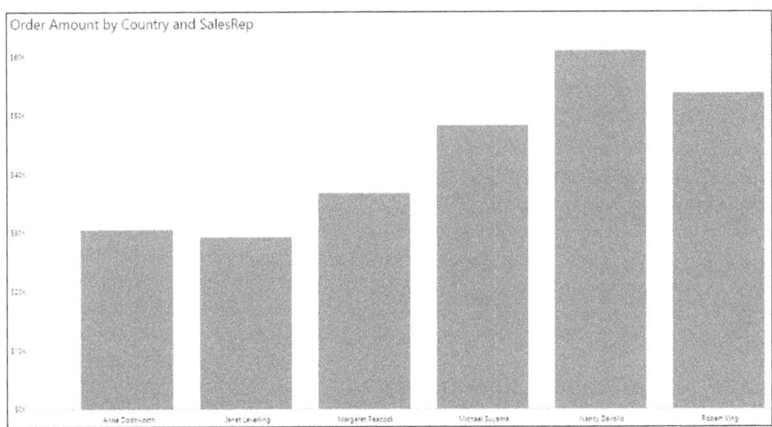

Figure 13-16 Drill down level of the chart

Line Chart Field Well

Figure 13-17 shows the options used to create a Line chart.

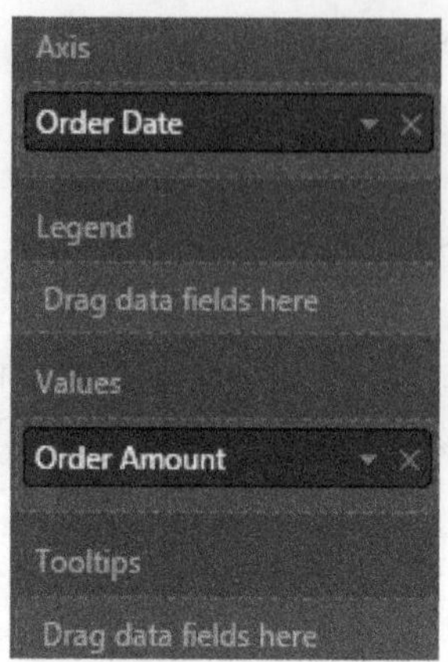

Figure 13-17 Line chart Field Well

Line Chart Formatting Options

The options covered in this section are specific to line charts.

Data Labels Options

The options shown in Figure 13-18 are used to customize the data labels.

The **LABEL DENSITY OPTION** is used to select how many data labels are displayed on the chart. A larger percent displays more data labels. The requirements to enable this option are:

① The **AXIS SECTION** on the Field Well must contain a date or number field.
② The X-Axis formatting **TYPE OPTION** must be set to Continuous, as shown below in Figure 13-19.

Figure 13-18 Line chart Data labels options

X-Axis Options

The **TYPE OPTION** is only available for **CARTESIAN CHARTS** (area, bar, column and line).

The **CATEGORICAL TYPE OPTION** is used to load more data when the scroll bar is enabled. This was demonstrated in Chapter 12, Exercise 12.7.

The **CONTINUOUS OPTION** is used to enable the Label Density option shown above in Figure 13-18.

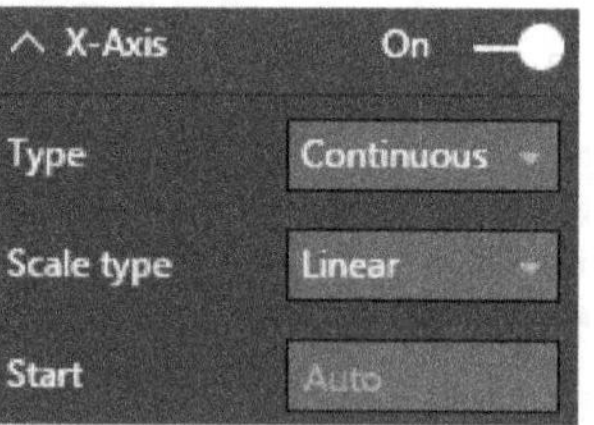

Figure 13-19 X-Axis formatting options

Figure 13-20 shows the Line chart created from the options shown above in Figures 13-17, 13-18 and 13-19.

Figure 13-21 shows the Line chart with the Label Density set to 95%.

The filter options used to create both charts are Order Amount greater than or equal to $10,000 and the year = 2014.

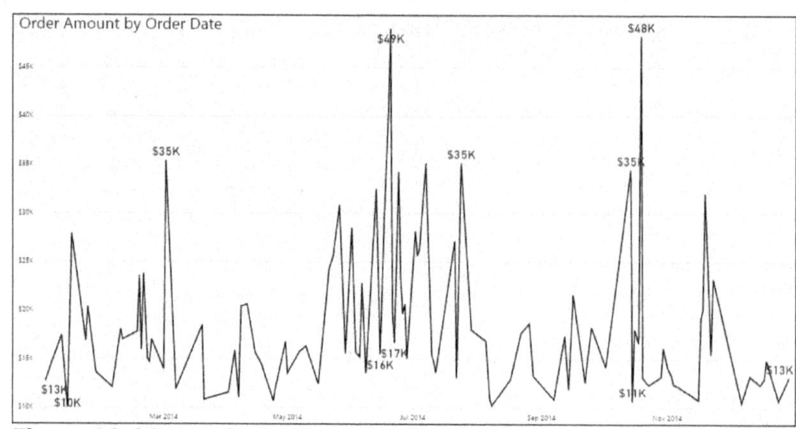

Figure 13-20 Line chart with a Label Density of 25%

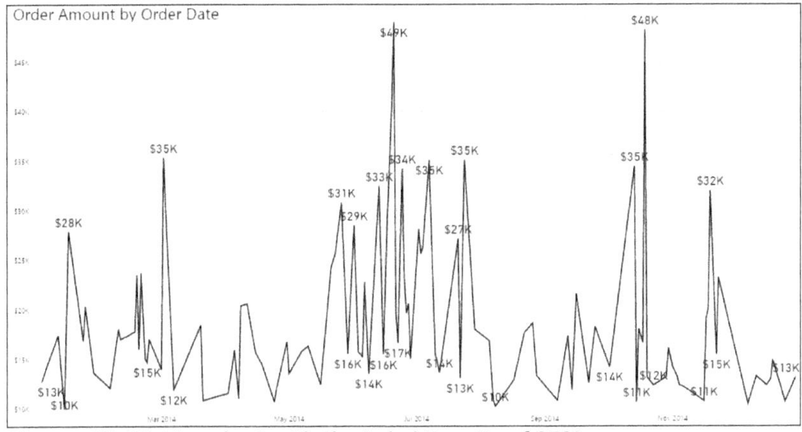

Figure 13-21 Line chart with the Label Density of 95%

Exercise 13.2: Create A Line Chart

In this exercise you will create a Line chart that sums the order amount by month.

1. Add the Line chart to the page.
2. Add the following fields to the chart.

   ☑ Add the Month And Year Abbr field to the Axis section
   ☑ Add the Order Amount field to the Values section

3. Create a filter to only display orders in 2014.
4. Display the Data Labels.

   Your chart should look like the one shown in Figure 13-22.

   If the data labels are not displayed, the values can still be viewed by holding the mouse pointer over a data marker on the chart, as illustrated in the figure.

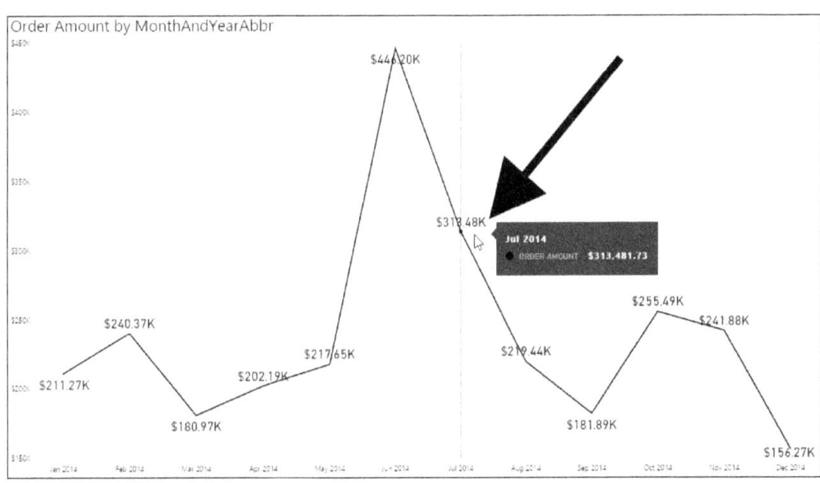

Figure 13-22 Line chart

Exercise 13.3: Create A Line Chart With Two Series Of Data

This exercise will show you how to display more than one data series on a chart.

1. Add the following fields to a Line chart: Order Amount and Sales Net fields.
2. Create a filter to only display orders in 2014.

3. Drag the Ship Via field to the Axis section.

   The chart should look like the one as shown in Figure 13-23.

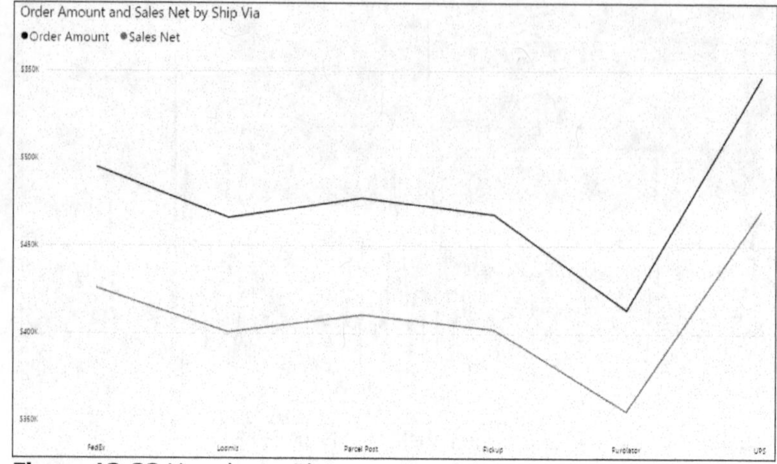

Figure 13-23 Line chart with two series of data

Exercise 13.4: Drill Down On A Line Chart

In this exercise you will learn how to drill down on a chart. The Ship Via, Sales Rep and a quarter field will be added to the chart, to create the drill down levels.

1. Duplicate page E13.3.

2. Delete the Sales Net field.

3. Add the Sales Rep and Quarter And Year Abbr fields to the Axis section below the Ship Via field.

4. Change the Data labels Display units option to Thousands ⇒
   Change the Data labels Decimal Places option to 0.

   The chart should look like the one shown in Figure 13-24.

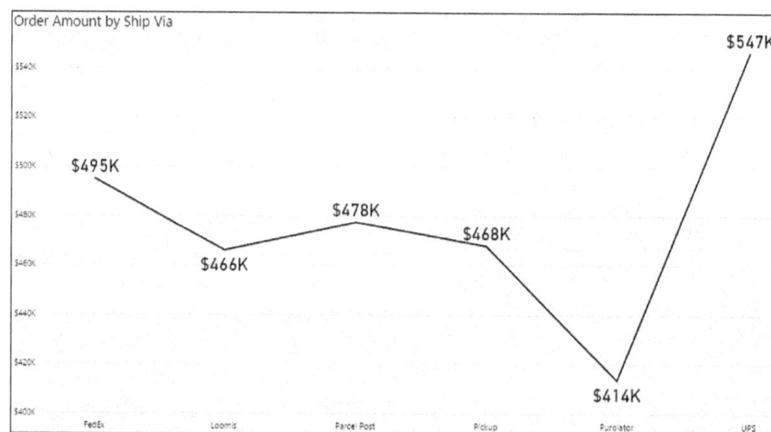

Figure 13-24 Line chart to be drilled down on

Enable Drill Down On A Line Chart

The drill down levels are in the Axis section for a line chart.

1. Enable drill down on the chart.

2. On the chart, click on the Pickup Up data point. You should see the chart shown in Figure 13-25. If you look at the chart title, you will see that it has changed from the title shown above in Figure 13-24. The chart now displays the total dollar amount of orders shipped via the Pick Up shipping option for each sales rep.

If you look in the Filters section on the Visualizations panel, you will see that there are two active filters, as shown at the bottom of Figure 13-26. They are the filters used to create the drill down level. The Ship Via filter was created to display the data shown in Figure 13-25. The year filter was created in the previous exercise.

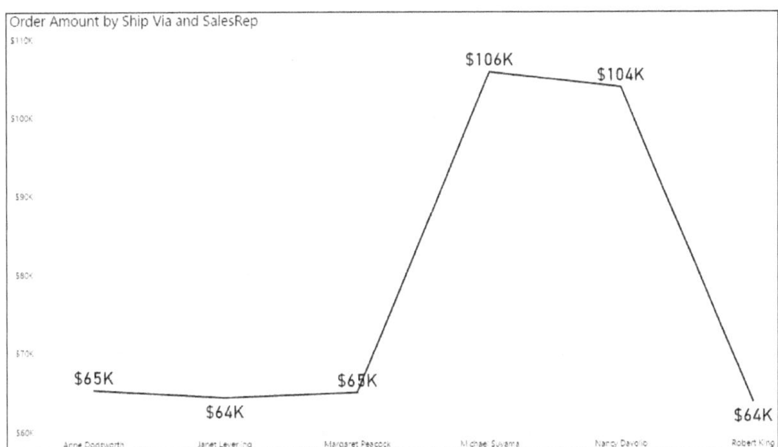

Figure 13-25 Sales rep drill down level of the chart

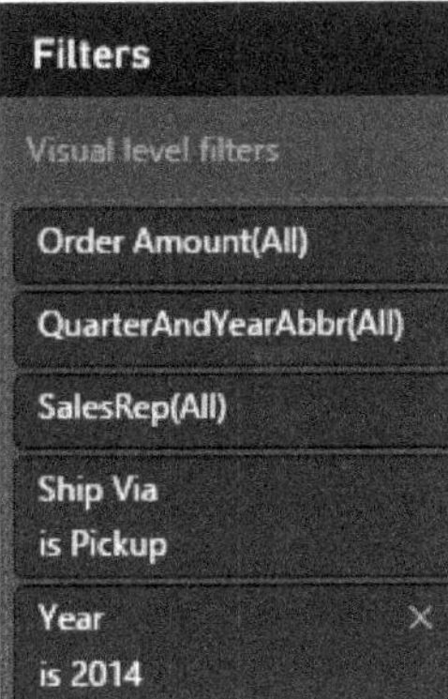

Figure 13-26 Active filters for the drill down

3. On the chart shown above in Figure 13-25, click on the data point for Michael Suyama.

   If you look in the Filters section, you will see a Sales Rep filter with this sales reps name.

   You will see the total amount of orders shipped via the Pick Up shipping option for this sales rep, as shown in Figure 13-27.

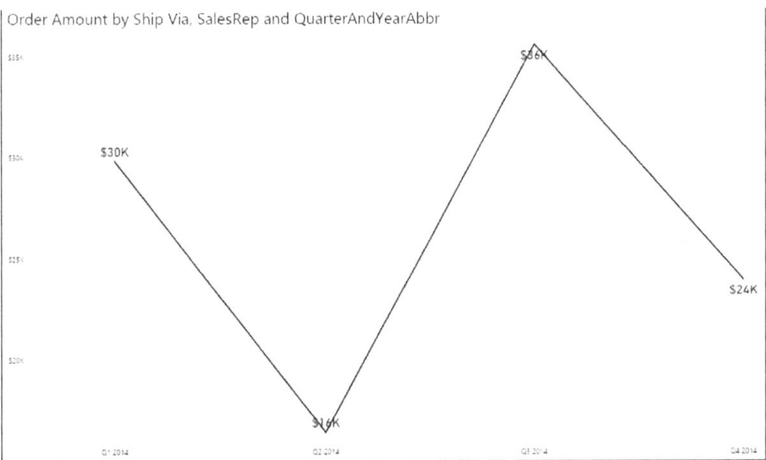

Figure 13-27 Quarter and Year drill down level of the chart

Exercise 13.5: Create An Area Chart

The chart that you will create in this exercise will display last years sales by region.

1. Add the Area chart to the page.

2. Check the Last Years Sales field ⇒ Check the Region field.

3. Create a filter for the Region field. Select the following states and province: BC, IL, MN, PA, WI.

   The chart should look like the one shown in Figure 13-28.

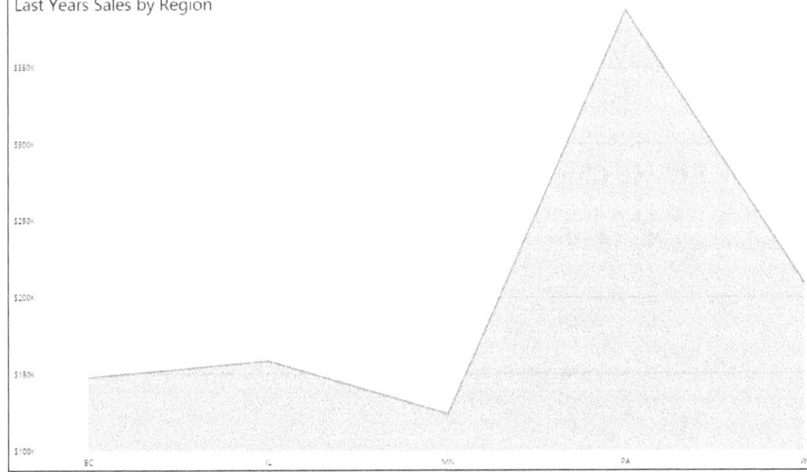

Figure 13-28 Area chart

Scatter Charts

This chart type needs two numeric values because the X and Y axis require numeric data. If you use a field that is not a numeric data type, Power BI Desktop will convert the data and use it as a Count aggregation. Scatter charts need three fields for the sections, on the Field Well, explained below. The order that the sections are listed in below, is also the order that the fields need to be added in, to create a scatter chart.

① **DETAILS** The field added to this section, often called the **DESCRIPTIVE FIELD**, is used to create the plot point (the intersection of the X and Y axis) on the chart.
② **X AXIS** The field added to this section is used to create the horizontal axis (the values across the bottom of the chart).
③ **Y AXIS** The field added to this section is used to create the vertical axis (the values on the left side of the chart).

If you are new to creating scatter charts, don't worry. If you can't figure out the correct section to place all of the fields in, add the fields that you can to a table visualization, then change the table to a Scatter chart, to view the output. Rearrange the fields as needed, then add any fields that may be missing.

Scatter And Bubble Chart Field Well

Figure 13-29 shows the options used to create Scatter and Bubble charts.

The **SIZE OPTION** is used to create the size of the bubble. When a value is added to this option, the Scatter chart becomes a Bubble chart.

The **PLAY AXIS OPTION** adds interactive functionality to the chart. This option is covered later in this chapter.

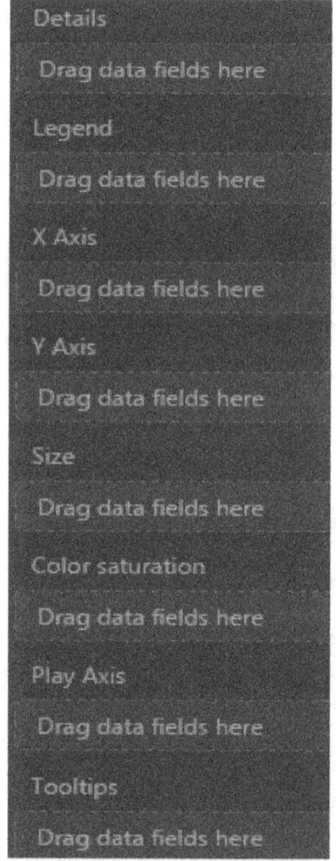

Figure 13-29 Scatter and Bubble chart Field Well

Scatter And Bubble Chart Formatting Options

The formatting options explained below work differently then they do in other chart types or they are exclusive to Scatter and Bubble charts.

Data Colors Options

The options shown in Figure 13-30 are used to change the color of the bubbles that represent the data.

The **DEFAULT COLOR OPTION** is the color that will be applied to each bubble that you do not apply a specific color to.

The **SHOW ALL OPTION** displays a data color option for each value from the field in the Details section, shown above in Figure 13-29. Once a field is added to the Details section, you can select a different color for each plot point on the chart, as shown at the bottom of Figure 13-30.

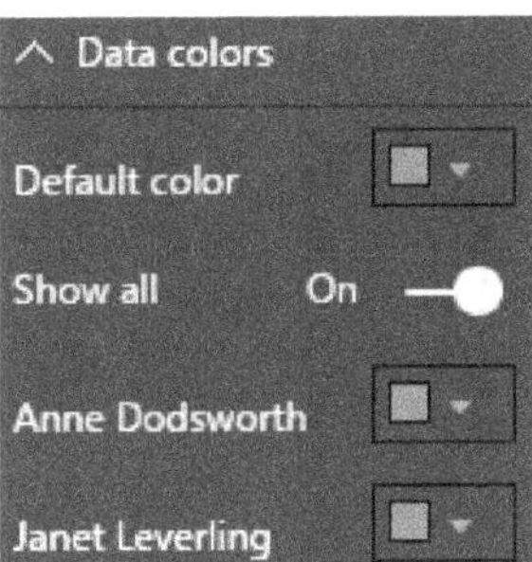

Figure 13-30 Data colors options

X-Axis Options

The **SCALE TYPE OPTION** is used to select between **LINEAR** and **LOG**. Log is not available if an X-Axis Constant Line analytic (reference line) is applied to the chart.

Category Labels Options

The options shown in Figure 13-31 are used to add data labels to the chart.

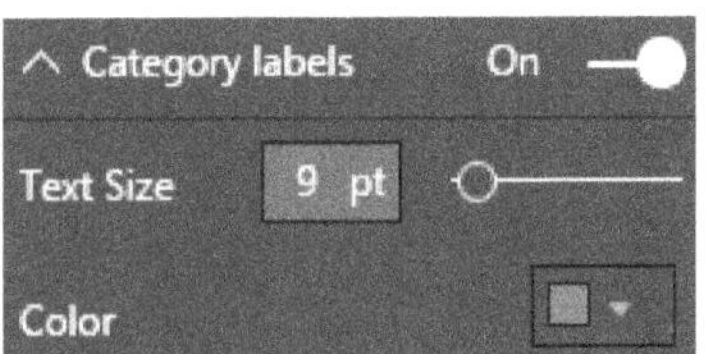

Figure 13-31 Category labels options

Fill Point Option

The option shown in Figure 13-32 is used to make the markers, on the chart, a solid color.

Figure 13-32 Fill point option

Color By Category Option

The option shown in Figure 13-33 is used to change the color of the markers (the bubbles), based on the value in the field in the Details field section.

Figure 13-33 Color by category option

Scatter And Bubble Chart Analytics Options

Figure 13-34 shows the analytics options that are specific to these two chart types. The options are explained below.

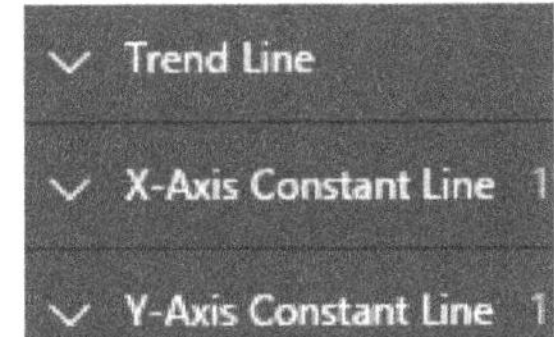

Figure 13-34 Scatter and Bubble chart analytics options

Trend Line Options

The options shown in Figure 13-35 are available once the Scatter or Bubble chart has been created. The options shown, create the dashed trend line, in the chart shown in Figure 13-36.

The **COMBINE SERIES OPTION** is used to select between displaying one trend line for all data series or one trend line per data series (based on the values in the field in the Legend section, shown earlier in Figure 13-29). Figure 13-35 shows the trend line with the Combine Series option enabled. Figure 13-37 shows the trend line with the Combine Series option disabled. This chart shows a trend line for each value in the field in the Legend section. As shown, the legend displays six values and there are six trend lines displayed on the chart.

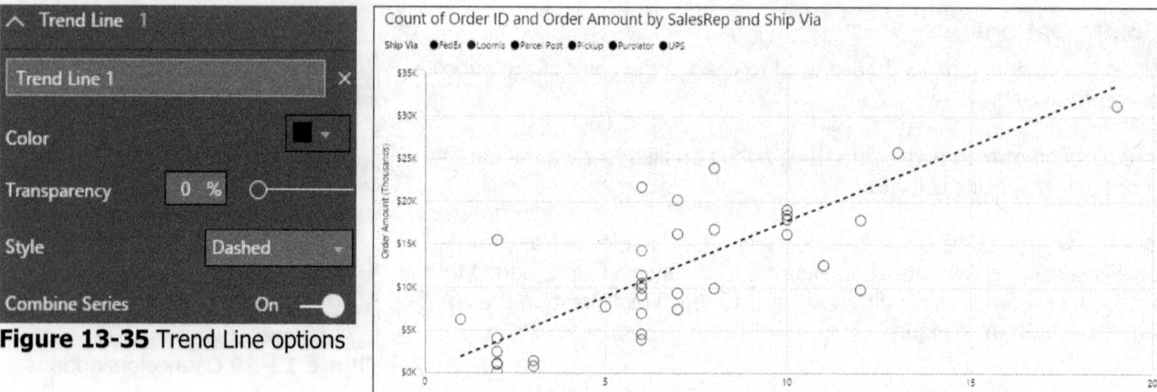

Figure 13-35 Trend Line options

Figure 13-36 Trend line added to a scatter chart

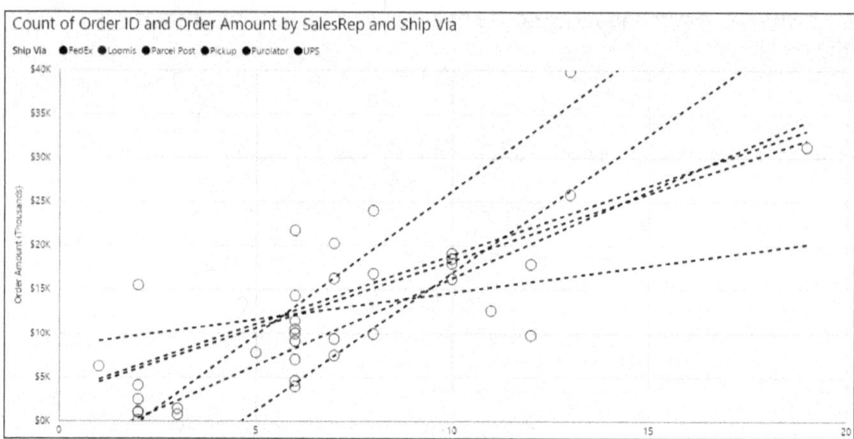

Figure 13-37 Scatter chart with a trend line for each series of data

X-Axis And Y-Axis Constant Line Options

The options shown in Figure 13-38 are used to create a reference line for the values on the X-Axis.

The **Y-AXIS CONSTANT LINE OPTIONS** are the same as the X-Axis Constant Line options. The difference is that the options are used to create a reference line for values on the Y-Axis.

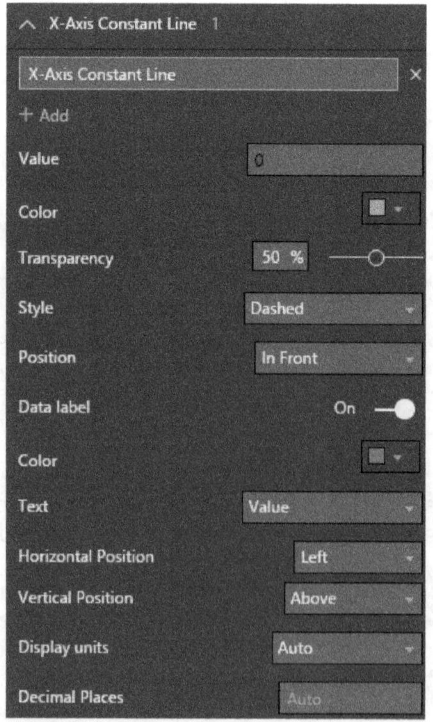

Figure 13-38 X-Axis Constant Line options

Exercise 13.6: Create A Scatter Chart

In this exercise you will learn how to create a scatter chart that will display a count of orders and total sales amount, per sales rep, for one month.

1. Add the Scatter chart.

2. Add the following fields to the chart.

   ☑ Add the Sales Rep field to the Details section
   ☑ Add the Order ID field to the X Axis section
   ☑ Add the Order Amount field to the Y Axis section

3. Change the Order ID field, in the X Axis section to the Count (Distinct) aggregation.

4. Create a filter to only display orders in June 2014.

5. Change the Y-Axis style formatting option to Show Both ⇒ Change the color to red ⇒

   Hold the mouse pointer over one of the bubbles on the chart, as shown in Figure 13-39.

   Because the chart does not display a lot of data, you could add category data labels to it.

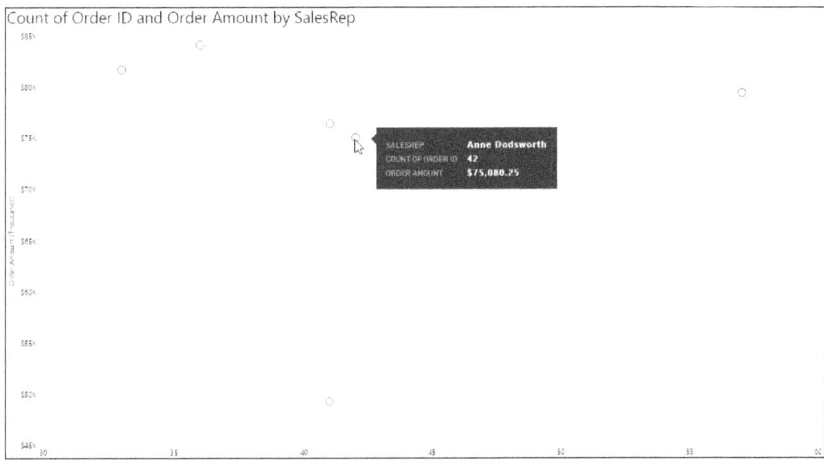

Figure 13-39 Scatter chart

Exercise 13.7: Create A Scatter Chart With Drill Down Functionality

1. Duplicate page E13.6.

2. Drag the Ship Via field to the Details section, below the Sales Rep field.

3. Enable the Category labels and Fill point formatting options.

4. Drill down on the data marker for Janet Leverling.

   You will see how her orders were shipped, as shown in Figure 13-40.

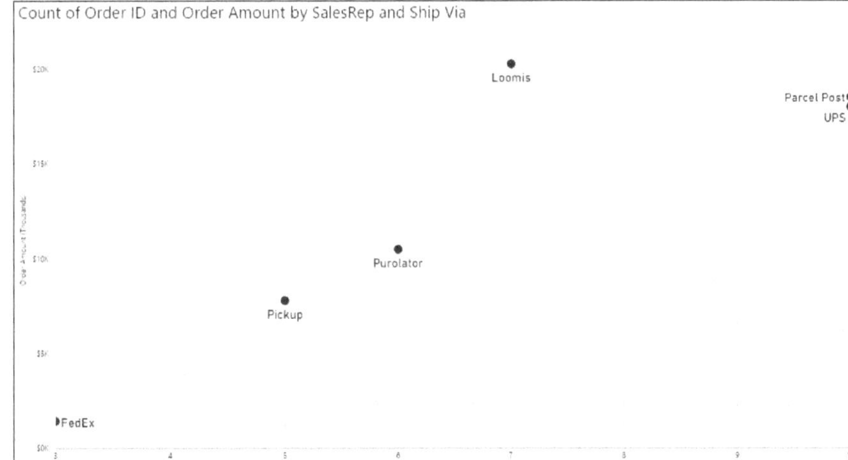

Figure 13-40 Drill down scatter chart with data labels

No Drill Down, Drill Down Charts

If you do not particularly care for drill down charts, the data from the drill down levels in a chart can be displayed on the top level of the chart. To me, this type of chart can be harder to read or use for analysis purposes. But in case your scatter chart does not have a lot of data, the next exercise shows you how to display the data from the top and drill down levels together.

Exercise 13.8: Another Way To Display Drill Down Data On A Scatter Chart

In this exercise you will create a scatter chart that also displays the data that you would see if the chart had drill down functionality.

1. Add the following fields to a Scatter chart.

    ☑ Add the Sales Rep field to the Details section
    ☑ Add the Ship Via field to the Legend section
    ☑ Add the Order ID field to the X Axis section
    ☑ Add the Order Amount field to the Y Axis section

2. Change the Order ID field to Count (Distinct).

3. Create a filter to only display orders in June 2014.

4. Display the Legend on the right.

    The chart should look like the one shown in Figure 13-41.

    I made the bubbles darker and filled in, so that they would be visible when printed.

    The chart displays a data point (bubble) for every sale in June 2014, for every option in the legend.

    This is the equivalent of the top and drill down levels combined.

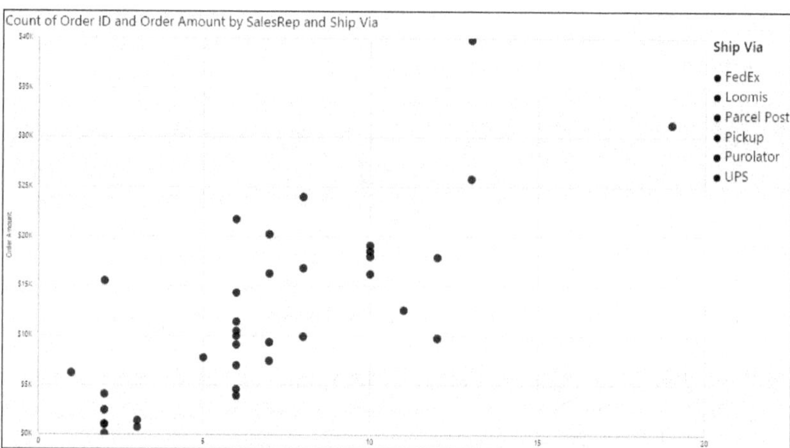

Figure 13-41 Scatter chart with the top level and drill down data displayed

Bubble Charts

For all practical purposes, a Bubble chart is a Scatter chart. The difference is that a Bubble chart requires an additional field (a fourth field). Like a Scatter chart, a Bubble chart uses one field to plot the values on the X axis and a different field to plot the values on the Y axis. The additional field is placed in the **SIZE SECTION** on the Field Well.

Bubble Chart Formatting Options

In addition to the Scatter chart formatting options that Bubble charts have in common, Bubble charts also have the option discussed below.

Color Border Option

The option shown in Figure 13-42, adds a border to each bubble on the chart.

Figure 13-42 Color border option

Exercise 13.9: Create A Bubble Chart

In this exercise you will create a chart that displays a count of orders and total sales amount for each sales rep.

1. Add the fields shown in Figure 13-43 to a Scatter chart.

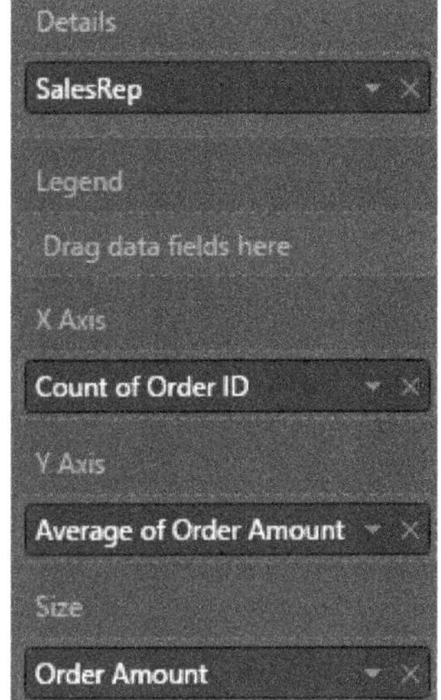

Figure 13-43 Fields for the Bubble chart

2. Change the Order ID field aggregation to Count (Distinct).

3. Create a filter to only display orders in 2014.

4. Enable the Category Labels formatting option ⇒ Change the Text Size to `12`.

   The chart should look like the one shown in Figure 13-44.

   Because the order totals for the year are almost the same for each sales rep, the bubbles are almost the same size.

   To me, this is an indication that a bubble or scatter chart may not be well suited for this data set, because none of the values really stand out.

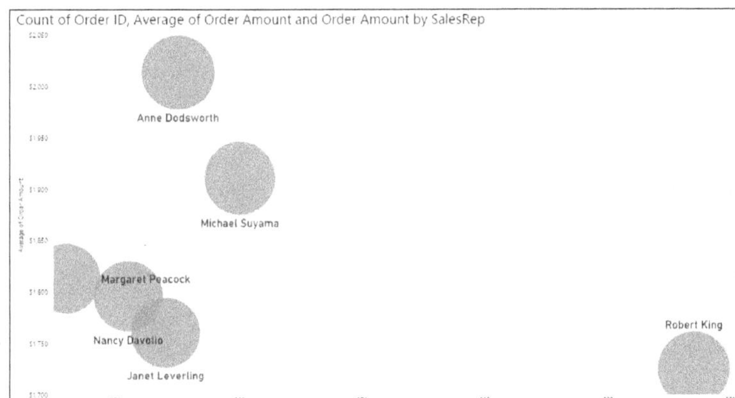

Figure 13-44 Bubble chart

Play Axis

This feature is used to add animation to scatter and bubble charts. It is best suited for charts that will display how data changes over time. An example would be using a date field or displaying the data by month or quarter on the Y axis. When a field is added to the Play Axis section on the Field Well, a second Y axis is added to the chart, below the Y axis that is already on the chart.

Play Axis Tips

① While a play axis does not have to be based on a date or time value, not using a date or time value makes it harder to see the data progression.

② The play axis has a pause button.

③ The play axis can be used as a filter by clicking on a value at the bottom of the play axis. This will pause the play mode and display the data for the value that is clicked on.

Exercise 13.10: Add A Play Axis To A Bubble Chart

In Exercise 13.9, you created a bubble chart that can be enhanced by adding a play axis to it.

1. Duplicate page E13.9.

2. Drag the Month And Year Abbr field to the **PLAY AXIS SECTION**, as shown in Figure 13-45. At the bottom of the chart, you should see the Play Axis with the month and year.

If you click the arrow button, illustrated in Figure 13-46, the bubbles on the chart will move to display the values for a specific month and year. Click the button again to pause/stop the animation.

The date appears as a watermark in the upper right corner of the chart. The data shown in Figure 13-46 is for September 2014. If you want to see a specific month and year, you can also drag the marker on the play axis to select it.

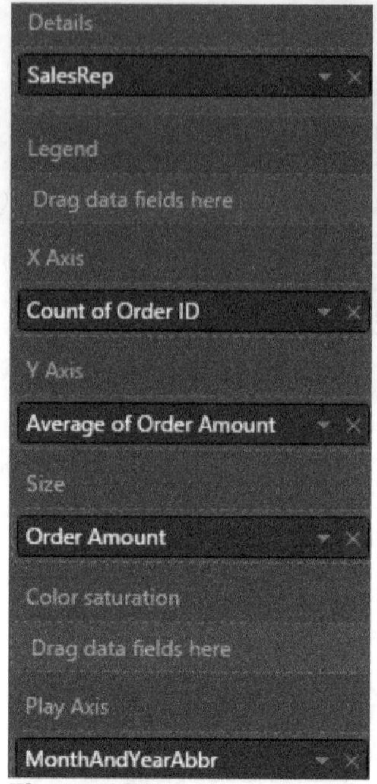

Figure 13-45 Play Axis options

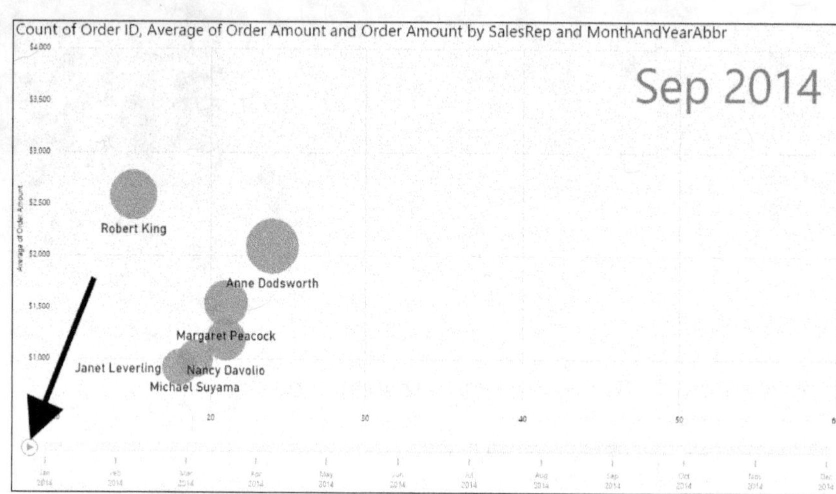

Figure 13-46 Chart with a play axis and a specific month selected

Exercise 13.11: Create A Stacked Column Chart

The charts that you have created so far, have only used one field in the Value section on the Field Well. In this exercise you will create a chart that will display totals for three fields that will be added to the **VALUE SECTION**.

1. Add the Stacked Column chart to the page.
2. Add the Sales Rep field to the Axis section.
3. Add the following fields to the Value section: Order Amount, Sales Cost and Sales Net.

   The chart should look like the one shown in Figure 13-47.

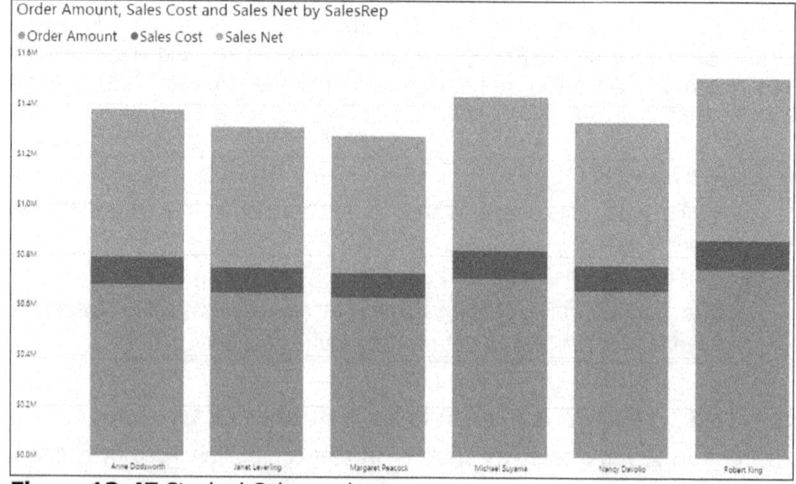

Figure 13-47 Stacked Column chart

X And Y Axis Font Size
Currently, there is no way to change the font size for the values on either axis of a Stacked Column chart.

Exercise 13.12: Filter Chart Data With Parameters

This exercise will show you how to use some of the date functions to create columns that you would find in a date table. These new date columns will be used as the values for parameters.

Duplicate And Modify A Table

To keep this manageable, two columns will be added to the new query that will store the order year and order month. These columns will be used to attach to the parameters, which will be used to filter the chart.

1. In the Query Editor, duplicate the Orders table ⇒ Rename it to `Parameter Orders`. The reason that I duplicated the query is to keep parameters from being used in the other exercises.
2. Select the Parameter Orders query ⇒ Click on the Order Date column.
3. Add Column tab ⇒ Date button ⇒ Year ⇒ Year.
4. Rename the column to `Order Year` ⇒ Change the Data Type to Text.
5. Click on the Order Date column ⇒ Add Column tab ⇒ Date button ⇒ Month ⇒ Name of Month ⇒ Rename the column to `Order Month`.

Create The Month Parameter

1. Create the parameter shown in Figure 13-48.

   Create an entry for each month.

   The order that parameters are created in, is the order that they are displayed in, on the Edit Parameters dialog box.

   Currently, there is no way to change the order on the Parameters dialog box, but the order can be changed on the Queries panel.

   In this exercise, the Country parameter will not be used, so it is better to display it at the bottom of the list.

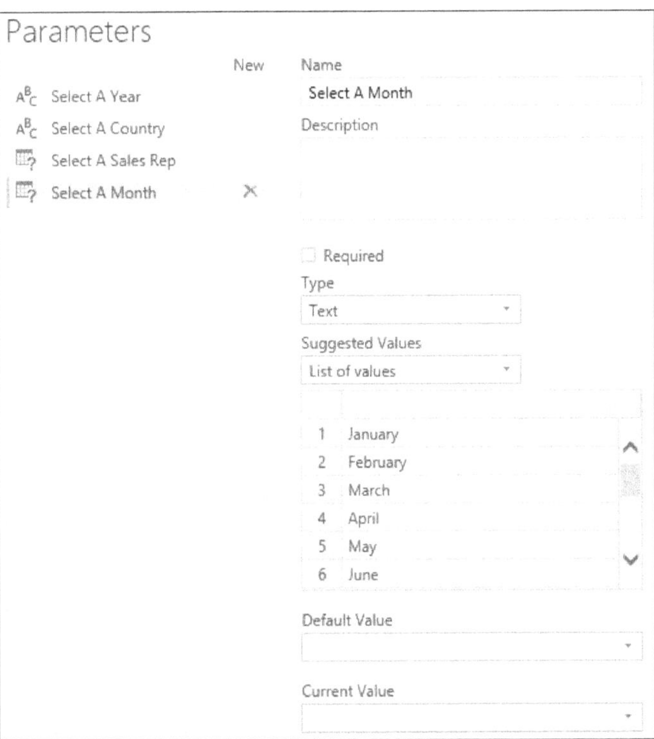

Figure 13-48 Select A Month parameter options

2. On the Queries panel, move the Select A Month parameter up above the Country parameter ⇒ Move the Country parameter to the bottom of the list of parameters.
3. Load the parameter to the data model and apply the changes.

Create The Filter

1. Display the Parameter Orders query.
2. Display the Filter Rows dialog box for the Order Year column ⇒ Select the Advanced option.

3. Create the filter criteria shown in Figure 13-49.

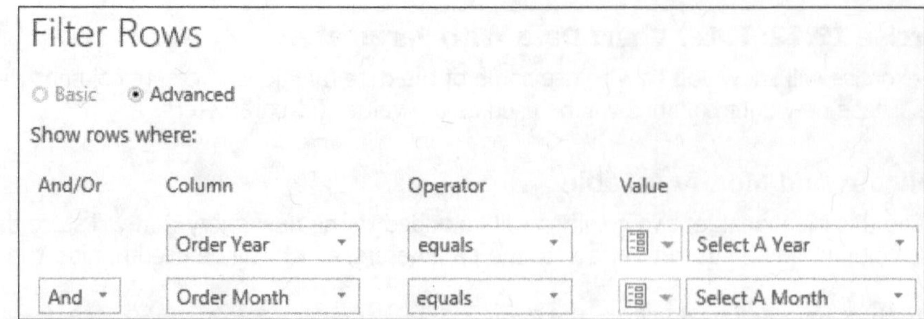

Figure 13-49 Parameter filter criteria

Create The Relationship For The Parameter Orders Table

The Parameter Orders table needs to be linked to the Dates table, so that the year and month columns on the Parameter Orders table can be used to filter the data.

1. Report view ⇒ Home tab ⇒ Manage Relationships button ⇒ Click the New button.

2. Select the Parameter Orders table ⇒ Select the Dates Table.

3. Click on the Order Date column in the Parameter Orders table ⇒ Click on the Date Key column in the Dates Table ⇒ Click OK ⇒ Save the changes.

Create The Chart

1. Add the Clustered column chart to the page.

2. Add the following fields to the chart.

   ☑ Add the Year field to the Axis section
   ☑ Add the Sales Rep to the Legend section
   ☑ Add the Order Amount field in the Parameter Orders table to the Value section

3. Change the following formatting options.

   ☑ X-Axis ⇒ Type ⇒ Categorical
   ☑ Data labels ⇒ On
   ☑ Data labels ⇒ Display units ⇒ Thousands
   ☑ Data labels ⇒ Decimal Places ⇒ 0

4. Make the chart the size of the page.

5. Home tab ⇒ Edit Queries button ⇒ Edit Parameters ⇒ Select the options shown in Figure 13-50.

   These options will filter the chart to only display orders for all sales reps in September 2014.

Enter Parameters

Select A Year
2014

Select A Month
September

Select A Sales Rep

Select A Country

Figure 13-50 Parameters for the chart

6. Click OK ⇒
   Click the Apply Changes button.

   The total order amount per sales rep in September 2014 will be displayed, as shown in Figure 13-51.

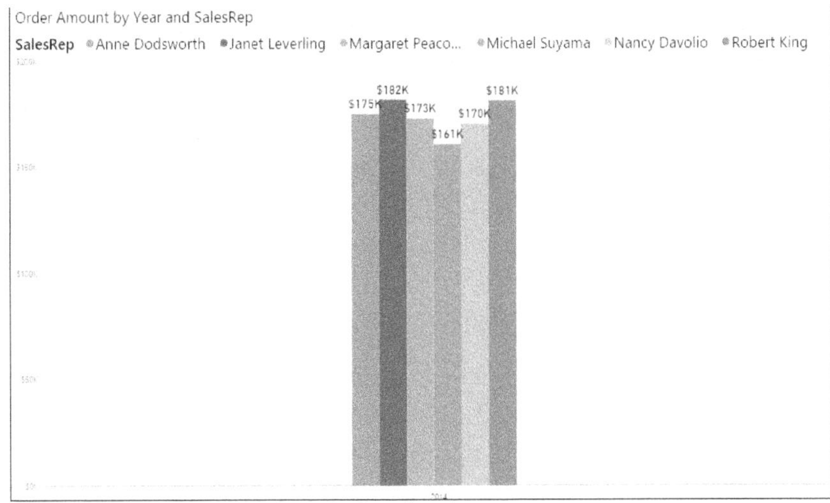

Figure 13-51 Parameters applied to the chart

Exercise 13.13: Import More Data

In this exercise you will import tables of data that are needed for the remaining chart exercises in this chapter. The goal for this data is explained in the Viewing Data In A Spreadsheet section.

1. Import the five tables that start with 01 in the More Data Files workbook.

2. Save the changes.

Modify The Balance Sheet Table

1. In the Data view, change the following formatting options for the Cash, Inventory and Receivables columns.

   ☑ Data Type = Fixed Decimal Number
   ☑ Format = Currency ⇒ $English (United States)

Modify The Financial Data Table

The two Line and column combination charts that are created later in this chapter need some date fields to be formatted differently. Figure 13-52 shows how the Order, Required and Ship Date fields are currently formatted. The format will be changed to match what is in the Dates Table.

Order Date	Required Date	Ship Date
February 27, 2013	March 10, 2013	February 27, 2013
February 27, 2013	March 09, 2013	March 06, 2013
December 16, 2013	December 28, 2013	December 25, 2013
December 16, 2013	December 25, 2013	December 18, 2013

Figure 13-52 Date columns before the formatting is changed

1. Click on the Order Date column ⇒
   Modeling tab ⇒
   Format button ⇒ Date Time ⇒
   Select the format illustrated in Figure 13-53.

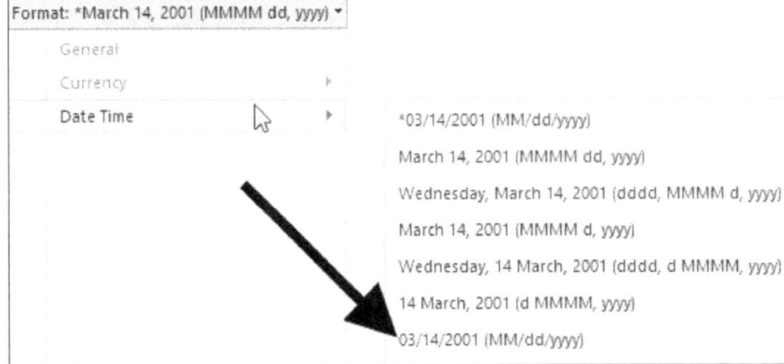

Figure 13-53 Date format illustrated

2. Repeat the step above for the Required Date and Ship Date fields.

   The fields should now look like the ones shown in Figure 13-54.

Order Date	Required Date	Ship Date
02/27/2013	03/10/2013	02/27/2013
02/27/2013	03/09/2013	03/06/2013
12/16/2013	12/28/2013	12/25/2013
12/16/2013	12/25/2013	12/18/2013
12/27/2013	01/07/2014	01/04/2014

Figure 13-54 Formatting changed for the date fields

3. Select the Order ID field ⇒ Change the Default Summarization option to Do Not Summarize.

4. Change the following formatting options for the Order Amount, Net Sales, Net Manager, Direct Costs and Sales Costs columns.

   ☑ Data Type = Fixed Decimal Number
   ☑ Format = Currency ⇒ $English (United States), no decimal places

Modify The Months On Market Table

1. Apply currency formatting with no decimal places to the Asking Price column.

Modify The Online vs Mail Order Table

1. Apply currency formatting with no decimal places to the Online and Mail Order columns.

Modify The Sales vs Market Growth Table

1. Change the Default Summarization option to Do Not Summarize for the Year column.

2. Change the Default Summarization option to Sum, for all of the Growth and Region columns.

Create The Relationship With The Dates Table

A relationship needs to be created between the Financial Data table and the My Date Table, so that fields in the latter can be used to create charts.

1. Click the Manage Relationships button ⇒ Delete all relationships for any of the tables that start with the prefix 01, because these tables were designed to be stand alone tables.

2. Click the New button ⇒ Select the 01 Financial Data table in the first drop-down list ⇒ Select the My Date Table in the second drop-down list.

3. Click on the Order Date and Date Key columns ⇒ Click OK ⇒ Click Close.

Multiple Series Of Data Formatting Options

The formatting options covered in this section are available when the chart displays more than one series of data, by adding more than one field to the Value section in the Field Well.

X-Axis Options

The options shown in Figure 13-55 are used to customize the values on the X-Axis.

The **TYPE OPTION** is used to select between **CONTINUOUS** (the values on the Axis change all the time and the number of different values can't be counted) and **CATEGORICAL** (is used to display a small number of categories. Age group is an example).

The following options shown in the figure, are removed when the Type option is set to Categorical: Scale type, Start, End, Display units and Decimal Places.

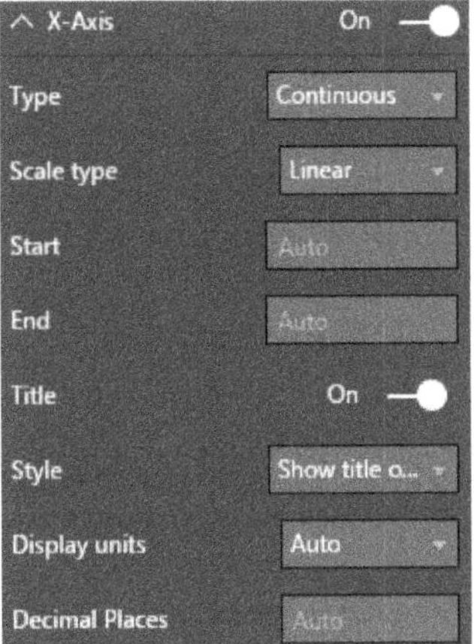

Figure 13-55 X-Axis options

Data Labels Options

If the **CUSTOMIZE SERIES OPTION** shown in Figure 13-56 is enabled, each series of data can be customized individually.

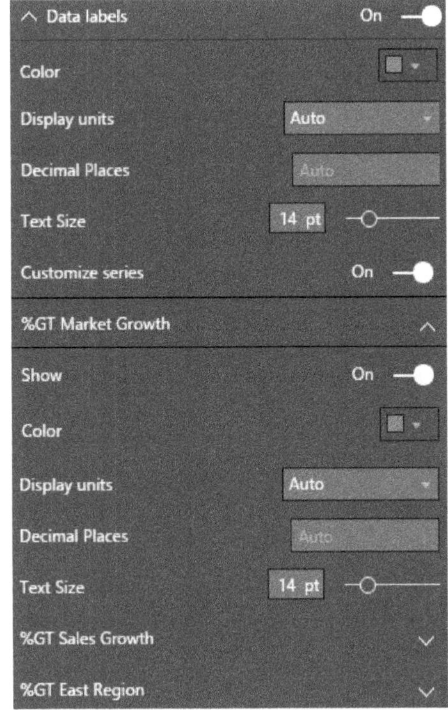

Figure 13-56 Data Labels options for multiple series of data

Viewing Data In A Spreadsheet

The goal of the remaining exercises in this chapter is to show what some of the raw data looks in a spreadsheet, that will be used to create a chart. The reason that I am doing this is because I think that a large percent of people using Power BI Desktop are importing data from spreadsheets. Often, being able to see the data in a layout that you are familiar with, helps make understanding how to create charts easier.

Keep in mind that the layout that the data is currently in, may not be in the correct layout to create charts, when it is imported into Power BI Desktop. The import will work, but trying to create a chart based on the layout may not work. As you have seen earlier in this book, you may have to change the layout, once the data is imported, so that it can be used to create charts. Hopefully, by seeing the data, the layout of the chart will be clearer.

Exercise 13.14: Display Multiple Series Of Data In Percent Format

Displaying multiple series of data on a chart is a way to compare data.

In this exercise you will create a chart that displays two series of data: Market growth and Sales growth. Figure 13-57 shows the data that will be used to create the chart.

	A	B	C	D	E
1	**Year**	**Market Growth**	**Sales Growth**	**East Region**	**West Region**
2	2009	7.00%	8.00%	4.00%	9.00%
3	2010	5.00%	11.00%	5.00%	11.00%
4	2011	8.00%	10.00%	9.00%	10.00%
5	2012	2.50%	13.00%	3.00%	3.00%
6	2013	7.00%	9.00%	8.00%	9.00%
7	2014	5.00%	7.00%	6.00%	7.00%
8	2015	5.00%	6.00%	5.00%	3.00%
9	2016	3.50%	5.00%	3.50%	4.00%

Figure 13-57 Data for a chart that uses multiple series of data

Often, when doing analysis, you need to see what percent a value is of the whole. Stacked column charts allow multiple series of data to be displayed in a readable layout.

1. Add the Stacked Column chart to the page.

2. Display the fields in the 01 Sales vs Market Growth table ⇒ Add the following fields to the Value section: Market Growth, Sales Growth, East Region and West Region.

3. Add the Year field to the Axis section.

Create The Percent Calculations

If the fields were going to always be used or displayed as a percent, you could change the display formatting to percent. When that is not the case, the fields need to be formatted on a chart by chart basis.

1. Use Quick Calc to create the percent calculation shown in Figure 13-58 for each of the fields in the Value section.

   The percent formula that will be created is for the percent of the category (the field, Market Growth, East Region, etc, not the Year column).

Figure 13-58 Percent calculation options

Format The Chart

1. Display the data labels.

   The chart should look like the one shown in Figure 13-59.

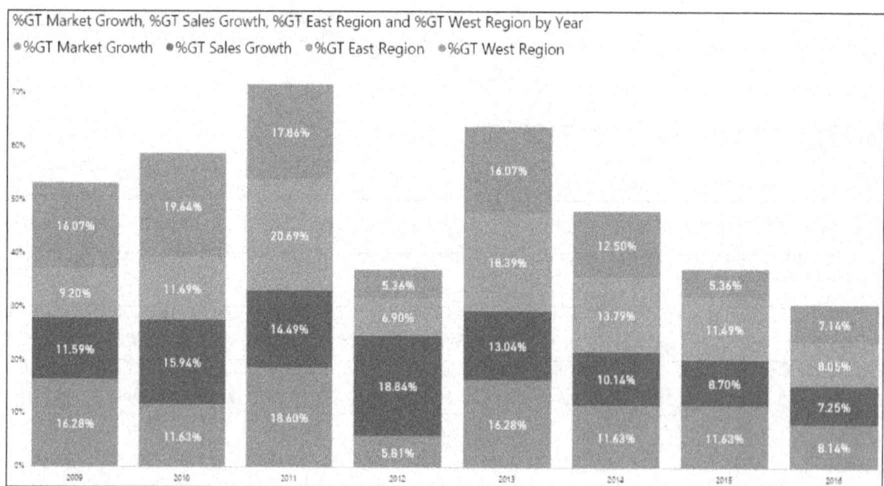

Figure 13-59 Stacked Column chart with percents and four series of data

Exercise 13.15: Display Two Series Of Data On An Area Chart

Earlier in this chapter you learned how to create a basic area chart. Like the percent chart created in the previous exercise, often, there is a need to display more than one series of data on a chart.

The area chart that you will create in this exercise will display two series of data: Online and Mail Order. Some of the data is shown in Figure 13-60.

	A	B	C
1	**Customer Name**	**Online**	**Mail Order**
2	Psycho-Cycle	$52,809	$82,809
3	The Great Bike Shop	$15,218	$55,218
		⋮	
14	Fred's Bikes	$7,874	$874
15	Phil's Bikes	$27	$15,927

Figure 13-60 Data for an Area chart

1. Add the Area chart to the page ⇒ Display the fields in the 01 Online vs Mail Order table.

2. Add the Mail Order and Online fields to the Values section.

3. Add the Customer Name field to the Axis section.

4. Enable the Y-Axis Title option.

   The chart should look like the one shown in Figure 13-61.

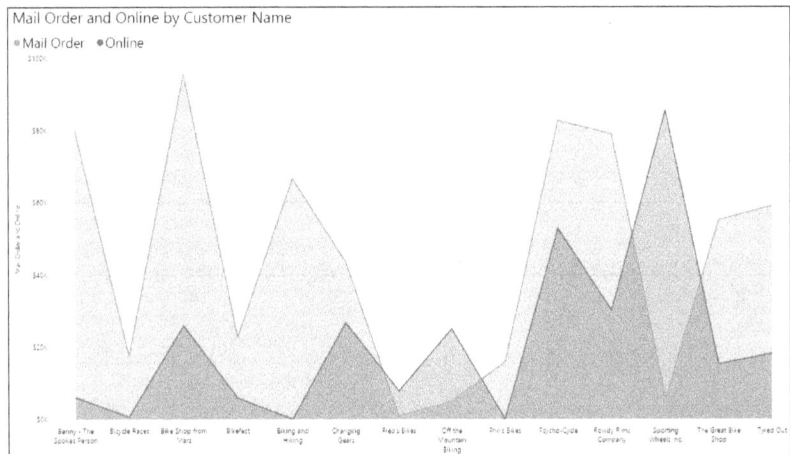

Figure 13-61 Area chart with multiple series of data (Y-Axis Scale type is Linear)

Figure 13-62 shows the same chart, as the one shown above in Figure 13-61.

The difference is that this chart has the Y-Axis scale type set to **LOG**.

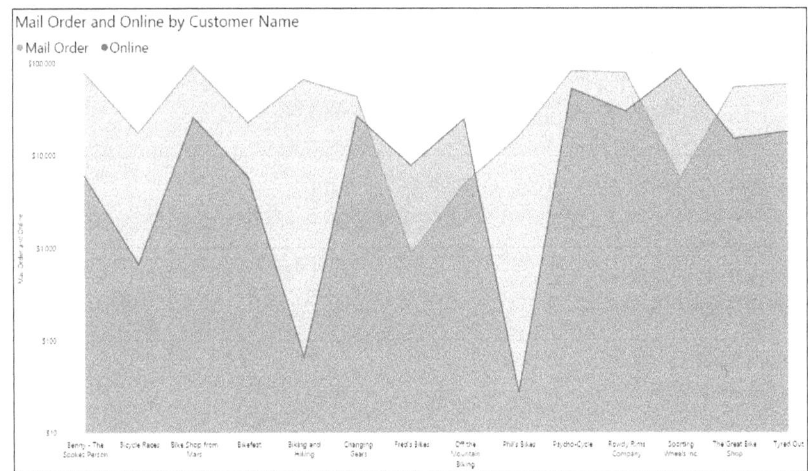

Figure 13-62 Area chart with multiple series of data (Y-Axis Scale type is Log)

Figure 13-63 shows the same values (as the chart in Figure 13-61) displayed using a Stacked Area chart.

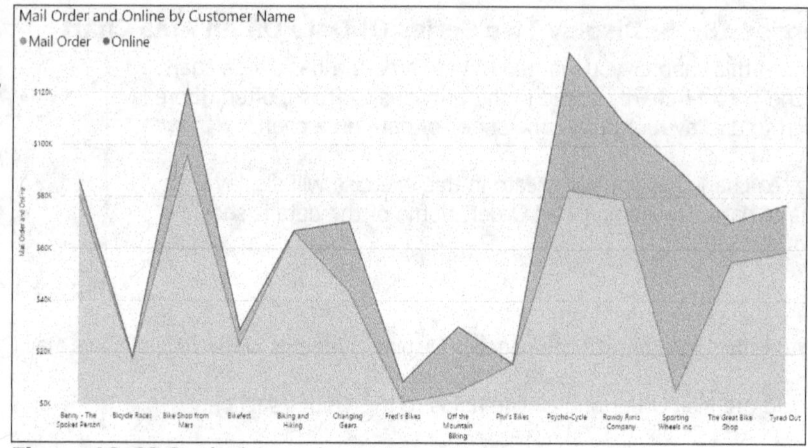

Figure 13-63 Stacked Area chart with multiple series of data

Exercise 13.16: Display Homes For Sale Data On A Bubble Chart

In this exercise you will create a bubble chart that will display how long homes have been on the market. Figure 13-64 shows the data for this exercise.

Bubble charts require numeric data for three axes, which are explained below.

The **X AXIS** will display the number of months that each home has been on the market.

The **Y AXIS** will display the asking price of the home.

The **SIZE** (also known as the **Z AXIS**) is used to calculate the size of the bubble for each column of data.

	A	B	C
1	**Months On Market**	**Asking Price**	**Qty**
2	35	$355,000	78
3	12	$160,000	19
4	6	$150,000	89
5	25	$400,000	36
6	28	$210,000	100
7	8	$175,000	47
8	22	$360,000	51
9	15	$223,000	22
10	33	$316,000	53
11	10	$500,000	10
12	8	$429,000	44
13	4	$279,900	77

Figure 13-64 Bubble chart data

1. Display the fields in the 01 Months On Market table ⇒ Add the Scatter chart to the page.

2. Add the following fields to the chart.

   ☑ Add the Months On Market field to the X Axis section
   ☑ Add the Asking Price field to the Y Axis section
   ☑ Add the Qty field to the Size section
   ☑ Add the Months On Market field to the Details section

3. Enable the Category labels formatting option.

   The chart should look like the one shown in Figure 13-65.

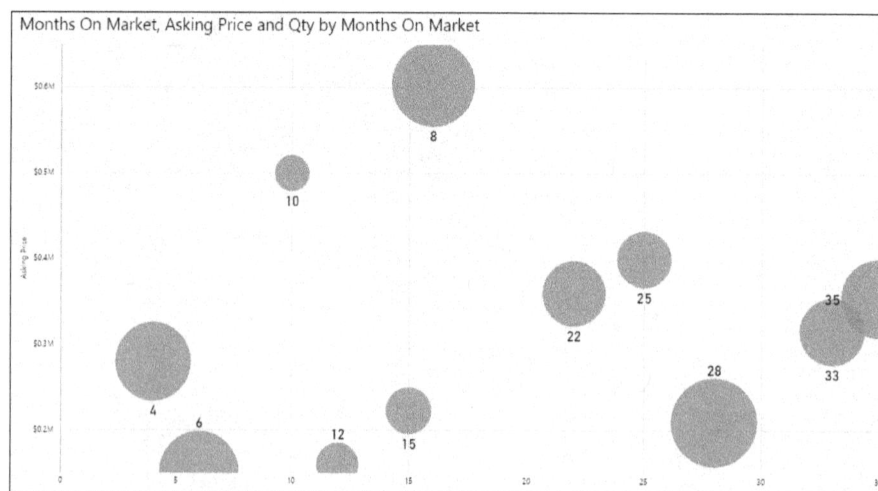

Figure 13-65 Bubble chart

Exercise 13.17: Display Balance Sheet Data On A Stacked Column Chart

Figure 13-66 shows a section of a yearly balance sheet. Figure 13-67 shows the same data in a layout that will work better in Power BI Desktop.

	A	B	C	D	E	F	G	H	I	J	K	L	M
1						**Balance Sheet**							
2						*Current Assets, Income & Expenses*							
3													
4		January	February	March	April	May	June	July	August	September	October	November	December
5													
6	**Current Assets**												
7	Cash	17580	12100	74770	44425	74770	17580	44425	12500	343434	17580	74770	17580
8	Inventory	31783	45700	21006	12230	21006	37874	12230	45700	12230	31783	21750	31783
9	Receivables	59560	27500	54321	34567	54321	59560	44567	27500	34567	12345	54321	59560

Figure 13-66 Section of a balance sheet

This exercise will show you how to display the balance sheet data shown in Figure 13-66, on a Stacked Column chart.

	A	B	C	D
1	**Month**	**Cash**	**Inventory**	**Receivables**
2	January	$17,580	$31,783	$59,560
3	February	$12,100	$45,700	$27,500
4	March	$74,770	$21,006	$54,321
5	April	$44,425	$12,230	$34,567
6	May	$74,770	$21,006	$54,321
7	June	$17,580	$37,874	$59,560
8	July	$44,425	$12,230	$44,567
9	August	$12,500	$45,700	$27,500
10	September	$343,434	$12,230	$34,567
11	October	$17,580	$31,783	$12,345
12	November	$74,770	$21,750	$54,321
13	December	$17,580	$31,783	$59,560

Figure 13-67 Same balance sheet data that is shown above in Figure 13-66

1. Display the 01 Balance Sheet table ⇒ Add the Stacked Column chart to the page.
2. Add the Cash, Inventory and Receivables fields to the Value section.
3. Add the Month Name field to the Axis section.
4. Display the Y-Axis title.
5. Display the data labels.

   The chart should look like the one shown in Figure 13-68.

   As you can see, the months are not in calendar order.

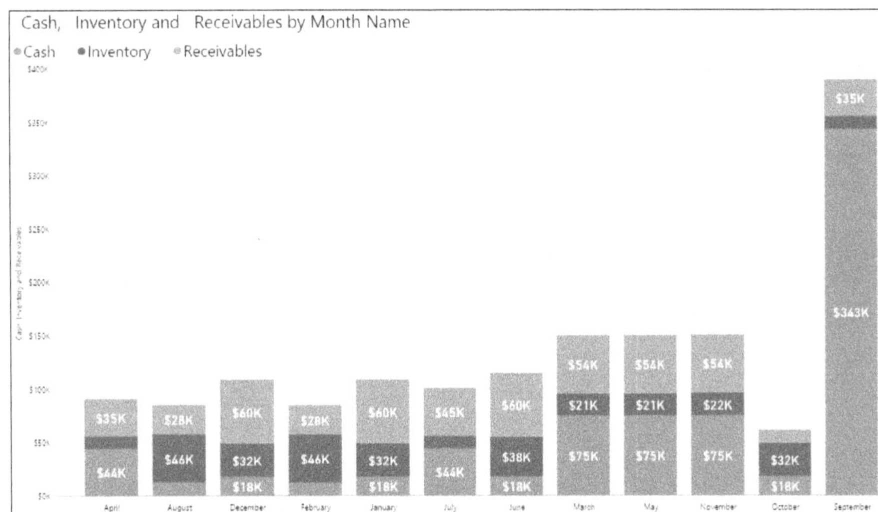

Figure 13-68 Balance sheet data displayed on a chart

Fix The Month Order

There is more than one way to force the months to appear in calendar month order. The easiest way, with the data in the Balance Sheet table, is to create an Index column.

1. Display the 01 Balance Sheet table in the Query Editor.

2. Add Column tab ⇒ Add Index Column button ⇒ From 1.

   The reason this will work is because the months in the table are in calendar month order. If they weren't, you would either have to go back to the data source and type the index numbers in manually, or use or create a field in the Dates Table that would cause the months to display in the order that you need.

   The next task is to sort the Month field in order, by the Index number.

3. Display the Balance Sheet table in the Data view.

4. Click on the Month Name column ⇒ Modeling tab ⇒ Sort By Column button ⇒ Select the Index field ⇒ Save the changes. The months should be sorted in calendar month order, as shown in Figure 13-69.

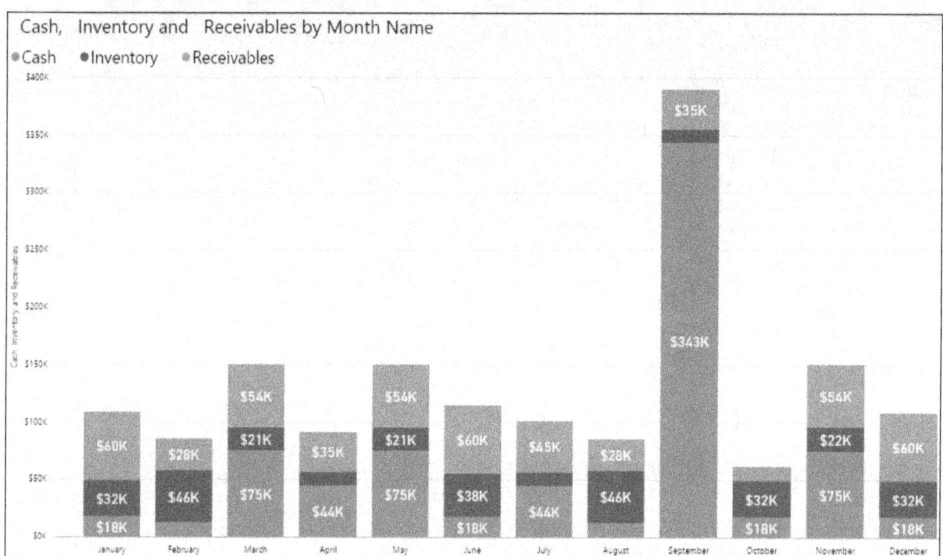

Figure 13-69 Months sorted in calendar month order

Combined Line Charts

There are two combined line chart options:

☑ Line and Stacked Column
☑ Line and Clustered Column

These chart types display a line chart and a column chart on the same chart. These charts display changes and the magnitude of the change over time.

Dual Axis Charts Tip
The Line and Stacked column chart and the Line and Clustered column chart share the X Axis values.

Line And Column Chart Field Well

Figure 13-70 shows the options used to create either dual axis chart type.

The **SHARED AXIS OPTION** is used to place values on the X axis.

The **COLUMN SERIES OPTION** is used to sub-divide the column values.

The **COLUMN VALUES OPTION** is used to select the fields that will be used to create the columns on the chart. Each field that is added to this section will be stacked on the column.

The **LINE VALUES OPTION** is used to select the fields that will be used to create the line chart. Each field that is added to this option will have its own line chart.

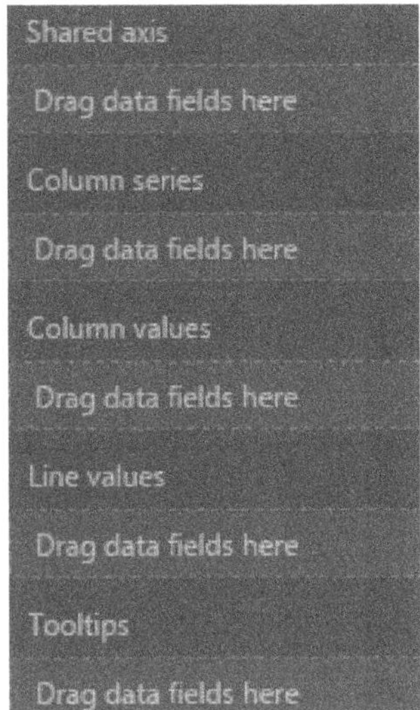

Figure 13-70 Line and column chart Field Well

Line And Column Chart Formatting Options

The options covered in this section are either unique to this chart type or function differently with this chart type.

Y-Axis Options

Figure 13-71 shows the Y-Axis options. These options format the column and line chart values on the Y-axis.

The options in the **Y-AXIS (COLUMN)** section are used to customize the Y-Axis for the column (the field(s) in the Column Values section).

The **SHOW SECONDARY OPTION** by default, displays a scale on the right side of the chart. (2)

The options in the **Y-AXIS (LINE)** section are used to customize the Y-Axis for the Line chart. (2)

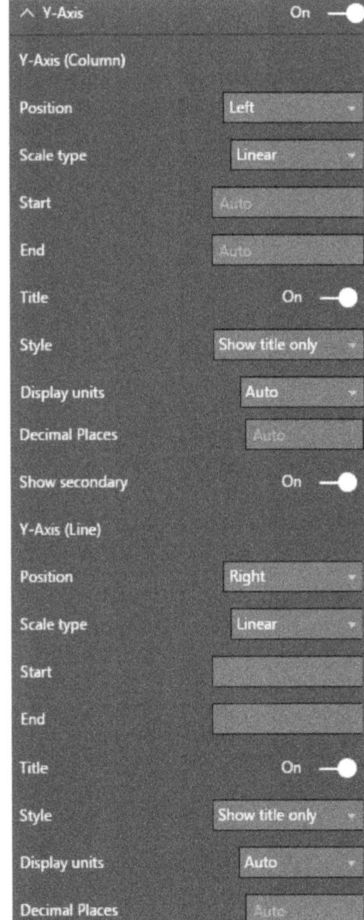

Figure 13-71 Y-Axis options

(2) This option uses the field in the Line values section on the Field Well.

Data Colors

The options in this section are used to select a color for each field in the Column values section.

Data Labels Options

Figure 13-72 shows the options for the data labels.

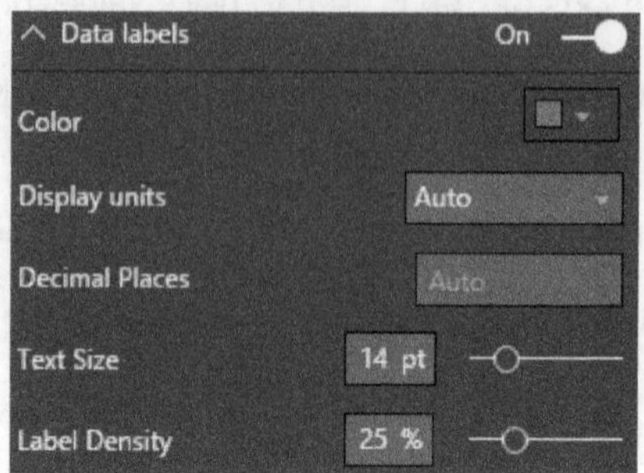

Figure 13-72 Data labels options

The **LABEL DENSITY OPTION** is used to select where the line chart data labels are placed. The higher the percent, the closer the labels are placed to the line.

Figure 13-73 illustrates the label placement when the label density is set to 25%.

Figure 13-74 illustrates the label placement when the label density is set to 100%.

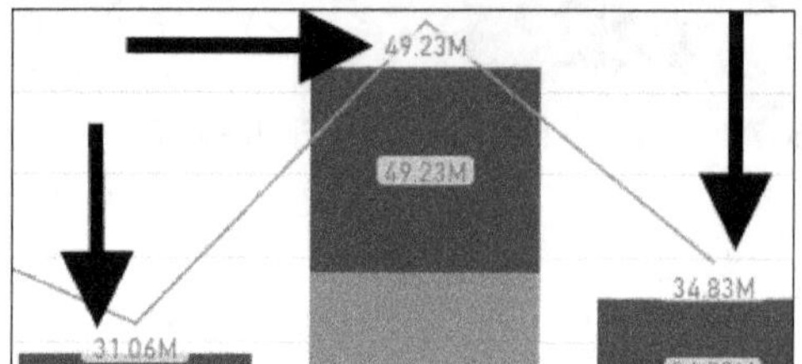

Figure 13-73 Label Density option set to 25%

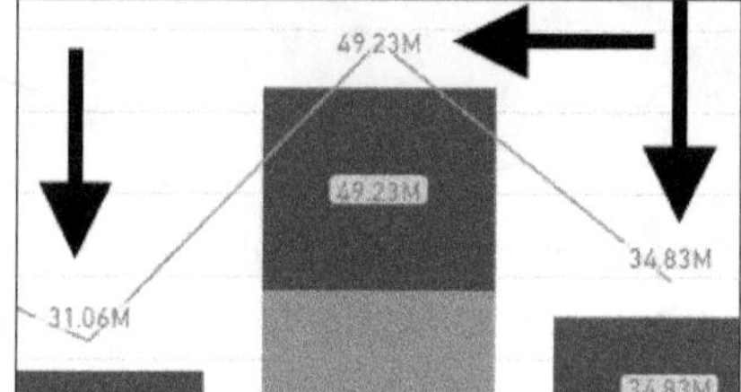

Figure 13-74 Label Density option set to 100%

Exercise 13.18: Create A Line And Stacked Column Chart

This exercise will show you how to create a chart that displays the Net Sales and Net Margin costs by year, using a combination chart. This type of chart makes it easy to see the correlation between the two series of data.

1. Display the 01 Financial Data table ⇒ Add the Line and Stacked Column chart to the page.
2. Add the following fields to create the chart.

   ☑ Add the Net Sales and Net Margin fields to the Column values section
   ☑ Add the Full Year field, in the MyDateTable, to the Shared axis section
   ☑ Add the Net Margin field to the Line values section

3. Display the data labels.

   The chart should look like the one shown in Figure 13-75.

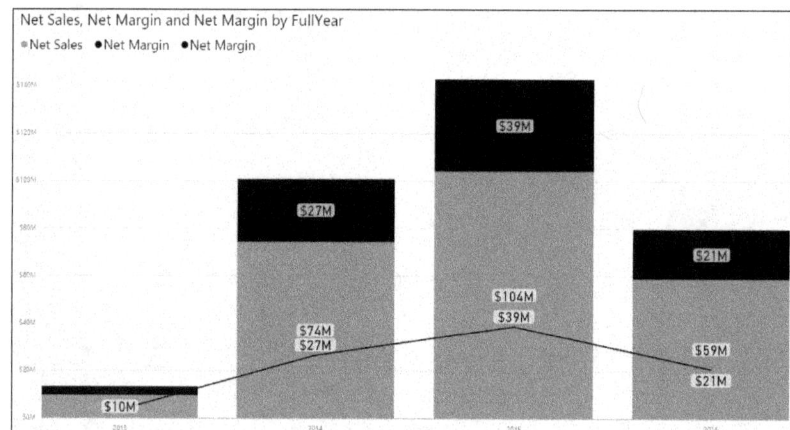

Figure 13-75 Combined Column Line chart

Line And Clustered Column Chart Analytics Options

Analytics are only available for this chart type if the Type X-Axis formatting option is set to Continuous.

Figure 13-76 shows the Trend Line options. The options that are unique for this chart type is explained below.

If the **COMBINE SERIES OPTION** is enabled, all of the trend lines will be combined into one trend line.

The **USE HIGHLIGHT VALUES OPTION** doesn't seem to change anything on the chart.

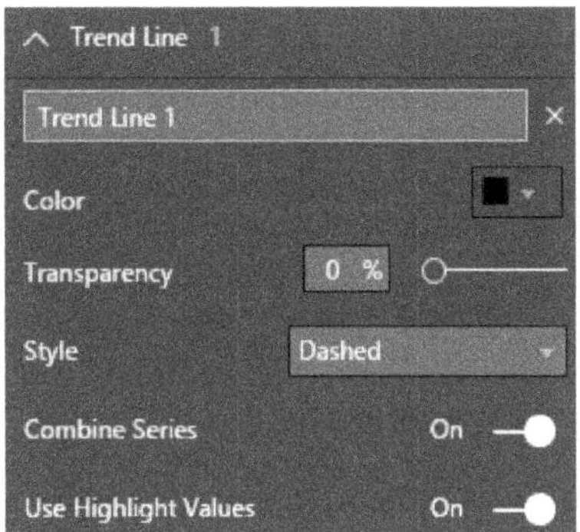

Figure 13-76 Trend Line options

Exercise 13.19: Create A Line And Clustered Column Chart

This exercise will show you how to create a combined column line chart with two Y axes, that will display two series of data (sales and direct costs) to see the correlation, if any.

1. Display the 01 Financial Data table ⇒ Add the Line and Clustered Column chart to the page.
2. Add the Sales Costs and Direct Costs fields to the Column values section.
3. Add the Quarter And Year Abbr field, in the MyDateTable, to the Shared axis section.
4. Add the Net Sales field to the Line values section. The chart should look like the one shown in Figure 13-77.

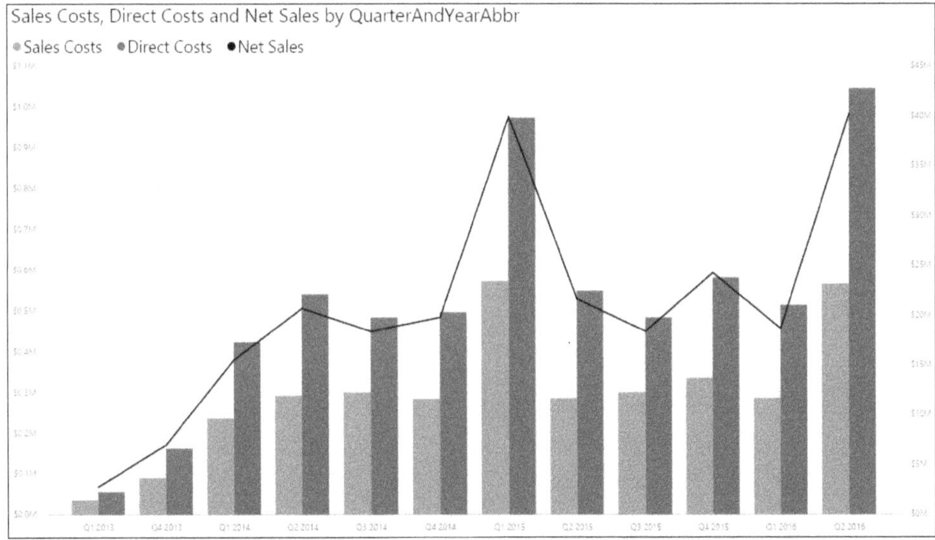

Figure 13-77 Sales and direct costs combined column line chart

Summary

In this chapter you learned how to create combination, line, area, scatter and bubble charts. Partial data sets were displayed for some exercises, so that you could see the data that creates the chart. The goal was to get you to look at the data before creating the visualization. Parameters were created and used on the Filter Rows dialog box. This is one place where parameters are very helpful.

The Analytics panel was also covered. The options on this panel are used to display a variety of reference or trend lines on a chart. Displaying trend lines, gives the charts the appearance of being a combination chart.

Did you think that there were so many ways to display data from the same seven tables <smile>. Adding drill down functionality to a chart enables a user to slice and dice the data, to display the view of the data that they need.

Trying To Display Too Much Data
Yes, it is possible that the combination of fields added to a chart will cause more data to be generated then what can be displayed. When that is the case, you will see the icon illustrated in Figure 13-78, in the upper left corner of the visualizations frame. Holding the mouse pointer over the icon, displays the message shown in the figure. One solution may be to create a filter to reduce the number of values being displayed or modify an existing filter for the chart.

Figure 13-78 Too much data message

CHARTS, MAPS AND CUSTOM VISUALS

After reading this chapter and completing the exercises you will be able to:

- ☑ Use more chart types
- ☑ Create a chart that uses a key performance indicator (KPI)
- ☑ Display data on maps
- ☑ Filter the data displayed on a map
- ☑ Use custom visuals

CHAPTER 14

Pie Charts

Pie charts are well suited for displaying small amounts of positive data. As you will see, each slice of a pie chart by default, is a different color. Each slice represents a percent of the data displayed on the chart. When percents need to be displayed on a chart, a pie chart is a good option.

Pie Chart Formatting Options

The options covered in this section are unique to pie charts.

Detail Labels Options

The options shown in Figure 14-1 are used to customize the labels displayed on the pie chart.

The **LABEL STYLE OPTION** can display the value in the field in the Legend section of the Field Well (the category), the data value (the sum of the field in the Values section) or both.

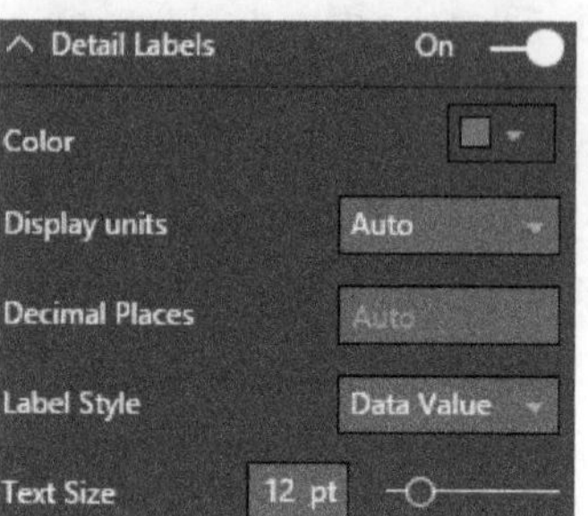

Figure 14-1 Detail labels options

Exercise 14.1: Create A Pie Chart To Display A Count Of Orders By Customer Type

1. Save the Report Data.pbix file as `Chapter 14 Charts and Custom Visuals.`
2. Add the Pie chart to the page.
3. Add the Customer Type field to the Legend section ⇒ Add the Order ID field to the Values section.
4. Display the legend on the right.

   The chart should look like the one shown in Figure 14-2.

   Notice the (Blank) option in the legend and on the chart.

   That means that currently all records in the Customer table have data in the Customer Type field.

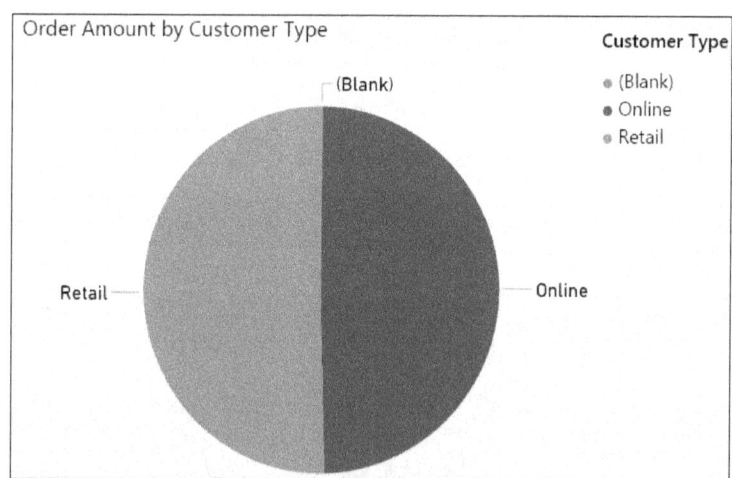

Figure 14-2 Pie chart

Using The Legend To Highlight Data
Clicking on an option in the legend, highlights the corresponding part(s) on the chart and disables the other parts of the chart. To clear the highlighting, click on a blank space on the page.

How Pie Charts Are Sorted

It is difficult to know how the data is sorted, on a pie chart.

Figure 14-3 shows a pie chart sorted on the Order Amount field, in descending order. The largest value is at the top of the chart.

The highest value (if sorted in ascending order) or the lowest value (if sorted in descending order) starts at the top of the pie chart.

The first entry in the legend denotes the "top" of the chart and continues clockwise with the next value.

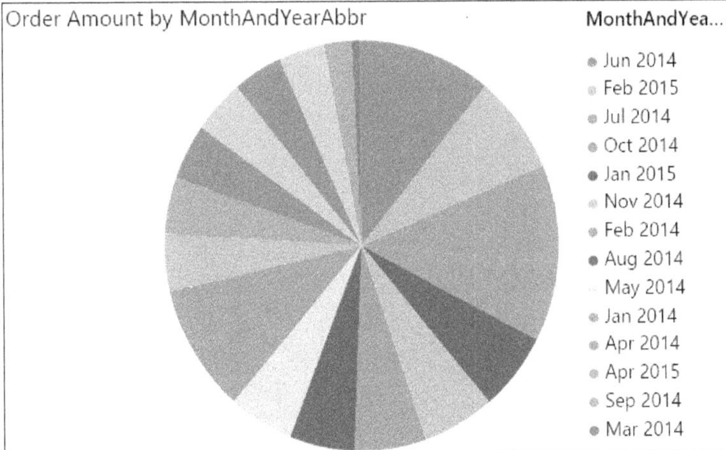

Figure 14-3 Pie chart sorted in descending order

If the Detail Labels options shown earlier in Figure 14-1 were enabled, each slice of the pie chart would display a value, as shown in Figure 14-4.

This would make the chart easier to understand.

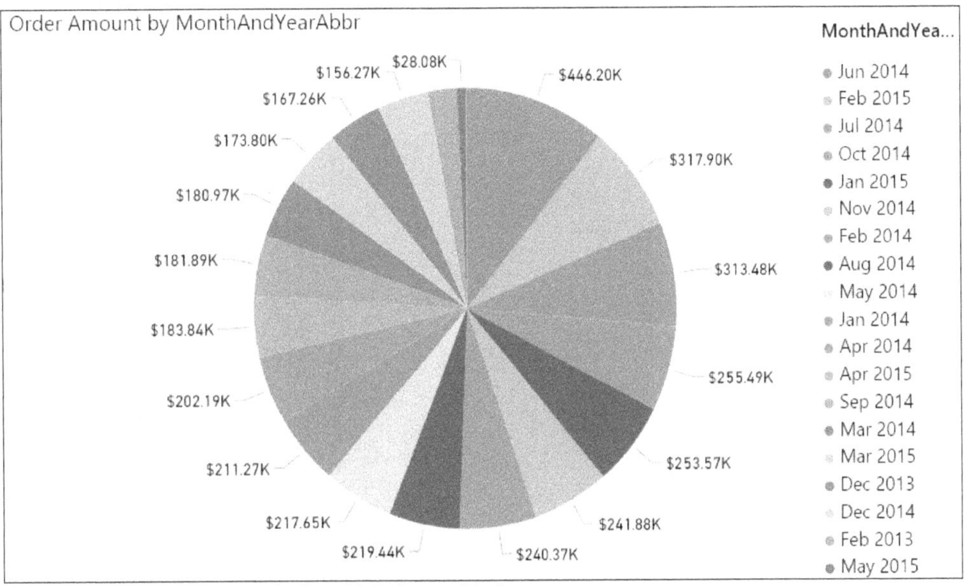

Figure 14-4 Pie chart with detail labels enabled

Missing Values In Pie Charts
It has been reported that Pie charts do not always display the smallest values on the chart.

Exercise 14.2: Use A Hierarchy Field To Create A Pie Chart

In this exercise you will create a chart that displays the order totals in 2014, by quarter.

1. Add the Pie chart to the page.
2. From the Dates Table, add the Select Quarter hierarchy field ⇒ Delete the Select Year field from the Legend section.
3. Add the Order Amount field to the Values section.
4. Create a filter to only display orders in 2014.
5. Enable the legend.

6. Enable the Detail Labels option ⇒

   Change the **LABEL STYLE** to Both ⇒

   Change the Text Size to 14.

   The chart should look like the one shown in Figure 14-5.

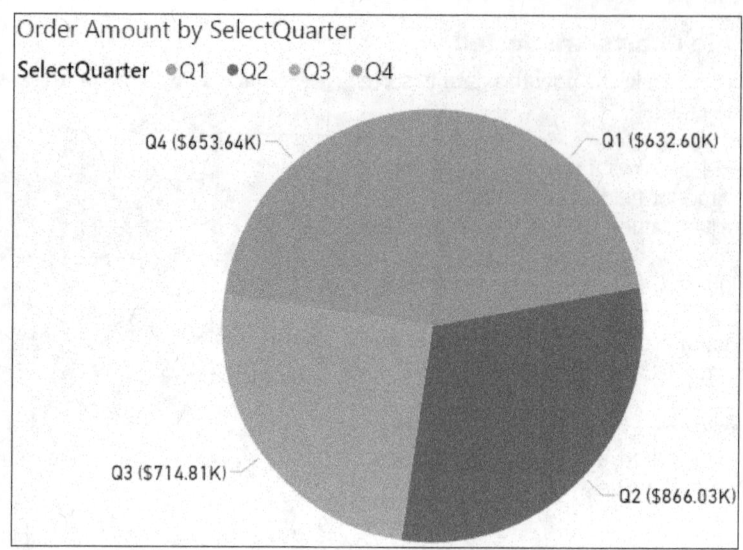

Figure 14-5 Pie chart created with a hierarchy field

Using the Quarter and Year field, instead of the Select Quarter hierarchy field, changes the values displayed in the legend, as shown in Figure 14-6.

The Quarter and Year field makes it easy to know what year and quarter the data displayed on the chart is for.

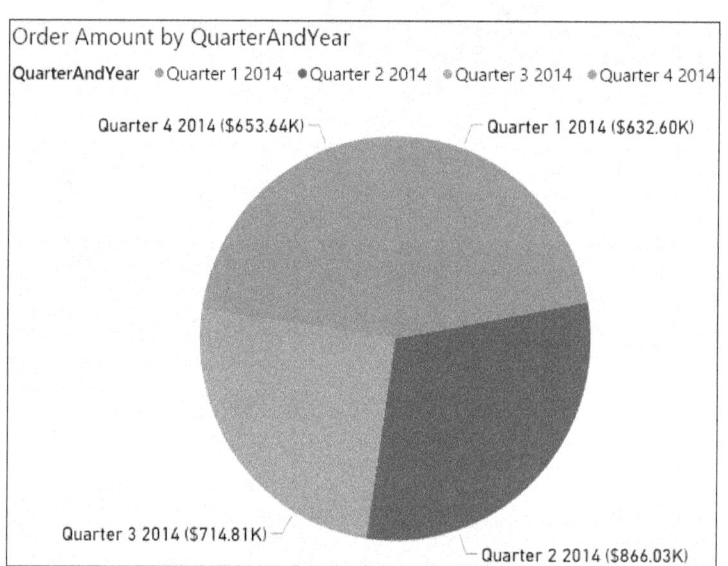

Figure 14-6 Pie chart displaying the Quarter and Year field in the legend

Handling Negative Values In Pie, Donut And Funnel Charts

Figure 14-7 shows a spreadsheet with the gross margin amount for each company. As you can see, some of the values are negative numbers.

A	B
Company	Gross Margin
company a	23
company b	62
company c	-20
company d	-54
company e	20
company f	40
company g	-60
company h	-57

Figure 14-7 Spreadsheet of data

Figure 14-8 shows the data displayed as a pie chart. Notice the message above the pie chart, that states that pie charts do not support negative values. While not obvious, the pie chart displays four values, but the legend has eight entries.

That is an indication that something is wrong, even if a message was not displayed. If you do not want to display negative values, create a filter that checks to see if the value in the field is greater than or equal to zero. Doing that removes the legend entries for records that have negative data. It would be a good idea to add a comment to the page, that indicates that negative values are not displayed on the chart.

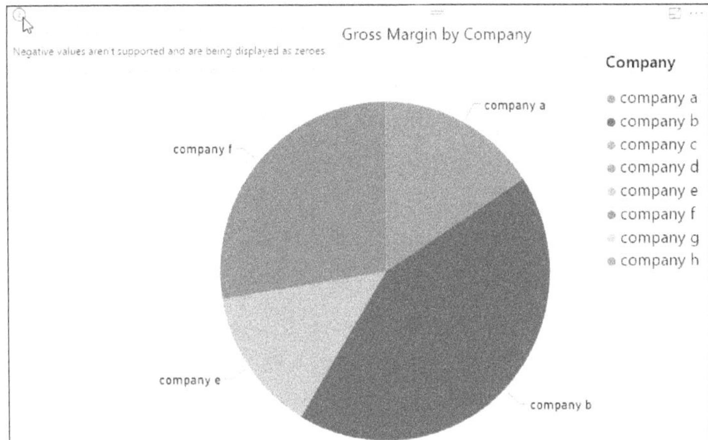

Figure 14-8 Pie chart based on data with negative values

Figure 14-9 shows the same data displayed on a Stacked Column chart.

Notice that the values on the Y axis display negative values and that the records that have negative values are displayed below the $0 marker.

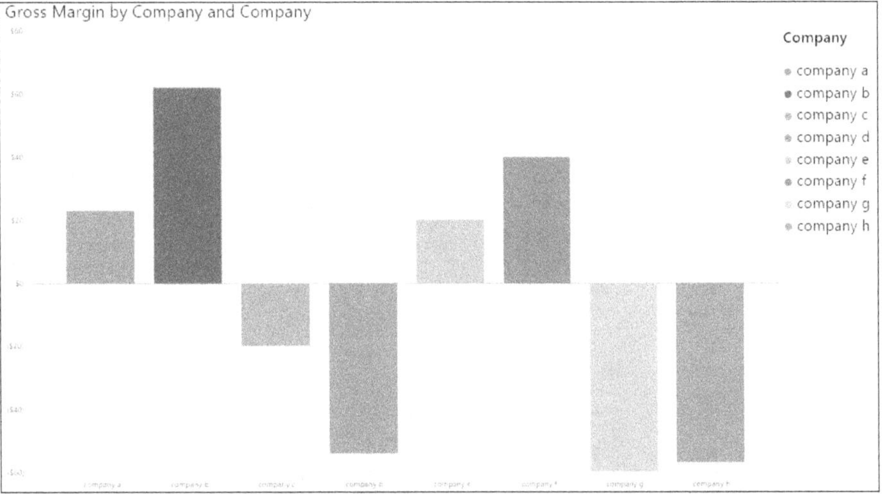

Figure 14-9 Stacked Column chart displaying negative data

Exercise 14.3: Create A Donut Chart

In this exercise, you will create a chart that displays the Order Amount by Month and Year.

1. Add the Donut chart to the page.
2. Add the Month And Year Abbr field to the Legend section.
3. Add the Order Amount field to the Values section.
4. Display the legend on the right side of the chart.
5. Display the Detail labels ⇒ Set the Label Style option to **DATA VALUE**.
6. Sort the chart by the Order Amount field. The chart should look like the one shown in Figure 14-10.
   In the lower right corner, below the legend is an arrow. It indicates that there are more values in the legend. Clicking this button will display more values in the legend.

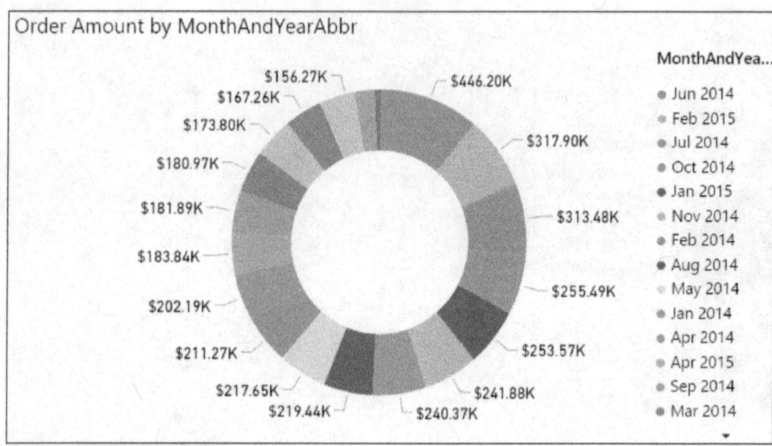

Figure 14-10 Donut chart

Funnel Chart Field Well

Figure 14-11 shows the field options.

The **GROUP OPTION** is used to select the field that will create the rings on the Funnel chart.

The **COLOR SATURATION OPTION** is used to select a value that will determine the color of the data points.

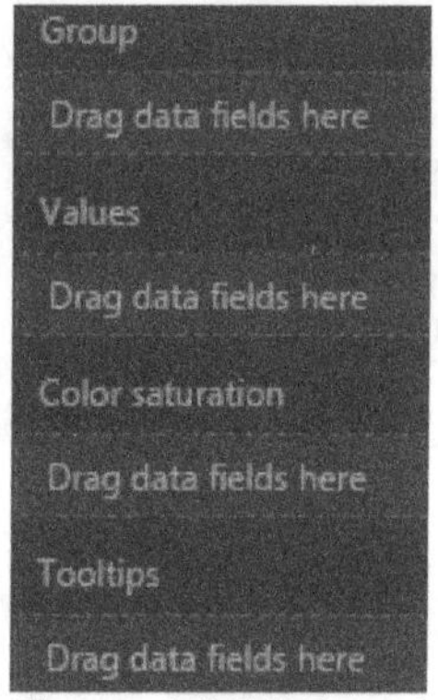

Figure 14-11 Funnel chart Field Well

Funnel Chart Formatting Options

Funnel charts do not have legend formatting options like some other charts have. The values that would go in the legend are automatically displayed on the left side of the funnel.

Data Labels Options

The majority of options shown in Figure 14-12 are the same as the Data Label options for other chart types.

The **POSITION OPTION** is used to select where the data values are placed, on each bar of the funnel.

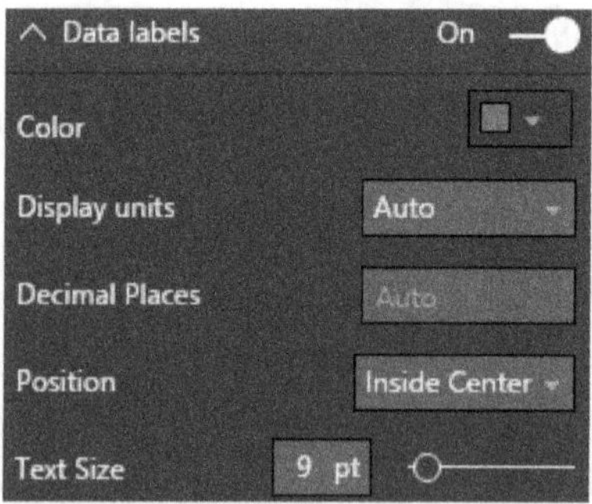

Figure 14-12 Data labels options

Conversion Rate Label Options

The options shown in Figure 14-13 are used to select the color options for the values displayed above and below the chart, as shown in Figure 14-14.

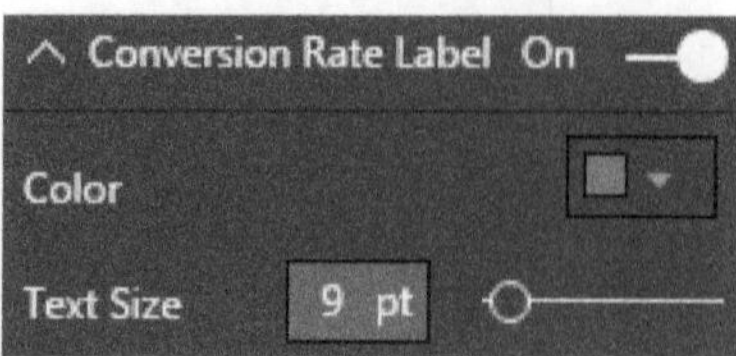

Figure 14-13 Conversion Rate Label options

Exercise 14.4: Create A Funnel Chart

This exercise will show you how to create a chart that displays a count of orders, by how they were shipped. If you have created a Funnel chart in other software, you will see that the Funnel chart in Power BI Desktop looks different.

1. Add the Funnel chart to the page.

2. Add the Ship Via field to the Group section.

3. Add the Order ID field to the Values section ⇒

   Change the Aggregation to Count(Distinct).

   The chart should look like the one shown in Figure 14-14.

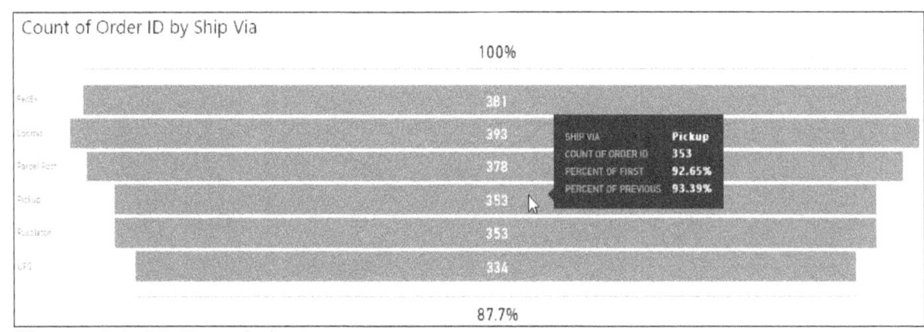

Figure 14-14 Funnel chart

Funnel Chart Tip
Notice that in addition to displaying the data from the field in the Group (also known as the **STAGE NAME**) and Values section, the tooltip also displays the comparison percents for the first (the top bar) and previous stage.

Waterfall Chart Field Well

Figure 14-15 shows the fields used to create a waterfall chart.

The **CATEGORY OPTION** is used to select the field with the values that will be displayed on the X axis.

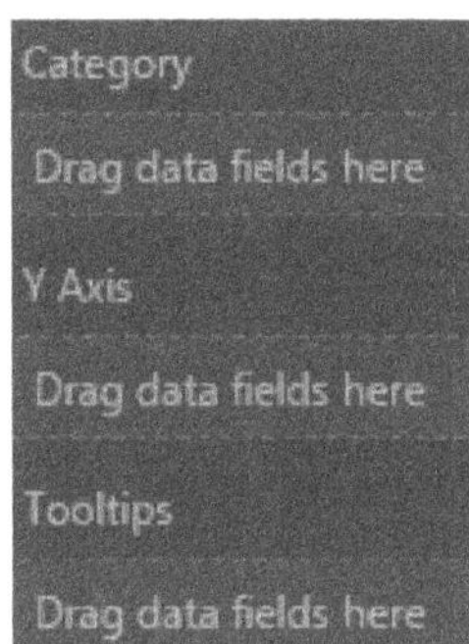

Figure 14-15 Waterfall chart Field Well

Waterfall Chart Formatting Options

The options covered in this section are unique to Waterfall charts.

Sentiment Colors Options

The **INCREASE AND DECREASE OPTIONS** shown in Figure 14-16 are used to select the colors that indicate if the value displayed for each element is greater than or less than the previous element. The colors selected will appear in the legend.

The **TOTAL OPTION** is used to select a color for the total value that is displayed as the last bar on the chart.

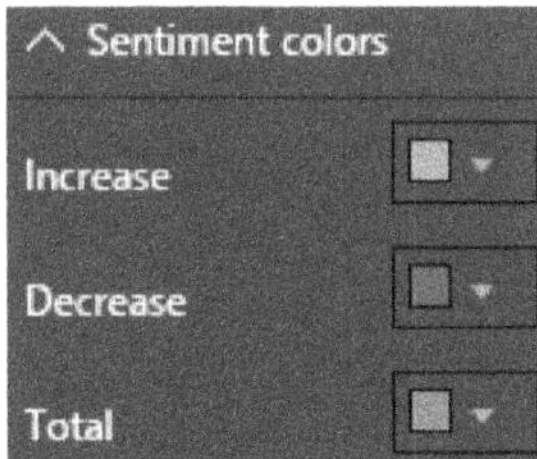

Figure 14-16 Sentiment colors options

Exercise 14.5: Create A Waterfall Chart

This exercise will show you how to create a chart that displays the total order amount for each year.

1. Add the Waterfall chart to the page.

2. Check the Order Amount field ⇒ Check the Year field.

3. Display the data labels.

   The chart should look like the one shown in Figure 14-17.

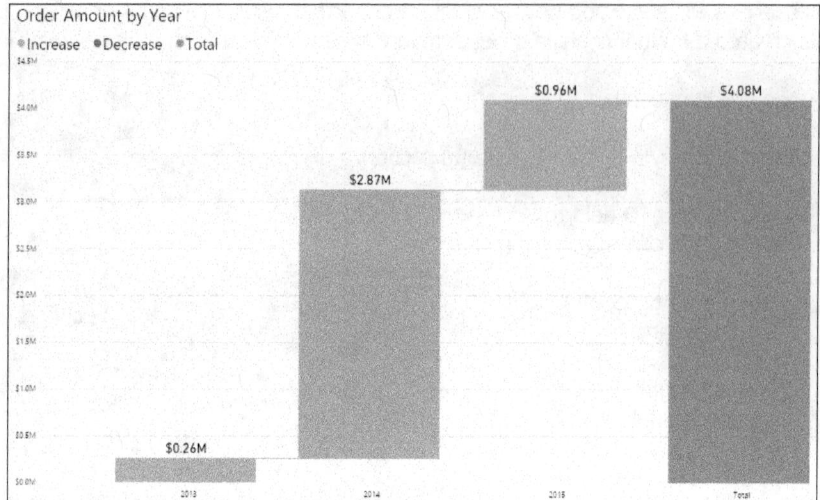

Figure 14-17 Waterfall chart

Exercise 14.6: Create A Waterfall Chart Using Negative Values

Earlier in this chapter, handling negative values on a chart was covered. In this exercise, you will use a modified version of the data shown earlier in Figure 14-7 to create the chart from. The chart will show how the gross margin changes from one company to the next.

1. Import the Negative Values table in the More Data Files workbook.

2. Add the Waterfall chart to the page.

3. In the Negative Values table, check the Gross Margin field ⇒ Check the Company field.

4. Display the data labels. The chart should look like the one shown in Figure 14-18. Even though the value for Companies C and I are positive, they are still displayed below zero because the (cumulative) running sum total at that point, is still a negative number.

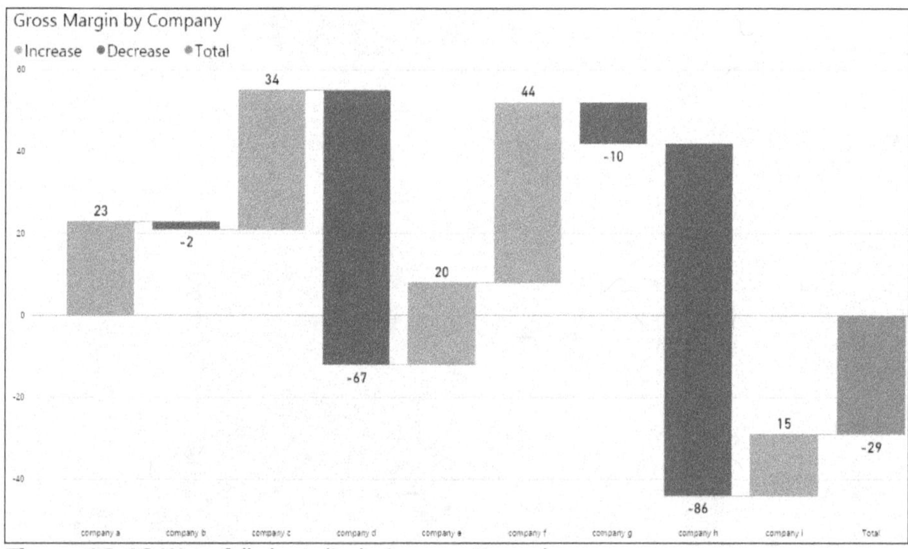

Figure 14-18 Waterfall chart displaying negative values

Adding Drill Down Functionality To A Waterfall Chart

If you want to walk through the drill down steps below, make a copy of page E14.5, then add the additional fields to the Category section, shown in Figure 14-19.

Each field added to the **CATEGORY SECTION** of the Field Well will create a drill down level. If the Category section was changed to the one shown in Figure 14-19, the drill down functionality would display the following in the Waterfall chart:

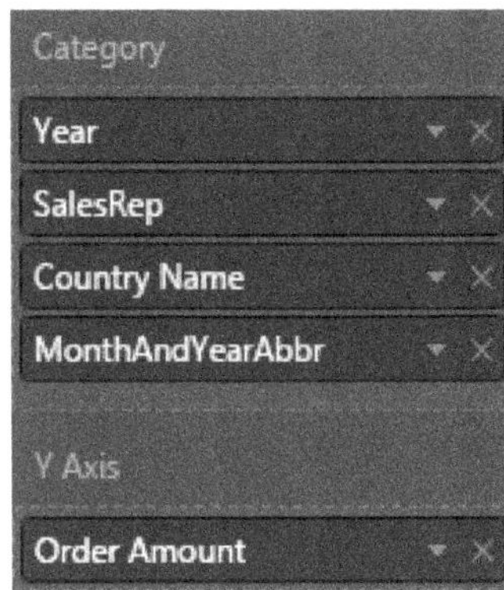

Figure 14-19 Categories to drill down on

① Figure 14-17 shown earlier, shows the top level.
② Drilling down (or selecting **EXPAND ALL**) on the 2014 column in Figure 14-17, displays the order totals for 2014, by sales rep, as shown in Figure 14-20. The Order amount is the dollar amount of sales made by the sales rep.
③ Drilling down on the column for the sales rep Robert King, then clicking the **SEE DATA BUTTON**, displays his sales by country for 2014, with the data shown below the chart, as shown in Figure 14-21.
④ Drilling down on the USA block, will display the total order amount by month and year for Robert King, as shown in Figure 14-22.

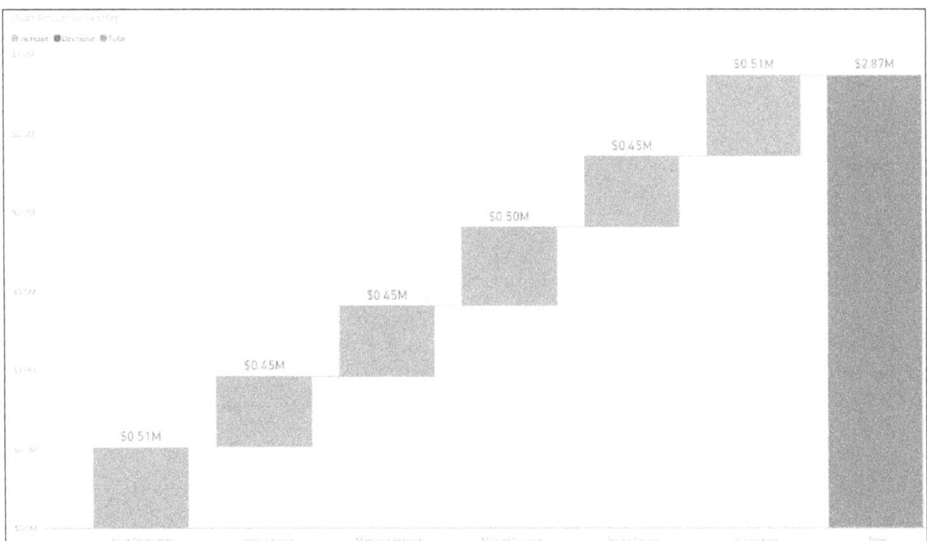

Figure 14-20 2014 Order amount by sales rep level

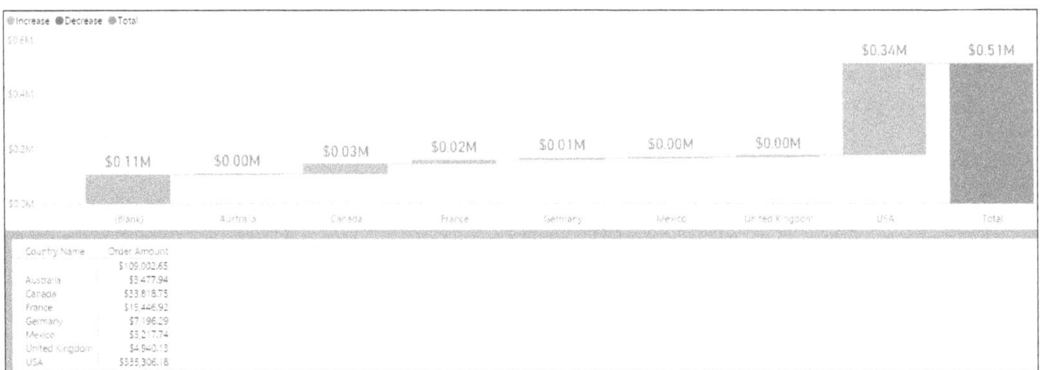

Country Name	Order Amount
	$109,002.65
Australia	$3,477.94
Canada	$33,818.75
France	$15,446.92
Germany	$7,196.29
Mexico	$3,217.74
United Kingdom	$4,940.13
USA	$335,306.16

Figure 14-21 Total order amount by country level

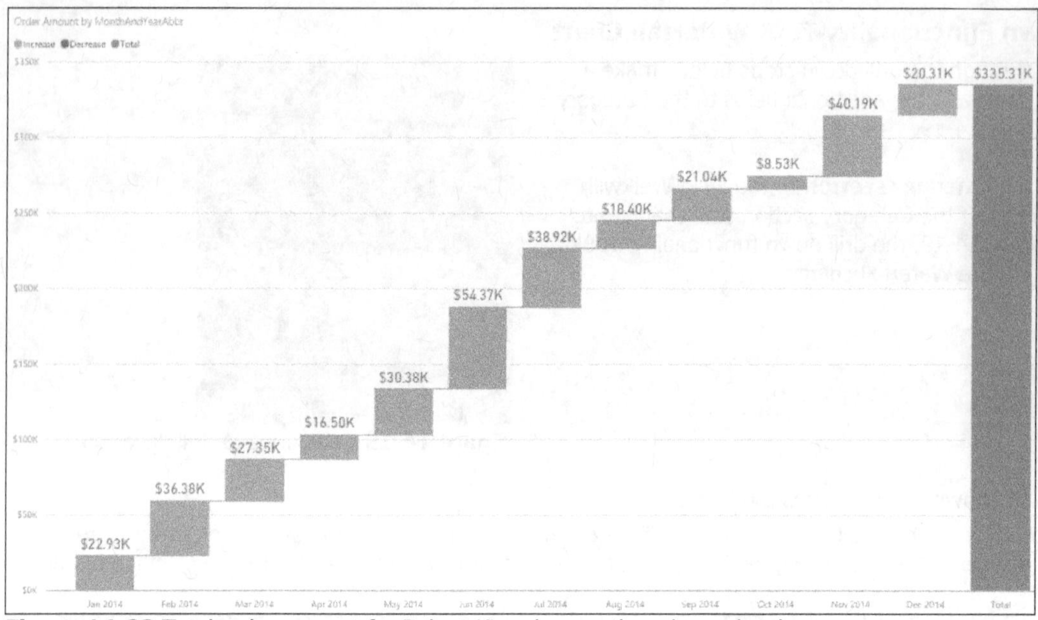

Figure 14-22 Total order amount for Robert King, by month and year level

Gauge Chart Field Well

The options shown in Figure 14-23 are used to select the fields to create a gauge chart.

The **MINIMUM VALUE OPTION** is used to select the lowest value that will be displayed on the chart.

The **MAXIMUM VALUE OPTION** is used to select the highest value that will be displayed on the chart.

Records that are outside of the minimum and maximum values will not be displayed on the chart. These fields, act like a filter.

The **TARGET VALUE OPTION** is used to select the field that contains the value that the field in the Value section will be compared to, to see if it meets or exceeds the target.

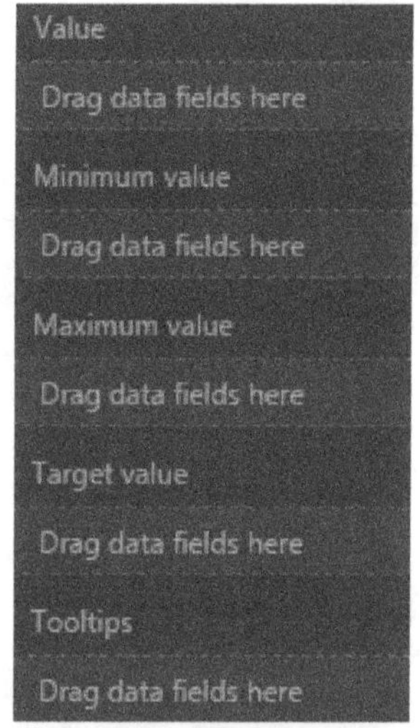

Figure 14-23 Gauge chart Field Well

Gauge Chart Formatting Options

The options explained in this section are specific to Gauge charts.

Gauge Axis Options

The options in this section vary, depending on how many fields have been added to create the chart. The options shown in Figure 14-24 are available, when only one field has been added to the Field Well.

The **MIN OPTION** is used to enter the smallest value that will be displayed on the gauge. This value will be displayed on the left side of the gauge.

The **MAX OPTION** is used to enter the largest value that will be displayed on the gauge. This value will be displayed on the right side of the gauge.

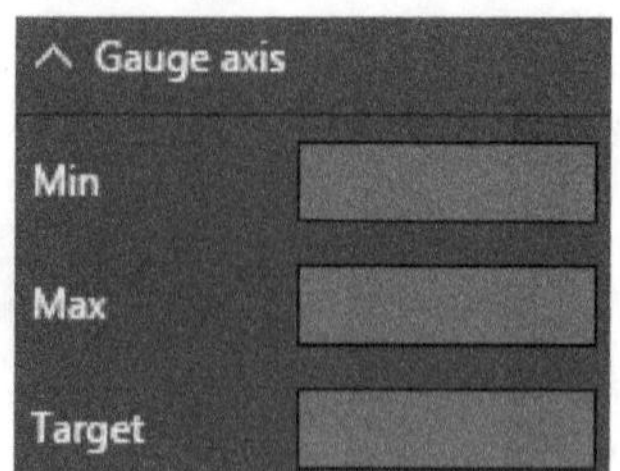

Figure 14-24 Gauge axis options

Callout Value Options

If the **CALLOUT VALUE OPTION** shown in Figure 14-25 is enabled, the options below it are used to customize the value displayed in the middle of the gauge. The value comes from the field in the Value section on the Field Well.

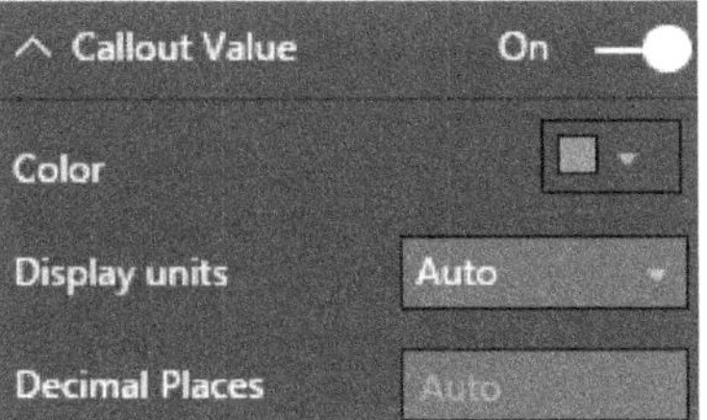

Figure 14-25 Callout Value options

Data Colors Options

The options shown in Figure 14-26 are used to select the colors for the values displayed on the gauge.

The **FILL OPTION** is used to select the color for the field in the Value section.

The **TARGET OPTION** is used to select the color for the field in the Target Value section.

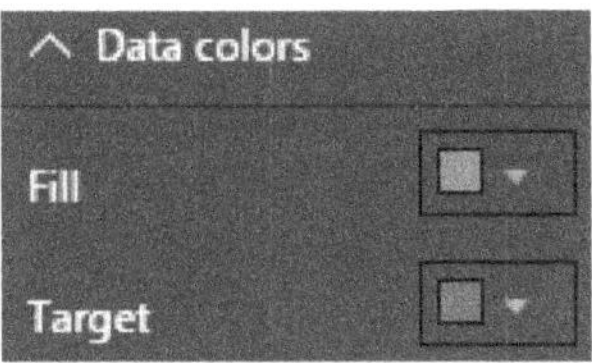

Figure 14-26 Data colors options

Exercise 14.7: Create A Gauge Chart

This exercise will show you how to display how actual sales compare to projected sales per region, on a gauge chart.

1. Import the Actual vs Projected table in the More Data Files workbook.

2. In the Data view, format both columns for 2016, to display the values with currency formatting.

3. In the Report view, add the Gauge chart.

4. Add the 2016 Projected Sales field to the Value section ⇒ Add the 2016 Actual Sales field to the Target Value section.

5. Add the Region field to the Filters section ⇒ Create a filter to only display data for the North region.

6. Make the following formatting changes. When finished, the chart should look like the one shown in Figure 14-27.

   ☑ Data Labels ⇒ Text Size ⇒ 10 pt
   ☑ Callout Value ⇒ Display units ⇒ Thousands
   ☑ Title ⇒ Title Text ⇒ Add the word `North` to the beginning of the title
   ☑ Title ⇒ Text Size ⇒ 14 pt

The $123,000 marker (the needle) on the North region gauge, is the actual sales for the year.

Currently, there is no option to change the font size of this value.

The $150,000 value in the center of the gauge is the projected value. It is represented by the color on the left side of the gauge. Any value in that portion of the gauge indicates that the goal was not met.

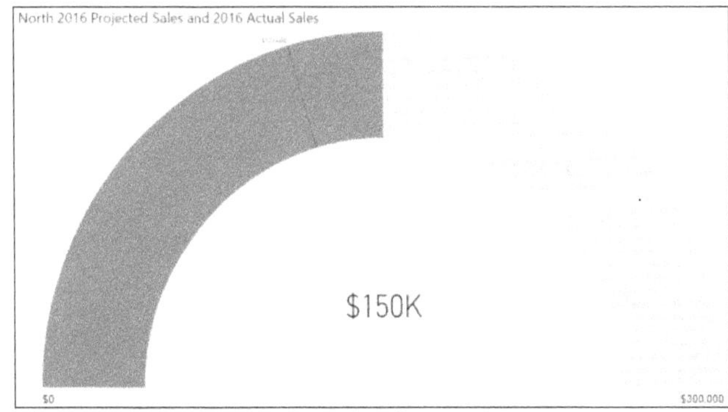

Figure 14-27 Gauge chart for the North region

Create A Gauge Chart For The South Region

1. Duplicate the gauge chart on the page.

2. Change the Region filter to South.

3. Change the Title Text to `South`.

   The chart should look like the one shown in Figure 14-28.

   The $424,000 marker on the South region gauge, is beyond the color (the projected value). This means that the South region exceeded the projected sales amount of $400,000.

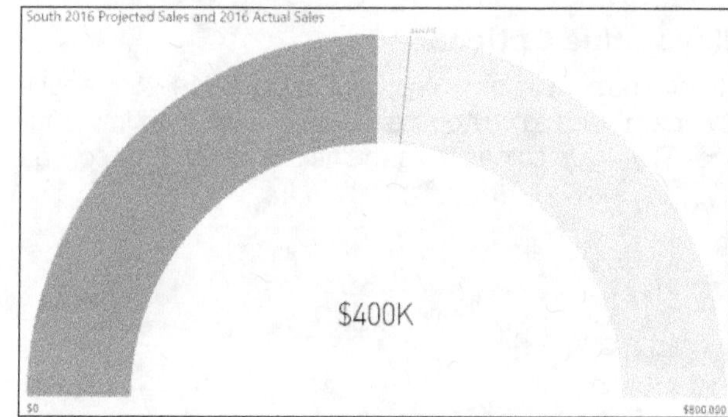

Figure 14-28 Gauge chart for the South region

Often, you will see the Data Colors Fill option color set to red. If the marker is in the red section, it means that the goal/target was not met. There is no option to change the gray color on the right side of the gauge.

Tree Map Chart Field Well

The options shown in Figure 14-29 are used to create a Tree Map chart. This chart type is created like a hierarchy.

Only one field can be added to each of the sections discussed below.

The field added to the **GROUP SECTION** is used to divide the blocks on the map (each group has a different color). The field added to this section is the highest level of the hierarchy.

The field added to the **DETAILS SECTION** will divide the values in the field in the Group section.

The field added to the **VALUES SECTION** creates a sum for the field in the Details section.

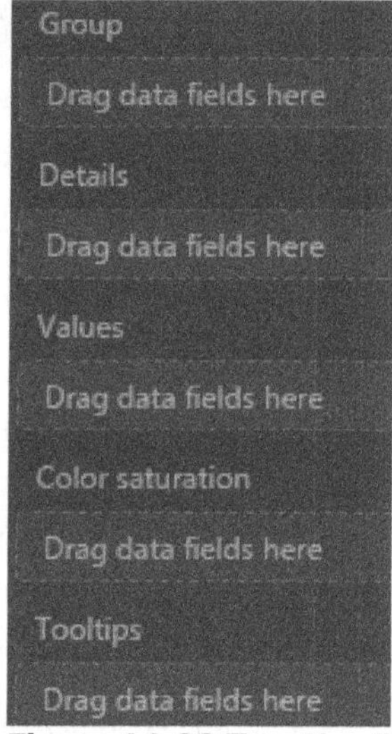

Figure 14-29 Tree Map Field Well

Tree Map Chart Formatting Options

The option covered in this section is unique to the Tree Map chart type.

Category Labels Option

The option shown in Figure 14-30 is used to display the value in the field in the Details section.

Figure 14-30 Category labels option

Exercise 14.8: Create A Tree Map

In this exercise you will learn how to create a chart that shows the sales cost and order amount by year and month. The order amount will be displayed on the tooltip for each block on the chart.

1. Add the Tree Map to the page.

2. Add the following fields to the chart.

   ☑ Add the Year field to the Group section
   ☑ Add the Month Full field to the Details section
   ☑ Add the Sales Cost field to the Values section
   ☑ Add the Order Amount field to the Tooltips section

3. Enable the data labels. The chart should look like the one shown in Figure 14-31.
   You will see the total order amount value for each month on the chart, as shown in the figure. Currently, there is no way to make the values displayed on the chart larger. Each block shows the sales costs for a specific month. Without even looking at the sales costs values displayed in each block, you can tell that June 2014 has the largest sales cost and February had the largest sales cost in 2015.

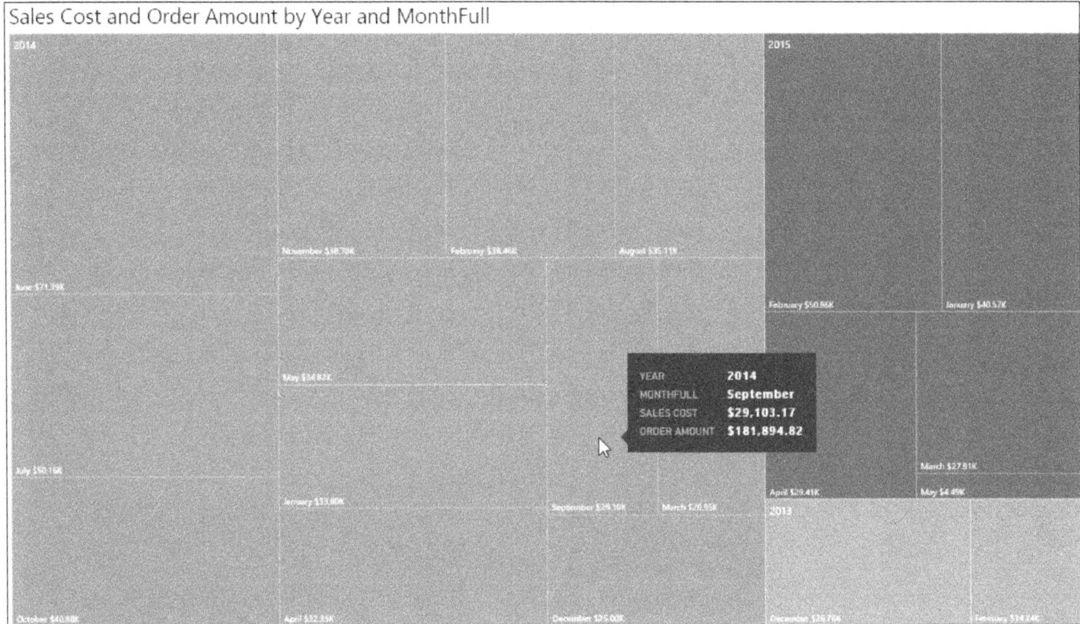

Figure 14-31 Tree Map chart

KPI's

(KPI stands for **KEY PERFORMANCE INDICATOR**). KPI's are a way to measure the performance of a process or objective. If you have seen or created a **SCORECARD**, you may already be familiar with KPI's. If you haven't seen a scorecard, it will remind you of a report card that students receive in school. In the workplace, a scorecard provides a summary of how the organization has performed during the last period. The goal of KPI's is to uncover performance that is not in the normal, acceptable range.

A KPI is an actual value that is measured against a target. This chart type uses color to indicate how a value compares to the target value. This array of colors depict the range of values that are considered, good (a value above the target value), acceptable (slightly above or below the target value) or poor (below the lowest acceptable target value).

Many dashboards are created around this concept because key performance indicators are one tool used to make business decisions, strategic or otherwise. KPI's are a measure of success, where you define what success is.
A measure is needed to create a KPI. While some measures require DAX to be used to create the formula, the Default Summarization options can also be used to create a measure, if the calculation needed is not very complex. If that is the case, no DAX is required.

KPI's are often used in dashboards because they make it easier to see trends, without having to read numbers. KPI's are also used to alert the reader to values that are outside of the extended range. For example, if sales reps have a monthly goal of $50,000 worth of orders, it is easier to tell which reps meet or exceed the expected goal, if there is a check mark icon, that indicates that goal was met, next to their name. This is easier then having to look at each reps total monthly order amount.

KPI Field Well

Figure 14-32 shows the options used to create a KPI chart.

The **INDICATOR OPTION** is used to select the field that has the values that need to be measured against the target.

The **TREND AXIS OPTION** is used to select the field that displays the time period.

The **TARGET GOALS OPTION** is used to select the field that has the expected result. Once a value is added to this field, the color of the chart will change from gray to green if the Indicator value is greater than the target value. If the Indicator value is lower than the target, the chart color will change to red. This means that the metric that is being tracked, is under performing.

Figure 14-32 KPI Field Well

Multiple target goals can be used. A chart that is yellow means that the value is between the lower and higher target values, but did not meet the higher target.

KPI Chart Formatting Options

The options covered in this section are used to format a KPI chart.

Indicator Options

The options shown in Figure 14-33 are used to select how the value in the field in the Indicator section is displayed.

These options work the same as the ones already covered. [See Chapter 11, Figure 11-48]

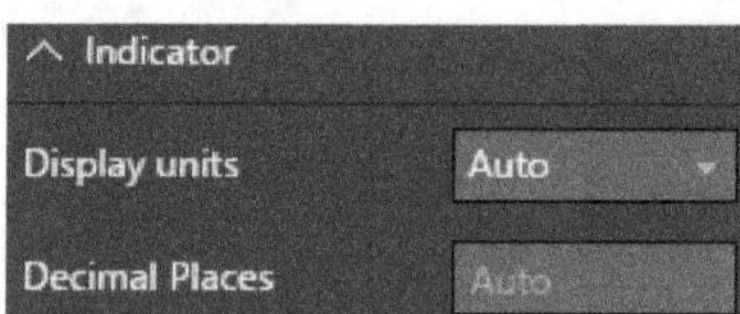

Figure 14-33 Indicator options

Trend Axis Option

The option shown in Figure 14-34 is used to display the data from the field in the Trend Axis section.

Figure 14-34 Trend axis option

Goals Options

The **GOAL OPTION** displays the value in the Target goals section, shown earlier in Figure 14-32.

The **DISTANCE OPTION** shown in Figure 14-35, displays a percent (positive or negative) of how close the Indicator value is to the Target goal value.

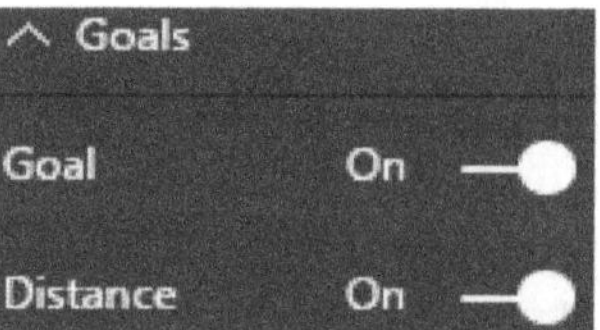

Figure 14-35 Goals options

Color Coding Options

The **DIRECTION OPTION** shown in Figure 14-36 is used to select whether the Indicator field value should be displayed based on whether low or high values are good.

The **GOOD COLOR** (green), **NEUTRAL COLOR** (yellow) and **BAD COLOR** (red) options are used to select what color to apply to which type of data values.

The default colors (listed above in parenthesis) represent the standard colors used to display KPI values. Notice that they are the same colors that traffic lights have, which represent what the values mean. You can change the colors as needed.

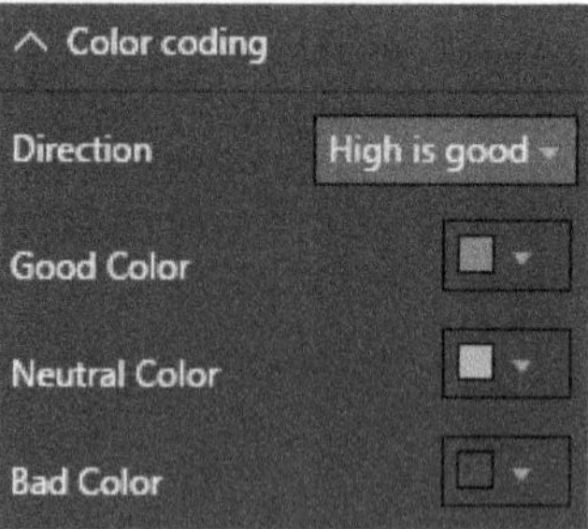

Figure 14-36 Color Coding options

Exercise 14.9: Create A KPI Chart

In this exercise you will learn how to create a KPI chart that displays whether or not the projected sales for the West region in 2015 was achieved.

1. Add the KPI chart to the page.

2. Add the following fields to the chart.

   ☑ Add the 2015 Actual Sales field, in the Actual vs Projected table, to the Indicator section
   ☑ Add the Region field to the Trend Axis section
   ☑ Add the 2015 Projected Sales field to Target Goals section

3. Create a filter to only use the West region.

4. Change the Indicator display units formatting option to Thousands. The chart should look like the one shown in Figure 14-37.

Because KPI charts do not have a data labels option, you can't tell what values are being displayed. There is no tooltip functionality.

You can add a Text Box to the page to explain the values. If you need to create a KPI chart on your own, I recommend using the KPI Indicator custom visual.

If you have trouble understanding the data, use the **SEE DATA OPTION** on the Drill tab.

The bottom of the figure shows the data used to create the KPI chart.

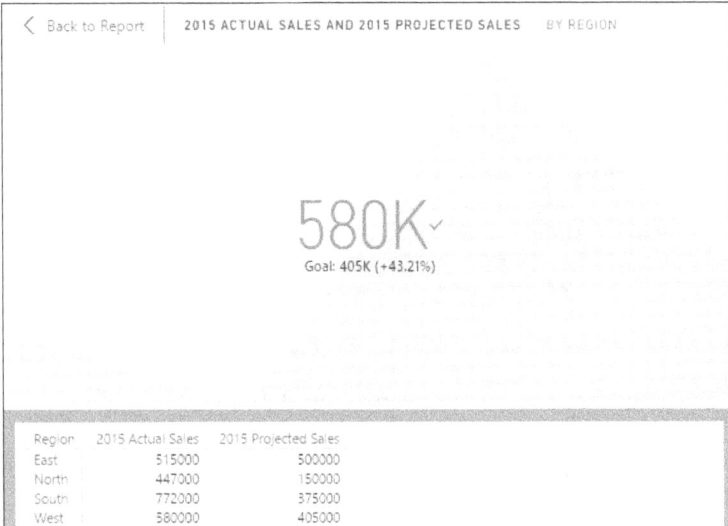

Region	2015 Actual Sales	2015 Projected Sales
East	515000	500000
North	447000	150000
South	772000	375000
West	580000	405000

Figure 14-37 KPI chart and the data used to create it

In addition to creating a KPI chart, KPI's that are created in Power Pivot for Excel or SSAS Tabular, can be imported into Power BI Desktop. Imported KPI elements can be used with tables, matrix tables and card visualizations.

If the images used to display the KPI elements are on a web site, the path to them will be in the table. To display the images, change the Data Category to **IMAGE URL**, on the Modeling tab, on the Data view.

Maps

As if being able to display data in tables and charts is not enough, Power BI Desktop also provides the ability to display data geographically on a map. All of the visualization techniques that you have learned so far in this book, including highlighting, filtering and drill down, can be applied to map visualizations. Like charts, maps can also be linked to charts. To be able to map data, a geographical field, like state or country is required, in the data that will be mapped. As long as you have a field like this, creating a map is as easy as creating other types of visualizations.

Creating maps is similar to creating charts. The biggest difference is that fields that have geographical data (like country, zip code, longitude and latitude) are required.

These fields need to be recognized by Bing maps. One way to know if a table has a geographical field, is if you see the globe icon before the field name (in the Fields panel), illustrated in Figure 14-38. There are two map types available in Power BI Desktop: Maps and Filled Maps.

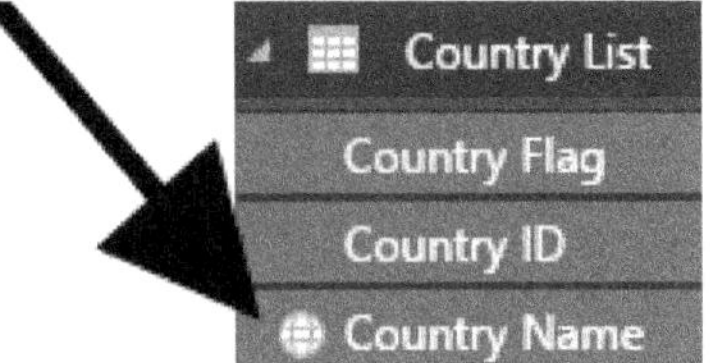

Figure 14-38 Globe icon illustrated

How Maps Work In Power BI Desktop

The map feature uses **BING MAPS**™, which is owned by Microsoft. The data is mapped in real time, which means that an Internet connection is required to view the maps that you create.

Bing Maps does not cover some parts of the world. An indication will be if no data is displayed on the map.

Geographical Information

Bing Maps needs to know what the geographical data is, without the data being ambiguous. For example, there is an Englewood, NJ and Englewood, CO. There is also a section of Chicago, IL named Englewood. Just using Englewood, Bing Maps would not know what part of the map to display. There are options to remove the confusion and ambiguity, as explained below.

① **UPDATE THE DATA MODEL IF NECESSARY** Using the Data view, the data type can be selected for each column, or more clarification of the data can be added.

② **USE THE GEOGRAPHICAL DATA CATEGORY OPTIONS** If the data category is correct in the data model, the correct data type will be selected. If not, Bing Maps will guess at the data category, but you can select a different data category. [See Chapter 8, Figure 8-7]

③ **USE SEVERAL LEVELS OF GEOGRAPHICAL DATA** In the example discussed at the beginning of this section, using the City and State fields would remove the ambiguity.

Map Field Well

Figure 14-39 shows the sections where fields can be placed.

The **LOCATION OPTION** is used to select the field that has the geographical locations (country, zip code, etc.) that you want to plot on the map. The locations are sometimes referred to as **PLOT POINTS.**

The **LEGEND OPTION** is used to select the categorical field to show color for.

The **LATITUDE OPTION** is used to select the field that has the latitude coordinate for the location that you want to plot on the map. Latitude is a geographic coordinate (location) that contains the north - south position of a point on earth.

The **LONGITUDE OPTION** is used to select the field that has the longitude coordinate for the location that you want to plot on the map. Longitude is a geographic coordinate (location) that contains the east - west position of a point on earth.

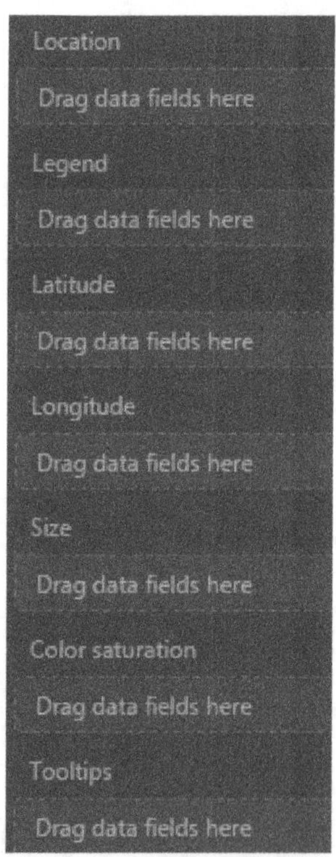

Figure 14-39 Map Field Well

Map Formatting Options

The options covered in this section are specific to map charts.

Data Colors Options

The options shown in Figure 14-40 are used to customize the color of the bubbles on the map. These options are helpful when you want certain values (bubbles) on the chart to stand out more than the others.

The **DEFAULT COLOR OPTION** will be applied to values that you do not select a custom color for. As shown at the bottom of the figure, there is an option for each value (bubble) on the chart.

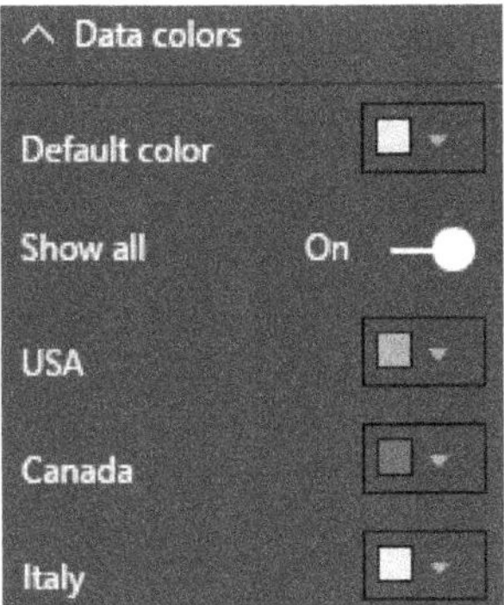

Figure 14-40 Data colors options

Category Labels Option

The options shown in Figure 14-41 are used to customize the data labels on the map.

The **COLOR OPTION** is used to change the font color of the data labels.

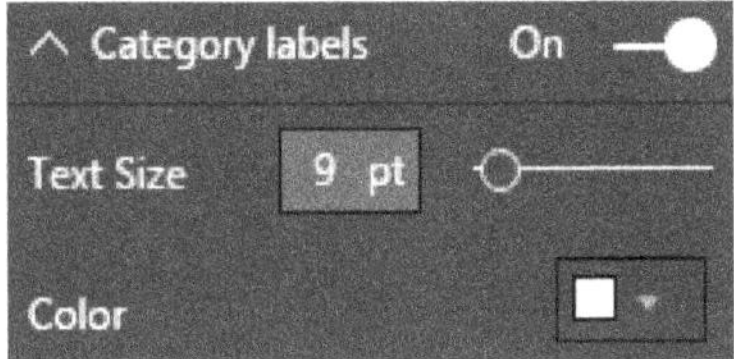

Figure 14-41 Category labels options

Exercise 14.10: Create A Basic Map

In this exercise you will create a map that displays the sum of orders by country.

1. Add the Map chart to the page.

2. Add the following fields to the chart.

   ☑ Add the Country field in the Customer table to the Location section
   ☑ Add the Order Amount field to the Color Saturation section

3. Make the map as large as the page ⇒ Click on the map near South America and drag that part of the map to the center of the page.

4. Move your mouse wheel forward.

   The circles indicate the order amounts. Hold the mouse pointer over a bubble on the map.

   You will start to see the data in the tooltip for the location.

   In this exercise, you will see the countries in South America, as shown in Figure 14-42.

Figure 14-42 Order amount by country map

Exercise 14.11: Filter Data On A Map

In this exercise you will filter the data displayed on the map, by year.

1. Duplicate page E14.10.

2. Create a date filter to only display orders in 2015.

   The map should look like the one shown in Figure 14-43.

   Compare it to the map shown above in Figure 14-42. Notice that there are fewer bubbles on the chart.

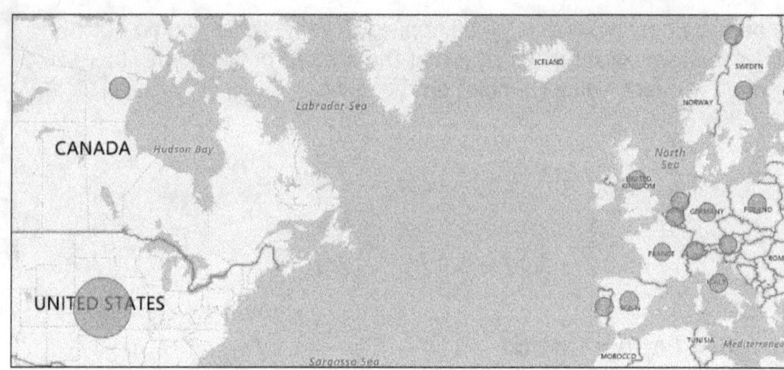

Figure 14-43 Order amount filtered by year on a map

Creating Maps That Display More Than One Series Of Data

The maps that you have created up to this point have displayed one series of data. Displaying more than one series of data, replaces the bubbles shown above in Figure 14-43, with the pie charts shown in Figure 14-44. The size of the pie chart represents the total, compared to the other pie charts on the map.

Holding the mouse pointer over a pie chart, displays the values (usually the location total counts or total amounts) for the geographic region that the mouse pointer is on.

Each slice of the pie chart will display different values.

Figure 14-44 Pie chart enlarged

Highlighting Data On A Map

This feature is available when a field is added to the Legend section. The options on the legend apply the highlighting to the map.

Exercise 14.12: Add A Legend And Highlighting To A Map

Creating a legend for a map is the same as creating one for a chart.

1. Duplicate page E14.10.

2. Click on the map ⇒ Add the Ship Via field to the **LEGEND** section. The map should look like the one shown above in Figure 14-44.

   Clicking on an option in the legend, highlights the corresponding data in the pie charts on the map. To remove the highlights, click on the legend option again or click on a blank space on the page.

Exercise 14.13: Add Drill Down Functionality To A Map

In this exercise you will create a map that will be used to view order amounts by state, then by city.

1. Add the Map chart to the page.

2. Add the following fields to the chart.

   ☑ Add the Region field to the Location section
   ☑ Add the City field to the Location section, below the Region field
   ☑ Add the Order Amount field to the Size section

3. Create a filter to only display records in the USA. The map shown in Figure 14-45, displays a bubble for each state that has at least one order.

4. Double-click on a bubble ⇒ Zoom in, until you can see the city names on the map. The chart drills down and shows all of the cities in the state that have an order, as shown in Figure 14-46.

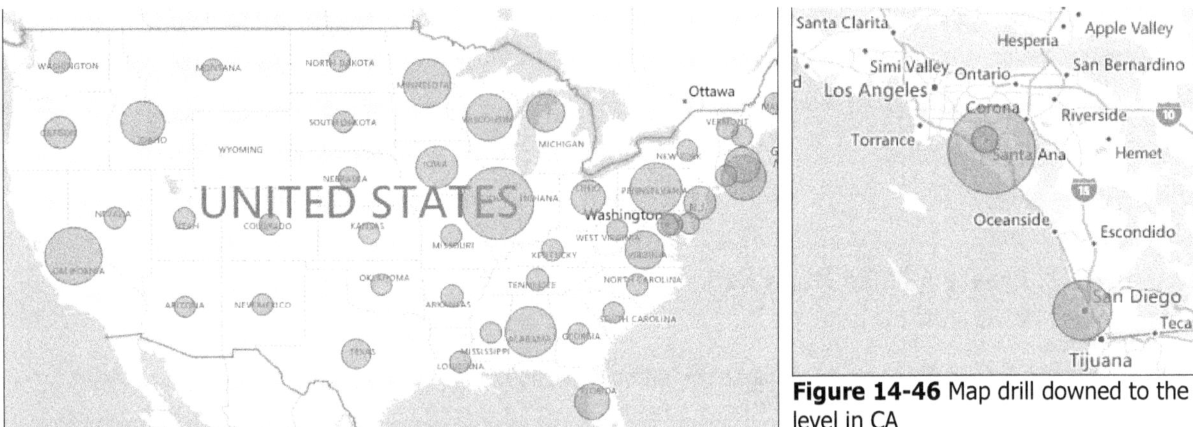

Figure 14-45 Map illustrating states that have orders

Figure 14-46 Map drill downed to the city level in CA

Exercise 14.14: Create A Map Using Coordinates

In this exercise, latitude and longitude coordinates will be used to plot points on the map. Using latitude and longitude coordinates provides a more accurate representation of the data.

1. Import the Latitude and Longitude table, in the More Data Files workbook.

2. Add the Map chart to the page.

3. Add the Latitude and Longitude fields to the corresponding sections in the Field Well.

4. Add the Net Sales field to the Size section ⇒

   Make the map larger, as shown in Figure 14-47.

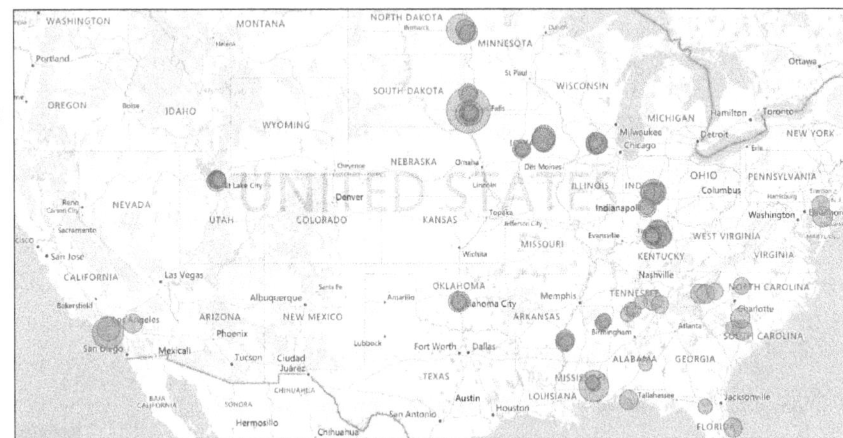

Figure 14-47 Map created using coordinates

Filled Map Formatting Options

The Data Colors options work different for the Filled Map chart, as explained below.

Data Colors Options

The options shown in Figure 14-48 are used to customize the range of colors displayed on the map.

The **DIVERGING OPTION** must be enabled to use the Center data color options.

The **MINIMUM, CENTER** and **MAXIMUM OPTIONS** with a color drop-down list are used to select a color for each value.

The **MINIMUM, CENTER** and **MAXIMUM FIELDS** are used to enter values to map colors to. Use these options when you need to exclude values from appearing on the map.

Once the options are selected, Power BI Desktop will apply the color changes.

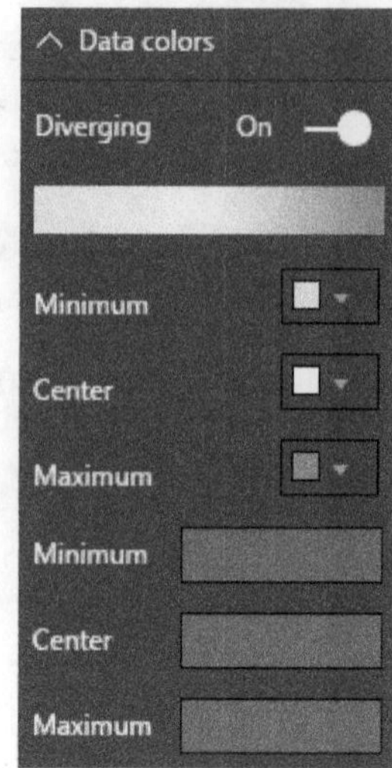

Figure 14-48 Data colors options

Exercise 14.15: Create A Filled Map Chart

1. Add the Filled Map chart to the page.

2. Add the Country field in the Customer table to the Location section.

3. Add the Order Amount field to the Color Saturation section.

   The map should look like the one shown in Figure 14-49.

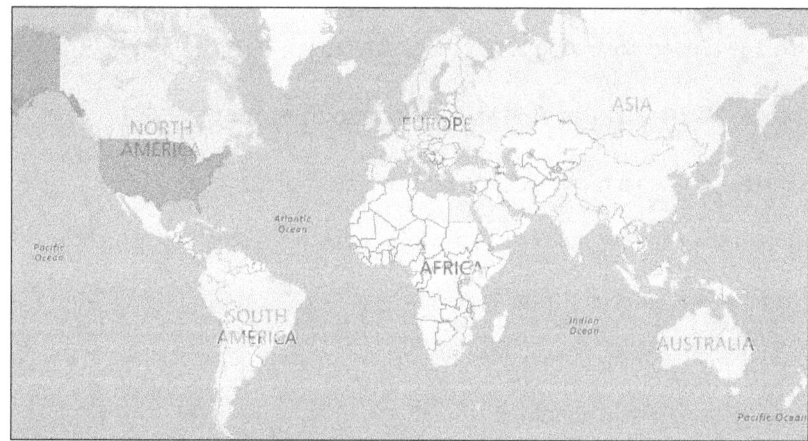

Figure 14-49 Filled map chart

Exercise 14.16: Create A Cross Filter Chart Using A Map

The page that you create in this exercise will have a bar chart and a map. **CROSS FILTERING** means that each object on the page can be used to filter other objects on the page.

1. Duplicate page E14.2.

2. Delete the Order Amount field ⇒ Add the Order ID field to the Size section ⇒ Change the aggregation of the Order ID field to Count (Distinct).

3. Make the following formatting changes.

   ☑ Change the legend to display on the right
   ☑ Disable the title

4. Create a Clustered Bar chart that displays the Order Amount totals by year ⇒ Place the bar chart below the map, as shown in Figure 14-50.

When you click on a pie chart on the map or a Ship Via option on the maps legend, the bar chart will change accordingly and vise versa.

For example, on the bar chart, click on the bar for the year 2015.

The pie charts on the map will change and the parts of the pie chart that do not have data for 2015, will be disabled.

Any options on the legend that do not have corresponding data will also be disabled.

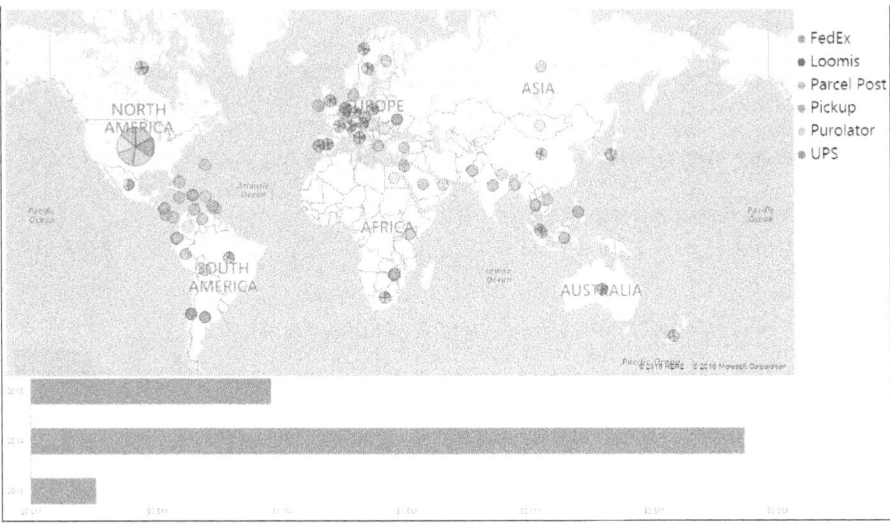

Figure 14-50 Cross filter chart with a map

Shape Map

This map works differently then the other maps, which display data on geographical locations. A Shape map shows comparisons of regions on a map, by displaying the data in different colors.

At the time this book went to print, this map was in preview mode, but I wanted to let you know about it.

Figure 14-51 shows the fields used to create the map shown in Figure 14-52.

Figure 14-53 shows the formatting categories.

Figure 14-51 Shape map Field Well

Figure 14-52 Shape map

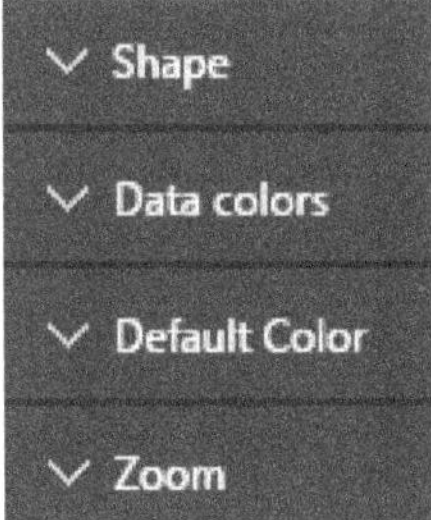

Figure 14-53 Shape map formatting categories

Using Custom Maps

If you have maps that are in **TOPOJSON FORMAT**, you can use them with the Shape map.

Click the **ADD MAP BUTTON** shown in Figure 14-54 to add the map.

To use the map, follow the steps below.

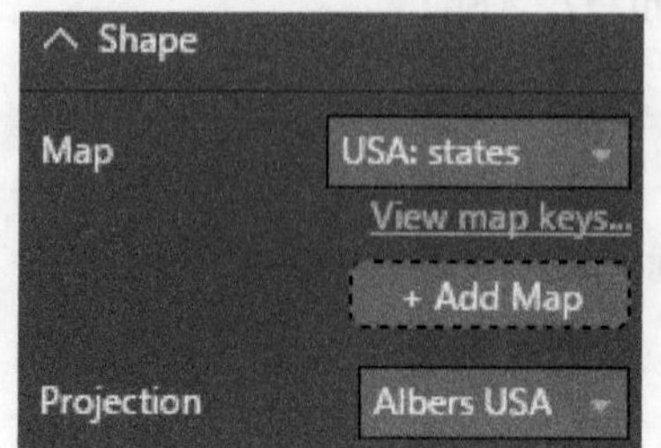

Figure 14-54 Shape formatting options

1. Add the Shape map visual to the page.

2. Add a field to the Location and Values sections, on the Field Well.

3. Format panel ⇒ Shape ⇒ Add map button ⇒ Select your map.

Custom Visuals

So far, all of the chart types covered in this book are built into Power BI Desktop. There is a growing gallery of custom visuals for Power BI Desktop that have been developed by Microsoft and approved third parties. The gallery contains a variety of charts and maps that you can import into Power BI Desktop. Down loading and installing them is easy. There are links in Power BI Desktop to get to the gallery. And yes, the custom visuals are free! The remaining exercises in this chapter show you how to download, install and use some of the custom visuals.

What you will see is that these visuals have the same interface, as Power BI Desktop. It is possible that a visual may not work as intended. I encountered one that would display a message that the visual had been successfully loaded, but there was no icon for it on the Visualizations panel, so I couldn't use it. I suspect that this was because an update to Power BI Desktop changed something behind the scenes that this custom visual wasn't designed to handle.

Keep in mind that the custom visuals can be modified at any time by the creator. This means that you may see different options then those shown in this book, when you use them on your own.

How To Download A Custom Visual File

This section and the next one are used to download and install all custom visuals. You will complete these steps for each custom visual exercise.

1. In your web browser, go to `https://app.powerbi.com/visuals/`

2. Scroll down the page and click on the visual that you want to download.

3. On the window shown in Figure 14-55, click the **DOWNLOAD VISUAL BUTTON** ⇒ Click the **I AGREE BUTTON** on the next screen.

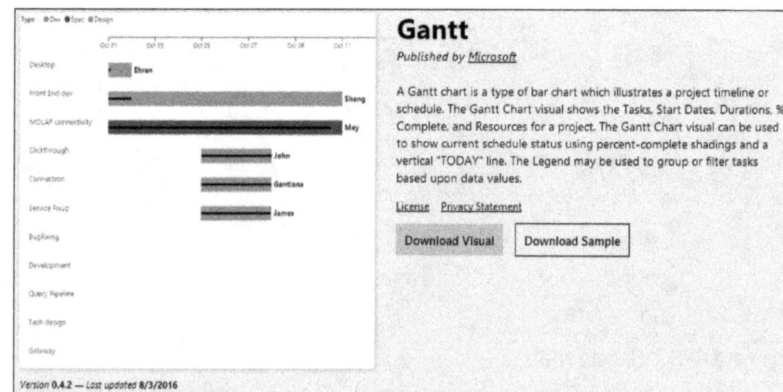

Figure 14-55 Window to download the custom visual from

4. Save the file to your hard drive. For the exercises in this book, save the file to your folder for this book.

Saving Custom Visuals
Custom visuals are added to the report file that is currently open. If you need to use the custom visual in another report file, you have to import it into that file also. If you are planning to create your own template report file to use as the starting point for all of your own projects, import the custom visual into your template file.

How To Access A Custom Visual That You Have Downloaded

There are two options in Power BI Desktop to import a custom visual that you have downloaded, as listed below.

① Report view ⇒ Visualizations panel ⇒ Click the ... icon, in the section where the chart and table styles are ⇒ Import a custom visual.
② Power BI Desktop workspace ⇒ File tab ⇒ Import ⇒ Power BI Custom Visual.

How To Install A Custom Visual

1. In the Report view, on the Visualization panel, click the Import from file button (the ... ellipses button), where the chart and map icons are ⇒ Select the Import a custom visual option.

2. On the Caution: Import Custom Visual message window, click the Import button ⇒ Navigate to the folder that you downloaded the custom visual file to ⇒ Double-click on the file.

3. You should see a message that says that the visual was successfully imported ⇒ Click OK. You will see a new icon on the Visualizations panel for the custom visual, right before the Import from file icon ⇒ Save the changes to the report file.

Gantt Charts

A Gantt chart is often used to display project management data in a horizontal bar chart like the start and end dates of tasks on a project plan. Gantt charts only work with date and date/time fields. For example, the vertical axis would display the project tasks and the horizontal axis would display the time frame for the tasks.

Gantt Chart Custom Visual Field Well

Figure 14-56 shows the fields used to create a Gantt chart.

The **TASK OPTION** is required.

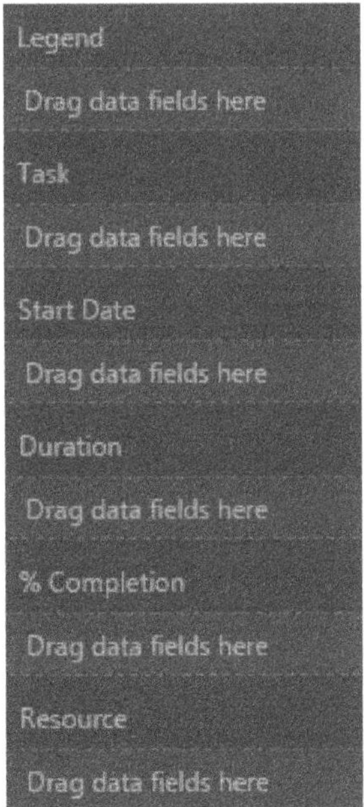

Figure 14-56 Gantt chart Field Well

Gantt Chart Custom Visual Formatting Options

Category Labels Options

The options shown in Figure 14-57 are used to customize the field in the Task section.

The **WIDTH OPTION** is used to make the field wider. This is helpful if you need to display longer values.

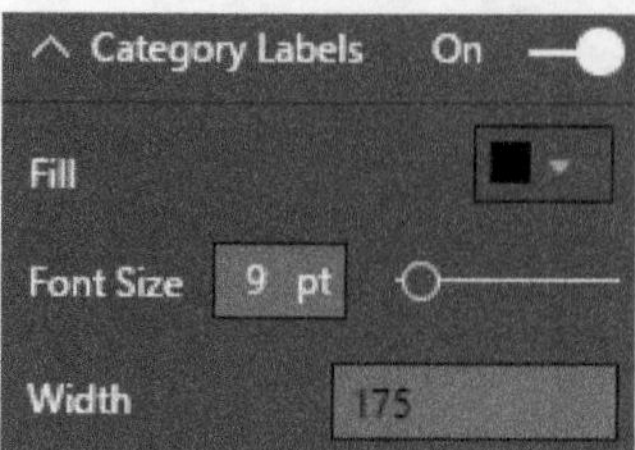

Figure 14-57 Category Labels options

Task Completion Options

The **COMPLETION COLOR OPTION** shown in Figure 14-58, is used to select a color for the field in the % Completion section.

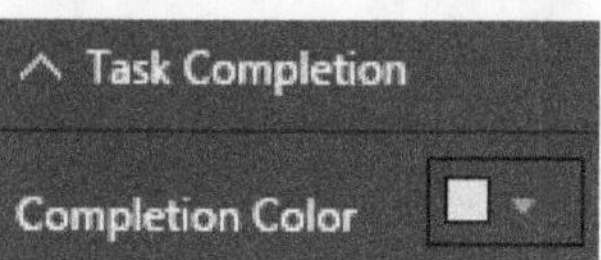

Figure 14-58 Task Completion options

Gantt Data Type Options

The **TYPE OPTION** shown in Figure 14-59, is used to select the increment (day, week, month, year) that the dates used to create the chart are displayed in.

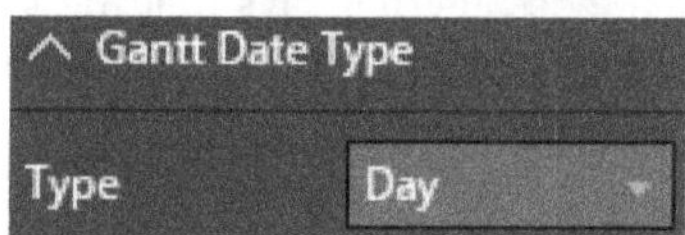

Figure 14-59 Gantt Data Type options

Exercise 14.17: Create A Gantt Chart

In Chapter 8, Exercise 8.3, you created a formula that calculates how many days it took to process customer orders. Gantt charts require a start and end date. In this exercise you will use the order date as the start date and the ship date as the end date.

The Gantt chart would not be readable if all of the records in the Orders table were displayed on the chart. To make the chart readable, you will select a date range to display on the chart.

1. Follow the steps earlier in this chapter to download and install the Gantt chart custom visual.
2. Add the Gantt chart to the page.
3. Create selection criteria that limits the order dates to the range 9/17/2014 to 9/21/2014.
4. Add the following fields to the chart.

   ☑ Add the Ship Via field to the Legend section
   ☑ Add the Customer Name field to the Task section
   ☑ Add the Order Date field to the Start Date section
   ☑ Add the Order Processing Time field to the Duration and Resource sections

Format The Gantt Chart

1. Position the legend on the right.
2. Category Labels ⇒ Width ⇒ Type `175`.
3. Gantt Data Type ⇒ Type ⇒ Day. The chart should look like the one shown in Figure 14-60. The bars show the date the order was placed and when it was shipped. The number at the end of the bar is how many days it took to process the order.

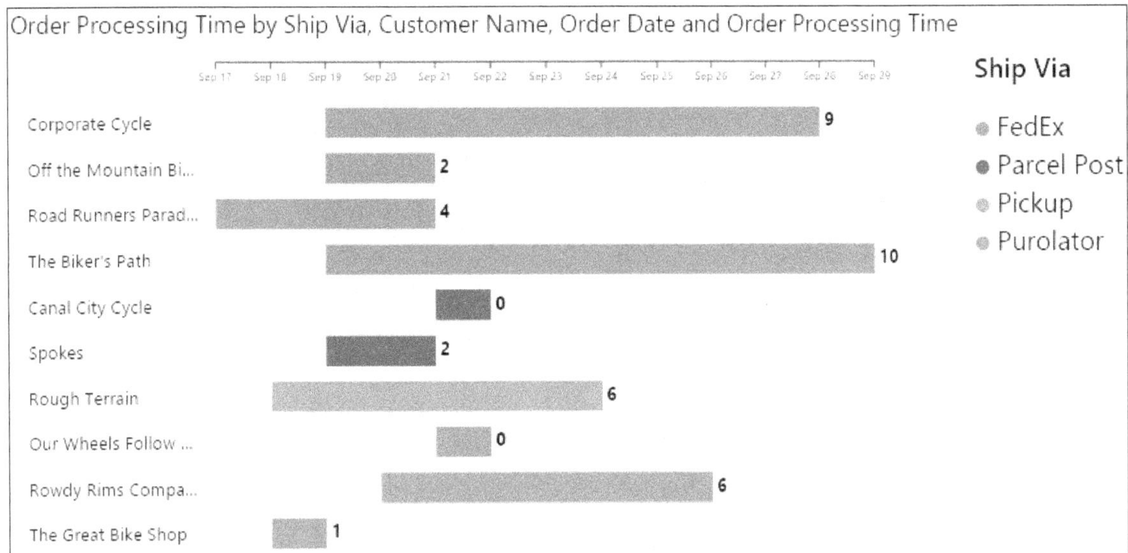

Figure 14-60 Gantt chart

Box And Whisker Charts

This chart type is similar to bar charts. The difference is that the bars in Box and Whisker charts do not have to touch the bottom of the chart. This chart type is also similar to chart types that are used to plot stock data. Another chart type that can be used to display stock data is a **CANDLESTICK CHART**. This type of chart is often used to display the minimum and maximum of stock prices, where each bar represents a different stock. Stock charts plot the first and last trade values of the day or the high and low values for each stock.

Box And Whisker Chart Field Well

Figure 14-61 shows the options used to create a Box and Whisker chart. All three are required.

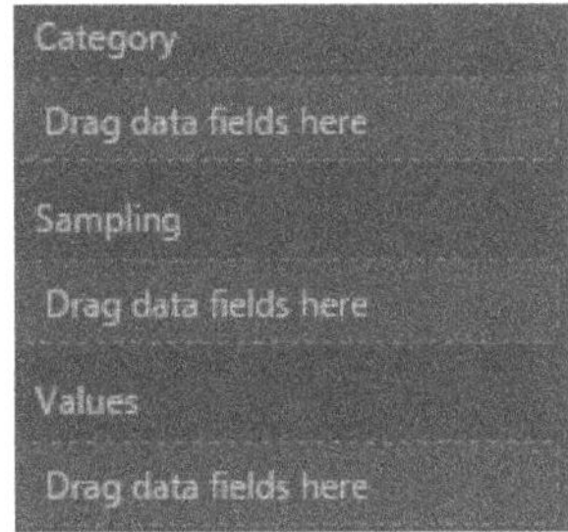

Figure 14-61 Box And Whisker chart Field Well

Box And Whisker Chart Formatting Options

Chart Options

The options shown in Figure 14-62 are used to select the chart type.

There are three chart types: Min/Max, Tukey and 1.5IQR.

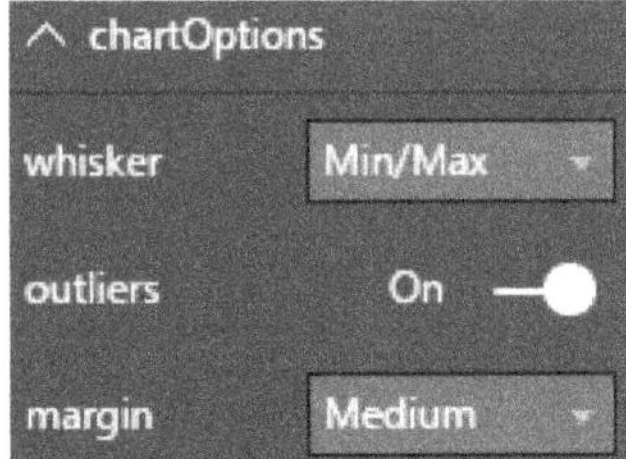

Figure 14-62 Chart options

X Axis And Y Axis Option

Figure 14-63 shows the option to customize the size of the values on the X and Y axis.

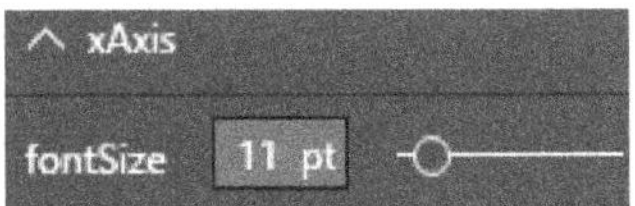

Figure 14-63 X Axis option

Gridlines Options

The options shown in Figure 14-64 are used to add and customize the gridlines on the chart.

Figure 14-64 Gridlines options

Exercise 14.18: Create A Stock Chart

Figure 14-65 shows the original spreadsheet layout that the stock data was in. Figure 14-66 shows the stock data in a modified layout, that will be easier to use to display on a chart.

	A	B	C	D	E	F
1		Stock 1	Stock 2	Stock 3	Stock 4	Stock 5
2	Open	$111	$55	$80	$70	$130
3	High	$78	$55	$99	$70	$168
4	Low	$5	$50	$23	$70	$145
5	Close	$42	$50	$25	$70	$165

Figure 14-65 Original stock data layout

	A	B	C
1	Stock	Level	Price
2	Stock 1	Open	$111
3	Stock 1	High	$78
4	Stock 1	Low	$5
5	Stock 1	Close	$42
6	Stock 2	Open	$55
7	Stock 2	High	$55

Figure 14-66 Modified stock data layout

Stock Levels Explained

OPEN Is the opening (beginning) price of the stock for the day.

HIGH Is the highest selling stock price for the day.

LOW Is the lowest selling stock price for the day.

CLOSE Is the closing (ending) price of the stock for the day.

Create The Stock Chart

The stock chart that you will create in this exercise will display the data for five stocks for a single day. While there currently isn't a Stock chart option in Power BI Desktop, the Box and Whisker custom visual can be used.

1. Download and install the Box and Whisker (Jan Pieter) custom visual.
2. Import the Stock Data table, in the More Data Files workbook.
3. Data view ⇒ Select the Price column in the Stock Data table ⇒ Change the Data type to Fixed Decimal Number ⇒ Change the Format to Currency ⇒ English (United States).
4. Add the Box and Whisker chart to the page.
5. Add the following fields to the chart.

   ☑ Add the Stock field to the Category section
   ☑ Add the Level field to the Sampling section
   ☑ Add the Price field to the Values section

Format The Stock Chart

1. Data Labels ⇒ On ⇒ Change the Text Size to 14. The chart should look like the one shown in Figure 14-67.

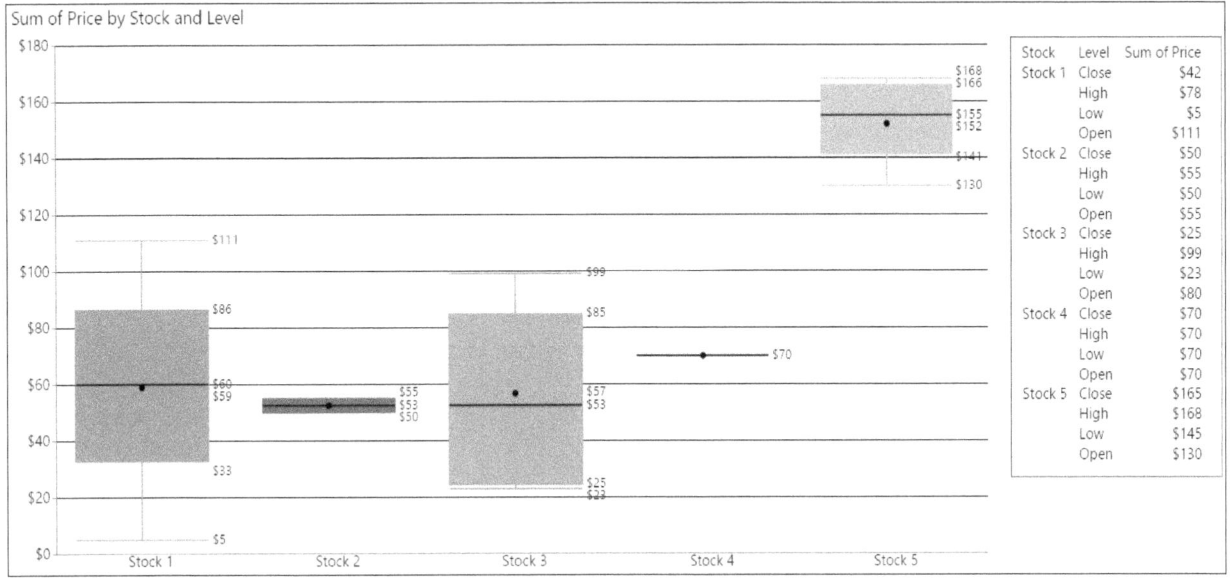

Stock	Level	Sum of Price
Stock 1	Close	$42
	High	$78
	Low	$5
	Open	$111
Stock 2	Close	$50
	High	$55
	Low	$50
	Open	$55
Stock 3	Close	$25
	High	$99
	Low	$23
	Open	$80
Stock 4	Close	$70
	High	$70
	Low	$70
	Open	$70
Stock 5	Close	$165
	High	$168
	Low	$145
	Open	$130

Figure 14-67 Stock chart

Because there is no way to display the Level field data next to the dollar amount, it would be helpful to display the three fields in the Stock Data table, next to the chart, as shown above, on the right side of the figure.

The reason that Stock 2 has a narrow price range is because the closing price is lower than the opening price. (See the data in Figure 14-65 for Stock 2). Yes, that means that the stock lost money that day.

The reason that Stock 4 is a line is because the closing price is the same as the other prices (open, high and low), as if there was no activity for the stock that day.

Radar Charts

This chart type compares sets of data relative to a center point and shows how far the data value is from the standard (the center point value). The values that are often used are group subtotals. The data from the X axis is usually plotted in a circle and the Y axis values are plotted from the center of the circle out.

Radar Chart Field Well

Figure 14-68 shows the options for a Radar chart. Both fields are required.

The **CATEGORY OPTION** is used to group the values on the Y axis.

The **Y AXIS OPTION** is used to select the values to group.

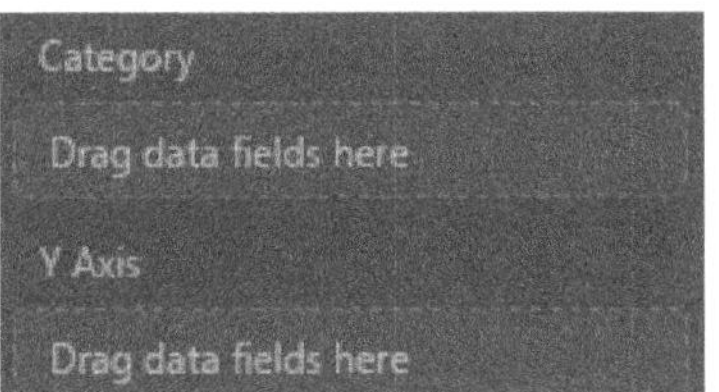

Figure 14-68 Radar chart Field Well

Radar Chart Formatting Options

The options shown in Figure 14-69 are used to display a line connecting the values for each field in the Y Axis section.

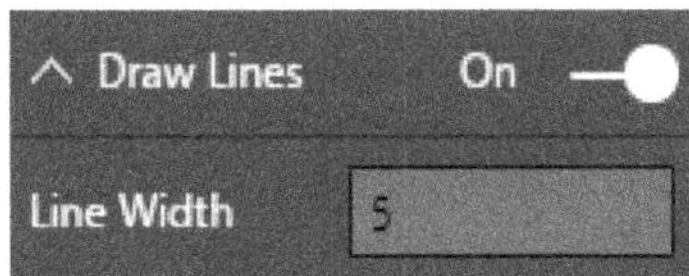

Figure 14-69 Radar chart Draw Lines options

Exercise 14.19: Create A Radar Chart

In this exercise you will create a chart that plots one years sales against another years sales.

1. Download and import the Radar chart custom visual.

2. Add the Radar chart.

3. Add the following fields from the Actual vs Projected table to the chart.

   ☑ Add the Region field to the Category section
   ☑ Add the 2015 Actual Sales field to the Y Axis section
   ☑ Add the 2016 Actual Sales field to the Y Axis section

4. Make the following formatting changes.

   ☑ Draw Lines ⇒ On
   ☑ Draw Lines ⇒ Line Width ⇒ Change to `10`
   ☑ Data Labels ⇒ Text Size ⇒ 12 pt
   ☑ Title ⇒ Title Text ⇒ Type `Radar Chart` at the beginning of the field

   When finished, the chart should look like the one shown in Figure 14-70.

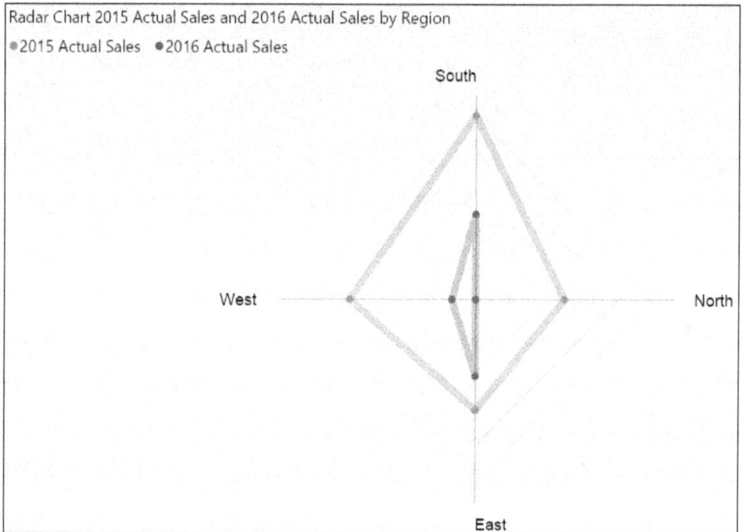

Figure 14-70 Radar chart

Summary

This chapter showed you how to create more types of charts and how to handle and negative values on charts. Setting up and using drill down functionality on a chart was covered. In a way, using drill down functionality is like displaying multiple charts in one.

Gauge and KPI charts may remind you of the Card table visualization, because they illustrate one value. Displaying data on several types of maps, with and without drill down functionality, was also covered. Last, but certainly not least, you were introduced to custom visuals.

CREATING AND USING SLICERS

After completing the exercises in this chapter you will be able to create and customize slicers.

CHAPTER 15

Slicers

Slicers were first introduced in Excel 2010. They are an interactive tool that is used to reduce the amount of data displayed on visuals in a report file. If you have used Power View for Excel, you are familiar with tiles. Power BI Desktop does not have tiles. Slicers can be used to emulate the tile functionality. They are also used to analyze data and create some types of "What If" scenarios. This is possible because slicers allow the data to be filtered, grouped and sorted. Slicers are also useful when creating dashboards. They are a tool of choice when the data needs to be sliced and diced. The results are displayed immediately. Even though slicers are filters, they are different from the filters on the Filters panel because:

① They are multi select. For example, multiple bars on a chart slicer can be selected to filter another visualization.
② They are placed on the page, opposed to on the Filters panel, and are always visible. This gives the user more flexibility, in terms of what data is selected to be displayed on the visualization.
③ By default, slicers cannot be based on ranges of data. If you need a range of data for each option on the slicer, the ranges (groups) have to be created in the data source. A range example would be order amounts between $1 - $50 or $50.01 - $75.

Slicer Tips
① If you save a report file with a slicer that is in use (active), then close and reopen the report file, the slicer is still active, with the last options that were selected.
② The field that the slicer uses does not have to be displayed on the visualization.
③ If a table, chart, page or report has filters, they are not removed when a slicer is added. Slicers filter the data that has already been filtered by the existing filters that have been applied to the page.

Slicer Field Well And Filter Options

Unlike tables and charts, slicers only have one field, as shown in Figure 15-1. Only one field can be added to the **FIELD SECTION**.

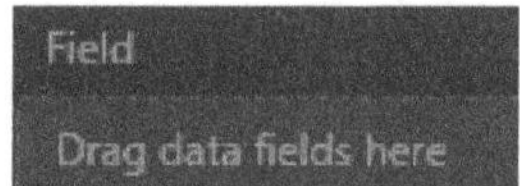

Figure 15-1 Slicer Field Well

Fields cannot be added to the **VISUAL LEVEL FILTERS OPTION**, which makes sense, because slicers are filters for objects that have data, on the page.

The Page level filters and Report level filters options can be used when a slicer object is selected.

Slicer Formatting Options

Figure 15-2 shows the slicer formatting categories. The Title, Background, Lock Aspect and Border categories work the same as they do for charts.

The categories that have options specifically for slicers are explained below.

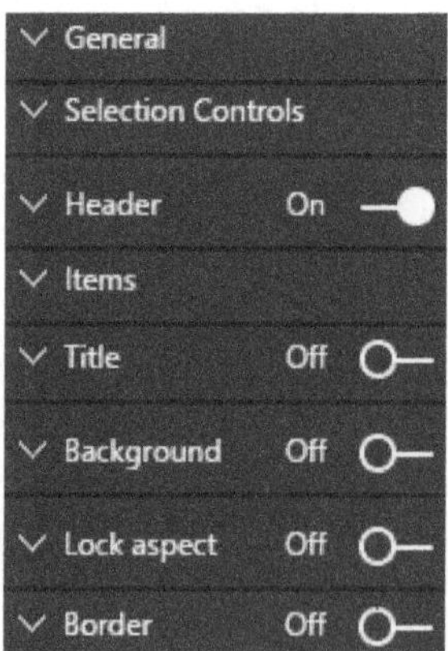

Figure 15-2 Slicer categories

General Options

The options shown in Figure 15-3 are used to change the structure of the slicer.

The **OUTLINE COLOR OPTION** is used to change the color of the line around the slicer header (the field name).

The **OUTLINE WEIGHT OPTION** is used to change the thickness of the line around the slicer header.

The **ORIENTATION OPTION** is used to change whether the options on the slicer are displayed horizontally or vertically.

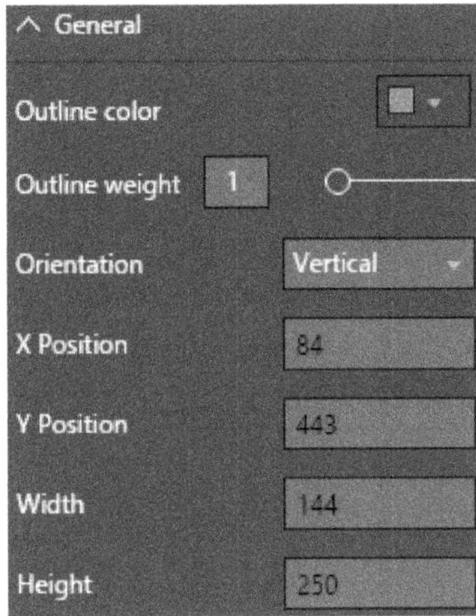

Figure 15-3 General options

Selection Controls Options

The options shown in Figure 15-4 are used to enable additional filter selection options, as explained below.

If enabled, the **SELECT ALL OPTION** adds the Select All option to the list of values on the slicer, as shown in Figure 15-5. Checking this option on the slicer, checks all of the other values on the slicer.

If enabled, the **SINGLE SELECT OPTION** only allows the slicer to filter on one value. This means that only one option on the slicer can be used at a time. The way that you know that this option is enabled, is that the check box of an item is black, as shown in Figure 15-5. Disable this option to allow more than one option to be selected on the slicer, at the same time, as shown later in Figure 15-9.

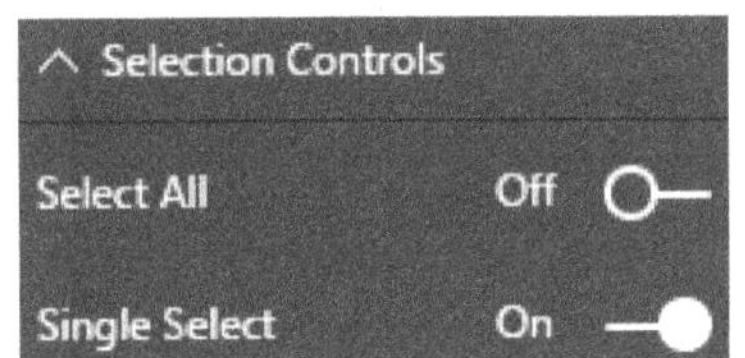

Figure 15-4 Selection Controls options

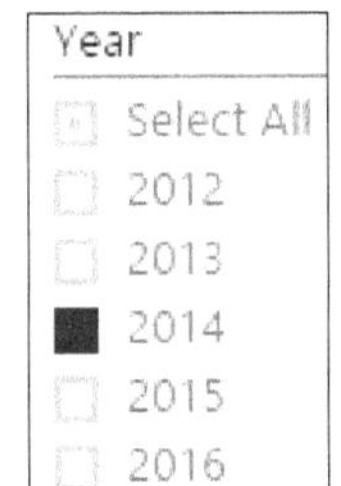

Figure 15-5 Slicer with the Single Select option enabled

Header Options

The options shown in Figure 15-6 are used to customize the header on the slicer.

The **OUTLINE OPTION** is used to select where, if any place, a line is placed around the header. The default is Bottom only, as shown above in Figure 15-5.

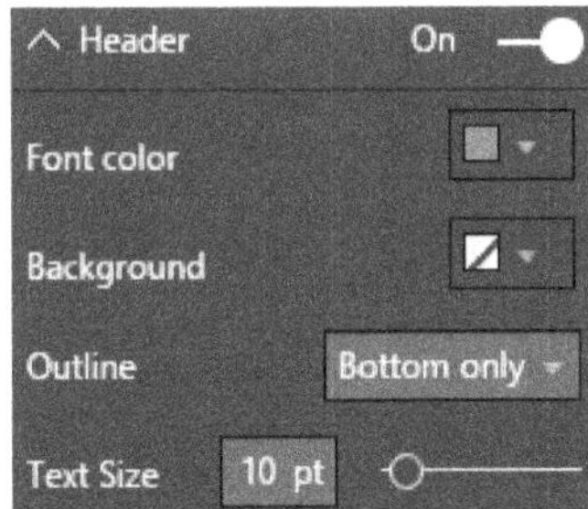

Figure 15-6 Header options

Items Options

The items in this category are the same as the Header options, shown above in Figure 15-6. The difference is that the options in this category are applied to the items on the slicer. This means that the text can be made larger or smaller, as needed.

Exercise 15.1: Create A Year Slicer

In this exercise you will create a slicer that will filter the data by the year of the order.

1. Save the Report Data.pbix file as `Chapter 15 Slicers`.

2. Duplicate the Order List page ⇒ Move the table to the right a little.

3. Click on a blank space on the page ⇒ Click the Slicer button ⇒ Add the Year field ⇒ Resize the slicer to make it smaller ⇒ Move it to the left of the table.

Format The Slicer

1. Display the formatting options for the slicer ⇒ Change the Header Text Size to 12.

   You should see the slicer shown on the left side of Figure 15-7.

Year	Customer Name	Order ID	Order Date	Order Amount
☐ 2012		3122	06/17/2014	$5,879.70
☐ 2013	7 Bikes For 7 Brothers	3054	05/26/2014	$53.90
☐ 2014	Against The Wind Bikes	3055	05/26/2014	$479.85
☐ 2015	AIC Childrens	3153	06/21/2014	$101.70
☐ 2016				

Figure 15-7 Slicer added to the report

Slicer Options

The slicer options are illustrated in Figure 15-8.

Clicking the **FOCUS MODE BUTTON** displays the slicer on a page by itself, as shown in Figure 15-9.

The **MORE OPTIONS BUTTON** is used to sort the items (values displayed) on the slicer, export the values in the slicer to a .csv file and search the values in the list, as shown in Figure 15-10.

The **CLEAR SELECTIONS BUTTON** changes the selected items in the slicer to not selected.

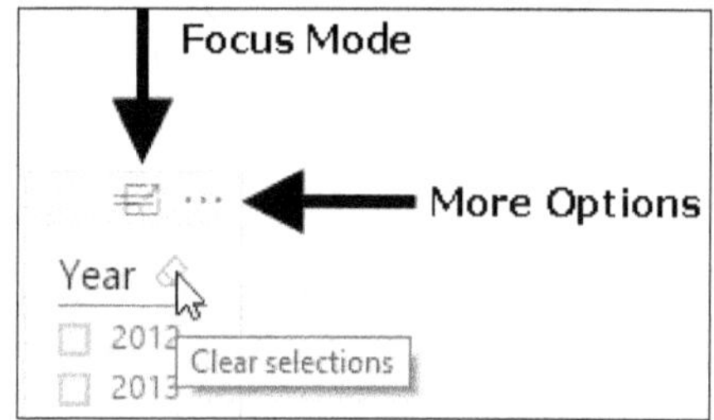

Figure 15-8 Slicer options

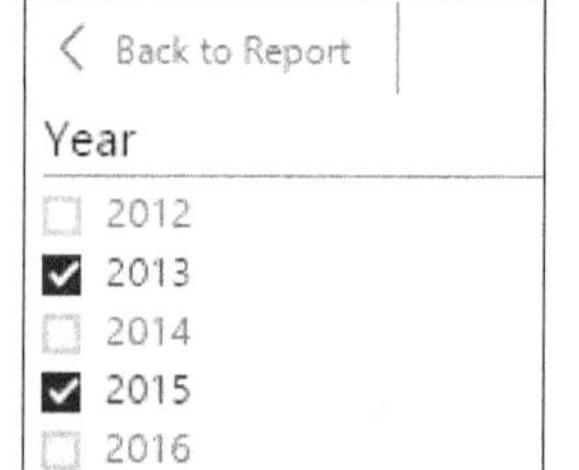

Figure 15-9 Slicer options in Focus Mode

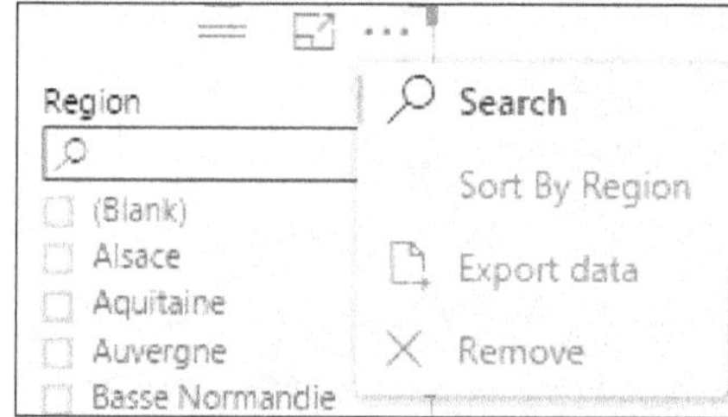

Figure 15-10 Slicer search options

Slicer Search Options

When a slicer contains a lot of items, the **SEARCH OPTION**, shown above in Figure 15-10 is available. Selecting this option displays a search field above the items on the slicer. As you type in the search field, the items in the slicer will be filtered, based on what you type.

1. Check the box for 2014. Only records with an order date in 2014 are displayed in the table.

After you create a slicer, you may decide that you need to use a different field for the slicer. If that is the case, drag the field that you now want to use over to the Field section, on the Field Well. The slicer on the page will be updated to reflect the new field and its values.

Exercise 15.2: Using More Than One Slicer

Pages in a report are not limited to one slicer. Just keep in mind that the order that the slicers are used in, makes a difference. The first slicer used, usually filters the data in the other slicers on the page. For example, you would use date related slicers in this order: year, quarter and month, but not in any other order to have the other slicers filtered properly. Slicers work the same as a hierarchy, in terms of the order that the slicers are used. Adding a second slicer will remind you of drill down functionality.

1. Duplicate page E15.1.

2. Move the table to the right, so that another slicer can be added to the left of the table. It is not a requirement that the slicers are placed next to the table or chart.

3. Click the Slicer button ⇒ Add the Month Full field to the slicer.

4. Move the month slicer next to the Year slicer ⇒

   Check the September option.

   Only records with an order date in September 2014 are displayed, as shown in Figure 15-11.

Customer Name	Order ID	Order Date
Alley Cat Cycles	2081	09/07/2014
Alley Cat Cycles	2153	09/27/2014
Alley Cat Cycles	2157	09/28/2014
Backpedal Cycle Shop	2171	09/30/2014
BBS Pty	2067	09/03/2014
Belgium Bike Co.	2155	09/28/2014
Belgium Bike Co.	2169	09/30/2014
Benny - The Spokes Person	2080	09/07/2014
Bike Shop from Mars	2144	09/25/2014

Figure 15-11 Table filtered by two slicers

It is not a requirement to select values in all of the slicers. If the Year slicer option was cleared, and January was selected on the Month filter, the table would display the rows shown in Figure 15-12.

As shown, all of the records have an order date in January, regardless of the year.

Customer Name	Order ID	Order Date
Alley Cat Cycles	1151	01/08/2014
Alley Cat Cycles	1204	01/19/2014
Alley Cat Cycles	1239	01/28/2014
Alley Cat Cycles	2644	01/27/2015
Alley Cat Cycles	2664	01/31/2015
Backpedal Cycle Shop	2560	01/04/2015

Figure 15-12 Table filtered by one slicer

Slicers That Do Not Display Data

As shown in Figure 15-13, no records are displayed in the table.

That is because there are no records with an order date in June 2013 or June 2015.

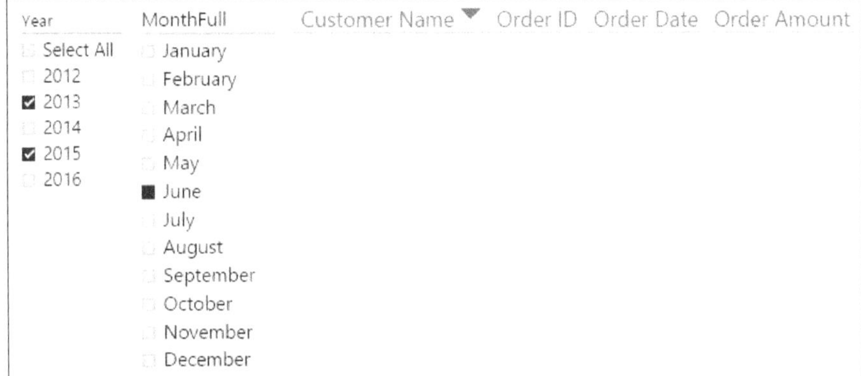

Figure 15-13 Table with no data

Slicer Placement From A Layout Perspective
It is not a good idea to place slicers below a table because the table can will grow and shrink, depending on the number of records that are retrieved when using a slicer.

Exercise 15.3: Use Multiple Slicers With A Matrix Table

The matrix table that you learned how to create in Chapter 11, Exercise 11.6, displays three years of data. As time goes on, the table will display more years of data, unless a filter is created to only display certain years. A better solution is to create slicers that will allow the person viewing the report to select the year(s) that they want to see data for.

1. Use the options shown in Figure 15-14 to create the matrix table.

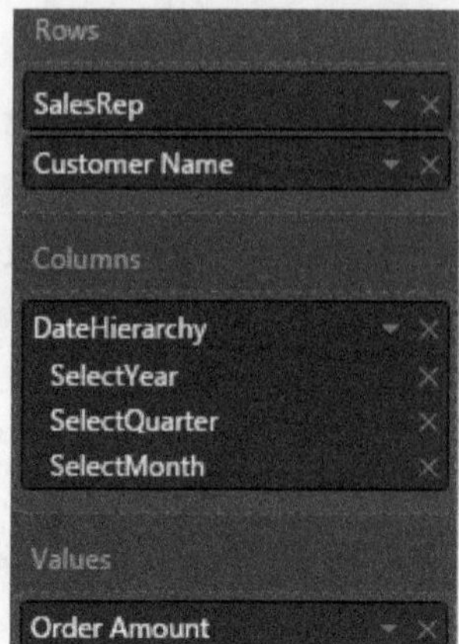

Figure 15-14 Options to create a matrix table

2. Move the table down, so that three slicers can be added across the top of the page.

3. Make the following formatting changes to the Matrix table.

☑ Matrix Style ⇒ Style ⇒ Minimal
☑ Grid ⇒ Vert grid ⇒ On
☑ Grid ⇒ Vert grid ⇒ Color ⇒ Select the third teal color (in the third column). It is the same color as the Outline Color options default color

Create And Customize Slicers

1. Click the Slicer button ⇒ Add the Sales Rep field to the slicer.

2. Format panel ⇒ Selection Controls ⇒ Enable the Select All option ⇒ Turn off the Single Select option.

3. Click the Slicer button ⇒ Add the Year field to the slicer.

4. Format panel ⇒ Selection Controls ⇒ Enable the Select All option ⇒ Turn off the Single Select option.

5. Click the Slicer button ⇒ Add the Quarter Full field to the slicer.

6. Format panel ⇒ Selection Controls ⇒ Enable the Select All option ⇒ Turn off the Single Select option.

7. Click the Slicer button ⇒ Add the Month Full field to the slicer.

8. Select the following formatting options for the Month Full slicer.

☑ General ⇒ Orientation ⇒ Horizontal
☑ Selection Controls ⇒ Enable the Select All option ⇒ Turn off the Single Select option

9. Rearrange the slicers, so that they look like the ones shown in Figure 15-15. The arrows at the beginning and end of the values on the Month Full slicer indicate that there are more values in the slicer. Clicking on an arrow on this slicer will display more values.

SalesRep	Year	QuarterFull	MonthFull
Select All	Select All	Select All	
(Blank)	(Blank)	(Blank)	
Albert Hellstern	2012	Quarter 1	Select All (Blank) January February March April May >
Andrew Fuller	2013	Quarter 2	
Anne Dodsworth	2014	Quarter 3	
Caroline Patterson	2015	Quarter 4	
Janet Leverling	2016		

Figure 15-15 Slicers for the matrix table

Use The Slicers

1. Select the following options on the slicers. The matrix table should look like the one shown in Figure 15-16.

☑ Sales Rep - Janet Leverling
☑ Year - 2014
☑ Quarter 2

	SelectYear	2014					Total
	SelectQuarter	Q2				Total	
SalesRep	Customer Name	April	May	June	Total		
Janet Leverling				$5,879.70	**$5,879.70**	**$5,879.70**	**$5,879.70**
	7 Bikes For 7 Brothers		$53.90		**$53.90**	**$53.90**	**$53.90**
	Ankara Bicycle Company			$959.70	**$959.70**	**$959.70**	**$959.70**
	Barbados Sports, Ltd.			$329.85	**$329.85**	**$329.85**	**$329.85**
	BBS Pty	$479.85			**$479.85**	**$479.85**	**$479.85**
	Belgium Bike Co.			$821.40	**$821.40**	**$821.40**	**$821.40**
	Benny - The Spokes Person	$1,680.94			**$1,680.94**	**$1,680.94**	**$1,680.94**
	Bicycle Basics			$539.85	**$539.85**	**$539.85**	**$539.85**

Figure 15-16 Result of slicer options applied to the matrix table

2. Clear all of the slicer options.

3. Select the following options on the slicers. The matrix table should look like the one shown in Figure 15-17.

☑ Year - 2014, 2015

	SelectYear	2014										
	SelectQuarter	Q1				Q2				Q3		
SalesRep	Customer Name	January	February	March	Total	April	May	June	Total	July	August	September
Anne Dodsworth	Alley Cat Cycles											
	Backpedal Cycle Shop		$3,544.20		**$3,544.20**			$35.00	**$35.00**	$5,099.25		
	BBS Pty							$8,819.55	**$8,819.55**			
	Belgium Bike Co.									$489.87	$2,786.45	$1,751.02
	Bendai Mountain Bikers							$15.00	**$15.00**			
	Benny - The Spokes Person										$125.70	
	Bicicletas de Montaña La Paz							$97.02	**$97.02**			
	Bike Shop from Mars	$43.50			**$43.50**						$2,944.35	
	Bike-A-Holics Anonymous		$5,879.70	$659.70	**$6,539.40**	$872.65			**$872.65**			

Figure 15-17 Result of slicer options applied to the matrix table

4. Clear all of the slicer options.

5. Select the following options on the slicers.

☑ Year - 2013, 2014, 2015
☑ Month Full - February, May, June, September

6. Create a filter for the matrix table. Use the Customer Name field ⇒ Select the Backpedal Cycle Shop. The matrix table should look like the one shown in Figure 15-18. Notice that there are no sales in 2013 for the customer. When data for multiple years is displayed, you can see how the data compares, from year to year.

	SelectYear	2014							2015			Total
	SelectQuarter	Q1		Q2		Q3		Total	Q1		Total	
SalesRep	Customer Name	February	Total	June	Total	September	Total		February	Total		
Anne Dodsworth	Backpedal Cycle Shop	$3,544.20	**$3,544.20**	$35.00	**$35.00**			**$3,579.20**				**$3,579.20**
	Total	**$3,544.20**	**$3,544.20**	**$35.00**	**$35.00**			**$3,579.20**				**$3,579.20**
Nancy Davolio	Backpedal Cycle Shop					$33.90	**$33.90**	**$33.90**	$8,819.55	**$8,819.55**	**$8,819.55**	**$8,853.45**
	Total					**$33.90**	**$33.90**	**$33.90**	**$8,819.55**	**$8,819.55**	**$8,819.55**	**$8,853.45**
Robert King	Backpedal Cycle Shop	$6,233.05	**$6,233.05**	$1,529.70	**$1,529.70**			**$7,762.75**				**$7,762.75**
	Total	**$6,233.05**	**$6,233.05**	**$1,529.70**	**$1,529.70**			**$7,762.75**				**$7,762.75**
Total		**$9,777.25**	**$9,777.25**	**$1,564.70**	**$1,564.70**	**$33.90**	**$33.90**	**$11,375.85**	**$8,819.55**	**$8,819.55**	**$8,819.55**	**$20,195.40**

Figure 15-18 Filter and slicer options applied to the matrix table

Exercise 15.4: Add A Slicer To A Chart

Slicers do not support Visual level filters. You could create a filter for the table, but it would not filter the slicer. One solution is to create a Page level filter.

1. On a new page, create a Clustered Bar chart, using the fields and filter below.

   ☑ Add the Customer Name field to the Axis section
   ☑ Add the Last Years Sales field to the Value section
   ☑ Create a Page level filter for the Country Name field to select records in the USA

2. Click the Slicer button ⇒ Add the Region field to the slicer ⇒ Select the following formatting options for the slicer.

   ☑ General ⇒ Orientation ⇒ Horizontal
   ☑ Selection Controls ⇒ Enable the Select All option

3. Resize the slicer so that it is almost as wide as the chart, as shown in Figure 15-19 ⇒

   Click on some of the Regions to see how the slicer works.

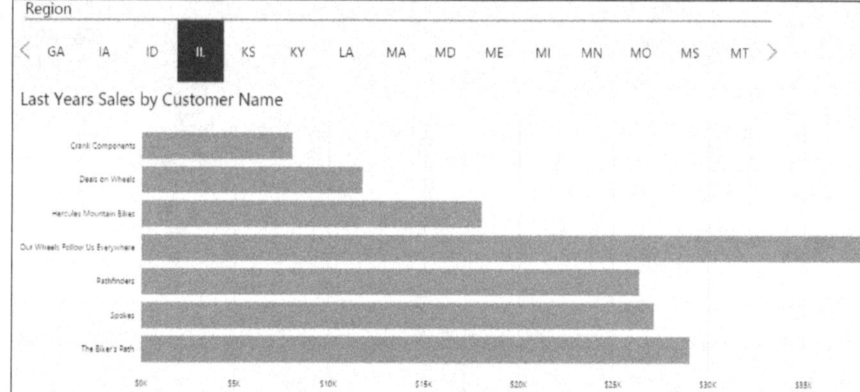

Figure 15-19 Chart with slicers

Exercise 15.5: Use Two Slicers With Two Tables

As you saw in Exercise 15.2, when two or more slicers are on a page, one slicer will filter the data displayed in another slicer, as long as there is a relationship between the fields used by the slicers. In this exercise, you will see how the slicers work with more than one table or chart on the page.

1. Duplicate the Customer List page.

2. Make the table smaller and move it to the lower left corner of the page.

3. Copy and paste the Order List table to the new page ⇒ Make it smaller and place it across from the Customer List table.

4. Add a slicer to the page ⇒ Add the Country Name field to it.

5. Make the following formatting changes to the slicer.

   ☑ General ⇒ Outline Weight ⇒ 3
   ☑ General ⇒ Orientation ⇒ Horizontal
   ☑ Selection Controls ⇒ Enable the Select All option
   ☑ Selection Controls ⇒ Turn off the Single Select option
   ☑ Border ⇒ Enable this option

6. Duplicate the slicer ⇒ Add the Region field to it. Doing this is easier then selecting all of the options in step 5 for this slicer. When finished, the page should look like the one shown in Figure 15-20.

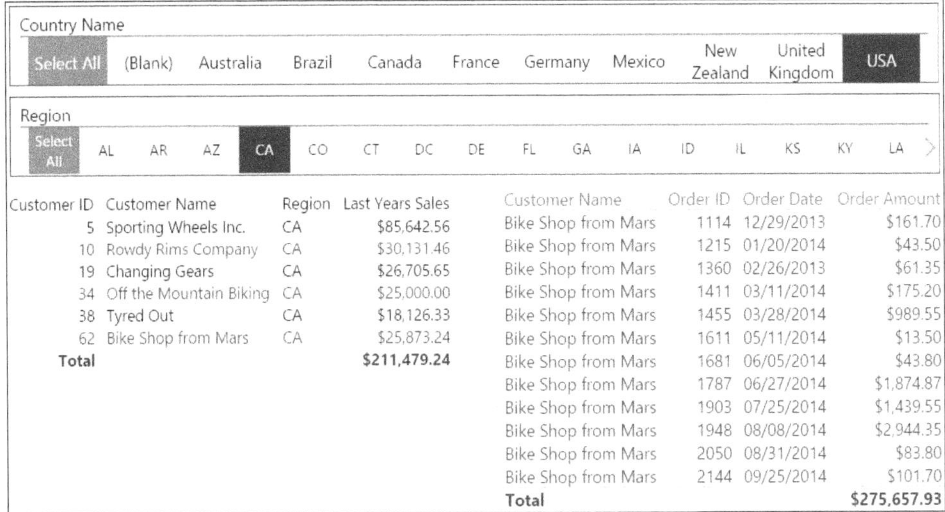

Customer ID	Customer Name	Region	Last Years Sales
5	Sporting Wheels Inc.	CA	$85,642.56
10	Rowdy Rims Company	CA	$30,131.46
19	Changing Gears	CA	$26,705.65
34	Off the Mountain Biking	CA	$25,000.00
38	Tyred Out	CA	$18,126.33
62	Bike Shop from Mars	CA	$25,873.24
Total			**$211,479.24**

Customer Name	Order ID	Order Date	Order Amount
Bike Shop from Mars	1114	12/29/2013	$161.70
Bike Shop from Mars	1215	01/20/2014	$43.50
Bike Shop from Mars	1360	02/26/2013	$61.35
Bike Shop from Mars	1411	03/11/2014	$175.20
Bike Shop from Mars	1455	03/28/2014	$989.55
Bike Shop from Mars	1611	05/11/2014	$13.50
Bike Shop from Mars	1681	06/05/2014	$43.80
Bike Shop from Mars	1787	06/27/2014	$1,874.87
Bike Shop from Mars	1903	07/25/2014	$1,439.55
Bike Shop from Mars	1948	08/08/2014	$2,944.35
Bike Shop from Mars	2050	08/31/2014	$83.80
Bike Shop from Mars	2144	09/25/2014	$101.70
Total			**$275,657.93**

Figure 15-20 Report with two slicers and two tables

7. Test the slicers.

Just like tables and charts can be copied and pasted from one page to another in the same report file, so can slicers.

Using Charts As A Slicer

In the slicer exercises up to this point, the slicers were created using the Slicer visualization. Power BI Desktop has the ability to use a chart as a slicer. While the chart slicer exercises demonstrate bar and pie charts, line charts can also be used as a slicer chart.

Exercise 15.6: Use Bar And Pie Charts As Slicers

In this exercise you will create a chart that displays order amounts by country. The slicer will display a list of countries that will be used to filter the chart.

Use A Bar Chart As A Slicer

1. Duplicate the Order List page ⇒ Move the table to the bottom of the page ⇒ Add the Country Name field to the bottom of the Values section.

   The reason that I am adding the Country Name field is so that you will be able to verify that the chart that will be created, is filtering the data in this table correctly. On your own, displaying the field that is filtered on, is not necessary.

2. Add a Stacked Bar chart to the top of the page.

3. Add the Country Name field to the Axis section ⇒ Add the Order Amount field to the Value section.

4. Click on the bar for Canada.

   The other bars on the chart should not be enabled, as shown in Figure 15-21.

   Notice that the table at the bottom of the page has been filtered and only displays orders in Canada.

   Multiple bars can be selected to filter data, by clicking on the first bar, then pressing and holding down the CTRL key and clicking on the other bar(s) that you want to filter on.

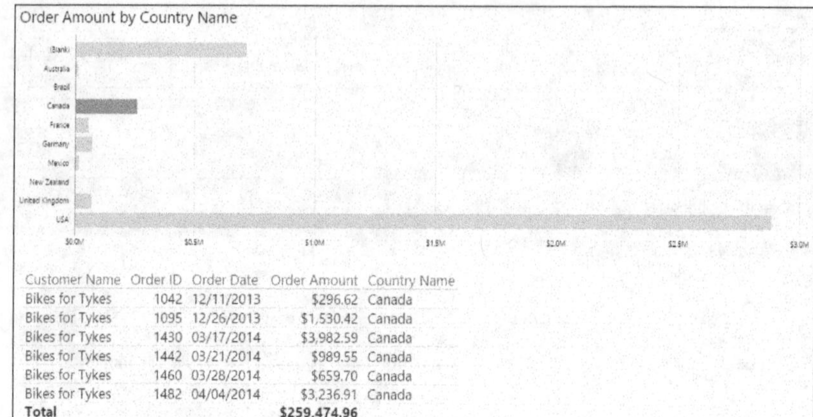

Customer Name	Order ID	Order Date	Order Amount	Country Name
Bikes for Tykes	1042	12/11/2013	$296.62	Canada
Bikes for Tykes	1095	12/26/2013	$1,530.42	Canada
Bikes for Tykes	1430	03/17/2014	$3,982.59	Canada
Bikes for Tykes	1442	03/21/2014	$989.55	Canada
Bikes for Tykes	1460	03/28/2014	$659.70	Canada
Bikes for Tykes	1482	04/04/2014	$3,236.91	Canada
Total			**$259,474.96**	

Figure 15-21 Bar chart used as a slicer

Use A Stacked Column Chart As A Slicer

1. Duplicate page E15.6 ⇒ Rename the page to `E15.6A`.
2. Select the table ⇒ Add the Ship Via field to the bottom of the Values section. I added this field so that you can see how the filter works. This field is not needed to complete the exercise.
3. Change the chart type to Stacked column.
4. Create a filter for the chart, for the Country Name field, to only display these countries: Canada, France, Germany, United Kingdom.
5. Add the Ship Via field to the Legend. The chart should look like the one shown in Figure 15-22.

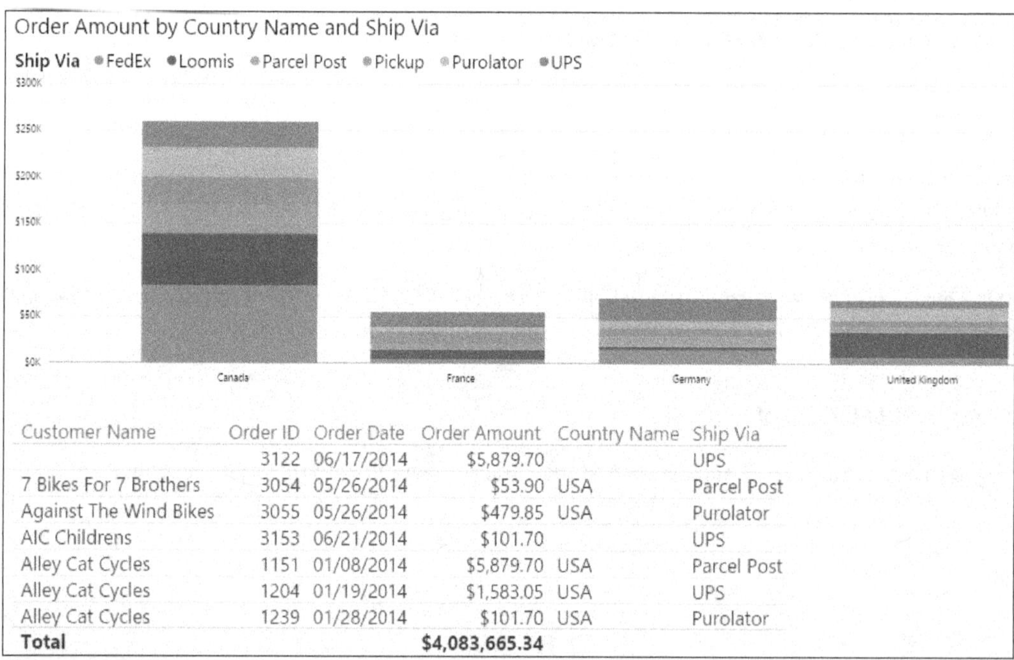

Customer Name	Order ID	Order Date	Order Amount	Country Name	Ship Via
	3122	06/17/2014	$5,879.70		UPS
7 Bikes For 7 Brothers	3054	05/26/2014	$53.90	USA	Parcel Post
Against The Wind Bikes	3055	05/26/2014	$479.85	USA	Purolator
AIC Childrens	3153	06/21/2014	$101.70		UPS
Alley Cat Cycles	1151	01/08/2014	$5,879.70	USA	Parcel Post
Alley Cat Cycles	1204	01/19/2014	$1,583.05	USA	UPS
Alley Cat Cycles	1239	01/28/2014	$101.70	USA	Purolator
Total			**$4,083,665.34**		

Figure 15-22 Stacked column chart that will be used as a filter

Clicking on a value in the legend will only display records in the table that have the value that was selected in the legend. The other sections on each bar on the chart will be disabled. Clicking on the same option again removes the filter.

Clicking on a section of a bar on the chart, disables all other sections, on all bars. The records displayed in the table are for the country and ship via value of the section, of the bar that you clicked on, as shown in Figure 15-23.
If the Ship Via field was removed from the Legend section, more than one column on the chart could be selected.

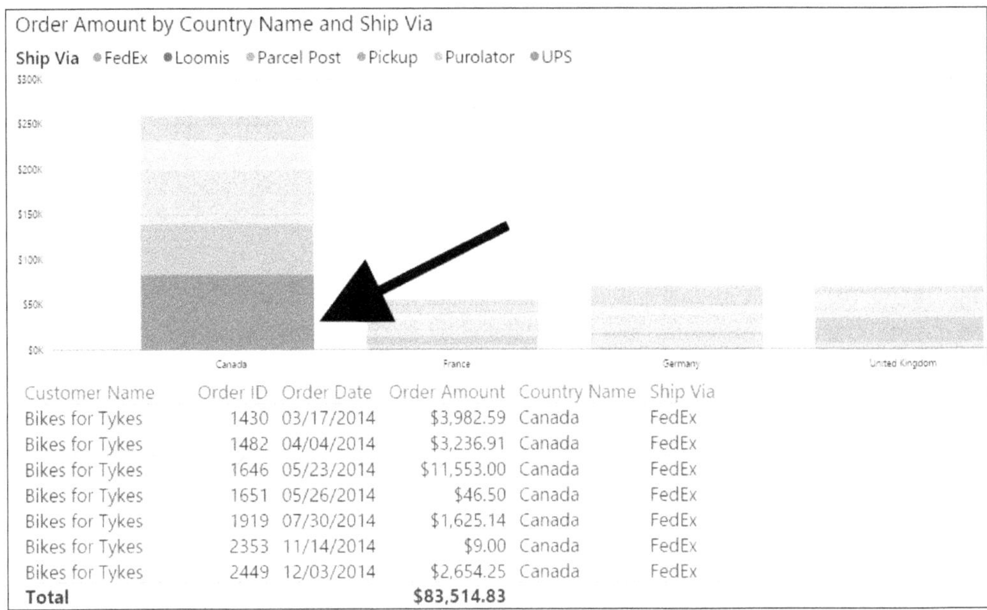

Customer Name	Order ID	Order Date	Order Amount	Country Name	Ship Via
Bikes for Tykes	1430	03/17/2014	$3,982.59	Canada	FedEx
Bikes for Tykes	1482	04/04/2014	$3,236.91	Canada	FedEx
Bikes for Tykes	1646	05/23/2014	$11,553.00	Canada	FedEx
Bikes for Tykes	1651	05/26/2014	$46.50	Canada	FedEx
Bikes for Tykes	1919	07/30/2014	$1,625.14	Canada	FedEx
Bikes for Tykes	2353	11/14/2014	$9.00	Canada	FedEx
Bikes for Tykes	2449	12/03/2014	$2,654.25	Canada	FedEx
Total			**$83,514.83**		

Figure 15-23 Data in a table filtered by the section selected on a bar

Use A Pie Chart As A Slicer

1. Duplicate page E15.6 ⇒ Rename the page to `E15.6B`.

2. Change the chart to a Pie chart.

3. Display the legend on the left side of the chart.

   Figure 15-24 shows the slicer chart changed to a pie chart.

   You can click on a slice of the pie chart or click on an option in the legend, to filter the data in the table.

   Notice that once a country is clicked on, the other values on the chart and legend are disabled.

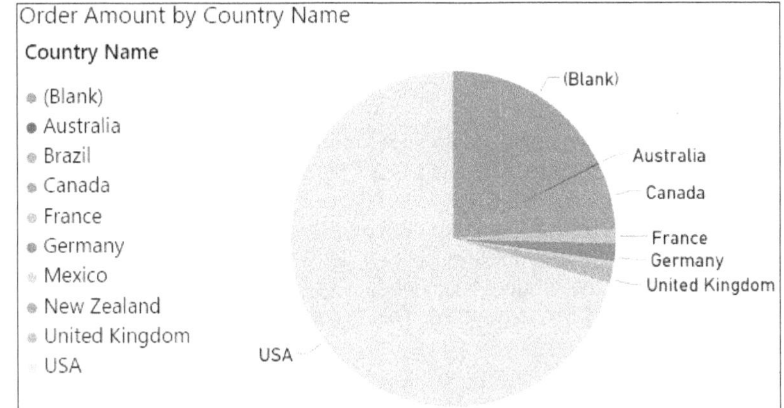

Figure 15-24 Pie chart slicer

Detach A Visual From A Slicer

In the exercises up to this point, when a slicer or chart was used as a filter, all of the other visuals had the slicer options applied automatically. There may be times when there is a visual on a page that does not need the slicer options applied to it.

Exercise 15.7: Detach A Visual From A Slicer

In this exercise you will learn how to prevent a visual on the page from being filtered by another chart.

1. Duplicate page E15.6A.

2. Make the chart smaller ⇒ Make a copy of the chart and place the copy to the right of the original chart. The copy will be the chart that you will detach.

3. Click on the first chart ⇒ Format tab ⇒ **EDIT INTERACTIONS BUTTON.**

   You will see the icons shown in Figure 15-25 in the upper right corner of the second chart. The buttons are explained below. Figure 15-26 shows the icons for the table.

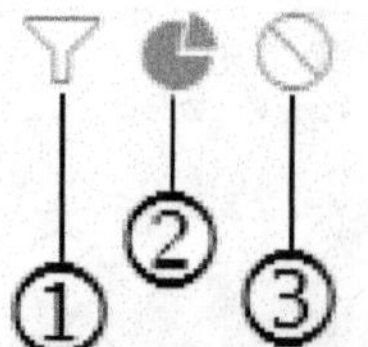

Figure 15-25 Interaction buttons for a chart

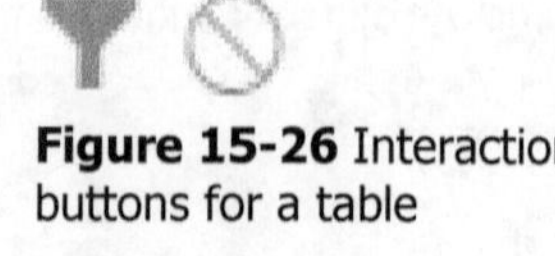

Figure 15-26 Interaction buttons for a table

   ① Click on the **FILTER BUTTON** to indicate that the visual can interact with the slicer.
   ② Click on the **HIGHLIGHT BUTTON** to indicate that the visual can interact with a chart slicer.
   ③ Click on the **NONE BUTTON** to prevent the visual from being filtered by any object on the page.

4. On the second chart, click the None button.

5. On the first chart, click on an item in the legend. Notice that the values on the table were filtered and the values on the second chart did not change.

6. On the first chart, clear the filter ⇒ On the second chart, click on the Highlight button ⇒ On the first chart, click on a section of a column. Notice that the second chart was filtered.

7. Add a slicer to the page ⇒ Add the Country field, in the Customer table, to the slicer.

8. On the second chart, click the None button.

9. On the slicer, select Canada. Notice that the second chart was not filtered, but the other chart and table were.

What Is The Difference Between Filtering And Highlighting Data?
A filter hides data in a table or chart, like slicers do. Highlighting, does not remove items, it changes how the data is displayed, by disabling items on the chart, which gives the appearance of being "highlighted".

Highlighting Data

Highlighting is used to make a data series stand out, while the entire data set is still displayed. Highlighting, is just a name given to the feature. The chart is not actually highlighted. This feature is helpful when a lot of data is displayed.

Highlighting data allows the user to click on a specific item on the visualization and only see related data for that item. For example, a chart that displays data for several product lines. If the page has three charts that display different information about the product lines, when a specific product line is selected (clicked on), all data that is not related to the selected product line is disabled. This makes it much easier to see and understand the data for the selected product line.

As you will see later in Exercise 15.9, highlighting can be the result of **CROSS FILTERING** (one visualization is the source and another visualization on the page, receives the highlighting).

Drill Down With Cross Filtering
Even with the Drill Down mode enabled, you can still do cross filtering between charts.

Exercise 15.8: Highlight A Chart Using The Legend

In this exercise, you will create a chart that will have highlighting applied by clicking on an option in the charts legend.

1. Create a Clustered Column chart and filter using the fields and filter listed below. The chart should look like the one shown in Figure 15-27.

   ☑ Add the Country Name field to the Axis section
   ☑ Add the following fields to the Value section: Sales Cost, Sales Net, Shipping Amount and Order Amount
   ☑ Create a filter to only display the following countries: Canada, France and United Kingdom

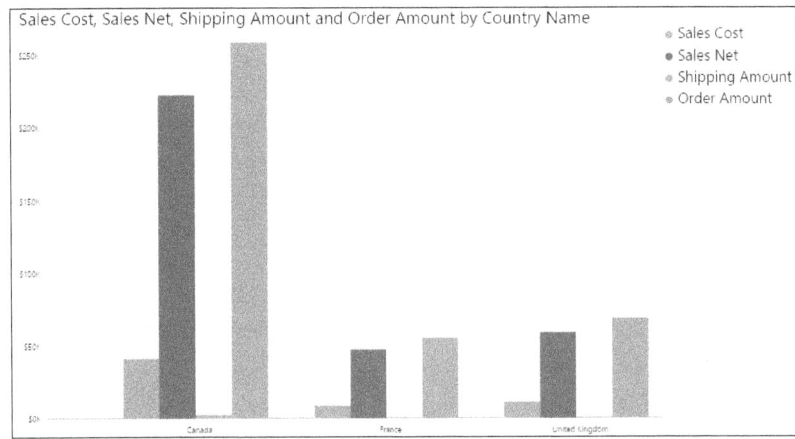

Figure 15-27 Clustered Column chart with highlighting

2. On the legend, click on the Sales Net option.

   This is the only value enabled on the chart, for each country, as shown in Figure 15-28.

   To enable all of the options on the legend and chart, click on the selected option on the legend again.

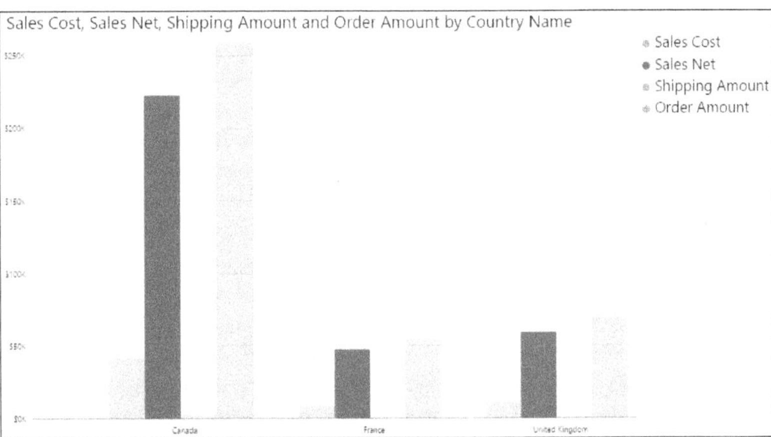

Figure 15-28 Chart filtered by the legend

Exercise 15.9: Use One Chart To Highlight Data In Another Chart

As the title of this exercise indicates, it is possible to use one chart to highlight data in another chart. You may be thinking that this type of chart highlighting only works one way. Just the opposite. Each chart can be used to highlight data in the other chart on the page. In this exercise you will create two charts to see how highlighting can be applied to either chart.

Create A Pie Chart

1. Add a Pie chart to the page.
2. Add the Sales Rep field to the Legend section ⇒ Add the Order Amount field to the Values section.
3. Display the legend to the right of the chart.
4. Disable the Detail Labels.

   The chart should look like the one shown in Figure 15-29.

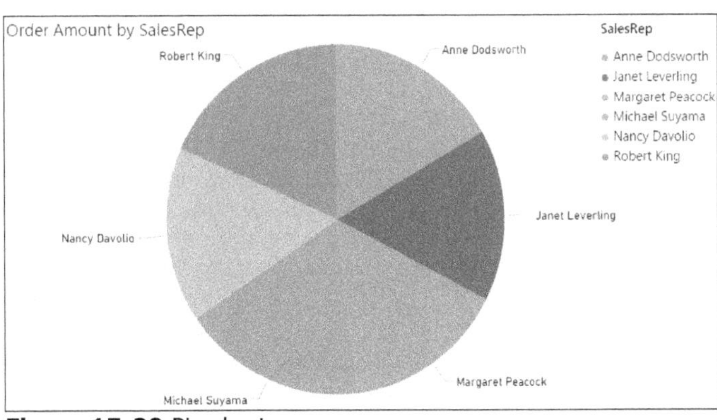

Figure 15-29 Pie chart

Create A Column Chart

1. Add a Clustered Column chart to the page.

2. Add the Country Name field to the Axis section ⇒ Add the Order Amount field to the Value section.

3. Create a filter for the column chart. Use the Country Name field to only display (Blank), Canada and USA records.

Highlight Data Displayed On The Column Chart Using The Pie Chart

1. Click on a sales reps name in the Pie chart legend. You will see that the other slices of the pie chart are disabled and that the column chart only displays amounts for the selected sales rep, as shown on the right side of Figure 15-30.

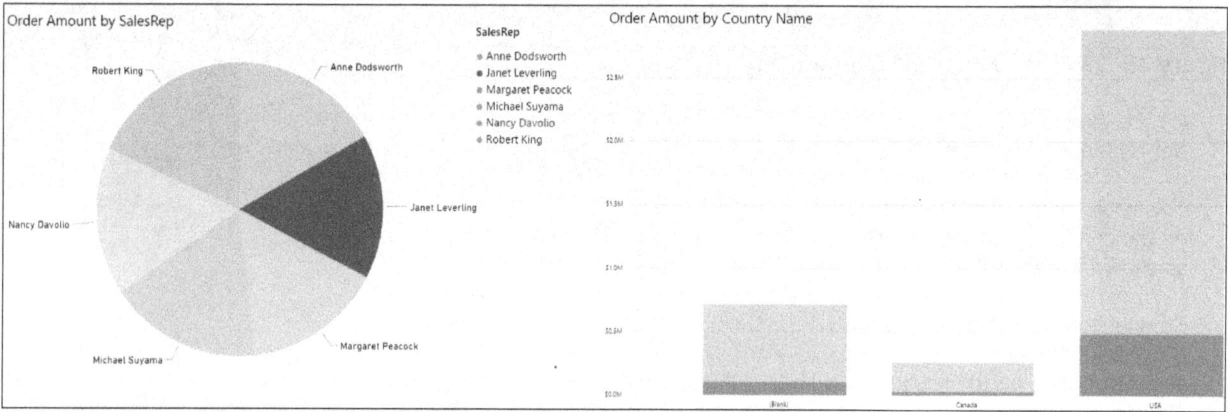

Figure 15-30 Pie and column chart highlighting for the selected sales rep

2. Click on the Sales Rep name again, so that neither chart has any highlighting.

3. On the column chart, click on the USA column. The pie chart now displays the USA total order amount per sales rep, as shown in Figure 15-31. The column chart also displays the USA total order amount per sales rep. If you click on the (Blank) column, in the column chart, the pie chart will look like the one shown in Figure 15-32. It displays sales reps orders that do not have data in the Country field.

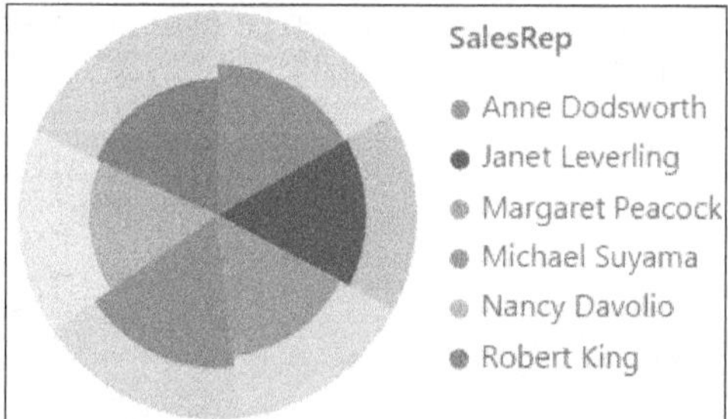

Figure 15-31 Pie chart filtered by the column chart

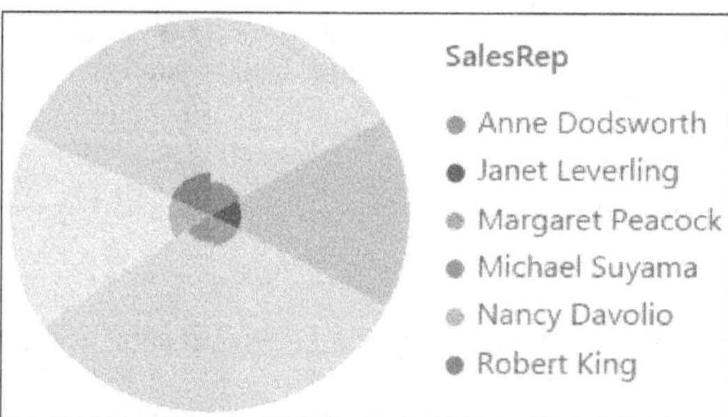

Figure 15-32 Pie chart filtered by a different column

Tips For Using Bar And Column Charts To Highlight Data
The previous exercise demonstrated how to use one chart (a pie chart) to highlight data in another chart (a column chart). Bar and column charts can use two values at the same time to highlight data on different visualizations. To create this scenario, at a minimum, the page needs a bar chart with one field in the Value section, a column chart with one field in the Value section (a different field from the one used in the other chart) and a table that displays the value fields that the bar and column chart use. The limitation to creating this scenario is only being able to use one value each, for the bar and column chart. Some things to be aware of are:

① On clustered bar and column charts, any bar or column in the group can be clicked on to highlight the data.

② On stacked bar and column charts, any section in the bar or column can be clicked on.

Exercise 15.10: Highlight Data In A Bubble Chart

In Exercise 13.9 you created a bubble chart. It did not have a lot of data, like the scatter chart that you created in Exercise 13.8 does. If a bubble chart has a lot of information, applying the highlighting feature will let you select which group of values to display. This is what you will learn how to do in this exercise.

1. Open a new page ⇒ Add the Scatter chart to the page.

2. Create the chart using the fields shown in Figure 15-33.

   Set the Order ID field to Count (Distinct).

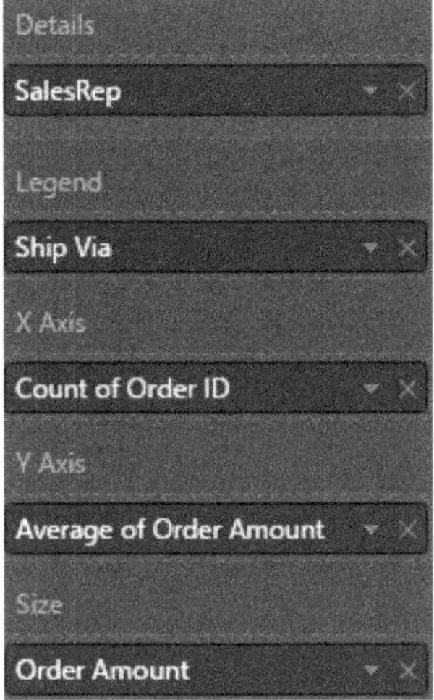

Figure 15-33 Options to create a Scatter chart

3. Display the legend to the right of the chart.

   The chart should look like the one shown in Figure 15-34.

   As you can see, the chart displays a lot of data.

   The legend displays the values that the chart can be highlighted on (filtered).

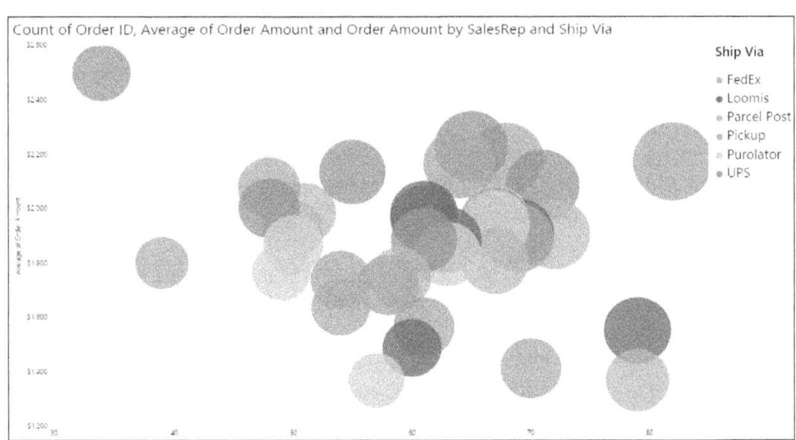

Figure 15-34 Bubble chart with highlighting capabilities

4. In the legend, click on the UPS option.

   All of the bubbles except UPS are no longer enabled. The chart should look like the one shown in Figure 15-35.

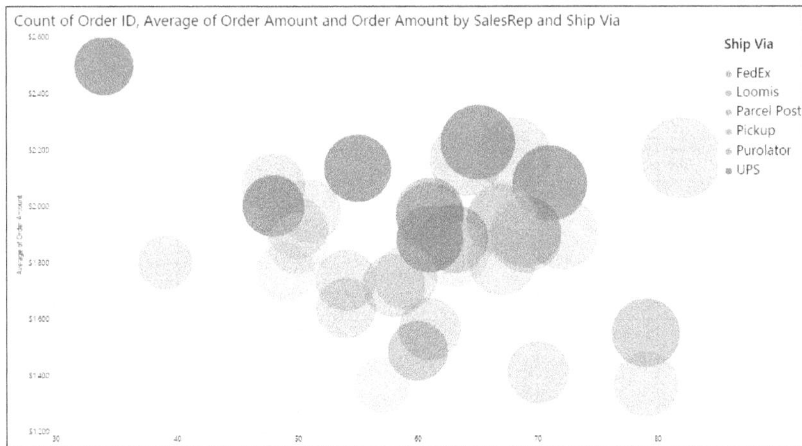

Figure 15-35 Highlighting applied to a Bubble chart

Exercise 15.11: Display Sales Reps By Total Order Amount

The table that will be created in this exercise will display a list of the sales reps in order, based on their total sales amount. Slicers will be added to filter the data.

1. Add the Table visual to the page.

2. Add the following fields to create the table.

   ☑ Sales Rep Rank (in the Orders table)
   ☑ Sales Rep
   ☑ Order Amount

3. Create a filter using the Order Amount field. The Order Amount should be greater than zero.

4. Sort the data in the table on the Sales Rep Rank column, in ascending order.

Format The Table

1. Change the following formatting options.

   ☑ General ⇒ Auto-Size column width ⇒ On
   ☑ General ⇒ Text Size ⇒ Change to 12
   ☑ General ⇒ Totals ⇒ Off

Create A Year Slicer

1. Add a slicer to the page.

2. Add the Year field.

3. Change the Selection Controls option ⇒ Change the Single Select option to Off.
   The table and slicer should look like the ones shown in Figure 15-36. The sales reps and order amounts will change when you filter by year, on the slicer.

Figure 15-36 displays the sales reps ranked, based on all of the data in the table.
Figure 15-37 displays the sales reps ranked, based on their 2015 sales.

Keep in mind that the rank is a formula. The filter selects the records that the formula ranks. If you duplicated the table shown in Figure 15-36 and changed it to a Stacked column chart, as shown in Figure 15-38, it may make it easier for some people that view the page to understand the data.

Year	SalesRepRank ▲	SalesRep	Order Amount
☐ (Blank)	1	Robert King	$748,755.94
☐ 2012	2	Michael Suyama	$710,401.48
☐ 2013	3	Anne Dodsworth	$682,849.21
☐ 2014	4	Nancy Davolio	$660,756.95
☐ 2015	5	Janet Leverling	$649,101.99
☐ 2016	6	Margaret Peacock	$631,799.77

Figure 15-36 Data displayed by the Sales Rep Rank field and year slicer

Year	SalesRepRank ▲	SalesRep	Order Amount
☐ (Blank)	1	Robert King	$215,255.59
☐ 2012	2	Michael Suyama	$158,715.78
☐ 2013	3	Janet Leverling	$157,745.16
☐ 2014	4	Margaret Peacock	$147,190.82
☑ 2015	5	Anne Dodsworth	$140,253.75
☐ 2016	6	Nancy Davolio	$138,028.42

Figure 15-37 Sales reps rank in 2015

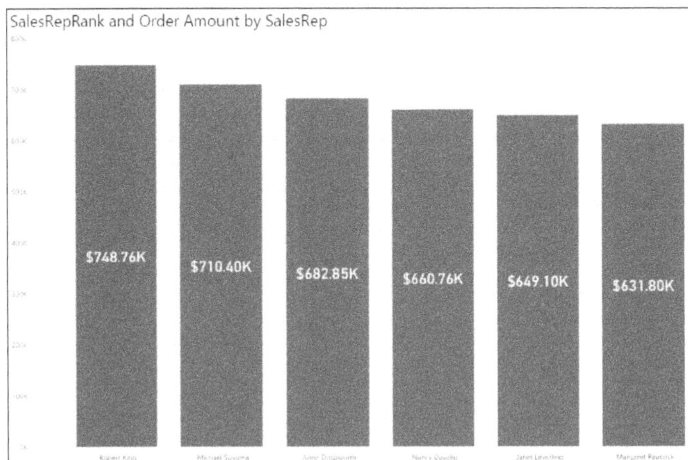

Figure 15-38 Stacked column chart with the sales reps ranked by order amount total

Timelines

A timeline is another way to filter the data displayed on a table or chart, similar to how slicers filter data. While slicers work with any field, timelines only work with a date field. When applied, the date range displayed on the timeline comes from the date field selected in the data source.

Truth be told, a timeline is easier to set up then using multiple slicers. In Exercise 15.2, two slicers were used to filter by year and month. Only one timeline object is needed to filter by year and month. While Power BI Desktop does not have an option for timelines, there is a timeline custom visual.

Timeline Custom Visual Field Well

Figure 15-39 shows the **TIME FIELD**. It requires a date field.

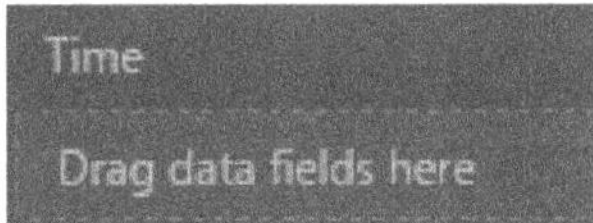

Figure 15-39 Timeline custom visual Field Well

Timeline Custom Visual Formatting Options

Figure 15-40 shows the format categories that are specific to this custom visual. The categories are explained below.

The **FISCAL YEAR START OPTIONS** are used to select the first month and day of month that you want displayed on the timeline.

The **FIRST DAY OF WEEK OPTIONS** are used to select the day that you want to use as the first day of the week. The default is Sunday.

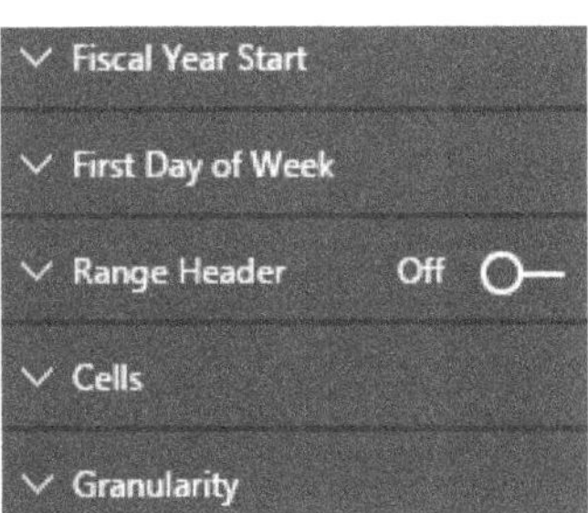

Figure 15-40 Timeline custom visual format options

The **RANGE HEADER OPTIONS** are used to select whether the range of dates in the field the timeline is based on, is displayed on the timeline.

The **CELLS OPTIONS** are used to change the color of the selected and unselected cells on the timeline.

The **GRANULARITY OPTIONS** are used to select how the dates are initially displayed on the timeline. Options include year, month and quarter. The slider displayed in the upper left corner of the timeline lets you change how the dates are displayed. The color options are used to change the colors of the slider in the upper left corner of the timeline.

Exercise 15.12: Use The Timeline Custom Visual

In this exercise you will create a clustered column chart that will be filtered by a timeline.

1. Download and import the Time Line custom visual.

2. Add the Clustered Column chart to the page.

3. Add the Month And Year Abbr field to the Axis section. The reason that I am using this field is because that while the timeline displays the data in the chart in calendar month order, it displays months from different years next to each other, as shown below, at the bottom of Figure 15-41. Using this field displays the month and year.

4. Add the Order Amount field to the Value section ⇒ Move the chart down a little.

Add The Timeline Visual To The Page

1. Add the Timeline visual to the top of the page ⇒ Make it as wide as the chart.

2. Add the Order Date field to the Time section.

3. Change the following formatting options. I selected a lot of colors, so that you can see what each option changes. When finished, the page should look like the one shown in Figure 15-41.

   ☑ Range Header ⇒ Font Color ⇒ Red
   ☑ Cells ⇒ Selected cell color ⇒ Yellow
   ☑ Cells ⇒ Unselected cell color ⇒ Purple
   ☑ Granularity ⇒ Scale color ⇒ Blue
   ☑ Granularity ⇒ Slider color ⇒ Orange

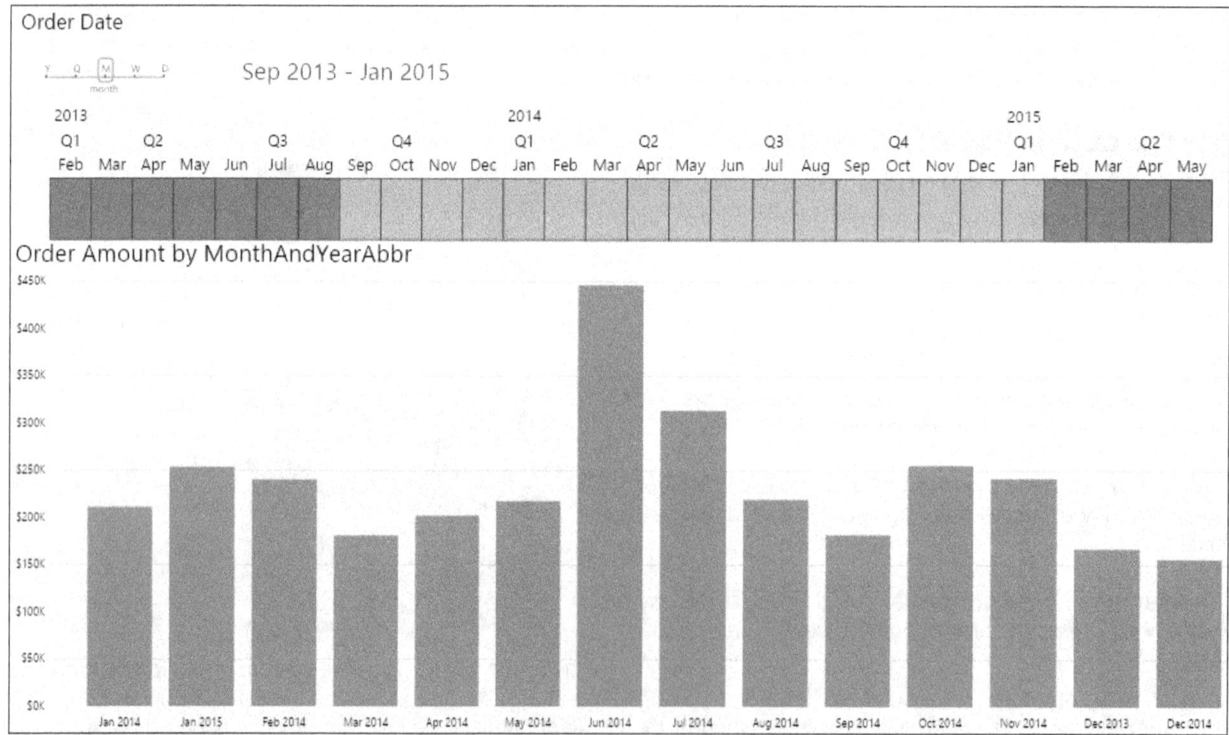

Figure 15-41 Timeline custom visual added to the page

The slider in the upper left corner of the timeline is used to select how the dates are displayed on the timeline. Currently, it is set to Month. The date range to the right of the slider is the date range that is currently selected on the timeline.

To select a different date range, drag the beginning or end of the timeline marker to select a new date range. Figure 15-42 shows the timeline options that will filter the chart to display three months of data in 2014.

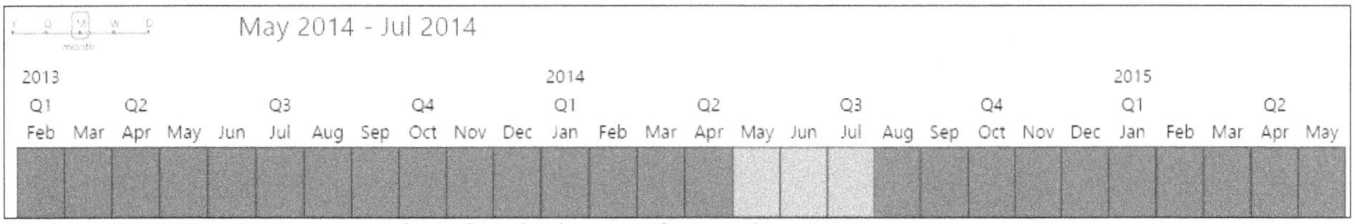

Figure 15-42 Timeline options selected to display specific months

If you click on the Y on the slider, the timeline will display the dates in years. When you click on a block, on the timeline slider for a year, the chart will display data for that year, as shown in Figure 15-43.

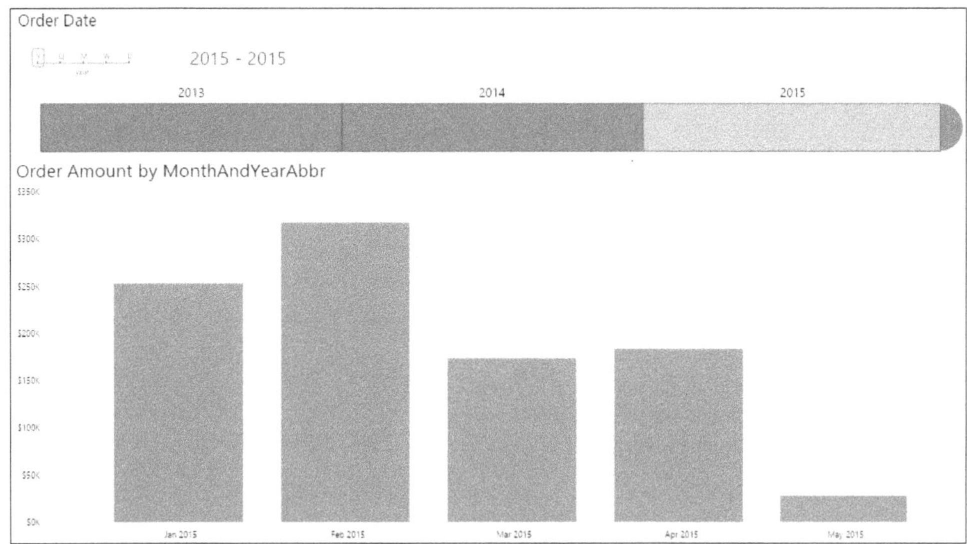

Figure 15-43 One year of data displayed on the chart

Summary

This chapter covered adding slicer interactive functionality to tables and charts. As you saw, slicers are another way to filter data. Having the ability to use more than one slicer is a way to add hierarchical filter functionality to a chart, without using a hierarchy. The primary use of the slicers is to allow users to be able to filter data, as needed.

INDEX

(blank) filter option (query editor), 4-2
(null) filter option (query editor), 4-2
(select all) filter option (query editor), 4-2, 6-30
(select all) filter option (report view), 10-3
.csv file import options, 2-9, 2-10
.json file import options, 2-12
.pbit template file, 1-10, 1-12, 10-16
.pbix file, 1-10
.tab file extension, 2-12
.txt file import options, 2-12
.xml file import options, 2-11
100% stacked bar chart, 12-2
100% stacked column chart, 12-2

A

access database connectors, 3-19
add as new query option, 3-12
add column tab options, 5-11
add conditional column dialog box, 5-21
add custom column dialog box, 4-12
add function, 3-11
add index column options, 4-13
add prefix function, 5-3
add suffix function, 5-3
advanced editor, 5-23
advanced filter criteria options, 4-8
age function, 5-14
aggregate button options, 6-4
aggregate functions (group by), 3-28
aggregate functions (pivot column), 6-23
aggregate functions (report view), 9-11
align options, 13-4
all rows operation, 6-20
always allow option, 5-23
analytics panel, 9-6, 13-2
analytics panel (line & clustered column charts), 13-31
analytics panel (scatter & bubble charts), 13-13
and operator (query editor), 4-3
and operator (report view), 10-6
any data type, 5-5, 7-4
append queries as new option, 6-3, 6-18
append queries options, 3-30, 6-3, 6-6
append queries with different column names, 6-18
append query to create new table, 6-18
append three or more tables, 6-19
appending data, 6-3
applied steps, 3-16, 3-18
area chart, 12-3, 13-11
assume referential integrity option, 7-13
auto detect option, 7-11
auto recovery options, 1-15
average function (query editor), 6-23
average function (report view), 9-12
average line chart formatting options, 13-3
Azure import options, 2-15
Azure Marketplace, 2-15

B

background formatting options, 11-6
bar chart, 12-10
basic filter criteria options, 4-3
blank query options, 2-17, 3-5
border formatting options, 11-6
box and whisker chart custom visual, 14-25
bridge chart, 12-3
bubble chart, 12-3, 13-16, 15-15
bubble chart formatting options, 13-12, 13-16
by delimiter options, 3-26, 5-9
by number of characters options, 3-27

C

calculated column (data view), 8-8
calculated tables, 8-12
callout value options, 14-11
candlestick chart, 14-25
canvas, 1-11, 9-3
card table, 9-5, 9-10, 11-15, 12-3
card table formatting options, 11-15
cardinality options, 7-7, 7-12
cartesian chart, 12-17, 13-8
cascade chart, 12-3
categorical option, 12-17, 13-8, 13-23
cell shortcut menu, 3-13, 3-14
change type option, 3-11
chart average line formatting options, 13-3
chart constant line formatting options, 13-2
chart data colors formatting options, 12-9
chart data labels formatting options, 12-9
chart formatting options, 12-7
chart general formatting options, 12-10
chart legend formatting options, 12-8
chart level filters, 12-15
chart max line formatting options, 13-3
chart median line formatting options, 13-3
chart min line formatting options, 13-3
chart percentile line formatting options, 13-3
chart plot area formatting options, 12-10
chart reference line formatting options, 13-3
chart title formatting options, 12-10
chart types, 12-2
chart x-axis formatting options, 12-8
chart y-axis formatting options, 12-8
child tables, 7-2, 7-3, 7-6, 7-14
clean function, 5-16
clipboard options, 9-4
close & apply options, 3-6, 3-22
clustered bar chart, 12-2
clustered column chart, 12-2
collapse all option (query editor), 3-9
collapse all option (report view & fields panel), 9-7
color saturation option, 12-7, 12-9, 12-12
column chart, 12-10
column data type shortcut menu (query editor), 3-14

column headers table formatting options, 11-5
column matrix table, 11-12
column shortcut menu (data view), 8-2
column shortcut menu (query editor), 3-10
combination chart, 12-4
combine binaries button, 3-31, 6-29
combine button, 6-29
combine columns of data, 4-11
combine date and time function, 5-14
comma-separated values (csv) connector options, 2-9, 2-11, 3-19
conditional columns, 5-20
conditional formatting, 9-14
connector options (access database file), 3-19
connector options (comma-separated values (csv) file), 2-9, 2-11, 3-19
connector options (text file), 2-9
constant line chart formatting options, 13-2
continuous option, 13-8, 13-23
conversion functions, 4-10, 6-13
convert to parameter option, 3-7
convert to query option, 3-7
copy entire list option, 3-13
copy entire table option, 3-6
copy table (data view), 8-3
count (all) function, 6-23
count (distinct) function (report view), 9-12
count (not blank) function, 6-6, 6-23, 6-24
count distinct values function, 5-18
count function (report view), 9-12
create function option, 3-7
create relationship dialog box, 7-12
create table dialog box, 8-13
cross filter direction options, 7-13
cross filtering charts, 14-20, 15-12
custom columns, 4-10
custom filter (query editor), 4-7
custom visuals, 1-12, 14-22
customize a slicer, 15-6

D

data analytics, 9-2
data category options (data view), 8-4
data colors chart formatting options, 12-9
data discovery, 2-2, 2-4, 3-2
data feed import options, 2-18
data labels chart formatting options, 12-9
data load options (current file), 1-16
data load options (global), 1-13
data loading, 3-2
data model defined, 7-2
data source settings (current file), 1-18, 3-6
data type icons, 8-5
data type options, 5-5
data view, 1-12, 8-2
database import options, 2-13
date & time functions (query editor), 4-4
date field filter options (report view), 10-4
date field operators, 10-5
date functions (add column tab), 5-14
date functions (transform tab), 5-3
date hierarchy fields, 10-6
date only function, 5-14
date table (create), 8-11
date table defined, 8-10
date table functions, 8-12
Date.From function, 6-13
Date.FromText function, 6-13
Date.ToText function, 6-13
datediff function (DAX), 8-9
DAX, 1-10, 8-8
day of week function, 3-12
days function, 5-14
default summarization options, 8-5
detach a visual from a slicer, 15-11
detect data type, 5-7
dimension table, 7-3
direct query option, 1-13, 2-14
display units, 11-15
diverging option, 9-14, 12-9, 14-20
do not detect data types option, 2-10
don't aggregate, 6-23
don't summarize (report view), 9-12
donut chart, 12-4, 14-5
drill down functionality (charts), 13-6
drill down mode, 13-6
drill down option (query editor), 3-10
drill down shortcut menu, 13-6
drill tab, 13-4
dual axis chart, 12-4
duplicate query option, 3-8
duration functions (add column tab), 5-16
duration functions (transform tab), 5-3
dynamic named ranges, 2-8

E

earliest function (add column tab), 5-14
earliest function (transform tab), 5-3
edit interactions button, 13-4
enable load option, 3-7
enable load to report option, 3-15
enable refresh of this query option, 3-15
enter data button, 3-4, 8-12
ETL, 3-3
Excel import option, 2-8
Excel workbook contents, 1-12, 3-34, 8-6
expand all option (query editor), 3-9
expand all option (report view & fields panel), 9-7
expand button options, 6-4
export chart data, 12-18
export template dialog box, 10-16
external data options, 2-2
extract options, 5-8
extract previous option, 3-17

F

fact table, 7-2, 7-14
field name shortcut menu (report view), 9-7
field well panel, 9-6
fields panel (data view), 8-3
fields panel (report view), 9-7
file import options, 2-8
file tab options (Power BI Desktop workspace), 1-12
file tab options (query editor), 3-6
fill option, 5-8

filled map chart, 12-3, 14-19
filled map chart formatting options, 14-19
filter options (query editor), 4-2
filter options (report view), 10-2
filter rows dialog box, 4-3, 4-9
flying bricks chart, 12-3
folder option (import), 2-8, 6-29, 6-32
foreign key, 7-6
format panel, 9-6
format tab, 13-3
function defined, 4-11
funnel chart, 12-3, 14-6
funnel chart formatting options, 14-6

G

gantt chart custom visual, 14-23
gauge chart, 12-3, 14-10
gauge chart formatting options, 14-10
general formatting options, 12-10
get data button options, 2-2
get data dialog box, 2-3
grid table formatting options, 11-4
group by options, 3-27, 5-10
group options (query editor), 3-8
grouping data, 6-7

H

hiding vs deleting columns, 7-9
hierarchies, 8-7, 9-14
highlighting data, 15-12
home tab options (Power BI Desktop workspace), 9-4
home tab options (query editor), 3-21
home table button, 8-4, 8-16

I

if function, 4-12
if then else statement, 4-12
image button, 9-4
image formatting options, 11-7
import from a csv file, 2-9, 2-10
import from a json file, 2-12
import from a text file, 2-9, 2-12
import from a xml file, 2-11
import from an access database, 2-14
import from Excel, 2-8
import from Excel data model, 3-34
import from file (chart), 12-4
import from the web, 2-5
import options, 1-12
import unlimited csv files, 6-28
import unlimited Excel files, 6-33
importing data, 2-2
include in report refresh option, 3-7
include relationship columns option, 3-19
inline hierarchy, 8-11, 13-6
insert link option, 11-6
insert options (home tab), 9-4
is even function, 5-3

J

join kind options, 6-3

K

keep duplicates, 3-24, 3-33
keep errors, 3-24, 6-31
keep rows options, 3-24
KPI chart, 12-4, 14-13
KPI chart formatting options, 14-14
KPI defined, 14-13

L

label density option, 13-8, 13-30
latest function (add column tab), 5-14
line & clustered column chart, 12-3, 13-31
line & clustered column chart analytics options, 13-31
line & column chart formatting options, 13-29
line & stacked column chart, 12-3, 13-30
line chart, 12-2, 13-9
line chart formatting options, 13-8
linear scale option, 12-8, 13-13
list data type, 2-13, 5-7
list tools transform tab, 3-12
load data while scrolling, 12-17
loading data, 2-2
local time function, 5-15
lock aspect formatting option, 11-6
log scale option, 12-8, 13-13

M

M Language, 3-4, 3-5, 3-35, 4-11, 5-9, 8-8
manage options, 3-23
manage parameters, 8-18, 8-20
manage relationships dialog box, 7-11
manage roles button/dialog box, 7-10
many-to-many relationship, 7-6, 7-7
map chart, 12-3, 14-15, 14-19
map formatting options, 14-16
maps, 14-15
matrix table, 9-5, 9-10, 11-8
matrix table formatting options, 11-9
max line chart formatting options, 13-3
maximum function (query editor), 6-23
maximum function (report view), 9-12
measures, 8-2, 8-8, 8-14
median function (query editor), 6-23
median function (report view), 9-12
median line chart formatting options, 13-3
merge columns (add column tab), 5-12
merge columns (transform tab), 5-12
merge queries as new option, 6-2, 6-15
merge queries options, 3-30, 6-2
merging data, 6-2, 6-7
metadata files, 2-5, 3-33, 6-28
min line chart formatting options, 13-3
minimum function (query editor), 6-23
minimum function (report view), 9-12
modeling tab (data view), 8-3
modeling tab (relationships view), 7-10
month function (DAX), 8-12
month function (query editor), 5-15
move options, 5-8
multiply function, 3-11, 5-13
multi-row card table, 9-5, 9-10, 11-14, 12-3
multi-row card table formatting options, 11-14

N

named ranges, 2-8
navigation step, 3-19
navigator window, 2-5
negative values in charts, 14-4
new group option, 3-9
new measure button, 9-5
new page button, 9-4
new query option, 3-7
new source options, 3-23
new visual button, 9-4
null value, 5-10
Number.FromText function, 6-13, 6-22
number.totext function, 4-10, 6-13, 6-22
numeric functions, 4-4

O

OData feed import options, 2-18
ODBC import options, 2-18
one-to-many relationship, 7-6
one-to-one relationship, 6-8, 7-6
options dialog box, 1-13
or operator (query editor), 4-3
or operator (report view), 10-6, 10-13

P

page background options, 11-3
page formatting options, 11-2
page information options, 11-2
page level filter, 10-2, 10-14, 12-16
page size options, 11-2
page view button options, 9-4
parallel loading of tables option, 1-16
parameter (create), 8-17
parameter (filter chart), 13-19
parameter list query, 8-19
parameter on filter rows dialog box, 8-21
parameter option, 5-20
parent-child relationship, 7-6
parse function (add column tab date button), 5-14
parse function (add column tab time button), 5-15
parse function (transform tab), 5-3
pending changes, 3-22
percent calculation (quick calc), 13-24
percent formatting formula, 6-22
percent functions, 5-19
percentile line chart formatting options, 13-3
pie chart, 12-3, 14-2, 15-13
pie chart formatting options, 14-2
pin to list option, 2-4, 2-15
pivot column dialog box, 6-23
pivot data, 6-22
pivot table (create), 6-24
play axis option, 13-12, 13-17
plot area chart formatting options, 12-10
Power BI, 1-11
Power BI Desktop workspace, 1-11
Power BI Mobile, 1-11
Power BI Template, 1-12, 10-15
preview features, 1-14
primary key fields, 7-6
primary table, 7-2, 7-14
privacy options (current file), 1-18
privacy options (global), 1-14
product option, 3-11
promoted headers step, 3-20
publish options, 1-13
publish to Power BI, 1-13

Q

q&a natural language, 3-8, 7-10, 11-2
quarter of year function (query editor), 5-15, 5-19
queries panel, 3-4, 3-7
query defined, 3-3
query editor, 3-2, 3-4
query editor options, 1-14
query function, 6-35
query parameters, 8-16
query properties dialog box, 3-15
query settings panel, 3-15
quick access toolbar (Power BI Desktop workspace), 1-21
quick access toolbar (query editor), 3-31
quick calc, 9-13, 13-24

R

R Script visual (chart), 12-4
R Scripting options, 1-13, 5-3
radar chart custom visual, 14-27
recent sources option, 2-3
record data type, 2-13, 5-6
record tools convert tab, 2-13, 5-7
recursive join, 7-7, 7-11
reference line chart formatting options, 13-3
reference query option, 3-8
refresh preview options, 3-23
regional settings options, 1-17
relationship defined, 7-5
relationships options, 1-17
relationships view, 1-12, 7-8
remove blank rows, 3-24
remove columns options, 3-24
remove duplicates, 3-25
remove empty option, 4-2
remove errors, 3-24, 6-33
remove rows options, 3-24
replace values, 3-30, 5-10
report level filter, 10-2, 10-14
report view, 1-12, 9-2
report view workspace, 9-3
reverse rows option, 6-24
round up function (query editor), 5-18
roundup function (DAX), 8-12
row headers table formatting options, 11-5
row level security, 7-10
row matrix table, 11-10, 11-13
row operation, 3-28

S

scale type options, 12-8
scatter chart, 12-3, 13-12, 13-15
scatter chart formatting options, 13-12
scientific functions (transform tab), 5-3
security options, 1-14
see data button, 13-4

see records button, 13-5
select related tables button, 2-15
self join, 7-7
self-service business intelligence, 1-5
shape map, 14-21
shapes button, 9-4
shapes formatting options, 11-7
shaping the data, 3-16, 4-6
share option, 9-5
show items with no data, 9-6
size option, 13-26
slicer (customize), 15-6
slicer formatting options, 15-2
slicers, 12-4, 15-2
sort by column, 8-4, 8-10
sort data in a table chart, 10-15
sorting (query editor), 3-25
sorting chart data, 12-14
source step, 3-18
split column by delimiter dialog box, 3-26
split column by number of characters dialog box, 3-27
split column options, 3-26
stacked area chart, 12-3
stacked bar chart, 12-2
stacked column chart, 12-2, 13-18
standard deviation function (report view), 9-12
standard functions (transform tab), 5-3
star schema, 7-2, 7-13
status bar (query editor), 3-5
status bar (report view), 9-5
stored procedures, 7-5
structured data types, 5-6
subtract days function, 5-14, 5-19
subtract function (add column tab duration button), 5-16
subtract function (add column tab time button), 5-15
sum function (query editor), 6-23
sum function (report view), 9-12
sum option, 3-11
summary type, 9-13

T

table button shortcut menu, 3-5, 3-6
table data type, 5-6
table formatting options, 11-3
table name shortcut menu (report view), 9-7
table style formatting options, 11-4
table view button, 2-6
table visualization, 9-5, 9-10
table.max function, 6-21
tabular format, 6-25
text box button, 9-4
text box formatting options, 11-6
text connector options, 2-9
text file import options, 2-9, 2-12
text functions, 4-4
text.start function, 4-12
time functions (add column tab), 5-15
time functions (transform tab), 5-3
time intelligence explained, 8-11
time intelligence option, 1-16
Time.ToText function, 6-13
timeline custom visual, 15-17
title chart formatting options, 12-10
title table formatting options, 11-6
to table options, 3-13
tooltips, 12-7, 12-18
total table formatting options, 11-5
total years function, 5-16
totalytd function, 8-10
transform option, 3-12
transform tab options, 5-2, 5-4
transforming data, 3-2, 5-2
tree map chart, 12-3, 14-12
tree map chart formatting options, 14-12
trend line analytic formatting options, 13-13
trend line chart, 12-4
trim function, 5-16
type detection, 1-16

U

ungroup option, 3-9
unpivot columns, 6-25
unpivot data, 6-25
unpivot other columns, 6-25
updates option, 1-14
url icon option, 11-5
use a query as a data source, 3-8
use first row as header options, 3-29
use original column name as prefix option, 6-4, 6-5
using locale option, 3-11, 3-19

V

values table formatting options, 11-5
variance chart, 12-4
variance function (report view), 9-12
view as roles button, 7-10
view native query option, 3-17
view tab (query editor), 5-23
views (in a database), 7-4
views (power bi desktop), 1-12
visual level filter, 10-2, 10-4, 10-11
visual tools tab, 13-3
visualizations panel, 9-5

W

waterfall chart, 12-3, 14-7
waterfall chart formatting options, 14-7
web connector import options, 2-4
web url option, 8-4
web view button, 2-7
wildcard search characters, 10-3
word wrap option, 11-16

X

x axis, 12-6, 13-12, 13-26
x-axis chart formatting options, 12-8
x-axis constant line options, 13-14
xy scatter chart, 12-3

Y

y axis, 12-6, 13-12, 13-26
y-axis chart formatting options, 12-8
y-axis constant line options, 13-14

year function (DAX), 8-12
year function (query editor), 5-15

Z

z axis, 13-26

www.ingramcontent.com/pod-product-compliance
Lightning Source LLC
LaVergne TN
LVHW060135070326
832902LV00018B/2800

* 9 7 8 1 9 3 5 2 0 8 3 4 1 *